the wiley reader

the wiley reader

DESIGNS
FOR
WRITING

CAROLINE D. ECKHARDT
THE PENNSYLVANIA STATE UNIVERSITY

JAMES F. HOLAHAN
THE PENNSYLVANIA STATE UNIVERSITY

DAVID H. STEWART
TEXAS A & M UNIVERSITY

WITH THE ASSISTANCE
OF PAUL SORRENTINO
THE PENNSYLVANIA STATE UNIVERSITY

JOHN WILEY & SONS, INC.
New York   London   Sydney   Toronto

This book was set in Times Roman by V & M
Typographical, Inc. and printed and bound by Quinn
and Boden Co., Inc. The text was designed by Suzanne
G. Bennett. The cover was designed by Blaise Zito
Associates Inc. The copy editor was Elaine Miller.
Reiko Okamura supervised production.

Library of Congress Cataloging in Publication Data:
The Wiley reader.

    Includes bibliographical references.
    1. College readers. 2. English language—Rhetoric.
I. Eckhardt, Caroline D., 1942–   II. Holahan,
James F. III. Stewart, David Hugh, 1926–   IV.
Wiley (John) and Sons, inc.
PE1417.W48   808'.04275   75-29499
ISBN 0-471-22970-9

Printed in the United States of America

10 9 8 7 6 5 4 3 2

preface

TO THE STUDENT

In the beginning is the title, and since ours summarizes the convictions behind this book, we would like to explain it. *The Wiley Reader: Designs for Writing* is based on the conviction that writing is a skill best learned not from rules but from examples. Anyone who is going to be a good writer will need to be an attentive reader as well, the kind of reader who sees what is said and also how it is said. This book shows you how 120 writers, whose professions range from logging to driving trucks to practicing law, have modeled and shaped the raw materials of their experience into the forms most likely to convey the dramatic power of their ideas. When you have seen how other writers have shaped their materials, you will find it easier to shape your own.

The book is based also on the conviction that good writing does not just "happen": it is a matter of design, not chance; of craftsmanship, not miracle. The process of writing is like the process of working clay with your hands. You need material to work with and a design to give the material meaning. If all goes well, the finished object will have exactly the effect you want. In writing, the material you work with comes from yourself. It may be your memory of a personal experience or your interpretation of what you have read or heard. The choice of the design is yours too. The purpose of *The Wiley Reader* is to offer you designs from which to choose.

THE FORMAT OF THIS BOOK

The introductory chapter, the section called "The Drama of Information," explains our conviction that information, knowledge of the world, can be as moving and powerful as a dramatic fictional story. "Human beings naturally desire to know," the Greek philosopher Aristotle said about 2500 years ago, and that statement is perhaps still the best description of our species. Knowledge is both pleasure and power. Have something to say, and people naturally will want to listen—if your way of expressing it helps them to see the dramatic quality of the information. The sections called "Prewriting" and "Rewriting" discuss the processes of choosing and organizing your information and revising your first drafts. The section called "Applications" will give you practice in beginning.

The book itself is divided into four parts, each beginning with an explanatory essay. The four parts present four kinds of writing: writing that aims to inform, to prove or argue, to judge or evaluate, and to recommend or persuade. Each part shows you several ways of achieving its particular objectives—several ways, rather than one, because in writing (as in most other forms of human interchange) there are many right ways of reaching a goal. Your personal preferences, your need to be faithful to your own style, will direct you to the right way for you for each writing occasion. This freedom to choose among alternatives permits you to say something about yourself: how you think, how you go about describing the world. Thus, every time you write you suggest a self-portrait that provides additional information for your readers.

The first kind of writing (Part 1) is called "Definition." This term includes, in this book, all writing whose primary purpose is to explain what the author means by X, to make his readers understand X—his subject, whatever that may be—as he himself understands it. Definitions, short or long, answer the question, "What is X?" They may call on a number of techniques such as clarification by example, comparison and contrast, and narration, as well as upon the type of defining you see in a dictionary.

Part 2, "Substantiation," presents writing whose primary intention is to support an opinion about X that goes beyond what is actually known. Definitions may appear here also, so that the writer is certain that X means the same thing to you as it does to him. The main purpose, however, is to prove that the further estimations ("educated guesses") about X are valid and well supported, that you can accept them as a responsible extension of the known into the unknown. Substantiations answer the question, "What is likely to be true or false about X?"

Part 3, "Evaluation," presents writing that establishes the writer's own value judgment of X: the ways he believes X is good or bad. Having defined his subject ("Definition"), and perhaps also shown what is probably true about it ("Substantiation"), he explains how he himself feels about it, and why. Of course, he does everything he can to make you feel the same way. Evaluations answer the question, "Is X good or bad?"

Part 4, "Recommendation," offers compositions in which the writer, having defined his subject, substantiated his interpretation of it, and evaluated it as good or bad, then presents a proposal for change. Recommendations answer the question, "What should we do about X?"

This fourfold division is simple and practical. It applies to almost all occasions for writing. The four categories, however, like all categories, are to some extent arbitrary. Each kind shades into the next, just as the colors of a rainbow do. Nevertheless the classification is useful, as the separate names for the parts of the rainbow's spectrum are, since it makes the wide range of nonfiction writing easier to understand, discuss, and practice.

In each section, the readings offered as examples are arranged in two series. In the first series, each selection has an introductory note, a commentary, an outline, and suggestions for writing. In the second series, each selection has an introductory note only, so that you and your instructor can approach it as best suits the progress of your own course. The sequence within each series is simple to complex and usually short to long; toward the end of the series the selections become more difficult and shade into the next major category.

The readings include letters, advertisements, and newspaper articles, as well as formal "essays." All demonstrate the variety and vitality of the written language today. You will notice that many authors represented here are not established writers. Indeed, some are anonymous; others are freelance writers—people who produce articles but often have other jobs as well. No special group or profession has a monopoly on good writing.

A glossary of terms, brief biographical notes on the more than 100 writers represented, and a thematic table of contents conclude the book.

WRITING IN A MASS SOCIETY

You may wonder why you need designs for writing at all. You have probably heard the claim that radio, television, and even body language are replacing the printed word. Defenders of this view cite statistics on the number of popular magazines that have ceased publication, on the declining per-capita book consumption, and on the falling examination scores—especially in verbal proficiency—among high school graduates.

At the same time, the "information explosion" has caused a tremendous increase in the quantity of printed material. Every industry, hobby, or religion in the nation supports several publications. From metallurgical journals to clothing patterns, from government reports to church-sponsored tracts, from income tax forms to commercial advertising, the flood of print pours through every home and office. If you were to read rapidly eight hours a day, five days a week, you could not keep pace with the supply of printed matter.

Although very little of this material invites attention to its stylistic polish, the level of competence is often high. Institutions of all kinds have discovered the power of language, and they employ writers to carry their message. Two hundred years ago, it was politicians who hired "hacks" to write for them. Now it is every agency and institution imaginable— and they want professonals, not hacks. Good writers are in demand and are rewarded. Of two equally competent chemists, accountants, or people involved in any occupation, the one who can write better will win quicker recognition. People with practical competence in writing will always have an advantage—in school, in civic activities, and in their profession.

Beyond this, the sensitivity to language that you gain through developing your skill as a writer can become a source of permanent enjoyment. The harder you work with words, the more comfortable you become with them and the more control you gain over them. You can make words and ideas behave for you; you can compel language to express accurately what's on your mind. The pleasure that this skill brings is very much like an athlete's satisfaction with a game well played. Novelist Thomas Mann described his own sense of the pleasure and power of words this way: ". . . language itself is a criticism of life: it names, it defines, it hits the mark, it passes judgment, and all by making things alive."

Preparing this book gave us a fine excuse to read a tremendous amount of good prose as we looked for selections to include. We hope that our pleasure in the endeavor shows and that you also will enjoy the book and find in it useful designs for giving shape to your own information. The material to work on is within the reach of your mind; the power to shape it is at the end of your fingers.

A NOTE OF THANKS

The editors are grateful to the following Pennsylvania State University colleagues (at the University Park and the Commonwealth Campuses) for examining and suggesting revisions of the text: Evelyn Buckalew, Wilma R. Ebbitt, Evelyn A. Hovanec, Cheryl J. Plumb, and Albert N. Skomra. Portions of the text were class-tested in pilot sections of English Composition at Pennsylvania State University, and we thank the students in those sections and their teachers, Timothy Conley, Michelle Knovic, Laurie Lieb, and Paul Sorrentino. The text could not have been prepared in time for deadlines without the industry of Barbara Bertram, Debra Quarato, and Nancy Royer.

Many others made helpful suggestions for improving the format and content of the text. We are especially grateful to John P. Broderick of Old Dominion University, Greg Cowan of Empire State College, C. Jeriel Howard of Bishop College, Russell Meyer of The University of Minnesota, Betty Renshaw of Prince George's Community College, Gary Tate of Texas Christian University, and Joseph F. Trimmer of Ball State University.

We would like to acknowledge Thomas Gay, Wiley's English editor, who was a lively critic and a helpful advisor, and his assistant Andrea Stingelin who greatly facilitated the effort in its closing days. We would particularly like to express our appreciation to the many staff members at John Wiley and Sons who consistently offered a uniquely high level of professional support.

CAROLINE D. ECKHARDT
JAMES F. HOLAHAN
DAVID H. STEWART

contents

EVALUATION
INTRODUCTORY ESSAY   295
Series One: Reading with Commentary

RECOMMENDATION

the wiley reader

introduction: the drama of information

How do you know the world? By seeing and hearing it, by tasting, smelling, and touching it. In short, you know the world by sensing it. You may reflect on what you sense; you may perform any number of intellectual operations on what you sense; but without the data that the senses provide, you can do nothing.

A few years before the first manned space flight, an aircraft manufacturer conducted an experiment to study how well people can withstand sensory deprivation. The subjects, young men between the ages of 18 and 25, were placed in an absolutely dark chamber. The air they breathed was filtered to remove even the barest trace of an odor. Their hands were encased in thick, soft mittens. The couch on which they reclined was filled with a soft gelatin-like substance that yielded instantly to the slightest body movement. They wore thickly padded earphones through which came only a low, constant whooshing sound—what scientists call "white noise"; they were to be denied even the sound of their own heartbeat. No one lasted in the chamber more than a few hours. One man emerged half-hysterical after what he thought was several days. He had been in the chamber for 18 minutes. All were severely disoriented; many required weeks to recover psychologically from the ordeal. The conclusion was plain: without data—without information—we go mad.

Good writing begins with information, with the raw material on which our minds feed: sights, sounds, smells, tastes, textures. The writer's task, as novelist Joseph Conrad put it, is to use the power of the written word to make us hear, to make us feel, to make us *see*.[1] In the following paragraphs about the 1969 moon landing, the intention is to make us realize how exciting an event that was.

Seventeen minutes later, Eagle had reached the low point of its orbit. The spacecraft was traveling feet first, its two triangular windows peering down as the barren surface of the Sea of Fertility rushed past less than ten miles below. If Armstrong and Aldrin had any doubts, it was still not too late to draw back and let Eagle remain safely in orbit. But neither the instruments crowding the tiny cabin nor the consoles back in Mission Control showed any signs of trouble, and Armstrong punched the "proceed" button to allow the computer to fire the descent engine. Flames blasted out of the big engine bell to slow the spacecraft down and send it dropping in a long arc toward the planned landing site three hundred miles to the east. Apollo 11 was past the point any previous flight had

---

1 Joseph Conrad, "The Condition of Art," in *The Portable Conrad,* Morton D. Zabel, ed. (New York: Viking, 1961), p. 708.

reached, plunging into the most dangerous and unpredictable twelve minutes of the mission.

Houston and Eagle exchanged terse, bullet-like packages of technical data as the seconds ticked away. The computer fired the little attitude control rockets clustered at each corner of the spacecraft to roll it gently over on to its back. A blue and white earth a quarter of a million miles away swung in front of the windows in place of the bare surface of the moon. The pace of events was quickening all the time. Pulses from the landing radar reflected from the surface below fed the astronauts with continuous information about their altitude and rate of descent.

"Eagle, Houston," said Mission Control. "You are go. Take it all at four minutes. Roger, you are go—you are to continue powered descent."[2]

The quotation is not an uncontrolled gush of superlatives. Neither is it a flat claim that man's first descent to the moon was "exciting." The writer does not say, "You wouldn't believe how exciting it was." If he said simply that, we *wouldn't* believe him. In order to convince us just how exciting the descent was, he must supply information. He selects items that he believes will evoke in us a sense of danger and urgency. The information, rather than being scattered, is arranged temporally—like the ticking of a clock. The first paragraph begins as we approach "the point of no return," the last 12 minutes of Eagle's flight, the moment after which the astronauts have no chance to change their minds. We begin traveling "feet first" (as if we were jumping down to the moon's surface) and "peering" at the Sea of Fertility 10 miles below. It all sounds very realistic, in fact almost familiar; but that is because language has translated unprecedented events into terms that we understand.

The effectiveness of the passage derives not only from the importance of the event itself and from the words (which are vigorous but commonplace: "pushed," "blasted," "terse") but also from the introduction of a spatial perspective that orients us as the seconds tick by. In the first paragraph, the crowded, tiny cabin gives us a reference point. It is here that Armstrong "punched" (*not* pushed or pressed) the "proceed" button. This fixes us in space. In the second paragraph, amid "bullet-like packages of technical data," we "gently" roll the spacecraft on its back—a breathtaking occurrence for two reasons: now we are falling backward toward the "ground"; and the earth, a "quarter of a million" (*not* 250,000) miles away, "swings" in front of the windows. That fixes us again in space and dramatizes our precarious situation. Now, feeding on pulses, we cannot turn back. Mission Control says, "You are go." And the verb "go" has a meaning new to the language, new to human experience. There was never a time or a place where we could "go" (in this sense) prior to the journey of Apollo. The writer has given us the

---

2 Hugo Young, Bryan Silcock, and Peter Dunn (we have collapsed the three authors into "the writer"), *Journey to Tranquility* (New York: Doubleday, 1970), p. 268.

crucial ingredients of the astronauts' world: the information we need to understand it, the data necessary to give the basic idea—the moon landing was exciting—dramatic impact.

How much information is contained in the following passage?

The door of the lunch room opened and two rough-looking characters came in. Both of them sat at the counter. One ordered a dinner, but since the dinner was not available for an hour yet, the man behind the counter calmly told them they'd have to make another choice.

The man who had ordered the meal became angry. The way he was dressed made him look like a "hit-man" and his quick temper and domineering attitude reinforced this impression. He argued loudly with the man behind the counter, whose name was George, belittling him to make it clear that he was not to be fooled with.

George didn't seem frightened; he answered the man's questions much as one might imagine he'd answer anybody. All the while, Nick Adams had been watching from the other end of the counter.

The two customers are described as "rough-looking." But how does a rough-looking man look? Is he big? Unshaven? Are his clothes old? New? Tattered? Too well tailored? How exactly does a "hit-man" dress? The man behind the counter (George) speaks to the customers "calmly" and does not "seem frightened." But it is hard to picture someone speaking calmly when you don't know what he's saying. One of the men becomes "angry." He has a "quick temper" and a "domineering attitude." These vague characteristics, applied here to a "hit-man"—a killer—could also apply to a middle-aged aunt told that there is no lemon for her tea.

The answer to the question "How much information is contained in the passage?" is really "Not very much." What substitutes for information are approximate judgments and lazy summaries. Such phrases as "rough-looking," "quick temper," and "domineering attitude" are summaries of whole complexes of observations that the writer denies us. It is the absence of the observations—of information—that robs the passage of drama, drama being the quality that allows us to participate intellectually *and* emotionally in the scene.

Here is the scene as Ernest Hemingway, who understood the drama of information, really wrote it.

The door of Henry's lunch-room opened and two men came in. They sat down at the counter.

"What's yours?" George asked them.

"I don't know," one of the men said. "What do you want to eat, Al?"

"I don't know," said Al. "I don't know what I want to eat." Outside it was getting dark. The streetlight came on outside the window. The two men at the counter read the menu. From the other end of the counter Nick Adams watched them. He had been talking to George when they came in.

"I'll have a roast pork tenderloin with apple sauce and mashed potatoes," the first man said.

"It isn't ready yet."

"What the hell do you put it on the card for?"

"That's the dinner," George explained. "You can get that at six o'clock." George looked at the clock on the wall behind the counter.

"It's five o'clock."

"The clock says twenty minutes past five," the second man said.

"It's twenty minutes fast."

"Oh, to hell with the clock," the first man said. "What have you got to eat?"

"I can give you any kind of sandwiches," George said. "You can have ham and eggs, bacon and eggs, liver and bacon, or a steak."

"Give me chicken croquettes with green peas and cream sauce and mashed potatoes."

"That's the dinner."

"Everything we want's the dinner, eh? That's the way you work it."

"I can give you ham and eggs, bacon and eggs, liver—"

"I'll take ham and eggs," the man called Al said. He wore a derby hat and a black overcoat buttoned across the chest. His face was small and white and he had tight lips. He wore a silk muffler and gloves.

"Give me bacon and eggs," said the other man. He was about the same size as Al. Their faces were different, but they were dressed like twins. Both wore overcoats too tight for them. They sat leaning forward, their elbows on the counter.

"Got anything to drink?" Al asked.

"Silver beer, bevo, ginger-ale," George said.

"I mean you got anything to *drink?*"

"Just those I said."

"This is a hot town," said the other. "What do they call it?"

"Summit."

"Ever hear of it?" Al asked his friend.

"No," said the friend.

"What do you do here nights?" Al asked.

"They eat the dinner," his friend said. "They all come here and eat the big dinner."

"That's right," George said.

"So you think that's right?" Al asked George.

"Sure."

"You're a pretty bright boy, aren't you?"

"Sure," said George.

"Well, you're not," said the other little man. "Is he, Al?"

"He's dumb," said Al. He turned to Nick. "What's your name?"

"Adams."

"Another bright boy," Al said. "Ain't he a bright boy, Max?"

"The town's full of bright boys," Max said.

George put the two platters, one of ham and eggs, the other of bacon and eggs, on the counter. He set down two side-dishes of fried potatoes and closed the wicket into the kitchen.

"Which is yours?" he asked Al.

"Don't you remember?"

"Ham and eggs."

"Just a bright boy," Max said. He leaned forward and took the ham and eggs. Both men ate with their gloves on. George watched them eat.

"What are you looking at?" Max looked at George.

"Nothing."

"The hell you were. You were looking at me."

"Maybe the boy meant it for a joke, Max," Al said.

George laughed.

"You don't have to laugh," Max said to him. "You don't have to laugh at all, see?"

"All right," said George.

"So he thinks it's all right," Max turned to Al. "He thinks it's all right. That's a good one."

"Oh, he's a thinker," Al said. They went on eating.[3]

Hemingway's "The Killers" is fiction which, along with poetry, is often labeled "creative" writing. Like most labels, "creative" can be useful—but also misleading. It seems to imply that other forms of writing are noncreative, dull and mechanical, somehow inferior. Some people are further misled into the notion that "creative" writing liberates the writer from the petty business of having to make sense—that the creative writer's job is to produce a vague and ambiguous mood of soft pastels, where connections are indistinct and edges blurred.

Both notions are wrong.

What *is* creative about creative writing? The writer of fiction seeks to create experience, to make us feel present in a place from which we are really absent. Knowing that the raw stuff of experience is what we see and hear and feel and touch and smell, he gives us these sensations, and if he gives us enough of the right kind in the right order, we will inevitably undergo the dramatic experience. Effective information transmission (from a shouted warning to a learned treatise) always dramatizes. The corollary, unfortunately, is also true: *in*effective information transmission deadens.

In the excerpt from "The Killers," Hemingway does not tell us (though he could) that the two strangers are dangerous and menacing. Nor does he tell us (though he could) what George or Nick thinks of them. Instead, he makes us feel present in the diner. We see what George and Nick see, hear what they hear. We grow uncomfortable (as George must) when Al purposely orders something he knows is not available.

"I can give you any kind of sandwiches," George said. "You can have ham and eggs, bacon and eggs, liver and bacon, or a steak."

"Give me chicken croquettes with green peas and cream sauce and mashed potatoes."

[3] Reprinted by permission of Charles Scribner's Sons from "The Killers" (Copyright © 1927 Charles Scribner's Sons) by Ernest Hemingway from *Men Without Women*.

"That's the dinner."

"Everything we want's the dinner, eh? That's the way you work it."

We learn that the strangers are dressed identically (a sort of uniform?), and that they eat with their gloves on (to avoid leaving fingerprints? to show their contempt for conventional manners?). We wince when Al calls George "bright boy," and when Max makes him pay for every casual remark.

"What are you looking at?" Max looked at George.
"Nothing."
"The hell you were. You were looking at me."
"Maybe the boy meant it for a joke, Max," Al said.
George laughed.
"You don't have to laugh," Max said to him. "You don't have to laugh at all, see?"
"All right," said George.
"So he thinks it's all right," Max turned to Al. "He thinks it's all right. That's a good one."
"Oh, he's a thinker," Al said. They went on eating.

Throughout, the drama of the scene builds by Hemingway's use of specific detail, pieces of information selected to extend and intensify the growing sense of menace these strangers radiate.

As a work of fiction, "The Killers" achieves its dramatic impact not by any mystical notion of creative inspiration but by information carefully selected and controlled. The same kinds of information, again carefully selected and controlled, can give nonfiction the same dramatic quality—the quality that gets us involved, makes us share in, and care about, the world the writer is creating. The major difference, really, is that the writer of fiction has greater initial latitude in choosing the information he wants to give us. (The word "initial" is crucial. Although a fictional character is not real, once he has been given certain attributes he must act as a real character with those attributes would act. The writer of fiction therefore has complete freedom only at the start.) The writer of nonfiction collects his information from the real worlds around and within him. What you know about yourself is information too.

The paragraphs below, from Lillian Ross' "Symbol of All We Possess," demonstrate the ability of information-based nonfiction to capture some of the drama inherent in life itself.

There are thirteen million women in the United States between the ages of eighteen and twenty-eight. All of them were eligible to compete for the title of Miss America in the annual contest staged in Atlantic City last month if they were high school graduates, were not and had never been married, and were not Negroes. Ten thousand of them participated in preliminary contests held in all but three of the forty-eight states. Then, one cool September day, a Miss from each of these states, together with a Miss New York City, a Miss Greater Philadelphia, a Miss Chicago, a Miss District of Columbia, a Miss Canada, a Miss Puerto Rico, and a Miss Hawaii, arrived in Atlantic City to display her beauty, poise, grace, physique, personality, and talent. The primary, and most obvious, stake in the contest was a twenty-five-thousand-dollar scholarship fund—a five-thousand-dollar scholarship for the winner and lesser ones for fourteen runners-up—which had been established by the makers of Nash automobiles, Catalina swimsuits, and a cotton fabric known as Everglaze. The winner would also get a new four-door Nash sedan, a dozen Catalina swimsuits, and a wardrobe of sixty Everglaze garments. The contest was called the Miss America Pageant. The fifty-two competitors went into it seeking, beyond the prizes, great decisions. Exactly what was decided, they are still trying to find out.

Miss New York State was a twenty-two-year-old registered nurse named Wanda Nalepa, who lives in the Bronx. She has honey-blond hair, green eyes, and a light complexion, and is five feet three. Some other statistics gathered by Miss American Pageant officials are: weight, 108; bust, 34; waist, 23; thighs, 19; hips, 34; calf, 12½; ankle, 7½; shoe size, 5; dress size, 10. She was asked in an official questionnaire why she had entered the Atlantic City contest. She answered that her friends had urged her to. The day before the contest was to start, I telephoned Miss Nalepa at her home to ask when she was leaving for Atlantic City. She said she was driving down the next morning, and invited me to go along.[4]

"Symbol of All We Possess" examines the Miss America Pageant in minute detail. Ross found the pageant crass and dehumanizing. But in 1948, when she wrote her description, the pageant was at the height of its popularity with the American public, and no explosion of indignation would have served to indict it. If the pageant were to be indicted it must indict itself. Therefore Ross simply supplies information: the discriminatory qualifications for contestants, the long —almost mindlessly long—list of "Misses" and the qualities they must display, the prizes, the measurements rattled off as though Wanda Nalepa were less a human being than a side of beef. Ross is not imposing drama on the situation she describes. Instead, she is making visible the drama inherent in the situation. She wants her readers to react negatively to the Miss America Pageant, and she has faith that a precise, factual, and honest description will produce that reaction.

Creative writers of nonfiction strive to make the drama of life visible. They do so by making us *see*. They recreate the real by making the abstract concrete, the general specific, the vague clear. Often the information they deal with is not new. In fact, it may be so old and so well known that we have forgotten its meaning, but creative writers can make us see old information with new eyes. For example, Loren Eiseley wanted to dramatize an idea common

4 From "Symbol of All We Possess" in *Reporting* (Simon & Schuster). Copyright © 1949 Lillian Ross. Originally in *The New Yorker*.

enough in our time: modern man's most dangerous enemy is himself. He put it this way:

> As a boy I once rolled dice in an empty house, playing against myself. I suppose I was afraid. It was twilight, and I forget who won. I was too young to have known that the old abandoned house in which I played was the universe. I would play for man more fiercely if the years would take me back.[5]

Eiseley was writing about the progress of the human species: man has conquered the sea, the land, the air; the antagonist he faces now is himself. This insight takes on a renewed dramatic power when Eiseley expresses it by means of a simple image of childhood. Because we have all been frightened children once, playing our games alone in the twilight, we can respond emotionally to this scene. The idea that man's enemy is himself has been stated so frequently lately that even Pogo's quip "We have met the enemy and he is us" is worn out. But the idea can be made new again and again by a careful choice of information, and information includes metaphors and comparisons. The most effective ones are often the simple shared experiences of life, because we can identify with them—they seem real to us—immediately.

Alvin Toffler's *Future Shock* illustrates another familiar viewpoint—that our world is changing very rapidly—in these dramatic terms:

> . . . if the last 50,000 years of man's existence are divided into lifetimes of approximately sixty-two years each, there have been about 800 such lifetimes. Of these 800, fully 650 were spent in caves.
>
> Only during the last seventy lifetimes has it been possible to communicate effectively from one lifetime to another—as writing made it possible to do. Only during the last six lifetimes did masses of men ever see a printed word. Only during the last four has it been possible to measure time with any precision. Only in the last two has anyone anywhere used an electric motor. And the overwhelming majority of all the material goods we use in daily life today have been developed within the present, the 800th, lifetime.[6]

When long stretches of time are rendered in terms of a unit that we can easily understand—a lifetime—we begin to see the extraordinary acceleration of change involved in human history. And we begin to see the meaning of all sorts of related matters. We may begin, for example, to comprehend the rate at which we now use up the earth's natural resources: developed over eons, they may be exhausted in decades. We see the human problems associated with rapid material progress as we realize that our lives are as different

---

[5] Loren Eiseley, *The Invisible Pyramid* (New York: Scribner's, 1970), pp. 2–3.
[6] From *Future Shock,* by Alvin Toffler. Copyright © 1970 by Alvin Toffler. Reprinted by permission of Random House, Inc., p. 13.

from those of our great-grandparents as their lives were different from those of the ancient Romans.

Toffler depicts in detail what he calls the "accelerative thrust" in one measure of progress: mobility, the speed with which people can move from one place to another.

. . . This acceleration is frequently dramatized by a thumbnail account of the progress in transportation. It has been pointed out, for example, that in 6000 B.C. the fastest transportation available to man over long distances was the camel caravan, averaging eight miles per hour. It was not until about 1600 B.C. when the chariot was invented that the maximum speed was raised to roughly twenty miles per hour.

So impressive was this invention, so difficult was it to exceed this speed limit, that nearly 3,500 years later, when the first mail coach began operating in England in 1784, it averaged a mere ten mph. The first steam locomotive, introduced in 1825, could muster a top speed of only thirteen mph, and the great sailing ships of the time labored along at less than half that speed. It was probably not until the 1880's that man, with the help of a more advanced steam locomotive, managed to reach a speed of one hundred mph. It took the human race millions of years to attain that record.

It took only fifty-eight years, however, to quadruple the limit, so that by 1938 airborne man was cracking the 400-mph line. It took a mere twenty-year flick of time to double the limit again. And by the 1960's rocket planes approached speeds of 4000 mph, and men in space capsules were circling the earth at 18,000 mph. Plotted on a graph, the line representing progress in the past generation would leap vertically off the page.[7]

Although filled with concrete words, these paragraphs show that dramatic information is not limited to the raw material of sensation. Our minds have been taught from infancy to process the information our senses provide into more complicated structures and symbols. Numbers are one example. The other animals with whom we share the earth are apparently incapable of numerical thinking (except perhaps in the rudimentary sense of recognizing the difference between "a little" and "a lot"), but all human beings can understand numbers. If you promise a small child three ice-cream cones, you will get an immediate response of astonishment and anticipation. Therefore Toffler can legitimately assume that the many numbers in his explanation of the accelerating pace of change will help make his writing dramatic. They constitute specific information just as Hemingway's phrases "ham and eggs" or "a black overcoat buttoned across the chest" do. Similarly, Toffler's concluding image, a line leaping upward on graph paper, assumes that we have become familiar with basic concepts in the graphic presentation of data.

The more that writing relies on universal experiences or on

7 Toffler, p. 24.

simple sensory evidence—what could be observed by anybody who was there—the more likely it is to be understood by everybody. But it is extremely hard to write completely in such terms without seeming trite or childish. Therefore most writers draw also upon more complex, less elemental, sources of information. The following paragraph from Harlow Shapley's *View from a Distant Star* requires that we recognize information from the fields of religion, chemistry, natural history, and geology.

. . . the breath of St. Francis is with us, and of Confucius, and of Mary of Nazareth. That knowledge may give you, I hope, a feeling of brotherhood with the great and holy past, for the nitrogen of the international air crosses the barriers of time as well as space. But each breath of yours, I should hasten to add, contains also nitrogen breathed by ancient sinners; and it probably contains at least six of the nitrogen atoms expelled in each ferocious snort of an ancient dinosaur, as he raised his head from the Mesozoic swamps 100 million years ago and sneered, in his vulgar way, at the primitive little mammals which were just beginning to grow into the most dominant animal form on earth.[8]

This example shows that the writer's decision as to exactly what information will convey the drama of his subject must be influenced by the background of the reading audience he has in mind. If you have never heard of St. Francis, or Confucius, or nitrogen, or dinosaurs, or the Mesozoic era, that paragraph is not likely to move you off dead center. Your response might be only "What on earth is he talking about?" Yet to the audience Shapley assumed he was writing for, an audience with a basic education in many fields, the paragraph is filled with precise information that successfully dramatizes his idea: all of us share kinship with the people who lived before us and with the creatures to whom the earth belonged before there were any people around at all.

Creative nonfiction, then, is writing that re-creates some part of the real world by supplying the right information: enough information, but not the surplus that would bore us; information that we will recognize, not obscurities that would merely puzzle us; information carefully arranged, not a hodgepodge. Enough of the right kind in the right order. Such creative nonfiction can achieve a drama equal to that of the finest fiction. It seems to capture reality itself and thus responds to our natural human desire to know, and to know more and more and always more about the world in which we live, a world which is defined partly by our presence in it.

PREWRITING

How does one write dramatic nonfiction? Alvin Toffler and Lillian Ross and other professional writers show us that it can be done— but not how.

[8] Harlow Shapley, *The View from a Distant Star* (New York: Dell, 1963), p. 90.

There isn't any simple answer (or we'd all be Alvin Tofflers and Lillian Rosses), but much of the success of a piece of writing depends on the process called preparation for writing, or "prewriting." Prewriting begins with our desires and attitudes and emotions and experiences; it ends with words on paper. In between occurs the crucial process of *discovery:* discovery of the significance, the value, the meaning of whatever information we have at hand. Mere information is both boring and useless. Nobody wants to read the telephone directory cover-to-cover; although it is densely packed with precise information, the information, taken as a whole, lacks meaning. Psychologists have become increasingly aware that the human mind naturally records information as patterns or structures rather than as isolated bits of data. We remember a face as a face, not as a list of facts such as "eyes with speckled irises, a nose with a low bridge, a tongue that sticks out most of the time, a shape of the face shorter than normal top-to-bottom." Information in that form, no matter how accurate and detailed, is meaningless because each item stands alone; there is no central point around which everything else is organized. The process of prewriting is the process of discovery of the center, the focal idea around which everything else falls into place to form a pattern that our minds accept as meaningful.

There is no set of rules, no magic formula, that can tell you how to find the meaning of information. Experienced writers say that they "think it through," or that they experience a flash of insight, or that they simply write and rewrite until somehow the act of putting words on paper seems to force the information to take shape. Perhaps you recognized that the speckled eyes, the low-bridged nose, the protruding tongue, and the wide face make a pattern known as Down's syndrome, a type of genetic damage sometimes called mongolism: that is the meaning of the information about the face.

The inexperienced writer, however, isn't helped much by being told to think it through, or to wait for a flash of insight, or to write and keep on writing. Here are two precise suggestions that work for some writers, although not for others. One technique is to assign arbitrarily a meaning to information and then to examine the ways in which that meaning seems wrong. In the course of this examination, the meaning that seems right may become more and more clear. For example, you might begin by declaring that your inability to get along with your brother shows that he is an unreasonable person. As you compare this hasty interpretation with the full range of your information—your total collection of memories, over many long years, about the relationship between the two of you, including the times when you briefly *did* get along—you may begin to see more and more clearly that sometimes he was unreasonable (just as you first thought), but that sometimes *you* were unreasonable, while sometimes it was the presence of other people that set the two of you against each other. Moreover, there is a changing pattern to your relationship. When you were small children, you squabbled ten times a day and made things up just as frequently. As you grew older, you spent less time together and quarreled less often but more seriously. Now that you spend even less time together than before, you disagree along a few familiar lines: you fight about money, about the need to have at least one of you visit your parents at holiday time, about which of you should have that car you once bought together. The more you examine this changing pattern, the more you realize that your initial statement about the meaning of the information was wrong. Your final judgment may be that the two of you are sharing a perfectly normal struggle for independence against the claims of family life. Both of you may seem unreasonable at times, but there is a consistent reason for your unreason: you both need to make it known, again and again, that you have your own lives to lead.

A second technique for finding the meaning of information is to plan from the beginning to present the subject to a specific audience. Imagine yourself in the audience's place: your readers are seeing the information for the first time, and they can see only what you tell them. As every new piece of information comes in, they automatically try to relate it to something you've already told them; and if they can't do so, they become bored or restless or annoyed. This technique requires that you first look not for an overall meaning but simply for the relationship between item 1 and item 2, item 1 or 2 and item 3, and so forth. Whatever does not fit is set aside to be tried again later; if it never fits, it is finally set aside for use in some other writing project, if at all.

Let's assume, for example, that you begin with the vague intention of writing about Sylvia's suicide. Now choose an audience: at least identify its age or educational level or occupational interests or personal situation. Should you define the audience by age and write either for people as old as Sylvia's parents or for her fellow students? As you consider this part of the problem, it occurs to you that Sylvia's age and educational level and occupational interests were not really critical in determining what happened to her; it was the tremendous frustration of her personal life that mattered most. Presumably, then, an understanding of what happened to her will be of most interest to other people suffering a similar frustration, whatever their age. They will be the audience.

You can now go back to where you began, to the intention to write "about Sylvia's suicide." You know now what it is that you need to understand—the process by which her frustration led her to do what she did. Now you know what you (and your audience) are looking for.

The next step is to sort through your information, selecting only what relates to this inquiry. You may find that you still have too much, which means that you will need to limit the subject by such boundary lines as time and space. You knew Sylvia for six years, but if you are to write only 500 words about her and give your audience a coherent picture, you may need to limit your subject to "An Afternoon in a Brooklyn Apartment: The Day Sylvia Killed Herself." After this decision, you will need to sort the information again, keeping only what still relates to the newly limited subject. Out go all those details about Sylvia's first boyfriend and her hobbies and her hairstyles. Although they may have something to do with her final frustration, they no longer fit the subject as defined. The details about her last boyfriend, the phone call she didn't get, and the end of her dreams stay in.

Everything now relates to everything else, but you still need to determine the *nature* of the relationship, the *meaning* of the pattern. Put yourself in the audience's place by asking the questions your readers would ask. "Are you trying to say it was her fault?" "Are you trying to say she didn't try hard enough?" "Are you trying to say that other people didn't care enough about her?" "Are you trying to make us see her as crazy?" "Are you trying to make us see the rest of the world as crazy?" (Perhaps you can find somebody to play the part of the audience at this point; if not, you will have to ask the questions yourself.) Each question suggests a possible meaning for the pattern. If you ask all the questions that your information permits, sooner or later you should come across the one that makes you answer "Yes! that's it." The right question makes the meaning of the information (a meaning that was really there all the time) suddenly stand out.

If none of the questions calls forth that response of discovery, you have probably made a wrong decision along the way. Look at the information you discarded, arrange *it* into patterns, and ask for their meanings too.

At the end of the prewriting process, then, you should have two things: a collection of information and a sense of what the information means. You may also have several pages full of jottings, or a neat outline, or some other form of words on paper. In any case, you are ready to write a first draft. Don't worry about elegance of phrasing; just begin to write words, sentences, paragraphs. If you always have trouble with introductions, begin in the middle and come back to the beginning afterward.

REWRITING

Very few writers are skilled enough to write a paper only once. Even professionals like Hemingway write, and rewrite, and rewrite, polishing off a rough edge here, accentuating a point there. Your first draft is probably a collection of sentences and paragraphs, not a composition. Some parts may be very dramatic, others repetitive or floundering or dull. As you rewrite it, you will have to do four things.

1. *Edit the language.* This involves making all aspects of style (grammar, spelling, punctuation, word choice, paragraphing, and so forth) correspond to standard American usage. Use a good dictionary and other reference books if you need help. No simple error of language should be permitted to undercut your paper's effect.

2. *Improve the organization.* Does the paper *go* somewhere? Does it have a recognizable sequence or order—for example, chronological order, a simple-to-complex sequence, a good-to-bad contrast, a near-to-far spatial development? A paper without a clear sense of organization will seem incomplete or confusing, like a road map without a north-south orientation: which way is up?

3. *Emphasize the major idea.* The major idea, usually called the thesis, expresses what you see as the meaning of your information, what you want your readers to remember. Most short compositions (500 to 800 words) dramatize one thesis rather than trying to present several. Even if your thesis consists of a group of related ideas, the overall impact will be greater if you make one idea the center of attention and keep the others clearly subordinate.

4. *Sort the information once again.* Which details deserve to be kept? Which can be done without? Which belong together? What is missing from the information you have included? Wherever possible, increase the drama of the information by using a concrete rather than a vague word, a new phrase rather than a cliché. Let "late afternoon" become "four-thirty."

Any change you make affects the whole piece of writing, so that you will need to make a final revision to adjust one change to another. If somewhere along the way you have revised the main idea, for instance, you will need to discard some information that is no longer relevant and insert new information to fill the blank spaces. If you first began to design a reindeer but discovered that the more you reworked it the more the reindeer looked like an ass with horns, you might end up choosing a camel instead. As you rewrite, you will have to eliminate the horns and add the hump to make the overall picture consistent.

Most writers find that they need help along the way, both in prewriting and in rewriting. Don't ask your best friend, however, because you're not likely to get the most honest evaluation. Ask other students who are struggling with the same writing problems. Some things will be easier for you, some easier for them, and so you should be able to help each other. Ask your instructor, who has been through all of this more times than he or she wants to remember.

And, indirectly, ask the writers whose work appears in this book. They can't tell you *how* they went about solving their writing problems, but they can show you the solutions they found.

They can also show you something else: you can't please all of the people all of the time. If information is to be dramatic, somebody must be on the receiving end. Otherwise, that striking fact so skillfully directed at its goal will merely disappear into limbo. Readers help determine what succeeds in being dramatic by their willingness to receive the subject matter. A superb article on guns or quasars might make someone say "Dull. I can't stand guns," or "Astronomy bores me." And a second-rate article on the sex lives of thirteenth-century European aristocrats might be read with avid interest by a reader who likes that sort of thing.

You are not trying, then, to conquer the world (although occasionally that happens). You are trying to reach a limited audience and to present your subject to that audience in the most effective way possible. Whether your subject is animal, mineral, or vegetable, reality or fantasy, dream or nightmare, tomorrow or yesterday, somebody out there is ready to listen. Somebody has listened to the essays in this book, which discuss everything from automobiles to zoology, with birth and death and love and spiders in between. Somebody out there is ready to listen, and the rest is up to you.

APPLICATIONS

1. *Enough Information.* Students often say that they run out of things to write about a topic. A student makes a point:

> Professor Smith is a very boring lecturer. He has nothing interesting to say. Nobody in his class pays the slightest attention to him. He puts us all to sleep. I'll never take another course from him.

The problem with this kind of writing is that it approaches the subject from the wrong end: the writer gives us his judgments rather than the information that produced them. The idea does not advance; the second sentence gives us no more information than the first, the third no more than the second. We know only that the writer thinks Professor Smith is boring. But why should we take his word (over and over) for it? Why won't he give us the information that will allow us to share his view, not merely take it or leave it?

Does this revision do the job?

> Professor Smith stands immobile behind his lectern. His eyes never lift from his notes. His voice, barely loud enough to be heard above the ticking of the wall clock, rises and falls in a rhythmic sing-song cadence:
> "The *role* of the teacher
> in this *age* of technology
> is per*haps* the most difficult
> in *all* of society."

Here and there, heads loll forward onto chests, then snap back spasmodically as someone noisily rearranges himself in his chair. At predictable intervals, Professor Smith asks for questions. There are never any.

Write a one-paragraph description of a person or scene or event with which you are familiar. Don't give your judgments; give the information that formed your judgments. Don't summarize. Allow the reader to see the person or scene or event as you did.

2. *Information of the Right Kind.* Good writing does not waste time. It includes nothing that would distract our attention from the subject. Nor does it give an exhaustive catalogue of information if a few telling details will do.

In the following paragraph, the writer's intention is to make us aware that local businesses exploit students.

Merchants in college towns are notorious for exploiting students. If you can believe the newspapers, prices are soaring in just about every town, big or little, college town or otherwise. But merchants in college towns really take advantage in every way they can. Places patronized mostly by students, such as movie theaters, bars, pizza parlors, bookstores, and record shops, inflate their prices in anticipation of student trade. Prices (to say nothing of the service) are truly outrageous because merchants take advantage of their knowledge that student money, mostly supplied by parents, is not valued as much as if the student had to earn it himself. But who can earn money with so few decent summer jobs available? Even though the main source of the town's income is student trade, students are rarely consulted on important town issues, and are not even allowed to participate in local elections unless some outside agency, such as the federal government, intervenes to allow students to vote. Towns that want student business should make students welcome, not change the price tags every time they see us coming.

How much of the information in that paragraph is irrelevant? How much, though relevant, is repetitious? In short, how much wastes our time?

3. *Information in the Right Order.* Imagine a description of a man that begins with the color of his hair, then mentions his shoe size, then his age, then the color of his eyes, then his preference in cigars, then the shape of his nose. Eventually, the description would be complete and accurate. It might even be free of irrelevance and repetition. But it would not be useful, since we couldn't follow it easily. The value of information depends on its being in the right place at the right time.

In the paragraph below, the information is arranged in a sequence which does not help us *see* what is meant. Sentences are in a hodgepodge order, and sometimes pieces of information which do not really belong together are linked in one sentence. Rewrite the paragraph.

A "glory" is a set of colors seen in the sky, somewhat like a rainbow. It may have given rise to the custom in painting of showing holy people with a halo of colors around their heads. The glory, like the rainbow, is caused by sunlight scattered by droplets of water, and is more commonly seen by passengers in airplanes than by observers on the ground. It consists of several concentric rings of color around a bright central region. The custom of painting holy people with haloes is known from Roman, Greek, and Oriental art; both gods and rulers may be painted that way. The innermost ring of color is violet, the outermost is red. There may be as many as four sets of such rings. Unlike the rainbow, a glory is not often seen, because perceiving it requires an unusual arrangement of the sun, the observer, and a cloud whose water droplets are all of one size. (Adapted from a publication copyright W. H. Freeman and Company.)

4. *Prewriting.* Below you will find a version of the Beaufort Wind Scale, a sailors' chart equating wind velocities with effects of the wind on sea and land. (The original Beaufort Scale was devised by Sir Francis Beaufort in 1806; our version is a U.S. Weather Bureau modernization.) Note that if you read the criteria downward, you witness the drama of an emerging hurricane. On the basis of the information given here, prewrite an essay about a storm. What does the storm mean? What idea will you focus on? What audience will you try to reach? What information should be kept? What discarded?

Table 1
Wind-Speed Equivalents [on Land]

DESCRIPTIVE WORD	MILES PER HOUR VELOCITY,	SPECIFICATIONS FOR ESTIMATING VELOCITIES
Calm	Less than 1	Smoke rises vertically.
	1 to 3	Direction of wind shown by smoke drift but not by wind vanes.
Light	4 to 7	Wind felt on face; leaves rustle; ordinary vane moved by wind.
Gentle	8 to 12	Leaves and small twigs in constant motion; wind extends light flag.
Moderate	13 to 18	Raises dust and loose paper; small branches are moved.
Fresh	19 to 24	Small trees in leaf begin sway; crested wavelets form on inland waters.
	25 to 31	Large branches in motion; whistling heard in telegraph wires; umbrellas used with difficulty.
Strong	32 to 38	Whole trees in motion; inconvenience felt in walking against the wind.
	39 to 46	Breaks twigs off trees; generally impedes progress.
Gale	47 to 54	Slight structural damage occurs (chimney pots and slate removed).
	55 to 63	Trees uprooted; considerable structural damage occurs.
Whole gale	64 to 75	Rarely experienced; accompanied by widespread damage.
Hurricane	Above 75	

Table 2

Specifications for Estimating the Force of the Wind at Sea

BEAUFORT NUMBER	GENERAL DE-SCRIPTION OF WIND	CRITERIA
0	Calm	Sea like a mirror.
1	Light air	Ripples with the appearance of scales are formed, but without foam crests.
2	Slight breeze	Small wavelets, still short but more pronounced; crests have a glassy appearance and do not break.
3	Gentle breeze	Large wavelets. Crests begin to break. Foam of glassy appearance. Perhaps scattered whitecaps.
4	Moderate breeze	Small waves, becoming longer; fairly frequent whitecaps.
5	Fresh breeze	Moderate waves, taking a more pronounced moderately long form; many whitecaps are formed. (Chance of some spray.)
6	Strong breeze	Large waves begin to form; the white foam crests are more extensive everywhere. (Probably some spray.)
7	Moderate gale	Sea heaps up and white foam from breaking waves begins to be blown in streaks along the direction of the wind.
8	Fresh gale	Moderately high waves of greater length; edges of crests begin to break into spindrift. The foam is blown in well-marked streaks along the direction of the wind.
9	Strong gale	High waves. Dense streaks of foam along the direction of the wind. Sea begins to "roll." Spray may affect visibility.
10	Whole gale	Very high waves with long, overhanging crests. The resulting foam, in great patches, is blown in dense white streaks along the direction of the wind. On the whole, the surface of the sea takes a white appearance. The rolling of the sea becomes heavy and shocklike. Visibility affected.
11	Storm	Exceptionally high waves. (Small and medium-sized ships might be for a time lost to view behind the waves.) The sea is completely covered with the long, white patches of foam lying along the direction of the wind. Everywhere the edges of the wave crests are blown into froth. Visibility affected.
12	Hurricane	The air is filled with foam and spray. Sea completely white with driving spray; visibility very seriously affected.

Source. From *Techniques of Observing the Weather* by B. C. Haynes. Copyright © 1947 by John Wiley & Sons, Inc. Reprinted by permission of the publisher.

5. *Rewriting*. Improve the following essay. Its subject is an immigrant's arrival in America, particularly one episode in a Canadian railroad station. The audience is intended to be anyone who has undergone the tension of being alone in a radically new situation (or anyone who wants to understand that experience). Its central idea is that a newcomer's success or failure can depend on whether anyone is willing to help him.

As you rewrite, strengthen the essay's organization, emphasize the major idea, eliminate unnecessary material, and add additional information (from the Data Chart following the essay) where it is needed.

"Off," said the conductor, inspecting Sam's ticket. He got off.

His name was Sam—Samuel Jankowski, in full—and he was twenty years old and two thousand miles from home. He knew nobody at all in America. His parents had told him that he had an aunt somewhere in "the Bronx," which was part of New York City, which was part of New York State. His aunt had taken the odd-sounding name of Mason. But the U.S.A. quota for the year had been filled. (There was a limit on the number of immigrants each year.) So Sam was going to Canada instead, so it didn't matter about his aunt anyway. In Canada he didn't even have an aunt he had never seen, hiding behind an Anglo-Saxon name.

He hadn't cared about that when he decided to leave home and come to the new world where, people said, if you could work you could be sure of eating, and there were no laws against people like him owning property or going to college. He had wanted to leave the dying little village in Poland so badly that he had quarreled with his parents over it. They said he should stay and live as they did; he said he couldn't stand it any more and had to get away. He just didn't want to live their kind of life. They said he could go, finally. (He would have gone anyway.) So here he was.

But as the train came to a stop in a small Canadian station whose name he could read but not pronounce, and as the babble of voices in English—speaking too fast for him to understand—turned into shouts of greeting, and everyone seemed to know what was going on except him, he wished he had never left home. The platform was full of people hugging and kissing. This town was a frequent destination of immigrants because there was factory work to be had. He could see the factory smokestacks against the sky. He was scared and just kept standing there looking around.

Then Sam saw that a man had detached himself from the dwindling crowd. The man was obviously poor. His clothes were torn and although it was winter, and bitterly cold, he had no gloves. There was a basket over his arm.

The man moved along the platform towards Sam. Sam had not eaten today, and he did not expect to unless he could get work right away and get an advance on his pay. He had spent the last of his money on a bit of food yesterday and on his train ticket this morning. He would have to sleep in the station, if they would let him. The man came nearer, looked at Sam, and said something Sam did not understand. Suddenly totally miserable, he simply stared back.

The man said something again.

For all of his twenty years, Sam was on the point of bursting onto tears. He fished around in his memory for the few English phrases he could say. Work, yes, no, tomorrow, I can do it, my aunt is named Mason. "My aunt is named Mason," he said, stupidly, since his aunt could not be anywhere around here.

The man didn't seem to hear. He was reaching into his basket. A loaf of bread came out, then a tomato. The man held them out to Sam. The food looked so good that Sam grabbed at it before he knew what he was doing. He started to eat and it tasted good too.

When he thought to look up the man was gone. Sam looked around for him and saw him getting off the end of the platform and starting to walk away down a street.

There was half the bread left yet. Save it for later.

"I guess I'm going to make it after all," he thought. He wasn't shaking any more. He fit the bread into his coat pocket and gathered his belongings and his emotions together. He felt so much better for having eaten that he couldn't believe the change.

Sixty years later, Sam Jankowsky, by then Sam Mason, had made it indeed. He had found a new life in Canada, and afterwards in New York. He had sent for his family to join him. He owned a store in the Bronx and became part of the American middle class. "But if it hadn't been for that man with the bread and tomato," he still likes to tell his grandchildren, "I just don't know if I would have survived."

"Did you ever see him again?" we grandchildren ask. It's part of our ritual.

"No. That afternoon I got a ride to the next town and got work there. But a fellow I worked with used to know him and said he was crazy. He used to meet all the trains from the coast, all day long, and give the immigrants—the ones who looked down-and-out, like me—a loaf of bread and a tomato."

I myself think that if everyone, just once, gave someone else a little something like a loaf of bread and a tomato when they needed it, the world would be a lot better place to live in for all of us.

Data Chart: How Much of This Additional Information Belongs in the Essay?

SAM   He is 5 feet 6 inches tall and weighs only 120 pounds but is strong. He has black hair and dark brown eyes. He wears a long brown wool coat that is too big for him, and underneath it a gray wool suit that is neatly patched and mended, but rather wrinkled and dirty. He carries a shabby khaki cloth drawstring bag and an old suitcase tied with a rope because the clasp is broken.

He has always been a quiet person, without many friends, but he knows what he wants and tries very hard to get it— for instance when he was 12 there was a contest in school for the child who got the highest score on a history exam (the prize was a book). He studied day and night for weeks, allowing himself just five hours' sleep at night, pestering his older brother to quiz him, walking 10 miles to borrow extra books from another town's library. He got absolutely every question right (the next nearest score was 88). He doesn't mind working hard if he knows what he is supposed to do.

SAM'S
FAMILY

Sam has one brother, Willie, two years older. In the village in Poland, most people have small farms and also a trade; Sam's father and mother work a garden plot and his father is a carpenter. Most of the young people want to leave the village because there seems to be no opportunity for them to do anything except join their parents in their trades. Everyone is poor: malnutrition is typical, the houses are little more than shanties, children share beds or lie on the floor, most people have only one or two garments, and almost nobody wears shoes except in the winter. The villagers do not know much about the rest of the world. Most of the older people have never been anywhere else, and the younger ones who go away don't often come back. Sam's parents want him to stay with them because Willie has already left (he went to Warsaw, a large city about 100 miles away) and they are afraid they will be alone and helpless in their old age if he goes away too.

THE SMALL
TOWN IN
CANADA

The name of the town is New Charlottetown. It has one main street; the railroad runs along it, so that from the station you can glance left and right along Main Street and see, to the left, the huge yellow brick factory building with "Johnson and Sons" painted in great black letters across half the length of the building, and, above, black smokestacks belching smoke into the gray January sky. Other streets run into Main Street, touching the railroad station. You can see houses, mostly yellow brick like the factory, and a building with a flag on a pole in front of it (a post office? a municipal building?), and, at about the end of the vista, a large house that must be used as a school because a group of children, perhaps a dozen of them, is playing wildly on the lawn—a mixture of grass and mud and snow —in front.

THE MAN
AT THE
STATION

The man's face is lined, his eyes are reddened and need wiping from time to time, and when he speaks you can see that he has no teeth—yet his walk is strong and rapid as if he were still fairly young. He wears a dirty blue-and-gold plaid cloak with a long rip on one side, and boots that do not match each other. He carries what looks like a wicker picnic basket; it must have been expensive once, as the outside is (or was once) decorated with painted designs, and when he opens the lid you can see the remnants of a gold-color satin lining. In the basket are four small loaves of bread—dark bread with shiny crust—and four tomatoes, their skins bright red but slightly puckered, as if they have dried somewhat during storage.

definition

Definition, the explanation of what we mean by the words we use, is a necessary preliminary to any kind of writing. A great many discussions are absolutely pointless because people do not first establish what their discussions are *about*—what exactly they mean by *X,* the subject they are considering. You may remember from your childhood the frustration of not knowing what words meant (did some relative ever offer to make you a "Nicholas pancake"?). Or you may remember reading, in *Through the Looking-Glass,* about Alice's puzzlement when she couldn't make sense of the strange ways in which other characters were using language.

> "I don't know what you mean by 'glory,' " Alice said.
> Humpty Dumpty smiled contemptuously. "Of course you don't— till I tell you. I meant 'there's a nice knock-down argument for you!' "
> "But 'glory' doesn't mean 'a nice knock-down argument,' " Alice objected.
> "When *I* use a word," Humpty Dumpty said in a rather scornful tone, "it means just what I choose it to mean—neither more nor less.". . .
> Alice was much too puzzled to say anything. . . .[1]

Unless our aim is to reduce other people to an astonished silence, we must make sure that the words we use are understood. The vast majority of words we do not stop to define, since (unlike Humpty Dumpty, who, you will remember, came to a bad end) we use them in their conventional meanings. But the central thing a writer wants to discuss often needs to be explained, so that writer and reader will have exactly the same concept in mind.

The shortest forms of definitions are single-sentence statements. Dictionary definitions of "mitosis" or "metaphor" or "metropolis" aim at no more than specifying the normal denotation of a word (on denotation see Altick, p. 146). Longer forms of definition may extend to several hundred pages, such as book-length presentations of the theory of relativity or the history of English literature, which

[1] Lewis Carroll (Charles L. Dodgson), *Through the Looking-Glass,* in *The Complete Works of Lewis Carroll,* illustrations by John Tenniel, introduction by Alexander Woollcott (New York: Modern Library, 1960), p. 214.

aim at explaining their subjects in full breadth and detail. Whether short or long, simple or complex, definitions always respond to the question, What is X?

X might be some aspect of an event, a process, a structure, a living organism, a theory, and so forth. It might be an episode in the writer's own experience, the method by which cancer kills, the form of a Shakespearean sonnet, the average size of the dinosaur *Tyrannosaurus rex,* the voting patterns of college students in the last presidential election, the provisions for birth control in medieval Europe, or the ways to maximize the yield of wheat per acre and the proportion of protein in that wheat. Regardless of its subject, definition intends primarily to present X so that readers can understand it too. It does not primarily intend to influence them for or against it. (That is the province of substantiation, evaluation, and recommendation, types of writing discussed later in this book.)

In many books about writing, formal definitions based on an "X = class term + distinguishing terms" pattern (see below, p. 27) are the only kind of presentation of X called "definition." More extended forms (see pp. 27–32) are called "description," "explanation," or "exposition." In this book, we include them all in the category "definition" because all have the same intention, all serve the same purpose: to provide the information necessary to a shared understanding of the subject.

When you write a definition, you face certain problems. First, you usually know much more about your subject than you can say in any single writing opportunity. You may be limited by space or the characteristics of your audience (their prior information about the subject and their interest in it). The first decisions, therefore, are matters of selection: of everything I know about the death of my father, what shall I say? Of everything I have learned about the practical applications of lasers, what shall I include? Second, because you are so familiar with your subject, you can comprehend it from a number of viewpoints simultaneously and begin almost anywhere without becoming confused. Your readers, however, probably know much less than you—which is why you are the one doing the explaining. They must be guided carefully through the field of information, or they will get lost. The second set of decisions, therefore, concerns matters of organization: What should be said first? Later? Why should the material in the fourth paragraph be there and not in the first or fifth?

Finally, you must accommodate your style to your readers so that the information you want to convey, once selected and organized into a logical sequence, will be fully comprehensible. Stylistic decisions concern vocabulary (does this term need to be explained? is it exactly the right one?), syntax (has this sentence become too complicated?), and tone of voice (do you sound well-informed without

seeming stuffy, friendly without seeming falsely chummy or conde-
scending?). Such questions as whether a given body of material needs
a diagram to clarify it, or whether references to the sources of information should be included, can also be considered matters of
style. And a good writing style must be free from distracting mechanical errors or surplus words. You don't want to throw your readers
off the track by saying "I found a man-eating dinosaur" when you
mean "I found a man, eating dinosaur," or insult their intelligence
by including the obvious as in "The sun was bright yellow in color"
(what else could it be "bright yellow" in?).

A well-written definition, whether brief or extended, resembles
a well-designed automobile. Efficiently and comfortably, with all its
parts cooperating, it functions to take someone from here (relative
ignorance of X) to there (relative familiarity with X). Normally, like
the automobile, it is not an end in itself, but the means by which
some further purpose can be accomplished. Sometimes, toward the
end of the definition, you suggest the potential uses for your material: how somebody else might benefit from understanding your response to your father's death, what relevance medieval birth-control
practices might have today. The primary task, however, is simply to
present X as you yourself understand it, so that your readers will
understand it that way also. Not that the gain is completely on their
part. It is good to be understood, as we all know, and the successful
definition brings its writer that satisfaction. In addition, the act of
reinvestigating X in order to make it comprehensible to somebody
else often makes it more fully comprehensible to you as well.

OBJECTIVE AND SUBJECTIVE DEFINITION

The general question, What is X? may be interpreted in either an
objective or *subjective* way. The difference between these two types
of definition is extremely important, for neither can do the job of
the other. *Objective definition* explains the normal or typical characteristics of X, characteristics that are public, apparent to anyone
who looks at the evidence, based on assumptions that our entire
society shares. Dictionary definitions—which record the conventional
meanings assigned to words—belong to this type, as do scientific
explanations of the natural world, descriptions of historical events,
and so forth. The purpose of the definition is to present X as it is
potentially accessible to everybody.

Subjective definition, on the other hand, explains characteristics
of X that are private, dependent on the experience of an individual,
based on one person's assumptions. The purpose of the definition is
to express what X means to *you,* whether it means the same thing
to anyone else or not. Harlow Shapley's definition "The Common
Breath of Humanity" (p. 122) belongs to this type. Shapley is not

trying to make us understand what a breath of air means chemically, or physiologically, but instead what it means to *him:* to him it means that we, and all the other breathing creatures past and present, are united by our dependence on the same air.

Subjective definition is not in opposition to objective. It would be pointless to call one true and the other false. They simply have different intentions. If we ever knew any X completely, we would discover that its total meaning consists of what it has meant to anybody and everybody, here and now as well as in every other time and place—the sum of all public and private experiences of it. In practice, our understanding of X is limited to the accepted public interpretations plus whatever private interpretations we are fortunate enough to be able to add. Both types enlarge our understanding of the world. Objective definition draws on the common perceptions that make us all human beings; subjective definition draws on the separate perceptions that make us individuals.

Occasionally the two types of definition coincide. When one person's private experience happens to be typical of everybody else's, the objective and subjective presentations, which normally run separate and parallel, merge. Greer (p. 94) explains what the female stereotype is (a public definition) and also her revulsion at that stereotype (a private response). Insofar as revulsion is the typical reaction among women, perhaps among men also, subjective definition enlarges toward objective, and she establishes not only what the female stereotype means to *her* but also what it means to many of us.

TECHNIQUES OF DEFINITION

How do you define something? It's usually not so easy as the finished product looks, but it's also not impossible. A good many time-tested techniques are available. We cannot divide every definition into a series of techniques, and it would not even be the best idea to try. Such an operation would wrongly imply that good writing is a patchwork quilt—here a formal dictionary definition, there two examples, next an analogy, all neatly stitched together. However, it does help to be aware of certain techniques that many writers have found useful so that you can see where, and how, and how well they work. No traditional technique of definition is inherently good or bad. Its value is always contextual—determined by whether it helps the writer do what he wants to at that particular time.

Formal Definition. A formal or lexical or dictionary definition consists of three parts: the word to be defined, the "genus" or "class term," and the "differentia" or "distinguishing terms." The class (that is, category) term relates X to other things by naming a larger category in which X belongs. This helps us to locate it in our previous universe of experience. The distinguishing terms separate it from other members of that category.

For example, a discussion of how a bimetallic strip in a thermostat works might include the statement that a bimetallic strip is *a short metal strip* (class term—now we know what sort of thing this is) *consisting of two different metals, bonded back-to-back* (distinguishing terms—now we know what makes this metal strip different from others). That example illustrates a useful formula:

$$X = \text{class term} + \text{distinguishing terms.}$$

Stewart (p. 162) defines a vulture's nest as *a broad and battered saucer* (class term, naming the category of shape to which X belongs) *of strong branches, topped with twigs and grass* (distinguishing terms, differentiating this saucer from others, which are normally made of china or plastic).

Occasionally the class term is self-evident, or has been made self-evident by previous parts of the discussion, and is therefore omitted. McMurtry (p. 76), having mentioned Satanta, does not need to tell us that this is an Indian leader (the class term), since he has been listing Indian leaders. He simply says Satanta, *the last great war chief of the Kiowa,* with that phrase functioning as the distinguishing term.

Formal definitions are useful especially in two situations: when X is totally unfamiliar, or when X is a familiar word being used in a new or special way. In the first case, we need the precision of formal definition to give us an initial understanding of what X is. In the second case, we also need it to give us a clear understanding of what X is not. Consider these examples:

1. An *argali* is a wild Asiatic sheep with unusually large horns.

2. A *bear* is someone who sells stocks and bonds in hopes of buying them back more cheaply later when their market price will have fallen.

In (*1*), most of us have no prior idea what the word "argali" means until the writer defines it. In (*2*), we almost certainly *do* have a prior idea what the word "bear" means—but, in this instance, that idea is irrelevant, and the formal definition helps to make it quite clear that for the moment a bear is *not* the large shaggy mammal we'd normally assume is meant. Without the formal definition, we might be confused by images of Smokey the Bear wandering around the New York Stock Exchange.

Illustration, or Definition by Example. Often the liveliest way to explain something is to give examples. Donald (p. 129) relies on a series of examples to explain the funny misuse of language called a "Spoonerism." E. B. White attempts to define democracy by a list of particular details:

We received a letter from the Writers' War Board the other day asking for a statement on "The Meaning of Democracy." It presumably is our duty to comply with such a request, and it is certainly our pleasure.

Surely the Board knows what democracy is. It is the line that forms on the right. It is the don't in Don't Shove. It is the hole in the stuffed shirt through which the sawdust slowly trickles; it is the dent in the high hat. Democracy is the recurrent suspicion that more than half of the people are right more than half of the time. It is the feeling of privacy in the voting booths, the feeling of communion in the libraries, the feeling of vitality everywhere. Democracy is the score at the beginning of the ninth. It is an idea that hasn't been disproved yet, a song the words of which have not gone bad. It's the mustard on the hot dog and the cream in the rationed coffee. Democracy is a request from a War Board, in the middle of a morning in the middle of a war, wanting to know what democracy is.[2]

White cites 13 examples to explain what democracy means to him (this is clearly a subjective definition). It would be easy enough to supply instead generalizations to correspond to these examples. "The line that forms on the right," for instance, suggests orderliness and cooperation, waiting your turn, as well as a system of priority based on when you get there, rather than on who you are. "The don't in Don't Shove" suggests restricting each person's freedom so that other people will not suffer. But White's presentation by means of illustrations is much more vivid—therefore, more dramatic—than such a list of generalizations would be.

A word of caution: when definition relies heavily on illustrations, it is usually advisable to state the common principle that underlies, and justifies, the illustrations. It might be said of White's "Democracy" statement, for instance, that the 13 separate items cited do not add up to a coherent whole. We know, to some extent, what it may be like to live in a democracy, but perhaps not what democracy *is*. For that, we still need a dictionary.

When in doubt, you can combine a formal definition with an example and have the best of both worlds—the logical clarity of the formal definition and the liveliness of the example. Here is Charlie Chaplin defining laughter (as Max Eastman recalls it):

"It seems to me," he said, "that there are two different kinds of laughter. Superficial laughter is an escape. The waiter comes in and the duck isn't cooked properly, and you pick it up and throw it at him— yes, and by God, he throws it back! That's an escape. It's a break in the monotony of normal conduct. That's superficial humor, slapstick. Subtle humor shows you that what you think is normal, isn't. This little tramp *wants* to get into jail. The audience thinks at first that he's ridiculous.

[2] From *The Wild Flag* (Houghton-Mifflin); Copyright © 1943 E. B. White. Originally in *The New Yorker*.

But he isn't. He's right. The conditions are ridiculous. If I make them laugh that way, it's what I call subtle laughter." [3]

That paragraph contains—unobtrusively, to be sure—the information for a formal definition and a definition by example, twice over. Let's take it just once over. We could rephrase the second half of the paragraph into a formal definition: subtle humor or subtle laughter (*X* to be defined) is *a form of comedy consisting of a funny incident* (class term) *that shows you that what you think is normal, isn't* (distinguishing term). We could then supply the example, the story of a little tramp who wants to get into jail, a story told in such a way that the audience gradually realizes that the tramp's enthusiasm for jail—not their distaste for it—is the right attitude. Charlie Chaplin's version, of course, is much more dramatic because it eliminates the obvious; once-over lightly is always more dramatic than once-over heavily.

Narration. Closely related to illustration, narration relies on a fuller development of one incident rather than the brief presentation of several. In order to do the work of definition, this single example must be very carefully controlled so that it will provide enough information of the right kind. It will need enough details to make us understand and care about *X*, but it must not be stuffed with extraneous material that would obscure the central issue, What is *X*? The best material for definition by means of narrative usually comes from our own experience, since we have all the information in mind and can therefore select the best possible data to dramatize the point. The human meaning of racial prejudice is made painfully clear by Elizabeth Eckford's narrative about the day that the guards and the mob kept her out of school (p. 127). The meaning of the 1969 moon landing (p. 103) is explained by narratives that recreate what happened and who said what, when, and where.

Narration is one of the most appealing of techniques. It has the intrinsic charm of fiction since it consists, quite simply, of a well-told story. The risk is that the story may not adequately clarify *X:* it may suggest too many meanings or perhaps none at all. To guard against this kind of failure, you can give your narrative a preface or an epilogue in which you explicitly define *X* by means of some other technique. Even so, you will have only a story and an artificially grafted-on "moral" unless the two fit naturally together.

Comparison and Contrast. Sometimes *X* is meaningful not so much in itself but in relation to other things and is best presented by showing how it resembles and differs from them. A description of the modern change in sexual mores, for instance, would need to com-

---

[3] Charlie Chaplin, quoted by Max Eastman, *Enjoyment of Laughter* (New York: Halcyon House, 1939), pp. 107–108.

pare current practices with previous ones or else we could not assess the "change." Hayakawa's essay on the kinds of statements people make (p. 136) depends on his ability to demonstrate how reports, inferences, and judgments, though superficially similar, are essentially different. Altick (p. 146) compares two types of connotation: personal and general.

The traditional name of "comparison and contrast" given to this technique of juxtaposing one thing with another suggests that there can be two emphases: comparison emphasizes the resemblance, contrast the difference. But the two are mutually reinforcing, since knowing the extent of the overlap between X and Y enables us to see the importance of the areas in which they do not overlap. A Manx cat is almost completely like any other cat—except at the end.

Analogy. When something is either totally unfamiliar to us or else so overfamiliar that we have no distinct awareness of it, it can often be clarified by analogy. Analogy is a particular type of comparison in which the two things compared are really quite different, but share some similarity that is useful to point out. Above, a written definition was compared to an automobile. Although different in almost every way, both exist in order to perform a task efficiently and conveniently, and their task is to take us from here to there. Hayakawa (p. 136) uses an analogy between a map and language; what they have in common—all that they have in common—is that both guide us through experience. Death is sometimes presented as if it were an extended sleep. It is not, but both states seem to share a peculiar unawareness of the body's surroundings. Orwell, describing pretentious speech (p. 522), says that a "mass of Latin words falls upon the facts like soft snow, blurring the outlines and covering up all the details." Words are hardly snow, but both can blot out reality's distinctness. Similarly, Orwell describes bad writing as consisting of conventional phrases "tacked together like the sections of a prefabricated hen-house" (p. 517). Cleaver draws an analogy between the Trinity and 3-in-1 oil (p. 363).

If it is going to help, an analogy must be something we are already acquainted with or can easily imagine (otherwise, it merely adds mystery to mystery). But it must not be something we are weary of (or we will not pay attention). To present death as if it were sleep is probably useful only to children, for whom that analogy is new. Orwell's hen-house analogy works because we have all seen a hen-house, or can easily imagine one, but we have not already wearied of thinking of language in that way. The dangers in using analogy, then, are obscurity and triteness.

Division and Classification. When the subject is complicated, it is often useful to divide it into parts, classify the parts according to some principle such as simple-to-complex or small-to-large, and then discuss each in turn. Thus, Stewart (p. 163) divides "vulture country" into what he sees as the three necessary parts of the idea:

> There are three essential qualities for vulture country: a rich supply of unburied corpses, high mountains, a strong sun. Spain has the first of these, for in this sparsely populated and stony land it is not customary, or necessary, to bury dead animals. Where there are vultures in action such burials would be a self-evident waste of labor, with inferior sanitary results. Spain has mountains, too, in no part far to seek; and the summer sun is hot throughout the country. But it is hottest in Andalusia, and that is the decisive factor.

Stewart uses this technique of analysis again (p. 164) in explaining how high a vulture will soar on a particular day: "His ceiling for this day is fixed by two factors. One is the strength and buoyancy of his chosen thermal. . . . But the more important factor, for it fixes his horizontal bearings as well, is the distribution of neighboring vultures in the sky, his colleagues and competitors."

An overuse of this technique can produce writing that sounds mechanical, unimaginative, anything but dramatic—a mere listing of parts ("there are two main types . . . there are four factors . . . there may be three reasons . . ." and so on). But division and classification need not be deadening if it is used occasionally as a means of organizing information rather than simply as an announcement.

Analysis of Causes or Effects. When X is scarcely known in itself, or is not of particular interest in itself, what we may really care about are its causes or its effects. At times, knowing the causes of something would permit us to control it. If we really understood the causes of crime, prejudice, and other social evils, we might be able to rid ourselves of them. McCarthy, in her examination of names (p. 156), is less interested in names themselves, which are simply words, than in their psychological impact on children, who equate their names with their identities.

Functional Definition. At times, the most important way to clarify the nature of X, as the writer sees it, is to explain its function: what it does, or what it is used for. Here is Percy Marks' definition of punctuation:

> Punctuation properly used is an analysis of thought. In effect, the writer says to the reader, "These commas indicate that this matter is parenthetical; this semicolon indicates that the thought in my first clause balances the thought in my second clause; this colon indicates that the clauses preceding it are equal in my mind to whatever may succeed it," and so forth. Only with punctuation can the writer make clear to the reader what one part of his sentence means to another part. . . .[4]

---

[4] Percy Marks, *The Craft of Writing* (New York: Harcourt Brace, 1932), p. 75.

Marks could also have defined punctuation by using division and classification: punctuation consists of commas, semicolons, colons, periods, and so forth. However, that would be telling us the obvious. The new information he has to tell us, the information that justifies one more definition of punctuation, concerns what he sees as punctuation's function: a signal from writer to reader about the logical relationships of parts of ideas.

A *negative functional definition* specifies what *X* does *not* do. "Far be it from God, that he should do wickedness," says the Bible (Job 34:10); almost by definition, it is the function of God to do good.

Two final suggestions. First, when you define something, keep the subject within bounds. (An old joke runs: "Define the universe and give two examples.") Second, don't be surprised if your effort to define what you mean seems to produce changes in the thing itself. When you begin, you will be starting with what you *think* you mean, but as you look closely—gathering the evidence, weighing the value of major and minor points, analyzing and classifying and comparing —you may discover that your first ideas about *X* no longer seem accurate. Writing is a gradual process of coming closer and closer to the essence of things. Most of the best writers keep revising and revising, and to revise means both to rewrite and to re-*see*. If each time you re-see, you see more and more clearly, then change will be progress. You may discover, as Alice did (to come back to Lewis Carroll), that what you at first thought was a most disagreeable baby is, in fact, a perfectly agreeable piglet. "It would have made a dreadfully ugly child," Alice remarks, "but it makes rather a handsome pig."

In the following readings you will find children and pigs, rifles and roadrunners, homing fish and whirling dervishes, even a well-boiled icicle. None of these pieces was written, by the way, solely as an example of definition. All were written because their authors had something to say, information they wanted to share, or—as Julian Huxley puts it—because "it is one of the duties and privileges of man to testify to his experience, to bear witness to the wonder and variety of the world in which he finds himself." [5]

---

[5] Julian Huxley, *From an Antique Land* (London: Max Parrish, 1954), p. 303.

series one

DEFINITION: READINGS WITH COMMENTARY

---

dadaism:
a definition

KARL BECKSON
AND ARTHUR GANZ

This short definition is an entry from a handbook. In fewer than 200
words, the authors offer a dictionary definition of their subject, an explanation of the peculiar name "dada," a list of general characteristics
(typical activities of followers of Dadaism), two illustrations, and finally a
quick summary of the rise and fall of this World War I protest movement.

How effective is this combination of techniques of definition?

1   **d**adaism: Founded by Tristan Tzara in Zurich during World War I,
Dadaism was a nihilistic movement in art and literature which protested
against logic, restraint, social convention, and literature itself. (Though
some Dadaists claimed that the word *dada* was selected arbitrarily, the
term is also believed to have expressed what the members of the group
wanted in literature and art—masculinity—instead of femininity, *dada* as
opposed to *mama*.)

2   To demonstrate their contempt for civilization, they painted shocking
pictures, wrote nonsensical poems, and arranged bizarre theatrical presentations in theaters and cabarets. One of [the group's] members, Marcel
Duchamps, sent a toilet bowl to be exhibited at a sculpture show in Paris,
but it was returned promptly. Hugo Ball, having composed a "sound

Source. Reprinted with the permission of Farrar, Straus & Giroux, Inc. from *A Reader's
Guide to Literary Terms* by Karl Beckson and Arthur Ganz, Copyright © 1970 by the
Noonday Press.

poem," read it in a cabaret while dressed with blue cardboard on his legs, a movable scarlet collar, and a blue-and-white-striped top hat. It begins "gadji beri bimba/glandridi lauli lonni cadori," but becomes less clear as it proceeds.

3   Dadaism, flamboyant and self-conscious, spread to Germany, Holland, France, Italy, and Spain but waned shortly after the end of the war.

COMMENTARY

In offering a brief definition of any unfamiliar X, a writer can choose to develop one technique of definition fully, or to combine several. When X is an unfamiliar word, as here, it is natural to begin with a formal definition (see p. 26) so that we can feel comfortable with the word itself before trying to see how it fits into our world. (You can test this statement by covering up the first sentence of the "Dadaism" article and seeing whether the rest is then more difficult to follow.) Since a dictionary definition rarely requires more than one sentence, it leaves space, even within a very short writing opportunity, for another approach to X, or for several.

The development in this case is from general to specific and then to general again. (Compare this technique with that of a cameraman who moves up close to his subject and then further away again.) Paragraph 1 has supplied a formal definition to explain the word "dada." Paragraph 2 begins with a statement of the general aim of the Dadaists: "to demonstrate their contempt for civilization." It then lists their typical activities. These generalizations, while accurate enough, might leave Dadaism rather vague, hence the paragraph then becomes more specific. We are told about Duchamps' toilet bowl and shown what Ball looked like reading his "sound poem," the first two lines of which we are permitted to hear. These two illustrations function to make our understanding of Dadaism vivid enough that the writer can then return to the general statements which cover ground rapidly. The final sentence summarizes the movement's characteristics, names five countries involved, and suggests the participation of many people over several years.

SUGGESTION FOR WRITING

You have been asked to explain, very briefly, some group to which you belong or some activity in which you participate. In 200 words or less, define your subject, using a formal definition (see p. 26) and then one or more other techniques. Examples: your grandmother, having learned that you belong to a rock music group, wants to know what that is; your younger brother asks you what a botany field trip is; you need to tell a prospective employer what your job last summer—as a recreation supervisor or a pharmacist's aide—involved. Or if you have made a definite career choice, define that career: what exactly does someone in "forestry," "pre-law," or "learning-disability therapy" do?

going to
the feelies

This short description of a device is based on a pattern that is also useful
for longer and more complete descriptions. Its first two paragraphs are
an introduction, which links this device to an earlier science-fiction
version (to show that the idea has been around for some time) and
then provides factual background about its development. Paragraphs
3 to 5 describe the parts of the device and then what it does (the
scientific principle involved is that a curve of any shape can be expressed
as an algebraic equation for a computer to read). The last paragraph
looks toward the future development of the device and summarizes
its purpose: "to make illusions tangible."

1   **t**he compulsive sybarites of Aldous Huxley's *Brave New World* were
    entertained by the "Feelies," which added a third sensory channel to the
    "talkies," themselves a recent innovation when the novel was published
    in 1932. In Huxley's Utopia one had only to grasp a metal globe to be
    tactually a party to sexual intercourse on a bearskin rug, "every hair of
    which . . . could be separately and distinctly felt."

2   A first tentative step toward the technology of the Feelies has been
    made by Michael Noll of the Bell Laboratories. For his doctoral disserta-
    tion at the Polytechnic Institute of New York, Noll designed and built a
    "tactile simulation device" that enables one to feel the contours of objects
    that exist only as mathematical concepts.

3   Noll's device consists of a large box with a stalk protruding through
    the top. The box is connected to a computer, and the stalk is fitted with a
    knob about the size of a billiard ball, which the user holds. When the
    machine is off or unprogrammed, the knob moves freely in all directions
    anywhere within a one-foot cube of space. The computer is programmed
    by entering an equation or a series of equations that describe the object
    to be simulated; once the program is established, the motion of the knob
    is limited by the boundaries of the object. When the knob touches the
    imaginary form, it slides along its surface or bounces off it, as it would
    if the object were real. By moving the knob throughout its range of
    excursion one can explore the entire surface of the mathematically con-
    structed form.

4   Inside the machine are three electric motors and three potentiometers;
    each controls the motion and senses the position of the knob on one of
    three axes. The computer continuously calculates the distance of the knob
    on each axis from the center of the empty cube. When the knob "touches"
    the edge of the object being simulated, the computer applies power to the

motors in such a way that the appropriate resistance or rebound is perceived.

5   When the machine is operated with the eyes closed, Noll says, the simulated three-dimensional object can be visualized. He suggests that one possible application of the device, which would take advantage of this capability, would be as an aid to the blind.

6   The present machine simulates tactile perception of the gross features of objects, of what would be felt by moving the hand and arm. It may be possible, Noll believes, to build a more sophisticated device that would also simulate what is felt by the palm and fingertips. Such a machine would provide a sense of texture as well as contour and would more closely approach the aim of the Feelies: to make illusions tangible.

COMMENTARY

In this short description—about 450 words—the writer cannot say everything he knows about the "Feelie" machine. Neither does he *want* to say everything. Since the device is still under development and not available to the public, it would be useless to most readers if he recorded every detail of Noll's "first tentative step." Therefore, two ideas are singled out: what the device can do for us and how, in a general way, it performs that function. This is the important information for us to know.

What X can do is suggested (only half seriously) at the beginning and again (seriously) at the end; how it works occupies most of the description's middle paragraphs.

SUGGESTION FOR WRITING

Write a brief description of a "quibilar"—a creature you have just discovered or a device you are in the process of inventing. Follow the pattern above (introduction to provide background, description of the quibilar's appearance and action, conclusion looking toward the future). Emphasize information that dramatizes your discovery: information that helps your readers see what the quibilar looks like (they should be able to recognize one if they meet one), and how it fits into their world (they should know what to do with or about it if they recognize one).

a charge of the camel-men

T. E. LAWRENCE

T. E. Lawrence was called "Lawrence of Arabia" because he was one of the few Westerners who knew Arabia well at the time of World War I and because he led Arab bands in revolt against their Turkish masters. This short section from one of his war chronicles is a description of an event, a downhill charge of soldiers mounted on camels. It is remarkable for its ability to capture the excitement of the moment in few words and for its blend of objective and subjective ingredients. Lawrence seems able both to record his subjective responses and to describe himself objectively as if he were someone else observing his own behavior.

Notice the twist at the end. Why is that information withheld?

Notice also the way the camel functions as a unifying device. Any attempt to describe a dramatic event very briefly must leave out many aspects and focus on only one or two; Lawrence focuses on himself and the animal he rides.

1   We rode all night, and when dawn came were dismounting on the crest of the hills between Batra and Aba el Lissan, with a wonderful view westwards over the green and gold Guweira plain, and beyond it to the ruddy mountains hiding Akaba and the sea. Gasim abu Dumeik, head of the Dhumaniyeh, was waiting anxiously for us, surrounded by his hard-bitten tribesmen, their grey strained faces flecked with the blood of the fighting yesterday. There was a deep greeting for Auda and Nasir. We made hurried plans, and scattered to the work, knowing we could not go forward to Akaba with this battalion in possession of the pass. Unless we dislodged it, our two months' hazard and effort would fail before yielding even first-fruits. . . .

2   The Arabs passed before us into a little sunken place, which rose to a low crest; and we knew that the hill beyond went down in a facile slope to the main valley of Aba el Lissan, somewhat below the spring. All our four hundred camel men were here tightly collected, just out of sight of the enemy. We rode to their head, and asked the Shimt what it was and where the horsemen had gone.

3   He pointed over the ridge to the next valley above us, and said, 'With Auda there': and as he spoke yells and shots poured up in a sudden torrent from beyond the crest. We kicked our camels furiously to the edge, to see our fifty horsemen coming down the last slope into the main valley like a run-away, at full gallop, shooting from the saddle. As we watched, two or three went down, but the rest thundered forward at

Source. Excerpts from *The Seven Pillars of Wisdom* by T. E. Lawrence. Copyright 1926, 1935 by Doubleday & Co., Inc. Used by permission of the publishers, Jonathan Cape, Ltd., and the Seven Pillars Trust.

marvellous speed, and the Turkish infantry, huddled together under the cliff ready to cut their desperate way out towards Maan, in the first dusk began to sway in and out, and finally broke before the rush, adding their flight to Auda's charge.

4   Nasir screamed at me, 'Come on', with his bloody mouth; and we plunged our camels madly over the hill, and down towards the head of the fleeing enemy. The slope was not too steep for a camel-gallop, but steep enough to make their pace terrific, and their course uncontrollable: yet the Arabs were able to extend to right and left and to shoot into the Turkish brown. The Turks had been too bound up in the terror of Auda's furious charge against their rear to notice us as we came over the eastward slope: so we also took them by surprise and in the flank; and a charge of ridden camels going nearly thirty miles an hour was irresistible.

5   My camel, the Sherari racer, Naama, stretched herself out, and hurled downhill with such might that we soon out-distanced the others. The Turks fired a few shots, but mostly only shrieked and turned to run: the bullets they did send at us were not very harmful, for it took much to bring a charging camel down in a dead heap.

6   I had got among the first of them, and was shooting, with a pistol of course, for only an expert could use a rifle from such plunging beasts; when suddenly my camel tripped and went down emptily upon her face, as though pole-axed. I was torn completely from the saddle, sailed grandly through the air for a great distance, and landed with a crash which seemed to drive all the power and feeling out of me. I lay there, passively waiting for the Turks to kill me, continuing to hum over the verses of a half-forgotten poem, whose rhythm something, perhaps the prolonged stride of the camel, had brought back to my memory as we leaped down the hill-side:

For Lord I was free of all Thy flowers, but I chose the world's sad roses,
And that is why my feet are torn and mine eyes are blind with sweat.

While another part of my mind thought what a squashed thing I should look when all that cataract of men and camels had poured over.

7   After a long time I finished my poem, and no Turks came, and no camel trod on me: a curtain seemed taken from my ears: there was a great noise in front. I sat up and saw the battle over, and our men driving together and cutting down the last remnants of the enemy. My camel's body had lain behind me like a rock and divided the charge into two streams: and in the back of its skull was the heavy bullet of the fifth shot I fired.

COMMENTARY

Many essays answer the question, What is X? by explaining how X looks (description) or how X works (explanation of a process). But when X is an event, most writers transform the question into What actually happened? and answer it with a narrative.

Lawrence first sets the scene: it is the moment of a surprise attack on the Turkish infantry by two units of Arabs—50 cavalrymen and 400 camel-men. Among the camel-men is Lawrence himself. He focuses on his personal experience: his own camel, the charge, his sensations when the animal falls. Afterward, in paragraph 7, he gives us the surprising explanation of what happened.

So many things happen so quickly in any violent event that you may have trouble capturing it in words. You may put in superfluous details or waste words on matters of secondary importance. Notice how Lawrence unifies his description by drawing our attention to camels again and again. Even the poem he remembers has the rhythm of a camel's stride. In paragraph 7 we see why he does this instead of concentrating, for example, on the desert setting or on the Arab or Turkish soldiers. Ironically, his racing camel, which he prized for its vitality, saved his life by its death—at his own hands.

SUGGESTIONS FOR WRITING

1. Describe a violent event (auto accident, fire in the kitchen, riot) as briefly as you can. Imitate Lawrence's device of singling out one crucial element in the event and keeping your reader's attention on it.

2. Write a short narrative using Lawrence's surprise pattern: recount what happened and at the end identify the cause. Your purpose is to take your readers through the same sequence of event-and-explanation that you yourself experienced.

what is a rifle?
JACK O'CONNOR

This definition of a class of items appears at the beginning of a book on rifles. The author defines his subject here in preparation for a more detailed analysis in subsequent chapters. His aim is thoroughly functional— he must make his definition of *X* perfectly clear; but his attention to "mere" detail also conveys his fascination with rifles. As he says in the introduction to the book, "I like a handgun. I hold a shotgun in high regard; but rifles—well, I love the darned things."

1 **m**ost readers of this book already know what a rifle is, but I suspect that any one of them would have to pause and consider if he was asked to give an airtight definition.

Source. From *The Rifle Book,* Second Edition, Revised, by Jack O'Connor Copyright 1949, © 1964 by Jack O'Connor. Reprinted by permission of Alfred A. Knopf, Inc.

2   Suppose he said: "It is a weapon with a rifled barrel." How would that be? Not very good. There are many weapons with rifled barrels besides those we commonly know as rifles—cannon used in the field, on airplanes, and on ships of war; heavy and light machine guns; the so-called submachine guns; even pistols and revolvers.

3   So let us work out a definition here.

4   *A rifle is a firearm with a rifled barrel, designed to fire one projectile at a time and to be operated by one man from the shoulder and with the use of both hands.*

5   That definition is fairly inclusive. It rules out shotguns, even though a few shotguns have been manufactured with rifled muzzles to spread the shot pattern, because shotguns shoot from a few large buckshot to several hundred small birdshot at a time. Actually, however, a British Paradox or other gun with a rifled muzzle is in fact a rifle when it is used with a conical bullet or a round ball. Our definition also rules out pistols and revolvers, since they are designed as one-hand firearms. Machine guns have rifled barrels, but they are operated by a crew of from two to several men. We might also try making our definition a bit tighter by saying that a rifle can be fired but once for each time the trigger is pressed, because no truly automatic *rifle* has ever been manufactured. Possibly this would be a wise addition to our definition, since the submachine gun or machine pistol fills all other requirements for the rifle except that it fires automatically. . . .

6   The typical feature of all rifles is, of course, the barrel, into which spiral grooves known as "rifling" have been cut. Barrels are a piece of steel with grooves cut to impart spin to a bullet. . . .

7   The barrel is the very heart and core of the rifle. It is from the barrel that the rifle gets its name. Important though it is, however, the barrel is but one part of the rifle.

8   In order to function, the barrel must be screwed into an *action,* which supports the rear of the cartridge and which causes it to fire through the trigger and firing-pin mechanism. The action may be repeating or single-shot, but at the present time few single-shot actions are made. It may be operated by a lever, of which the trigger guard is part, as in the Winchester, Marlin, and Savage lever-action rifles. It may be operated by a bolt, as with all Mauser-type actions, with the Savage sporter actions, and the many seen on .22 rifles and on various military rifles. A slide-handle may be the means of inserting fresh cartridges and ejecting fired cases, as in the Remington line of pump- or "trombone"-action high-power rifles and in .22 repeating rifles manufactured by almost all American makers.

9   In addition, semiautomatic, self-loading or autoloading mechanisms are manufactured in calibers from the tiny .22 to the powerful .30/06. In that case the rifleman needs only to pull the trigger. The mechanism ejects the fired case, inserts a new cartridge, and cocks the firing pin. All "automatic" .22 rifles, the Winchester self-loading big-game rifles (.32, .35, .351, and .401), and the Remington autoloading rifle in .30 and .35

Remington rimless are operated in one way or another by recoil. The Johnson semiautomatic rifle is also recoil-operated.

10   Every rifle must have a barrel, an action, and also a stock. Lever- and pump-action rifles have two-piece stocks; so do single-shot rifles like the Winchester 85, the Stevens 44 and 44½, and the former Stevens Walnut Hill line, the Sharps Borchardt. The Remington pump and autoloading high-power rifles have two-piece stocks, and so do some .22 self-loading rifles. All things being equal, the one-piece stock is the most satisfactory, since it supports barrel and action and welds the whole rifle together. However, the actions that are held to the butt stock by a long strong bolt as in the Savage 99 actions and some of the single-shots compare very favorably with the bolt actions for accuracy.

THE CLASSIFICATION OF RIFLES

11   Here I might as well explain some of the various terms used in relation to rifles. Among the most common are "small bore" and its opposite, "big bore." In the United States the term "small bore" usually refers to the .22 rim-fire caliber. Indeed, an official small-bore match is always a .22 match. For sporting purposes the term is extended to include rifles of .25 caliber. A rifle that is anywhere from .22 to .25 may legitimately be called "small bore." The "big bore" rifle, in the United States anyway, can refer to anything from a .270 up to .375 Magnum or .45/70 but official big-bore matches are fired with rifles using the .30/06 cartridge, which is the government military rifle cartridge.

12   Rifles can also be classified by their use. A "small game rifle" for use on edible game animals like cottontails and squirrels is always a .22 light enough to be portable as compared with the very heavy target .22's, which often weigh ten or eleven pounds. The term "deer rifle" usually refers to a light rifle of medium power to be used on deer at short and medium ranges. Such a rifle is the Model 141 Remington pump in .30 Remington caliber, the Model 99 Savage in .250/3000, or the Model 94 Winchester for the .30/30 cartridge. The term "big game rifle" usually refers to a rifle to be used on animals larger than deer at longer ranges. Such a term can apply to the .30/06, the .270, or the .348 Winchester Model 71.

13   "Varmint rifle" refers to a specialized rifle to be used at relatively long ranges on inedible pests like jackrabbits, woodchucks, prairie dogs, crows, and harmful hawks. Varmint rifles are usually chambered for cartridges which drive light bullets at high velocity so that the explosive effect of the bullet will make one-shot kills even though the game is badly torn up and also so that these bullets will disintegrate when they hit the ground and not be dangerous in thickly settled farming country, where varmints are so often hunted. Often varmint rifles are made quite heavy and use scopes of 6-X or even higher because precise aim must be taken at small marks rather far away. The term "bull gun" simply means a target rifle with an especially

heavy barrel. A bull gun will weigh twelve to fifteen pounds. It is used only on the range and is not carried as is a hunting rifle.

COMMENTARY

There is nothing particularly elegant about the style of this article. The author handles language the same way a gunsmith might handle a rifle: as a relatively simple mechanism designed for accuracy. It is as if the article were produced at a workbench rather than a desk. A perfectionist might point out that there is a certain clumsiness in the question and answer of paragraph 2, and that where precision is not essential, approximation suffices, as in paragraph 6, where barrels are defined as "a piece of steel," shape unspecified, grammatical agreement ignored.

But the article "works." O'Connor proceeds methodically from definition to a presentation of the crucial parts and then two classifications: one by size, the other by function. The roll call of names conveys authority and, for some readers, drama: the Stevens Walnut Hill line, the Sharps Borchardt, Savage 99, Model 94 Winchester, .375 Magnum. All in all, it's a respectable job. We certainly know what a rifle is; and we know, in addition, that the author is full of enthusiasm for his subject. This is not to say that all of us necessarily share that enthusiasm. People who dislike guns will not have their minds changed by this article. They can still learn from it, however, and one of the things they can learn is how the mind of a gun-lover works.

OUTLINE

    I. Introduction: the problem of definition—paragraphs 1–2
    II. Definition—paragraphs 3–5
   III. Parts of a rifle
      A. Barrel—paragraphs 6–7
      B. Action—paragraphs 8–9
      C. Stock—paragraph 10
   IV. Classification
      A. Bore size—paragraph 11
      B. Function—paragraphs 12–13

SUGGESTIONS FOR WRITING

1. Define a category of items that you understand, for example subcompact cars, exceptional children, grospoint needlework, or organically grown vegetables. Differentiate your *X* from related ones (subcompact from compact cars, exceptional children from normal, etc.), discuss its major characteristics, and identify and classify the smaller units within the category (like O'Connor's types of rifles) if there are any. Your purpose is to make sure that your readers will never confuse an *X* with anything else—or one type of *X* with another.

2. Define an imaginary ideal *X* as if it were real. Imagine, for example, the ideal chair, or motorcycle, or pizza, or country cabin. Relate it to existing items of the same general type (as O'Connor begins by setting a rifle among other firearms), and then differentiate it, that is, identify its special characteristics, unique parts, and so forth. Try to be so specific that someone could make it for you (assuming that he could obtain the materials).

the costume
of women in mostar
REBECCA WEST

We often need to describe, and understand, objects we see around us— from shoes and ships to sealing wax, from cabbages to kings (to paraphrase Lewis Carroll).

Traveling through Yugoslavia, Rebecca West noticed that the women of the town of Mostar wore an extraordinary garment, a costume "idiotically unpractical," apparently owing its existence to the attitudes of the local people rather than to any functional characteristics. West first describes what the Mostar women wore and then offers her interpretation of this strange costume.

1   **t**he traditional Mostar costume for women consists of a man's coat, made in black or blue cloth, immensely too large for the woman who is going to wear it. It is cut with a stiff military collar, very high, perhaps as much as eight or ten inches, which is embroidered inside, not outside, with gold thread. It is never worn as a coat. The woman slips it over her, drawing the shoulders above her head, so that the stiff collar falls forward and projects in front of her like a visor, and she can hide her face if she clutches the edges together, so that she need not wear a veil. The sleeves are allowed to hang loose or are stitched together at the back, but nothing can be done with the skirts, which drag on the ground.

2   We asked the people in the hotel and several tradesmen in Mostar, and a number of Moslems in other places, whether there was any local legend which accounted for this extraordinary garment, for it seemed it must commemorate some occasion when a woman had disguised herself in her husband's coat in order to perform an act of valour. But if there was ever such a legend it has been forgotten. The costume may have some value as a badge of class, for it could be worn with comfort and cleanli-

ness only by a woman of the leisured classes, who need not go out save when she chooses. It would be most inconvenient in wet weather or on rough ground, and a woman could not carry or lead a child while she was wearing it. But perhaps it survives chiefly by its poetic value, by its symbolic references to the sex it clothes.

3   It has the power of a dream or a work of art that has several interpretations, that explains several aspects of reality at one and the same time. First and most obviously the little woman in the tall man's coat presents the contrast between man and woman at its most simple and playful, as the contrast between heaviness and lightness, between coarseness and fragility, between that which breaks and that which might be broken but is instead preserved and cherished, for the sake of tenderness and joy. It makes man and woman seem as father and daughter. The little girl is wearing her father's coat and laughs at him from the depths of it, she pretends that it is a magic garment and that she is invisible and can hide from him. Its dimensions favour this fantasy. The Herzegovinian* is tall, but not such a giant as this coat was made to fit. I am barely five-foot-four and my husband is close on six-foot-two, but when I tried on his overcoat in this fashion the hem was well above my ankles; yet the Mostar garment trails about its wearer's feet.

4   But it presents the female also in a more sinister light: as the male sees her when he fears her. The dark visor gives her the beak of a bird of prey, and the flash of gold thread within the collar suggests private and ensnaring delights. A torch is put to those fires of the imagination which need for fuel dreams of pain, annihilation, and pleasure. The austere yet lubricious beauty of the coat gives a special and terrifying emphasis to the meaning inherent in all these Eastern styles of costume which hide women's faces. That meaning does not relate directly to sexual matters; it springs from a state of mind more impersonal, even metaphysical, though primitive enough to be sickening. The veil perpetuates and renews a moment when man, being in league with death, like all creatures that must die, hated his kind for living and transmitting life, and hated woman more than himself, because she is the instrument of birth, and put his hand to the floor to find filth and plastered it on her face, to affront the breath of life in her nostrils. There is about all veiled women a sense of melancholy quite incommensurate with the inconveniences they themselves may be suffering. Even when, like the women of Mostar, they seem to be hastening towards secret and luxurious and humorous love-making, they hint of a general surrender to mortality, a futile attempt of the living to renounce life.

COMMENTARY

West begins with an objective description of the Mostar women's garment (paragraph 1). She then moves (paragraphs 2 to 4) to her subjective explanation of the "poetic value," the "symbolic references" which

* [Herzegovina is a region in Yugoslavia; Mostar is a town in that region—Eds.]

she decides must be responsible, if not for the costume's origin, at least for its survival. These symbolic references are of two kinds: suggestions of playfulness, fragility, and tenderness associated with women (paragraph 3) and "more sinister" suggestions of fear, pain, and hatred of women (paragraph 4). The garment that women wear in the male-dominated society of Mostar thus reflects, West believes, the contradictory attitudes of men—both the male appreciation of woman as a pretty little plaything and the male resentment of woman as "the instrument of birth," the mother of new life.

OUTLINE

I. Description of the garment—paragraph 1
II. Absence of a rational explanation—paragraph 2
III. The symbolic function of the garment
    A. Appreciation of woman as child—paragraph 3
    B. Resentment of woman as mother—paragraph 4

SUGGESTIONS FOR WRITING

1. Using West's pattern (beginning with objective definition and moving into subjective interpretation), consider some current American costume and its meaning. For example: "In America, the most common garment for young women, especially those who are college students, is the type of trousers called 'blue jeans.' These trousers fit almost skintight from the hips to the knees, and then may be cut straight or else flare slightly to the ankles. They are made of dark blue denim, which is a heavy, twill-woven, rather stiff fabric otherwise used mostly for working-men's garments such as the overalls of farmers, and for similar 'blue jeans' worn by young men" (etc.).

2. Examine the costumes worn at an earlier period, perhaps when your parents or grandparents were your age. You might look at family photographs, back issues of newspapers or magazines in the library, old Sears catalogues, old paintings, a book about the history of costume, and so forth. For example, during the Victorian period (the latter half of the nineteenth century and the first few years of the twentieth), "respectable" women usually wore garments that concealed their natural shapes and covered virtually all skin except that on the hands and face. What does such a style imply? Describe an earlier style and interpret its meaning.

3. Apply West's pattern of description to some aspect of our lives other than clothing (household furnishings, cars, recreation equipment, "labor-saving" devices, whiskey-bottle shapes, etc.). Move from a brief objective definition into subjective interpretation. "Most middle-class homes in America have at least one television, an electronic device that provides instant audio-visual entertainment" (etc.).

the roadrunner

This selection offers two definitions of a living thing: a technical identification and an informal description, both of the bird called the roadrunner.

The ornithologist's technical account (taken from a field guide) differs from the informal description in a number of ways. One is length. The technical account is kept very brief. Another is intention. Readers consult a field guide in order to be able to identify a bird. Thus the technical description divides into "field marks," "voice," and "range," so that we will know what to look for and in what likely places.

Hollister's informal description (from a popular journal), though somewhat fuller, is also brief, with short sentences and paragraphs that create a "staccato" rhythm. How much more do we learn about roadrunners here than in the technical field guide? If the answer is "not much," then what is the purpose of Hollister's account?

the cuckoo family, the roadrunner species
ROGER TORY PETERSON

1   **b**irds of this family are slender, long-tailed. Feet zygodactyl (2 toes forward, 2 behind). Sexes usually similar. Our cuckoos are slim, brown above, whitish below. Roadrunners are large streaked cuckoos that travel on the ground. Anis are loose-jointed and slender, coal-black, with deep, high-ridged bills. **Food:** Caterpillars, other insects. Anis may eat seeds, fruits, grasshoppers; roadrunners eat insects, reptiles, etc. **Range:** Nearly all warm and temperate parts of world. **No. of species:** World, 128; West, 4 (+1 accidental).

ROADRUNNER *Geococcyx Californianus*

2   **Field marks:** A cuckoo that runs on the ground (tracks show 2 toes forward, 2 backward). Slender, heavily streaked; long, maneuverable, white-tipped tail, shaggy crest, strong legs. In flight the short rounded wings display a white crescent.

Voice: Song, 6–8 dovelike *coo*'s descending in pitch (last note about pitch of Mourning Dove). The bird makes a clattering noise by rolling mandibles together.
Where found: Sw. U.S. (east to e. Oklahoma, nw. Louisiana); south to c. Mexico. **West:** *Resident* from n. Californa (n. Sacramento Valley), s. Nevada, s. Utah, c. Colorado, sw. Kansas south. **Habitat:** Open country with scattered cover, stony deserts, dry brush, open piñon-juniper. **Nest:** A shallow saucer in bush, cactus, low tree. Eggs (3–8; 12) white.

with legs like these...
who needs wings?

GEORGE E. HOLLISTER

1   **h**e's half tail and half feet. The rest of him is head and beak. When he runs, he moves on blurring wheels. He can turn on a dime and leave change. He doesn't need to fly because he can run faster. He kicks dirt in a snake's face, and then eats the snake. He chases lizards, and watches hawks with one eye.

2   He's "Meep-meep" and a cartoon favorite of three generations. He's an odd bird, but a real one—the roadrunner.

3   Early southwestern settlers were surprised to see a wildly colored bird dart onto a trail, race ahead of a lone horse and rider, slide to a dusty halt and then bob and bow in salute. Scientists later labeled him *Geococcyx californianus,* a member of the cuckoo family, but settlers aptly named him "roadrunner."

4   Because of his foot structure, Indians of the Southwest believed he had special power. His toes form an X, with two pointed forward and two backward. This arrangement held special meaning to the Indians, who scratched duplicate X figures near new graves and, for extra protection from evil spirits, decorated infant cradleboards with roadrunner feathers.

5   The footprint X's are unique in a more concrete way—they show the roadrunner may take 22-inch strides in high gear. He's been clocked at fifteen miles per hour (the rate of a four-minute miler). This means his thin muscular legs are taking 12 steps every second.

6   The combination of fast feet and a flat, wide tail serving as rudder gives the roadrunner a double advantage over lizards and low-flying insects. He simply darts and twists after his prey, screeching into ninety-degree turns, careening around sagebrush and spurting into a straightaway as he catches his meals on the run.

7   In the roadrunner's hot, dry desert environment, all this hyper-activity would seem likely to dehydrate the bird. (He also frequents many plains, prairies and oak-hickory forests.) But he has adapted remarkably well to temperatures over one hundred degrees and dry winds. His biggest problem—water—is solved by careful budgeting. He rests in the shade during the hottest part of the day, and replenishes body water through his diet; he eats things like lizards, whose bodies have a high water content, and then manufactures liquid by oxidation of the food into carbon dioxide

8   The remainder of his diet is no problem, mainly because he eats most anything he can catch that's smaller than he is. He prefers insects (high water content), plants, lizards, snakes, and mammals like mice and rats.

9   His manner of catching a snake is especially noteworthy. He dashes in circles around a coiled snake, stops within striking distance, shuffles his feet, swishes his tail in the dirt and stirs up a blinding cloud of dust.

10   Then begins Act II. Roadrunner ruffles his feathers to reduce penetration from a direct strike, and leaps back into a dizzying series of circles around the bewildered snake. He often reverses directions in mid-stride, catches the snake going the other way, and clouts him with his long, sharp beak. Finally, the tired, wounded snake catches several pecks to the brain and succumbs.

11   Eating the snake requires almost as much talent as catching it; the bird is dealing with a dinner frequently longer than itself. Roadrunner swallows his prey headfirst, forcing the snake as far down his gullet as possible. If there is excess snake, the bird simply waits for his superactive digestive juices to do their part, and in a matter of hours the snake is completely eaten.

12   Compared to snakes, insects are easy pickings. Most are simply snapped off mesquite and cacti, or flushed from under rocks with a tail flick. To catch cicadas, so erratic in flight that man can hardly catch them, Roadrunner simply dogs their odd flight pattern.

13   Roadrunner's eyesight is spectacular. He can spot a lizard skittering out of reach and watch an enemy hawk overhead at the same time. When he really wants to concentrate, he can focus all attention through one eye. Roadrunners have been observed standing entranced with head tilted sideways, one eye focused on the ground, and the other scanning the sky for airborne enemies.

14   In the spring, Roadrunner gets restless, grows a few sporty new feathers in his head crest and begins stepping out. When he finds a likely prospect for his affections, he starts acting like a normal roadrunner—odd. His call to establish territory is normal: his series of six or eight calls descends in pitch until the last one resembles a mourning dove's plaintive coo.

15   He'll offer some food, flutter his tail, shuffle his feet in another dust-stirring dance, then end the performance with a graceful bow and more coos. If the hen thinks he's acceptable, she takes the food, they dance and bow, then begin to look for a suitable place to build a nest.

16   Nest building, roadrunner style, usually results in a disorganized pile

of sticks, feathers, old snake skins and rubble. The hen tramples a slight hollow in the center of this debris and lays three to eight white eggs at infrequent intervals. This haphazardly planned parenthood usually results in the first hatched young stumbling over a freshly laid egg or two.

17   It remained for Warner Brothers to enshrine the incredible roadrunner. From cartoons, the screwball bird and "meep-meep" branched out to emblems, decals and patches. And not only for the toddler set—unofficial military insignia also bears his picture.

18   And he's not done yet. Next time you see a whirling cloud of dust, watch for some fast soft-shoe, a little artful bobbing and weaving. In the center of that cloud will be a roadrunner, the king of the cuckoos, doing his bit to enliven your hours on the road.

COMMENTARY

Peterson prefaces his account of the roadrunner with scientific information about the family to which this bird belongs. Hollister, in contrast, uses a "high-speed" opening paragraph that deliberately misrepresents the facts—or indulges in poetic license. A bird that is half tail and half feet literally cannot have a body or head. No bird has wheels nor can it "leave change." But this metaphoric language brings a new vitality to the "cuckoo that runs on the ground." It dramatizes.

The two styles of the pieces on the roadrunner are well suited to their different purposes. Peterson can use incomplete sentences because in a very brief technical description, both the subject and the verb "to be" can sometimes be taken for granted: "Feet zygodactyl. . . ." "Slender, heavily streaked. . . ." Hollister, on the other hand, writes complete sentences that are as lively as he can make them. For example, he uses contractions (he's) and incorporates colorful words wherever possible: screeching, careening, dizzying, skittering. No technical account would say that roadrunners "dog" the odd flight pattern of a grasshopper. Nor would it include a minidrama in two acts (paragraphs 9 and 10).

Hollister not only dramatizes the bird by showing it in action (we see not the nest but the *building* of the nest and the courting ritual) but also provides a familiar context at the beginning and end: the Warner Brothers screwball cartoon with its "meep-meep." Paragraphs 1—2 and 17—18 provide a relationship between us and a bird that few of us have actually seen.

As an outline indicates, there is little amplification or development of individual elements in either version. Each item is self-contained.

OUTLINE
Peterson
      I. The larger context: the cuckoo family—paragraph 1
     II. The roadrunner—paragraph 2
         A. Field marks (what you would see)

    B. Voice
    C. Range
Hollister
    I.   Introduction: the roadrunner in action—paragraphs 1–2
    II. Name—paragraph 3
    III. Feet and locomotion—paragraphs 4–6
    IV. Diet—paragraphs 7–12
            (interpolated "play"—paragraphs 9–10)
    V.   Sight—paragraph 13
    VI. Courting—paragraphs 14–15
    VII. Nesting—paragraph 16
    VIII. Conclusion: roadrunner's value—paragraphs 17–18

SUGGESTIONS FOR WRITING

1. Write a field guide entry for an animal, fish, reptile, or bird with which you are familiar and also a brief descriptive essay on the same subject. In the first, your intention is to identify and inform *only;* in the second, your purpose is also to entertain.

2. Compare the two descriptions of the roadrunner. What information or misinformation appears in one but not the other? Notice that this difference is partly determined by the connotative value of language (read Altick, p. 146). Is it possible to say *exactly* the same thing in two different ways? Try to prepare a new version of another piece of writing in this book, a version that combines Peterson's concern for specific detail with Hollister's concern for liveliness. You will find that this hybrid is itself a new species.

why an airplane flies
WOLFGANG LANGEWIESCHE

This article shows how a device description can reduce apparent chaos to sense. You watch a jet airliner take off and ask an engineer how it works. It works, you are told, because a hundred valves, miles of wire, thousands of whirling blades all operate simultaneously to produce flight. The answer is truthful but not very satisfying. It remains apparent chaos.

But how do we order chaos? How do we write sequentially about things that happen simultaneously?

Langewiesche's method is to pull one idea out of the chaos and clarify it. Then he pulls out another, clarifies it, and relates it to the first. He pulls out a third, and a fourth. Most important, he starts with the simplest idea, the fundamental principle—that of shape—from which the rest grows.

1   **W**hat makes an airplane fly is not its engine nor its propeller. Nor is it, as many people think, some mysterious knack of the pilot, nor some ingenious gadget inside. What makes an airplane fly is simply its shape. This may sound absurd, but gliders do fly without engines and model airplanes do fly without pilots. As for the insides of an airplane, they are disappointing for they are mostly hollow. No, what keeps an airplane up is its shape—the impact of the air upon its shape. Whittle that shape out of wood, or cast it out of iron, or fashion it, for that matter, out of chocolate and throw the thing into the air. It will behave like an airplane. It will *be* an airplane.

2   This—that its shape is what counts—is what makes the airplane so beautiful. It also makes it easy to understand. You don't have to open it up and look at "the works" inside as one has to do with a watch, a refrigerator or an automobile. An airplane's outside appearance is its "works." If you want to understand it, simply have a look.

3   Look at the wing. It holds the airplane up entirely by its shape. A wing is nothing but an air deflector, curved so and set at such an angle that it will catch the air and push it down. The air, resisting, pushes back up against the wing's bottom surface and that gives it some lift. At the same time—and this is more important—the wing also creates a lack of air on its top surface because of the way it is curved there. Thus it sucks air down from above. That air, resisting, sucks back upward on the wing's top surface and this is what gives the wing most of its lift.

4   And that's all there is to a wing! Man's greatest invention since the wheel and the boat—the thing that carries weights through thin air—is just a shape. As for the exact shape that will make the best wing, a whole science is concerned with that—aerodynamics. What counts most is the wing's cross section—what you would see if you sawed off the tips. Some 15,000 different shapes have been tested in the world's laboratories. It has been found that the wing with the highly arched top surface and a concave, scooped-out under surface will carry the most weight. The early airplanes had that kind of wing. But a more nearly streamlined cross section will carry good weight too and slide through the air more easily. Hence modern fast airplanes' wings don't have that hollowed-out under surface. But all such engineering refinements don't change the main idea of the wing: a wing is a shape that holds itself up by acting on the air.

AIR IS STRANGE STUFF

5   It is simple. If flight seems just the same a little miraculous and, to many people, still a little unsound, it is not because the natural law involved is at all strange. The law is the old one of action and reaction: if

you push against *anything,* that thing resists and pushes back against you. As the gun pushes the bullet forward, the bullet kicks the gun backward making it recoil. What seems so strange about flying is merely that the thing we work against is air. And air is strange stuff. Because we cannot see it, we think of it as a nothing. Because we cannot pinch it between our fingers, we think of it as empty space. And thus an airplane seems to sit up there in empty space, held up by nothing.

6   Actually, air is real stuff, just as real as water. It has density and body. It is a thick and slightly sticky fluid, molasses-like, though very thin molasses. Its tendency to stick to the skin of an airplane causes much headache to the engineers. It has weight. A cubic yard of air (a bathtubful) weighs about 2 lb. Thus if we could only see the air, all the mystery would go out of flying at once. We could then see the fierce attack with which the wing smashes into that stuff. We could see the terrific downward wallop which the wing gives to thousands of pounds of air every minute. And we could see that everywhere in the wake of an airplane, the air is in downward flow and keeps swirling and eddying for many minutes when the airplane itself is already miles farther on.

7   The magic shape of the wing can't have effect, of course, unless it keeps continually attacking new air. If an airplane is to keep flying, it must keep moving. It can't ever stop or even slow down much. If it slows down it sinks; if it slows down too much it sinks too fast. The wings then can no longer catch the air at the proper angle. The lift goes out of the wings like air out of a punctured tire; the airplane drops. That is what is called a stall. A "tailspin" is nothing but a fancy stall. One wing makes lift and wants to fly, the other wing is stalled and keeps dropping. Between them they twist the airplane down in a corkscrew motion. Normally, pulling

What a wing does is shown in the impressionistic drawing below. The bottom surface pushes air down, like a hand pushing through the air. The upper surface lifts the wing, like hand pulling down at the air. (Illustrated by Fred Cooper.)

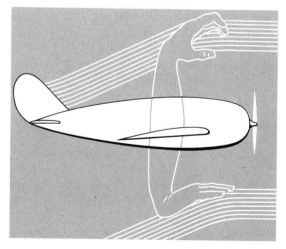

back on the stick makes the airplane go up. But in the spin or stall, the harder the pilot pulls back, the more obstinately the airplane goes down. The more it goes down, the harder the pilot's self-preservation instinct makes him pull back on the stick. The way to recover from a stall or spin is to get the stick forward, diving at the ground to pick up new speed. But that takes courage. A stall or spin means quite a drop—dozens of feet in a Cub, thousands of feet in a bomber. It is because a wing needs speed that airplanes need big airports. They can't fly until they have gathered speed, and they dare not slow up again until they are firmly on the ground. It is because a wing needs speed that the first rule of the art of piloting, contrary to all common sense, is this: keep your speed. If you want to be safe, *don't* go slow, go fast. When in doubt, speed up.

8   Just how fast must an airplane fly in order to be safe? This depends on the airplane's shape. If in proportion to its weight the plane has big wings, it can fly slowly; if it has small wings, it must fly fast. That's what "wing loading" means, the proportion between an airplane's weight and the size of its wings. A very speedy medium bomber has a square foot of wing for every 60 lb. of its weight; a slow Cub has ten square feet of wing for every 60 lb. of its weight. The bomber needs 110 m.p.h. or it will stall; the Cub will hang on at 35 m.p.h. A heavily wing-loaded airplane is fast but "hot," needs big airports and, if stalled, it will drop hard and deep. A lightly wing-loaded airplane is slow but more forgiving of pilot mistakes. But all airplanes must keep moving.

9   There are many ways to keep an airplane going. A motor and propeller are not the only way. The gliders, for instance, are pulled by a rope, the rope in turn being pulled by another airplane or by an automobile, or even (as was done in Russia) by galloping horses. Any airplane can also always maintain its speed simply by nosing down a little and coasting. This is called a glide and is the reason why an airplane doesn't crash simply because its engine quits. But a glide means a steady loss of altitude and the airplane must eventually land. Sometimes an airplane can glide in an updraft of air and, though it noses downward, the updraft may at the same time carry it up, much as a piece of paper is sometimes lifted high above the roofs. This sort of gliding is called soaring and is the most delightful of all types of flight. But updrafts are hard to find and unreliable and it takes a slow, light glider to stay in them. The sensible and businesslike way to keep the airplane going is to give it its own source of power, an engine and propeller.

10   Propellers are weird, doubly so, because at work they become invisible. They whirl too fast. Hence many people don't understand what a propeller really does. Some think that the propeller pulls the airplane always upward as well as forward and that this is really what keeps an airplane up. This is not true. The propeller drives the airplane forward, the wings take care of the lift. In a blimp the propeller drives the ship forward and the balloon takes care of the lift. Again, some people think that the propeller's purpose is to blow air against the wings and that this is how the wings

develop lift. That isn't true either. The propeller does throw a blast of air backward, but the engineers would be only too happy to keep that air from hitting any part of the airplane. It is a nuisance. Moreover, the wings don't need a blast of air. If the airplane keeps moving they get plenty of air to work on.

11   And that's what the propeller does: it keeps the airplane moving forward. It doesn't lift, it drives. Mount one on a sled and it will drive the sled; mount one on a hydroplane and it will drive the hydroplane. And if you mounted one on a trolley car, it would run the trolley car.

THE PROPELLER IS LIKE A WING

12   The propeller, just like the wing, works upon the air by shape. Each propeller blade is nothing but an "air foil," a shape much like an airplane wing to catch and make use of the air. In fact, a propeller blade's cross section has exactly the same curves as a wing's cross section. The propeller blade catches the air and throws it backward and by so doing gets a forward force.

13   Because the propeller is driven by a motor, it is almost the same thing as an electric fan; the two look slightly different only because they are used differently. In the propeller you don't use the backward blast of air, but you use the kick and you allow it to make plenty of noise. The electric fan is designed not to make too much noise; you use the blast of air and you don't use the "kick-back." In fact, most people don't know that an electric fan has a kick just like a propeller. But just set your electric fan on a toy wagon and watch it propel.

14   How big a propeller, how powerful an engine does it take to keep the airplane going fast enough so that it will fly? The amazing, the at first quite incredible thing is that it takes very little force. A one-man glider weighing 500 lb. can be pulled through the air by a force of only 25 lb. A child in the rumble seat of the tow car could easily hold the tow rope in his hand and keep it flying. For ordinary airplanes, the figures are only a little less favorable; to keep a 10,000-lb. airplane flying takes only about 1,000 lb. of propeller pull.

15   The force that holds an airplane back, the force which the propeller has to overcome to keep the airplane going, is called the drag. Like everything else about the airplane it depends on the shape, and hence you can see it, if you know where to look.

16   The wing itself makes a drag: the plowing down of air requires force. This drag—the price which we must pay for lift—is called the induced drag, and it depends much on the shape of the wing. A narrow wing of long span catches much air, gives it a gentle push and requires little force. A broad wing of short span catches less air, gives it more of a push and requires more force. This is why patrol bombers and other long-distance airplanes have long narrow wings; they get more miles per gallon that

way. That is also why gliders have long narrow wings; they slide more easily. Wing-tip shape, too, has much to do with this induced drag: on a square wing, the tip plows too hard, and some of the rest not hard enough; a tapered wing works more easily, slides more easily.

17   Another drag is skin friction: the air, molasses-like, clings to the skin, and the airplane can't move without dragging a lot of air around. An airplane actually won't dust itself off in flight; if it goes up dusty, it comes down still dusty. The reason is that next to the skin, the air hardly slides at all.

18   That's why it is important that the shape of an airplane be absolutely smooth: in an airliner or a bomber even the tiny roughness of the rivet heads on the skin causes a drag force of a couple of hundred pounds. Racers and soaring gliders are polished with a cloth before each flight. Skin friction is the reason why some airplanes are of odd shape. In very fast airplanes, the designer sometimes will rather have a less efficient shape simply because it will give him less total skin surface and hence less friction.

19   But the biggest thing that holds the airplane back is so obvious that one doesn't think of it: the many parts of the airplane that are not wing. The wing is the airplane's essential part—it makes the lift. Yet an airplane also needs space for passengers and cargo, a pilot seat with windshield, a radiator, a radio mast. It needs a landing gear, perhaps struts and wires to stiffen the wings. It needs tail fins.

20   Each of these parts causes a drag. It takes definite force to push each of them through the air, for the air, sticky dense stuff, resists their passage. But unlike the drag of the wings, drag of those parts is not associated with the making of lift. It is pure evil. It is useless and bears the contemptuous name of parasite drag.

Four forces work like giant hands on the airplane in flight. Lift pulls the plane up and weight pulls it down. Thrust from the propeller pulls the plane forward, drag of plane through the air holds it back. (Illustration by Fred Cooper.)

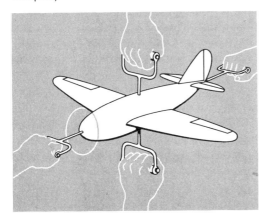

21   The airplane is shaped to keep parasite drag small. Hence, that shark-like look—sharks, too, are shaped to move through a dense fluid fast. And hence all the little things that aren't there. The most remarkable thing about a modern airplane is what you *don't* see, and what in older airplanes you used to see. The engine is hidden under a smooth cowl, pilot and passengers are inside, the landing gear is tucked away in flight, the wings stick out without any struts and wires. Just as those things are out of your sight, so they are out of the way of the air, and cause no drag. The dream ship of aeronautical engineers is the Flying Wing, the all-wing airplane that hasn't even a fuselage any more. Everything has been pulled into the wing and the wing is all there is.

22   Those then, as every student pilot learns, are the four forces that act on an airplane in flight: 1) weight pulls it down, but 2) lift of its wings holds it up; 3) drag holds it back, but 4) pull of the propeller keeps it going. In steady flight, the four forces balance and all is serene.

COMMENTARY

This section from "Why An Airplane Flies" is a classic example of analysis by division. "Analysis" means literally "a breaking up," a separation of the whole into its component parts. It is one of the basic techniques by which we acquaint ourselves with the unfamiliar, especially the complicated unfamiliar: we take it one part at a time. Into what parts does Langewiesche divide the airplane? Even the most technically naive reader knows that an airplane employs many parts Langewiesche doesn't explain, for instance, a fuel pump and an instrument panel. Why does he omit them? What does he gain or lose by their omission?

"Why An Airplane Flies" was first published in *Life* magazine in 1943, when probably 80 to 90 percent of *Life's* readers had never been aboard an airplane. Does this fact explain the simplicity of its language? Simplicity of language which might help one reader might insult another. Discuss the ways in which Langewiesche simplifies complex phenomena (especially paragraphs 6, 9, 14, and 17).

Notice that Langewiesche uses a number of techniques of definition. He begins with a negative statement of cause (see p. 51): "What makes an airplane fly is *not*. . . ." and, having cleared some misconceptions out of the way, moves to a positive statement of cause: "What makes an airplane fly *is*" (paragraph 1). The second paragraph offers a contrast (see p. 51) between an airplane and other machines; the third paragraph compares the airplane—on the basis of its importance—to other inventions. Paragraph 5 uses an example (see p. 52), the recoil of a gun, to clarify a general principle of physics. Paragraph 6 introduces an analogy (see p. 52) between air and molasses. How many techniques does Langewiesche use in all, and why do you think he seems to need so many?

OUTLINE

SUGGESTIONS FOR WRITING

1. Analyze a device with which you are familiar.

    a. Identify the fundamental principle that the device is constructed to exploit. (For example, the jet engine exploits the physical principle that every action produces an equal and opposite reaction.)

    b. Divide the device into its major parts. (In analyzing an internal combustion engine, you would certainly explain the electrical and fuel systems. You might, however, omit emission-control systems, since they are not crucial to the engine's operation.)

    c. Show the device in action.

2. Langewiesche recognizes that some of his readers may be suspicious of technology (in paragraph 5, he notes that many people regard flight as "a little unsound"). Therefore he takes special care to show that an airplane is a beautiful, simple, normal thing; that it operates on familiar natural principles; that it can indeed be understood ("simply have a look"); that it can be approached with a sense of humor (the illustrations seem, and are meant to seem, a little silly)—in short, that an airplane is not an enemy but a friend.

The following brief explanation of how an airplane wing works (covering the same subject matter as Langewiesche's paragraphs 3 and 4) comes from a

The explanation of the lift of an airplane wing.

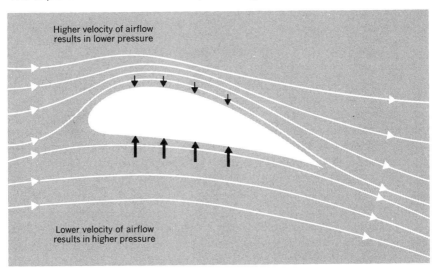

Higher velocity of airflow
results in lower pressure

Lower velocity of airflow
results in higher pressure

physics textbook. Here the authors do not feel that they must overcome potential suspicion or hostility, and therefore they offer a straightforward analysis without attempting to convey affection for the device.

Bernoulli's principle [that the pressure of a flowing liquid increases when its velocity decreases, and vice versa] is quite general and applies to all kinds of fluid motion. Consider, for example, the stream of air around the wing of a flying plane. The profile of the wing and the lines of air flowing around it are shown in [the figure on page 57]. Airplane wings are shaped in such a way that the total distance traveled by the air flowing over the wing is longer than that of the air flowing under it. Thus, the velocity of airflow above the wing must be higher, and the pressure correspondingly lower, than that of the airflow under the wing. This difference of pressure above and below the wing results in an upward force that supports the flying airplane in the air.*

Write two short descriptions of anything—a snake, for instance, or a toad, or a hypodermic syringe, or rabbit stew. In one, assume that your audience is neutral or favorable toward your subject; simply present it. In the other, assume that your audience is suspicious or hostile and that you want to overcome this attitude; present your subject with evident affection. Don't just say "I like it." Make your *readers* like it.

* George Gamow and John M. Cleveland, *Physics: Foundations and Frontiers,* Copyright © 1960, pp. 69–70. Reprinted by permission of Prentice-Hall, Inc., Englewood Cliffs, N.J.

---

pavlova
AGNES DE MILLE

Capturing a personality in words is not easy; in a short piece we can usually capture only one facet because people are so complex. This selection presents a person as performer.

Most of us have seen someone execute a difficult task superbly. Whether the performer is a musician, actor, athlete, surgeon, or stevedore, we who listen and watch have shared the excitement that the perfect performance of any action inspires. De Mille's task is to make her readers —who will never be able to see the Russian ballerina Pavlova—experience the excitement of watching her dance.

1   **a**nna Pavlova! My life stops as I write that name. Across the daily preoccupation of lessons, lunch boxes, tooth brushings and quarrelings with Margaret flashed this bright, unworldly experience and burned in a single afternoon a path over which I could never retrace my steps. I had wit-

nessed the power of beauty, and in some chamber of my heart I lost forever my irresponsibility. I was as clearly marked as though she had looked me in the face and called my name. For generations my father's family had loved and served the theater. All my life I had seen actors and actresses and had heard theater jargon at the dinner table and business talk of box-office grosses. I had thrilled at Father's projects and watched fascinated his picturesque occupations. I took a proprietary pride in the profitable and hasty growth of "The Industry." But nothing in his world or my uncle's prepared me for theater as I saw it that Saturday afternoon.

2   Since that day I have gained some knowledge in my trade and I recognize that her technique was limited; that her arabesques were not as pure or classically correct as Markova's, that her jumps and batterie were paltry, her turns not to be compared in strength and number with the strenuous durability of Baronova or Toumanova. I know that her scenery was designed by second-rate artists, her music was on a level with restaurant orchestrations, her company definitely inferior to all the standards we insist on today, and her choreography mostly hack. And yet I say that she was in her person the quintessence of theatrical excitement.

3   As her little bird body revealed itself on the scene, either immobile in trembling mystery or tense in the incredible arc which was her lift, her instep stretched ahead in an arch never before seen, the tiny bones of her hands in ceaseless vibration, her face radiant, diamonds glittering under her dark hair, her little waist encased in silk, the great tutu balancing, quickening and flashing over her beating, flashing, quivering legs, every man and woman sat forward, every pulse quickened. She never appeared to rest static, some part of her trembled, vibrated, beat like a heart. Before our dazzled eyes, she flashed with the sudden sweetness of a hummingbird in action too quick for understanding by our gross utilitarian standards, in action sensed rather than seen. The movie cameras of her day could not record her allegro. Her feet and hands photographed as a blur.

4   Bright little bird bones, delicate bird sinews! She was all fire and steel wire. There was not an ounce of spare flesh on her skeleton, and the life force used and used her body until she died of the fever of moving, gasping for breath, much too young.

5   She was small, about five feet. She wore a size one and a half slipper, but her feet and hands were large in proportion to her height. Her hand could cover her whole face. Her trunk was small and stripped of all anatomy but the ciphers of adolescence, her arms and legs relatively long, the neck extraordinarily long and mobile. All her gestures were liquid and possessed of an inner rhythm that flowed to inevitable completion with the finality of architecture or music. Her arms seemed to lift not from the elbow or the arm socket, but from the base of the spine. Her legs seemed to function from the waist. When she bent her head her whole spine moved and the motion was completed the length of the arm through the elongation of her slender hand and the quivering reaching fingers. I believe there has never been a foot like hers, slender, delicate and of such an astonishing

aggressiveness when arched as to suggest the ultimate in human vitality. Without in any way being sensual, being, in fact, almost sexless, she suggested all exhilaration, gaiety and delight. She jumped, and we broke bonds with reality. We flew. We hung over the earth, spread in the air as we do in dreams, our hands turning in the air as in water—the strong forthright taut plunging leg balanced on the poised arc of the foot, the other leg stretched to the horizon like the wing of a bird. We lay balancing, quivering, turning, and all things were possible, even to us, the ordinary people.

6   I have seen two dancers as great or greater since, Alicia Markova and Margot Fonteyn, and many other women who have kicked higher, balanced longer or turned faster. These are poor substitutes for passion. In spite of her flimsy dances, the bald and blatant virtuosity, there was an intoxicated rapture, a focus of energy, Dionysian in its physical intensity, that I have never seen equaled by a performer in any theater of the world. Also she was the *first* of the truly great in our experience.

7   I sat with the blood beating in my throat. As I walked into the bright glare of the afternoon, my head ached and I could scarcely swallow. I didn't wish to cry. I certainly couldn't speak. I sat in a daze in the car oblivious to the grownups' ceaseless prattle. At home I climbed the stairs slowly to my bedroom and, shutting myself in, placed both hands on the brass rail at the foot of my bed, then rising laboriously to the tips of my white buttoned shoes I stumped the width of the bed and back again. My toes throbbed with pain, my knees shook, my legs quivered with weakness. I repeated the exercise. The blessed, relieving tears stuck at last on my lashes. Only by hurting my feet could I ease the pain in my throat.

8   Standing on Ninth Avenue under the El, I saw the headlines on the front page of the *New York Times*. It did not seem possible. She was in essence the denial of death. My own life was rooted to her in a deep spiritual sense and had been during the whole of my growing up. It mattered not that I had only spoken to her once and that my work lay in a different direction. She was the vision and the impulse and the goal.

COMMENTARY

The intensity of the author's excitement strikes the reader at once because of the exclamatory (and verbless!) first sentence. Then, in three paragraphs, De Mille sketches her own personal connection with the theater (thus establishing her "credentials" as a writer on this subject), and the limitations and impact of Pavlova's performance. This background prepares us for paragraph 4, which elaborates the first sentence, "Anna Pavlova!" The exclamatory tone returns. In this brief climactic paragraph, De Mille both focuses on Pavlova's immense vitality and introduces its opposite, death. The paragraph is therefore like a fulcrum balancing equal (symmetrical) halves of the essay.

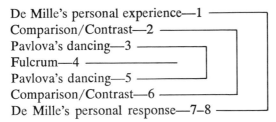

De Mille's personal experience—1
Comparison/Contrast—2
Pavlova's dancing—3
Fulcrum—4
Pavlova's dancing—5
Comparison/Contrast—6
De Mille's personal response—7–8

Part of the success of De Mille's description derives from this symmetry. Another part comes from the comparisons with other dancers, more sophisticated performers whose superiority in little matters heightens Pavlova's superiority in more important ones. De Mille's style, however, is crucial. She turns the everyday reality of physical movement (most of us *do* stump around in our shoes) into images of flying and floating, so that Pavlova becomes almost supernaturally birdlike. And she transmits this impression to us in nervous, abbreviated sentences and phrases. In addition, she presents her own excitement in terms of familiar symptoms: the sensations that her life is stopping (paragraph 1), the blood is beating in her throat, her head is aching (paragraph 7).

SUGGESTIONS FOR WRITING

1. Describe the best performance you have ever witnessed—anything from a cowboy riding at a rodeo to a clergyman preaching. Devise a style that will communicate your sense of excitement to the reader. Use a central metaphor (as De Mille uses the metaphor of a bird) if this helps.

2. Consider what the source of excitement is in some activity. To De Mille, what made Pavlova's performance so marvelous was the dancer's extraordinary energy and "intoxicated rapture" (paragraph 6). What makes a drill team's performance exciting is the perfect coordination of the team's members. What makes a particular football game exciting may be the physical and mental agility of one individual star.

Explain what quality makes watching a certain kind of performance exciting for you.

3. De Mille sees Pavlova as a dancer. Does she also seem aware of Pavlova as a person? Is the public image that a performer offers to spectators the same as his or her private identity?

If you have ever known a performer personally, or have yourself been in the position of offering a public image (as performer, as speaker to a group of strangers, as teacher, etc.), write a description comparing the personality that the spectators see with the personality that the performer himself, or a close friend, would see: follow your equivalent of Pavlova offstage.

science fiction: the term defined

HARRY HARRISON

Diagrams and formulas are, in a way, definitions. This essay uses both in an effort to pin down the slippery term "science fiction." In addition, Harrison has fun as he goes through the routine of formal definition: he scorns inferior descriptive terms by calling them "pretenders" (paragraph 3), he teases about foreign equivalents of science fiction, then he plays arithmetic as a substitute for the expected "term, genus, differentia" procedure. Along the way, he also provides specific examples to show which books qualify as science fiction and which don't according to his own "scientific" (also fictional?) definition.

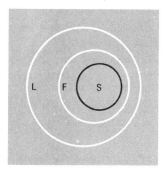

1   I have never seen a definition of the term "science fiction" that completely pleased me. They all err to one extreme or the other, either being too narrow in definition ("stories about rocket ships and time machines") or so broad they bring in most of modern fiction ("the impact of science upon people" or "stories that might be true" as opposed to fantasy which consists of stories that could not be true).

2   Not that there has been a want of trying. Science fiction writers have been approached to write definitions for dictionaries and encyclopedias and have rushed into the fray. I have heard many panel discussions at science fiction conventions about the meaning of this term. It is strange, but all of them reached similar conclusions. Either they found a definition so short that it didn't work—or produced a page of qualifications that might work if you could wend your way through them.

3   Though I doubt if I shall lay this fascinating controversy to rest forever, I can at least make a try. Firstly we must toss aside all of the pre-

Source. "The Term Defined," from *Science Fiction: The Academic Awakening,* ed. Willis E. McNelly, copyright © 1974 Harry Harrison and The College English Association, Inc. Reprinted by permission of the author and The College English Association.

tenders to the name. ("Scientifiction" should be dead by now, *pace* its creator, the noble Hugo Gernsback.) Nor can we hide behind "speculative fiction" or "science fantasy" or any of the others. I rather like the Italian *fantascienza;* it rolls off the tongue so smoothly, but I am afraid it doesn't work in English. It is interesting to note that many other languages, after trying to create a term on their own, simply drop back to using the correct English one. Except the Germans, of course, who with their joyous love of organization have at least a dozen different terms for what they think are the different types of science fiction, a species of Linnean camouflage for the fact that they simply don't have a single one that works. The Russians on the other hand—how our language reflects our culture—refuse to have even a single term for sf; perhaps they will come to it some day, but now they simply lump the stuff under the general heading of fantasy and let it go at that.

4   In order to see if we can arrive at a simple definition, let us begin by defining our subject. What exactly *is* science fiction? Getting answers is many times the art of answering the right question, and this is a right question. Let us go to the beginning and narrow down on our target.

5   In the beginning there is literature, world literature, and, in the diagram that opens this piece, it will be seen as the large circle L which encloses everything. We shall attach specific definitions to terms for the sake of this argument so that literature here is defined as the totality of all written world literature that is fiction, works of the imagination. Within this circle you will find the French novel, the English gothics, Russian, Japanese, Basque fiction of all kinds. It is all there.

6   Within the larger circle L there is a smaller one which is F. This is fantasy, part of the greater whole of fiction. And, within fantasy, we have the smaller circle that encloses the area known as science fiction, circle S.

7   I do not think any of these statements can be contested. Science fiction is fantasy and fantasy is certainly fiction—so there we are.

8   Well, just where are we? Coming close to the promised definition. But not quite there yet. Before we reach it I would like you to consider an axiom. Not the axiom that the dictionaries define as "a recognized truth" but the one with the mathematical definition. A proposition which is assumed without proof for the sake of studying the consequences that follow from it. So here is the axiom, and let the consequences fall where they may.

$$SFQ = \frac{F + L + 6}{S}$$

SFQ is our Science Fiction Quotient which, leaving humility aside for the moment, I shall call Harrisons' Axiom, the measure of the science fiction content of a story. (The plural Harrison is explained by the fact that, while the theory is mine, the actual construction of the axiom owes a great deal to my son Todd who is much more at home with mathematics.) S is science fiction, F fiction and L is literature, as they apply in the diagram.

9   The reasoning behind this axiom, as can be seen in the diagram, is that science fiction is a new thing in the world, a construction of man just like his culture and his automobiles. New things define themselves by existing. We invent them, we know what they are, then apply a new term to a referent that has just come into existence. The dictionary says that an automobile is "a vehicle, especially one for passengers, carrying its own power-generating and propelling mechanism for travel on ordinary roads." Ohh, like a motorcycle or a streamroller? Well, no, we'll have to define a bit more . . . thereby falling into the same endless sf definition trap. The only short sf definition that works, like the one for the automobile, is "sf is what I am pointing at when I say this is sf." But this is too subjective and we should have some definition that is a bit more rigorous, one that can be applied by constant rules. Therefore this axiom which attempts to determine the "science fictionness" of a story.

10   Let us determine how it works and begin with an unarguable sample of hardcore, solid fuel sf. Any one of Van Vogt's stories of the war against the Rull will fit; "Cooperate Or Else" is a fine example. No one would deny that all of this story falls within the science fiction circle—there are no gnomes or elves and the story would never be published in *Harper's.* If we say that any story has six parts to be divided up then this story gets the full six and emerges with an SFQ of 1. Unity, the real thing.

11   Now let us venture away from the hardcore a bit and consider the Aldiss story "Hothouse." At least half science fiction for a 3 in that category, because this is a scientific prediction of the state of the world in the far future when the sun gets a good bit warmer and causes a number of mutations. But cobwebs to the moon must be fantasy, as lovely as the concept is, and, since no part of the story is out there in L, the mainstream, the other 3 parts go to fantasy alone to produce an SFQ of 3.

12   Now take *Tarzan,* pride of the Burroughs' bibliophiles. A slight whiff of sf with the scientific gimmickry here and there, but worth no more than a 1 in that category. And at least a 1 for the L category for it really is pure action adventure fiction a good part of the time. And a well deserved 4 in F for talking apes (they don't), hidden cities, total unreality of Africa and such. The SFQ is 11.

13   Consider next *Arrowsmith.* I mention this novel because Robert Heinlein once attempted to define science fiction in an essay. His definition is one hundred and seventy words long and still doesn't work. One reason it does not work, as has been pointed out, is that *Arrowsmith* is an sf novel according to this definition. Let's see how it shapes up by the SFQ. It certainly has no science fiction or fantasy content and sits firmly in the realm of L as a mainstream novel about a hardworking doctor. Its SFQ is 0.

14   A pattern has been formed—as well as a recognition that there is hardcore science fiction, fringe sf and a number of variations in between. 1 is science fiction, the pure quill. The science fictional content diminishes

numerically up to 11 which is fringe sf that barely qualifies. All else is 0 and does not belong, for the answer falls into the null set and is beyond the realm of science fiction (assuming that the possible values of S, F and L fall within the set [0, 1, 2, 3, 4, 5, 6]).

15   The SFQ is a very useful tool to work out whether those borderline cases have any sf content at all. In this way the Hobbit stories are pure fantasy and rate a 12, nothing to do with sf at all. If one cares to call them sf to any degree, assigning a meagre 1, the area that is sf must be clearly defined to creep into the outermost fringe sf category. A book like *On the Beach* must surely rate a 2 or a 3 for its extrapolation of the effects of nuclear bomb warfare so it has an SFQ of 5 or 3, thus reassuring our intuition that it is indeed sf.

16   Using the SFQ we begin to realize that the trouble with many earlier definitions of science fiction is that they attempted a *yes* or *no* description. It either is or is not science fiction. This does not work. The definition of sf is very firm at the center and gets more and more ragged until it gets out to the very edge and ceases having a science fictional content at all.

17   The definition of science fiction is:
Science fiction is.

COMMENTARY

The question in every reader's mind is: can Harrison be serious? The tongue-in-cheek humor throughout the article makes us wonder about his sincerity. (Consider the sardonic first sentence of paragraph 2, the "smooth" Italian word *fantascienza,* the mockery in paragraph 9 about "traps," or the final sentence of the article, which hardly qualifies as a definition.) Behind the playfulness, however, Harrison does follow the standard procedure, as we see from his diagram: the term "sf" belongs to the genus "fiction" (or fantasy) which belongs to the general category "literature." Harrison then differentiates sf from all other fictions (fantasies) and all other kinds of literature.

This helps clarify the problem, but it also creates new ones. We may not accept his idea that "fantasy" is fiction containing gnomes or elves, or that "literature" is what gets published in *Harper's* magazine. And it's impossible to use the formula without knowing in advance what sf is—in which case why use the formula?

As a definition, then, the article clarifies some things but obscures others. Well aware of the dilemma, Harrison refuses to make grand claims about his definition. He evidently means for it to be provocative, to assist us in thinking straight about sf.

OUTLINE
I. Unsatisfactory definitions of sf—paragraphs 1–3
II. Determining the genus of sf—paragraphs 4–9

III. Differentiating sf from other members of the genus—paragraphs 10–14

IV. Justification of the formula—paragraphs 15–17

SUGGESTIONS FOR WRITING

1. Develop a formula to describe another type of writing: western American literature, outdoor adventure fiction, sports fiction, "true romance" fiction (or a type of TV program: westerns, soaps, documentaries, social comedies, talk shows). Apply your formula.

2. Analyze the following definitions of sf: are they more (or less) successful than Harrison's? Then write one of your own, using examples of stories you have read to clarify it.

A. "Science fiction is really sociological studies of the future, things that the writer believes are going to happen by putting two and two together."—Ray Bradbury

B. "Science fiction, in its purest sense, should mean entertaining colorful fiction that either extrapolates what logically, or possibly, will take place in the future, or creates a more or less logical alien culture, or cultures, and records the probable impact upon it by an extrapolated Terran civilization. Successful science fiction, hopefully, brings temporary suspension of disbelief and a sense of identification with either the humans of the likeable or offbeat alien entities involved. Along with this should be the feeling of: WHAT IF? and WHY NOT? The seeds of speculative thought are sprouted—hopefully, the reader is hooked on science fiction. . . ."—Basil Wells

C. "SF is a controlled way to think and dream about the future. An integration of the mood and attitude of science (the objective universe) with the fears and hopes that spring from the unconscious. Anything that turns you and your social context, the social you, inside out. Nightmares and visions, always outlined by the barely possible."—Gregory Benford.

D. "Science fiction expresses the dreams that, varied and modified, later become the visions and then the realities in scientific progress. Unlike fantasy, they present probabilities in their basic structure and create a reservoir of imaginative thought that sometimes can inspire more practical thinking."—Vincent H. Gaddis

E. "Science Fiction is that branch of literature which deals with the reaction of human beings to changes in science and technology."—Isaac Asimov

the death of the moth

VIRGINIA WOOLF

In this subjective presentation of an event, Virginia Woolf demonstrates
that the most common occurrences of our everyday lives—incidents we
usually dismiss as trivial, if we notice them at all—can represent the
most serious aspects of existence. In the course of this short narrative,
an ordinary moth is associated with the vigor, energy, light, and activity
which (to Woolf) are the essence of life itself, and then it dies: a miniature
enactment of humanity's own life-into-death drama.

1   **m**oths that fly by day are not properly to be called moths; they do
not excite that pleasant sense of dark autumn nights and ivy-blossom
which the commonest yellow-underwing asleep in the shadow of the curtain never fails to rouse in us. They are hybrid creatures, neither gay like
butterflies nor sombre like their own species. Nevertheless the present
specimen, with his narrow hay-coloured wings, fringed with a tassel of the
same colour, seemed to be content with life. It was a pleasant morning,
mid-September, mild, benignant, yet with a keener breath than that of the
summer months. The plough was already scoring the field opposite the
window, and where the share had been, the earth was pressed flat and
gleamed with moisture. Such vigour came rolling in from the fields and
the down beyond that it was difficult to keep the eyes strictly turned
upon the book. The rooks too were keeping one of their annual festivities;
soaring round the tree tops until it looked as if a vast net with thousands
of black knots in it had been cast up into the air; which, after a few moments, sank slowly down upon the trees until every twig seemed to have
a knot at the end of it. Then, suddenly, the net would be thrown into the
air again in a wider circle this time, with the utmost clamour and vocifera-
tion, as though to be thrown into the air and settle slowly down upon
the tree tops were a tremendously exciting experience.

2   The same energy which inspired the rooks, the ploughmen, the horses,
and even, it seemed, the lean bare-backed downs, sent the moth fluttering
from side to side of his square of the window-pane. One could not help
watching him. One was, indeed, conscious of a queer feeling of pity for
him. The possibilities of pleasure seemed that morning so enormous and
so various that to have only a moth's part in life, and a day moth's at that,
appeared a hard fate, and his zest in enjoying his meagre opportunities to
the full, pathetic. He flew vigorously to one corner of his compartment,
and, after waiting there a second, flew across to the other. What remained
for him but to fly to a third corner and then to a fourth? That was all
he could do, in spite of the size of the downs, the width of the sky, the

Source. From *The Death of the Moth and Other Essays* by Virginia Woolf, Copyright ©
1942, by Harcourt Brace Jovanovich, Inc., renewed, 1970, by Marjorie T. Parsons. Reprinted
by permission of the publishers.

far-off smoke of houses, and the romantic voice, now and then, of a steamer out at sea. What he could do he did. Watching him, it seemed as if a fibre, very thin but pure, of the enormous energy of the world had been thrust into his frail and diminutive body. As often as he crossed the pane, I could fancy that a thread of vital light became visible. He was little or nothing but life.

3   Yet, because he was so small, and so simple a form of the energy that was rolling in at the open window and driving its way through so many narrow and intricate corridors in my own brain and in those of other human beings, there was something marvellous as well as pathetic about him. It was as if someone had taken a tiny bead of pure life and decking it as lightly as possible with down and feathers, had set it dancing and zig-zagging to show us the true nature of life. Thus displayed one could not get over the strangeness of it. One is apt to forget all about life, seeing it humped and bossed and garnished and cumbered so that it has to move with the greatest circumspection and dignity. Again, the thought of all that life might have been had he been born in any other shape caused one to view his simple activities with a kind of pity.

4   After a time, tired by his dancing apparently, he settled on the window ledge in the sun, and, the queer spectacle being at an end, I forgot about him. Then, looking up, my eye was caught by him. He was trying to resume his dancing, but seemed either so stiff or so awkward that he could only flutter to the bottom of the window-pane; and when he tried to fly across it he failed. Being intent on other matters I watched these futile attempts for a time without thinking, unconsciously waiting for him to resume his flight, as one waits for a machine, that has stopped momentarily, to start again without considering the reason of its failure. After perhaps a seventh attempt he slipped from the wooden ledge and fell, fluttering his wings, on to his back on the window sill. The helplessness of his attitude roused me. It flashed upon me that he was in difficulties; he could no longer raise himself; his legs struggled vainly. But, as I stretched out a pencil, meaning to help him to right himself, it came over me that the failure and awkwardness were the approach of death. I laid the pencil down again.

5   The legs agitated themselves once more. I looked as if for the enemy against which he struggled. I looked out of doors. What had happened there? Presumably it was midday, and work in the fields had stopped. Stillness and quiet had replaced the previous animation. The birds had taken themselves off to feed in the brooks. The horses stood still. Yet the power was there all the same, massed outside indifferent, impersonal, not attending to anything in particular. Somehow it was opposed to the little hay-coloured moth. It was useless to try to do anything. One could only watch the extraordinary efforts made by those tiny legs against an oncoming doom which could, had it chosen, have submerged an entire city, not merely a city, but masses of human beings; nothing, I knew had any chance against death. Nevertheless after a pause of exhaustion the legs

fluttered again. It was superb this last protest, and so frantic that he succeeded at last in righting himself. One's sympathies, of course, were all
on the side of life. Also, when there was nobody to care or to know, this
gigantic effort on the part of an insignificant little moth, against a power
of such magnitude, to retain what no one else valued or desired to keep,
moved one strangely. Again, somehow, one saw life, a pure bead. I lifted
the pencil again, useless though I knew it to be. But even as I did so, the
unmistakable tokens of death showed themselves. The body relaxed, and
instantly grew stiff. The struggle was over. The insignificant little creature
now knew death. As I looked at the dead moth, this minute wayside
triumph of so great a force over so mean an antagonist filled me with
wonder. Just as life had been strange a few minutes before, so death was
now as strange. The moth having righted himself now lay most decently
and uncomplainingly composed. O yes, he seemed to say, death is stronger
than I am.

COMMENTARY

Woolf's narrative is superficially about a moth but fundamentally
about life and death: what happens to the moth represents what must
happen to every living thing. (Why does she choose a moth rather than
a flower or a puppy?) This idea is first suggested by a deliberate series of
associations of the moth with images of movement, energy, and warmth.
For example, the sentence "The same energy which inspired the rooks,
the ploughmen, the horses, and even, it seemed, the lean bare-backed
downs, sent the moth fluttering from side to side of his square of the
windowpane" (paragraph 2) identifies the moth as participating in the
vigorous natural activities of birds, people, animals, and the earth itself.
This process of equating the moth with life becomes explicit at the end
of paragraph 2 and in paragraph 3: "He was little or nothing but life"
and "It was as if someone had taken a tiny bead of pure life. . . ."

In paragraph 4 the moth, now representing life, begins to accumulate
negative associations. He is "stiff," "awkward," his attempts at flying
fail, his efforts seem "futile." Something is clearly wrong with life, and
by the end of the paragraph we are told what it is: "the approach of
death." In order to ensure that this change is not interpreted as applying
to the moth alone, Woolf tells us that the whole outside world also seems
to have lost its activity. Its strength has been transformed into an
antagonistic "power," a force that kills.

The cosmic drama of tiny helpless life struggling against such an
enemy can end only one way, and Woolf is interested not so much in
what is happening—what *must* happen—as in what that outcome means.
In its final posture, the moth is "uncomplainingly composed."

Does this lack of complaint suggest that death is a final peace or
merely the last inevitability? Does Woolf's narrative make her concept
of the meaning of death clear?

SUGGESTIONS FOR WRITING

1. You have probably watched a living creature die, even if only an insect. Describe that event in such a way as to emphasize what it seemed to mean: death is horrible, death is merely the stopping of a machine, death is a release from pain, and so forth.

2. Woolf knows how to find the significance of an apparently trivial event. Describe a "trivial" event that seemed important to you, and make us see the meaning also. For example, what incident first proved to you that parents are fallible?

3. Describe the attitudes toward death expressed in the following poems. How are they different from that in Woolf's essay?

DESIGN—Robert Frost

I found a dimpled spider, fat and white,
On a white heal-all, holding up a moth
Like a white piece of rigid satin cloth—
Assorted characters of death and blight
Mixed ready to begin the morning right,
Like the ingredients of a witches' broth—
A snow-drop spider, a flower like a froth,
And dead wings carried like a paper kite.

What had that flower to do with being white,
The wayside blue and innocent heal-all?
What brought the kindred spider to that height,
Then steered the white moth thither in the night,
What but design of darkness to appall?—
If design govern in a thing so small.*

DIRGE WITHOUT MUSIC—Edna St. Vincent Millay

I am not resigned to the shutting away of loving
        hearts in the hard ground.
So it is, and so it will be, for so it has been, time
        out of mind:
Into the darkness they go, the wise and the lovely.
        Crowned
With lilies and with laurel they go; but I am not
        resigned.

Lovers and thinkers, into the earth with you.
Be one with the dull, the indiscriminate dust.

---

* From *The Poetry of Robert Frost* edited by Edward Connery Latham. Copyright © 1936 by Robert Frost. Copyright © 1964 by Lesley Frost Ballantine. Copyright © 1969 by Holt, Rinehart and Winston, Inc.

A fragment of what you felt, of what you knew,
A formula, a phrase remains,—but the best is lost.

The answers quick and keen, the honest look, the
    laughter, and love,—
They are gone. They are gone to feed the roses.
    Elegant and curled
Is the blossom. Fragrant is the blossom. I know.
    But I do not approve.
More precious was the light in your eyes than all
    the roses of the world.

Down, down, down into the darkness of the grave
Gently they go, the beautiful, the tender, the kind;
Quietly they go, the intelligent, the witty, the brave.
I know. But I do not approve. And I am not
    resigned.*

* From *Collected Poems*, Harper & Row. Copyright © 1929, 1955 by Edna St. Vincent Millay and Norma Millay Ellis.

my search for roots: a black american's story

ALEX HALEY

One of the most exciting kinds of information is information about yourself. In such cases, the question, What is *X*? becomes What am *I*? Sometimes the search for self focuses on the past, because all of us are, in part, what we have been earlier and what our people were before us. Haley, deprived of part of his past, set out to recover it. He wanted to know where in Africa his people had come from and who his ancestors had been.

    This article (the introduction to a book on the African roots of black Americans) describes the search that led Haley to an emotional moment that "can never again be equaled . . ." (paragraph 11): the identification of his great-great-great-great-grandfather and his reunion with his African relatives. The article is dramatic both because of its subject matter (the story of a person in search of himself is perennially appealing, since all of us enact our own such story in some way) and because of Haley's ability to make us share his tremendous emotional involvement.

Source. "My Search for Roots: A Black American's Story," copyright © 1974 by Reader's Digest Association, Inc., from *Roots* by Alex Haley. Used by permission of Doubleday & Co., Inc.

1 **m**y earliest memory is of Grandma, Cousin Georgia, Aunt Plus, Aunt Liz and Aunt Till talking on our front porch in Henning, Tenn. At dusk, these wrinkled, graying old ladies would sit in rocking chairs and talk, about slaves and massas and plantations—pieces and patches of family history, passed down across the generations by word of mouth. "Old-timey stuff," Mamma would exclaim. She wanted no part of it.

2 The furthest-back person Grandma and the others ever mentioned was "the African." They would tell how he was brought here on a ship to a place called "Naplis" and sold as a slave in Virginia. There he mated with another slave, and had a little girl named Kizzy.

3 When Kizzy became four or five, the old ladies said, her father would point out to her various objects and name them in his native tongue. For example, he would point to a guitar and make a single-syllable sound, *ko*. Pointing to a river that ran near the plantation, he'd say "Kamby Bolongo." And when other slaves addressed him as Toby—the name given him by his massa—the African would strenuously reject it, insisting that his name was "Kin-tay."

4 Kin-tay often told Kizzy stories about himself. He said that he had been near his village in Africa, chopping wood to make a drum, when he had been set upon by four men, overwhelmed, and kidnaped into slavery. When Kizzy grew up and became a mother, she told her son these stories, and he in turn would tell *his* children. His granddaughter became my grandmother, and she pumped that saga into me as if it were plasma, until I knew by rote the story of the African, and the subsequent generational wending of our family through cotton and tobacco plantations into the Civil War and then freedom.

5 At 17, during World War II, I enlisted in the Coast Guard, and found myself a messboy on a ship in the Southwest Pacific. To fight boredom, I began to teach myself to become a writer. I stayed on in the service after the war, writing every single night, seven nights a week, for eight years before I sold a story to a magazine. My first story in the Digest was published in June 1954: "The Harlem Nobody Knows." At age 37, I retired from military service, determined to be a full-time writer. Working with the famous Black Muslim spokesman, I did the actual writing for the book *The Autobiography of Malcom X*.

6 I remembered still the vivid highlights of my family's story. Could this account possibly be documented for a book? During 1962, between other assignments, I began following the story's trail. In plantation records, wills, census records, I documented bits here, shreds there. By now, Grandma was dead; repeatedly I visited other close sources, most notably our encyclopedic matriarch, "Cousin Georgia" Anderson in Kansas City, Kan. I went as often as I could to the National Archives in Washington, and the Library of Congress, and the Daughters of the American Revolution Library.

7 By 1967, I felt I had the seven generations of the U.S. side docu-

mented. But the unknown quotient in the riddle of the past continued to be those strange, sharp, angular sounds spoken by the African himself. Since I lived in New York City, I began going to the United Nations lobby, stopping Africans and asking if they recognized the sounds. Every one of them listened to me, then quickly took off. I can well understand: me with a Tennessee accent, trying to imitate African sounds!

8   Finally, I sought out a linguistics expert who specialized in African languages. To him I repeated the phrases. The sound "Kin-tay," he said, was a Mandinka tribe surname. And "Kamby Bolongo" was probably the Gambia River in Mandinka dialect. Three days later, I was in Africa.

9   In Banjul, the capital of Gambia, I met with a group of Gambians. They told me how for centuries the history of Africa has been preserved. In the older villages of the back country there are old men, called *griots,* who are in effect living archives. Such men know and, on special occasions, tell the cumulative histories of clans, or families, or villages, as those histories have long been told. Since my forefather had said his name was Kin-tay (properly spelled Kinte), and since the Kinte clan was known in Gambia, they would see what they could do to help me.

10   I was back in New York when a registered letter came from Gambia. Word had been passed in the back country, and a *griot* of the Kinte clan had, indeed, been found. His name, the letter said, was Kebba Kanga Fofana. I returned to Gambia and organized a safari to locate him.

11   There is an expression called "the peak experience," a moment which, emotionally, can never again be equaled in your life. I had mine, that first day in the village of Juffure, in the back country in black West Africa.

12   When our 14-man safari arrived within sight of the village, the people came flocking out of their circular mud huts. From a distance I could see a small, old man with a pillbox hat, an off-white robe and an aura of "somebodiness" about him. The people quickly gathered around me in a kind of horseshoe pattern. The old man looked piercingly into my eyes, and he spoke in Mandinka. Translation came from the interpreters I had brought with me.

13   "Yes, we have been told by the forefathers that there are many of us from this place who are in exile in that place called America."

14   Then the old man, who was 73 rains of age—the Gambian way of saying 73 years old, based upon the one rainy season per year—began to tell me the lengthy ancestral history of the Kinte clan. It was clearly a formal occasion for the villagers. They had grown mouse-quiet, and stood rigidly.

15   Out of the *griot's* head came spilling lineage details incredible to hear. He recited who married whom, two or even three centuries back. I was struck not only by the profusion of details, but also by the Biblical pattern of the way he was speaking. It was something like, "—and so-and-so took as a wife so-and-so, and begat so-and-so. . . ."

16   The *griot* had talked for some hours, and had got to about 1750 in our calendar. Now he said, through an interpreter, "About the time the

king's soldiers came, the eldest of Omoro's four sons, Kunta, went away from this village to chop wood—and he was never seen again. . . ."

17   Goose pimples came out on me the size of marbles. He just had no way in the world of knowing that what he told me meshed with what I'd heard from the old ladies on the front porch in Henning, Tenn. I got out my notebook, which had in it what Grandma had said about the African. One of the interpreters showed it to the others, and they went to the *griot,* and they all got agitated. Then the *griot* went to the people, and *they* all got agitated.

18   I don't remember anyone giving an order, but those 70-odd people formed a ring around me, moving counterclockwise, chanting, their bodies close together. I can't begin to describe how I felt. A woman broke from the circle, a scowl on her jet-black face, and came charging toward me. She took her baby and almost roughly thrust it out at me. The gesture meant "Take it!" and I did, clasping the baby to me. Whereupon the woman all but snatched the baby away. Another woman did the same with her baby, then another, and another.

19   A year later, a famous professor at Harvard would tell me: "You were participating in one of the oldest ceremonies of humankind, called 'the laying on of hands.' In their way, these tribespeople were saying to you, 'Through this flesh, which is us, we are you and you are us.' "

20   Later, as we drove out over the back-country road, I heard the staccato sound of drums. When we approached the next village, people were packed alongside the dusty road, waving, and the din from them welled louder as we came closer. As I stood up in the Land Rover, I finally realized what it was they were all shouting: "Meester Kinte! Meester Kinte!" In their eyes I was the symbol of all black people in the United States whose forefathers had been torn out of Africa while theirs remained.

21   Hands before my face, I began crying—crying as I have never cried in my life. Right at that time, crying was all I could do.

22   I went then to London. I searched and searched, and finally in the British Parliamentary records I found that the "king's soldiers" mentioned by the *griot* referred to a group called "Colonel O'Hare's forces," which had been sent up the Gambia River in 1767 to guard the then British-operated James Fort, a slave fort.

23   I next went to Lloyds of London, where doors were opened for me to research among all kinds of old maritime records. I pored through the records of slave ships that had sailed from Africa. Volumes upon volumes of these records exist. One afternoon about 2:30, during the seventh week of searching, I was going through my 1023rd set of ship records. I picked up a sheet that had on it the reported movements of 30 slave ships, my eyes stopped at No. 18, and my glance swept across the column entries. This vessel had sailed directly from the Gambia River to America in 1767; her name was the *Lord Ligonier;* and she had arrived at Annapolis (Naplis) the morning of September 29, 1767.

24   Exactly 200 years later, on September 29, 1967, there was nowhere

in the world for me to be except standing on a pier at Annapolis, staring sea-ward across those waters over which my great-great-great-great-grand-father had been brought. And there in Annapolis I inspected the micro-filmed records of the *Maryland Gazette.* In the issue of October 1, 1767, on page 3, I found an advertisement informing readers that the *Lord Ligonier* had just arrived from the River Gambia, with "a cargo of choice, healthy SLAVES" to be sold at auction the following Wednesday.

25   In the years since, I have done extensive research in 50 or so libraries, archives and repositories on three continents. I spent a year combing through countless documents to learn about the culture of Gambia's villages in the 18th and 19th centuries. Desiring to sail over the same waters navigated by the *Lord Ligonier,* I flew to Africa and boarded the freighter *African Star.* I forced myself to spend the ten nights of the crossing in the cold, dark cargo hold, stripped to my underwear, lying on my back on a rough, bare plank. But this was sheer luxury compared to the inhuman ordeal suffered by those millions who, chained and shackled, lay in terror and in their own filth in the stinking darkness through voyages averaging 60 to 70 days.

COMMENTARY

Haley's organization seems calculated to heighten the drama of his search for facts. Beginning familiarly with reminiscences of his elderly relatives, he then goes to Africa to hear a *griot* (paragraphs 10 to 17), the bard who has memorized his tribe's formal history. This leads to a climactic recognition scene (paragraphs 18 and 19) in which Haley is received into the community of his ancestors. But the process of validating oral tradition still remains. Haley tells the story with great precision ("one afternoon at 2:30, during the seventh week of search"; "in the issue of October 1, 1767, on page 3") in order to maximize and authenticate the dramatic effect of his moments of discovery.

        The chronological development is swift (except for a pause in paragraph 5 where Haley provides his "credentials" as a writer and authority on black issues). It also moves in opposite directions at the same time: while the article proceeds forward in time, describing the progress of Haley's research, it is moving backward in time to 1767. In a quest for the past, to go backward is to advance.

        But the principle of organization in Haley's article is not only chronological. It is also spatial, as an outline of the contents shows. Crucial events occur in specific places, without which there would be no discovery. It is appropriate that the most intense passage (and the longest one) occurs in Gambia (paragraphs 9 to 21), the location of Haley's "roots," which are the object of his search. Yet the narrative ends back in America, suggesting that the searcher, having found his past, is able to continue the life he was born into in the present. He sees himself, as the subtitle says, as a "black American."

OUTLINE

SUGGESTIONS FOR WRITING

1. Describe a journey in which you went to find, or obtain, something. Emphasize the meaning of the quest to you and give the most time and detail to its climactic moment.

2. Where are your roots? Interview your oldest relatives (you might even send a questionnaire) in order to discover the facts (or legends) about the origins of your family. Describe the most distant ancestor known to you or, as Haley does, describe your attempt to identify him.

take my saddle
from the wall: a valediction
LARRY MCMURTRY

Two segments of a chapter from McMurtry's book of essays on Texas represent two different forms of definition that often work well together: personal memoir and essay on some aspect of society. The first segment is a narrative about the author's family. This leads naturally into the second, an essay on the cowboy, because McMurtry's uncles all worked on the range. In the personal narrative, McMurtry describes a group of people; in the essay he sets out to define a way of life.

Pioneers didn't hasten to west Texas like they hastened to the southern and eastern parts of the state. At first glance, the region seemed neither safe nor desirable; indeed, it wasn't safe, and it took the developing cattle industry to render it desirable. My grandparents arrived in 1877 and prudently paused for ten years in Denton County, some sixty miles west of Dallas and not quite on the lip of the plains. The fearsome Comanche had

Source. Copyright © 1968 The Encino Press, 510 Baylor, Austin, Texas.

been but recently subdued—in fact, it was still too early to tell whether they *were* subdued. The last battle of Adobe Walls was fought in the Panhandle in 1874, and Quanah Parker surrendered himself and his warriors in 1875. The very next year, sensing a power vacuum, Charles Goodnight drove his herds into the Palo Duro; Satanta, the last great war chief of the Kiowa, killed himself in prison in 1878. Remnants of the two nations trickled into the reservation for the next few years; there were occasional minor hostilities on the South Plains as late as 1879. The Northern Cheyenne broke out in 1878—who could be sure the Comanches wouldn't follow their example? To those brought up on tales of Comanche terror the psychological barrier did not immediately fall. The Comanche never committed themselves readily to the reservation concept, and for a time there remained the chance that one might awaken in the night in that lonely country to find oneself and one's family being butchered by a few pitiless, reactionary warriors bent on a minor hostility.

2   At any rate, in the eighties William Jefferson and Louisa Francis and their first six children moved a hundred miles farther west, to Archer County, where, for three dollars an acre, they purchased a half-section of land. They settled near a good seeping spring, one of the favorite watering places on a military road that then ran from Fort Belknap to Buffalo Springs. The forts that the road connected soon fell from use, but cattle drivers continued to use the trail and the spring for many years. The young McMurtry boys had only to step out their door to see their hero figures riding past.

3   Indeed, from the pictures I have seen of the original house, they could have ignored the door altogether and squeezed through one of the walls. Life in such a house, in such a country, must surely have presented formidable difficulties and the boys (there were eventually nine, as against three girls) quite sensibly left home as soon as they had mastered their directions.

4   The median age for leave-taking seems to have been seventeen, and the fact that the surrounding country was rapidly filling up with farmers merely served as an added incentive to departure. The cowboy and the farmer are genuinely inimical types: they have seldom mixed easily. To the McMurtrys, the plow and the cotton-patch symbolized not only tasks they loathed but an orientation toward the earth and, by extension, a quality of soul which most of them not-so-covertly despised. A "one-gallus farmer" ranked very low in their esteem, and there were even McMurtrys who would champion the company of Negroes and Mexicans over the company of farmers—particularly if the farmers happened to be German. The land just to the north of the McMurtry holdings was settled by an industrious colony of German dairymen, and the Dutchmen (as they were called) were thought to be a ridiculous and unsightly thorn in the fair flesh of the range.

5   In later years two or three of the McMurtry brothers increased their

fortunes through farming, but this was a fact one seldom heard bruited about. Indeed, I heard no discussion of the matter until fairly recently, when one of the farms sold for an even million dollars, a figure capable of removing the blight from almost any scutcheon.

6   The cowboy's contempt of the farmer was not unmixed with pity. The farmer walked in the dust all his life, a hard and ignominious fate. Cowboys could perform terrible labors and endure bone-grinding hardships and yet consider themselves the chosen of the earth; and the grace that redeemed it all in their own estimation was the fact that they had gone a-horseback. They were riders, first and last. I have known cowboys broken in body and twisted in spirit, bruised by debt, failure, loneliness, disease and most of the other afflictions of man, but I have seldom known one who did not consider himself phenomenally blessed to have been a cowboy, or one who could not cancel half the miseries of existence by dwelling on the horses he had ridden, the comrades he had ridden them with, and the manly times he had had. If the cowboy is a tragic figure, he is certainly one who will not accept the tragic view. Instead, he helps his delineators wring pathos out of tragedy by ameliorating his own loss into the heroic myth of the horseman.

7   To be a cowboy meant, first of all, to be a horseman. Mr. Dobie was quite right when he pointed out that the seat of the cowboy's manhood is the saddle. I imagine, too, that he understood the consequences of that fact for most cowboys and their women, but if so he was too kindly a man to spell out the consequences in his books. I would not wish to make the point crudely, but I do find it possible to doubt that I have ever known a cowboy who liked women as well as he liked horses, and I know that I have never known a cowboy who was as comfortable in the company of women as he was in the company of his fellow cowboys.

8   I pointed out in Chapter 4 that I did not believe this was the result of repressed homosexuality, but of a commitment to a heroic concept of life that simply takes little account of women. Certainly the myth of the cowboy is a very efficacious myth, one based first of all upon a deep response to nature. Riding out at sunup with a group of cowboys, I have often felt the power of that myth myself. The horses pick their way delicately through the dewy country, the brightness of sunrise has not yet fallen from the air, the sky is blue and all-covering, and the cowboys are full of jokes and morning ribaldries. It is a fine action, compelling in itself and suggestive beyond itself of other centuries and other horsemen who have ridden the earth.

9   Unfortunately, the social structure of which that action is a part began to collapse almost a hundred years ago, and the day of the cowboy is now well into its evening. Commitment to the myth today carries with it a terrible emotional price—very often the cowboy becomes a victim of his

own ritual. His women, too, are victims, though for the most part acqui-
escent victims. They usually buy the myth of cowboying and the ideal of
manhood it involves, even though both exclude them. A few even buy it
to the point of attempting to assimilate the all-valuable masculine qualities
to themselves, producing that awful phenomenon, the cowgirl.

10   If, as I suggested earlier, the cowboy is a tragic figure, one element of
the tragedy is that he is committed to an orientation that includes but does
not recognize the female, which produces, in day-to-day life, an extraordinary range of frustrations. Curiously, the form the cowboy's recognition
does take is literary: he handles women through a romantic convention.
The view is often proffered by worshippers of the cowboy that he is a
realist of the first order, but that view is an extravagant and imperceptive
fiction. Cowboys are romantics, extreme romantics, and ninety-nine out of
a hundred of them are sentimental to the core. They are oriented toward
the past and face the present only under duress, and then with extreme
reluctance.

11   People who think cowboys are realists generally think so because the
cowboy's speech is salty and apparently straight-forward, replete with the
wisdom of natural men. What that generally means is that cowboy talk
sounds shrewd and perceptive, and so it does. In fact, however, both the
effect and the intention of much cowboy talk is literary: cowboys are aphorists. Whenever possible, they turn their observations into aphorisms. Some
are brilliant aphorists, scarcely inferior to Wilde or La Rochefoucauld; one
is proud to steal from them. I plucked a nice one several years ago, to wit:
"A woman's love is like the morning dew: it's just as apt to fall on a horse-
turd as it is on a rose." In such a remark the phrasing is worth more than
the perception, and I think the same might be said for the realism of most
cowboys. It is a realism in tone only: its insights are either wildly romantic,
mock-cynical, or solemnly sentimental. The average cowboy is an excellent
judge of horseflesh, only a fair judge of men, and a terrible judge of
women, particularly "good women." Teddy Blue stated it succinctly forty
years ago:

> I'd been traveling and moving around all the time and I can't say I ever
> went out of my way to seek the company of respectable ladies. We (cowboys)
> didn't consider we were fit to associate with them on account of the company
> we kept. We didn't know how to talk to them anyhow. That was what I meant
> by saying that the cowpunchers was afraid of a decent woman. We were so
> damned scared that we'd do or say something wrong . . .[1]

That was written of the nineteenth century cowboy, but it would hold good
for most of their descendants, right down to now. Most of them marry,
and love their wives sincerely, but since their sociology idealizes women
and their mythology excludes her the impasse which results is often little
short of tragic. Now, as then, the cowboy escapes to the horse, the range,

---

[1] *We Pointed Them North,* p. 188.

the work, and the company of comrades, most of whom are in the same unacknowledged fix.

12   Once more I might repeat what cannot be stressed too often: that the master symbol for handling the cowboy is the symbol of the horseman.[2] The gunman had his place in the mythology of the West, but the cowboy did not realize himself with a gun. Neither did he realize himself with a penis, nor with a bankroll. Movies fault the myth when they dramatize gunfighting, rather than horsemanship, as the dominant skill. The cowboy realized himself on a horse, and a man might be broke, impotent, and a poor shot and still hold up his head if he could ride.

COMMENTARY

The bridge between the two segments of McMurtry's chapter is paragraph 5, where he notes that, although farming was disdained by his ranching ancestors, a *rich* farmer became acceptable. This leads to an explanation of the cowboy's dislike of farmers and thence to a definition of "cowboy."

McMurtry equates cowboy with horseman (paragraph 7). He supports that definition by citing an authority, J. Frank Dobie, who taught for many years at the University of Texas and wrote many books on the West. By looking beneath the surface of the cowboy's romanticized life-style, McMurtry discloses internal conflicts that have unfortunate social and psychological consequences. Because many people have been deceived by false definitions of the cowboy, McMurtry uses "negative detail" as he differentiates his subject from others of the genus "male hero." Thus the cowboy is *not* homosexual, *not* a lady's man, *not* a gunman.

OUTLINE

    I. Reminiscence—paragraphs 1–5
       A. McMurtry's pioneer grandparents' arrival in west Texas—paragraphs 1–3
       B. Their childrens' departure—paragraph 4
       C. The cause of this emigration: displacement by farmers of cowboys—paragraph 5
    II. The cowboy—paragraphs 6–12
       A. A chosen man "a-horseback"—paragraphs 6–7
       B. Womanless—paragraphs 8–9

---

[2] *Singing Cowboy,* ed. Margaret Larkin, Oak Publications, N.Y., 1963, p. 60. See in this regard the well-known song "My Love is a Rider," a song said to have been composed by Belle Starr: He made me some presents among them a ring. The return that I made him was a far better thing. 'Twas a young maiden's heart I would have you all know, He won it by riding his bucking bronco. Now listen young maidens where e're you reside, Don't list to the cowboy who swings the rawhide. He'll court you and pet you and leave you and go Up the trail in the spring on his bucking bronco.

    C. Tragic—paragraphs 10–11
    D. Without a gun—paragraph 12

SUGGESTIONS FOR WRITING

1. Select some career that is popularly believed to be glamorous (artist, doctor, writer, pilot, lumberjack, professional athlete) and show how the reality may differ from the illusion.

2. Describe a person or an event in the life of your own family (migration, work or profession such as farming, mining, practicing law). Then generalize the particular into a broader definition of a class or kind of people: integrate your own experience with the experience of others.

3. Many definitions attempt to describe "what something *is*." There are also "functional definitions" that describe "what something *does*." McMurtry's main point about the cowboy is that his central "action" (paragraphs 8 and 9) is riding horses. Define some activity in terms of the most prominent actions that are performed, for example, a student, athlete, soldier, engineer, musician, and so forth. Show how the central forms of behavior may determine what else is, or is not, possible.

4. Do you agree with McMurtry's statement (paragraph 9) that the cowgirl is "an awful phenomenon"? What limitations of the myth of the cowboy may make it inapplicable to women—or to other groups? Do you know of other occupations which by their very natures seem to exclude certain categories of people? If so, describe and explain; if not, show how some occupation traditionally limited to men, to women, to the rich, to the young (etc.) can, in fact, be appropriate beyond its traditional group. If you think, for example, that a woman can be a soldier, or that an octogenarian can be a college student, explain how this currently atypical situation might work out.

the grey beginnings
RACHEL CARSON

Carson has two purposes in this essay. First, she wants to present a brief account of a very extended event—the history of our earth and the evolution of life on it. Second, she wants to make us see the connections between this past history and the present, not in a utilitarian sense (she is not concerned with the fact that we can use the remains of ancient dinosaurs as fuel oil) but in an emotional sense (she *is* concerned with

Source. From *The Sea Around Us,* Revised Edition, by Rachel L. Carson. Copyright © 1950, 1951, 1961 by Rachel L. Carson. Reprinted by permission of Oxford University Press, Inc.

helping us to feel at home in our natural environment). Our culture suffers from a stereotyped separation between science, seen as a coldly rational approach to life without regard for values and emotional understanding, and humanistic studies, seen as concerning themselves with values and understanding but in a vague and unrealistic way. Carson designs her writing to show that the two can come together, that a scientific interest in facts is quite compatible with a humanistic interest in emotional values.

And the earth was without form, and void; and darkness was upon the face of the deep.

Genesis

1 **b**eginnings are apt to be shadowy, and so it is with the beginnings of that great mother of life, the sea. Many people have debated how and when the earth got its ocean, and it is not surprising that their explanations do not always agree. For the plain and inescapable truth is that no one was there to see, and in the absence of eyewitness accounts there is bound to be a certain amount of disagreement. So if I tell here the story of how the young planet Earth acquired an ocean, it must be a story pieced together from many sources and containing whole chapters the details of which we can only imagine. The story is founded on the testimony of the earth's most ancient rocks, which were young when the earth was young; on other evidence written on the face of the earth's satellite, the moon; and on hints contained in the history of the sun and the whole universe of star-filled space. For although no man was there to witness this cosmic birth, the stars and the moon and the rocks were there, and, indeed, had much to do with the fact that there is an ocean.

2 The events of which I write must have occurred somewhat more than 2 billion years ago. As nearly as science can tell that is the approximate age of the earth, and the ocean must be very nearly as old. It is possible now to discover the age of the rocks that compose the crust of the earth by measuring the rate of decay of the radioactive materials they contain. The oldest rocks found anywhere on earth—in Manitoba—are about 2.3 billion years old. Allowing 100 million years or so for the cooling of the earth's materials to form a rocky crust, we arrive at the supposition that the tempestuous and violent events connected with our planet's birth occurred nearly 2½ billion years ago. But this is only a minimum estimate, for rocks indicating an even greater age may be found at any time.

3 The new earth, freshly torn from its parent sun, was a ball of whirling gases, intensely hot, rushing through the black spaces of the universe on a path and at a speed controlled by immense forces. Gradually the ball of flaming gases cooled. The gases began to liquefy, and Earth became a molten mass. The materials of this mass eventually became sorted out in a definite pattern: the heaviest in the center, the less heavy surrounding

them, and the least heavy forming the outer rim. This is the pattern which persists today—a central sphere of molten iron, very nearly as hot as it was 2 billion years ago, an intermediate sphere of semi-plastic basalt, and a hard outer shell, relatively quite thin and composed of solid basalt and granite.

4   The outer shell of the young earth must have been a good many millions of years changing from the liquid to the solid state, and it is believed that, before this change was completed, an event of the greatest importance took place—the formation of the moon. The next time you stand on a beach at night, watching the moon's bright path across the water, and conscious of the moon-drawn tides, remember that the moon itself may have been born of a great tidal wave of earthly substance, torn off into space. And remember that if the moon was formed in this fashion, the event may have had much to do with shaping the ocean basins and the continents as we know them.

5   There were tides in the new earth, long before there was an ocean. In response to the pull of the sun the molten liquids of the earth's whole surface rose in tides that rolled unhindered around the globe and only gradually slackened and diminished as the earthly shell cooled, congealed, and hardened. Those who believe that the moon is a child of earth say that during an early stage of the earth's development something happened that caused this rolling, viscid tide to gather speed and momentum and to rise to unimaginable heights. Apparently the force that created these greatest tides the earth has ever known was the force of resonance, for at this time the period of the solar tides had come to approach, then equal, the period of the free oscillation of the liquid earth. And so every sun tide was given increased momentum by the push of the earth's oscillation, and each of the twice-daily tides was larger than the one before it. Physicists have calculated that, after 500 years of such monstrous, steadily increasing tides, those on the side toward the sun became too high for stability, and a great wave was torn away and hurled into space. But immediately, of course, the newly created satellite became subject to physical laws that sent it spinning in an orbit of its own about the earth.

6   There are reasons for believing that this event took place after the earth's crust had become slightly hardened, instead of during its partly liquid state. There is to this day a great scar on the surface of the globe. This scar or depression holds the Pacific Ocean. According to some geophysicists, the floor of the Pacific is composed of basalt, the substance of the earth's middle layer, while all other oceans are floored with a thin layer of granite. We immediately wonder what became of the Pacific's granite covering and the most convenient assumption is that it was torn away when the moon was formed. There is supporting evidence. The mean density of the moon is much less than that of the earth (3.3 compared with 5.5), suggesting that the moon took away none of the earth's heavy iron core, but that it is composed only of the granite and some of the basalt of the outer layers.

7   The birth of the moon probably helped shape other regions of the world ocean besides the Pacific. When part of the crust was torn away, strains must have been set up in the remaining granite envelope. Perhaps the granite mass cracked open on the side opposite the moon scar. Perhaps, as the earth spun on its axis and rushed on its orbit through space, the cracks widened and the masses of granite began to drift apart, moving over a tarry, slowly hardening layer of basalt. Gradually the outer portions of the basalt layer became solid and the wandering continents came to rest, frozen into place with oceans between them. In spite of theories to the contrary, the weight of geologic evidence seems to be that the locations of the major ocean basins and the major continental land masses are today much the same as they have been since a very early period of the earth's history.

8   But this is to anticipate the story, for when the moon was born there was no ocean. The gradually cooling earth was enveloped in heavy layers of cloud, which contained much of the water of the new planet. For a long time its surface was so hot that no moisture could fall without immediately being reconverted to steam. This dense, perpetually renewed cloud covering must have been thick enough that no rays of sunlight could penetrate it. And so the rough outlines of the continents and the empty ocean basins were sculptured out of the surface of the earth in darkness, in a Stygian world of heated rock and swirling clouds and gloom.

9   As soon as the earth's crust cooled enough, the rains began to fall. Never have there been such rains since that time. They fell continuously, day and night, days passing into months, into years, into centuries. They poured into the waiting ocean basins, or, falling upon the continental masses, drained away to become sea.

10   That primeval ocean, growing in bulk as the rains slowly filled its basins, must have been only faintly salt. But the falling rains were the symbol of the dissolution of the continents. From the moment the rains began to fall, the lands began to be worn away and carried to the sea. It is an endless, inexorable process that has never stopped—the dissolving of the rocks, the leaching out of their contained minerals, the carrying of the rock fragments and dissolved minerals to the ocean. And over the eons of time, the sea has grown ever more bitter with the salt of the continents.

11   In what manner the sea produced the mysterious and wonderful stuff called protoplasm we cannot say. In its warm, dimly lit waters the unknown conditions of temperature and pressure and saltiness must have been the critical ones for the creation of life from non-life. At any rate they produced the result that neither the alchemists with their crucibles nor modern scientists in their laboratories have been able to achieve.

12   Before the first living cell was created, there may have been many trials and failures. It seems probable that, within the warm saltiness of the primeval sea, certain organic substances were fashioned from carbon dioxide, sulphur, phosphorus, potassium, and calcium. Perhaps these were transition steps from which the complex molecules of protoplasm arose—molecules

that somehow acquired the ability to reproduce themselves and begin the endless stream of life. But at present no one is wise enough to be sure.

13 Those first living things may have been simple microorganisms rather like some of the bacteria we know today—mysterious borderline forms that were not quite plants, not quite animals, barely over the intangible line that separates the non-living from the living. It is doubtful that this first life possessed the substance chlorophyll, with which plants in sunlight transform lifeless chemicals into the living stuff of their tissues. Little sunshine could enter their dim world, penetrating the cloud banks from which fell the endless rains. Probably the sea's first children lived on the organic substances then present in the ocean waters, or, like the iron and sulphur bacteria that exist today, lived directly on inorganic food.

14 All the while the cloud cover was thinning, the darkness of the nights alternated with palely illumined days, and finally the sun for the first time shone through upon the sea. By this time some of the living things that floated in the sea must have developed the magic of chlorophyll. Now they were able to take the carbon dioxide of the air and the water of the sea and of these elements, in sunlight, build the organic substances they needed for life. So the first true plants came into being.

15 Another group of organisms, lacking the chlorophyll but needing organic food, found they could make a way of life for themselves by devouring the plants. So the first animals arose, and from that day to this, every animal in the world has followed the habit it learned in the ancient seas and depends, directly or through complex food chains, on the plants for food and life.

16 As the years passed, and the centuries, and the millions of years, the stream of life grew more and more complex. From simple, one-celled creatures, others that were aggregations of specialized cells arose, and then creatures with organs for feeding, digesting, breathing, reproducing. Sponges grew on the rocky bottom of the sea's edge and coral animals built their habitations in warm, clear waters. Jellyfish swam and drifted in the sea. Worms evolved, and starfish, and hardshelled creatures with many-jointed legs. The plants, too, progressed, from the microscopic algae to branched and curiously fruiting seaweeds that swayed with the tides and were plucked from the coastal rocks by the surf and cast adrift.

17 During all this time the continents had no life. There was little to induce living things to come ashore, forsaking their all-providing, all-embracing mother sea. The lands must have been bleak and hostile beyond the power of words to describe. Imagine a whole continent of naked rock, across which no covering mantle of green had been drawn—a continent without soil, for there were no land plants to aid in its formation and bind it to the rocks with their roots. Imagine a land of stone, a silent land, except for the sound of the rains and winds that swept across it. For there was no living voice, and nothing moved over its surface except the shadows of the clouds.

18 Meanwhile, the gradual cooling of the planet, which had first given the

earth its hard granite crust, was progressing into its deeper layers; and as the interior slowly cooled and contracted, it drew away from the outer shell. This shell, accommodating itself to the shrinking sphere within it, fell into folds and wrinkles—the earth's first mountain ranges.

19   Geologists tell us that there must have been at least two periods of mountain building (often called "revolutions") in that dim period, so long ago that the rocks have no record of it, so long ago that the mountains themselves have long since been worn away. Then there came a third great period of upheaval and readjustment of the earth's crust, about a billion years ago, but of all its majestic mountains the only reminders today are the Laurentian hills of eastern Canada, and a great shield of granite over the flat country around Hudson Bay.

20   The epochs of mountain building only served to speed up the processes of erosion by which the continents were worn down and their crumbling rock and contained minerals returned to the sea. The uplifted masses of the mountains were prey to the bitter cold of the upper atmosphere and under the attacks of frost and snow and ice the rocks cracked and crumbled away. The rains beat with greater violence upon the slopes of the hills and carried away the substance of the mountains in torrential streams. There was still no plant covering to modify and resist the power of the rains.

21   And in the sea, life continued to evolve. The earliest forms have left no fossils by which we can identify them. Probably they were soft-bodied, with no hard parts that could be preserved. Then, too, the rock layers formed in those early days have since been so altered by enormous heat and pressure, under the foldings of the earth's crust, that any fossils they might have contained would have been destroyed.

22   For the past 500 million years, however, the rocks have preserved the fossil record. By the dawn of the Cambrian period, when the history of living things was first inscribed on rock pages, life in the sea had progressed so far that all the main groups of backboneless or invertebrate animals had been developed. But there were no animals with backbones, no insects or spiders, and still no plant or animal had been evolved that was capable of venturing onto the forbidding land. So for more than three-fourths of geologic time the continents were desolate and uninhabited, while the sea prepared the life that was later to invade them and make them habitable. Meanwhile, with violent tremblings of the earth and with the fire and smoke of roaring volcanoes, mountains rose and wore away, glaciers moved to and fro over the earth, and the sea crept over the continents and again receded.

23   It was not until Silurian time, some 350 million years ago, that the first pioneer of land life crept out on the shore. It was an arthropod, one of the great tribe that later produced crabs and lobsters and insects. It must have been something like a modern scorpion, but, unlike its descendants, it never wholly severed the ties that united it to the sea. It lived a strange life, half-terrestrial, half-aquatic, something like that of the ghost crabs that speed

along the beaches today, now and then dashing into the surf to moisten their gills.

24 Fish, tapered of body and stream-molded by the press of running waters, were evolving in Silurian rivers. In times of drought, in the drying pools and lagoons, the shortage of oxygen forced them to develop swim bladders for the storage of air. One form developed an air-breathing lung and by its aid could live buried in the mud for long periods.

25 It is very doubtful that the animals alone would have succeeded in colonizing the land, for only the plants had the power to bring about the first amelioration of its harsh conditions. They helped make soil of the crumbling rocks, they held back the soil from the rains that would have swept it away, and little by little they softened and subdued the bare rock, the lifeless desert. We know very little about the first land plants, but they must have been closely related to some of the larger seaweeds that had learned to live in the coastal shallows, developing strengthened stems and grasping, rootlike holdfasts to resist the drag and pull of the waves. Perhaps it was in some coastal lowlands, periodically drained and flooded, that some such plants found it possible to survive, though separated from the sea. This also seems to have taken place in the Silurian period.

26 The mountains that had been thrown up by the Laurentian revolution gradually wore away, and as the sediments were washed from their summits and deposited on the lowlands, great areas of the continents sank under the load. The seas crept out of their basins and spread over the lands. Life fared well and was exceedingly abundant in those shallow, sunlit seas. But with the later retreat of the ocean water into the deeper basins, many creatures must have been left stranded in shallow, landlocked bays. Some of these animals found means to survive on land. The lakes, the shores of the rivers, and the coastal swamps of those days were the testing grounds in which plants and animals either became adapted to the new conditions or perished.

27 As the lands rose and the seas receded, a strange fishlike creature emerged on the land, and over the thousands of years its fins became legs, and instead of gills it developed lungs. In the Devonian sandstone this first amphibian left its footprint.

28 On land and sea the stream of life poured on. New forms evolved; some old ones declined and disappeared. On land the mosses and the ferns and the seed plants developed. The reptiles for a time dominated the earth, gigantic, grotesque, and terrifying. Birds learned to live and move in the ocean of air. The first small mammals lurked inconspicuously in hidden crannies of the earth as though in fear of the reptiles.

29 When they went ashore the animals that took up a land life carried with them a part of the sea in their bodies, a heritage which they passed on to their children and which even today links each land animal with its origin in the ancient sea. Fish, amphibian, and reptile, warm-blooded bird and mammal—each of us carries in our veins a salty stream in which the

CHART OF THE HISTORY OF

ERAS	PERIODS c. million years ago Holmes Scale (Revised 1959)	MOUNTAINS	VOLCANOES
CENOZOIC	Pleistocene 0–1	Coast ranges, western United States: this disturbance probably still in progress	
CENOZOIC	Tertiary 1–70	Alps, Himalayas, Apennines, Pyrenees, Caucasus	Great vulcanism in western United States formed Columbia Plateau (200,000 square miles of lava) Vesuvius and Etna began to erupt
MEZOZOIC	Cretaceous 70–135	Rocky Mountains, Andes Rising of Panama Ridge: indirect result — Gulf Stream	
MEZOZOIC	Jurassic 135–180	Sierra Nevadas	
MEZOZOIC	Triassic 180–225		Many volcanoes in western North America, also in New England
PALEOZOIC	Permian 225–270	Appalachians south of New England	Volcanic outpourings produced Deccan Plateau of India
PALEOZOIC	Carboniferous 270–350		
PALEOZOIC	Devonian 350–400	Northern Appalachians (this area never again covered by sea)	
PALEOZOIC	Silurian 400–440	Caledonian Mountains (Great Britain, Scandinavia, Greenland — only their roots remain)	Volcanoes in Maine and New Brunswick
PALEOZOIC	Ordovician 440–500		
PALEOZOIC	Cambrian 500–600		
PROTEROZOIC	600–3000 ±	Grenville Mountains of eastern North America (only their roots remain) — age 1000 million Penokean Mountains (Minnesota, Ontario) formerly Killarney — age 1700 million	
ARCHEOZOIC	3000 ±	Earliest known mountains (Laurentian of Minnesota and Ontario — only traces remain) — age 2600 million Earliest known sedimentary and volcanic rocks, much altered by heat and pressure, their history obscure	

THE EARTH AND ITS LIFE

GLACIERS	SEAS	DEVELOPMENT OF LIFE
Pleistocene glaciation — ice sheets over vast areas of North America and northern Europe	Sea level fluctuating because of glaciers	Rise of man Modern Plants and animals
	Great submergence of lands. Nummulitic limestone formed — later used in Pyramids	Higher mamals, except man Highest plants
	Much of Europe and about half of North America submerged. Chalk cliffs of England formed	Last of dinosaurs and flying reptiles Reptiles dominant on land
	Last invasion of sea into eastern California and Oregon	First birds
		First dinosaurs Some reptiles return to sea Small, primitive mammals
Glaciers in broad equatorial belt: India, Africa, Australia, South America	Extensive seas over western United States; world's largest salt deposits formed in Germany	Primitive reptiles Amphibians declining Earliest cycads and conifers
	Central United States covered by sea for last time. Great coal beds formed	Amphibians developing rapidly First insects Coal—making plants
		Fishes dominate seas First amphibian fossils
	Repeated invasions by sea. Salt beds formed in eastern United States	First life appeared on continents
	Greatest known submergence of North America — more than half of continent covered	Earliest known vertebrates Cephalopods common in seas
	Seas advance and withdraw, at one time covering most of United States	First clear fossil record dates from this period; all major groups of invertebrates established
Earliest known ice age		Rise of invertebrates (inferred)
		Earliest life (inferred)

elements sodium, potassium, and calcium are combined in almost the same proportions as in sea water. This is our inheritance from the day, untold millions of years ago, when a remote ancestor, having progressed from the one-celled to the many-celled stage, first developed a circulatory system in which the fluid was merely the water of the sea. In the same way, our lime-hardened skeletons are a heritage from the calcium-rich ocean of Cambrian time. Even the protoplasm that streams within each cell of our bodies has the chemical structure impressed upon all living matter when the first simple creatures were brought forth in the ancient sea. And as life itself began in the sea, so each of us begins his individual life in a miniature ocean within his mother's womb, and in the stages of his embryonic development repeats the steps by which his race evolved, from gill-breathing inhabitants of a water world to creatures able to live on land.

30   Some of the land animals later returned to the ocean. After perhaps 50 million years of land life, a number of reptiles entered the sea in Mesozoic time. They were huge and formidable creatures. Some had oarlike limbs by which they rowed through the water; some were webfooted, with long, serpentine necks. These grotesque monsters disappeared millions of years ago, but we remember them when we come upon a large sea turtle swimming many miles at sea, its barnacle-encrusted shell eloquent of its marine life. Much later, perhaps no more than 50 million years ago, some of the mammals, too, abandoned a land life for the ocean. Their descendants are the sea lions, seals, sea elephants, and whales of today.

31   Among the land mammals there was a race of creatures that took to an arboreal existence. Their hands underwent remarkable development, becoming skilled in manipulating and examining objects, and along with this skill came a superior brain power that compensated for what these comparatively small mammals lacked in strength. At last, perhaps somewhere in the vast interior of Asia, they descended from the trees and became again terrestrial. The past million years have seen their transformation into beings with the body and brain and the mystical spirit of man.

32   Eventually man, too, found his way back to the sea. Standing on its shores, he must have looked out upon it with wonder and curiosity, compounded with an unconscious recognition of his lineage. He could not physically re-enter the ocean as the seals and whales had done. But over the centuries, with all the skill and ingenuity and reasoning powers of his mind, he has sought to explore and investigate even its remote parts, so that he might re-enter it mentally and imaginatively.

33   He fashioned boats to venture out on its surface. Later he found ways to descend to the shallow parts of its floor, carrying with him the air that, as a land mammal long unaccustomed to aquatic life, he needed to breathe. Moving in fascination over the deep sea he could not enter, he found ways to probe its depths, he let down nets to capture its life, he invented mechanical eyes and ears that could re-create for his senses a world long lost, but a world that, in the deepest part of his subconscious mind, he had never wholly forgotten.

34   And yet he had returned to his mother sea only on her own terms. He cannot control or change the ocean as, in his brief tenancy of earth, he has subdued and plundered the continents. In the artificial world of his cities and towns, he often forgets the true nature of his planet and the long vistas of its history, in which the existence of the race of men has occupied a mere moment of time. The sense of all these things comes to him most clearly in the course of a long ocean voyage, when he watches day after day the receding rim of the horizon, ridged and furrowed by waves; when at night he becomes aware of the earth's rotation as the stars pass overhead; or when, alone in this world of water and sky, he feels the loneliness of his earth in space. And then, as never on land, he knows the truth that his world is a water world, a planet dominated by its covering mantle of ocean, in which the continents are but transient intrusions of land above the surface of the all-encircling sea.

COMMENTARY

Carson's essay is distinguished by two qualities: a marvelous control over masses of information, so that a 34-paragraph history of the earth and of life is shaped into sense rather than chaos; and the ability to humanize information about the nonhuman world, so that we respond to the story of a past which none of our kind witnessed as easily as if it were a story of yesterday. Let's look at these two qualities in turn.

    The skill of controlling masses of information consists of (1) the ability to summarize, and (2) the ability to select details, to emphasize one or two aspects, in order to give the summaries drama and prevent them from seeming vague. In the paragraph on human evolution (paragraph 31), for example, more than a million years of continuous change are compressed into four sentences. This compression is achieved by bypassing many of the complexities of the story, complexities that would delay Carson longer than she can afford here and would make no difference to the overall course of human history which she is describing. Thus the very tangled issue of just *where* the first human beings lived, and exactly *when* they became what we call "human," is ignored in her summary. About the place and time of the appearance of man she tells us only that it occurred "At last, perhaps somewhere in the vast interior of Asia . . ." That is all we need to know for this purpose. In the other direction, she gives a disproportionate amount of time to the two specific biological changes she feels are crucial: the modification of the hand and the increase in brain power. There were, of course, a great many other changes too, but she chooses those that are the most crucial to our being human. She mentions the change in our hands rather than the change in our feet (which are equally different from those of other primates) because she feels that our hands are crucial to the way of life we call human.

    The skill of humanizing nonhuman information consists of what rhetoricians call "personification," using words whose connotations refer to the lives of people so that nonhuman entities almost *become* people. We personify, for example, when we say "Necessity is the mother of invention," because "mother" is a word suggesting the human family. (If we said instead "Necessity is the source of invention," the personification—and the drama—would disappear.) Thus, Carson calls the sun the earth's "parent," refers to the moon as "a child of earth" and to its creation as its "birth," calls the sea "the great mother of life" and the first microorganisms "the sea's first children." The first creature to live on the land, an arthropod, is called a "pioneer" and a member of a "great tribe"; the movement onto the land is called "colonizing," the seas are said to have "crept" out of their basins. At the end of the essay, we watch man returning to "his mother sea."

The implication is that the entire ecosystem of the earth is one family, and that, like the members of one family, we can understand one another and feel at home together. Carson's ability to humanize the nonhuman world recalls that of the medieval mystic St. Francis, who wrote poetry about his "brother moon" and "sister wind." It is a powerful weapon in the battle to make people *care* about their natural environment.

OUTLINE

   I. The earth's beginnings: how the earth acquired an ocean—paragraphs 1–10

  II. The first biological formations—paragraphs 11–15

 III. Progressive complexity of evolution—paragraphs 16–34

     A. The lifeless continents—paragraphs 17–20

     B. Early life in the sea—paragraphs 21–22

     C. Colonizing the land and then the air—paragraphs 23–28

     D. Dependence of the land—and air—creatures on the sea—paragraph 29

     E. Return of some creatures to aquatic life—paragraph 30

     F. The evolution of man and his continuing ties to the sea—paragraphs 31–34

SUGGESTIONS FOR WRITING

1. Practice humanizing nonhuman information. Locate a straightforward description either of an event or of an object that moves or changes (these will be the easiest because you can use human verbs of motion). There are several in this book. Rewrite the description to emphasize the similarities between *X* and the way people think and behave. But be careful not to overdo it. The following overdone description of a flower, for instance, is merely silly.

"The infant daisy snuggles comfortably against the breast of its mother earth. Day by day it yearns upwards, reaching for the comforting smiling face of its nurse-maid the sun, and stretches its elongated toes in the soil. With its bright expression and haloed head, its neat green garments and clean sweet smell, it is as lovely a child as any of us could hope to bring up."

That won't make anyone protect our wild flowers. Any writing technique carried to excess defeats its purpose.

Before you write, consider the following narrative. Is its use of personification excessive, or effective?

DEATH OF AN ATLANTIC SALMON—Nelson Bryant

1   YORK COUNTY, New Brunswick—Bright as an angler's dream of a far away pool, the Atlantic salmon twisted out of the dark water and into the morning air when it felt the pressure of my line.

2   A few minutes later it lay gleaming on the rocky shore of Sister's Pool on the South West Miramichi River. It was only a three-pound grilse (an early returning salmon) but the miracle of its presence was in no way diminished, and I was once again reminded that a century-old tradition decrees that one "kills" rather than "catches" an Atlantic salmon. "Catching" does not carry the emotional freight of the deed.

3   Some five years before, that salmon's parents had come in from the ocean and moved up the river and into a secluded pool in Sister's Brook to spawn. Although they arrived in summer, spawning did not take place until October when the female formed a redd, or depression, in the gravelly bottom of the pool with violent contortions of her body. When she was ripe, she deposited her eggs in that redd, perhaps taking two or three days to accomplish this, and the male was always on hand to fertilize the eggs with his milt. The eggs, which were then covered with several inches of gravel, lay dormant until spring—the 10-pound female had deposited more than 5,000 eggs—when most of them hatched out and wriggled way up into open water. For a few weeks, these fry, as they are called, lived on the food provided by the yolk sacs of the eggs, then began to feed on the aquatic life of the stream.

4   The young salmon, my fish among them, remained in Sister's Brook for three years, and during most of that period they were so-called parr, the size of small brook trout, red-spotted and marked with vertical brown bands. Near the end of the time of their stay in the brook, the parr began to resemble mature salmon. Their bars and spots faded and their bodies took on a silver hue as they dropped down the brook and down the river to its mouth. They remained in the estuary for a few days, then swam out into the vast Atlantic through Cabot Straight or the Strait of Belle Isle.

5   In the years my fish spent in the brook, his mother returned twice more. His father, weakened by months of no food—for salmon do not feed after entering a river—and the stress of procreation and guarding the redd, had died the spring the young were hatched. A weakly swimming kelt, or spent, salmon, he had worked his way part of the distance downstream to the sea, his once-powerful and silvery body lank and black, before dying in a small eddy on a remote rocky shore where the crows soon found him.

6   At the time of his departure into the ocean, my fish had lost most of his brothers and sisters. About 90 per cent of them had perished, some eaten by mergansers, others by kingfishers, otters, eels and trout. Larger fish, including cod, dined on them as they swam through the Atlantic, but later, the rapidly growing salmon (some attain a weight of 15 pounds after two years at sea) would feed on the young of the cod.

7   Reaching the Davis Strait off Greenland, my salmon managed to remain alive, and at the end of 13 months at sea the urge to return to his natal river to spawn could not be denied, although other salmon, born in the same spring as he, might remain at sea for two more years.

8   Eluding drift nets, gill nets, and a variety of natural hazards including seals and larger predatory fish, my grilse (the word of a salmon that leaves

the ocean after only a little more than a year at sea) worked his unerring way back to Miramichi Bay and the river and swam upstream. He moved past other tributaries until he arrived at Rocky Brook Pool, which is on the main river, where he paused before beginning his ascent of the brook itself. He was the first of his "family" to return, and probably no more than a dozen of the original 5,000 would get as far as he did.

9   To kill a salmon is no small thing.*

2. Reduce a large body of information about an extended event to the size of a short essay. Perhaps you have just finished a course in American history: present American history in 700 words. Read an encyclopedia article on, for example, the French Revolution and condense it to a fifth of its length. Summarize the history of your family for three generations—in 700 words. Include the information necessary to make us see the meaning and direction of the extended event.

* Copyright © 1974 by *The New York Times* Company. Reprinted by permission.

the stereotype
GERMAINE GREER

This selection is a combination: it describes a concept (the female stereotype), an extended event (the history of the female stereotype), a personal reaction (the writer's disgust with the stereotype), and a current event (the career of "April Ashley").

Greer's rage at what she takes to be the female role in modern society prompts her to assemble an extraordinary collection of information. Everything about the essay is extravagant (rhetoricians would call it hyperbolic). The startling imagery and diction, the interpolated quotations, the final illustration: all are intended to astonish. The purpose of depicting the stereotype in the boldest, most colorful style possible is to make it preposterous, to make us raise the common sense objection that a *real* woman is not like that. The stereotype must be a lie. This is exactly the response that Greer wants. She despises the illusory woman manufactured by advertising and popular romantic art, because this illusory woman becomes the criterion by which men judge real women and real women judge themselves.

This subjective definition of the female stereotype, substantiated by such dramatic and selective use of details, functions also as an evaluation. It is a denunciation of what Greer sees as bad about society's expectations of women.

Source. From *The Female Eunuch* by Germaine Greer. Copyright © 1970, 1971 by Germaine Greer. Used with permission of McGraw-Hill Book Company.

In that mysterious dimension where the body meets the soul the stereotype is born and has her being. She is more body than soul, more soul than mind. To her belongs all that is beautiful, even the very word beauty itself. All that exists, exists to beautify her. The sun shines only to burnish

---

Taught from infancy that beauty is woman's sceptre, the mind shapes itself to the body, and roaming round its gilt cage, only seeks to adorn its prison.

Mary Wollstonecraft,
Vindication of the Rights of Women, 1792, p. 90

---

her skin and gild her hair; the wind blows only to whip up the color in her cheeks; the sea strives to bathe her; flowers die gladly so that her skin may luxuriate in their essence. She is the crown of creation, the masterpiece. The depths of the sea are ransacked for pearl and coral to deck her; the bowels of the earth are laid open that she might wear gold, sapphires, diamonds and rubies. Baby seals are battered with staves, unborn lambs ripped from their mothers' wombs, millions of moles, muskrats, squirrels, minks, ermines, foxes, beavers, chinchillas, ocelots, lynxes, and other small and lovely creatures die untimely deaths that she might have furs. Egrets, ostriches and peacocks, butterflies and beetles yield her their plumage. Men risk their lives hunting leopards for her coats, and crocodiles for her handbags and shoes. Millions of silkworms offer her their yellow labors; even the seamstresses roll seams and whip lace by hand, so that she might be clad in the best that money can buy.

The men of our civilization have stripped themselves of the fineries of the earth so that they might work more freely to plunder the universe for treasures to deck my lady in. New raw materials, new processes, new machines are all brought into her service. My lady must therefore be the chief spender as well as the chief symbol of spending ability and monetary success. While her mate toils in his factory, she totters about the smartest streets and plushiest hotels with his fortune upon her back and bosom, fingers and wrists, continuing that essential expenditure in his house which is her frame and her setting, enjoying that silken idleness which is the necessary condition of maintaining her mate's prestige and her qualification to demonstrate it.[1] Once upon a time only the aristocratic lady could lay claim to the title of crown of creation: only her hands were white enough, her feet tiny enough, her waist narrow enough, her hair long and golden enough; but every well-to-do burgher's wife set herself up to ape my lady and to follow fashion, until my lady was forced to set herself out like a gilded doll overlaid with monstrous rubies and pearls like pigeons' eggs. Nowadays the Queen of England still considers it part of her royal female role to sport as much of the family jewelry as she can manage at any one time on all public occasions, although the male monarchs have escaped such showcase duty, which devolves exclusively upon their wives.

---

[1] Thorstein Veblen [*The Theory of the Leisure Class*], *passim*.

3   At the same time as woman was becoming the showcase for wealth and caste, while men were slipping into relative anonymity and "handsome is as handsome does," she was emerging as the central emblem of western art. For the Greeks the male and female body had beauty of a human, not necessarily a sexual, kind; indeed they may have marginally favored the young male form as the most powerful and perfectly proportioned. Likewise the Romans showed no bias towards the depiction of femininity in their predominantly monumental art. In the Renaissance the female form began to predominate, not only as the mother in the predominant emblem of *madonna col bambino,* but as an aesthetic study in herself. At first naked female forms took their chances in crowd scenes or diptychs of Adam and Eve, but gradually Venus claims ascendancy, Mary Magdalene ceases to be wizened and emaciated, and becomes nubile and ecstatic, portraits of anonymous young women, chosen only for their prettiness, begin to appear, are gradually disrobed, and renamed Flora or Primavera. Painters begin to paint their own wives and mistresses and royal consorts as voluptuous beauties, divesting them of their clothes if desirable, but not of their jewelry. Susanna keeps her bracelets on in the bath. and Hélène Fourment keeps ahold of her fur as well!

4   What happened to women in painting happened to her in poetry as well. Her beauty was celebrated in terms of the riches which clustered around her: her hair was gold wires, her brow ivory, her lips ruby, her teeth gates of pearl, her breasts alabaster veined with lapis lazuli, her eyes as black as jet.[2] The fragility of her loveliness was emphasized by the inevitable comparisons with the rose, and she was urged to employ her beauty in love-making before it withered on the stem.[3] She was for consumption; other sorts of imagery spoke of her in terms of cherries and cream, lips as sweet as honey and skin white as milk, breasts like cream uncrudded, hard as apples.[4] Some celebrations yearned over her finery as

[2] E.g.,

> I thought my mistress' hairs were gold,
> And in her locks my heart I fold;
> Her amber tresses were the sight
> That wrapped me in vain delight;
>
> Her ivory front, her pretty chin,
> Were stales that drew me on to sin;
> Her starry looks, her crystal eyes
> Brighter than the sun's arise.
>
> [Robert Greene, *Francesco's Fortunes*]

[3] E.g.,

> When I admire the rose,
> That Nature makes repose
> In you the best of many,
> And see how curious art
> Hath decked every part,
> I think with doubtful view
> Whether you be the rose or the rose be you.
>
> [Thomas Lodge, *William Longbeard*]

[4] E.g.,

> Her cheeks like apples which the sun hath rudded,
> Her lips like cherries charming men to bite,
> Her breasts like to a bowl of cream uncrudded . . .
>
> [Edmund Spenser, *Epithalamion*]

well, her lawn more transparent than morning mist, her lace as delicate as gossamer, the baubles that she toyed with and the favors that she gave.[5] Even now we find the thriller hero describing his classy dames' elegant suits, cheeky hats, well-chosen accessories and footwear; the imagery no longer dwells on jewels and flowers but the consumer emphasis is the same. The mousy secretary blossoms into the feminine stereotype when she reddens her lips, lets down her hair, and puts on something frilly.

5   Nowadays women are not expected, unless they are Paola di Liegi or Jackie Onassis, and then only on gala occasions, to appear with a king's ransom deployed upon their bodies, but they are required to look expensive, fashionable, well-groomed, and not to be seen in the same dress twice. If the duty of the few may have become less onerous, it has also become the duty of the many. The stereotype marshals an army of servants. She is supplied with cosmetics, underwear, foundation garments, stockings, wigs, postiches and hairdressing as well as her outer garments, her jewels and furs. The effect is to be built up layer by layer, and it is expensive. Splendor has given way to fit, line and cut. The spirit of competition must be kept up, as more and more women struggle towards the top drawer, so that the fashion industry can rely upon an expanding market. Poorer women fake it, ape it, pick up on the fashions a season too late, use crude effects, mistaking the line, the sheen, the gloss of the high-class article for a garish simulacrum. The business is so complex that it must be handled by an expert. The paragons of the stereotype must be dressed, coifed and painted by the experts and the style-setters, although they may be encouraged to give heart to the housewives studying their lives in pulp magazines by claiming a lifelong fidelity to their own hair and soap and water. The boast is more usually discouraging than otherwise, unfortunately.

6   As long as she is young and personable, every woman may cherish the dream that she may leap up the social ladder and dim the sheen of luxury by sheer natural loveliness; the few examples of such a feat are kept before the eye of the public. Fired with hope, optimism and ambition, young women study the latest forms of the stereotype, set out in *Vogue, Nova, Queen* and other glossies, where the mannequins stare from among the advertisements for fabulous real estate, furs and jewels. Nowadays the uniformity of the year's fashions is severely affected by the emergence of

---

[5]E.g.,

> The outside of her garments were of lawn,
> The lining purple silk, with gilt stars drawn,
> Her wide sleeves green and bordered with many a grove . . .
> Buskins of shells all silvered used she
> Branched with blushing coral to the knee,
> Where sparrows perched, of hollow pearl and gold,
> Such as the world would wonder to behold;
> Those with sweet water oft her handmaid fills,
> Which as she went would chirrup through the bills.
> [Christoper Marlowe, *Hero and Leander*]

It is only proper to point out that in this passage Marlowe is setting Hero up as a foil to the natural beauty of Leander, beloved of the gods, who is presented quite naked. Hero as a stereotype might be considered one of the themes of the poem.

the pert female designers who direct their appeal to the working girl, emphasizing variety, comfort, and simple, striking effects. There is no longer a single face of the year: even Twiggy has had to withdraw into marketing and rationed personal appearances, while the Shrimp works mostly in New York. Nevertheless the stereotype is still supreme. She has simply allowed herself a little more variation.

7 The stereotype is the Eternal Feminine. She is the Sexual Object sought by all men, and by all women. She is of neither sex, for she has herself no sex at all. Her value is solely attested by the demand she excites in others. All she must contribute is her existence. She need achieve nothing, for she is the reward of achievement. She need never give positive evidence of her moral character because virtue is assumed from her loveliness, and her passivity. If any man who has no right to her be found with her she will not be punished, for she is morally neuter. The matter is solely one of male rivalry. Innocently she may drive men to madness and war. The more trouble she can cause, the more her stocks go up, for possession of her means more the more demand she excites. Nobody wants a girl whose beauty is imperceptible to all but him; and so men welcome the stereotype because it directs their taste into the most commonly recognized areas of value, although they may protest because some aspects of it do not tally with their fetishes. There is scope in the stereotype's variety for most fetishes. The leg man may follow miniskirts, the tit man can encourage see-through blouses and plunging necklines, although the man who likes fat women may feel constrained to enjoy them in secret. There are stringent

---

The myth of the strong black woman is the other side of the coin of the myth of the beautiful dumb blonde. The white man turned the white woman into a weak-minded, weak-bodied, delicate freak, a sex pot, and placed her on a pedestal; he turned the black woman into a strong self-reliant Amazon and deposited her in his kitchen. . . . The white man turned himself into the Omnipotent Administrator and established himself in the Front Office.

Eldridge Cleaver,
"The Allegory of the Black Eunuchs,"
Soul on Ice, 1968, p. 162

---

limits to the variations on the stereotype, for nothing must interfere with her function as sex object. She may wear leather, as long as she cannot actually handle a motorbike: she may wear rubber, but it ought not to indicate that she is an expert diver or waterskier. If she wears athletic clothes the purpose is to underline her unathleticism. She may sit astride a horse, looking soft and curvy, but she must not crouch over its neck with her rump in the air.

She was created to be the toy of man, his rattle, and it must jingle in his ears whenever, dismissing reason, he chooses to be amused.

Mary Wollstonecraft,
Vindication of the Rights of Women, 1792, p. 66

---

8 Because she is the emblem of spending ability and the chief spender,

she is also the most effective seller of this world's goods. Every survey ever held has shown that the image of an attractive woman is the most effective advertising gimmick. She may sit astride the mudguard of a new car, or step into it ablaze with jewels; she may lie at a man's feet stroking his new socks; she may hold the petrol pump in a challenging pose, or dance through woodland glades in slow motion in all the glory of a new shampoo; whatever she does her image sells. The gynolatry of our civilization is written large upon its face, upon hoardings, cinema screens, television, newspapers, magazines, tins, packets, cartons, bottles, all consecrated to the reigning deity, the female fetish. Her dominion must not be thought to entail the rule of women, for she is not a woman. Her glossy lips and mat complexion, her unfocused eyes and flawless fingers, her extraordinary hair all floating and shining, curling and gleaming, reveal the inhuman triumph of cosmetics, lighting, focusing and printing, cropping and composition. She sleeps unruffled, her lips red and juicy and closed, her eyes as crisp and black as if new painted, and her false lashes immaculately curled. Even when she washes her face with a new and creamier toilet soap her expression is as tranquil and vacant and her paint as flawless as ever. If ever she should appear tousled and troubled, her features are miraculously smoothed to their proper veneer by a new washing powder or a bouillon cube. For she is a doll: weeping, pouting or smiling, running or reclining, she is a doll. She is an idol, formed of the concatenation of lines and masses, signifying the lineaments of satisfied impotence.

Her essential quality is castratedness. She absolutely must be young, her body hairless, her flesh buoyant, and *she must not have a sexual organ*. No musculature must distort the smoothness of the lines of her body, although she may be painfully slender or warmly cuddly. Her expression must betray no hint of humor, curiosity or intelligence, although it may signify hauteur to an extent that is actually absurd, or smoldering lust, very feebly signified by drooping eyes and a sullen mouth (for the stereotype's lust equals irrational submission), or, most commonly, vivacity and idiot happiness. Seeing that the world despoils itself for this creature's benefit, she must be happy; the entire structure would topple if she were not. So the image of woman appears plastered on every surface imaginable, smiling interminably. An apple pie evokes a glance of tender beatitude, a washing machine causes hilarity, a cheap box of chocolates brings forth meltingly joyous gratitude, a Coke is the cause of a rictus of unutterable

---

Discretion is the better part of Valerie
though all of her is nice
lips as warm as strawberries
eyes as cold as ice
the very best of everything
only will suffice
not for her potatoes
and puddings made of rice

Roger McGough, *Discretion*

brilliance, even a new stick-on bandage is saluted by a smirk of satisfaction. A real woman licks her lips and opens her mouth and flashes her teeth when photographers appear: *she* must arrive at the premiere of her husband's film in a paroxysm of delight, or his success might be murmured about. The occupational hazard of being a Playboy Bunny is the aching facial muscles brought on by the obligatory smiles.

10   So what is the beef? Maybe I couldn't make it. Maybe I don't have a pretty smile, good teeth, nice tits, long legs, a cheeky arse, a sexy voice. Maybe I don't know how to handle men and increase my market value, so that the rewards due to the feminine will accrue to me. Then again, maybe I'm sick of the masquerade. I'm sick of pretending eternal youth. I'm sick of belying my own intelligence, my own will, my own sex. I'm sick of peering at the world through false eyelashes, so everything I see is mixed with a shadow of bought hairs; I'm sick of weighting my head with a dead mane, unable to move my neck freely, terrified of rain, of wind, of dancing too vigorously in case I sweat into my lacquered curls. I'm sick of the Powder Room. I'm sick of pretending that some fatuous male's self-important pronouncements are the objects of my undivided attention, I'm sick of going to films and plays when someone else wants to, and sick of having no opinions of my own about either. I'm sick of being a transvestite. I refused to be a female impersonator. I am a woman, not a castrate.

11   April Ashley was born male. All the information supplied by genes, chromosomes, internal and external sexual organs added up to the same thing. April was a man. But he longed to be a woman. He longed for the stereotype, not to embrace, but to be. He wanted soft fabrics, jewels, furs,

---

To what end is the laying out of the embroidered Hair, embared Breasts; vermilion Cheeks, alluring looks, Fashion gates, and artfull Countenances, effeminate intangling and insnaring Gestures, their Curls and Purls of proclaiming Petulancies, boulstered and laid out with such example and authority in these our days, as with Allowance and beseeming Conveniency?

    Doth the world wax barren through decrease of Generations, and become, like the Earth, less fruitful heretofore? Doth the Blood lose his Heat or do the Sunbeams become waterish and less fervent, than formerly they have been, that men should be thus inflamed and persuaded on to lust?

         Alex. Niccholes, *A Discourse of Marriage and Wiving,*
               1615, pp. 143–52

---

makeup, the love and protection of men. So he was impotent. He couldn't fancy women at all, although he did not particularly welcome homosexual addresses. He did not think of himself as a pervert, or even as a transvestite, but as a woman cruelly transmogrified into manhood. He tried to die, became a female impersonator, but eventually found a doctor in Casablanca who came up with a more acceptable alternative. He was to be castrated, and his penis used as the lining of a surgically constructed cleft, which would be a vagina. He would be infertile, but that has never affected the attribution of femininity. April returned to England, resplendent.

Massive hormone treatment had eradicated his beard, and formed tiny breasts: he had grown his hair and bought feminine clothes during the time he had worked as an impersonator. He became a model, and began to illustrate the feminine stereotype as he was perfectly qualified to do, for he was elegant, voluptuous, beautifully groomed, and in love with his own image. On an ill-fated day he married the heir to a peerage, the Hon. Arthur Corbett, acting out the highest achievement of the feminine dream, and went to live with him in a villa in Marbella. The marriage was never consummated. April's incompetence as a woman is what we must expect from a castrate, but it is not so very different after all from the impotence of feminine women, who submit to sex without desire, with only the infantile pleasure of cuddling and affection, which is their favorite reward. As long as the feminine stereotype remains the definition of the female sex, April Ashley is a woman, regardless of the legal decision ensuing from her divorce.[6] She is as much a casualty of the polarity of the sexes as we all are. Disgraced, unsexed April Ashley is our sister and our symbol.

COMMENTARY

Greer wants to write about herself and also about other women, since she feels that her personal life is very much affected by the situation of women in general. Her essay begins with the others, continues with herself, and ends with another person who includes them all: a person who functions, in Greer's view, as "our sister and our symbol." (Why do you think she does not want to end simply with herself?)

In the first six paragraphs, Greer lists the accoutrements of femininity: clothing, jewelry, cosmetics, the ingredients of good grooming as dictated by the modern "fashion industry." The next three paragraphs (7 to 9) explain how women, thus turned into the "Eternal Feminine," function as sexless sex objects.

In paragraph 10, Greer anticipates questions by stating her own point of view, explaining and justifying the intemperance of the preceding paragraphs. She is "sick of" complying with the stereotype, and this article is her manifesto. She refuses to be a female impersonator. Now it is clear that the first nine paragraphs have served not only to describe but also to indict. They were a catalogue of charges and grievances. Paragraph 10 is filled with the declarative first person singular: "I am," in rejection of the unreal "she is."

As a final vindication of her personal declaration, Greer relates the tale of April Ashley, a story Greer makes so unnatural and revolting that *any* effort to prevent its repetition seems legitimate.

Greer's involvement with her subject is so intense that at times it may almost seem as if hysteria, rather than reason, directs the surge of language.

---

[6] *Corbett* v. *Corbett* (otherwise Ashley) before Mr. Justice Ormerod (Law Report, February 2, 1970, Probate, Divorce and Admiralty Division). *News of the World,* February 8, 1970, *Sunday Mirror,* February 3, 8, 15, 1970.

The vocabulary ranges from formal (simulacrum, gynolatry, rictus) to slangy (ahold, tit man, gimmick). The use of present-tense verbs and the author's frankness about her own frustration (paragraph 10) give a sense of immediacy to the article, as if the personal here-and-now were the whole world. The dramatic power of this presentation is undeniable. Greer, and others like her, are indeed changing the way men think of women and women think of themselves. We may nevertheless question the accuracy of making a single stereotype of woman seem universal and of oversimplifying the course of the history of ideas (paragraphs 3 and 4).

Does intensity necessarily mean narrowness of view?

OUTLINE

    I. The historical beautification of "woman"—paragraphs 1–6
       A. By ornamentation—paragraph 2
       B. In art—paragraph 3
       C. In poetry—paragraph 4
    II. Today's woman as product of this history—paragraphs 5–9
       A. Class implications of the stereotype—paragraphs 5–6
       B. Woman's commercialization—paragraphs 8–9
   III. Exposure and illustration of the "lie"—paragraphs 10–11
       A. Greer's protest "I'm sick of pretending"—paragraph 10
       B. April Ashley, a casualty of the stereotype—paragraph 11

SUGGESTIONS FOR WRITING

1. Write a description of a female stereotype based on specific characteristics that Greer ignores. For example, describe the mother (or grandmother), the professional woman, or the athletic woman.

2. Is there a male stereotype also? (Perhaps there are several.) Write a definition that, like Greer's, establishes both the details that belong to the stereotype and your attitude toward it.

3. Define what you see as the stereotype of parents, sons, or daughters, and explain how the illusory model interferes with honest relationships between the generations.

the eagle has landed

Sometimes truth (like the proverbial beauty) is in the eye of the beholder: we define the world the way it looks to us. No two people see it through the same pair of eyes or record it exactly the same way.

The final selection in this series consists of three quite different descriptions of the same thing, specifically an event, man's first landing on the moon. In this case, the subject is intrinsically dramatic, as most genuine "firsts" are, probably because of the inherent human hunger for new experiences. These writers therefore have some of the best material imaginable. Their task is to make the best of that best.

They try to make the best of it by different methods. The first account simply selects certain sections of the recorded conversation between the astronauts and their earthbound guides during the tense moments before landing. The voices of the participants constitute the entire description of that first touchdown on the moon. The second account fleshes out this dialogue with a running commentary that identifies what is going on, explains why the voices say what they do, and widens the scope by adding information about "the listening millions back on earth." The third account invokes many of the techniques of fiction: the device of metaphor, the introduction of a narrator who seems able to read minds, a remarkable variability in diction and syntax, a novelist's backward manipulation of time. What results is an impressionistic account, not only of what happened and what it was like but also of how one intensely involved spectator—the writer himself—felt: shaken, apprehensive, tremendously excited at the spectacle of people doing what people had never done before.

Which presentation is the best?

Sources. Excerpted from *Life* Special Edition, "To the Moon and Back," Copyright © 1969 Time, Inc.
"The Eagle Landing," from *Journey to Tranquility* by Hugo Young, Bryan Silcock, and Peter Dunn. Copyright © 1970 Doubleday & Company, Inc.
Copyright © 1969, 1970 by Norman Mailer. Dialogue in Mailer excerpted from *First Man on the Moon* by Neil Armstrong, Michael Collins, Edwin E. Aldrin, Jr. Copyright © 1970 by Little, Brown and Company.

a Life magazine account

*E*agle's *powered let-down to the moon on Sunday afternoon was a surpassingly suspenseful maneuver. The dialogue between Eagle, whose onboard computer kept ringing false alarms, and Houston—with occasional interpolations by Apollo Control—was heard by tens of millions. A part of the sequence follows.*

CONTROL: Altitude about 46,000 feet, continuing to descend. . . . 2 minutes 20 seconds [into the burn of the descent engine]. Everything looking good.

EAGLE: Our position checks downrange here seem to be a little long.

HOUSTON: Eagle, you are go—you are go to continue power descent.

EAGLE: We've got good [radar] lock on. Altitude lights out. . . . And the earth right out our front window.

EAGLE: 1202, 1202!

CONTROL: Good radar data. Altitude now 33,500 feet.

EAGLE: Give us the reading on the 1202 program alarm.

HOUSTON: Roger. We got—we're go on that alarm.

CONTROL: Still go. Altitude 27,000 feet.

EAGLE: [We] throttle down better than in the simulator.

CONTROL: Altitude now 21,000 feet. Still looking very good. Velocity down now to 1,200 feet per second.

HOUSTON: You're looking great to us, Eagle.

EAGLE: Good, roger.

HOUSTON: Eagle, you're looking great, coming up 9 minutes.

CONTROL: We're now in the approach phase, looking good. Altitude 5,200 feet.

EAGLE: Manual auto attitude control is good.

CONTROL: Altitude 4,200.

HOUSTON: You're go for landing. Over.

EAGLE: Roger, understand. Go for landing. 3,000 feet.

EAGLE: 12 alarm. 1201.

HOUSTON: Roger, 1201 alarm.

EAGLE: We're go. Hang tight. We're go. 2000 feet. 47 degrees.

HOUSTON: Eagle looking great. You're go.

CONTROL: Altitude 1,600 . . . 1,400 feet.

EAGLE: 35 degrees. 35 degrees. 750, coming down at 23. 700 feet, 21 down. 33 degrees. 600 feet, down at 19 . . . 540 feet . . . 400 . . . 350 down at 4. . . . We're pegged on horizontal velocity. 300 feet, down 3½ . . . a minute. Got the shadow out there . . . altitude-velocity lights. 3½ down, 220 feet. 13 forward, 11 forward, coming down nicely . . . 75 feet, things looking good.

HOUSTON: 60 seconds.

EAGLE: Lights on. Down 2½. Forward. Forward. Good. 40 feet, down 2½. Picking up some dust. 30 feet. 2½ down. Faint shadow. 4 forward. Drifting to the right a little.

HOUSTON: 30 seconds.

EAGLE: Drifting right. Contact light. Okay, engine stop.

HOUSTON: We copy you down, Eagle.

EAGLE: Houston, Tranquility Base here.

The Eagle has landed.

HOUSTON: Roger, Tranquility, we copy you on the ground. You got a bunch of guys about to turn blue. We're breathing again. Thanks a lot.

journey to tranquility
HUGO YOUNG,
BRYAN SILCOCK,
PETER DUNN

1   Seventeen minutes later, Eagle had reached the low point of its orbit. The spacecraft was traveling feet first, its two triangular windows peering down as the barren surface of the Sea of Fertility rushed past less than ten miles below. If Armstrong and Aldrin had any doubts, it was still not too late to draw back and let Eagle remain safely in orbit. But neither the instruments crowding the tiny cabin nor the consoles back in Mission Control showed any signs of trouble, and Armstrong punched the "proceed" button to allow the computer to fire the descent engine. Flames blasted out of the big engine bell to slow the spacecraft down and send it dropping in a long arc toward the planned landing site three hundred miles to the east. Apollo II was past the point any previous flight had reached, plunging into the most dangerous and unpredictable twelve minutes of the mission.

2   Houston and Eagle exchanged terse, bullet-like packages of technical data as the seconds ticked away. The computer fired the little attitude control rockets clustered at each corner of the spacecraft to roll it gently over on to its back. A blue and white earth a quarter of a million miles away swung in front of the windows in place of the bare surface of the moon. The pace of events was quickening all the time. Pulses from the landing radar reflected from the surface below fed the astronauts with continuous information about their altitude and rate of descent.

3   "Eagle, Houston," said Mission Control. "You are go. Take it all at four minutes. Roger, you are go—you are to continue powered descent."

But a crisis was at hand. The job of processing the flood of data needed to control the spacecraft's descent was getting too much for its computer. At about 33,500 feet above the surface an alarm light flashed on, and the warning number 12 02 appeared on the computer keyboard just by Armstrong's right hand.

4   During their long training, the astronauts had been through simulations of every alarm in the lunar module the designers had been able to imagine. They had memorized the drill for dealing with the most likely emergencies and scribbled memos about others and attached them to the instrument panel. But the alarms that now lit up during Eagle's descent were not among them. They were completely unfamiliar. The success of the whole mission hung on the judgment, nerve and co-ordination between the men in the spacecraft and those back at Mission Control. Four times during the descent the alarm was repeated. Each time the guidance officer in Houston —Stephen Bales, an engineer still in his twenties—had to make an instant decision that the alarm was not mortally dangerous, and give Eagle a "go."

5   For five minutes the astronauts wrestled with their almost critically overloaded computer as their spacecraft gradually tipped over toward an upright position, ready for landing under the control of the automatic guidance system.

MISSION COMMENTATOR: Fido says we're go, altitude 9200 feet.
CAPCOM: 8300. You're looking great.
EAGLE: Good. Roger.
MISSION COMMENTATOR: Descent rate 129 feet per second.
CAPCOM: Eagle. You're looking great. Coming up nine minutes.
MISSION COMMENTATOR: We're now in the approach phase of it, looking
    good. Altitude 5200 feet.
EAGLE: Manual auto attitude control is good.
CAPCOM: Roger. Copy.
MISSION COMMENTATOR: Altitude 4200.
CAPCOM: Houston. You're go for landing. Over.
EAGLE: Roger, understand. Go for landing. 3000 feet.

6   Not until Eagle reached this point, 3000 feet from the surface, did Armstrong get the chance to look out of the window and get his bearings. The view was quite different from what he expected. Instead of the smooth landing ground Eagle needed he saw a crater the size of a football field, filled with big boulders and surrounded by rocks. A navigational error had brought Eagle into the final phase of the descent four miles away from the intended landing site, to a place where the ground was so uneven that the craft might easily have tipped over on landing.

7   The listening millions back on earth got no hint of how close the mission was to an abort, or an even more disastrous failure, from the clipped tones of the astronauts as they maneuvered down the last three thousand feet, the computer still perilously close to seizing up, and periodically flashing alarms.

EAGLE: 12 alarm. 12 01.
CAPCOM: Roger. 12 01 alarm.
EAGLE: We're go. Hang tight. We're go. 2000 feet. 47 degrees.
CAPCOM: Eagle looking great. You're go.

8   Armstrong, realizing that the automatic guidance system was going to carry Eagle down among the boulders, took over control from the computer. With Aldrin reading off the vital figures from the control panel he was able to give his whole attention to the controls and the terrain below.

EAGLE: 35 degrees [*the angle of approach*]. 35 degrees. 750 feet [*altitude*]. Coming down at 23 [*feet per second*]. 700 feet, 21 down. 33 degrees. 600 feet, down at 19. 540 feet, down at 30. Down at 15. 400 feet down at 9 (garbled).

9   By moving the attitude control handle in his right hand Armstrong could tilt the spacecraft in any direction. Using the thrust control handle in his left hand he could travel horizontally. The computer still had control over the rate of descent.

EAGLE: 8 forward. 350, down at 4. 330, 3½ down. We're pegged on horizontal velocity. 300 feet, down 3½. 47 forward (garbled). Down 1 a minute. 1½ down. 70. Got the shadow out there. 50, down at 2½. 19 forward. Altitude-velocity lights. 3½ down, 220 feet. 13 forward. 11 forward, coming down nicely. 200 feet, 4½ down. 5½ down. 160, 6½ down, 5½ down, 9 forward. 5 percent. Quantity light. [*A warning that the fuel was almost exhausted*].

10   Several times as Eagle skimmed westward from the football field crater, Armstrong had seen possible landing sites, only to reject them on coming closer. Back in Houston, Mission Control knew how desperately close Eagle was to the mandatory abort line, where with his landing fuel tanks virtually empty Armstrong would have had to fire the ascent engine to hurl the spacecraft back into orbit without landing. The lunar module, almost untried, with the weight of fuel allowed for contingencies pared to a minimum, was the weakest link of the chain forged to lift men to the moon. It almost broke at that moment.

EAGLE: 75 feet, things looking good. Down a half. 6 forward.
CAPCOM: 60 seconds.
EAGLE: Lights on. Down 2½. Forward. Forward. Good. 40 feet, down 2½. Picking up some dust.

Eagle's exhaust blasting the soil of the moon was throwing out dust on either side, making it difficult to judge the spacecraft's speed over the ground.

EAGLE: 30 feet, 2½ down. Faint shadow. 4 forward. 4 forward, drifting to the right a little 6 (garbled) down a half.
CAPCOM: 30 seconds.

EAGLE: (garbled). Forward. Drifting right. (garbled). Contact light [*meaning that the sensors under the landing pads had touched the moon's surface*]. Okay, engine stop. ACA out of detent. Modes control both auto. Descent engine command override, off. Engine arm, off. 413 is in.

CAPCOM: We copy you down Eagle.

EAGLE: (Armstrong). Houston, Tranquility Base here. The Eagle has landed.

CAPCOM: Roger. Tranquility. We copy you on the ground. You've got a bunch of guys about to turn blue. We're breathing again. Thanks a lot.

11   In the press center's auditorium the newspapermen were jigging wildly, waving their arms and yelling. The astronaut's wives were asked what they thought. Mrs. Joan Aldrin, an actress, said, "It's like a dramatic television show, but it seems unreal. There are just no words. Don't you agree?" She said her husband had taken a piece of the blessed bread from Webster Presbyterian Church but didn't know when he planned to eat it.

12   Mrs. Pat Collins said, "It was positively marvelous. From what I can tell everything is going like clockwork." Was she disappointed that her husband would not be walking on the moon? "Don't you think he's probably right there with them in spirit?" said Mrs. Collins brightly.

13   Mrs. Jan Armstrong, formidable short-haired sportswoman who lives with every heartbeat of her husband's flights into space, had followed Eagle's descent on a moon chart saying aloud, "Good . . . good . . . good . . . good . . ." Mrs. Armstrong said she planned to stay up until the two men were safely back on board the lunar module.

# of a fire on the moon
NORMAN MAILER

1   **b**oxed in their bulky pressure suits, tied in and swaddled like Eskimo children in baskets, all moves bulky, always in fear of rapping a bank of switches with the insensitive surface of their suits—"You're so clumsy and there's so much force required to move inside the suit," Aldrin had said, "that everything is WHAM! I could bump right into you and maybe I wouldn't know it"—constrained in vision, they began their powered descent. The motors of the descent stage were fired. Once again they braked. Once again the reduction of their speed began to bring them down from high velocity to low. Now they came below the orbital parameter of fifty thousand feet. They were committed. They would land, or they would

crash, or they would abort and return to Columbia, but they could not try it again.

2   It is worth a moment to consider the complexities of the descent. The Lem, we recall, had started at a speed of thirty-six hundred miles an hour when it left the Command Module and would come hovering to the lunar soil at three feet a second or less. Its first burn had braked its speed enough to reduce its orbit, but this was relatively a small reduction. Now at fifty thousand feet it would go from approximately three thousand and more miles an hour down to six hundred miles an hour at 13,500 feet, a steady forceful braking of the motors for two hundred and fifty miles. Conceive of them on this long brake, two hundred and fifty miles with their rocket motors burning in front of them in order to take their speed down to no more than the speed of a jet plane, and that is but the beginning. They have lost but five miles of altitude in this period of braking—their route has been near to parallel to the curve of the moon—they will descend yet another half-mile and cover another ten miles before their horizontal speed is relevant to the speeds of an automobile, sixty miles an hour, fifty miles an hour, there, slowed, ready for the last descent, they are at high gate, seven thousand feet, not a mile and a half above the moon. Yet all this while, for all of this trip, from a point forty-five thousand feet up, down to high gate at seven thousand feet, there in their bulky-wham suits, they have been riding on their backs, feet forward, eyes looking up through their windows, so that they see nothing of the moon ground, but instead are staring up at the earth. What a curious position for descent. But the landing radar is on the other side of the Lem (it would require a huge outrigger to install it in a position more comfortable for them) and the landing radar is now their eyes as it bounces signals off the moon and returns them estimates of altitude. So they will ride from forty-five thousand feet to seven thousand feet flat on their backs, unable even to see the moon. Yet there has been additional cause for worry already. At the beginning of powered descent, at fifty thousand feet, before they turned over, they had been lying face down, looking out backward on the Sea of Tranquility as it receded through their windows, and their first mark of orientation, the crater Maskelyne W, did not appear on time and in the place where it should be. A fatefully long second passed. A second at three thousand miles an hour is nearly a mile, another second passed. Were they lost? Maskelyne W came under the window two full seconds and then a little more late. They were already two miles off the mark. At forty-five thousand feet, motor burning all the way in front of them, the Lem rolled them over on their backs. The moon was now invisible, the earth above their window—their hands reached up to the instrument panel overhead, they floated, held in position by cables and restraints for there were, we may remember, no couches in the Lem. How must the earth have looked in the quiet anxiety of the moment. Their toes were leading them to the moon, their eyes were looking at the earth—would they ever see it again, or was this the hour of signing off? So descended the Lem, weird unwieldy flying

machine, vehicle on stilts and never before landed, craft with a range of shifting velocities more than comparable to the difference from a racing car down to an amphibious duck, a vehicle with huge variations in speed and handling as it slowed, a vehicle to be flown for the first time in the rapidly changing field of gravity of the moon, going from weightlessness to one-sixth gravity, and one-sixth gravity had never been experienced before in anything but the crudest simulations, and mascons beneath, their location unknown, their effect on moon gravity considerable, angles of vision altering all the time and never near to perfect, the weight of the vehicle reducing drastically as the fuel was consumed, and with it all, the computer guiding them, allowing them to feel all the confidence a one-eyed man can put in a blind man going down a dark alley, and when, at the moment they would take over themselves to fly it manually, a range of choices already tried in simulation but never in reality would be open between full manual and full computer. Armstrong could, if he wished, control the attitude of the Lem and its forward progress, but allow the computer to manage the rate of descent. The only difficulty was that the hand controls of the Lem were curious indeed. To his right was a short thick red pistol grip like a small club of a joy stick, and it could be cocked left and right, forward and back, or be turned like a screwdriver to translate separate commands for roll, pitch, and yaw—it had even a push-to-talk switch, and this control (Attitude Controller Assembly) by pitching the Lem forward or back, could serve to increase or retard the forward speed once the ship was slowed for the final descent; it could also twist her, sidle her, waddle her, or cant her into new positions for skimming over boulders. What a swivel, what phallus!

3   At the left hand was a control which altered the speed of descent, a Thrust-Translater Controller, a glorified toggle switch which changed the rate of descent one foot per second every time one clicked it. Armed with this set of instruments, they would come in over ground never seen closely before, in an unfamiliar field of gravity, flying a ship which had never been landed, there to come down on four legs rather than wheels, all the while directing their vehicle with two hand controls as difficult of manipulation as some sophisticated version of patting the head with one hand while rubbing a circle on the belly with the other. All of this to be done in the bulky-wham suit.

4   It was not easy. No question of that. Many of the simulations on the ground had ended in mock crashes or mock aborts. Not all problems were solvable on the spot. Only Armstrong in fact was trained to take the Lem all the way in, and he had the memory of smashing the LLRV. But let us listen to an account of the difficulties by Aldrin.

> Neil will take it down. He has the controls on his side. I don't have them on my side. There's a throttle on my side, but I don't have this rate of descent control, and I don't have this redesignation capability. . . . But during the actual landing there is a fairly neat division of labor. Neil will be looking more and more out the window with his hand on that stick. He's not able to

look much at the displays on board. This is where we have to have a finely tuned teamwork, so that Neil gets the information he needs to transfer whatever he sees into something meaningful. I'll have to relay this information. If Neil has to take his attention away from looking out the window, look down to the keyboard and then back again, this is wasteful.

5   There were items sufficient for tension, yes. It was the measure of the trip to the moon that the more one knew of the difficulties, the more intense was the anxiety. Now we can add to the failures of communication and the difficulties of flying the Lem that extraordinary moment in the descent when the alarm light went on and the number 1202 blinked on the Display and Keyboard.

6   We can go back to the point not four minutes after ignition when the Lem turned over on its back and the astronauts approaching the moon looked across a quarter of a million miles to earth. The comments are laconic, the difficulties are doubtless still ahead, but the radio is giving trouble again. They have passed through a minute where their remarks are garbled.

CAPCOM: Eagle, Houston. You are GO. Take it all at four minutes. Roger, you are GO—you are GO to continue power descent.
ALDRIN: Roger.
PAO: Altitude 40,000.
CAPCOM: And Eagle, Houston. We've got data dropout. You're still looking good.
ALDRIN: PGNCS. We got good lock on. Altitude light is out. Delta H is minus 2900.
CAPCOM: Roger, we copy.
ALDRIN: Got the earth right out our front window.

7   How powerful must have been such a sight to draw comment when the radio is working poorly, and a garbled remark can throw confusion back and forth. Perhaps it suggests some hint of happiness that they are finally at the beginning of the entrance to the last tunnel.

8   In the next moment Aldrin's voice speaks. "Houston, you're looking at our Delta H program alarm?"

9   "That's affirmative," replies the Capcom. "It's looking good to us. Over."

10   Aldrin's voice calls out, "1202, 1202." It was an alarm from the computer—"Executive Overflow" was its title. What a name! One thinks of seepage on the corporation president's bathroom floor. In fact it meant the computer was overloaded, and so unable to perform all its functions. In such a case the computer stops, then starts over again. It has recalculated its resources. Now it will take on only the most important functions, drop off the others. But what a moment at Mission Control! They have worked on this alarm in the day Kranz devoted to emergency situations. They know that if 1202 keeps blinking, the activities of the computer will soon deteriorate. The automatic pilot will first be lost, then control over the thrust

of the engine, then Navigation and Guidance—the pilots will have to abort. In fifteen seconds it can all happen.

11   Picture Aldrin on his back looking up at the DSKY. "Give us the reading on the 1202 program alarm." It is his way of saying, "Is it serious?"

12   Thirty seconds go by. Duke speaks up the quarter of a million miles. "Roger, we got. . . ." Pause. "We're GO on that alarm."

13   Kranz has been quizzing his Guidance officers and his Flight Dynamics officers. It is a ten-second roll call, and each one he queries says GO. The words come in, "GO. GO. GO. GO." The key word is from Guidance Officer Stephen G. Bales. It is on his console that the 1202 is also blinking. But they have been over the permissible rate of alarm on which they can continue to fly a mission, and the 1202 is coming in not that fast—the Executive Overflow is not constant. So Bales' voice rings out GO. Listening to it on a tape recorder later, there is something like fear in the voice, it is high-pitched, but it rings out. In the thirty seconds between Aldrin's request for a reading and the reply that they were GO, the decision has been taken.

14   Capcom: "Eagle, Houston. We'll monitor your Delta H." Mission Control would take over part of Pings. Data from the landing radar would no longer be fed to the computer on the Eagle, it would be sent uniquely to the ground. Eagle would be able to continue with the computer eased of some of its burden. But if telemetry failed again, and Pings could not reassume the burden, they would still have to turn back.

15   So they were obliged to proceed through the long braking burn with their minds on thoughts of Abort all the way, their eyes on the instrument panel, Armstrong's eyes as much as Aldrin's, searching for a clue to what had caused the overload, six hundred dials and switches to consider and eliminate in blocks and banks—a hopeless activity: the cause of the malfunction might reveal itself on no dial, and in fact could derive from the load of the rendezvous radar in addition to the landing radar, and that introduced still another fear, for the rendezvous radar would have even more work on the trip up from the moon. As Duke said: "Here we are with a computer that seems to be saturated during descent and my gosh, we might be asking it to perform a more complicated task during ascent." And periodically Kranz queried his FIDO, his GUIDO, his TelCom and his EECOM, and the voices came back, "GO, GO, GO, GO," and Eagle descended, now at twenty-one thousand feet, now at sixteen thousand, thirteen thousand five hundred. "Stand by," said the Capcom, "You're looking great at eight minutes." Altitude ninety-two hundred feet.

16   In another twelve seconds they were at high gate. Now their horizontal speed was very low, their thrust was reduced, and they began to sit up from their near horizontal position. Slowly the astronauts' legs inclined with the legs of the Lem toward the ground, slowly their heads came up. And as they did, so returned a view of the moon through the bottom of the window now that the Lem inclined back toward the vertical. There were markings on their windows, horizontal lines to line up against the horizon of the

moon and so serve to pinpoint the area where they would land, but as the ground of the Sea of Tranquility came into sight from four thousand feet, from three thousand feet, as their angle shifted and more and more of the moon was visible through that slanted window, so to their distress was the terrain unrecognizable. Quick glimpses showed no landmarks, no particular craters on the flat desert of Tranquility which might bear familiar relation to the photographs and charts Apollo 10 had prepared for them, and Armstrong memorized, no, now they were in another place, whether four miles or fourteen away from the selected landing site was impossible to tell. And at that instant a new alarm blinks on the computer. "Twelve alarm," says Aldrin, "1201." The Capcom answers, "Roger. 1201 alarm."

17 When nothing further is said, Aldrin's voice comes in again. "We're GO. Hang tight. We're GO. Two thousand feet. . . ."
CAPCOM: "Roger."
EAGLE: "Forty-seven degrees."
CAPCOM: "Eagle looking great. You're GO."

18 And the flight controllers at Mission Control are screwed to the parameters of the consoles, the roll calls come in for GO. There is always attention to Bales' answer to Kranz's query. "GO," Bales' voice will pipe out against the alarms.

19 Kranz is a leader. He is a man who gives others the feeling that they are about to go through the door together into the stadium where they are each going to play the best game of their life. Kranz, like Slayton, has the look of a man who had lived for years in space, and Bales is a young engineer with a large round face and large horn-rimmed glasses, destiny sits on him with a moist touch, but the limits of decision had been clarified that June morning a month ago and Bales had done the work to separate a total crisis from a partial crisis on 1202 and 1201, and now, distinguishing the differences—no time to ask for confirmation—calls GO. The mission continues.

20 But the astronauts continue without the division of labor Aldrin has specified as tidy. They come down toward the gray wife of the earth's ages with their eyes riveted to the instruments. There are no more than peeps and glimpses of the oncoming ground. At two thousand feet, Armstrong finally leaves the dials, studies the view from the window. He can land by hand if necessary now.

21 But he cannot locate himself. No landmarks are familiar. From one thousand feet up it is apparent that Eagle is headed for a wretched crater with a boulder field of rocks and "the rocks seemed to be coming up at us awfully fast." Fast and mean are those rocks accelerating to the eye like the zoom of a camera down to the ground. "The clock runs about triple speed in a situation like that." And now Aldrin is calling out relevant computer and instrument readings. Here they come at Armstrong! "750, coming down at 23." That was altitude seven hundred and fifty feet, rate of descent twenty-three feet per second. "700 feet, 21 down. 600 feet,

down at 19. 540 feet down at 30—down at 15." In the tension Aldrin has miscalled a number for an instant. "400 feet, down at 9." Something is now garbled. Then the voice again. It is quiet, it is almost sad. "350, down at 4. 330 feet, 3½ down. We're pegged on horizontal velocity."

22   They are drifting horizontally over the boulder fields, skittering like a water bug debating which pad it will light on. Armstrong has taken over all of attitude control and part of throttle control—his commands are now inserted in with computer commands. The descent rate has reduced from ten feet a second to three feet, then only a foot a second. They hover, Armstrong searching for a spot in the boulder field, "because I'm sure some of the ejecta coming out of such a large crater would have been lunar bedrock, and as such, fascinating to the scientists. I was tempted, but my better judgment took over. . . ." No, he is not rushing in. He has gone through the computer alerts, the loss of all landmarks, has descended into that narrow field of vision where the horizon of the moon is always near, now drops down toward those boulders, hovers and skims, he has not had his recurring dreams as a boy night after night without tutoring the synapses of his growth into a thousand simulations of deliberate entrance into a dark space.

23   At last there is a place, "the size of a big house lot" between craters and a boulder field, and drifting almost done, they see the shadow of their Lem slanting across the moon ground like a giant prehistoric bird of destiny and "200 feet," says Aldrin, "4½ down, 5½ down. 160, 6½ down, 5½ down, 9 forward. 5 percent. Quantity light. 73 feet. Things looking good. Down a half. 6 forward."

24   "Sixty seconds," says the Capcom. That is the limit of their fuel.

25   "Lights on," returns Eagle. Now their landing lights burn down on the sunlit moon ground to beam through the dust, and now comes the dust. At thirty feet above the ground, a great amount blows out in all directions like an underwater flower of the sea and the ground is partially visible beneath as if "landing in a very fast-moving ground fog," and the fuel gauges almost empty, and still he drifts forward. "Thirty seconds," calls out the Capcom for warning. And in a murk of dust and sunlight and landing lights, the Eagle settles in. Contact lights light up on the board to register the touch of the probes below her legs. Aldrin's voice speaks softly, "Okay, engine stop. ACA out of detente. Modes control both auto. Descent engine command override off. Engine arm off. 413 is in."

26   CAPCOM: "We copy you down, Eagle"

27   ARMSTRONG: "Houston, Tranquility Base here. The Eagle has landed."

28   Then was it that the tension broke for fifty million people or was it five hundred million, or some sum of billions of eyes and ears around a world which had just come into contact with another world for what future glory, disaster, blessing or curse nobody living could know. And Armstrong and Aldrin, never demonstrative, shook hands or clapped each other on the back—they did not later remember—and back at Mission Control, Charley

Duke said, "Roger, Tranquility, we copy you on the ground. You've got a bunch of guys about to turn blue. We're breathing again. Thanks a lot."

29   And Kranz, who had issued every order to Duke, and queried his controllers in a voice of absolute calm for the entire trip down, now tried to speak and could not. And tried to speak, and again could not, and finally could unlock his lungs only by smashing his hand on a console so hard his bones were bruised for days. But then if his throat had constricted and his lungs locked, his heart stopped, he would have been a man who died at the maximum of his moments on earth and what a spring might then have delivered him to the first explorers of the moon. Perhaps it is the function of the dream to teach us those moments when we are GO or NO GO for the maximum thrust into death. They were down, they were on the moon ground, and who could speak?

30   "All right," said Kranz. "Everybody settle down, and let's get ready for a T-1 Stay—No Stay."

COMMENTARY

All of the moon-landing descriptions use the structure natural to the presentation of an event, chronological development. However, the three narratives differ in two ways: they include different amounts of material and material of different kinds. The dialogue between the astronauts and the NASA personnel functions as an essential core (in the first version, this core is all that is judged essential). Even here, however, where the kind of material is identical, the writers include different segments of the total record available. Thus at one point the *Life* writer chooses

> HOUSTON: "Eagle, you are go—you are go to continue power descent."

Young, Silcock, and Dunn choose, more fully,

> "Eagle, Houston," said Mission Control. "You are go. Take it all at four minutes. Roger, you are go—you are go to continue power descent."

Mailer chooses, more excitedly,

> CAPCOM: "Eagle, Houston. You are GO. Take it all at four minutes. Roger, you are GO—you are GO to continue power descent."

The *Life* writer, aiming primarily at a sense of rapid progression, does not want the triple repetition of "you are go" that the other two versions take time for. Young, Silcock, and Dunn, aiming at a fuller but "objective" account, do not want the emotionalism of Mailer's capitalized "GO" series.

As for different kinds of material, at one point the Eagle's computer sends out an alarm ("1202") which could abort the landing. *Life* records this crisis with only an exclamation point to indicate its importance:

> EAGLE: 1202! 1202!
> CONTROL: Good radar data. Altitude now 33,500 feet.

> EAGLE: Give us a reading on the 1202 program alarm.
> HOUSTON: Roger. We got—we're go on that alarm.

Both of the other versions emphasize the incident of the 1202 alarm by stopping the chronological progress to explain. In order to fill this pause and identify its meaning, Young, Silcock, and Dunn choose a statement describing the astronauts' preparations for handling such alarms, the inadequacy of those preparations now, the necessity for interaction between the spacecraft and ground control, the fourfold repetition of the alarm, the decision of engineer Bales—"still in his twenties"— that the mission should continue. All of this could be called "external background," information that permits us to sense the duration of the alarm period and to assess its significance.

Mailer pauses much longer over the 1202 alarm and includes a wider range of information. The first thing we learn, in fact, is his own awareness of the incongruity of scientific terminology.

> Aldrin's voice calls out "1202, 1202." It was an alarm from the computer—"Executive Overflow" was its title. What a name! One thinks of seepage on the corporation president's bathroom floor.

With that witticism he gets a laugh, and so dispels tension. We don't worry too much about a leaky toilet. But tension is not dispelled for long: we learn next that in a mere 15 seconds (the time it took for the joke about the bathroom), the Eagle's equipment could have failed and aborted the landing. While we were laughing, everything might have been lost.

Mailer next concentrates on the actions and emotions of people. We learn a good deal more about Stephen Bales, for example. He acquires a title, a middle initial, and a high-pitched voice which betrays "something like fear." We watch the encapsulated astronauts in a frantic attempt to make 600 dials tell them what's gone wrong. We are made to store away tension for the eventual ascent from the moon by Charley Duke's remark that even if the Eagle can make it down, it might not be able to make it back up. We encounter again the incongruous mixture of technical terms (FIDO, GUIDO, TelCom, EECOM), and the simplest and most excited of everyday words (the "GO, GO, GO, GO" is the chant of a high-school cheerleader)—and the crisis is past. After a pause of some 500 words, we are on our way again: the Eagle descends the next 11,000 feet in a mere 27 words.

Mailer's account of the 1202 alarm plays on our emotions, creates and releases and re-creates tension, includes images of everyday reality (the leaky plumbing, the shouting cheerleaders) to heighten our sense of how different this experience is from all others and yet how much it consists of the same words, the same human responses. From all of this emerges the unstated thesis that, on the moon as well as on earth, people are people: there is nothing dehumanizing about going where no one has ever gone before. It seems as if people become most dramatically human precisely by sharing in the quest for new experiences. Mailer's definition of the effect of the moon landing therefore functions also as an endorsement of the spirit of adventure and verges upon evaluation.

SUGGESTIONS FOR WRITING

1. Write three accounts of the same event, with different intentions: simply to tell someone what happened; to tell someone what happened and how it came about; to tell someone what happened, how it came about, and how you feel about it. In this incremental process you will use new ranges of material each time. The final version will define the effect of the event upon you.

2. Read several published accounts of another dramatic event, a genuine "first" or "only"—for example, the assassination of President Kennedy or Martin Luther King (events occurring for *both* the first and the only time), the attempted assassination of Governor Wallace, a key play in a crucial athletic contest, the first day of a war (Germany's invasion of Poland in 1939, the bombing of Pearl Harbor in 1941), or the last day of a war (V-E Day, V-J Day, the return of the first prisoners from North Vietnam).

Write a commentary in which you explain the writers' different intentions and methods of fulfilling them.

3. Attempt to share the astronauts' experience of doing something for the first time, without familiar surroundings, without the familiar means by which we gather information. Have someone blindfold you and then direct you through an area filled with obstacles; allow only a short time, perhaps 60 seconds. Ask someone in the class to write down the conversation, which will consist of your guide's directions and your questions and responses.

Afterward, describe the experience. Use the transcript as a basis, but (1) eliminate unnecessary material, and (2) go beyond it both objectively (to explain what happened) and subjectively (to explain how you felt). Before you write, read (below) a section of the actual transcript of the Apollo landing published by the National Aeronautics and Space Administration (NASA). It covers the last five minutes. Note the extraordinary amount of detail. Why do all three of our versions above eliminate certain parts of it?

TRANSCRIPTS OF LANDING SEQUENCE*

APOLLO 11 MISSION COMMENTARY, 7-20-69, GET 102:43:00, CDT 15:15 307/1

CapCom: Roger, copy.
Pao: Altitude 4200.
CapCom: Houston. You're go for landing. Over.
Eagle: Roger, understand. Go for landing. 3000 feet.
CapCom: Copy.
Eagle: 12 alarm. 1201.

---

*Courtesy of the National Aeronautics and Space Administration.

EAGLE: 1201.

CAPCOM: Roger. 1201 alarm.

EAGLE: We're go. Hang tight. We're go. 2,000 feet. 2,000 feet into the AGS. 47 degrees.

CAPCOM: Roger.

EAGLE: 47 degrees.

CAPCOM: Eagle looking great. You're go.

PAO: Altitude 1600. 1400 feet. Still looking very good.

CAPCOM: Roger. 1202. We copy it.

EAGLE: 35 degrees. 35 degrees. 750, coming down at 23. 700 feet, 21 down. 33 degrees. 600 feet, down at 19. 540 feet, down at 30— down at 15. 400 feet, down at 9. (garbled) 8 forward. 350, down at 4. 330, 3½ down. We're pegged on horizontal velocity. 300 feet, down 3½. 47 forward. (garbled) Down 1 a minute. 1½ down. 70. Got the shadow out there. 50, down at 2½. 19 forward. Altitude-velocity lights. 3½ down, 220 feet. 13 forward. 11 forward, coming down nicely. 200 feet, 4½ down. 5½ down. 160, 6½ down, 5½ down, 9 forward. 5 percent. Quantity light. 75 feet, things looking good. Down a half. 6 forward.

CAPCOM: 60 seconds.

EAGLE: Lights on. Down 2½. Forward. Forward. Good. 40 feet, down 2½. Picking up some dust. 30 feet, 2½ down. Faint shadow. 4 forward. 4 forward, drifting to the right a little. 6 (garbled) down a half.

CAPCOM: 30 seconds.

EAGLE: (garbled) forward. Drifting right. (garbled) Contact light. Okay, engine stop. ACA out of detent. Modes control both auto, descent engine command override, off. Engine arm, off. 413 is in.

CAPCOM: We copy you down, Eagle.

EAGLE: (Armstrong) Houston, Tranquility base here. The Eagle has landed.

CAPCOM: Roger, Tranquility, we copy you on the ground. You've got a bunch of guys about to turn blue. We're breathing again. Thanks a lot.

TRANQUILITY: Thank you.

CAPCOM: You're looking good here.

TRANQUILITY: I tell you. We're going to be busy for a minute. Master arm on. Take care of the descent. (garbled) Very smooth touchdown. Looks like we're venting the oxidizer now.

CAPCOM: Roger, Eagle. And you are stay for T1. Over. Eagle, you are stay for T1.

END OF TAPE

(Press Kit, Release No. 74–75, pp. 66–67.)

series two

DEFINITION: READINGS WITHOUT COMMENTARY

---

the hurricane
RICHARD HUGHES

This short description of the process by which a hurricane is born, grows, and dies emphasizes the underlying natural principles (the effective immobility of huge amounts of a fluid, the tendency of spinning substances to fly outwards from their center), so that we will be able not only to see what is happening but also to understand why it happens. Since the writer cannot show us *X* itself, and yet wants us to see it, he calls upon analogies with which we are familiar: a balloon, for example, and a revolving motor.

1   **t**he thing to remember about the atmosphere is its size. A little air is so thin, so fluid; in small amounts it can slip about so rapidly, that the conditions which give rise to a hurricane cannot be reproduced on a small scale. In trying to explain a hurricane, therefore, one must describe the large thing itself, not a model of it. For it is only when one thinks of the hugeness of a parcel of air on the world, the big distance it may have to shift to equalise some atmospheric difference, that one can realise how slow and immobile, regarded on a *large* scale, the air is.

2   It happens like this. The air above a warm patch of sea, somewhere near the Canaries, is warmed: so it will tend to be pushed up and replaced by the colder, weightier air around. In a warm room it would rise in a continuous gentle stream, and be replaced by a gentle draught under the door—no excitement. But on a large scale it cannot: that is what is different. It rises in a single lump, as if it were encased in a gigantic balloon—

Source. From *In Hazard* by Richard Hughes. Copyright © 1962. Reprinted by permission of David Higham Associates, Ltd.

being actually encased in its own comparative sluggishness. Cold air rushes in underneath not as a gentle draught but as a great wind, owing to the bodily lifting of so great a bulk of air.

3 Air moving in from all round towards a central point: and in the middle, air rising: that is the beginning. Then two things happen. The turning of the earth starts the system turning: not fast at first, but in a gentle spiral. And the warm air which has risen, saturated with moisture from the surface of the sea, cools. Cooling, high up there, its moisture spouts out of it in rain. Now, when the water in air condenses, it releases the energy that held it there, just as truly as the explosion of petrol re-leases energy. Millions of horse-power up there loose. As in a petrol-motor, that energy is translated into motion: up rises the boundless balloon still higher, faster spins the vortex.

4 Thus the spin of the Earth is only the turn of the crank-handle which starts it: the hurricane itself is a vast motor, revolved by the energy gen-erated by the condensation of water from the rising air.

5 And then consider this. Anything spinning fast enough tends to fly away from the centre—or at any rate, like a planet round the sun, reaches a state of balance where it cannot fly inwards. The wind soon spins round the centre of a hurricane so fast it can no longer fly into that centre, how-ever vacuous it is. Mere motion has formed a hollow pipe, as impervious as if it were made of something solid.

6 That is why it is often calm at the centre of a hurricane: the wind actually cannot get in.

7 So this extraordinary engine, fifty miles or more wide, built of speed-hardened air, its vast power generated by the sun and by the shedding of rain, spins westward across the floor of the Atlantic, often for weeks together, its power mounting as it goes. It is only when its bottom at last touches dry land (or very cold air) that the throttle is closed; no more moist air can be sucked in, and in a few days, or weeks at most, it spreads and dies.

the dance of the dervishes
JULIAN HUXLEY

Most of us have heard the phrase "a whirling dervish." This short description of an activity shows what dervishes really do when they whirl and what this whirling—certainly a peculiar way to behave, in the opinion of Westerners—means to the people who do it.

Huxley writes from the viewpoint of an objective observer, a "casual

Source. From an Antique Land. Reprinted by permission of A. D. Peters and Company.

visitor" as he puts it, and therefore the information he gives us is limited to what he was able to see.

1 **t**here are very few dancing dervisheries left in the region. The one at Tripoli stands among olive groves just outside the city, on the banks of the Kadesha river. The Sheikh of the community, a dignified little man with a greying beard, led us through the various domed dwellings to the separate building set aside for the ceremonial dancings, or turnings as they might better be called. This was a square hall, open on the valley side, with balconies round the other three, supported on wide white arches. We took our places to the left of the Sheikh, with the musicians on his right. The rest of the seats were soon filled up with privileged spectators. After a time the dozen or so dervishes walked in slowly with folded hands, and sat down cross-legged on carpets. They were wearing tall khaki fezzes protruding from small turbans, and brown abbas—sleeved robes like heavy dressing-gowns, but without a belt, and made of camel's hair. The musicians began chanting chants full of semi-tones, and prayers were intoned. The dancers rose and began to walk slowly round and round in a heavy ritualized step, with a solemn pause at each forward pace, and a turn and a bow each time they passed one corner of the hall. A flute and drums struck up, and after some twenty minutes the dervishes took off their abbas, disclosing full white skirts with weighted hems, reaching from waist to feet. Then, each in his appointed spot, they began their turning.

2 Turning consists essentially in pivoting on the left foot, with two or three steps of the right foot to each full turn. As the speed of turning increases, the white skirt flares out into a great rotating cone. One handsome young dervish elaborated the movement by making a graceful dip during each turn, and by varying the position of head and arms. His most beautiful pose was one with arms and hands fully extended in line, one diagonally upwards, the other downward, with head inclined against the upward arm, and a serene, absorbed, prayer-like expression on his face. Then there was a stoutish middle-aged little turner, who spun round with head thrown back. He lacked the effortless grace of the young man, but achieved the same look of rapt serenity. He was a policeman by profession.

3 The turning went on for an hour or more, its monotony remaining strangely beautiful and fascinating instead of becoming boring. Most of the dancers stopped at intervals for a short rest, but the policeman and the graceful young dervish never broke their turning. The Sheikh later told us that the policeman had a weak heart, and that his deepest desire was that he might die while dancing.

4 At the private ceremonies of the community, turning may go on for many hours, until the dancers fall immobile on the floor in a state of exalted and complete exhaustion. The Sheikh covers them with their abbas, and there they lie until they recover.

5 I had got it into my head that the dances we were to see would be

orgies of violent and frenzied motion, but I had been confusing the dancing dervishes with a quite different confraternity, the howling dervishes.
The turning ritual seems designed to give a sense of liberation and ecstasy,
but a serene and orderly one. It was clear that the turners could, through
their controlled and long-continued rotation, spin themselves into a state
in which the world of everyday was transcended. We are apt to look down
on such simple physical methods of achieving a sense of ecstasy or trans-
cendence as barbarous or childish. I can only say that, to the casual
visitor like myself, it looked like a satisfying form of ritual and, for some
of the participants at least, seemed to provide a quality of real fulfilment.

the common breath
of humanity
HARLOW SHAPLEY

In this subjective definition, Shapley answers the question, What is a
breath of air? with the response that it is evidence of "the one world
of mankind." He is, of course, aware of objective definitions also (he
reports, for instance, that a breath weights about three-quarters of a gram,
and that it consists of about 78 percent nitrogen and 21 percent oxygen).
His real purpose, however, is to make us see such an everyday item as
a breath of air in a new way: as a symbol of the fact that all people,
indeed all breathing creatures of past and present, depend on the same
natural environment for their survival. We're all in this thing together.
This idea is, by now, hardly a novel one; but Shapley gives it new dramatic
impact by his information about the breath of air. Thus two familiar
ingredients—the breath and the fact of our interdependence—gain power
by being associated together.

to put ourselves in a proper mood for optimistic thoughts, we need a
new evaluation. Take a deep breath, please, and hold tight, for I am taking you on a tour of the universe, on a quick trip to the corners of the
world, on an exploration of unusual perspectives—all in the interest of
a discussion of the one world of mankind. We shall talk of simple things,
starting with that deep breath, which you may now distribute into surrounding space.

Source. "The Common Breath of Humanity," from Chapter 7, "Stars, Ethics, and Coexistence," from *The View from a Distant Star*, by Harlow Shapley, © 1963 by Basic
Books, Inc., Publishers, New York.

2   That breath, which you found so necessary and natural, unites you quietly with the rest of us all over the earth. It was a volume of the moving air of your immediate locality, and most of it has now gone forth to join again the winds of the planet, to join the international stock of terrestrial atmosphere.

3   A year from now I shall breathe in and out a good many thousands of the nitrogen molecules which a minute ago were in the Deep Breaths of all of you; and wherever you are, on whatever continent, you, too, will be rebreathing some of the Deep Breath of a minute ago. I shall, unknowingly, have intimate association with you, and, of course, you with me. This may sound unhygienic, a little more intimate than you like, but it is true. Let us consider further the simple arithmetic and argument that concern internationalism in breathing.

4   Some breaths are big, some are small; a deep, full breath weighs a little less than three-fourths of a gram. That is, there are about 600 breaths in a pound of air. Good air is about 78 per cent nitrogen gas and about 21 per cent oxygen. (There are also small amounts of carbon dioxide, argon, and other gases.)

5   Knowing that the breath weighs something like three-fourths of a gram, I can easily compute the approximate number of nitrogen atoms in that breath. The number is inconceivably large, because atoms are inconceivably small. The number is so large that it is hard to pronounce. One way of expressing the number of nitrogen atoms in a deep breath is to say that it is two point four times ten to the twenty-second power. That is the hard way. Another way is to say 24 thousand million million million. It's an appalling number. There were, in fact, in your Deep Breath more than ten million million times as many nitrogen atoms as there are people living on this planet. There were more than a hundred billion times as many nitrogen atoms as there are stars in our galaxy. You do, indeed, whenever you breathe, take on more numerically than you may have appreciated. And now, where are those 24 thousand million million million nitrogen atoms that you expelled? They are mingling with other nitrogen and oxygen atoms of the atmosphere, and in the course of time they will be so thoroughly mixed by the winds of the land and the seas that every person on the surface of the planet—every man, woman, and child—will be using some of the same nitrogen atoms that you used in that one Deep Breath.

6   You may wonder how I know such things. It is simple to deduce, from knowledge of the diffusion of gases and the speeds and habits of the winds, that the thorough mixing will take place. It is also easy to calculate how much air there is on the earth. I could tell it to you in tons, or in the numbers of nitrogen and oxygen atoms, or in terms of breaths. I find that there are three times as many nitrogen atoms in one breath as there are breaths in the whole atmosphere. That means, for example, that every breath of yours at the present time contains, on the average, three of the nitrogen atoms from any given ancient human breath—three atoms, for

example, from every one of the breaths that William Shakespeare took throughout his life. The breath that you are just now going to take contains many thousands of the atoms that were used by Shakespeare during the writing of Hamlet—a wonderful *inspiration* it should be, at least in one sense of the word.

7   To the same extent, the breath of St. Francis is with us, and of Confucius, and of Mary of Nazareth. That knowledge may give you, I hope, a feeling of brotherhood with the great and holy past, for the nitrogen of the international air crosses the barriers of time as well as space. But each breath of yours, I should hasten to add, contains also nitrogen breathed by ancient sinners; and it probably contains at least six of the nitrogen atoms expelled in each ferocious snort of an ancient dinosaur, as he raised his head from the Mesozoic swamps 100 million years ago and sneered, in his vulgar way, at the primitive little mammals which were just beginning to grow into the most dominant animal form on the earth.

homecoming
DANIEL K. INOUYE

In about a thousand words, this selection recreates the age-old experience of a soldier's homecoming. Inouye was not only a war hero (he lost his arm in the Italian campaign of World War II) but also a man who overcame racial prejudice to become the first American of Japanese ancestry elected to the U.S. Senate. The selection printed here, from his book *Journey to Washington,* tells the story of his return home after the war. The narrative begins in San Francisco with his attempt to get a seat on a Hawaii-bound plane. In this excellent example of defining by personal experience, Inouye captures the complexity of homecoming: he is a changed person now, inevitably affected by the loss of his arm, and yet home is still home.

1   **I**n the end, of course, I did get to the coast, but still had to wangle a flight on that last, long trans-Pacific leg. I managed to hitch a jeep ride from San Francisco to the Air Corps base at Hamilton Field, and promptly ran into fresh trouble. As I checked through the guard post at the entrance, a captain—I suppose he was officer of the day—noticed that I returned the M.P. sentry's salute with a nod of my head, and he came storming through the door.

Source. From *Journey to Washington* by Senator Daniel K. Inouye with Lawrence Elliott.
Copyright © 1967 by Prentice-Hall, Inc.

2   "Where'd you learn your military courtesy, Lieutenant?" he bellowed at me. "That guard is entitled to a salute. It's officers like you that make it so tough to maintain any sense of discipline in this man's army . . ."

3   He ranted on and on while, in the narrow confines of the jeep seat, I tried to get my overcoat open. Then he noticed what I was doing:

4   "Listen, don't show me your ribbons. They don't excuse . . ."

5   "Captain," I finally broke in, "you haven't given me a chance to say anything so I was trying to show you, not my ribbons"—here I finally got my coat open and pulled my hook out—"but the fact that I don't have an arm to salute with. I don't think you'd want me doing it with a hook, would you?"

6   I thought the poor man was going to burst into tears. He started to apologize, couldn't make it, leaned close and just touched my shoulder. "I didn't know," he whispered at last. "I . . . didn't know."

7   "Forget it, sir. No harm done."

8   "No, listen, where are you bound? Is there anything I can do for you?"

9   Well, that's how I got my ride home. I told that captain my problem and he just about broke his back to get me a seat on a troop carrier flight bound for Hickam Field that very day. That's what I call really atoning for an error.

10   And sometimes when your luck changes, it really changes. I had to wait to board the plane, since it was done by rank and I was very nearly the most junior passenger. And somewhere in the lounge, the most senior officer, a brigadier general, noticed me. Anyway, once we were aboard, he sent his aide back to my seat to ask if I'd like to join him up forward. And so he was my seatmate on the trip, and given his rank, the service was as good as the company. We chatted about Hawaii—this was to be his first visit—and I told him a little about the ins and outs of Honolulu. He asked if this was my first trip back and I said yes. He asked if I had a ride home and I said no, and thought no more about it until we bumped down at Hickam, just past midnight. No sooner had the props stopped spinning than a staff car with a gleaming single star on the front bumper came tearing up under the wing.

11   "There's your ride, Lieutenant," the general said with a smile. "Just tell the sergeant where to take you."

12   "But . . . but that's your car, sir," I stammered. "How will you . . ."

13   "Oh, I imagine I'll get a lift somehow. But I want you to take my car tonight." And he didn't look at my hook when he said, "It's little enough for what you've given."

14   And so Dan Inouye, who'd barely made it into the army and had gone off to war with a uniform that didn't fit and high hopes of making corporal, came home in a general's car, a staff sergeant carrying his bag. I had called from the terminal—"Hello, Papa, I'm sorry to wake you up, but I'm at Hickam Field and I'll be there in twenty minutes"—and now as I stood outside the house in the still, deserted street I suddenly couldn't believe it. Was I really home? Had all those incredible things happened to

me in the more than two and a half years that had passed since I last saw this place? Then the door opened and light poured into the dark street and my mother was saying, "Ken?"

15   I had my arm around her and felt her tears. I had my arm around all of them, my father, my sister May who had been a child when I left and was now grown and beautiful, my brothers John and Robert flushing with embarrassment and the pride plain in their faces. It was a sublimely happy moment, that homecoming, those few first minutes when we dispelled the long years with our joy and gratitude.

16   John took my bag from the sergeant, who saluted smartly as he left. Robert took my coat and May brought me a chair. "Shall I bring you something?" my mother whispered. "Tea? You're hungry! I'll make . . ."

17   "No, no Mama. I'm fine."

18   I was. I looked around the house, my home, suddenly grown smaller and yet just the same. There was the picture of President Roosevelt on the wall, with one of me next to it. A blue star hung in the window. When I turned back, they were all looking at me, at my uniform and the ribbons on my chest, and, of course, at the hook. Now there had come that moment of awkward silence, the fumbling for a thought after the first heedless and loving greeting.

19   I lit a cigarette—tense, stomach tight—and had taken a deep-down drag before I realized what I was doing. May's eyes widened. My father, who must have had a pretty clear idea about my little vices—he'd once sent me a cigarette lighter, cautioning me never to mention it to my mother —tried to pretend he was in another city. And Mother came to her feet as though pinched.

20   "Daniel Ken Inouye!" she said in exactly the old way.

21   I looked sheepishly at the cigarette, then at her, then at the rest of them. And then we all began to laugh, my mother, too, and I knew that I was home.

elizabeth eckford, the guards, and the mob

DAISY BATES

The event defined here belongs to the painful story of school desegregation in America. In 1957, a court order granted nine black students the right to enter Central High School in Little Rock, Arkansas, but when they tried to do so they found their way blocked both by angry white towns-people and by Arkansas National Guardsmen. One of the nine students, 15-year-old Elizabeth Eckford, later described that experience to writer Daisy Bates. Elizabeth's narrative is remarkable for three qualities: first, its realism (such details as "I was pressing my black and white dress— I had made it to wear on the first day of school"—make her an individual rather than a name in a newspaper); second, its balance (she remembers to mention the white people who helped her as well as the ones who were cruel); third, its control (she never gives way to childish emotionalism such as name calling). These qualities of maturity in the telling of the story imply maturity in her own character and offer a dramatic contrast to the behavior of the mob. The style of the narrative is therefore as important as its substance in explaining the kinds of people who participated in this confrontation.

1   She remained quiet for a long time. Then she began to speak.

2   "You remember the day before we were to go in, we met Superintendent Blossom at the school board office. He told us what the mob might say and do but he never told us we wouldn't have any protection. He told our parents not to come because he wouldn't be able to protect the children if they did.

3   "That night I was so excited I couldn't sleep. The next morning I was about the first one up. While I was pressing my black and white dress— I had made it to wear on the first day of school—my little brother turned on the TV set. They started telling about a large crowd gathered at the school. The man on TV said he wondered if we were going to show up that morning. Mother called from the kitchen, where she was fixing breakfast, 'Turn that TV off!' She was so upset and worried. I wanted to comfort her, so I said, 'Mother, don't worry.'

4   "Dad was walking back and forth, from room to room, with a sad expression. He was chewing on his pipe and he had a cigar in his hand, but he didn't light either one. It would have been funny, only he was so nervous.

5   "Before I left home Mother called us into the living-room. She said

we should have a word of prayer. Then I caught the bus and got off a block from the school. I saw a large crowd of people standing across the street from the soldiers guarding Central. As I walked on, the crowd suddenly got very quiet. Superintendent Blossom had told us to enter by the front door. I looked at all the people and thought, 'Maybe I will be safer if I walk down the block to the front entrance behind the guards.'

6   "At the corner I tried to pass through the long line of guards around the school so as to enter the grounds behind them. One of the guards pointed across the street. So I pointed in the same direction and asked whether he meant for me to cross the street and walk down. He nodded 'yes.' So, I walked across the street conscious of the crowd that stood there, but they moved away from me.

7   "For a moment all I could hear was the shuffling of their feet. Then someone shouted, 'Here she comes, get ready!' I moved away from the crowd on the sidewalk and into the street. If the mob came at me I could then cross back over so the guards could protect me.

8   "The crowd moved in closer and then began to follow me, calling me names. I still wasn't afraid. Just a little bit nervous. Then my knees started to shake all of a sudden and I wondered whether I could make it to the center entrance a block away. It was the longest block I ever walked in my whole life.

9   "Even so, I still wasn't too scared because all the time I kept thinking that the guards would protect me.

10   "When I got right in front of the school, I went up to a guard again. But this time he just looked straight ahead and didn't move to let me pass him. I didn't know what to do. Then I looked and saw that the path leading to the front entrance was a little further ahead. So I walked until I was right in front of the path to the front door.

11   "I stood looking at the school—it looked so big! Just then the guards let some white students go through.

12   "The crowd was quiet. I guess they were waiting to see what was going to happen. When I was able to steady my knees, I walked up to the guard who had let the white students in. He too didn't move. When I tried to squeeze past him, he raised his bayonet and then the other guards closed in and they raised their bayonets.

13   "They glared at me with a mean look and I was very frightened and didn't know what to do. I turned around and the crowd came toward me.

14   "They moved closer and closer. Somebody started yelling, 'Lynch her! Lynch her!'

15   "I tried to see a friendly face somewhere in the mob—someone who maybe would help. I looked into the face of an old woman and it seemed a kind face, but when I looked at her again, she spat on me.

16   "They came closer, shouting, 'No nigger bitch is going to get in our school. Get out of here!'

17   "I turned back to the guards but their faces told me I wouldn't get help from them. Then I looked down the block and saw a bench at the

bus stop. I thought, 'If I can only get there I will be safe.' I don't know why the bench seemed a safe place to me, but I started walking toward it. I tried to close my mind to what they were shouting, and kept saying to myself, 'If I can only make it to the bench I will be safe.'

18   "When I finally got there, I don't think I could have gone another step. I sat down and the mob crowded up and began shouting all over again. Someone hollered, 'Drag her over to this tree! Let's take care of the nigger.' Just then a white man sat down beside me, put his arm around me and patted my shoulder. He raised my chin and said, 'Don't let them see you cry.'

19   "Then, a white lady—she was very nice—she came over to me on the bench. She spoke to me but I don't remember now what she said. She put me on the bus and sat next to me. She asked me my name and tried to talk to me but I don't think I answered. I can't remember much about the bus ride, but the next thing I remember I was standing in front of the School for the Blind, where Mother works.

20   "I thought, 'Maybe she isn't here. But she has to be here!' So I ran upstairs, and think some teachers tried to talk to me, but I kept running until I reached Mother's classroom.

21   "Mother was standing at the window with her head bowed, but she must have sensed I was there because she turned around. She looked as if she had been crying, and I wanted to tell her I was all right. But I couldn't speak. She put her arms around me and I cried."

---

will someone please hiccup my pat?
WILLIAM SPOONER DONALD

Donald has two purposes: to define the term "Spoonerism," and to present the personality of the man whose comic misuse of language gave rise to that term. In this brief account of Spooner's life, conventional biographical data (date of birth, etc.) are kept to a minimum, while the incidents during which Spooner made his silly remarks such as "Will someone please hiccup my pat?" are emphasized. The collection of Spoonerisms worked chronologically into the narrative functions as a definition by example. The narrative itself serves to connect and explain the separate Spoonerisms and to help us see the man behind the mistakes. The resultant combination is neither standard biography nor standard definition of a term, but a delightful hybrid of the two.

Source. Copyright © 1968 *Horizon Magazine.* Reprinted by permission of William Spooner Donald, Troutlets, Church Street, Keswick, Cumbria, England.

1   **O**ne afternoon nearly a hundred years ago the October wind gusted merrily down Oxford's High Street. Hatless and helpless, a white-haired clergyman with pink cherubic features uttered his plaintive cry for aid. As an athletic youngster chased the spinning topper, other bystanders smiled delightedly—they had just heard at first hand the latest "Spoonerism."

2   My revered relative William Archibald Spooner was born in 1844, the son of a Staffordshire county court judge. As a young man, he was handicapped by a poor physique, a stammer, and weak eyesight; at first, his only possible claim to future fame lay in the fact that he was an albino, with very pale blue eyes and white hair tinged slightly yellow.

3   But nature compensated the weakling by blessing him with a brilliant intellect. By 1868 he had been appointed a lecturer at New College, Oxford. Just then he would have been a caricaturist's dream with his freakish looks, nervous manner, and peculiar mental kink that caused him—in his own words—to "make occasional felicities in verbal diction."

4   Victorian Oxford was a little world of its own where life drifted gently by; a world where splendid intellectuals lived in their ivory towers of Latin, Euclid, and Philosophy; a world where it was always a sunny summer afternoon in a countryside, where Spooner admitted he loved to "pedal gently round on a well-boiled icicle."

5   As the years passed, Spooner grew, probably without himself being aware of the fact, into a "character." A hard worker himself, he detested idleness and is on record as having rent some lazybones with the gem, "You have hissed all my mystery lessons, and completely tasted two whole worms."

6   With his kindly outlook on life, it was almost natural for him to take holy orders; he was ordained a deacon in 1872 and a priest in 1875. His unique idiosyncrasy never caused any serious trouble and merely made him more popular. On one occasion, in New College chapel in 1879, he announced smilingly that the next hymn would be "Number One seven five—Kinkering Kongs their Titles Take." Other congregations were treated to such jewels as ". . . Our Lord, we know, is a shoving Leopard . . ." and ". . . All of us have in our hearts a half-warmed fish to lead a better life. . . ."

7   Spooner often preached in the little village churches around Oxford and once delivered an eloquent address on the subject of Aristotle. No doubt the sermon contained some surprising information for his rustic congregation. For after Spooner had left the pulpit, an idea seemed to occur to him, and he hopped back up the steps again.

8   "Excuse me, dear brethren," he announced brightly, "I just want to say that in my sermon whenever I mentioned Aristotle, I should have said Saint Paul."

9   By 1885 the word "Spoonerism" was in colloquial use in Oxford circles, and a few years later, in general use all over England. If the dividing line between truth and myth is often only a hairsbreadth, does it really

matter? One story that has been told concerns an optician's shop in London. Spooner is reputed to have entered and asked to see a "signifying glass." The optician registered polite bewilderment.

10   "Just an ordinary signifying glass," repeated Spooner, perhaps surprised at the man's obtuseness.

11   "I'm afraid we haven't one in stock, but I'll make inquiries right away, sir," said the shopkeeper, playing for time.

12   "Oh, don't bother, it doesn't magnify, it doesn't magnify," said Spooner airily, and walked out.

13   Fortunately for Spooner, he made the right choice when he met his wife-to-be. He was thirty-four years old when he married Frances Goodwin in 1878. The marriage was a happy one, and they had one son and four daughters. Mrs. Spooner was tall, good-looking girl, and on one occasion the family went on a short holiday in Switzerland. The "genial Dean," as he was then called, took a keen interest in geology, and in no time at all he had mastered much information and many technical definitions on the subject of glaciers.

14   One day at lunchtime the younger folk were worried because their parents had not returned from a long walk. When Spooner finally appeared with his wife, his explanation was: "We strolled up a long valley, and when we turned a corner we found ourselves completely surrounded by erotic blacks."

15   He was, of course, referring to "erratic blocks," or large boulders left around after the passage of a glacier.

16   In 1903 Spooner was appointed Warden of New College, the highest possible post for a Fellow. One day walking across the quadrangle, he met a certain Mr. Casson, who had just been elected a Fellow of New College.

17   "Do come to dinner tonight," said Spooner, "we are welcoming our new Fellow, Mr. Casson."

18   "But, my dear Warden, I *am* Casson," was the surprised reply.

19   "Never mind, never mind, come along all the same," said Spooner tactfully.

20   On another occasion in later years when his eyesight was really very bad, Spooner found himself seated next to a most elegant lady at dinner. In a casual moment the latter put her lily-white hand onto the polished table, and Spooner, in an even more casual manner, pronged her hand with his fork, remarking genially, "My bread, I think."

21   In 1924 Spooner retired as Warden. He had established an astonishing record of continuous residence at New College for sixty-two years first as undergraduate, then as Fellow, then Dean, and finally as Warden. His death in 1930, at the age of eighty-six, was a blushing crow to collectors of those odd linguistic transpositions known by then throughout the English-speaking world as Spoonerisms.

the functions of the
urban black church

JAMES P. COMER

An institution can be defined in several ways—in terms of its history, structure, or functions. This selection is a functional definition of one modern social institution, the urban black church. In trying to explain what their church meant to the black families in the East Chicago neighborhood where he grew up (and in other similar neighborhoods), Comer begins and ends with his own family. Within this framework, he expands his scope to include the experiences of other people while he discusses two major functions the church fulfilled: "the church was the place to discharge frustration and hostility," and "it was a place for participation and belonging," offering "a little bit of respect for everybody." He also explains the church's weaknesses, the ways it did *not* function: it failed to respond to the needs of educated people, and it failed to resist white dominance.

1   **t**he church played a big role in the development of the black man's self-respect and dignity. Because of the church's dominant role, Sunday was always a big day at our house. We awoke to the smell of bacon and the sound of gospel music. Every house down the street seemed to be tuned in to the same station. Our favorite vocal group was the "Wings over Jordan." My father was a deacon, a position of great importance in the black church, and a deeply religious man. He said a very long grace and we often got a little restless around the table. Sometimes my two brothers and I would make faces and I could hardly keep from laughing— my younger sister would get mad at us and we would look up and find our mother giving us a withering glance. All eyes closed and there was silence again. She would not tolerate any disrespect for our father. The black woman often zealously protected the dignity of the black man, because his dignity was under such constant assault outside the home.

2   The major roots of our family were in the church; ours was the Zion Baptist. Some of the ministers could touch the congregation deeply. One approach always caused people to shout and cry: these were the sermons that were full of assurances that conditions would be better in the hereafter. They were also designed to help a rejected and abused people feel good about themselves and enjoy a sense of purpose and worth.

3   During such sermons, the minister would gradually build to a high emotional pitch and then in a repetitive fashion cry out, "He's a Rock in a weary land! He's a Shelter in a mighty storm! He rescued Daniel from

Source. Reprinted by permission of Quadrangle/The New York Times Book Co. From *Beyond Black and White* by Dr. James P. Comer. Copyright © 1972 by James P. Comer, M.D.

the lion's den! He's a Father to the fatherless! He's a Light in the darkness! He's Eyes to the blind and a Cane to the cripple! He brought the children of Israel out of bondage and He'll take care of you!" With each assertion, the "Amens," "Yes, Reverends," and "Yes, Lords" would become more frequent and the excitement would grow. When he reached "He'll take care of you," the shouting and crying would start.

4   Some of the women would lurch back in the pews, as if having a fit, their arms flailing back and forth. I often thought the force against the pews would pull them from their moorings. Two or three ushers would rush up to control them. One man in our church shouted and others would occasionally weep quietly with one hand over their eyes. I often wondered why grown men would cry. As a child, I never did quite understand the shouting and crying and the explanations I received always left me more curious: "Well, Negroes have had it hard"; "Some people have to let it all out." Later, when I met many of these people in the steel mills and in the world beyond the church, I began to understand what the shouting and weeping were all about. While an element of African and even Southern black and white religious culture was involved, the intensity of the response reflected the sense of frustration and helplessness the people felt. The church was the place to discharge frustration and hostility so that one could face injustice and hardship the rest of the week.

5   The black church had another important function: it was a place for participation and belonging. The deacons, trustees and ushers were ten feet tall on Sunday. This was not Inland Steel, Miss Ann's Kitchen nor the bank. This—the church—was theirs. In retrospect, the trustees were like the city board of finance and the deacons were like the city council. There was a little bit of respect for everybody.

6   One Sunday I visited a storefront church with a friend of mine. Several of the choir members and ushers were people I knew from school. It seemed to me odd that some of these people were quite withdrawn in school and were hardly known to the teachers and staff, but in their church they were lively, active participants. At the storefront church that day, I found at least part of the answer. The choir gave a rousing rendition of a spiritual. The soloist responded to the audience's enthusiasm with these words, "One thing I like about this church is that if you have a speck of talent you can use it, and the people will love you and respect you for it." I had noticed this in my own church as well. In the Baptist Young People's Training Union Bible Drill, girls who barely participated in school could quickly find the chapter and verse. Many black children were not respected in school even when they attempted to use their talent. I still observe that many black children who are turned off in school and considered dull are turned on in church and in other less alien places.

7   The biblical and hereafter sermons bothered my mother. "What's he talking about David, John, Moses and Paul and all those people for? . . . Why does he talk about golden streets and rewards in Heaven? . . . I'm worried about these cement sidewalks I have to walk down every day. He

ought to be teaching our people about saving their money and buying homes and taking care of their families."

8   Occasionally a minister would come to town who could preach two sermons—one spiritual and one intellectual. Then many of the educated people, old and young, who had abandoned church would come back. But it would never last. Soon the people who wanted to hear the spiritual sermon would complain that he "wasn't preaching." These people were the backbone of the church: the church was their major investment and they were the major contributors. They did not want the church branching out and getting into areas like business, education, or even recreation. I recall that one of the major debates in my church was over a plan to have a youth night. The officers would not have any dancing in our church! Some members argued that it would be better to have the youth dancing in the church than in some "smoke-filled den of iniquity." Others countered that if young people are going to sin, they should not sin in the House of the Lord. The church was for listening to the Word of God!

9   Divisions of this sort were usually between the group who turned toward the values and interests of the total society and those who remained primarily tied to the substitute culture—the black church. Education and opportunities in the "outside world" enabled some to keep their feet in two cultures—the church and the total society. Others, for various reasons, remained enmeshed in the culture of the church alone.

10   One Sunday, a sixteen-year-old girl brought her born-out-of-wedlock baby to church and created quite a stir. A few women fussed over the baby. The minister talked about forgiveness and understanding. Most of the women did not see it that way—they grumbled about "people carrying on over the baby like it had a daddy." Some of the women who complained were of the "black puritan" background. This "better class of Negroes," as some have referred to themselves, attempted to "out-middle-class" or "out-decent" the white middle and upper classes in vain efforts to win respectability. Because of the stereotype of the immoral Negro, sexual morality was an issue of special concern. In the academy my father had attended as a youngster, girls were always accompanied by a matron in front of the line and at the rear. Until very recently, supervision of female students was much stricter at black colleges than at white.

11   Because the minister and the church could gratify so many social and psychological needs, he and the institution were very powerful.

12   My parents occasionally disagreed about the church. I sometimes thought my mother was less religious than my father. I asked her about it once. She replied that it was not that she was less religious, just that she did not trust all the people who claimed they were called to spread the gospel. Gradually I came to understand what she meant. One Sunday the minister was preaching a "race sermon." This is a sermon in which the minister "gives white folks the business." The congregation responds with loud and enthusiastic "Amens," as the sins and wrongs of white America are spelled out. Just as the minister was warming up to the subject, the

head usher rushed down the aisle and onto the pulpit and whispered something in the minister's ear. This was highly unusual; nobody ever disturbed the minister after he started his sermon. The usher returned to the vestibule and brought two white visitors to the rostrum. They were given the honored seats of the assistant pastors and the minister continued his sermon. But there was an abrupt change in his tone. He began to preach about love and brotherhood and how white folks and colored folks could get along together.

13   The visitors were from the Inland Steel Company. As I recall, Inland Steel gave a large check to the church every Christmas. (Some say it was as much as $1,000.)

14   My mother's distrust of certain ministers was again vindicated when I was in the seventh grade. The older black students asked me to talk with a minister I knew to get his support for our side in a disagreement in our school. There was a black Paul Robeson Glee Club and a white glee club. The black students did not think we needed both. When I explained the argument to the minister, he paused thoughtfully and said, "Well you see there's a difference in our voices. We have richer, stronger voices and that's the reason for separate glee clubs." Although I had been taught to respect my elders, particularly ministers, I argued that if our voices were stronger and richer it would appear that the white glee club could use our help. He did not appreciate my point of view and told me that some day I would understand. I understood at the end of the year when I saw him on the school stage giving the benediction at the high-school graduation. He was the only Negro on the stage; in fact, I am told it was a black first for East Chicago. He had had to "go along with 'the Man's' program" to appear on the program—to take one step forward.

15   In the recent flurry of major studies of the black experience, only E. Franklin Frazier and Carter Woodson, both blacks, have given more than a passing glance at the role of the black church. The director of a black-studies program told me that he could not find collections of church sermons in the libraries of major universities. Some young students would like to ignore it all together. But how can we? The root, heart and soul of black culture in America are in the black church—whether we blacks like it or not.

reports, inferences, judgments

S. I. HAYAKAWA

Hayakawa defines the kinds of statements we make. He begins by
classifying statements into three types: reports, inferences, and judgments.
To explain each type, he uses formal definition, a great many specific
examples, and a recurrent analogy that compares life to a territory through
which we might move and language to the map we would make of that
territory so that other people could locate themselves within it.

Hayakawa's governing idea is that we can make an accurate map of
experience only if we describe it impartially or, in his terms, only if we
offer "reports" of what we see, hear, feel, and so forth, rather than
"inferences" and "judgments." He is asking us to write objectively, to let
others see X as X is and to avoid writing subjectively, to avoid asking
others to see X "our way." To what extent is such neutrality possible?
When might it not be desirable? What do you make of Hayakawa's own
partiality on behalf of impartiality?

To put it briefly, in human speech, different sounds have different meanings.
To study this co-ordination of certain sounds with certain meanings is to study
language. This co-ordination makes it possible for man to interact with great
precision. When we tell someone, for instance, the address of a house he has
never seen, we are doing something which no animal can do.

LEONARD BLOOMFIELD

Vague and insignificant forms of speech, and abuse of language, have so long
passed for mysteries of science; and hard or misapplied words with little or
no meaning have, by prescription, such a right to be mistaken for deep learning and height of speculation, that it will not be easy to persuade either those
who speak or those who hear them, that they are but the covers of ignorance
and hindrance of true knowledge.

JOHN LOCKE

for the purposes of interchange of information, the basic symbolic act is
the *report* of what we have seen, heard, or felt: "There is a ditch on each
side of the road." "You can get those at Smith's hardware store for $2.75."
"There aren't any fish on that side of the lake, but there are on this side."
Then there are reports of reports: "The longest waterfall in the world is
Victoria Falls in Rhodesia." "The Battle of Hastings took place in 1066."
"The papers say that there was a smash-up on Highway 41 near Evans-
ville." Reports adhere to the following rules: first, they are *capable of veri-
fication;* second, they *exclude,* as far as possible, *inferences* and *judgments.*
(These terms will be defined later.)

Source. From *Language in Thought and Action,* Second Edition, by S. I. Hayakawa, Copyright © 1964 by Harcourt Brace Jovanovich, Inc. and reprinted with their permission.

2   Reports are verifiable. We may not always be able to verify them ourselves, since we cannot track down the evidence for every piece of history
we know, nor can we all go to Evansville to see the remains of the
smash-up before they are cleared away. But if we are roughly agreed on
the names of things, on what constitutes a "foot," "yard," "bushel," and so
on, and on how to measure time, there is relatively little danger of our
misunderstanding each other. Even in a world such as we have today, in
which everybody seems to be quarreling with everybody else, *we still to a
surprising degree trust each other's reports.* We ask directions of total
strangers when we are traveling. We follow directions on road signs without
being suspicious of the people who put them up. We read books of information about science, mathematics, automotive engineering, travel, geography,
the history of costume, and other such factual matters, and we usually
assume that the author is doing his best to tell us as truly as he can what
he knows. And we are safe in so assuming most of the time. With the
interest given today to the discussion of biased newspapers, propagandists,
and the general untrustworthiness of many of the communications we receive, we are likely to forget that we still have an enormous amount of
reliable information available and that deliberate misinformation, except in
warfare, is still more the exception than the rule. The desire for self-preservation that compelled men to evolve means for the exchange of information
also compels them to regard the giving of false information as profoundly
reprehensible.

3   At its highest development, the language of reports is the language of
science. By "highest development" we mean greatest general usefulness.
Presbyterian and Catholic, workingman and capitalist, East German and
West German, *agree* on the meanings of such symbols as $2 \times 2 = 4$,
$100°$ *C.*, HNO_3, *3:35* A.M., *1940* A.D., *1000 kilowatts, Quercus agrifolia,*
and so on. But how, it may be asked, can there be agreement about even
this much among people who disagree about political philosophies, ethical
ideas, religious beliefs, and the survival of my business *versus* the survival
of yours? The answer is that circumstances *compel men to agree,* whether
they wish to or not. If, for example, there were a dozen different religious
sects in the United States, each insisting on its own way of naming the time
of the day and the days of the year, the mere necessity of having a dozen
different calendars, a dozen different kinds of watches, and a dozen sets of
schedules for business hours, trains, and television programs to say nothing
of the effort that would be required for translating terms from one nomenclature to another, would make life as we know it impossible.[1]

---

[1] According to information supplied by the Association of American Railroads, "Before
1883 there were nearly 100 different time zones in the United States. It wasn't until November 18 of that year that . . . a system of standard time was adopted here and in Canada.
Before then there was nothing but local or 'solar' time. . . . The Pennsylvania Railroad in
the East used Philadelphia time, which was five minutes slower than New York time and
five minutes faster than Baltimore time. The Baltimore & Ohio used Baltimore time for
trains running out of Baltimore, Columbus time for Ohio, Vincennes (Indiana) time for

4   The language of reports, then, including the more accurate reports of science, is "map" language, and because it gives us reasonably accurate representations of the "territory," it enables us to get work done. Such language may often be dull or uninteresting reading: one does not usually read logarithmic tables or telephone directories for entertainment. But we could not get along without it. There are numberless occasions in the talking and writing we do in everyday life that *require that we state things in such a way that everybody will be able to understand and agree with our formulation.*

INFERENCES

5   The reader will find that practice in writing reports is a quick means of increasing his linguistic awareness. It is an exercise which will constantly provide him with his own examples of the principles of language and interpretation under discussion. The reports should be about first-hand experience—scenes the reader has witnessed himself, meetings and social events he has taken part in, people he knows well. They should be of such a nature that they can be verified and agreed upon. For the purpose of this exercise, inferences will be excluded.

6   Not that inferences are not important—we rely in everyday life and in science as much on *inferences* as on reports—in some areas of thought, for example, geology, paleontology, and nuclear physics, reports are the foundations, but inferences (and inferences upon inferences) are the main body of the science. An inference, as we shall use the term, is *a statement about the unknown made on the basis of the known.* We may *infer* from the material and cut of a woman's clothes her wealth or social position; we may *infer* from the character of the ruins the origin of the fire that destroyed the building; we may *infer* from a man's calloused hands the nature of his occupation; we may *infer* from a senator's vote on an armaments bill his attitude toward Russia; we may *infer* from the structure of the land the path of a prehistoric glacier; we may *infer* from a halo on an unexposed photographic plate that it has been in the vicinity of radioactive materials; we may *infer* from the sound of an engine the condition of its connecting rods. Inferences may be carelessly or carefully made. They may be made on the basis of a broad background of previous experience with the subject matter, or no experience at all. For example, the inferences a good mechanic can make about the internal condition of a motor by listening to it are often startlingly accurate, while the inferences made by an amateur (if he tries to make any) may be entirely wrong. But the common characteristic of inferences is that they are statements about matters which

those going out of Cincinnati. . . . When it was noon in Chicago, it was 12:31 in Pittsburgh; 12:24 in Cleveland; 12:17 in Toledo; 12:13 in Cincinnati; 12:09 in Louisville; 12:07 in Indianapolis; 11:50 in St. Louis; 11:48 in Dubuque; 11:39 in St. Paul, and 11:27 in Omaha. There were 27 local time zones in Michigan alone. . . . A person traveling from Eastport, Maine, to San Francisco, if he wanted always to have the right railroad time and get off at the right place, had to twist the hands of his watch 20 times en route." Chicago *Daily News* (September 29, 1948).

are not directly known, statements made on the basis of what has been observed.

7   The avoidance of inferences in our suggested practice in report-writing requires that we make no guesses as to what is going on in other people's minds. When we say, "He was angry," we are not reporting; we are making an inference from such observable facts as the following: "He pounded his fist on the table; he swore; he threw the telephone directory at his stenographer." In this particular example, the inference appears to be fairly safe; nevertheless, it is important to remember, especially for the purposes of training oneself, that it is an inference. Such expressions as "He thought a lot of himself," "He was scared of girls," "He has an inferiority complex," made on the basis of casual social observation, and "What Russia really wants to do is to establish a world communist dictatorship," made on the basis of casual newspaper reading, are highly inferential. We should keep in mind their inferential character and, in our suggested exercises, should substitute for them such statements as "He rarely spoke to subordinates in the plant," "I saw him at a party, and he never danced except when one of the girls asked him to," "He wouldn't apply for the scholarship although I believe he could have won it easily," and "The Russian delegation to the United Nations has asked for *A*, *B*, and *C*. Last year they voted against *M* and *N*, and voted for *X* and *Y*. On the basis of facts such as these, the newspaper I read makes the inference that what Russia really wants is to establish a world communist dictatorship. I agree."

8   In spite of the exercise of every caution in avoiding inferences and reporting only what is seen and experienced, we all remain prone to error, since the making of inferences is a quick, almost automatic process. We may watch a car weaving as it goes down the road and say, "Look at that *drunken driver*," although what we *see* is only *the irregular motion of the car*. The writer once saw a man leave a one-dollar tip at a lunch counter and hurry out. Just as the writer was wondering why anyone should leave so generous a tip in so modest an establishment, the waitress came, picked up the dollar, put it in the cash register as she punched up ninety cents, and put a dime in her pocket. In other words, the writer's description to himself of the event, "a one-dollar tip," turned out to be not a report but an inference.

9   All this is not to say that we should never make inferences. The inability to make inferences is itself a sign of mental disorder. For example, the speech therapist Laura L. Lee writes, "The aphasic [brain-damaged] adult with whom I worked had great difficulty in making inferences about a picture I showed her. She could tell me what was happening at the moment in the picture, but could not tell me what might have happened just before the picture or just afterward." [2] Hence the question is not whether or not we make inferences; the question is whether or not we are aware of the inferences we make.

2 "Brain Damage and the Process of Abstracting: A Problem in Language Learning," *ETC.: A Review of General Semantics,* XVI (1959), 154–62.

JUDGMENTS

10 In our suggested writing exercise, judgments are also to be excluded. By judgments, we shall mean *all expressions of the writer's approval or disapproval of the occurrences, persons, or objects he is describing.* For example, a report cannot say, "It was a wonderful car," but must say something like this: "It has been driven 50,000 miles and has never required any repairs." Again statements such as "Jack lied to us" must be suppressed in favor of the more verifiable statement, "Jack told us he didn't have the keys to his car with him. However, when he pulled a handkerchief out of his pocket a few minutes later, a bunch of car keys fell out." Also a report may not say, "The senator was stubborn, defiant, and uncooperative," or "The senator courageously stood by his principles"; it must say instead, "The senator's vote was the only one against the bill."

11 Many people regard statements such as the following as statements of "fact": "Jack *lied* to us," "Jerry is a *thief*," "Tommy is *clever*." As ordinarily employed, however, the word "lied" involves first an inference (that Jack knew otherwise and deliberately misstated the facts) and second a judgment (that the speaker disapproves of what he has inferred that Jack did). In the other two instances, we may substitute such expressions as, "Jerry was convicted of theft and served two years at Waupun," and "Tommy plays the violin, leads his class in school, and is captain of the debating team." After all, to say of a man that he is a "thief" is to say in effect, "He has stolen *and will steal again*"—which is more of a prediction than a report. Even to say, "He has stolen," is to make an inference (and simultaneously to pass a judgment) on an act about which there may be difference of opinion among those who have examined the evidence upon which the conviction was obtained. But to say that he was "convicted of theft" is to make a statement capable of being agreed upon through verification in court and prison records.

12 Scientific verifiability rests upon the external observation of facts, not upon the heaping up of judgments. If one person says, "Peter is a deadbeat," and another says, "I think so too," the statement has not been verified. In court cases, considerable trouble is sometimes caused by witnesses who cannot distinguish their judgments from the facts upon which those judgments are based. Cross-examinations under these circumstances go something like this:

WITNESS: That dirty double-crosser Jacobs ratted on me.
DEFENSE ATTORNEY: Your honor, I object.
JUDGE: Objection sustained. (Witness's remark is stricken from the record.) Now, try to tell the court exactly what happened.
WITNESS: He double-crossed me, the dirty, lying rat!
DEFENSE ATTORNEY: Your honor, I object!
JUDGE: Objection sustained. (Witness's remark is again stricken from the record.) Will the witness try to stick to the facts.

WITNESS: But I'm telling you the facts, your honor. He did double-cross me.

This can continue indefinitely unless the cross-examiner exercises some ingenuity in order to get at the facts behind the judgment. To the witness it is a "fact" that he was "double-crossed." Often patient questioning is required before the factual bases of the judgment are revealed.

13   Many words, of course, simultaneously convey a report and a judgment on the fact reported, as will be discussed more fully in a later chapter. For the purposes of a report as here defined, these should be avoided. Instead of "sneaked in," one might say "entered quietly"; instead of "politicians," "congressmen" or "aldermen" or "candidates for office"; instead of "bureaucrat," "public official"; instead of "tramp," "homeless unemployed"; instead of "dictatorial set-up," "centralized authority"; instead of "crackpots," "holders of nonconformist views." A newspaper reporter, for example, is not permitted to write, "A crowd of suckers came to listen to Senator Smith last evening in that rickety firetrap and ex-dive that disfigures the south edge of town." Instead he says, "Between seventy-five and a hundred people heard an address last evening by Senator Smith at the Evergreen Gardens near the South Side city limits."

SNARL-WORDS AND PURR-WORDS

14   Throughout this book, it is important to remember that we are not considering language as an isolated phenomenon. Our concern, instead, is with language in action—language in the full context of the nonlinguistic events which are its setting. The making of noises with the vocal organs is a muscular activity and, like other muscular activities, often involuntary. Our responses to powerful stimuli, such as to things that make us very angry, are a complex of muscular and physiological events: the contracting of fighting muscles, the increase of blood pressure, a change in body chemistry, clutching of our hair, *and* the making of noises, such as growls and snarls. We are a little too dignified, perhaps, to growl like dogs, but we do the next best thing and substitute series of words, such as "You dirty double-crosser!" "The filthy scum!" Similarly, if we are pleasurably agitated, we may, instead of purring or wagging the tail, say things like "She's the sweetest girl in all the world!"

15   Speeches such as these are, as direct expressions of approval or disapproval, judgments in their simplest form. They may be said to be human equivalents of snarling and purring. "She's the sweetest girl in all the world" is not a statement about the girl; it is a purr. This seems to be a fairly obvious fact; nevertheless, it is surprising how often, when such a statement is made, both the speaker and the hearer feel that something has been said about the girl. This error is especially common in the interpretation of utterances of orators and editorialists in some of their more excited denunciations of "Reds," "greedy monopolists," "Wall Street," "radicals,"

"foreign ideologies," and in their more fulsome dithyrambs about "our way of life." Constantly, because of the impressive sound of the words, the elaborate structure of the sentences, and the appearance of intellectual progression, we get the feeling that something is being said about something. On closer examination, however, we discover that these utterances merely say, "What I hate ('Reds,' 'Wall Street,' or whatever) I hate very, very much," and "What I like ('our way of life') I like very, very much." We may call such utterances "snarl-words" and "purr-words." They are not reports describing conditions in the extensional world in any way.

16   To call these judgments "snarl-words" and "purr-words" does not mean that we should simply shrug them off. It means that we should be careful to *allocate the meaning correctly*—placing such a statement as "She's the sweetest girl in the world" as a revelation of the speaker's state of mind, and not as a revelation of facts about the girl. If the "snarl-words" about "Reds" or "greedy monopolists" are accompanied by verifiable reports (which would also mean that we have previously agreed as to who, specifically, is meant by the terms "Reds" or "greedy monopolists"), we might find reason to be just as disturbed as the speaker. If the "purr-words" about the sweetest girl in the world are accompanied by verifiable reports about her appearance, manners, character, and so on, we might find reason to admire her too. But "snarl-words" and "purr-words" as such, unaccompanied by reports, offer nothing further to discuss, except possibly the question, "Why do you feel as you do?"

17   It is usually fruitless to debate such questions as "Is President Kennedy a great statesman or merely a skillful politician?" "Is the music of Wagner the greatest music of all time, or is it merely hysterical screeching?" "Which is the finer sport, tennis or baseball?" "Could Joe Louis in his prime have licked Bob Fitzsimmons in his prime?" To take sides on such issues of conflicting judgments is to reduce oneself to the same level of stubborn imbecility as one's opponents. But to ask questions of the form, "Why do you like (or dislike) Kennedy (or Wagner, or tennis, or Joe Louis)?" is to learn something about one's friends and neighbors. After listening to their opinions and their reasons for them, we may leave the discussion slightly wiser, slightly better informed, and perhaps slightly less one-sided than we were before the discussion began.

18   A judgment ("He is a fine boy," "It was a beautiful service," "Baseball is a healthful sport," "She is an awful bore") is a conclusion, summing up a large number of previously observed facts. The reader is probably familiar with the fact that students almost always have difficulty in writing themes of the required length because their ideas give out after a paragraph or two. The reason for this is that those early paragraphs contain so many judgments that there is little left to be said. When the conclusions are carefully excluded, however, and observed facts are given instead, there is never any trouble about the length of papers; in fact, they tend to become too long, since inexperienced writers, when told to give facts, often

give far more than are necessary, because they lack discrimination between the important and the trivial.

19   Still another consequence of judgments early in the course of a written exercise—and this applies also to hasty judgments in everyday thought—is the temporary blindness they induce. When, for example, a description starts with the words, "He was a real Madison Avenue executive," or "She was a typical sorority girl," if we continue writing at all, we must make all our later statements consistent with those judgments. The result is that all the individual characteristics of this particular "executive" or this particular "sorority girl" are lost sight of; and the rest of the account is likely to deal not with observed facts but with the writer's private notion (based on previously read stories, movies, pictures, and so forth) of what "Madison Avenue executives" or "typical sorority girls" are like. The premature judgment, that is, often prevents us from seeing what is directly in front of us, so that clichés take the place of fresh description. Therefore, even if the writer feels sure at the beginning of a written account that the man he is describing is a "real leatherneck" or that the scene he is describing is a "beautiful residential suburb," he will conscientiously keep such notions out of his head, lest his vision be obstructed. He is specifically warned against describing *anybody* as a "beatnik"—a term (originally applied to literary and artistic Bohemians) which was blown up by sensational journalism and movies into an almost completely fictional and misleading stereotype. If a writer applies the term to any actual living human being, he will have to spend so much energy thereafter explaining what he does *not* mean by it that he will save himself trouble by not bringing it up at all.

20   In the course of writing reports of personal experiences, it will be found that in spite of all endeavors to keep judgments out, some will creep in. An account of a man, for example, may go like this: "He had apparently not shaved for several days, and his face and hands were covered with grime. His shoes were torn, and his coat, which was several sizes too small for him, was spotted with dried clay." Now, in spite of the fact that no judgment has been stated, a very obvious one is implied. Let us contrast this with another description of the same man. "Although his face was bearded and neglected, his eyes were clear, and he looked straight ahead as he walked rapidly down the road. He seemed very tall; perhaps the fact that his coat was too small for him emphasized that impression. He was carrying a book under his left arm, and a small terrier ran at his heels." In this example, the impression about the same man is considerably changed, simply by the inclusion of new details and the subordination of unfavorable ones. Even if explicit judgments are kept out of one's writing, implied judgments will get in.

21   How, then, can we ever give an impartial report? The answer is, of course, that we cannot attain complete impartiality while we use the language of everyday life. Even with the very impersonal language of science, the task is sometimes difficult. Nevertheless, we can, by being aware of the

favorable or unfavorable feelings that certain words and facts can arouse, attain enough impartiality for practical purposes. Such awareness enables us to balance the implied favorable and unfavorable judgments against each other. To learn to do this, it is a good idea to write two accounts of the same subject, both strict reports, to be read side by side: the first to contain facts and details likely to prejudice the reader in favor of the subject, the second to contain those likely to prejudice the reader against it. For example:

FOR	AGAINST
He had white teeth.	His teeth were uneven.
His eyes were blue, his hair blond and abundant.	He rarely looked people straight in the eye.
He had on a clean white shirt.	His shirt was frayed at the cuffs.
His speech was courteous.	He had a high-pitched voice.
His employer spoke highly of him.	His landlord said he was slow in paying his rent.
He liked dogs.	He disliked children.

22   This process of selecting details favorable or unfavorable to the subject being described may be termed *slanting*. Slanting gives no explicit judgments, but it differs from reporting in that it deliberately makes certain judgments inescapable. Let us assume for a moment the truth of the statement "When Clyde was in New York last November he was seen having dinner with a show girl. . . ." The inferences that can be drawn from this statement are changed considerably when the following words are added: ". . . and her husband and their two children." Yet, if Clyde is a married man, his enemies could conceivably do him a great deal of harm by talking about his "dinner-date with a New York show girl." One-sided or biased slanting of this kind, not uncommon in private gossip and backbiting, and all too common in the "interpretative reporting" of newspapers and news magazines, can be described as a technique of lying without actually telling any lies.

DISCOVERING ONE'S BIAS

23   Here, however, a caution is necessary. When, for example, a newspaper tells a story in a way that we dislike, leaving out facts we think important and playing up important facts in ways that we think unfair, we are tempted to say, "Look how unfairly they've slanted the story!" In making such a statement we are, of course, making an inference about the newspaper's editors. We are assuming that what seems important or unimportant to us seems equally important or unimportant to them, and on the basis of that assumption we infer that the editors "deliberately" gave the story a misleading emphasis. Is this necessarily the case? Can the reader, as an outsider, say whether a story assumes a given form because the editors "deliberately slanted it that way" or because that was the way the events appeared to them?

24   The point is that, by the process of selection and abstraction imposed on us by our own interests and background, experience comes to all of us (including newspaper editors) already "slanted." If you happen to be pro-labor, pro-Catholic, and a stock-car racing fan, your ideas of what is important or unimportant will of necessity be different from those of a man who happens to be indifferent to all three of your favorite interests. If, then, some newspapers often seem to side with the big businessman on public issues, the reason is less a matter of "deliberate" slanting than the fact that publishers are often, in enterprises as large as modern urban newspapers, big businessmen themselves, accustomed both in work and in social life to associating with other big businessmen. Nevertheless, the best newspapers, whether owned by "big businessmen" or not, do try to tell us as accurately as possible what is going on in the world, because they are run by newspapermen who conceive it to be part of their professional responsibility to present fairly the conflicting points of view in controversial issues. Such newspapermen are *reporters* indeed.

25   The writer who is neither an advocate nor an opponent avoids slanting, except when he is seeking special literary effects. The avoidance of slanting is not only a matter of being fair and impartial; it is even more importantly a matter of making good maps of the territory of experience. The profoundly biased individual cannot make good maps because he can see an enemy *only* as an enemy and a friend *only* as a friend. The individual with genuine skill in writing—one who has imagination and insight—can look at the same subject from many points of view. The following examples may illustrate the fullness and solidity of descriptions thus written:

Adam turned to look at him. It was, in a way, as though this were the first time he had laid eyes on him. He saw the strong, black shoulders under the red-check calico, the long arms lying loose, forward over the knees, the strong hands, seamed and calloused, holding the reins. He looked at the face. The thrust of the jawbone was strong, but the lips were heavy and low, with a piece of chewed straw hanging out one side of the mouth. The eyelids were pendulous, slightly swollen-looking, and the eyes bloodshot. Those eyes, Adam knew, could sharpen to a quick, penetrating, assessing glance. But now, looking at that slack, somnolent face, he could scarcely believe that.

ROBERT PENN WARREN, *Wilderness*

Soon after the little princess, there walked in a massively built, stout young man in spectacles, with a cropped head, light breeches in the mode of the day, with a high lace ruffle and a ginger-coloured coat. This stout young man [Pierre] was the illegitimate son of a celebrated dandy of the days of Catherine, Count Bezuhov, who was now dying in Moscow. He had not yet entered any branch of the service; he had only just returned from abroad, where he had been educated, and this was his first appearance in society. Anna Pavlovna greeted him with a nod reserved for persons of the very lowest hierarchy in her drawing-room. . . .

Pierre was clumsy, stout and uncommonly tall, with huge, red hands; he did not, as they say, know how to come into a drawing-room and still less how to get out of one, that is, how to say something particularly agreeable on going away. Moreover, he was dreamy. He stood up, and picking up a three-cornered hat with the plume of a general in it instead of his own, he kept hold of it, pulling the feathers until the general asked him to restore it. But all his dreaminess and his inability to enter a drawing-room or talk properly in it were atoned for by his expression of good-nature, simplicity and modesty.

COUNT LEO TOLSTOY, *War and Peace*
(Translated by Constance Garnett)

connotation
RICHARD D. ALTICK

Altick's essay is useful because it discusses *words,* the smallest tools of writing. It defines the different kinds of meanings attached to words, moving from what connotations are (in contrast, largely, to denotations), to what the subdivisions of connotations are (personal and general), to how connotations work. In each section, Altick's main explanatory technique is illustration, the presentation of multiple examples to clarify a point. These examples—over a hundred of them, not counting the words in the prose and poetry excerpts at the end—are Altick's data, his information, the flesh and blood by which he attempts to make a rather abstract concept come alive.

1   Incidents like this are happening every day. A teacher in a college English course has returned a student's theme on the subject of a poem. One sentence in the theme reads, "Like all of Keats's best work, the 'Ode to Autumn' has a sensual quality that makes it especially appealing to me." The instructor's red pencil has underscored the word *sensual,* and in the margin he has written "Accurate?" or whatever his customary comment is in such cases. The student has checked the dictionary and comes back puzzled. "I don't see what you mean," he says. "The dictionary says *sensual* means 'of or pertaining to the senses or physical sensation.' And that's what I wanted to say. Keats's poem is filled with words and images that suggest physical sensation."

2   "Yes," replies the instructor, "that's what the word *means*—according to the dictionary." And then he takes his copy of the *American College Dictionary,* which contains the definition the student quoted, and turns to the word *sensual.* "Look here," he says, pointing to a passage in small type just after the various definitions of the word:

SENSUAL, SENSUOUS, VOLUPTUOUS refer to experience through the senses. SENSUAL refers, usually unfavorably, to the enjoyments derived from the senses,

Source. From *Preface to Critical Reading,* fifth edition by Richard D. Altick. Copyright © 1946, 1951, © 1956, 1960, 1969 by Holt, Rinehart and Winston, Inc. Reprinted by permission of Holt, Rinehart and Winston, Inc.

generally implying grossness or lewdness: *a sensual delight in eating, sensual excesses.* SENSUOUS refers, favorably or literally, to what is experienced through the senses: *sensuous impressions, sensuous poetry.* VOLUPTUOUS implies the luxurious gratification of sensuous or sensual desires: *voluptuous joys, voluptuous beauty.*[1]

3   The student reads the passage carefully and begins to see light. The word *sensual* carries with it a shade of meaning, an unfavorable implication, which he did not intend; the word he wanted was *sensuous.* He has had a useful lesson in the dangers of taking dictionary definitions uncritically, as well as in the vital difference between denotation and connotation.

4   The difference between the two is succinctly phrased in another of those small-type paragraphs of explanation, taken this time from *Webster's New Collegiate Dictionary:*

Denote implies all that strictly belongs to the definition of the word, *connote* all of the ideas that are suggested by the term; thus, "home" *denotes* the place where one lives with one's family, but it usually *connotes* comfort, intimacy, and privacy. The same implications distinguish *denotation* and *connotation.*[2]

The denotation of a word is its dictionary definition, which is what the word "stands for." According to the dictionary, *sensuous* and *sensual* have the same general denotation: they agree in meaning "experience through the senses." Yet they *suggest* different things. And that difference in suggestion constitutes a difference in connotation.

5   For another elementary example, take the word *tabloid,* the denotation of which refers to small size. For that reason, newspapers with pages that are half as large as regular ones and which specialize in very brief news articles are regularly called tabloids. But because the average tabloid newspaper emphasizes the racy and the bizarre in its attempt to appeal to a certain class of readers, the word's connotation introduces the idea of sensationalism, of "yellow journalism." Thus *tabloid,* not surprisingly, is applied to newspapers in a negative, or pejorative, sense. In such a fashion many words acquire additional meanings which are derived from common experience and usage. (Similarly, the term *prima donna* refers, strictly speaking, to the leading woman in an opera company. By what process has it come to be applied to a certain kind of man or woman, with no reference to opera?)

6   Nothing is more essential to intelligent, profitable reading than sensitivity to connotation. Only when we possess such sensitivity can we understand both what the author *means,* which may be quite plain, and what he wants to *suggest,* which may actually be far more important than the superficial meaning. The difference between reading a book, a story, an essay, or a poem for surface meaning and reading it for implication is the difference between listening to the New York Philharmonic Symphony Orchestra on

a battered old transistor radio and listening to it on a high-fidelity stereophonic record player. Only the latter brings out the nuances that are often more significant than the obvious, and therefore easily comprehended, meaning.

7   An unfailing awareness of the connotative power of words is just as vital, of course, to the writer. His ceaseless task is to select the word which will convey exactly what he wants to say. The practiced writer, like the practiced reader, derives his skill from his awareness that though many words may have substantially the same denotation, few are exactly synonymous in connotation. The inexperienced writer, forgetting this, often has recourse to a book like Roget's *Thesaurus,* where he finds, conveniently assembled, whole regiments of synonyms; not knowing which to choose, he either closes his eyes and picks a word at random or else chooses the one that "sounds" best. In either case he is neglecting the delicate shadings in implication and applicability which differentiate each word in a category from its neighbors. Wishing to refer to the familiar terse expressions of wisdom in the Bible, for example, he has a number of roughly synonymous words at his disposal: *maxim, aphorism, apothegm, dictum, adage, proverb, epigram, saw, byword, motto,* among others. But if he chooses *saw* or *epigram* he chooses wrongly; for neither of these words is suitable to designate biblical quotations. (Why?) The way to avoid the all too frequent mistake of picking the wrong word from a list is to refer to those invaluable paragraphs in the dictionary which discriminate among the various words in a closely related group. (If the definition of the word in question is not followed by such a paragraph, there usually is a cross reference to the place where the differentiation is made.) For further help, consult the fuller discussions, illustrated by examples quoted from good writers, in *Webster's Dictionary of Synonyms.* But cheap pocket and desk dictionaries should always be avoided in any work involving word choice. They are frequently misleading because they oversimplify entries which are already reduced to a minimum in the larger, more authoritative dictionaries.

8   What has been said so far does not mean that the conscientious reader or writer is required to take up every single word and examine it for implications and subsurface meanings. Many words—articles, conjunctions, prepositions, and some adverbs—have no connotative powers, because they do not represent ideas but are used to connect ideas or to show some other relationship between them. Still other words, such as (usually) polysyllabled scientific or technical terms, have few if any connotations; that is, they call forth no vivid pictures, no emotional responses. *Psychomotor* and *cardiovascular* are neutral words in this sense; so are *acetylsalicylic acid* (asprin) and *crustacean* (shellfish). The single word *eschatology* is colorless compared with the words for its chief concerns: *heaven, hell, death, judgment.* The fact remains, however, that most words which stand for ideas have some connotation, however limited, simply because ideas themselves have connotations. Some technical words, especially when they

affect our daily lives, take on more and more connotation as they become familiar: *intravenous, angina pectoris, anxiety neurosis,* for example.

CONNOTATIONS: PERSONAL AND GENERAL

9 There are two types of connotation: personal and general. Personal connotations result from our individual experience. The way we react to ideas and objects, and thus to the words that refer to them (this is why the ideas are often called "referents"), is determined by the precise nature of our earlier experience with these referents. Taken all together, the connotations that surround most of the words in our vocabulary are, though we may not recognize the fact, a complex and intimate record of our life. Our present reaction to a word may be the cumulative result of all our experiences with the word and its referent. In the case of another word, our reaction may have been determined once and for all by an early or a particularly memorable experience with it. A student's reaction to the word *teacher,* for instance, may be determined by all his experience with teachers, which has been subtly synthesized, in the course of time, into a single image or emotional response. In it are mingled memories of Miss Smith, the first-grade teacher who dried his tears when he lost a fight in the schoolyard at recess; of Miss Jones, the sixth-grade teacher who bored her pupils with thrice-told tales of her trip to Mexico ten years earlier; of Mr. Johnson, the high-school gym teacher who merely laughed when he saw the angry red brush burns a boy sustained when he inexpertly slid down a rope; of Mr. Miller, the college professor who somehow packed a tremendous amount of information into lectures that seemed too entertaining to be instructive. Or, on the other hand, when the student thinks of *teacher* he may think of a particular teacher who for one reason or another has made an especially deep impression upon him—such a person as the chemistry teacher in high school who encouraged him, by example and advice, to make chemistry his life work.

10 A moment's thought will show the relationship between personal and general connotations as well as the fact that there is no firm line of demarcation between the two types. Since "the mass mind" is the sum total of the individual minds that comprise it, general connotations result when the reaction of the great majority of people to a specific word is substantially the same. The reasons why one word should possess a certain connotation, while another word has a quite different connotation, are complex. We shall spend a little time on the subject later. Here it need only be said that differences in general connotation derive from at least two major sources. For one thing, the exact shade of meaning a word possesses in our language is often due to the use to which it was put by a writer who had especially great influence over the language because he was, and in some cases, is, so widely read. The King James version of the Bible, for instance, is responsible for the crystallizing of many connotations.

People came to know a given word from its occurrence in certain passages in the Bible, and thus the word came to connote to them on *all* occasions what it connoted in those familiar passages; it was permanently colored by particular associations. Such words include *trespass, money changers, manger, Samaritan* (originally the name of a person living in a certain region of Asia Minor), *salvation, vanity, righteous, anoint,* and *charity.* The same is true of many words used in other books which, being widely read and studied, influenced the vocabularies of following generations— Shakespeare's plays, or *Paradise Lost,* or the essays of Addison and Steele.

11   But general connotation is not always a matter of literary development. It can result also from the experience that men as a social group have had with the ideas which words represent. Before 1938, the word *appease* had an inoffensive connotation. In the edition of *Webster's Collegiate Dictionary* current in that year it was defined simply as "to pacify, often by satisfying; quiet; calm; soothe; allay." But then the word became associated with the ill-fated attempts of Neville Chamberlain to stave off war with Hitler by giving in to his demands, and that association has now strongly colored its meaning. The latest edition of the same dictionary adds to the meaning quoted above this newer one: "to conciliate by political, economic, or other considerations;—now usually signifying a sacrifice of moral principle in order to avert aggression." Laden as the word is with its suggestions of the disaster of Munich, no British or American official ever uses it in referring to a conciliating move in foreign policy for which he wants to win public acceptance. On the other hand, opponents of that move use the word freely to arouse sentiment against it, even though the situation in question may have little or no resemblance to that of Munich. In other words, events have conditioned us to react in a particular way to the verb *appease* and the noun *appeasement.* If our support is desired for a policy of *give and take, live and let live,* or *peaceful coexistence* in international relations, its advocates will use the terms just italicized, as well as *negotiation* and *compromise,* which convey the idea of mutual concessions without sacrifice of principle; or *horse trading,* which has a homely American flavor, suggesting shrewd bargaining with the additional implication that good profit can be made on the deal.

12   All general connotations thus have their origin in private connotations —in personal, individual, but generally shared reactions to words and the ideas for which they stand. But later, after general connotations have been established, the process works the other way: the individual, who may have had no personal experience with the idea represented by a given word, may acquire a personal attitude toward it by observing how society in general reacts to the word. In the future, men and women who were not yet born when Winston Churchill was delivering his famous Second World War speeches in Britain, or when Adolf Hitler was presiding over mass executions of the Jews, supposedly will continue to react admiringly or with revulsion to their names. In addition, some words pass into and then out of connotative "atmospheres." The word *quisling* probably inspires no

feeling whatever in today's student, yet not too long ago it was synonymous with *traitor*. Yet the much older name of Benedict Arnold still serves the same purpose.

13   Every writer must cultivate his awareness of the distinction between general connotations and personal ones. It is the general ones—those he can be reasonably sure his readers share with him—on which he must rely to convey the accurate spirit of his message. If he uses words for the sake of the additional connotations they have to him alone, he runs the risk of writing in a private shorthand to which he alone holds the key. Since there is no clear dividing line between general and personal connotations, it would, of course, be unrealistic to require that a writer absolutely confine himself to the former. Moreover, some of the subtle richness of poetry, and to some degree of imaginative prose, is derived (assuming that the reader discovers the secret) from the author's use of words in private senses. But in most forms of practical communication, the writer does well to confine himself to words whose connotations, he has reason to assume, are approximately the same to his readers as they are to him.

THE USES OF CONNOTATIONS

14   What forms do our reactions to words take? As we have observed, by no means do all words evoke any distinguishable emotional response; *delusion* and *illusion,* for instance, probably do not do so for most people. Here the response is largely an intellectual one, a recognition that the two words are customarily used in different contexts, that they imply slightly different things.

15   But for our purposes the most important words are those which appeal to the emotions, words which stir people to strong (but not always rational) judgment and may arouse them to action. Mention of *militarist* or *atheist* or *capitalist* or *communist* evokes deep-seated prejudice, for or against the ideas or ideologies behind the words, for or against the people who are called by those names. The adjectives *atomic* and *nuclear,* until 1945 purely technical terms in physics, have since acquired a variety of connotations—on the one hand, of unspeakably capacity for destruction (think how often the words are linked with and therefore colored by such nouns as *annihilation* and *holocaust*), and, on the other hand, of a certain measure of hope for human progress through medical applications and increased industrial efficiency.

16   Many words lose much of their clear connotation, and in some instances much of their evocative power, through indiscriminate application. The word *bohemian* has been so overused that now it hazily covers nearly any form of untidy existence, as long as the "bohemians" in question are not genuinely poor and are living in unkempt quarters because they choose to do so. The term now has only vague connections, which once were much stronger, with the artist's life. For the same reason *streamlined* has lost its once-pleasant connotation; no advertising man would now consider

using the word to describe the latest Pontiac model. *Streamlined* now suggests instead a slapdash glossing over or cutting corners (as in *streamlined* business operation or educational curriculum), because the word has so often been loosely applied in such contexts. A few years ago *space age,* which became current when the Russians orbited their first sputnik, contained the awe appropriate to a development which soon thereafter witnessed man himself voyaging into the cosmos. But within a decade of its introduction *space age* was being applied to such mundane trivia as cosmetics, with the inevitable result that its initial power was entirely lost. It became merely another too-handy, threadbare word in the vocabulary of advertising and journalism.

17   Often the connotative power of a word is dependent on circumstances: who uses it, who is intended to read or hear it, and where. The connotations of the adjectives *hot* and *cold,* as slang terms, differ with the age of the user. *Debutante* means one thing to a New York society girl, who is actually going to have a costly debut, and another to the girl on an Iowa farm who buys *sub-deb* clothing from a mail order catalogue. *Nigger* connotes very different things to a diehard Mississippi segregationist and a member of the National Association for the Advancement of Colored People. *Draft, selective service,* and *conscription* mean the same thing, but one of these is never used in the United States, and of the remaining two, one has a more unpleasant connotation than the other. Both are widely used; who is likely to use which?

18   Intimately associated with emotional response, and often directly responsible for it, are the images that many words inspire in our minds. The commonest type of image is the visual: that is, a given word habitually calls forth a certain picture on the screen of our inner consciousness. Mention of places we have seen and people we have known produces a visual recollection of them. Of course the precise content of these pictures is determined by the sort of experience one has had with their originals. *Mary* may not recall the picture of one's childhood sweetheart, but it may evoke instead a picture of a pink hair ribbon which Mary must once have worn. *Boston* may recall only the picture of a street accident, which was the most vivid memory one carried away from that city. It is a fascinating game to examine in this fashion the mental images thus spontaneously conjured up by words. Equally rewarding is the effort to explain why many words evoke images which on first thought seem so completely irrelevant to their denotations.

19   It is not only words referring to concrete objects that have this power of evoking imaginative responses. Our picture-making faculty also enables us to visualize abstractions in concrete terms—and, as we shall see, it sometimes gets us into trouble on that account. Abstractions have little meaning unless we can concretize them in mental images; but we must take care not to allow abstractions, thus visualized, to become distorted by preconceptions or ingrained prejudices, which are inculcated emotionally rather than learned from our own experience. *Dictator* denotes a person

who has absolute authority in any state; it does not necessarily mean that he is a tyrannical megalomaniac. But the most memorable dictators of history—Napoleon, Mussolini, Hitler—have also been ambitious egotists and demagogues. And so our understanding of the abstract word *dictator* is colored by a composite picture of the most flamboyant of the past's dictators: we perhaps envision a gesturing, ranting military figure, mesmerizing the crowd with four-hour-long appeals to national pride and hatred of enemies, watching with puffed-up chest an interminable military review complete with exaggerated parade step and fearsome weapons of war flashing in the sun. The truth is that dictators from Caesar to Franco, in fact the great majority, have been far less colorful men than those mentioned. And in any case, personal flamboyance is not nearly as significant as a dictator's substantive actions. Our mental image of the dictator, then, is composed of what really amounts only to irrelevant window dressing. The word *dictator* serves to pull out many emotional stops in our minds; and emotion clouds any reasonable response we might be able to make to the idea. Therein lies the danger of connotation.

20   A further example: The picture that the word *artist* almost automatically calls forth in the imagination is of a pale, gaunt figure laboring fruitlessly in skylighted garret, scornful and defiant of a philistine society. His hands are long, sensitive looking (and bedaubed with paint), his eyes hollow, a little wild; his hair long and innocent of comb and brush. We envision him dying young through self-neglect, dissipation, and disappointment—the world has failed to recognize his genius. Such an image of "the artist" obviously is not fair; it may apply to a few individual specimens, but hardly to the profession of artists as a whole. It is a stereotype, a stock response cultivated in our minds by countless books, poems, and pictures: by the opera *La Bohème,* by what is told of the "decadent" figures in the England of the 1890s and the Greenwich Villagers of our own century.

21   Out of similar materials, a fortuitous mixture of the truly typical with a great deal that is not typical but exceptional, are made the stereotypes which usually govern our ideas of nationalities, races, parties, professions—in fact, of all kinds of groups—and our attitudes toward them.

22   In addition to visual responses in the imagination, words evoke responses associated with the other senses. Many have connotations that appeal most directly to our inward ear: *tick-tock, be-bop, slap, whir, squeak, splash, trumpet, dirge, shrill, thunder, shriek, croon, lisp, boom.* Others appeal to our sense of touch: *greasy, gritty, woolly, slick, silky, nettle, ice-cold, hairy, furry.* Another class invites palatal responses—*peppery, creamy, mellow, sugary, olive oil, menthol, salty, bitter.* Another brings olfactory responses, as in *burning rubber, incense, new-mown grass, pine forest, rancid, coffee roaster, ammonia, stench, diesel fumes, coal smoke.* Many words, of course, appeal to two or more senses at once; in addition to some of the above (which ones?) they are, for instance, *dry, effervescent, satin, lather, plastic, mossy, winy, slimy, wrinkle, sewage, frothy, sea breeze, misty, cigar.*

23   Because our sensory experience may be either pleasant or unpleasant, the words that evoke their imaginative equivalents have the power to sway us to accept or reject an idea. "So soft, yet manageable . . . so sweetly clean! Come-hither loveliness—that's what your hair has after a luxurious Prell shampoo! It's caressably soft, yet so *obedient!* Yes, angel-soft, smooth as satin, glowing with that 'Radiantly Alive' look *he'll* love!" Thus exclaims the advertising man who wants millions of women to buy a certain preparation for washing their hair. Or: "It's a foul, evil-smelling mess!" says a minority-party congressman who is dissatisfied with something the administration has done.

24   In some of the following pages, we shall concentrate upon this persuasive power of words, especially as found in advertising and political discussion. There is perhaps no simpler or better way of showing how connotation works. But this preliminary emphasis on the ways in which language may be manipulated for selfish purposes must not lead to the assumption that all, or even most, writers have wicked designs on their readers. On the contrary, the greater part of what people read has the sole purpose of informing or entertaining them—of giving them new knowledge, or fresh food for the imagination and the emotions. And here connotative language is used to heighten the effectiveness, the accuracy, and the vividness of the writer's communication.

25   Take the best of today's journalism—not routine newspaper reporting, but, say, feature stories and magazine articles. Really good descriptive journalism requires a high degree of skill in the use of words; and the more skillfully and attentively we read what the author has set down, the greater will be our pleasure. Examine the sure sense of connotative values employed in this description of a Pennsylvania industrial town:

> Donora is twenty-eight miles south of Pittsburgh and covers the tip of a lumpy point formed by the most convulsive of the Monongahela's many horseshoe bends. Though accessible by road, rail, and river, it is an extraordinarily secluded place. The river and the bluffs that lift abruptly from the water's edge to a height of four hundred and fifty feet enclose it on the north and east and south, and just above it to the west is a range of rolling but even higher hills. On its outskirts are acres of sidings and rusting gondolas, abandoned mines, smoldering slag piles, and gulches filled with rubbish. Its limits are marked by sooty signs that read, "Donora. Next to Yours the Best Town in the U.S.A." It is a harsh, gritty town, founded in 1901 and old for its age, with a gaudy main street and a thousand identical gaunt gray houses. Some of its streets are paved with concrete and some are cobbled, but many are of dirt and crushed coal. At least half of them are as steep as roofs, and several have steps instead of sidewalks. It is treeless and all but grassless, and much of it is slowly sliding downhill. After a rain, it is a smear of mud. Its vacant lots and many of its yards are mortally gullied, and one of its three cemeteries is an eroded ruin of gravelly clay and toppled tombstones. Its population is 12,300.[3]

Here, in carefully chosen everyday words, the reporter has produced a

---

[3] From "The Fog" by Berton Roueché. Copyright © 1950 Berton Roueché. Originally in *The New Yorker.*

graphic impression of a dismal community. He was clearly depressed by what he saw—a feeling he means us to have, too. And, were we to read on past the passage quoted, we would discover that even the seemingly casual reference to the population and the cemeteries is part of his plan; for the article as a whole is about the poison-laden smog that descended on Donora some years ago and killed at least a score of its inhabitants. The quoted passage, with its single-minded stress on language suggestive of griminess, ugliness, deterioration, prepares us for the disaster to come.

26   In the same way, but on a less ephemeral plane of interest, with more exalted purpose and greater intensity of feeling, poets too utilize the connotative potentialities of language. They employ words lovingly, unschemingly, wishing to delight and move the reader through an imparting of their own vivid experience:

Here, where the reaper was at work of late—
    In this high field's dark corner, where he leaves
        His coat, his basket, and his earthen cruse,
    And in the sun all morning binds the sheaves,
        Then here, at noon, comes back his stores to use—
            Here will I sit and wait,
    While to my ear from uplands far away
        The bleating of the folded flocks is borne,
        With distant cries of reapers in the corn—
All the live murmur of a summer's day.

Screen'd is this nook o'er the high, half-reap'd field,
    And here till sun-down, shepherd! will I be.
        Through the thick corn the scarlet poppies peep
    And round green roots and yellowing stalks I see
        Pale blue convolvulus in tendrils creep;
            And air-swept lindens yield
    Their scent, and rustle down their perfumed showers
        Of bloom on the bent grass where I am laid,
        And bower me from the August sun with shade;
And the eye travels down to Oxford's towers.

Or:

    It is a beauteous evening, calm and free,
    The holy time is quiet as a Nun
    Breathless with adoration; the broad sun
    Is sinking down in its tranquility;
    The gentleness of heaven broods o'er the Sea:
    Listen! the mighty Being is awake,
    And doth with his eternal motion make
    A sound like thunder—everlastingly.

names

MARY McCARTHY

Technically, names are just words, but they are an unusual class of words because of the importance we give them: we accept our names as our identities. If someone asks, Who are you? we respond by naming our name. People who want to erase their past identities and start anew express this intention by changing their names.

In this subjective definition, Mary McCarthy discusses the importance of names among the Catholic children who were her schoolmates. The episode about her "perfectly absurd situation" (paragraphs 8 through 12) stresses the problem of personal identity that is the underlying theme. Because she felt insecure in other ways, McCarthy permitted her fellow students to force upon her a name—a label, an identity—that she neither wanted nor understood.

1   **a**nna Lyons, Mary Louise Lyons, Mary von Phul, Emilie von Phul, Eugenia McLellan, Marjorie McPhail, Marie-Louise L'Abbé, Mary Danz, Julia Dodge, Mary Fordyce Blake, Janet Preston—these were the names (I can still tell them over like a rosary) of some of the older girls in the convent: the Virtues and Graces. The virtuous ones wore wide blue or green moire good-conduct ribbons, bandoleer-style, across their blue serge uniforms; the beautiful ones wore rouge and powder or at least were reputed to do so. Our class, the eighth grade, wore pink ribbons (I never got one myself) and had names like Patricia ("Pat") Sullivan, Eileen Donohoe, and Joan Kane. We were inelegant even in this respect; the best name we could show, among us, was Phyllis ("Phil") Chatham, who boasted that her father's name, Ralph, was pronounced "Rafe" as in England.

2   Names had a great importance for us in the convent, and foreign names, French, German, or plain English (which, to us, were foreign, because of their Protestant sound), bloomed like prize roses among a collection of spuds. Irish names were too common in the school to have any prestige either as surnames (Gallagher, Sheehan, Finn, Sullivan, McCarthy) or as Christian names (Kathleen, Eileen). Anything exotic had value: an "olive" complexion, for example. The pet girl of the convent was a fragile Jewish girl named Susie Lowenstein, who had pale red-gold hair and an exquisite retroussé nose, which, if we had had it, might have been called "pug." We liked her name too and the name of a child in the primary grades: Abbie Stuart Baillargeon. My favorite name, on the whole, though, was Emilie von Phul (pronounced "Pool"); her oldest sister, recently graduated, was called Celeste. Another name that appealed to me was Genevieve Albers, Saint Genevieve being the patron saint of Paris who turned back Attila from the gates of the city.

3   All these names reflected the still-pioneer character of the Pacific Northwest. I had never heard their like in the parochial school in Minneapolis, where "foreign" extraction, in any case, was something to be ashamed of, the whole drive being toward Americanization of first name and surname alike. The exceptions to this were the Irish, who could vaunt such names as Catherine O'Dea and the name of my second cousin, Mary Catherine Anne Rose Violet McCarthy, while an unfortunate German boy named Manfred was made to suffer for his. But that was Minneapolis. In Seattle, and especially in the convent of the Ladies of the Sacred Heart, foreign names suggested not immigration but emigration—distinguished exile. Minneapolis was a granary; Seattle was a port, which had attracted a veritable Foreign Legion of adventurers—soldiers of fortune, younger sons, gamblers, traders, drawn by the fortunes to be made in virgin timber and shipping and by the Alaska Gold Rush. Wars and revolutions had sent the defeated out to Puget Sound, to start a new life; the latest had been the Russian Revolution, which had shipped us, via Harbin, a Russian colony, complete with restaurant, on Queen Anne Hill. The English names in the convent, when they did not testify to direct English origin, as in the case of "Rafe" Chatham, had come to us from the South and represented a kind of internal exile; such girls as Mary Fordyce Blake and Mary McQueen Street (a class ahead of me; her sister was named Francesca) bore their double-barreled first names like titles of aristocracy from the ante-bellum South. Not all our girls, by any means, were Catholic; some of the very prettiest ones—Julia Dodge and Janet Preston, if I remember rightly—were Protestants. The nuns had taught us to behave with special courtesy to these strangers in our midst, and the whole effect was of some superior hostel for refugees of all the lost causes of the past hundred years. Money could not count for much in such an atmosphere; the fathers and grandfathers of many of our "best" girls were ruined men.

4   Names, often, were freakish in the Pacific Northwest, particularly girls' names. In the Episcopal boarding school I went to later, in Tacoma, there was a girl called De Vere Utter, and there was a girl called Rocena and another called Hermoine. Was Rocena a mistake for Rowena and Hermoine for Hermione? And was Vere, as we called her, Lady Clara Vere de Vere? Probably. You do not hear names like those often, in any case, east of the Cascade Mountains; they belong to the frontier, where books and libraries were few and memory seems to have been oral, as in the time of Homer.

5   Names have more significance for Catholics than they do for other people; Christian names are chosen for the spiritual qualities of the saints they are taken from. Protestants used to name their children out of the Old Testament and now they name them out of novels and plays, whose heroes and heroines are perhaps the new patron saints of a secular age. But with Catholics it is different. The saint a child is named for is supposed to serve, literally, as a model or pattern to imitate; your name is your fortune and it tells you what you are or must be. Catholic children ponder their names

for a mystic meaning, like birthstones; my own, I learned, besides belonging to the Virgin and Saint Mary of Egypt, originally meant "bitter" or "star of the sea." My second name, Therese, could dedicate me either to Saint Theresa or to the saint called the Little Flower, Soeur Thérèse of Lisieux, on whom God was supposed to have descended in the form of a shower of roses. At Confirmation, I had added a third name (for Catholics then rename themselves, as most nuns do, yet another time, when they take orders); on the advice of a nun, I had taken "Clementina," after Saint Clement, an early pope—a step I soon regretted on account of "My Darling Clementine" and her number nine shoes. By the time I was in the convent, I would no longer tell anyone what my Confirmation name was. The name I had nearly picked was "Agnes," after a little Roman virgin martyr, always shown with a lamb, because of her purity. But Agnes would have been just as bad, I recognized in Forest Ridge Convent—not only because of the possibility of "Aggie," but because it was subtly, indefinably *wrong* in itself. Agnes would have made me look like an ass.

6   The fear of appearing ridiculous first entered my life, as a governing motive, during my second year in the convent. Up to then, a desire for prominence had decided many of my actions and, in fact, still persisted. But in the eighth grade, I became aware of mockery and perceived that I could not seek prominence without attracting laughter. Other people could, but I couldn't. This laughter was proceeding, not from my classmates, but from the girls of the class just above me, in particular from two boon companions, Elinor Heffernan and Mary Harty, a clownish pair—oddly assorted in size and shape, as teams of clowns generally are, one short, plump, and babyfaced, the other tall, lean, and owlish—who entertained the high-school department by calling attention to the oddities of the younger girls. Nearly every school has such a pair of satirists, whose marks are generally low and who are tolerated just because of their laziness and nonconformity; one of them (in this case, Mary Harty, the plump one) usually appears to be half asleep. Because of their low standing, their indifference to appearances, the sad state of their uniforms, their clowning is taken to be harmless, which, on the whole, it is, their object being not to wound but to divert; such girls are bored in school. We in the eighth grade sat directly in front of the two wits in study hall, so that they had us under close observation; yet at first I was not afraid of them, wanting, if anything, to identify myself with their laughter, to be initiated into the joke. One of their specialties was giving people nicknames, and it was considered an honor to be the first in the eighth grade to be let in by Elinor and Mary on their latest invention. This often happened to me; they would tell me, on the playground, and I would tell the others. As their intermediary, I felt myself almost their friend and it did not occur to me that I might be next on their list.

7   I had achieved prominence not long before by publicly losing my faith and regaining it at the end of a retreat. I believe Elinor and Mary questioned me about this on the playground, during recess, and listened with

serious, respectful faces while I told them about my conversations with the Jesuits. Those serious faces ought to have been an omen, but if the two girls used what I had revealed to make fun of me, it must have been behind my back. I never heard any more of it, and yet just at this time I began to feel something, like cold breath on the nape of my neck, that made me wonder whether the new position I had won for myself in the convent was as secure as I imagined. I would turn around in study hall and find the two girls looking at me with speculation in their eyes.

8   It was just at this time, too, that I found myself in a perfectly absurd situation, a very private one, which made me live, from month to month, in horror of discovery. I had waked up one morning, in my convent room, to find a few small spots of blood on my sheet; I had somehow scratched a trifling cut on one of my legs and opened it during the night. I wondered what to do about this, for the nuns were fussy about bedmaking, as they were about our white collars and cuffs, and if we had an inspection those spots might count against me. It was best, I decided, to ask the nun on dormitory duty, tall, stout Mother Slattery, for a clean bottom sheet, even though she might scold me for having scratched my leg in my sleep and order me to cut my toenails. You never know what you might be blamed for. But Mother Slattery, when she bustled in to look at the sheet, did not scold me at all; indeed, she hardly seemed to be listening as I explained to her about the cut. She told me to sit down: she would be back in a minute. "You can be excused from athletics today," she added, closing the door. As I waited, I considered this remark, which seemed to me strangely munificent, in view of the unimportance of the cut. In a moment, she returned, but without the sheet. Instead, she produced out of her big pocket a sort of cloth girdle and a peculiar flannel object which I first took to be a bandage, and I began to protest that I did not need or want a bandage; all I needed was a bottom sheet. "The sheet can wait," said Mother Slattery, succinctly, handing me two large safety pins. It was the pins that abruptly enlightened me; I saw Mother Slattery's mistake, even as she was instructing me as to how this flannel article, which I now understood to be a sanitary napkin, was to be put on.

9   "Oh, no, Mother," I said, feeling somewhat embarrassed. "You don't understand. It's just a little cut, on my leg." But Mother, again, was not listening; she appeared to have grown deaf, as the nuns had a habit of doing when what you were saying did not fit in with their ideas. And now that I knew what was in her mind, I was conscious of a funny constraint; I did not feel it proper to name a natural process, in so many words, to a nun. It was like trying not to think of their going to the bathroom or trying not to see the straggling iron-gray hair coming out of their coifs (the common notion that they shaved their heads was false). On the whole, it seemed better just to show her my cut. But when I offered to do so and unfastened my black stocking, she only glanced at my leg cursorily. "That's only a scratch, dear," she said. "Now hurry up and put this on or you'll be late for chapel. Have you any pain?" "No, no, Mother!" I cried. "You

don't understand!" "Yes, yes, I understand," she replied soothingly, "and you will too, a little later. Mother Superior will tell you about it some time during the morning. There's nothing to be afraid of. You have become a woman."

10   "I know all about that," I persisted. "Mother, please listen. I just cut my leg. On the athletic field. Yesterday afternoon." But the more excited I grew, the more soothing, and yet firm, Mother Slattery became. There seemed to be nothing for it but to give up and do as I was bid. I was in the grip of a higher authority, which almost had the power to persuade me that it was right and I was wrong. But of course I was not wrong; that would have been too good to be true. While Mother Slattery waited, just outside my door, I miserably donned the equipment she had given me, for there was no place to hide it, on account of drawer inspection. She led me down the hall to where there was a chute and explained how I was to dispose of the flannel thing, by dropping it down the chute into the laundry. (The convent arrangements were very old-fashioned, dating back, no doubt, to the days of Louis Philippe.)

11   The Mother Superior, Madame MacIllvra, was a sensible woman, and all through my early morning classes, I was on pins and needles, chafing for the promised interview with her which I trusted would clear things up. *"Ma Mère,"* I would begin, "Mother Slattery thinks . . ." Then I would tell her about the cut and the athletic field. But precisely the same impasse confronted me when I was summoned to her office at recess-time. *I* talked about my cut, and *she* talked about becoming a woman. It was rather like a round, in which she was singing "Scotland's burning, Scotland's burning," and I was singing "Pour on water, pour on water." Neither of us could hear the other, or, rather, I could hear her, but she could not hear me. Owing to our different positions in the convent she was free to interrupt me, whereas I was expected to remain silent until she had finished speaking. When I kept breaking in, she had hushed me, gently, and took me on her lap. Exactly like Mother Slattery, she attributed all my references to the cut to a blind fear of this new, unexpected reality that had supposedly entered my life. Many young girls, she reassured me, were frightened if they had not been prepared. "And you, Mary, have lost your dear mother, who could have made this easier for you." Rocked on Madame MacIllvra's lap, I felt paralysis overtake me and I lay, mutely listening, against her bosom, my face being tickled by her white, starched, fluted wimple, while she explained to me how babies were born, all of which I had heard before.

12   There was no use fighting the convent. I had to pretend to have become a woman, just as, not long before, I had had to pretend to get my faith back—for the sake of peace. This pretense was decidedly awkward. For fear of being found out by the lay sisters downstairs in the laundry (no doubt an imaginary contingency, but the convent was so very thorough), I reopened the cut on my leg, so as to draw a little blood to stain the napkins, which were issued me regularly, not only on this occasion, but every twenty-eight days thereafter. Eventually, I abandoned this bloodletting,

for fear of lockjaw, and trusted to fate. Yet I was in awful dread of detection; my only hope, as I saw it, was either to be released from the convent or to become a woman in reality, which might take a year at least, since I was only twelve. Getting out of athletics once a month was not sufficient compensation for the farce I was going through. It was not my fault; they had forced me into it; nevertheless, it was I who would look silly—worse than silly; half mad—if the truth ever came to light.

13   I was burdened with this guilt and shame when the nickname finally found me out. "Found me out," in a general sense, for no one ever did learn the particular secret I bore about with me, pinned to the linen band. "We've got a name for you," Elinor and Mary called out to me, one day on the playground. "What is it?" I asked, half hoping, half fearing, since not all their sobriquets were unfavorable. "Cye," they answered, looking at each other and laughing. "Si?" I repeated, supposing that it was based on Simple Simon. Did they regard me as a hick? "C.Y.E.," they elucidated, spelling it out in chorus. "The letters stand for something. Can you guess?" I could not and I cannot now. The closest I could come to it in the convent was "Clean Your Ears." Perhaps that was it, though in later life I have wondered whether it did not stand, simply, for "Clever Young Egg" or "Champion Young Eccentric." But in the convent I was certain that it stood for something horrible, something even worse than dirty ears (as far as I knew, my ears were clean), something I could never guess because it represented some aspect of myself that the world could see and I couldn't, like a sign pinned on my back. Everyone in the convent must have known what the letters stood for, but no one would tell me. Elinor and Mary had made them promise. It was like halitosis; not even my best friend, my deskmate, Louise, would tell me, no matter how much I pleaded. Yet everyone assured me that it was "very good," that is, very apt. And it made everyone laugh.

14   This name reduced all my pretensions and solidified my sense of *wrongness*. Just as I felt I was beginning to belong to the convent, it turned me into an outsider, since I was the only pupil who was not in the know. I liked the convent, but it did not like me, as people say of certain foods that disagree with them. By this, I do not mean that I was actively unpopular, either with the pupils or with the nuns. The Mother Superior cried when I left and predicted that I would be a novelist, which surprised me. And I had finally made friends; even Emilie von Phul smiled upon me softly out of her bright blue eyes from the far end of the study hall. It was just that I did not fit into the convent pattern; the simplest thing I did, like asking for a clean sheet, entrapped me in consequences that I never could have predicted. I was not bad; I did not consciously break the rules; and yet I could never, not even for a week, get a pink ribbon, and this was something I could not understand, because I was trying as hard as I could. It was the same case as with the hated name; the nuns, evidently, saw something about me that was invisible to me.

15   The oddest part was all that pretending. There I was, a walking mass

of lies, pretending to be a Catholic and going to confession while really I had lost my faith, and pretending to have monthly periods by cutting myself with nail scissors; yet all this had come about without my volition and even contrary to it. But the basest pretense I was driven to was the acceptance of the nickname. Yet what else could I do? In the convent, I could not live it down. To all those girls, I had become "Cye McCarthy." That was who I was. That was how I had to identify myself when telephoning my friends during vacations to ask them to the movies: "Hello, this is Cye." I loathed myself when I said it, and yet I succumbed to the name totally, making myself over into a sort of hearty to go with it—the kind of girl I hated. "Cye" was my new patron saint. This false personality stuck to me, like the name, when I entered public high school, the next fall, as a freshman, having finally persuaded my grandparents to take me out of the convent, although they could never get to the bottom of my reasons, since, as I admitted, the nuns were kind, and I had made many nice new friends. What I wanted was a fresh start, a chance to begin life over again, but the first thing I heard in the corridors of the public high school was that name called out to me, like the warmest of welcomes: "Hi, there, Si!" That was the way they thought it was spelled. But this time I was resolute. After the first weeks, I dropped the hearties who called me "Si" and I never heard it again. I got my own name back and sloughed off Clementina and even Therese—the names that did not seem to me any more to be mine but to have been imposed on me by others. And I preferred to think that Mary meant "bitter" rather than "star of the sea."

vulture country
JOHN D. STEWART

Stewart's subject is vultures or, more precisely, the way they live in Spain, that country with the three requirements of "vulture country": "a rich supply of unburied corpses, high mountains, a strong sun." In the center of the essay is a narrative, partly a factual description of a particular episode (paragraphs 15 to 29), partly an extension of that episode into its sequel which the author did not witness but knows must have taken place (paragraphs 31 and 32). Stewart's purpose in writing about the vultures is not simply to present scientific observation about them, but more fundamentally to understand how they fit into his world, and he into theirs.

1   **S**pain is the stronghold of the vultures. There are four listed species in Europe, two common and two rare; if they are anywhere, they are in Spain. The bearded vulture and the black survive there, the Egyptian flourishes, and the great griffon swarms. The further south you go the more numerous they become, until you reach the hot grazing plains of Andalusia. There, summer and winter through, they hang in hordes in the roofless sky, for Andalusia is the vulture country.

2   There are three essential qualities for vulture country: a rich supply of unburied corpses, high mountains, a strong sun. Spain has the first of these, for in this sparsely populated and stony land it is not customary, or necessary, to bury dead animals. Where there are vultures in action such burial would be a self-evident waste of labor, with inferior sanitary results. Spain has mountains, too, in no part far to seek; and the summer sun is hot throughout the country. But it is hottest in Andalusia, and that is the decisive factor.

3   The sun, to the vulture, is not just something which makes life easier and pleasanter, a mere matter of preference. His mode of life is impossible without it. Here in Andalusia the summer sun dries up every pond and lake and almost every river. It drives the desperate frogs deep into the mud cracks and forces the storks to feed on locusts. It kills the food plants and wilts the fig trees over the heads of the panting flocks. Andalusia becomes like that part of ancient Greece, "a land where men fight for the shade of an ass."

4   All animals, both tame and wild, weaken in these circumstances, and the weakest go to the wall and die. The unpitying sun glares down on the corpses and speeds their putrefaction, rotting the hide and softening the sinews and the meat, to the vulture's advantage. But the sun plays a still greater part in his life. Its main and vital function, for him, is the creation of thermal currents in the atmosphere, for without these he would be helpless.

5   The vulture must fly high—high enough to command a wide territory, for, except at times of catastrophe, dead animals are never thick on the ground. His task is to soar to ten thousand feet, more or less, two or three times in a day, and to hang there and keep constant survey. A male griffon weighs up to sixteen pounds, so that to hoist himself up to that necessary viewpoint would call for fifty-three thousand calories, the equivalent of fifty pounds of meat. To find and eat three times his own weight in a day is clearly impossible; a short cut must be made. In the dawn of any day, in Andalusia, you may see the vulture discovering that short cut.

6   The eagles, buzzards, kites, and falcons are already on the wing, quartering the plain fast and low, seeking reptiles and small game. But the vulture sits on a crag and waits. He sees the sun bound up out of the sierra, and still he waits. He waits until the sun-struck rocks and the hard earth heat up and the thermal currents begin to rise. When the upstream is strong enough, he leaps out from the cliff, twists into it, and without one laborious wingbeat, spirals and soars.

7   By the time the vulture reaches his station, a half hour later and maybe

more, the sun is blazing down on the plain and betraying every detail to his telescopic eye, and the updraft is strengthening as the day approaches its zenith. His ceiling for this day is fixed by two factors. One is the strength and buoyancy of his chosen thermal, which will vary with the strength of the sun and the behavior of the upper winds. But the more important factor, for it fixes his horizontal bearings as well, is the distribution of neighboring vultures in the sky, his colleagues and competitors.

8   He cocks his head from side to side and checks their various positions. There they hang, dotted across the clear sky at intervals of a mile or so— at the corners of one-mile squares. Height and lateral distances all adjusted, the vulture settles, circling slowly on his invisible support, and begins his long and lonely vigil.

9   This griffon vulture, which I select from the four species as being by far the most prevalent and typical, is almost sure to be a male. The female rarely leaves her nest from early March, when she lays her rough white egg, until August, when her huge poult is fledged and flying. The father has to feed and carry for all three.

10   At first glance, from below, he appears as one great wing, ten feet from tip to tip and two feet broad. His tail is square and very short, which is all it needs to be, for there are no sharp or sudden quirks in his flight that would call for a strong rudder. His movements are premeditated, stressless, and leisurely, for his energy must be conserved at all costs and never wasted on aerobatics.

11   The vulture's head and neck, too, protrude very little in front of his wing plane, and this distinguishes his flight silhouette from the eagle's. His neck is, in fact, some two feet long, but since it is bare—and must be bare —he folds it back into his collar to keep it warm. His head, apart from its nakedness, is like an eagle's; his yellow claws, which never kill and rarely carry, are shorter and not so strong. His plumage is a uniform sandy color, faded and tattered by work and waiting and, perhaps, by old age. It is relieved only by his coffee-colored ruff and the broad black primary wing feathers fingering the air.

12   The vulture sails in silence, for no vocal signals could serve him at such a distance from his fellows. He croaks, growls, and whistles only in his family circle, and at his feasts. He circles by almost imperceptible adjustments of his wing planes, aided by slight twists of his tail. But his head is in constant and active movement. He swivels it from one side to the other, bringing each eye in turn to bear on the earth. Then he bends his neck to right or left to check on one of his neighbors to north, south, east, or west.

13   The whole vulture network is interdependent. Each vulture can give and receive two signals or, as the scientists call them, "visual stimuli." Circling means "Nothing doing"; dropping, or its resultant hole in the sky, calls "Come here!" Like all other vultures, he rests reassured by the first and is rapidly and relentlessly drawn by the second.

14   It is demonstrable how, with a special density of nerve endings on his retina, the vulture can see a small animal from a great height. Many other birds—gannets, for example—have the same propensity. Their eyesight is surprising only when we compare it with the poor standards of our own. But a mystery remains: how does the bird know that the animal is dead? The sense of smell is to be ruled out straightway. It is impossible that it would operate at such a distance, even allowing for the upward current of air. Birds are not, generally, well endowed in this respect, and in the vulture's case this may be especially fortunate.

15   No book, no expert, could answer this question for me, and I carried it through the vulture country for years, the one tantalizing imponderable, the broken link. Then, one hot afternoon, I lay down beside an old swineherd in the shade of a cork oak on the foothills overlooking the great plain of La Janda. For fifty years, he told me, he had watched pigs on that plain —the pigs, yes, and the vultures. I put my problem to him.

16   The swineherd's theory is not to be proved, but it is a wise one and I shall hold it until I find a better. No, he said, it is not the white belly skin that distinguishes the dead animals. White fur may fix the vulture's eye, but it does not offer him evidence of death. All herds and flocks, said the old man, lie down together and at one time. They have their place and their hour of rest. When a vulture sees an animal lying alone and apart, he is bound to notice it. The next time he crosses, the same image strikes his eye and startles him again. Over and over again he marks it and waits and watches; but now, alerted, he watches it more closely.

17   The next day the animal is still there; his attention is fixed upon it now, so he circles a little lower, his eye riveted, seeking the slightest movement of limb or lung. He sees none, but he continues to wait, said the old man. It takes him two days, at least, to confirm death. He goes on circling, but lower. He becomes more engrossed, and more sure. The other vultures note his behavior and move over a little in the sky. Every time he falls, they move closer. Now he is very low. He seeks the heaving of the flanks or eye movements; he sees neither. At some point, perhaps, he receives a visual stimulus in some death sign—the protruding tongue or the wide and whitened eye. Then he falls quickly, landing heavily at a little distance from the corpse.

18   The swineherd and I watched the first vulture land. We watched him sidling and circling the dead goat, standing erect to see better, wing tips trailing, naked neck stretched to the full, head swiveling rapidly to bring alternate eyes to bear. He hopped closer and paused, peering intently. If he could smell, even as well as we, his doubts would have been over. But he stood there, irresolute, famished yet fearful, with his bill open and his wings ready for use.

19   Then a big shadow swept across the brown grass, and the vulture glanced upwards. His involuntary signal had been answered, and a tall column of vultures wheeled overhead. He hopped to close quarters,

stretched forward, pecked the corpse, and leapt back. He watched it for a second more; no movement. Then he croaked once, as though to bless himself, and threw himself on the body. He struck his heavy beak into the flank, flapped for balance, and thrust backwards with feet and wings to strip the hide from the ribs and belly.

20   Almost immediately there were eight more vultures at the corpse, and we saw that all of them sought and fought for the same place. Their aim was to penetrate, their object the viscera. Watching them thrusting their long necks deep into the belly cavity and withdrawing them befouled and bloodstained, I saw why those necks must be bare. Yes, said the swineherd, and that is the one part the vulture cannot reach to clean. His mate may clean it for him later, for pure greed, but if he had feathers there he would have maggots in them.

21   Now sixteen more vultures swept down, landing heavily in their haste and flap-hopping to the feast—the second square from the sky pattern. The corpse was covered, submerged in a heaving, struggling mass of broad brown wings. A new column wheeled above us, circling lower. There should be twenty-four up there, I reckoned. There were twenty-three.

22   The latecomers landed on nearby trees, including ours, and their weight bent thick limbs to the ground. From points four miles distant, we could expect thirty-four more, and at the height of the carnival I counted just short of one hundred birds.

23   A mule lasts two hours, said the old man, and an ox, three. This goat became bones in the sun in half an hour.

24   As the hundred fed, or hoped and waited, many more vultures circled high above, assessing the situation and the prospects and treasuring their altitude. Toward the end, when the feasters scattered and exposed the small skeleton, the watchers flapped and drifted wearily away to resume their distant stations. But they had fulfilled their function. They had marked the spot and drawn the Egyptian vultures and the kites.

25   Now the little Egyptian vultures landed daintily and dodged nimbly through the throng of giants. They are bare on the face and throat only, with well-feathered head and neck, and so, perforce, they are cleaner feeders. The dirty work has been done; now the long and delicate beak comes into play. The Egyptian vultures attack the skull, the large joints, and the crevices of the pelvic girdle—all parts inaccessible to the griffon's heavy beak. They extract brains, membranes, and the spinal cord, and clip out tendons and ligaments. They dodge out through the encircling griffons with their spoils, gobble them swiftly, and dance back for more. The griffons, gorged with meat and panting in the sun, pay them scant attention.

26   Finally, when all but the whistling kites have left the scene, comes the great solitary bearded vulture, the fierce lammergeier. His whole head is feathered, so he despises carrion. He lives aloof from all the rest of the vulture tribe, but they serve his interests, so he keeps them within sight. The old swineherd calls him *Quebrantahuesos*—the bone smasher—and Aeschylus noted him, long ago, for the same behavior. The lammergeier

seizes the largest bones, carries them high, in his claws, and drops them on the rocks. Then he swoops down and rakes out the marrow.

27　Like an eagle, he can kill as well as carry with his claws, and he has not the true vulture's patient, soaring habit. He attacks flocks and herds and carries off the lambs and kids and piglets. After his work has been done nothing will remain except an empty skull and some small bones, which the ants and carrion beetles pick and polish.

28　Our griffon, first on the scene, will not be the first to leave it. He is sure to have gorged himself with his advantage. Crop, throat, and neck distended, he squats back on his tail, with his wings spread to steady him and his beak hanging open. From time to time he chokes and belches and gags, and it is an hour, maybe, before the meat subsides in him.

29　When he is ready, the griffon runs and leaps across the plain, thrashing heavily with his big wings, and labors into the air. He finds a thermal, circles in it to his altitude, then slips sideways and sweeps gently across the sierra to his distant nest.

30　The griffon vultures are gregarious in nesting, with colonies throughout the mountains at fairly regular intervals of thirty miles. They are said to pair for life. Certainly they return every year to the same nest. In January they begin to repair the nest, a broad and battered saucer of strong branches, topped with twigs and grass. They are careless builders, and many nests have bare rock protruding in them. No attempt is made to cover it. The egg is laid in late February and incubated for forty days. The new chick is bare and blue-skinned and looks as though he might become a dragon, but soon he sprouts white down and begins to assert the characteristics of his race. In a month he is voracious, and by the end of April he will demand four pounds of meat every day. Before he is fledged he will need eight pounds. Providentially, his demands coincide with the heyday of death.

31　When the male vulture arrives at the nest he settles on a nearby ledge, vomits, and sorts out the result with his beak. The female helps with this assessment, feeding herself hungrily on the larger relics. Then she offers her gape and crop to her cowering, whistling infant. The chick gobbles madly. With vultures it can never be "little and often," for animals die irregularly, as they must, so the birds, young and old, must gorge to the neck when opportunity offers. That is their instinct and their nature.

32　A male vulture with family responsibilities cannot rest for long. Now that his load is delivered and eaten, he is likely to be the hungriest of the family. This, too, is as it should be, for the hunger sends him out and up again, however little daylight may remain, to circle in the sky until the sunset reddens the sierra.

33　Time was when the summer drought killed thousands of beasts every year and the floods of winter hundreds more. Nowadays there are fewer casualties, but the vultures still have a fairly constant food supply in the charnel gorges, which lie below most mountain villages.

34　Grazalema, Arcos, Casares, and a hundred more were built, for protection from the raiding Moors, on the edge of the precipice. All dead and dying animals, as well as all the garbage of the town, are simply pushed over the cliff and left to the birds. There is a bird in Andalusia for every class and size of refuse. From the escarpment you can watch all the scavengers of the air, soaring below you or fighting on the feast. The great black vulture may be here, the griffon and Egyptian for sure, and two kinds of kites. The cunning ravens and carrion crows wait on the outskirts, dashing in to snatch their choice. Clouds of choughs and jackdaws wheel and cry above them.

35   There is a new feeding ground in the unfenced highways of Andalusia. As motor traffic increases, these offer more and more dead dogs, cats, kids, pigs, and rabbits. If you are abroad at dawn, it is a common thing to run down a vulture intent on scraping a dead dog off the asphalt. Even so, with an apparently limitless population of these great birds, each looking for some thirty pounds of meat every day, one wonders how they flourish.

36   Their wonderful feeding system has, it seems to me, one fatal flaw. They can signal "Food here," but not how much. At the feast which I have described only some succeeded in feeding at all, and only two or three ate their fill. A majority came the distance and lost their height for little or for nothing.

37   In Africa, also vulture country, there is no such difficulty, for there all the game is big game, and every funeral is worth attending. It may be that some of our Andalusian vultures go there in the winter. Certainly our vulture population increases here, but that is because the vultures from further north crowd in as the heat decreases and the air currents weaken in their homelands. Fortunately, there is a seasonal food supply ready for them all, for it is the time of birth, with all its failures and fatalities. After the winter storms, too, the torrents offer up their toll of corpses. And in winter, each bird has only himself to feed. But you would not doubt, if you knew the constant panic for food which dominates him summer and winter alike, that the vulture leads a competitive and anxious life. He has strong forces for survival. It is held—and we know it to be true of eagles—that the vulture has a very long life. If this longevity is a fact, then the solitary chick each year may add up to a good replacement rate.

38   The nest is inaccessible, and the hen guards it constantly against the only possible natural enemy—other vultures or raptors. So the survival rate must be high, as is proved by the evident increase toward saturation point.

39   At times, lying on my back on the plain with binoculars trained on the sky, I have seen vultures circling in two or three layers, each one high above the other. What can this mean? A hungry duplication, or triplication, hopelessly covering the same feeding ground and using the only available thermals? Or the opposite—idle and well-fed reserves standing by for surplus?

40   No one can tell me. But here in the vulture country there are no birds more spectacular, more fascinating to watch and to study. In time we may find out the last of their secrets. I lie on the plains and keep on watching them. And they, I know, keep on watching me.

substantiation

In one of G. K. Chesterton's mystery stories, a detective, Father Brown, is called to Scotland to investigate the disappearance of the Earl of Glengyle. At the earl's castle, Father Brown finds a puzzling collection of items: a pile of jewels without settings; little heaps of snuff (a form of tobacco sniffed up the nose); piles of small metal springs, tiny wheels, and so forth; and 25 candles, without a single candlestick. A police inspector declares in frustration that no theory could account for this assortment of oddities. Rising to the challenge, Father Brown promptly provides three separate theories to account for the evidence:

1. The earl was a burglar who carried candles in a portable lantern, threw snuff into the faces of his pursuers, and used the diamonds and small steel pieces to cut out panes of glass.

2. The earl was a madman who tried to reenact the lives of the French royal family just before the French Revolution. He kept snuff because it was a luxury, candles because they were the method of lighting then, bits of metal because King Louis XVI had played at being a locksmith, the jewels because Queen Marie Antoinette had had a famous diamond necklace.

3. The earl was the victim of con men who had planted the loose jewels to persuade him that there was buried treasure on his estate. The pieces of steel were to be used for cutting the jewels, the snuff for bribing local shepherds to secrecy, the candles for light as the earl explored caves and other likely hiding places.

The problem, as Father Brown points out, is not a shortage of theories. "Ten false philosophies will fit the universe. Ten false theories will fit Glengyle Castle. But we want the *real* explanation of the castle and the universe." [1]

Real explanations are the province of substantiation. When we want to know something about X and have partial information but not the full story, substantiation is the process of determining which among any number of available theories is the one most likely to be true.

Essays of substantiation respond to the question, What is likely to be true about X? They differ from essays of definition in that the purpose is no longer to clarify what something *is* (or how it looks to us). The purpose is to demonstrate that some further assertion about X, in other words, some claim about its relationship to other things in the world, is justified.

TYPES OF ASSERTIONS

Most assertions belong to one of the following three classes.

1. *Causal explanations.* Assertions that X was caused by something else. (Father Brown is looking for the right one of this class: the correct cause of the collection of objects he sees.)

2. *Predictions.* Assertions that X will happen at some time in the future. ("Do you think it will stop?" inquired a friend of Mark Twain, looking out at a pouring rainstorm. "Why yes—it always *has*," Twain is supposed to have answered.)

3. *Attributions.* Assertions that some action or characteristic can be assigned to X, either now or at some time in the past. This class is sometimes divided into *generalizations,* in which X is a whole category ("College students are less physically fit than high school students"—two categories are concerned here); and *specifications,* in which X is an individual ("Roger Bannister ran the first four-minute mile").

Each class includes both positive and negative assertions. A causal explanation may assert that X was or was not caused by something; a prediction may claim that X will or will not occur; an attribution may state that George did or did not do it.

Occasionally, an assertion may belong to more than one category. Consider "College students are less physically fit than high school students, because they get less sleep." The first part of that assertion is an attribution (more narrowly, a generalization); the second part is a causal explanation.

---

[1] Gilbert Keith Chesterton, "The Honour of Israel Gow," in *The Amazing Adventures of Father Brown* (New York: Dell, 1958, and other editions; originally published 1910).

STEPS IN THE PROCESS OF SUBSTANTIATION

Every assertion is the answer to some question. "Nero fiddled while Rome burned" answers the question "What was Nero doing while Rome burned?" In theory, the question always comes before the answer, and the logical process of substantiation consists of the following four steps.

1. Awareness of a question and statement of the question in a well-defined form;

2. Collection of information;

3. Formation of a tentative assertion (a hypothesis or thesis) in answer to the question;

4. Verification of the hypothesis: a check to make sure that it accounts for all the evidence, that it does so better than any competing hypotheses do, and that it does not conflict with any other facts or concepts accepted as true.

In practice, however, these logical steps often get out of sequence. Father Brown begins with a question (step 1): "What happened to the Earl of Glengyle?" He is then shown the peculiar evidence (step 2), and the police inspector revises the question (back to step 1) to "What could account for this stuff?" Immediately Father Brown constructs three hypotheses (step 3). But he takes none of them on to verification (step 4), since he simply made them up to prove that he could, and he feels they are silly. Then more evidence is presented (step 2): a walking-stick from which the top knob is missing and some old Bibles with the haloes cut out of the pictures. While Father Brown is devising new hypotheses (step 3 again), further evidence is discovered (step 2): the body of the earl, with no head.

Sometimes you may begin not with a question but with an answer. You might hear someone assert "labor unions are responsible for inflation" (a causal explanation), or "we will never see a lasting peace in the Middle East" (a prediction), or "UFO's are nonsense" (a general attribution), or "the last horse race at Belmont yesterday was fixed" (a specific attribution). If you wanted to substantiate one of these assertions—or substantiate your suspicion that it is false—you might well begin by putting it into question form.

Who (or what) is responsible for inflation?
Will we ever see a lasting peace in the Middle East?
What are UFO's?
Was the last horse race at Belmont fixed?

Shifting the assertion, which is really the logical end point of an inquiry, into the form of a question, the logical beginning of an inquiry, usually makes it easier to organize the investigation. You can now follow, more or less, the four-step process outlined above. That process, by the way, is a simplified version of what is called the Scientific Method. It might better be called the Rational Method, since it describes a method for problem solving not only in scientific research but also in every inquiry where we want the most rational solution.

DIFFERENT DEGREES OF CERTAINTY

The process of substantiation tries to clarify the relationship between a body of evidence and an assertion (thesis) being made on the basis of it. Usually, what you want to know is whether the assertion is *true*—an accurate representation of reality. But the best we can ordinarily do is determine whether the assertion is *valid*—the most accurate representation of the evidence as we have it.

We can rarely arrive at absolute certainty, at truth itself. Our basic question recognizes this in asking not, What is true about *X*? but instead, What is likely to be true? Our legal system also recognizes this by requiring not absolute proof but only proof "beyond a reasonable doubt." Philosophers have repeatedly pointed out the unreliability of our equipment for knowing the world: our senses can deceive us. A traditional example is that if you insert half the length of a ruler into a glass of water, you will "see" a bent ruler although no bent ruler is there.

Though absolute certainty is rarely achieved, approximate knowledge is often useful, and we can approach more closely to the actual truth of things as the amount of evidence we have increases. It is better to make an educated guess (as Sagan does, p. 253), or to present the evidence and the range of possible answers (as Kramer does, p. 192), or at least to state the problem clearly and invite other people to work on it (as Gamow does, p. 186), than not to embark on the process of problem solving at all.

It usually helps to distinguish degrees of our less-than-absolute certainty. Questions to which we can be (reasonably) certain of having the right answer now are traditionally called *matters of fact*. These tend to be issues involving reports of our experiences. Questions to which we must regard any answer made now as only probably, not almost certainly, right are called *matters of opinion* or *matters of inference*. These tend to be issues involving the interpretation (not just the report) of our experiences (see Hayakawa, p. 136).

You can tell rather easily whether any question you are trying to answer concerns a matter of fact or a matter of opinion. The following set of diagnostic questions, rather like a biological key, will differentiate one species from the other.

1. Is the question to be answered free from definition problems?

2. Is it clear what the evidence should consist of, and is that evidence available?

3. Is the evidence free from internal contradiction?

4. Is the evidence explained best by only one hypothesis (rather than equally well by several)?

If the answer to all of these questions is yes, you are dealing with a matter of fact. If the answer to any question, or any part of a question, is no, you are dealing with a matter of opinion. Predictions, for instance, will always be in this second category because the evidence for their accuracy lies in the future and is not (diagnostic question 2) available now.

This distinction between matters of fact and matters of opinion is useful because it enables you to see in advance whether you can expect to settle your issue or only to advance a well-supported opinion. If your issue belongs to the second category, you can be, in fact you *must* be, satisfied with something less than a resounding verdict.

The distinction is useful also because it enables you to judge whether another writer has done his job. If his issue is a matter of fact and he does not seem able to arrive at reasonable certainty, or if his issue is a matter of opinion and he thinks he *has* arrived at certainty—something's wrong.

Finally, the distinction enables you to tell whether having a disagreement over something makes sense. If people are arguing about a matter of fact, disagreeing doesn't make sense; they're being either ornery or opinionated. There's no point in arguing whether Montana is north of Utah or vice versa, or whether Sweden's suicide rate is higher than ours. All you need to do is look up the evidence, present it coherently, make the answer explicit, and sign off. If people are arguing about a matter of opinion, on the other hand, and they come to different conclusions and don't seem able to convince each other, the fact that disagreement persists makes excellent sense. That condition is necessitated by the subject itself.

TECHNIQUES OF SUBSTANTIATION

Given a question of the type What is likely to be true about *X*?, a certain amount of information, and a number of theories that bear some relationship to the evidence, how do you determine which theory best fits the data and deserves to be presented as your thesis? The two traditional types of reasoning used to bring information and theses together are called *deduction* and *induction*. Chances are that you will use both of them, because they do rather different things.

Deduction is the process of bringing together an already accepted statement or principle (the major premise), a second statement (the minor premise), and drawing from these two a third statement (the conclusion) which joins parts of the two premises in a new way. The complete pattern is called a syllogism. The classic example is the following argument:

1. All men are mortal (major premise).

2. Socrates is a man (minor premise).

3. Therefore, Socrates is mortal (conclusion).

Deductive reasoning is a way of clarifying what *must,* given certain statements, follow from them. It does not add new information. Instead, it rearranges existing information so that all of the relationships implicit in our knowledge come out in the open. It resembles algebra, another system for clarifying the meaning implicit in what we already know. If you combine the algebraic premises $a + b = 12$ and $a = 2b,$ the conclusion *must* be that $a = 8, b = 4.$

The validity of deductive arguments depends on two factors: (1) whether the premises are, in fact, correct and (2) whether the conclusion joins their parts properly. As for the correctness of the premises, the deductive pattern does not establish that. It simply takes it for granted. Consider the argument of the following paragraph.

The main characteristic of the modern American is his perpetual restlessness. This may take the form of an endless moving-on to some new part of the country, a search for those greener pastures which always seem just beyond wherever we are now; or the American restlessness may manifest itself in a continuing search for a new philosophy which will explain our perplexing world better than the last one did. Each of us must come to terms with this problem as best we can. If the impulse seizes us physically we must move on, uprooted again and again; if it seizes us mentally we must move our minds on, uprooting our ideas again and again. In either case, there can be no final peace, no ultimate complacency, for you—or for me.

The flow of the prose here somewhat conceals the deductive pattern. In syllogism form, it would look like this:

1. The main characteristic of the modern American is his perpetual restlessness.

2. You are a modern American. (This second premise is not stated but is implied by the pronouns: "we," "each of us," "us," etc. The argument takes it for granted that the readers are Americans.)

3. You will never be at peace for very long.

A matter of opinion at best—not fact—because to be "at peace," and other key terms, are only vaguely defined. In addition, it is probably not a true conclusion because the major premise may well be untrue. We "modern Americans" are repeatedly told that this, that, or the other is our distinguishing characteristic ("We are the world's most violence-prone people"; "Americans are mad for power"; "You can tell an American by the bulge in his wallet, the bulge in his belly, and the bulge in his ego"). Until it is really established that "the main characteristic of the modern American is his perpetual restlessness," you might as well unpack your bags and put the road-maps away.

The deductive argument we have just looked at is weak because it includes an inaccurate (or suspicious) premise. A deductive argument can also be flawed because the premises, accurate in themselves, are improperly connected in the conclusion. To explain fully what connections are proper would require a course in logic. Such an explanation is beyond the scope of this book, and your own common sense will often smell a rat when one is lurking in the corners of a dirty syllogism. Let's look at a single example. Alice, having eaten a bit too much of the Wonderland mushroom that made people grow, became taller than the treetops and found herself addressed as "Serpent!" by a very grumpy pigeon. When she protested that she was a little girl, not a serpent, the pigeon replied:

"I've seen a good many little girls in my time, but never *one* with such a neck as that! No, no! You're a serpent; and there's no use denying it. I suppose you'll be telling me next that you never tasted an egg!"

"I *have* tasted eggs, certainly," said Alice, who was a very truthful child; "but little girls eat eggs quite as much as serpents do, you know."

"I don't believe it," said the Pigeon; "but if they do, then they're a kind of serpent: that's all I can say." [2]

Alice's egg-eating confession settles her identity for this birdbrain because it has constructed this syllogism:

1. Serpents eat eggs.

2. Alice and other little girls eat eggs.

3. Alice and other little girls are serpents.

There is nothing inaccurate about the premises here. Unfortunately for birds, both snakes and children *do* eat eggs. Where the syllogism goes astray is in the conclusion.

To go anywhere at all—even astray—a set of premises must include a *common term,* in other words, some phrase or idea that appears in both of them. If there is no common term to hitch the premises together, nothing at all follows from them. A remark like "Professor Lefkowitz is a hard grader—I hate eight o'clock classes" is only a grumble, not an argument.

But the pigeon's syllogism about Alice has a common term ("eat eggs"), so that's not the problem here. The problem is that this

2 Lewis Carroll (Charles L. Dodgson), *Alice's Adventures in Wonderland* in *The Complete Works of Lewis Carroll,* illustrated by John Tenniel, introduction by Alexander Woollcott (New York: Modern Library, 1960), pp. 60–61.

common term, which the pigeon takes as diagnostic, that is, as proof of what a thing's nature is, is not really diagnostic. The quality of eating eggs applies to too many creatures to be useful in deciding what any given creature is.

Only if premise 1 said that serpents and *only* serpents eat eggs (and if that were true) would it be legitimate to equate Alice with serpents. The pigeon's premises now leave open the possibility that there are many egg-eaters who do not fall within the category "serpents" *or* within the category "Alice and other little girls" (there are, for example, marmoset monkeys). Therefore the conclusion to the argument is not valid, and Alice need not practice hissing.

The same logical problem invalidates such arguments as "American white racists are flocking to the suburbs to escape the blacks within the cities; Senator Johnson recently moved from Washington D.C. to a quiet Maryland suburb; Johnson is another white racist type." The argument breaks down to

1. Racists move to the suburbs.
2. Senator Johnson has moved to the suburbs.
3. Johnson is a racist.

That conclusion is no more reliable than the pigeon's classification of Alice.

In dealing with deductive arguments, then, try to reduce their claims to a syllogism (a set of premises containing a common term and a conclusion). Next, try to check whether the premises are accurate. Finally, check whether the connection being made in the conclusion is a reasonable one. If your sense of smell isn't very acute, ask for some help here or check a handbook of logic.

If the deductive argument passes all these checkpoints, you can accept its conclusion with as much confidence as you can give to anything in this world. If the premises are accurate and the connection between them valid, the conclusion *must* be right.

Induction is the process of bringing together a set of observations and seeing what they mean. It is unlike deduction in a number of ways. It rarely provides the same level of certainty, since it shows not what must be true (given what you're starting with), but instead what the most likely interpretation is (given what you're starting with). On the other hand, because it begins with observations of reality rather than with accepted premises, it provides a way of dealing with genuinely new information.

The basic pattern of deduction is recombination, the rearrangement of parts of the premises. The basic pattern of induction is simple addition—observation 1 plus observation 2 plus observation 3 (any number can play) add up to what? The evidence Father

Brown finds at Glengyle Castle adds up to what? The complete inductive pattern consists of a body of evidence and a conclusion that interprets the evidence: identifies its meaning, explains it, states what it adds up to. In this case, the whole is always greater than the sum of the parts because the conclusion, in interpreting, goes beyond the evidence itself. The jump from evidence to conclusion is called the inductive leap.

The validity of inductive reasoning depends on two factors: (1) the quality of the evidence (its accuracy and its sufficiency—we will come back to these terms) and (2) the size of the inductive leap. High-quality evidence and a small inductive leap produce reliable inductions.

Naturally the evidence must be accurate, since any impurity in the data will contaminate the whole system. Unfortunately, we usually have no way of checking the accuracy of the evidence someone else presents. If we read in the newspaper that 3000 people have been rendered homeless by an earthquake in Mexico, or that the unemployment rate rose .6 percent last month, we must assume that these figures have not been falsified. There is no feasible way for us to check on them. The same applies to a larger body of evidence presented as part of an inductive argument. When du Bois tells us that several people died as the result of an innocent fantasy involving the name "America" (p. 251), virtually none of her readers is in a position to say whether her evidence is accurate or not.

In dealing with other people's evidence, we tend to assume that it is accurate unless it seems intrinsically preposterous or unless we have reason to suspect the honesty of the people from whom it comes. A case in point is the body of evidence about UFO's. If all of the reports submitted are accurate, we would have to conclude that the United States has been repeatedly visited by intelligent beings from another planet, and that some earthlings have communicated with these beings, have been inside their space vehicles, and so forth. However, many of the UFO reports have been discounted for precisely the two reasons mentioned. The evidence has sometimes been —in the judgment of our experts—intrinsically preposterous. And the people from whom it comes have sometimes been—again, in the judgment of our experts—unreliable, not to say intentionally dishonest. But you should use your own judgment as well as the experts'. It is always possible that things that seem preposterous are really happening and that the unreliable witness *did* see little green men this time.

As for checking the accuracy of your own evidence, that is easier. You don't need to cope with the possibility of somebody else's dishonesty or hysteria. If you have measured, measure again; if you are remembering, verify your recollection with someone else who was there too; if you are running an experiment, run it once or twice more. Sometimes, of course, it's not that simple. If you are collecting evidence about people, the accuracy of your evidence depends on whether they have answered your questions truthfully, and figuring that out may not be easy. In such special situations, ask for a professional's help.

In any case, if you have reservations about the accuracy of your data but have made every reasonable effort to check it, just level with your readers about the possible errors (notice that du Bois explains she is relying on a letter from a stranger). Then go forward with the inductive process.

The criterion of "sufficiency" can be met in one of two ways. The evidence will certainly be sufficient if you get all of it. If someone asks "How many of the students in your class are women?" you can count them. If you want to know where your congressman stands on aid to higher education, you can get the *Congressional Record* and see how he voted on every higher education bill.

But if the evidence cannot be sufficient in this sense of completeness, it may be instead a representative sample of the whole. If you are running for a student government office and want to know whether calling for the abolition of grades is likely to help your chances, you probably can't get all the evidence (every student's response to such a proposal). You can, however, ask some of the students; if you select them properly, your incomplete evidence will be sufficient. It would be a mistake to ask only students who are on academic probation, and not much better (do you see why?) to ask only students who are on the honor roll, or have enrolled in engineering curricula, or hold part-time jobs. Evidence based on a sample, rather than on the whole universe you are concerned with, can be sufficient only if the sample is a miniature replica of the whole, representing, in proper proportion, all elements of the whole. If your problem is complicated, you will need help from someone who knows the statistical techniques for deciding whether the sample is biased (unrepresentative), what errors the sample is likely to introduce, and how great the margin of error is likely to be. Huff (p. 494) provides useful suggestions.

Occasionally, the only evidence available is your own experience. From the viewpoint of the discussion above, such a small sample is not likely to be sufficient. People are so different from each other that nobody's experience is representative of everybody's. That does not mean, however, that arguments based on individual experience are worthless. Each person is contributing one piece of evidence to a gradually growing amount. So if you have testimony to give, speak up. Chesterton, for instance, asserts, on the basis of his own experience, that the color white has marvelous meaning (p. 245). Just be sure that, in basing an argument on personal experience, you do not try to make your story do the work of a larger sample. Don't present it as more than it is. Rather than talking in terms of "the child who grows up in a small rural town," talk in terms of yourself, if your own childhood in Hicksville, Ohio is your evidence. Your logic will be stronger as a result, and your style will probably be more dramatic too.

Once your evidence is in good shape (accurate and sufficient), what next? How do you decide what it adds up to?

This is the hard part, the part over which experts disagree. As the old saying goes, "that's what makes horse races." If different people looking at the same horses (the same data) didn't come to different conclusions and place their bets different ways, there wouldn't be any contest. Traditionally, it has been thought that when there are several hypotheses which account for the evidence, the one you should choose is the one with the following characteristics: it is the simplest hypothesis that accounts for all the evidence; it not only fits this body of evidence but also corresponds to, or at least does not contradict, everything else we know; and it goes beyond merely explaining its own body of evidence to illuminate other observations as well. If you have doubts about this list of characteristics, you are in good company. The principle of simplicity, for one, may not really apply to logical inquiries involving human beings. People do not always work in simple ways. If your friend comes in soaking wet on a rainy day, the simplest explanation is that he got caught in the rain. The truth may be that (having taken along an umbrella) he was perfectly dry until coming in the front door, at which time an automatic ceiling-mounted fire extinguisher, set off by his prankster girlfriend, doused him head to foot.

The one sure guide in dealing with inductive argument is the principle that the smaller the inductive leap is, the more reliable the whole argument will be. Let us assume that you are investigating whether Shakespeare's plays have as many lines for female characters as for male. There will be no difficulty in managing the evidence. You can get a standard edition of Shakespeare's plays, count all the lines for male and female characters (the evidence will be sufficient because complete), recheck your count (the evidence should be accurate, unless you keep falling asleep at the task), and total things up with the aid of an adding machine. Once the two totals have been rung up, you can give a one-word answer to the question. The inductive leap here is extremely small. The conclusion is little more than a statistical *summary* of the evidence; it involves almost no *interpretation* of the evidence. It interprets—goes beyond the evidence—only in adding the assumptions that your edition is accurate in its assignment of lines to characters, that those plays were indeed written by Shakespeare, and that those plays were the only ones Shakespeare wrote.

But if your question is whether Shakespeare was antifeminist and you are trying to answer *that* on the basis of your line-count evidence, your induction will require a kangaroo's leap.

You can avoid the need for a kangaroo by increasing the range of evidence. You can collect evidence on other kinds of male-female comparisons, for instance, from Shakespeare's plays. You can also decrease the scope of the question and decide to consider not whether "Shakespeare was antifeminist" but only whether "Shakespeare's plays as represented in this book are antifeminist." Both of these techniques will narrow the gap between the evidence and the conclusion and increase the chances that your readers will be willing and able to follow your logical gymnastics.

In dealing with inductive arguments, then, check to see whether the evidence is accurate, if you can. Next, check whether it is sufficient (all of it is there, or a representative sample is there); and then whether the size of the inductive leap requires only a moderate crouch-and-spring. You may also want to apply the traditional tests referred to above (whether the proposed thesis is the simplest one that accounts for the evidence, whether it corresponds to what else is known, and whether it serves to illuminate further data as well as that with which you began).

Some essays of substantiation are primarily deductive, others inductive, but usually the two techniques of substantiation are found together. Sagan (p. 253), for example, uses inductive reasoning when he recites the evidence showing that four billion years ago the earth was not frozen but had liquid oceans as it does now:

There are in old mud deposits ripple marks caused by liquid water. There are pillow lavas produced by undersea volcanoes. There are enormous sedimentary deposits that can only be produced on ocean margins. There are biological products, called algal stromatolites, that can only be produced in water.

In the next paragraph, he uses deductive reasoning to resolve the contrast between this evidence, which shows that the earth was not frozen, and other evidence, which shows that the sun was not shining brightly enough then to keep the earth's temperature above freezing:

Either our theory of the evolution of the sun is wrong or our assumption that the early earth was like the present earth is wrong. The theory of solar evolution seems to be in good shape. What uncertainties exist do not appear to affect the question of the sun's early luminosity.

The most likely resolution of this apparent paradox is that something was different on the early earth.

In syllogism form, this argument would read

1. Either our theory of the evolution of the sun is wrong, or our assumption that the early earth was like the present earth is wrong.

2. Our theory of the evolution of the sun is not wrong.

3. Therefore, our assumption that the early earth was like the present earth is wrong: something was different on the early earth.

THE LOGICAL IMPORTANCE OF INSPIRATION

You may think, by now, that defending your concept of what is likely to be true—proving your thesis—is a wholly objective process. To be sure, there are objective systems for determining which logical arguments are reliable. But there is still room, in the process of substantiation, for more subjective input. You always bring your personal assumptions and expectations to bear on any problem, and solving it sometimes requires a dash of the intellectual magic that we call inspiration or intuition or creative insight.

Father Brown got nowhere with his problem of the Earl of Glengyle until he suddenly realized, in a flash of inspiration, that each piece of evidence he had seen was *half* a piece of evidence. The answer was hidden in the missing halves. Each item he had been shown was missing a container or trimming made of gold. The jewels should have had gold settings, the snuff should have been in gold snuff-boxes instead of lying around in heaps on the furniture, the candles should have had gold candlesticks, the little metal pieces should have been inside gold watchcases, the walking-stick should have had a gold knob at the top, and the mutilated pictures in the old Bibles should have had haloes made of gold leaf. Even the headless body of the earl was missing its gold: the gold in the filling of the teeth.

After this realization, everything else was easy. The earl had died a natural death as it turned out—no mystery there. But before he died, he had promised "all the gold of Glengyle" to a simpleminded village boy, who seemed to be the only absolutely honest person he had ever met. So when the earl died, the boy followed up that promise. He took everything made of gold, but nothing else. After extracting the gold from the teeth, he replaced the earl's head in its coffin.

This last act confirmed Father Brown's hunch that, of all the theories that seemed to fit the evidence, he finally had the one most likely to be true. No thievery was involved, no insane fixation on the French royal family, no con men's schemes (to go back to the first three theories). What explained Glengyle Castle was merely an honest and simple person taking, bit by bit, precisely what had been given to him.

In the selections that follow, you will find writers working with various parts of the process of substantiation. Some presentations (for example, Gamow's "Four Colors," p. 186) simply establish the existence of a problem (step 1). If you can get no further than that,

that's the place to stop. Other presentations go on to offer collections of evidence, hypotheses, and confirmations (steps 2, 3, and 4). Even in these arguments, however, you will sense different levels of certainty: the near-absolute certainty we can accord when the issue concerns a matter of fact, the partial certainty we should accord when the issue concerns a matter of opinion.

You will find people providing causal explanations: explaining why it seems that inner-city blacks do not work for a living, why a growing number of married couples are deciding that they do not want any children. And people providing predictions: predicting that the all-American hot dog may well not survive, that it's not going to be easy to find someone to do society's dirty work tomorrow. And people providing generalizations: asserting that if we are normal we do not want to hear the truth, that "no man is an island," that witchcraft is a religion, that the comics have gone relevant. And, finally, specifications: that long ago the earth had ammonia in its atmosphere, that growing up rich has made a certain person unhappy, that a piece of chalk embodies the secrets of the universe.

You may be thoroughly convinced by some of these essays of substantiation and have reservations about others. But if you come away feeling that the writers have made good cases for their claims, then the job of substantiation has been accomplished.

series one

growing up rich

In this selection, which appeared as a letter to the editor of *Ms.* magazine, the writer uses personal experience to substantiate her claim that growing up rich can produce a hatred of oneself and of the world quite like the hatred produced by growing up poor. Growing up rich meant, to this child, growing up knowing that she was ugly and bad. Even now she feels rejected by people who blame her for the wealth of her family.

1   **m**uch is said about the pain of growing up in poverty, but not much about the pain of growing up rich. My wealthy family never had to worry about a lack of material possessions. Growing up in this environment, especially as a woman, was a deadening experience. Because she had money, Mom hired other people to live for her: to take care of her children, to wash the clothes, to clean the house. She hated herself. There was nothing for her to be except a social ornament for Dad to introduce to his business friends. She never had a job—didn't know how to go about getting a job, didn't even consider that she was capable of working or of supporting herself.

2   Dad was the provider. I have a gut hatred for ruthlessness and competitiveness because both killed my father. He didn't die of starvation, in jail, or in a fight; he died from alcoholism.

3   When Dad died, Mom almost died. All of her repressed anger tore her up inside when her main identity as a wife was taken away. After Mom got home from a mental hospital, her upper-class "proper" facade was totally

Source. Reprinted from *Ms.* Magazine, September, 1974.

destroyed. She went crazy. For 10 years she was crazy angry. She became an alcoholic. No one could be near her.

4   When I was a little girl, I was, in many ways, like Mom was when she was crazy. I was angry all the time. I didn't have any friends. I didn't know how to be a friend. All I could hope for was to be recognized by people, and the only way I knew to be recognized was to be angry. If I hit you, you knew I was there. And your anger at me for hitting you reinforced my feeling of not being able to have any friends. Mom knew deep inside that she was ugly and bad; and I knew I was, too.

5   In the last five years I have really been struggling to tear down the walls of my isolation—not only to be seen, but also to be heard.

6   Most of my friends these days didn't grow up in a wealthy environment. One aspect of my relationship with these friends throws me back into the painful isolation I am trying to overcome. I feel a subtle rejection from some of them because I grew up in a family with money. I belong to the class of the oppressors. I will "never really know what the pain of poverty is like." And I want to say to these friends, "Do you know what the pain of wealth is like? Do you know how it crippled my mother, and, through her, me? Don't push me away. Money didn't keep me from suffering. Your pain and my pain may be different, but the pain I feel is as intense as the pain you feel."

7   Dad made his money by being able to ignore the pain of others, and this ignorance (the same ignorance which causes racism and war) eventually killed him.

8   My father's insensitivity isn't restricted to wealthy people. I've seen the same insensitivity and desire to exploit others in the actions of people without money. Take the money away from all the wealthy people and give it to all the poor; unless there is a corresponding change in attitudes, the violence and exploitation will still remain. Wealthy or poor, until we can share our pain together, the world will remain a cold and brutal place.

(name withheld)

COMMENTARY

This letter to the editor shows how personal experience can be used—how information about yourself can be selected, controlled, and presented in effective order—as evidence to substantiate a thesis that goes well beyond that experience. The writer has available some 20 or 25 years' worth of memories, a collection of data far too large and varied for her to be able to use all of it. Some of it must be discarded because it is irrelevant to the subject at hand, or not quite clear in itself (many of our memories are shadowy), or repetitive of other material to be kept, or perhaps too painful to be stated in words to be read by strangers. What appears here is a small portion of the original body of evidence, focused around two people only (the writer herself and her mother, with subordinate attention given to her father) and organized into two chronological blocks. The writer's childhood is presented as one period of indefinite duration because it would be irrelevant to keep introducing details of months and years. The writer's present situation is called simply "these days." (The verb tenses move from past to present to indicate the chronological development.)

A very strict process of elimination has resulted in the exclusion of every piece of information that is not evidence for the point to be made. In the section about "these days," for example, we find out nothing about the writer's life beyond what the thesis requires: she is still suffering the pain of growing up rich. We don't even know whether she is still wealthy or whether, as she suggests in the last paragraph, she has tried to end her pain by giving her money away.

Would you be more convinced of the writer's point, more willing to agree that growing up rich causes tremendous emotional distress, if you knew more about her? Or has she told you enough?

Is her personal experience adequate to support her generalization?

OUTLINE

I. Introduction: statement of the subject, establishment of the comparison to being poor—paragraph 1

II. Evidence: narrative about her life
   A. Childhood—paragraphs 1–4
   B. Transition toward the present—paragraph 5
   C. The present ("these days")—paragraph 6

III. Development of thesis: summary of the damage that wealth did to her father, extension of the problem beyond wealth itself to the attitudes behind it—insensitivity, desire to exploit—which appear among the poor also—paragraphs 7–8

SUGGESTIONS FOR WRITING

1. In about 500 words (about the same length as the letter above), state and substantiate some thesis relating to your personal experience in growing up. Keep the introduction very brief and move rapidly into the presentation of the evidence. The difficult part will be compressing all the years of your memories into 500 words or, more accurately, choosing the particular memories you can present in 500 words.

If your thesis is as wide ranging as the one in the letter—which discusses such large concepts as poverty and wealth—you may find that no selection of your evidence leaves you satisfied. If so, try a more narrow thesis, for instance "living in a trailer makes for a close-knit family," or "growing up on an Air Force base causes a warped personality: you stiffen and salute at the sight of blue."

2. If you have read F. Scott Fitzgerald's *The Great Gatsby* (or seen the film), summarize the evidence in it to show how that story makes a point about wealth similar to the one made in the letter above.

the problem of the four colors

GEORGE GAMOW

In this short selection, Gamow goes no further than step 1 of the logical process (see p. 171): the presentation of a problem. He is looking for a causal explanation of the observed fact that four colors will suffice to color any map—real or imaginary—without any two adjacent territories being the same color. (Two maps are included as representative evidence.) Why should this fact be so? Gamow doesn't have the answer and apparently neither does anyone else.

Simply to establish that a problem exists is useful, however, because that is an invitation to other people to try to solve it.

1   **S**uppose we have a surface of a sphere subdivided into a number of separate regions, and we are asked to color these regions in such a way that no two adjacent regions (that is, those having a common boundary) will have the same color. What is the smallest number of different colors we must use for such a task? It is clear that two colors only will in general not suffice since, when three boundaries come together in one point (as, for example, those of Virginia, West Virginia, and Maryland on a map of the United States, Figure 1) we shall need different colors for all of the three states.

2   It is also not difficult to find an example (Switzerland during the German annexation of Austria) where four colors are necessary (Figure 1).

Topological maps of Maryland, Virginia, and West Virginia (on the left) and Switzerland, France, Germany, and Italy (on the right).

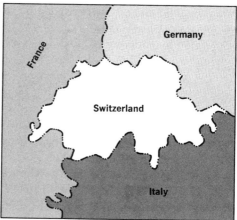

3   But try as you will, you never will be able to construct an imaginary map, be it on the globe or on a flat piece of paper, for which more than four colors would be necessary. It seems that no matter how complicated we make the map, four colors always suffice to avoid any confusion along the boundaries.

4   Well, if this last statement is true one should be able to prove it mathematically, but in spite of the efforts of generations of mathematicians this has not yet been done. Here is a typical case of a mathematical statement that practically nobody doubts, but that nobody has been able to prove. The best that has been accomplished mathematically has been to prove that five colors are always sufficient. That proof is based on the Euler relationship, which has been applied to the number of countries, the number of their boundaries, and the number of triple, quadruple, etc. points in which several countries meet.

5   We do not demonstrate this proof, since it is fairly complicated and would lead us away from the main subject of the discussion, but the reader can find it in various books on topology and spend a pleasant evening (and perhaps a sleepless night) in contemplating it. Either he can try to devise the proof that not only five, but even four colors are sufficient to color any map, or, if he is skeptical about the validity of this statement, he can draw a map for which four colors are not enough. In the event of success in either of the two attempts his name will be perpetuated in the annals of pure mathematics for centuries to come.

COMMENTARY

Gamow's procedure in presenting his problem is simple. He moves from summary of what has been observed (anyone asked to color a map has always found that four colors are sufficient) to a statement of the difficulty: "Here is a typical case of a mathematical statement that practically nobody doubts, but that nobody has been able to prove." After referring to the partial success of the specialists (their ability to prove that *five* colors should be sufficient), he closes with an open challenge to the reader. You are invited to try your own luck in either discovering the explanation for the data or devising a piece of evidence that contradicts the existing data —a map requiring not four but five colors—and thus makes the five-color proof of the specialists good enough.

If you were tempted to draw a map of your own or color the maps in Figure 1, Gamow succeeded in his purpose.

OUTLINE

I. Description of the map situation, with two real maps as illustration —paragraphs 1–3

II. Statement of the logical problem: nobody has been able to explain the map situation —paragraph 4

III. Invitation to the reader to work on it—paragraph 5

SUGGESTIONS FOR WRITING

In an essay of about the same length as Gamow's selection (450 to 500 words), follow his procedure: summarize your observations, state the unresolved problem, and invite the reader to work on it too. For example, you may often have observed that women tend to sit in the front of the room, men in the back; that cats, male and female, rub against peoples' ankles and arch their backs; that if you say hello to someone who is eating alone in the cafeteria, he or she usually gulps his food and looks embarrassed rather than glad for your company (while if one other person is sitting there already, you are welcomed); or that people seem to resent your calling them by the wrong name much more than your saying that you have forgotten their name altogether.

In each case, you don't know why, but perhaps someone else does.

the origin of life: spontaneous generation

GEORGE WALD

Wald examines what logicians call a "false dichotomy": a situation in which a question has been asked, and everyone assumes that the answer must be one of two choices. Because neither choice is satisfactory, the effort to solve the problem gets nowhere until somebody points out that there are other answers from which to choose.

As Wald says in paragraph 1, for a long time everyone assumed that the answer to the question "How did life begin?" must be either that life was created supernaturally or that it arises spontaneously from nonliving matter. Scientists found both of these choices unsatisfactory and therefore stopped asking the question. Wald's own reasoning shows that a third possibility is available: life "may have arisen spontaneously under different conditions in some former period," although it does not arise spontaneously *now* (paragraph 9).

1   **a**bout a century ago the question, How did life begin?, which has interested men throughout their history, reached an impasse. Up to that time two answers had been offered: one that life had been created supernaturally, the other that it arises continually from the nonliving. The first explanation lay outside science; the second was now shown to be untenable. For a time

scientists felt some discomfort in having no answer at all. Then they stopped asking the question.

2   Recently ways have been found again to consider the origin of life as a scientific problem—as an event within the order of nature. In part this is the result of new information. But a theory never rises of itself, however rich and secure the facts. It is an act of creation. Our present ideas in this realm were first brought together in a clear and defensible argument by the Russian biochemist A. I. Oparin in a book called *The Origin of Life,* published in 1936. Much can be added now to Oparin's discussion, yet it provides the foundation upon which all of us who are interested in this subject have built.

3   The attempt to understand how life originated raises a wide variety of scientific questions, which lead in many and diverse directions and should end by casting light into many obscure corners. At the center of the enterprise lies the hope not only of explaining a great past event—important as that should be—but of showing that the explanation is workable. If we can indeed come to understand how a living organism arises from the nonliving, we should be able to construct one—only of the simplest description, to be sure, but still recognizably alive. This is so remote a possibility now that one scarcely dares to acknowledge it; but it is there nevertheless.

4   One answer to the problem of how life originated is that it was created. This is an understandable confusion of nature with technology. Men are used to making things; it is a ready thought that those things not made by men were made by a superhuman being. Most of the cultures we know contain mythical accounts of a supernatural creation of life. Our own tradition provides such an account in the opening chapters of *Genesis.* There we are told that beginning on the third day of the Creation, God brought forth living creatures—first plants, then fishes and birds, then land animals and finally man.

5   The more rational elements of society, however, tended to take a more naturalistic view of the matter. One had only to accept the evidence of one's senses to know that life arises regularly from the nonliving: worms from mud, maggots from decaying meat, mice from refuse of various kinds. This is the view that came to be called spontaneous generation. Few scientists doubted it. Aristotle, Newton, William Harvey, Descartes, van Helmont, all accepted spontaneous generation without serious question. Indeed, even the theologians—witness the English Jesuit John Turberville Needham —could subscribe to this view, for *Genesis* tells us, not that God created plants and most animals directly, but that He bade the earth and waters to bring them forth; since this directive was never rescinded, there is nothing heretical in believing that the process has continued.

6   But step by step, in a great controversy that spread over two centuries, this belief was whittled away until nothing remained of it. First the Italian Francesco Redi showed in the 17th century that meat placed under a screen, so that flies cannot lay their eggs on it, never develops maggots. Then in the following century the Italian abbé Lazzaro Spallanzani showed

that a nutritive broth, sealed off from the air while boiling, never develops microorganisms, and hence never rots. Needham objected that by too much boiling Spallanzani had rendered the broth, and still more the air above it, incompatible with life. Spallanzani could defend his broth; when he broke the seal of his flasks, allowing new air to rush in, the broth promptly began to rot. He could find no way, however, to show that the air in the sealed flask had not been vitiated. This problem finally was solved by Louis Pasteur in 1860, with a simple modification of Spallanzani's experiment. Pasteur too used a flask containing boiling broth, but instead of sealing off the neck he drew it out in a long, S-shaped curve with its end open to the air. While molecules of air could pass back and forth freely, the heavier particles of dust, bacteria and molds in the atmosphere were trapped on the walls of the curved neck and only rarely reached the broth. In such a flask the broth seldom was contaminated; usually it remained clear and sterile indefinitely.

7   This was only one of Pasteur's experiments. It is no easy matter to deal with so deeply ingrained and common-sense a belief as that in spontaneous generation. One can ask for nothing better in such a pass than a noisy and stubborn opponent, and this Pasteur had in the naturalist Félix Pouchet, whose arguments before the French Academy of Sciences drove Pasteur to more and more rigorous experiments. When he had finished, nothing remained of the belief in spontaneous generation.

8   We tell this story to beginning students of biology as though it represents a triumph of reason over mysticism. In fact it is very nearly the opposite. The reasonable view was to believe in spontaneous generation; the only alternative, to believe in a single, primary act of supernatural creation. There is no third position. For this reason many scientists a century ago chose to regard the belief in spontaneous generation as a "philosophical necessity." It is a symptom of the philosophical poverty of our time that this necessity is no longer appreciated. Most modern biologists, having reviewed with satisfaction the downfall of the spontaneous generation hypothesis, yet unwilling to accept the alternative belief in special creation, are left with nothing.

9   I think a scientist has no choice but to approach the origin of life through a hypothesis of spontaneous generation. What the controversy reviewed above showed to be untenable is only the belief that living organisms arise spontaneously under present conditions. We have now to face a somewhat different problem: how organisms may have arisen spontaneously under different conditions in some former period, granted that they do so no longer.

COMMENTARY

Wald works with the following logical situation: a question has been asked; the answers offered are A and B; answer A conflicts with scientific premises; answer B is disproven by scientific evidence. As a scientist, then, what can Wald do? Unlike some of his colleagues, he is unwilling to ignore the question and hope it will go away.

The solution is to expose the falseness of the original dichotomy (division of the possible answers into only two) by demonstrating that a third answer is possible. This third answer turns out to be a revised version of one of the earlier ones, the theory that life arose through a process of spontaneous generation. Wald revises it to claim not that this process goes on all the time, but instead that it went on at an earlier point in time but does not occur any longer. This revised theory is not contradicted by scientific evidence, nor is it in conflict with scientific premises. Therefore, Wald, a Nobel prize-winning biologist, accepts it.

(The article from which this selection was chosen goes on to explain exactly how the process of spontaneous generation would have worked under the conditions that apparently existed on the earth some four billion years ago.)

OUTLINE

    I. Introduction: statement of the problem leads to acknowledgement of Oparin's work—paragraphs 1–3

    II. Theory A (supernatural creation) is unsatisfactory to a scientist—paragraph 4

    III. Theory B (continuous spontaneous generation) corresponds to the evidence of our senses but not to the evidence produced by careful research—paragraphs 5–7

    IV. What now? Some scientists are left with nothing; Wald himself proposes *Theory C* (a revision of B)—paragraphs 8–9

SUGGESTIONS FOR WRITING

1. Apply Wald's logical process to a problem in your own experience. A question arises. People assume that the answer is either A or B, but neither A nor B is really acceptable. Show that the answer might be C (or D or E, etc.) instead, so that you are no longer caught in the logical trap of the false dichotomy. For example, the question has arisen as to whether men or women are more intelligent. Most people assume that the answer must be either that men are more intelligent or that women are more intelligent. But we need not get caught in this logical trap. Another answer is that men and women are equally intelligent; another is that one group is more intelligent in some ways, less in other ways, so that the net result is a balance. Still another answer is that on the *average* one group surpasses the other, but that the very brightest (or dumbest) *individuals* belong to the other group, and so forth.

Your task is not to demonstrate that C or D or E is really the right answer, but only, for the moment, to break out of the false dichotomy. You want to establish that although A or B are both unsatisfactory, we need not be "left with nothing," as Wald puts it (paragraph 8).

2. Does Wald deal fairly with Theory A (supernatural creation)? He equates "rational people" and "reasonable people" (watch how he uses those words) with people who prefer the evidence of their senses to the evidence of

the Bible. Certainly he is being honest about his own system of beliefs, and he is careful to say that the logical predicament he is dealing with applies to scientists, not necessarily to everybody.

If Theory A appeals to you more than it does to Wald, explain how it (or a revision of it) could be logically compatible with his Theory C. Your task is to demonstrate *not* that any theory is true, but that some version of Theory A can be logically integrated with Theory C. (Note that in paragraph 5 Wald explains how earlier religious thinkers were able to logically integrate Theory A with Theory B.)

the no-child family: going against 100,000 years of biology

RITA KRAMER

This article looks for a causal explanation of an aspect of human behavior. It raises the question of whether married couples who decide not to have children do so because they are "immature, self-centered egotists," or because they are "responsible adults considering the consequences of their decisions" (paragraph 18). Two kinds of evidence are presented: the statements of the childless wives and husbands themselves, given in their own words so that we can judge whether they sound like immature egotists or responsible adults; and the opinions of experts on human behavior—psychiatrists, psychoanalysts, psychologists—presented in their own words so that we can judge them also. Kramer herself avoids giving any answer to a question about which the experts disagree. Her conclusion is only that the increasing frankness about such issues ought to help people make the decisions that will be best for their individual lives.

Does the evidence she presents warrant any stronger conclusion? What do you think the motives of the "childfree" couples are?

1   **C**athy and Wayne N. are in their late 20's, have been married five years, and are childless. The last time a member of Cathy's family asked, "When are you going to start a family?" her answer was, "*We're* a family!"

2   Cathy and Wayne belong to a growing number of young married couples who are deciding not to have children. A recent survey showed that in the last five years the percentage of wives aged 25 to 29 who did not want children had almost doubled and among those 18 to 24 it had almost

tripled. What lies behind this decision which seems to fly in the face of biology and society?

3   Perhaps the most publicly outspoken childless (or "childfree" as they like to put it) couple are Ellen Peck, author of "The Baby Trap," and her husband William, an advertising executive who is president of the National Organization for Non-Parents, which the Pecks founded last year to defend the social and economic interests of what they feel is a discriminated-against minority group: couples without children. The Pecks insist neither they nor the organization are against parenthood, just against the social pressures that push people into parenthood whether it is what they really want and need or not.

4   "It's a life-style choice," Ellen says. "We chose freedom and spontaneity, privacy and leisure. It's also a question of where you want to give your efforts—within your own family or in the larger community. This generation faces serious questions about the continuity of life on earth as well as its quality. Our grandchildren may have to buy tickets to see the last redwoods or line up to get their oxygen ration. There are men who complain about being caught in a traffic jam for hours on their way home to their five kids but can't make the association between the children and the traffic jam. In a world seriously threatened by the consequences of overpopulation we're concerned with making life without children acceptable and respectable. Too many children are born as a result of cultural coercion. And the results show up in the statistics on divorce and child-abuse."

5   Her husband adds, "Every friend, relative and business associate is pressuring you to have kids 'and find out what you're missing.' Too many people discover too late that what they were missing was something they were totally unsuited for."

6   And Ellen again: "From the first doll to soap operas to cocktail parties, the pressure is always there to be parents. But let's take a look at the rate of parental failure. Perhaps parenthood should be regarded as a specialized occupation like being a doctor. Some people are good at it and they should have children; others aren't, and they should feel they have other alternatives."

7   Less evangelical than the Pecks, who appear regularly in the media extolling the virtues of nonparenthood, but equally convinced that having children is not for them, a number of young husbands and wives who were asked about their decision not to have children made these comments:

8   *The main reason we enjoy our lives together is because we are together. I am not in the kitchen washing baby bottles while he thinks of an excuse to get out of the house because the baby is screaming.*

9   *The thing I find amusing is there are people our age with two or three children, struggling along, and they tell us we are missing something. Meanwhile we ride in a new car, own our own lakefront home, spend our summers on our boat, go away every weekend, and spend every Christmas holiday skiing in Europe. And they tell us we are missing something.*

10   *I'm sure there are some very happy families with children, but the*

unhappy ones far outnumber the happy ones. I don't want to take that chance.

11   *Most married people I know had no choice. They were programed to have three children and be Cub Scout leaders. Then there are those of us who stop to think about the big fantastic world out there waiting to be explored. I feel that most people are so busy washing diapers and trying to balance the budget that they merely exist and look around them, but never see. They're too busy wiping runny noses.*

12   *After five years, both sets of parents are putting on the pressure for us to have kids. They have taken to calling our cat and two dogs their "grandchildren."*

13   *A man's life isn't anywhere near as greatly altered as a woman's once the baby arrives. He may need to increase his earnings, but there is still the job, a productive life outside. The woman will have to sacrifice many things. I would feel trapped in that role.*

14   *It's depressing how crucial my sister and I are to my mother—she more or less lives for us. I will never let that happen to me.*

15   *I want to live my life while I'm young. My parents were always telling me that after my younger brother and I were out of school they would do all the things they wanted to do. My father will be 60 by the time my brother's out of college.*

16   *I don't think it's selfish to stay childless. Who are you hurting? It would be worse to become pregnant and not really want the baby. It might start out as a great ego trip, but all you'd wind up with would be problems.*

17   *When we say we don't want kids, people ask us, "What if everyone felt the way you do?" What a silly question.*

18   Are these the voices of immature, self-centered egotists or of responsible adults considering the consequences of their decisions?

19   Professional observers agree that many people have children for the wrong reasons, sometimes for no reason at all. Men often drift into fatherhood without ever making a deliberate choice. For many women pregnancy can be a way to escape from unresolved conflicts, to achieve instant identity or strengthen a poor self image, to gratify a need for the attention and affection they feel they never had as children.

20   I talked with a number of specialists in the field of human behavior about what these couples had said. Their reactions varied widely. A family therapist described the decision not to have children as "a basic instinctual response to the world situation today," implying that something like the herd instinct in animals was operating as a response to the dangers of overpopulation, crowding, pollution and nuclear war, causing women to feel a reluctance to reproduce and leading them to seek new ways of realizing themselves outside of family life.

21   More than one psychiatrist suggested that those who want to remain childless are narcissistic—making a virtue out of necessity by rationalizing their inner conflicts about giving care *vs.* being taken care of. "These are people who can't tolerate the idea of caring for children, who have no

margin of love to spare them," said one, adding, "You're going against something with 100,000 years of biology behind it." A colleague of his chimed in, "Well, we all rationalize our deficits, and these people probably *shouldn't* have children whatever their real motives are, for the same reason there ought to be liberal abortion laws. There should only be enthusiastic parents in this world."

22 Some observers suggest that perhaps what we are seeing is not a real change at all, that, like the sexual revolution, it is not really a revolution in behavior but in expression. "It may be," says one Connecticut psychoanalyst, "that an identifiable group that has existed all along is simply coming out of the closet, like homosexuals or swingers. The spirit of the time is to do your own thing and not hide it, and these people may reflect an increased frankness and openness rather than any real change."

23 Dr. Helen Kaplan, associate professor of psychiatry at The New York Hospital—Cornell Medical Center and head of its Sexual Disorder Program, thinks there has been a kind of sexual revolution and that what it amounts to is the separation of morality and sexuality. "Sex used to be permissible only for purposes of procreation in marriage. We no longer think it is immoral to have sex without having children and that leaves couples with a choice about whether they want to have them or not. They no longer have to feel guilty about not wanting it."

24 Dr. Kaplan believes there is a strong maternal urge in many women from early childhood on—"and it's not just culturally determined, either"— but that women vary tremendously in their degree of maternal need. And while women who experience deep maternal drives can't give up having children without feeling a real sense of deprivation, not all women feel this way.

25 Psychologist Donald M. Kaplan (no relation to Helen) believes that while some people have always opted not to have children, the increased frequency we are seeing is in those children of the nineteen-forties and fifties who were raised by parents whose character style had shifted from what sociologist David Riesman called "inner-directed" to "other-directed," and that these other-directed parents had two relevant effects on their children. One was to give them a greater feeling of "narcissistic entitlement"—what one expects from life. The other was the loss of a sense of certainty. They are more open to self-doubt, he says, more preoccupied with their bodies, their life-styles, less able to maintain stable attachments to others. The decision to have a baby, he thinks, is the kind of decision such people might be most likely to postpone. It can't be modified, can't be undone.

26 "Many of these young adults are ambivalent about relinquishing the role of the one who is cared for and taking on that of the one who does the caring," says Dr. Kaplan.

27 Dr. E. James Anthony is professor of child psychiatry at Washington University School of Medicine and co-author of "Parenthood, Its Psychology and Psychopathology." In a recent conversation Dr. Anthony said,

"Many people I've talked to are very concerned about their own future and the future of children in this rather troubled world. In the past there was always a feeling implicit in the culture that parenthood was something very significant, attractive, enriching, creative. Now it seems to be going by the board. There seem to be so many other opportunities for women to express themselves creatively and family life requires them to give up so many things that the emphasis on family life as a good and creative thing, a way to contribute to the future of the world, doesn't really ring a bell with many young people.

28   "I think that part of what's happening is that the ambivalence of parents today is being passed on unconsciously to their children. Children are a great deal of trouble, and perhaps more so today than ever before. They can be a pain in the neck. Their precocious development, adolescent acting-out, drug-taking, all loom as problems. The young people feel, 'If they don't really want us, why should *we* want to have children?' Then they rationalize this feeling in terms of the external questions like what the world has to offer. They ask questions like, 'Why add to the population explosion? Why create people who will have to face all the problems that are approaching in the next century?'

29   "Just how deeply ingrained are mothering and fathering? Does such a thing as fatherliness really activate men? Can they do without it easily? Some suggest it's just a question of having a fling and then nine months later having to think about the responsibilities of a family. Many young men say they don't feel the need to immortalize themselves in children.

30   "With women, there's the question of what has been called 'the disappointed womb'—whether there is a real need in women to experience something in what Erikson calls that 'inner space.' Many women I talk with are conscious of this kind of enrichment, they talk about being fulfilled in pregnancy, of feeling complete and better than they have ever felt in their lives—but, later, many find handling children is a bit of a nuisance. Still, having a child has been experienced as marvelous, miraculous. What happens if a woman abrogates this experience? It's a much more serious decision for her than for a man. There is something powerful about this basic biological means of creation. To deny oneself may be a little like Beethoven having this powerful talent and being told you must never use it.

31   "Despite their stated motives for not having children, the question arises whether young people really in fact lead richer lives today. I find that many college students today feel strangely empty. They live in a world full of stimuli of all sorts but lack a sense of inner satisfaction that may relate to these basic biologic things."

32   Whatever else they disagree on, the experts all seem to be saying that it's not whether you have children or don't that really matters, what matters is that you are comfortable about what you do. If you don't have children and you have much inner conflict about it, you'll be miserable in your childlessness; if you have children and regret it, you'll be miserable and your children will be miserable too. The point seems to be to know your-

self, to accept your deeper feelings and not make such an important life decision because it's the thing to do or to satisfy unrealistic fantasies, or to give your parents what they want or to escape from other responsibilities.

33   Some people are afraid to admit their own feelings of the kind many of the childless couples interviewed could accept about themselves—what they called being "selfish." They are ashamed to admit they would rather travel than bring up children. But what if that *is* what would make them happiest? Deeply held feelings are not easily changed and if you do not recognize what yours really are, you will not make the choices that are right for you.

34   For many, if not most people, the joys of parenthood as well as its problems are what life is all about. To see one's children grow and develop into individuals, and to see oneself continue on in them, can be the richest experience between one's own birth and death. But there are also people for whom living a full life and realizing themselves take other routes. And we live in a time in which attitudes seem to be freeing up in a way which enables increasing numbers of men and women to question the way "everybody" lives if that is not the way that is right for them. The more people continue to ask themselves such questions as whether or not they really want to raise a family before they begin to do so, the fewer unhappy parents and troubled children there will be.

COMMENTARY

Kramer's procedure is first to introduce us to some of the people who call themselves "childfree": Cathy and Wayne N., who apparently did not want their last name used (why?); Ellen and William Peck, who are positively evangelical about "the virtues of nonparenthood"; and ten other people who are represented only by their voices, not their names. It is only after this part of the evidence has been presented that Kramer puts her question: What kind of people are these? The question has been withheld this long to force us to meet them as people, to listen to their own explanations. Had we been asked to categorize them before meeting them, we might have jumped too soon to a conclusion, one way or the other. Kramer wants us to avoid a premature judgment.

She herself seems to avoid *all* judgment. She turns at once from a statement of the question to a selection of the opinions of experts, and then ends on a note of optimism about the good effects of greater frankness. We never do find out which kind of people she thinks the "childfree" couples are. The implication of this decision on the writer's part to abstain from a conclusion is that the evidence—what we have of it—is not sufficient to justify a conclusion. The essay will probably leave you unsatisfied, but it is more intellectually honest to abstain from concluding when you feel that the evidence is insufficient than to apply a conclusion just for the sake of having one.

Kramer's presentation of the problem of the no-child family is, in a way, a criticism of the experts, the "professional observers" who seem only too ready to tell us why we are doing what we are doing. "Fools rush in where angels fear to tread," as the proverb says. Is this implied attack on the experts for rushing to judgment justified? Or do you suspect that the experts have access to much more evidence than Kramer herself does and that their greater willingness to answer the question is legitimate?

OUTLINE

    I. Introduction: examples—paragraphs 1–2

    II. Evidence: the statements of the "childfree"—paragraphs 3–17

    III. Thesis question—paragraph 18

    IV. Professional testimony: theories explaining childlessness—paragraphs 19–31

    V. Conclusion: the benefits of honesty about one's desire (or lack of desire) for children—paragraphs 32–34

SUGGESTIONS FOR WRITING

1. Imitate Kramer's logical pattern: present part of the evidence, then state the question you are trying to answer, then present the rest of the evidence. Choose a subject where this organization is appropriate, in other words, a subject that you want your readers to *see* first, before they begin to answer a specific question. For example, describe what goes on in one of your classes, then ask "Is this learning, or just sounding off?" and then supply the rest of the evidence necessary to answer the question (or, like Kramer, supply further evidence but abstain from answering the question).

2. Confront the problems in substantiation that Kramer does by writing about some other aspect of human behavior where you are trying to interpret people's motives—*why* they behave or talk the way they do. Use your own observations as evidence. If you have been a camp counselor, try to explain why nine- and ten-year-olds divide themselves up into groups of two and three. Are they trying to return to the security of their family units, where they had a brother or sister or two as consistent companions, or are they looking forward to more adult relationships such as sexual pair-bonds or teen-age groups and gangs? If you played high school sports, try to explain why the team sometimes cooperated perfectly, sometimes dissolved into individuals pulling in different directions. If you changed schools, try to explain the motivations behind the way the people at your new school—students, teachers, counselors—received you.

You can't, of course, really know what lies behind the behavior of others (do you even know what lies behind your own?), but you can, like Kramer, present your observations and offer one or more theories to account for them.

good-bye to all t--t!

WALLACE STEGNER

This is an essay about calling spades "spades." Stegner dislikes both the prudish suppression of profanity and the constant use of it in print. As a teacher of creative writing and a successful novelist, he is concerned about effective language. His thesis is that too much obscenity defeats its own purpose. It loses its flavor. His crucial evidence is the little story (paragraph 9) where language turns a somersault from obscenity back to the meekest gentility—in order to recover its force.

Stegner's title indicates that he may intend to tease as well as be serious—a reminder that good titles are important.

1 **n**ot everyone who laments what contemporary novelists have done to the sex act objects to the act itself, or to its mention. Some want it valued higher than fiction seems to value it; they want the word "climax" to retain some of its literary meaning. Likewise, not everyone who has come to doubt the contemporary freedom of language objects to strong language in itself. Some of us object precisely because we value it.

2 I acknowledge that I have used four-letter words familiarly all my life, and have put them into books with some sense that I was insisting on the proper freedom of the artist. I have applauded the extinction of those d----d emasculations of the Genteel Tradition and the intrusion into serious fiction of honest words with honest meanings and emphasis. I have wished, with D. H. Lawrence, for the courage to say shit before a lady, and have sometimes had my wish.

3 Words are not obscene: naming things is a legitimate verbal act. And "frank" does not mean "vulgar," any more than "improper" means "dirty." What vulgar does mean is "common"; what improper means is "unsuitable." Under the right circumstances, any word is proper. But when any sort of word, especially a word hitherto taboo and therefore noticeable, is scattered across a page like chocolate chips through a tollhouse cookie, a real impropriety occurs. The sin is not the use of an "obscene" word; it is the use of a loaded word in the wrong place or in the wrong quantity. It is the sin of false emphasis, which is not a moral but a literary lapse, related to sentimentality. It is the sin of advertisers who so plaster a highway with neon signs that you can't find the bar or liquor store you're looking for. Like any excess, it quickly becomes comic.

4 If I habitually say shit before a lady, what do I say before a flat tire at the rush hour in Times Square or on the San Francisco Bay Bridge? What do I say before a revelation of the inequity of the universe? And what if the lady takes the bit in her teeth and says shit before *me*?

Source. "Good-Bye to All T--t" by Wallace Stegner. Copyright © 1965 by The Atlantic Monthly Company. Reprinted by permission of Brandt & Brandt.

5   I have been a teacher of writing for many years and have watched this problem since it was no bigger than a man's hand. It used to be that with some Howellsian notion of the young-girl audience one tried to protect tender female members of a mixed class from the coarse language of males trying to show off. Some years ago Frank O'Connor and I agreed on a system. Since we had no intention whatever of restricting students' choice of subject or language, and no desire to expurgate or bowdlerize while reading their stuff aloud for discussion, but at the same time had to deal with these young girls of an age our daughters might have been, we announced that any stuff so strong that it would embarrass us to read it aloud could be read by its own author.

6   It was no deterrent at all, but an invitation, and not only to coarse males. For clinical sexual observation, for full acceptance of the natural functions, for discrimination in the selection of graffiti, for boldness in the use of words that it should take courage to say before a lady, give me a sophomore girl every time. Her strength is as the strength of ten, for she assumes that if one shocker out of her pretty mouth is piquant, fifty will be literature. And so do a lot of her literary idols.

7   Some acts, like some words, were never meant to be casual. That is why houses contain bedrooms and bathrooms. Profanity and so-called obscenities are literary resources, verbal ways of rendering strong emotion. They are not meant to occur every ten seconds, any more than—Norman Mailer to the contrary notwithstanding—orgasms are.

8   So I am not going to say shit before any more ladies. I am going to hunt words that have not lost their sting, and it may be I shall have to go back to gentility to find them. Pleasant though it is to know that finally a writer can make use of any word that fits his occasion, I am going to investigate the possibilities latent in restraint.

9   I remember my uncle, a farmer who had used four-letter words ten to the sentence ever since he learned to talk. One day he came too near the circular saw and cut half his fingers off. While we stared in horror, he stood watching the bright arterial blood pump from his ruined hand. Then he spoke, and he did not speak loud. "Aw, the dickens," he said.

10   I think he understood, better than some sophomore girls and better than some novelists, the nature of emphasis.

COMMENTARY

The major thesis in this essay is that too much of anything loses its impact. Stegner's thesis appears in paragraph 3: "When any sort of word . . . is scattered across a page like chocolate chips through a toll-house cookie, a real impropriety occurs." He attempts repeatedly to show us what happens when language is abused, either by evasion or by overuse. His "genteel dashes" (d----d) in paragraph 2 and in the title are evidence for the point that an excess of prudery is silly. His anecdotes about his classroom experience and his uncle are evidence for the point that an excess of four-letter words renders them meaningless: language is power, but any given word or device of language will "lose its sting" if it is overworked.

Are Stegner's examples sufficient evidence to convince you? If he provided more, would he himself be overworking *that* device of writing?

OUTLINE

    I. Introduction: the subject identified and the author's attitude stated —paragraphs 1–2

    II. Thesis: propriety of language determined by circumstances—paragraph 3

    III. Evidence: hypothetical examples ("If I say . . ."); classroom experience—paragraphs 4–6

    IV. Thesis restated and affirmed—paragraphs 7–8

    V. Evidence: the uncle who cut his hand—paragraph 9

    VI. Summary: referring to paragraphs 5–6 and paragraph 1—paragraph 10

SUGGESTIONS FOR WRITING

1. Revise a passage that overuses some technique of style. Attempt to make it more dramatic by eliminating some examples of that device. For example, watch for too much slang, too many adjectives or exclamation marks, too many unintelligible words. You will be attempting to confirm Stegner's thesis that not using a device may be better than overusing it, that restraint may have its own power.

When you have completed your revision, write a short essay using the before-and-after versions as evidence to confirm (or perhaps to refute) Stegner's thesis.

2. Does Stegner himself rely excessively on some characteristic of style? Use his essay, especially paragraphs 4 to 8, as evidence to substantiate the thesis that he overworks the female stereotype.

the witches and their god

GILBERT HIGHET

The popularity of films such as *Rosemary's Baby* and *The Exorcist* testifies to our continuing interest in witchcraft and the supernatural, even though we supposedly live in an age of science. We remain curious about voodoo although we can watch men walk on the moon. By switching channels, we can look almost simultaneously at "The Twilight Zone" and at live space shots at Cape Canaveral.

Thus, Highet's first sentence strikes a familiar chord: "We still remember the witches. . . ." After all that science and engineering and technology and industry have accomplished over the past centuries, after all the indoctrination we receive in school about the dangers of superstition and the advantages of rationality—"we still remember the witches." Highet tries to tell us why.

1   **W**e still remember the witches—as we remember the nursery rhymes we heard when we were children, and the fairy stories we were told. They seem to belong to the far past, to the childhood of our world. They come out of it once a year, on Hallowe'en: on that evening ghosts also appear—cut out of pumpkins or cardboard, but still looking like skulls glowing with an unnatural inner life; our own children turn into evil spirits with strange clothes and blackened faces, to run about after sunset doing mischief; and the decorations for Hallowe'en parties always include pictures of witches, thin women with peaked hats, in black clothes, talking to a sinister black cat or riding a broomstick through the air. After that night (the night of the Dead, All Souls' Night), the witches vanish for another year. In other countries, they have other festivals. In Germany the night before May Day is a witches' sabbath, the Walpurgis-Nacht which Dr. Faust attended; and all over western Europe there is something uncanny about St. John's Eve, the 21st of June, the night before Midsummer: you remember the spirit of confusion and witchery which spreads over the darkling town of Nuremberg, in Wagner's *Mastersingers,* on that same enchanted night.

2   But apart from one or two dates in the year and one or two vestigial memories like hex marks, we have almost forgotten the witches. We think of them as a delusion typical of the Middle Ages, when people thought the sun went round the earth.

3   Yet, if we think over it, we shall begin to see that we are a little vague about the whole question. What *was* witchcraft? Mumbo-jumbo, hocus-pocus . . . no doubt. A delusion . . . yes, but who was deluded? The

Source. From *A Clerk of Oxenford: Essays on Literature and Life* by Gilbert Highet. Copyright © 1954 by Gilbert Highet. Reprinted by permission of Oxford University Press, Inc.

witches? Or the people who believed they were witches and persecuted them? Or both the witches and the public? Or neither, but only a few witch-hunting officials? Whenever you read the straight historical evidence, you find that it is more and more difficult to find a single, rational explanation of the witches, their power, their punishment, and their beliefs.

4   Take the first, the simplest explanation. There never was any such thing as witchcraft. Nobody can do magic. Nobody can fly through the air on a broomstick or conjure up the devil or cast spells on a neighbor. Anyone who *believed* that he or she could do such things was simply a crackpot. Even today we see many people who might well have been thought to be witches a few hundred years ago. Nobody can walk through the streets of a big city without seeing three or four really sinister-looking men and women, their faces distorted by savage inner pressures and conflicts, their pace irregular as though they were engaged in some hideous secret rite, their gestures fierce and unnatural, their mouths moving with half-audible words, usually malevolent, always repellent and pitiful. They seem to wish evil to the surrounding world. Perhaps the witches of whom we hear in the past were only mentally disturbed people who thought they were talking with unseen spirits (produced by their own troubled minds), and who did practice complicated ceremonies meant by them to hurt other people, although in fact the ceremonies did have and could have no objective effect whatever. If that is the true explanation of witchcraft, then the witches were only mental sufferers, and their mistreatment was one aspect of the long-standing failure of society to look after the insane.

5   That could well be a partial explanation; but it cannot be the complete explanation. Many of the people charged with witchcraft were outwardly sane and sensible: in Europe, they included eminent statesmen and scholars, and professional soldiers with long records of competent behavior; in America, one of the accused was a dignified Bostonian, son of the famous John Alden and his wife Priscilla.

6   Therefore there must be another solution. The first was that the accused witches were mad and the public was sane. The second possible explanation is that the accused were sane and the public was mad. Hysterical exhibitions took place at some of the trials, and it is often said nowadays that the men and women who stood in court to watch a witch trial were suffering from "collective hysteria," and that the judges were simply swept along on the irresistible tide of their emotion—in fact, that the whole thing was like a riot, or a lynching where the entire mob was wildly excited, and drunk, and virtually insane. This is the theme of a recent comedy, Christopher Fry's *The Lady's Not for Burning,* and of a still more recent tragedy, Arthur Miller's *The Crucible.*

7   Yet it is not easy to accept this solution either. For one thing, the hysteria was usually manifested not by the general public but by the people accused of being witches or said to have been bewitched—usually the

latter. At most of the witch trials the public was kept in the background, and was quiet, passive, and gloomy, the reverse of a lynching mob. For instance, at the Salem trials and at the examination of the nuns of Loudun, it was the so-called victims who screamed and twitched and had rigors, not their relatives or the audience. And furthermore, in many trials nobody got excited at all: the whole thing was as sober and gloomy as a modern prosecution for income-tax evasion.

8   But what is most disturbing is that large numbers of accused witches confessed; that some of them at least seem to have confessed without torture (for instance, Major Weir, in Scotland in 1670); and that they confessed the same sort of thing in widely different and far distant countries such as southern France and Sweden and eastern England; and that some of them refused to withdraw their confessions but defied their accusers and died laughing, proclaiming that they were right and renouncing the Christian religion. One of the slogans which they are said to have repeated is "Out, out of my house all Crosses and cares!" Yes, but what did they really confess?

9   I could never see my way into this problem until I looked up the article on witchcraft in the *Encyclopædia Britannica,* and later went on to read several books on primitive religion. One of these is essential for everyone interested in the subject: *The God of the Witches,* by an eminent anthropologist of London University, Margaret Murray. Then there are valuable sidelights on primitive religion today in a book on the voodoo religion of Haiti, called *Divine Horsemen,* by Maya Deren: not a pleasant book, but a powerful and thoughtful book. It is filled with stories of performances which you and I would call magical, actually seen by the authoress, and of powerful spirits, which a Puritan would call devils and which Miss Deren calls non-Christian elemental gods, possessing men and women at voodoo ceremonies, and one at least possessing Miss Deren herself.

10   There is one reasonable and systematic explanation of witchcraft which does not assume that the witches or the public were mad. It is that witchcraft was simply a religion—a non-Christian religion, an anti-Christian religion, which was practiced in Europe and elsewhere before the introduction of Christianity, which survived as it were "underground," and which is fundamentally opposed to Christianity, as to Judaism and Islam also. It was a religion of this world: of pleasure and carnal satisfaction; it was a cult of the animal element in man. When people confessed that they were witches, they sometimes meant that they were not Christians but adherents of this religion. When they said that the devil had appeared to them and made a pact with them, they meant that they had seen and talked to the god of this religion, renounced Christianity, and been baptized and accepted by this other god into his own cult. The devil, the god of the witches, was not a disembodied spirit from heaven or hell. He was simply a man, a human being, wearing a disguise, very often an animal disguise such as a

horned mask so that he would appear as half-man and half-goat, or half-man and half-bull: sometimes also in special shoes that looked like cloven hooves. He was a man, but—as in most primitive religions—in this costume he was a god incarnate.

11   The worship of the beast-man-god was an old, old religion, going back to the Stone Age hunters and the cattle breeders for whom the horned animals were vitally important and sacred. There are many traces of it as a genuine cult, throughout history: paintings on the walls of the caves where our ancestors lived; legends of sacred monsters like the Minotaur and the satyrs and the god Pan; festival dances, still surviving, where the dancers wore animal masks; even the name of the devil in Scotland, Auld Hornie. From this perspective, witchcraft begins to be understandable. It was apparently an organized underground religion far older and far more carnally enjoyable than Christianity. And it was persecuted because its creed and practices were diametrically opposed to Christianity: its rites were not sober meetings to sing hymns and hear sermons and attend Mass, but festivals often held at night, with eating and drinking and wild dancing and sexual adventure—both because sexual adventure was forbidden in the Christian church and because the religion of the witches was a fertility cult.

12   But how about magic? Did the witches really fly, on broomsticks? Dr. Murray explains: according to their own evidence, they often rubbed themselves with a flying ointment which would produce effects like those of marihuana today. (Sometimes, in New York, you can see a marihuana-smoker in the condition described as 'floating': doped up, he thinks he is flying, and he walks across the street with huge strides, as though he were leaping or soaring over the cars which just miss him.) And did witches cause illness and death to others by magic, simply by casting spells? Dr. Murray does not go fully into this, but it seems clear that the old religion carried with it a considerable knowledge of powerful drugs—remedies and poisons: if you wanted to cure a sick child or to produce abortion or to kill your neighbor's cows, the old woman in the tumble-down cottage would give you a brew of herbs which (although administered with a lot of hocus-pocus) would have the same effect as an efficient prescription today. The use either of drugs or of carefully directed hatred is implied in the remarkable Danish film about witchcraft, *Day of Wrath*. Some of the trials of the so-called witches might have contained more convincing evidence if a medical examiner had dissected the cattle they were supposed to have bewitched; and probably some of the scoundrels who peddle marihuana to school children today would, in the sixteenth century, have thought of themselves as witches—opening the way into a new and forbidden universe of sensual satisfaction with its own secret language, persecuted by the God-fearing world outside.

13   This looks reasonable. Many witches were unjustly accused; but others appear to have been adherents of a primitive, anti-Christian religion with quite different conceptions of morality and family life and the laws of thought. We can understand this more easily because on this continent,

no further away than New Mexico and Guatemala and Haiti, such primitive religions survive actively and energetically, today. (All the authorities on the witch trials of Salem agree in saying that the thing started with a woman called Tituba, part Indian and part Negro, who taught the little girls something—something like voodoo?)

14   But the thing which is left out of most rational explanations is the hysteria suffered by the girls in the Salem trials and by the nuns at Loudun. Why did they squirm and scream and stiffen and become apparently deaf and blind and start acting wickedly and unnaturally? And why did this happen most often in the presence, or at the mention, of the persons accused of enchanting them? Here Miss Maya Deren's book on Haiti will help us. She says again and again that one of the essences of the primitive religion of voodoo is possession; the climactic experience of that cult is that its devotees are "mounted" by spirits who ride them and dominate them. "The self must leave if the loa is to enter; one cannot be man and god at once." She describes how, after much drumming and ritual and prayer and singing and dreaming and dancing, a man will suddenly fall down as though dead, and then jerk violently, catapulted from side to side, mastered by the spirit Ogoun—to be left afterward, exhausted and limp. She says she herself was possessed by the charming female spirit Erzulie, and she prints photographs of several worshipers possessed by spirits and transfigured.

15   You and I probably do not believe in the Haitian god Ogoun, or in Baron Saturday and The Siren and Marinette-Congo and such elementals; but we can easily believe that there are powerful subliminal psychical forces which Christianity and other reasonable spiritual religions help us to keep under control, and which a really irrational cult, calling on the historic forces of sex, and blood, and the night, and the animal ancestors, would set free within us. In Haiti the man who knows how to preside over the rites which evoke such forces is entitled a *houngan* (chief of the spirits); in the sixteenth and seventeenth centuries he was called a chief wizard, or a priest of the devil; and twenty or fifty centuries before that, he was himself the priest, and the chief dancer, and the chief male, and the king, and the bull, the stag, the goat, the life of the herd and of the primitive human beings who followed it and depended on it; and so, himself personifying all that life, he was divine.

Maya Deren, *Divine Horsemen: The Living Gods of Haiti* (Thames and Hudson, 1953).

Christopher Fry, *The Lady's Not for Burning* (Oxford, 1949).

Pennethorne Hughes, *Witchcraft* (Longmans, Green, 1952).

Aldous Huxley, *The Devils of Loudun* (Harper, 1952).

Arthur Miller, *The Crucible* (Viking, 1953).

Margaret Murray, *The Witch-Cult in Western Europe* (Oxford, 1921).

Margaret Murray, *The God of the Witches* (Oxford, 1953).

W. S. Nevins, *Witchcraft in Salem Village in 1692* (North Shore Publishing Company, 1892).

M. L. Starkey, *The Devil in Massachusetts* (Knopf, 1949).
C. W. Upham, *Salem Witchcraft* (Wiggin & Lunt, 1867).

COMMENTARY

Highet's essay involves the refutation (disproving) of theories that are wrong—in the writer's view—in order to clear the way for his own. After the introductory summary of modern vestiges of witchcraft (paragraphs 1–2), Highet sets forth two explanations that seem objective and satisfying—except that he cites evidence that disproves them (paragraphs 4–9). He is halfway through before he states his thesis, "that witchcraft was simply a religion" (paragraph 10). Then he proceeds to substantiate this thesis, to make witchcraft "understandable" (paragraph 11). One by one, he answers the vexing questions about magic, spells, and possession. He ends with a reasonable description of unreasonable events, but at no point does he try to debunk or discredit the events themselves.

Does Highet deal with his own theory as critically as he deals with others? Or has he left certain aspects vulnerable to objections? Consider the statement that the witches' god "was simply a man, a human being, wearing a disguise. . ." (paragraph 10). How does Highet know that? Does the evidence demonstrating that people have long worshipped a beast-man-god (paragraph 11) prove that the witches' god *was* simply a man in fancy dress?

Highet ends by providing us with a bibliography, in effect inviting us to "check up" on him, to see whether his substantiation of a thesis is sound. He, at least, believes that he has found the most likely explanation of what witchcraft is, and why we do not forget it.

OUTLINE

     I. Introduction: the modern survivals; the question: "What was witchcraft?"—paragraphs 1–3
    II. Rejection of theories (that the witches were insane; that the public was insane)—paragraphs 4–8
   III. Highet's thesis: witchcraft as a religion
       A. Books on primitive religion—paragraph 9
       B. Characteristics of early witchcraft as a religion—paragraphs 10–11
       C. Explanation of magic—paragraph 12
       D. Restatement of thesis—paragraph 13
       E. Explanation of hysteria—paragraph 14
   IV. Conclusion: the appeal of the irrational—paragraph 15

SUGGESTIONS FOR WRITING

1. If you have had direct or induced experience with the "inexplicable" (in a dream, a vision, etc.), describe the experience and offer an explanation —or discuss the range of possible explanations if no single one satisfies you.

2. Apply Highet's logical process to a problem of your own: introduce the subject, define one or two theories that may be popular but that you do not accept, present the evidence to refute them, and then define and defend your own theory. Consider, for example, "Why don't most 18-year-olds make use of their right to vote?" Some people think the reason is that the newly enfranchised group (the 18- to 20-year-old group) doesn't know enough about the process of registering and voting; other people think that this group doesn't care enough about its representation in local, state, and federal government to bother; other people think . . . and so forth; your thesis is different from all these. Use yourself and your friends in this age category as evidence to refute the incorrect theses and to substantiate yours.

3. In April 1974, the magazine *MS.* published an article on witchcraft. The following letters to the editor, written in response to that article, confirm —20 years later—Highet's basic thesis that witchcraft is a religion.

But do these letters substantiate Highet's viewpoint (paragraph 15) that witchcraft is a "really irrational cult, calling on the historic forces of sex, and blood, and the night, and the animal ancestors"? If not, what theory or what revision of Highet's theory do the letters suggest to you?

I

1   I am a Witch. I was initiated into my first coven in 1967 and have been a student and active practitioner of the Craft ever since. I am a charter member of the Council of American Witches (having nothing except spiritual connections with the Women's International Terrorist Conspiracy from Hell). So, having stated my credentials, I have a bone to pick with Andrea Dworkin about her article, "What Were Those Witches Really Brewing?" (April, 1974).

2   She writes of our rites and practices, using Pennethorne Hughes and Jules Michelet as her only sources, who are not only *men* but *Christians* as well, which is enough to ruffle any Wiccan's feathers! There was not *one* mention of the Goddess: the Great Earth Mother, the Maiden Flora of the Plant Kingdom, Diana/Hecate Queen of Sorcery and Night. The primary Deity of the Craft was and is the Goddess. The Horned God, Faunus, Her consort, is Lord of Animals, the Sun, and the Underworld. None of this has anything to do with the Christian devil, in whom only Christians believe. Witchcraft is a religion with a primarily matriarchal orientation. The Great Triple Goddess was the Primal Deity for most of the world at one time. The practice of Witchcraft and numerous other pagan and neo-pagan fertility religions is based on Her worship.

3   Witchcraft and the other matriarchal neo-pagan earth religions exist today, and are constantly growing. They are a viable spiritual alternative to the dogmatic, patriarchal, and authoritarian systems such as Christianity, Islam, Hinduism, and Judaism. Witchcraft is also the only religion which has a female avatar: Aradia.

4   In the midst of the current male-aggression-generated eco-catastrophe, what could be more beautifully logical than a return to our Holy Mother Nature? Thou are Goddess! Blessed Be . . .

Morning G'Zell, Church of All Worlds (5th Circle)
Maiden for the Coven of Gwynvod, St. Louis, Mo.*

*Ms., June 1974, p. 7.

II

I was heartened to note that Andrea Dworkin took an objective and rather accurate look at the Old Religion. What with so much of the media still babbling on about witches being anti-Christian and involved in black magic, satanism, and demons, and witches being just a shabby excuse for drug or swinging parties, it was a rare treat.

But it is folly to assume that witchcraft died with the persecutions. You cannot murder a philosophy or a belief, and there are many very active witchcraft covens today. The number of people seeking out the old pagan gods as an alternative to other religions is astounding. Where witches of yore were concerned with fertility of crops, today we are more concerned with the fertility of thoughts and the mind. Where witches of old performed rituals to aid the seasons in changing to replenish the earth, today many of us are active in ecological and environmental programs.

Within a modern coven, the Great Mother predominates over the Horned God. The high priestess represents the Great Mother and she is the primary leader of the coven. It is she who leads all of the rituals, assisted by the high priest of the coven; it is she who has the final say over all other members of the coven, including the high priest.

Covens usually have equal numbers of male and female members. It always seems to surprise outsiders that the male coven members seldom feel that their masculinity is threatened or that they are being emasculated because the leadership of the coven rests in female hands. We like to feel that this is because our intiates have emotionally and spiritually matured to where there need no longer be a tug-of-war between male and female for supremacy. Blessed Be . . .

Theos, High Priestess,
L.I. Gardnerian Coven, Commack, N.Y.*

*Ms., June 1974, p. 8.

the body in the bog
GEOFFREY BIBBY

This is an essay in logical inference from an extremely limited amount of data: a naked body, male, its throat slit, found in a peat bog in Denmark. There would be no point in looking for witnesses since whatever happened took place 1500 years ago.

Bibby describes the process of investigation which establishes what can be known with certainty about X and what, in addition, can be logically inferred. The investigation involves assembling medical, botanical, and chemical evidence, and comparing this body with others recovered

Source. Copyright © 1968, American Heritage Publishing Company, Inc. Reprinted by permission from Horizon (Winter, 1968).

from the peat bogs in northern Europe. The range of information brought to bear upon this particular murder mystery then widens to include facts about the burial customs of prehistoric peoples, artifacts found in the bogs, early histories of Germanic tribes, surviving remnants of pagan religious practices, and finally—returning to the bodies themselves—the contents of their stomachs (the kinds of food the victims ate at their last meals). On the basis of this accumulated evidence, Bibby offers an explanation of the murder.

1   **t**he business of the archaeologist is the digging up of the past, the reconstruction of remote history. He does his best to find out what our remote ancestors did and thought and felt from the material remains they left in the ground. A distinguished archaeologist has unflatteringly described himself and his colleagues as surgeons probing into the workings of the human brain with picks, shovels, and builders' trowels. "Fortunately," he adds, "our patients are already dead."

2   This comparison must not be taken too literally. When Sir Mortimer Wheeler describes the archaeologist as investigating people who are dead, he means, I am afraid, that we are trying to find out about these dead-and-gone people by studying the things they left behind them, their implements and weapons and coins and pots and pans. The nearest we normally get to the people themselves is their skeletons, and there is a limit to what can be deduced from dry bones.

3   I wish to tell an archaeological detective story that is different—a detective story that begins with a body and no artifacts.

4   My part in the story began on Monday, April 28, 1952, when I arrived at the Prehistoric Museum of Aarhus, in mid-Denmark, to find a dead body on the floor of my office. On an iron sheet stood a large block of peat, and at one end of it the head and right arm of a man protruded, while one leg and foot stuck out from the other end. His skin was dark brown, almost chocolate colored, and his hair was a brownish red.

5   He had been found on Saturday afternoon by workers cutting peat in a little bog near Grauballe, about twenty miles away. He lay a yard below the surface, but peat had been dug for generations there so that the "surface" had lain much higher, even within living memory. The finders had informed the local doctor of their discovery, not so much because he was a doctor but because he was known to be an antiquary of repute. And he had informed Professor Peter Glob, who was the director of our museum.

6   This was not Professor Glob's first "bog body"; he knew what to expect and made preparations accordingly. The next day he drove out to the bog, cut a section through the peat exposing the lie of the body, drew and photographed that section, took samples of the peat surrounding the body, and then cut out the whole block in which the body lay and brought it in to the museum in a truck.

7   That Monday we carefully dug away the peat covering the body, tak-

ing samples every two inches. The body lay face down, with one leg drawn up and the arms twisted somewhat behind it. It was completely naked. When we removed the peat from below the body (after turning it over in a plaster cast to preserve its original position), we still found nothing, no trace of clothing, no artifacts—nothing except the naked body.

8   At this point we turned for help to the professor of forensic medicine at Aarhus University, who carried out a thorough autopsy and presented us with a lengthy and detailed report:

9   "This most unusually well-preserved body has, as a result of the particular composition of the earth in which it has lain, undergone a process of conservation which appears to resemble most closely a tanning. This has made the skin firm and resistant, and has to a high degree counteracted the various processes of decay which normally commence soon after death. . . . The subject is an adult male, and the condition of the teeth suggests that he was of somewhat advanced age. . . . On the front of the throat was found a large wound stretching from ear to ear. . . . This wound may with certainty be interpreted as an incised lesion, probably caused by several cuts inflicted by a second person. The direction of the wound and its general appearance make it unlikely that it could be self-inflicted or accidentally inflicted after death. . . . The investigation of the hair suggests that the subject was dark-haired. The reddish coloration is presumably accounted for by the body having lain in peat."

10   So the man from Grauballe had had his throat cut, and we had a murder mystery on our hands.

11   The investigation went on. The police expert reported: "There is nothing unusual about the fingerprints obtained. I myself possess the same type of pattern on the right thumb and middle finger—without therefore claiming any direct descent from Grauballe Man. Among the present-day Danish population the two patterns occur with a frequency of, respectively, 11.2 and 68.3 per cent."

12   More important were the results we got from the peat samples and from a portion of the liver region that we had excised and sent to the radioactive-carbon laboratory.

13   It happens that the botanists of Scandinavia have worked out in great detail the changing composition of the vegetation of the region since the last ice age ended more than ten thousand years ago. They do this by means of the thousands of infinitesimal grains of pollen to be found in any cubic centimeter of peat. The time within this sequence when any particular specimen of peat was formed is shown by the proportion of certain types of pollen grains, particularly of tree pollen. And the pollen analysts could tell us that the peat immediately below Grauballe Man had been formed early in the period the Danes call the Roman Iron Age, a period extending from the beginning of the Christian Era to about A.D. 300.

14   But they could tell us more. The peat *above* the body was of *earlier* date than that directly below and around the body, and the peat at a little distance to either side of the body was earlier still. The body had clearly

been buried in a hole cut in the peat—but not in a hole cut to receive it. The only explanation to fit the facts was that a hole had been cut, probably to obtain peat for fuel, had stood open for some years (long enough for new peat to form in the water at the bottom of the hole), and then Grauballe Man had been thrown into this new peat and the hole had been filled in with peat from the surface layers.

15   The radio-carbon laboratory—which determines the age of organic substances by measuring the residual carbon-14 in the specimen—could tell us that this had occurred and that Grauballe Man had died in A.D. 310, with a possible error of a hundred years in either direction. This did not surprise us; for, though local newspapers and gossip had made much of a certain "Red Christian," a drunkard farmhand who was said to have disappeared one night some sixty years before, not far from the Grauballe peat bog, we should have been very surprised indeed if the pollen laboratory and the radio-carbon laboratory had *not* given us a date in the region of 100 B.C.—A.D. 300.

16   For Grauballe Man was far from being an isolated example. Bodies have always been turning up in the peat bogs of Denmark—and not only in Denmark. They are frequently found in northwest Germany and even as far south as Holland. In that area there are records of something like two hundred bog bodies. Since the earlier records are not very detailed, sometimes merely an entry in a parish registry of the "body of a poor man drowned in such and such a bog," the statistics are far from exact. The earliest doubtful record of this nature is from 1450, at Bonstorf in Germany. And the first detailed report is from 1773, when a completely preserved body of a man was found three feet deep in the peat at Ravnholt on the Danish island of Fünen. The body lay on its back with its arms crossed behind it—"as though they had been bound," says the parish clerk. Apart from a sheepskin around the head, it was naked. When the sheepskin was removed, it could be seen that the man had had his throat cut.

17   In 1797, in southwest Jutland, another well-preserved male body was found, naked save for one oxhide moccasin but covered with two calfskin cloaks. The cause of death is not recorded, and the body was hurriedly buried in a nearby churchyard when it began to dry out and decompose.

18   And so it went. Every few years a body would be found, would be a nine-day wonder in its immediate locality because of its surprising state of preservation, and would be buried again when it began to smell.

19   A few of the bodies achieved more than local fame. In 1853, about fifty miles south of Copenhagen a body was found, probably that of a woman, though there was little left besides the skeleton and the long, fair hair. The body was noteworthy because it was accompanied by a bronze brooch and seven glass beads, which even then could be dated to the Iron Age and which we can now date to about A.D. 300.

20   Eight years earlier a much more complete female body had been found at Haraldskaer, in south Jutland, not far from the burial mounds of

Gorm, the last heathen king of Denmark, and his queen, nor from the site of the first Christian church in Denmark, built about A.D. 950 by Gorm's son, Harald Bluetooth. The body lay in the peat with its hands and feet held down by forked sticks, and it achieved some notoriety in Denmark because some learned antiquaries claimed that it was Queen Gunhild of Norway, who, according to legend, had been enticed to Denmark by Harald Bluetooth and drowned by him in a morass. Even at the time of discovery, though, the evidence for this identification was regarded as too slender.

21   The first photograph of a peat-bog body dates from 1873 and is of a body found near Kiel. It was a man's body with a triangular hole in the forehead. He was naked except for a piece of leather bound around the left shin, but his head was covered with a large square woollen blanket and a sewn skin cape. An attempt was made to preserve him for exhibition by smoking, and several photographs were taken, some extravagantly posed. The first photograph of a body *in situ* was taken in 1892. The body was found not many miles away from where Grauballe Man was discovered sixty years later, and very close indeed to another recent find, the Tollund Man.

22   The list could be continued almost indefinitely. But it is only within recent years that pollen analysis has been developed to a stage where the bodies can be accurately dated. And all the bodies found since have proved to date to the same restricted period of Danish prehistory, the first three centuries of the Christian Era. This fact makes it possible—indeed essential —to regard them as a single "case."

23   Apart from Grauballe Man, four bodies have been found in the peat bogs of Denmark since World War II, and all have been subjected to the same thorough analysis that we gave Grauballe Man. Three came from the same bog, the large peat area of Borremose in north Jutland. The first was a man, naked like so many of the others but with two cloaks of skin beside him. Around his neck was a rope noose, which may have been the cause of death, although the body was too badly preserved to be certain. There were odd features about the noose; it had been knotted at the neck, and both of the fairly short ends had been bent over and lashed with leather thongs to prevent them from unraveling, surely an unduly elaborate treatment for an ordinary hangman's noose.

24   The second body was that of a woman, again poorly preserved. The upper part of the body appeared to have been naked, while the lower part was covered with a blanket, a shawl, and other bits of clothing. There was a leather cord around the neck, but the cause of death was apparently a crushing blow on the skull.

25   The third body was also a woman's, a rather stout lady who lay face downward in the peat with only a blanket wrapped around her middle and held in place by a leather strap. She was no sight for squeamish archaeologists—she had been scalped and her face battered to pieces, though perhaps after death.

26   It is with quite unjustified relief that one turns from the rather macabre

Borremose bodies to the well-know Tollund Man, whose portrait has been in the press of the world and who has had the honor of appearing on British television. Tollund Man was discovered in 1950, two years before Grauballe Man and under the same circumstances, by farmers cutting peat. The discovery was reported to the police, and they called in Professor Glob, who described what he saw:

27   "In the peat cut, nearly seven feet down, lay a human figure in a crouched position, still half-buried. A foot and a shoulder protruded, perfectly preserved but dark-brown in color like the surrounding peat, which had dyed the skin. Carefully we removed more peat, and a bowed head came into view.

28   "As dusk fell, we saw in the fading light a man take shape before us. He was curled up, with legs drawn under him and arms bent, resting on his side as if asleep. His eyes were peacefully shut; his brows were furrowed, and his mouth showed a slightly irritated quirk as if he were not overpleased by this unexpected disturbance. . . ."

29   Tollund Man was found to be naked except for a leather belt around his waist and a leather cap upon his head, a cap made of eight triangular gussets of leather sewn together. There was one other item. Around his neck was the elaborately braided leather rope with which they had hanged him.

30   It is clear, I think, that we have a case of mass murder. There are too many points of similarity between the killings for it to be possible to consider each independently of the others. I should point out, though, that their generally fantastic state of preservation is not one of these points of similarity. It is merely our good fortune. The preservation is due to the fact that the peat bogs contain sufficient humic acid and tannic acid to halt the processes of decay and start a tanning process that can preserve the body. (This process, incidentally, we have carried to its logical conclusion with Grauballe Man. Eighteen months in an oak vat in a concentrated solution based on oak shavings has completed the tanning process that nature commenced some eighteen hundred years ago. Grauballe Man, on exhibition at the Prehistoric Museum in Aarhus, needs only a little linseed oil now and then in order to last indefinitely.)

31   There is one condition for preservation, however, for otherwise the peat bogs would be full of the bodies of every animal that falls into them. The body must be *buried* in the peat, deep enough down to be below the oxygen-containing surface levels. And this—the fact that all these bodies were disposed of in old cuttings in the peat—*is* one of the common factors that cause us to regard all the killings as a single phenomenon.

32   Another is the fact that all the bodies are naked. Though it is the rule rather than the exception for articles of clothing to be found with the bodies, and sometimes wrapped around the bodies, they are never regularly clothed in the garments. But the most obvious similarity is that all have died violent deaths and that all are found in bogs.

33   And that leads to the next step in the inquiry: the question of motive. Why are these bodies there at all?

34   These are not ordinary burials. Archaeologists are very well acquainted with the burials of this period of Danish prehistory. They were elaborate, clearly showing evidence of belief in an afterlife in which the dead would have need of material things. The graves are large and edged with stones. The body lies carefully arranged on its side, together with a whole set of pottery vessels, or in the case of the wealthy, with glass and silver ware imported from the Roman Empire. The vessels must have held provisions for the journey to the afterworld, for there is often a leg of pork or of mutton with the rest of the provisions, and even a knife to carve the joint.

35   It is clear that whatever it was that resulted in the deaths of the bodies in the bogs also deprived them of regular, ritual burial.

36   We must dismiss the most obvious explanation—that the bodies were victims of robbery with violence. All are dated to the comparatively short period of three hundred years at the beginning of our era. It may have been a lawless time—though farther south it is the period of the Pax Romana—but certainly it was no more lawless than many other periods: the period before, of the great Celtic and Germanic wanderings; or the period after, when the Roman Empire was breaking up and all the vultures flocked to the kill; or the Viking period; or much of the Middle Ages. We should expect a much greater spread in date if the bodies are to be explained as the victims of robber bands.

37   We must widen our scope and look not so much at the bodies as at the bogs. What do we find there?

38   Any Danish archaeologist can answer that question at length. And he can illustrate his answer at the Danish National Museum in Copenhagen, where room after room is full of things found in bogs. More than half of the best treasures of Danish prehistory have been found in bogs, and the archaeologist will tell you that these treasures were offerings to the gods.

39   Now, archaeologists have often been accused of calling in hypothetical gods and cult practices whenever they find anything they cannot explain by obvious mundane means. A theory of offerings in the peat bogs must not be accepted uncritically. But how else is one to explain why a Stone Age farmer, some four thousand years ago, very carefully laid seven large, new, unused stone axes side by side in a row in a peat bog? How is one to explain why several pairs of the big bronze trumpets known as lurs, the finest known products of the Danish Bronze Age, have been found in the bogs in good working order?

40   It begins to look as though anything of prehistoric date found in the bogs of Denmark is a priori likely to be an offering to the gods. If we move forward to the actual period of the bog bodies, we find the offerings in the bogs getting more numerous and more varied and richer. In the early 1950's I spent three years a few miles south of our museum, helping to dig out an immense offering of weapons—several thousand iron swords

and spearheads and arrowheads and shield bosses—all of them burned, bent, hacked to pieces, and then deposited in a lake in the middle of a peat bog. They had been deposited at various times—it was a regular place of offering—but all during the period A.D. 150—300. Among the weapons lay the skeletons of two horses—and here perhaps we approach quite close in spirit to the bog bodies, for the horses had been beheaded before they were offered, and marks on the bones showed quite clearly where spears had been stuck into the carcasses, before or after death.

41   We are entering a dark region. Our probings into the minds of our distant ancestors are lifting a corner of a veil that seems to cover an area of deep superstition, a time when the peat bogs were the abodes of gods and spirits, who demanded sacrifice. When we look now at the bodies in the bogs it seems by no means impossible that they, too, were offerings; that the sacrifices to the gods also included human sacrifices.

42   We must ask ourselves what we know about the gods and goddesses of this period.

43   At the northern end of that very bog at Borremose in which three of the bodies were found, there was discovered in 1897 a large caldron of solid silver. In itself the Gundestrup caldron is far and away the most intrinsically valuable of all the bog offerings. But it is more than that; it is a picture book of European religion around the beginning of the Christian Era. Its sides are decorated, inside and out, with a series of panels bearing pictures, in relief, of gods and goddesses, of mythical animals, and of ritual scenes. Admittedly the caldron is believed to have been manufactured in southeast Europe and to have been brought to Denmark as booty, but the deities portrayed are like the native Danish gods of the period.

44   It is particularly noteworthy that each one of these deities, although otherwise naked, bears a torque, or broad necklet, at the throat, which appears to have been a symbol of kingship and of divinity. It has even been suggested—perhaps not entirely fancifully—that the oddly elaborate nooses around the necks of Tollund and Borremose Man in some way set them apart as consecrated to the gods. We know from the sagas, not many hundreds of years later, that in Viking times hanged men were sacred to Odin, the chief god of the Viking pantheon.

45   One of the interior caldron panels shows clearly that the idea of human sacrifice was not alien to the religion of the time. It is admittedly a different ceremony of sacrifice, with the victim dropped headfirst into, or perhaps slaughtered above, a caldron, perhaps the Gundestrup caldron itself. The cutting of the throats of animal victims and the draining of their blood into a caldron was not unknown even among the civilized Greeks and Romans —and Grauballe Man, like many of the victims in the Danish bogs, had had his throat cut.

46   Speculation concerning details of ritual, though fascinating, can hardly be justified by the slender evidence at our disposal. But the general picture cannot be questioned: the Danes of the early Christian centuries worshiped

torque-bearing gods and goddesses; they were not averse to human sacrifice; and the holy places of the divinities were the peat bogs.

47   There is one source of information that we have not yet tapped. The historians and geographers of the Roman Empire wrote books, some of which describe the manners and customs of peoples beyond the imperial frontiers. The books must be used with caution; few of the authors had visited the regions they describe, and their accounts may well be as full of misunderstandings and fanciful explanations as anything the modern archaeologist can invent to explain what he finds.

48   But there is a passage in Tacitus's *Germania,* an account of the peoples beyond the Rhine written in A.D. 98, that bears on our study of the Danish bog bodies. Tacitus names seven tribes to the north of Germany, including the Angles, who are known to have lived in south Jutland before they invaded England in the fifth century together with the Saxons and Jutes. And he says: "these people . . . are distinguished by a common worship of Nerthus, or Mother Earth. They believe that she interests herself in human affairs and rides through their peoples. In an island of Ocean stands a sacred grove, and in the grove stands a car draped with a cloth which none but the priest may touch. The priest can feel the presence of the goddess in this holy of holies, and attends her, in deepest reverence, as her car is drawn by oxen. Then follow days of rejoicing and merrymaking in every place that she honors with her advent and stay. No-one goes to war, no-one takes up arms; every object of iron is locked away; then, and only then, are peace and quiet known and prized, until the goddess is again restored to her temple by the priest, when she has had her fill of the society of men. After that, the car, the cloth and, believe it if you will, the goddess herself are washed clean in a secluded lake. This service is performed by slaves who are immediately afterwards drowned in the lake. Thus mystery begets terror and a pious reluctance to ask what that sight can be which is allowed only to dying eyes."

49   Here we may be getting close to an answer. Nerthus—Mother Earth—is clearly a goddess of fertility; she may be the "goddess with the torque." And the time of peace and rejoicing when the goddess is driven around the countryside in her draped carriage will be the time of sowing, the vernal equinox. Pagan survivals of this spring festival still exist in many parts of Europe, in mummers' plays and Maypole dancing and Queens of the May. And in the National Museum in Copenhagen may be seen one of the ox-drawn carriages that almost certainly was used to carry the image of the fertility goddess around the fields. It was found—inevitably—in a peat bog, at Dejbjerg in east Jutland, in the 1880's. Richly carved and decorated with ornaments of bronze, it is far too fine a wagon to have been used for mundane purposes. Upon it stands a palanquin, a carrying chair with a canopy, within which the image of the goddess must have rested.

50   A final point brings the evidence full circle to the bodies in the bogs. Microscopic examination of the stomach contents of the men from Borre-

mose, Tollund, and Grauballe shows that their food for several days before death had been vegetarian. It seems to have consisted of some sort of porridge or mash composed of various kinds of corn, of sorrel and heart's-ease (both cultivated during the Iron Age), and of the seeds of such weeds as were accidentally harvested along with the corn. It has been suggested that this was a ritual diet, part of the ceremony needed to make the corn grow. Be that as it may, it is significant that there was no trace of any of the edible plants or fruits of summer in the stomach contents. So whatever our uncertainty about the precise year of death, we can say with confidence that the season of the year was winter or early spring.

51   Further we cannot go. We have been probing, with our picks and shovels and builders' trowels, not merely into the brains but perhaps also into the souls of men, and we must be content if our diagnosis is imprecise and inconclusive. But it does take us a little way beyond the conventional archaeological picture of the material lives of the simple peasants of barbarian Europe. Behind the material life, interleaved with it and perhaps dominating it, was the world of taboos and magic and superstition, the spirits of the earth and of the heavens, who had to be bribed or placated or bought off. One of the occupational risks of Iron Age Europe, right up to the end of the Viking period scarcely a thousand years ago, was that of being chosen as victim, as the price to be paid for prosperity in the next harvest or victory in the next war. It was only with the coming of Christianity that human sacrifice ceased in Europe; looking on the bodies from the Danish bogs we should do well to realize that there, but for the grace of God, lie we.

COMMENTARY

After a brief introduction about the work of archaeologists, who "dig up the past" and attempt to understand it, Bibby describes the particular case he is interested in: a body of a murdered man, found preserved in a Danish peat bog. After summarizing the information that can be gathered from this body (radiocarbon analysis, for example, shows that the victim was killed in approximately the fourth century A.D.), Bibby expands the mystery by reviewing several other cases of murder victims found in bogs, and states the problem: why were these people killed and buried in peat bogs?

The question can be answered only by gathering other kinds of data. One of the crucial aspects of any logical investigation is the decision about what kinds of information are to be considered. Bibby's inquiry has reached the point where no further progress can be made by examining the bodies themselves, and he therefore turns to other sources of data about the society in which the victims lived. He is on less certain ground here, since someone might object that these other sources are inappropriate, misleading, or irrelevant, and his dependence on them means that his conclusion about the bodies can be only tentative. However, when an inquiry reaches an impasse, the investigator has no choice except to involve new kinds of information or leave the problem unresolved.

Bibby's information about primitive European peoples, gathered from various sources—some, as he acknowledges, less reliable than others—permits him to reach the tentative conclusion that the murder victims were the human sacrifices in pagan religious ceremonies. This interpretation allows him to make sense of one final observation about the bodies themselves, the contents of their stomachs, which indicate that the victims were killed in the winter or early spring. They were probably sacrificed, then, to a fertility goddess, perhaps to a god of battle, "as the price to be paid for prosperity in the next harvest or victory in the next war."

The mystery has been only partially solved. We still do not know exactly when or by whom the man with whose body we began was murdered; we do not even know who he was. Bibby realizes the incompleteness of his answer, remarking, "we must be content if our diagnosis is imprecise and inconclusive."

The essay illustrates both the process by which one can go from information to a conclusion and the need to refrain from making that conclusion seem more definite than it really is. A less responsible writer might have concealed the incompleteness of his data and presented an answer with a fraudulent aura of certainty.

OUTLINE

    I. Introduction: the archaeologist's business—paragraphs 1–3
   II. The body in the bog and what can be learned directly from it—paragraphs 4–15
 III. Other bog bodies—paragraphs 16–29
 IV. Common elements in all the cases—paragraphs 30–36
  V. Other kinds of information about primitive European society—paragraphs 37–49
 VI. A final fact about the bodies—paragraph 50
VII. Conclusion: summary of the interpretation and of its limits—paragraph 51

SUGGESTIONS FOR WRITING

1. The discovery of new evidence often requires reinterpretation of the whole body of material. Suppose that you were to discover several more bog bodies. Their stomach contents include foods available at various times of the year (not only winter or early spring). The people have been killed by a number of methods, but each body has tied onto it some valuable object—a piece of jewelry, a gold cup, a decorated bronze bowl. What reinterpretation of the whole bog-body problem would this new evidence suggest? Write Bibby a letter describing the new discoveries and presenting your revised resolution of the mystery.

2. Apply Bibby's investigative process—what is known about *X*, what must be added from related areas of knowledge, conclusion—to some problem in your experience. For example, you might attempt to predict what would happen if students were to organize into unions (as faculty members have at some institutions). You have some information about students and about their behavior in groups. However, no data on students organized into unions is available, and your inquiry can go no further unless you turn to related kinds of material: the behavior of faculty members organized into unions or the behavior of students united into less formal or less inclusive interest groups (action movements, foreign students' associations, etc.). You will need to do some library research unless you have had personal experience to use as evidence. Avoid, as Bibby does, suggesting any unwarranted certainty for your conclusion.

the bathtub hoax
H. L. MENCKEN

Mencken's thesis, in this two-part selection, is that "No normal human being wants to hear the truth" (paragraph 20). People much prefer lies, as long as the lies are agreeable. This rather odd assertion is substantiated by some curious evidence from Mencken's own experience as a writer. His procedure is to present the evidence first, in the section called "A Neglected Anniversary" (published in 1917), and then to develop his thesis in "Hymn to the Truth" (1926).

Is Mencken's cynical assessment of the American public accurate today? Do you think it was accurate then?

A NEGLECTED ANNIVERSARY

1   On December 20 there flitted past us, absolutely without public notice, one of the most important profane anniversaries in American history—to wit: the seventy-fifth anniversary of the introduction of the bathtub into these states. Not a plumber fired a salute or hung out a flag. Not a governor proclaimed a day of prayer. Not a newspaper called attention to the day.

2   True enough, it was not entirely forgotten. Eight or nine months ago one of the younger surgeons connected with the Public Health Service in Washington happened upon the facts while looking into the early history of public hygiene, and at his suggestion a committee was formed to celebrate the anniversary with a banquet. But before the plan was perfected Washington went dry, and so the banquet had to be abandoned. As it was, the day passed wholly unmarked, even in the capital of the nation.

3   Bathtubs are so common today that it is almost impossible to imagine a world without them. They are familiar to nearly every one in all incorporated towns; in most of the large cities it is unlawful to build a dwelling house without putting them in; even on the farm they have begun to come into use. And yet the first American bathtub was installed and dedicated so recently as December 20, 1842, and, for all I know to the contrary, it may be still in existence and in use.

4   Curiously enough, the scene of its setting up was Cincinnati, then a squalid frontier town, and even today surely no leader in culture. But Cincinnati, in those days as in these, contained many enterprising merchants, and one of them was a man named Adam Thompson, a dealer in cotton and grain. Thompson shipped his merchandise by steamboat down the Ohio and Mississippi to New Orleans, and from there sent it to England in sailing vessels. This trade frequently took him to England, and in that country, during the 30s, he acquired the habit of bathing.

5   The bathtub was then still a novelty in England. It had been introduced in 1828 by Lord John Russell and its use was yet confined to a small class of enthusiasts. Moreover, the English bathtub, then as now, was a puny and inconvenient contrivance—little more, in fact, than a glorified dishpan —and filling and emptying it required the attendance of a servant. Taking a bath, indeed, was a rather heavy ceremony, and Lord John in 1835 was said to be the only man in England who had yet come to doing it every day.

6   Thompson, who was of inventive fancy—he later devised the machine that is still used for bagging hams and bacon—conceived the notion that the English bathtub would be much improved if it were made large enough to admit the whole body of an adult man, and if its supply of water, instead of being hauled to the scene by a maid, were admitted by pipes from a central reservoir and run off by the same means. Accordingly, early in 1842 he set about building the first modern bathroom in his Cincinnati home—a large house with Doric pillars, standing near what is now the corner of Monastery and Oregon streets. . . .

7   The tub itself was of new design and became the grandfather of all the bathtubs of today. Thompson had it made by James Guiness, the leading Cincinnati cabinet maker of those days, and its material was Nicaragua mahogany. It was nearly seven feet long and fully four feet wide. To make it water tight the interior was lined with sheet lead, carefully soldered at the joints. The whole contraption weighed about 1,750 pounds, and the floor of the room in which it was placed had to be reinforced to support it. The exterior was elaborately polished.

8   In this luxurious tub Thompson took two baths on December 20, 1842 —a cold one at 8 a.m. and a warm one some time during the afternoon. The warm water, heated by the kitchen fire, reached a temperature of 105 degrees. On Christmas day, having a party of gentlemen to dinner, he exhibited the new marvel to them and gave an exhibition of its use, and four of them, including a French visitor, Col. Duchanel, risked plunges into it. The next day all Cincinnati—then a town of about 100,000 people—had heard of it, and the local newspapers described it at length and opened their columns to violent discussions of it.

9   The thing, in fact, became a public matter, and before long there was bitter and double-headed opposition to the new invention, which had been promptly imitated by several other wealthy Cincinnatians. On the one hand it was denounced as an epicurean and obnoxious toy from England, designed to corrupt the democratic simplicity of the republic, and on the other hand it was attacked by the medical faculty as dangerous to health and a certain inviter of "phthisic, rheumatic fevers, inflammation of the lungs, and the whole category of zymotic diseases." (I quote from the *Western Medical Repository* of April 23, 1843.)

10   The noise of the controversy soon reached other cities, and in more than one place medical opposition reached such strength that it was reflected in legislation. Late in 1843, for example, the Philadelphia common council considered an ordinance prohibiting bathing between November 1 and March 15, and it failed of passage by but two votes. During the same year the legislature of Virginia laid a tax of $30 a year on all bathtubs that might be set up, and in Hartford, Providence, Charleston, and Wilmington, Del., special and very heavy water rates were levied upon those who had them. Boston early in 1845 made bathing unlawful except upon medical advice, but the ordinance was never enforced and in 1862 it was repealed.

11   This legislation, I suspect, had some class feeling in it, for the Thompson bathtub was plainly too expensive to be owned by any save the wealthy. Indeed, the common price for installing one in New York in 1845 was $500. Thus the low caste politicians of the time made capital by fulminating against it, and there is even some suspicion of political bias in many of the early medical denunciations. But the invention of the common pine bathtub, lined with zinc, in 1847, cut off this line of attack, and thereafter the bathtub made steady progress.

12   The zinc tub was devised by John F. Simpson, a Brooklyn plumber, and his efforts to protect it by a patent occupied the courts until 1855. But the decisions were steadily against him, and after 1848 all the plumbers of New York were equipped for putting in bathtubs. According to a writer in the *Christian Register* for July 17, 1857, the first one in New York was opened for traffic on September 12, 1847, and by the beginning of 1850 there were already nearly 1,000 in use in the big town.

13   After this medical opposition began to collapse, and among other eminent physicians Dr. Oliver Wendell Holmes declared for the bathtub, and vigorously opposed the lingering movement against it in Boston. The Amer-

ican Medical Association held its annual meeting in Boston in 1849, and a poll of the members in attendance showed that nearly 55 per cent of them now regarded bathing as harmless, and that more than 20 per cent advocated it as beneficial. At its meeting in 1850 a resolution was formally passed giving the imprimatur of the faculty to the bathtub. The homeopaths followed with a like resolution in 1853.

14 But it was the example of President Millard Fillmore that, even more than the grudging medical approval, gave the bathtub recognition and respectability in the United States. While he was still Vice President, in March, 1850, he visited Cincinnati on a stumping tour, and inspected the original Thompson tub. Thompson himself was now dead, but the bathroom was preserved by the gentleman who had bought his house from his estate. Fillmore was entertained in this house and, according to Chamberlain, his biographer, took a bath in the tub. Experiencing no ill effects, he became an ardent advocate of the new invention, and on succeeding to the presidency at Taylor's death, July 9, 1850, he instructed his secretary of war, Gen. Charles M. Conrad, to invite tenders for the construction of a bathtub in the White House.

15 This action, for a moment, revived the old controversy, and its opponents made much of the fact that there was no bathtub at Mount Vernon or at Monticello, and that all the Presidents and other magnificoes of the past had got along without any such monarchical luxuries. The elder Bennett, in the *New York Herald,* charged that Fillmore really aspired to buy and install in the White House a porphyry and alabaster bath that had been used by Louis Philippe at Versailles. But Conrad, disregarding all this clamor, duly called for bids, and the contract was presently awarded to Harper & Gillespie, a firm of Philadelphia engineers, who proposed to furnish a tub of cast iron, capable of floating the largest man.

16 This was installed early in 1851 and remained in service in the White House until the first Cleveland administration, when the present enameled tub was substituted. The example of the President soon broke down all that remained of the old opposition, and by 1860, according to the newspaper advertisements of the time, every hotel in New York had a bathtub, and some had two and even three. In 1862 bathing was introduced into the army by Gen. McClellan, and in 1870 the first prison bathtub was set up at Moyamensing prison in Philadelphia.

17 So much for the history of the bathtub in America. One is astonished, on looking into it, to find that so little of it has been recorded. The literature, in fact, is almost nil. But perhaps this brief sketch will encourage other inquirers and so lay the foundation for an adequate celebration of the centennial in 1942.

(December 28, 1917)

HYMN TO THE TRUTH

18 On May 23 last, writing in this place, I told the strange, sad story of an article that I printed in the *New York Evening Mail,* a paper now hap-

pily extinct, on December 28, 1917. The article, thrown off as a relief from the patriotic libido of war time, was, in substance, a burlesque history of the bathtub. I may confess that, when it was done, I fancied it no little. It was artfully devised, and it contained some buffooneries of considerable juiciness. I had confidence that the customers of the *Evening Mail* would like it.

19   Alas, they liked it only too well. That is to say, they swallowed it as gospel, gravely and horribly. Worse, they began sending clippings of it to friends east, west, north, and south, and so it spread to other papers, and then to the magazines and weeklies of opinion, and then to the scientific press, and finally to the reference books. Its transparent wheezes got themselves converted into sober history. It accumulated corroborative detail. To this day it is in circulation, and, as I say, has broken into the reference books, and is there embalmed for the instruction and edification of posterity.

20   On May 23, writing here, I exposed it at length. I pointed out some of the obvious absurdities in it. I confessed categorically that it was all buncombe. I called upon the historians of the land to take it out of their books. This confession and appeal was printed simultaneously in nearly thirty great American newspapers. One of them was the eminent Boston *Herald,* organ of the New England illuminati. The *Herald* printed my article on page 7 of its editorial section, under a four column head, and with a two column cartoon labeled satirically, "The American public will swallow anything." And then on June 13, three weeks later, in the same editorial section but promoted to page 1, this same *Herald* reprinted my 10 year old fake—soberly and as a piece of news!

21   Do not misunderstand me: I am not seeking to cast a stone at the *Herald* or at its talented and patriotic editors. It is, I believe, one of the glories of American journalism. It labors unceasingly for virtue and the flag. If it were suppressed by the Watch and Ward society tomorrow New England would revert instantly to savagery, wolves and catamounts would roam in Boylston street, and the Harvard Law school would be engulfed by bolshevism. Little does the public reck what great sums such journals expend to establish and disseminate the truth. It may cost $10,000 and a reporter's leg to get a full and accurate list of the guests at a Roxbury wake, with their injuries.

22   My point is that, despite all this extravagant frenzy for the truth, there is something in the human mind that turns instinctively to fiction, and that even journalists succumb to it. A German philosopher, Dr. Hans Vaihinger, has put the thing into a formal theory, and you will find it expounded at length in his book, *The Philosophy of As If.* It is a sheer impossibility, says Dr. Vaihinger, for human beings to think exclusively in terms of the truth. For one thing, the stock of indubitable truths is too scanty. For another thing, there is the instinctive aversion to them that I have mentioned. All of our thinking, according to Vaihinger, is in terms of assumptions,

many of them plainly not true. Into our most solemn and serious reflections fictions enter—and three times out of four they quickly crowd out all the facts.

23   That this is true needs no argument. Every man, thinking of his wife, has to assume that she is beautiful and amiable, else despair will seize him and he will be unable to think at all. Every American, contemplating Dr. Coolidge, is physically bound to admire him: the alternative is anarchy. Every Christian, viewing the clergy, is forced into a bold theorizing to save himself from Darwinism. And all of us, taking stock of ourselves, must resort to hypothesis to escape the river.

24   What ails the truth is that it is mainly uncomfortable, and often dull. The human mind seeks something more amusing, and more caressing. What the actual history of the bathtub may be I don't know: digging it out would be a dreadful job, and the result, after all that labor, would probably be a string of banalities. The fiction I concocted back in 1917 was at least better than that. It lacked sense, but it was certainly not without a certain charm. There were heroes in it, and villains. It revealed a conflict, with virtue winning. So it was embraced by mankind, precisely as the story of George Washington and the cherry tree was embraced, and it will live, I daresay, until it is displaced by something worse—and hence better.

25   In other words, it was poetry. And what is poetry? Poetry is simply a mellifluous statement of the obviously untrue. The two elements are both important, and perhaps equally. It is not sufficient that the thing said be untrue: it must also be said with a certain grace—it must soothe the ear while it debauches the mind. And it is not sufficient that it be voluptuous: it must also offer a rock and a refuge from the harsh facts of every day. All poetry embodies a lie. It may be an objective lie, as in "God's in His heaven; all's well with the world." Or it may be a subjective lie, as in "I am the master of my fate." But it must be a lie—and preferably a thumping one.

26   Poets, in general, protest against this doctrine. They argue that they actually deal in the truth, and that their brand of truth is of a peculiarly profound and esoteric quality—in other words, that their compositions add to the sum of human wisdom. It is sufficient answer to them to say that chiropractors make precisely the same claim, and with exactly the same plausibility. Both actually deal in fictions. Those fictions are not truth; they are not even truths in decay. They are simply better than truths. They make life more comfortable and happy. They turn and dull the sharp edge of reality.

27   It is commonly held that the vast majority of men are anesthetic to poetry, as they are alleged to be anesthetic to other forms of beauty, but this is a fiction, devised by poets to dignify their trade, and make it seem high toned and mysterious. The fact is that the love of poetry is one of the most primitive of human traits, and that it appears in children almost as

soon as they learn to speak. I do not refer here to the love of verbal jingles, but to the love of poetry properly so-called—that is, to the love of the agreeably not so. . . .

28   The more simple minded the individual, indeed, the greater his need of poetry, and hence the more steady his demand for it. No poet approved by the intelligentsia ever had so many customers as Edgar A. Guest. Guest's dithyrambs are laughed at by the intelligentsia, not because the things they say are not so, but because the fiction in them is of a kind not satisfying to sniffish and snooty men. It is fiction suitable to persons of a less critical habit. It preaches the joys open to the humble. It glorifies their dire necessities. It cries down their lacks. It promises them happiness, and if not happiness, then at least contentment. No wonder it is popular! No wonder it is intoned every time Kiwanians get together and the reassuring slapping of backs begins. It is itself a sort of back slapping.

29   And so is all other poetry. The strophes of Robert Browning elude the Kiwanian, but they are full of soothing for the young college professor, for they tell him that it is a marvelous and exhilarating thing to be as intellectual as he is. This, of course, is not true—which is the chief reason why it is pleasant. No normal human being wants to hear the truth. It is the passion of a small and aberrant minority of men, most of them pathological. They are hated for telling it while they live, and when they die they are swiftly forgotten. What remains to the world, in the field of wisdom, is a series of long tested and solidly agreeable lies.

(July 25, 1926)

COMMENTARY

Mencken's "A Neglected Anniversary" shows what you can do with a little imagination and the ability to present evidence in a convincing manner. The history of the bathtub found believers everywhere, probably because it was packed with "exact" information. Such an array of names and dates and realistic details, cleverly linked to good guys and bad guys and nostalgia for the past when life was simpler than it is now, catches our fancy.

"A Neglected Anniversary" demonstrates the thesis of this book: dramatic presentation of information has a power all its own. For another example, Orson Welles' radio program "The War of the Worlds" frightened millions of Americans who were convinced that Martians had invaded Earth. Less amusing examples can be found in advertising and political oratory.

Mencken takes advantage of the fact that the dramatic power of information can be used to deceive people. He first deceives us and then turns the deception into an object lesson. His thesis (paragraph 22) is that despite the "frenzy for truth, there is something in the human mind that turns instinctively to fiction." He quotes an authority, Vaihinger, to support his point (paragraph 22) and gives several illustrations to drive it home (paragraph 23). But his major piece of evidence is that he has just succeeded in "hooking" us with the article on the bathtub.

Mencken concludes by widening his subject to cover all kinds of pleasant pretending, all forms of "the agreeably not so." In this section he concentrates on poetry, claiming that the explanation for its appeal is that it responds to our need for attractive lies. People who think they admire poetry for other reasons are likely to take violent exception to Mencken's reasoning here.

OUTLINE

"A Neglected Anniversary"

    I. Introduction: ignoring the bathtub anniversary—paragraphs 1–3

    II. History of the bathtub, presented as a series of anecdotes in chronological order—paragraphs 4–16

    III. Conclusion: a call for an adequate celebration of the bathtub's centennial in 1942—paragraph 17

"Hymn to the Truth"

    I. Introduction: exposure of the bathtub-history hoax—paragraphs 18–21

    II. Thesis: people prefer fiction—paragraph 22

    III. Evidence: reference to an authority; examples from daily life; the bathtub-history hoax as an example from Mencken's experience (and ours)—paragraphs 22–24

    IV. Expansion of the subject: causal explanation of why we like poetry—paragraphs 25–29

    V. Conclusion: restatement of thesis—paragraph 29

SUGGESTIONS FOR WRITING

1. Describe a hoax perpetrated daily through advertising and explain why the deception seems to work. (You may find it helpful to consult Ogilvy's essay on advertising, p. 460).

2. Using your own experience as evidence, support or reject Mencken's claim that there is a "pathological" elite, "a small and aberrant minority of men" who want to know the truth. (Is Mencken being serious or ironic? Why does he call his second section "Hymn to the Truth"?)

3. The "Drama of Information" essay (p. 1) asserts that people want to know, without distinguishing between fact and fiction as to *what* they want to know.

Using the selections you have read in this book as evidence, support or refute the thesis that most writers think their readers want "the truth, the whole truth, and nothing but the truth." What techniques do the writers use to persuade you that they are telling the truth? How do you explain Thurber's quest for the truth about Shakespeare's *Macbeth* (p. 281)?

penny capitalism on an urban streetcorner

ELLIOT LIEBOW

Liebow attempts to answer a question sometimes asked about inner-city people: Why don't they work for a living? Some of them *do,* he says; but he is more interested in the reasons why others do not and why working is a low-priority activity. In this selection from *Tally's Corner,* Liebow combines two types of evidence: what he himself saw on that Washington, D. C. streetcorner, and the more comprehensive data he found in published sources. His conclusion is that many of the streetcorner people do not care much about working because, purely objectively, they cannot make enough money at the jobs available to them for working to be worthwhile.

1   **a** pickup truck drives slowly down the street. The truck stops as it comes abreast of a man sitting on a cast-iron porch and the white driver calls out, asking if the man wants a day's work. The man shakes his head and the truck moves on up the block, stopping again whenever idling men come within calling distance of the driver. At the Carry-out corner, five men debate the question briefly and shake their heads no to the truck. The truck turns the corner and repeats the same performance up the next street. In the distance, one can see one man, then another, climb into the back of the truck and sit down. It starts and stops, the truck finally disappears.

2   What is it we have witnessed here? A labor scavenger rebuffed by his would-be prey? Lazy, irresponsible men turning down an honest day's pay for an honest day's work? Or a more complex phenomenon marking the intersection of economic forces, social values, and individual states of mind and body?

3   Let us look again at the driver of the truck. He has been able to recruit only two or three men from each twenty or fifty he contacts. To him, it is clear that the others simply do not choose to work. Singly or in groups, belly-empty or belly-full, sullen or gregarious, drunk or sober, they confirm what he has read, heard and knows from his own experience: these men wouldn't take a job if it were handed to them on a platter.[1]

4   Quite apart from the question of whether or not this is true of some of the men he sees on the street, it is clearly not true of all of them. If it were, he would not have come here in the first place; or having come, he

[1] By different methods, perhaps, some social scientists have also located the problem in the men themselves, in their unwillingness or lack of desire to work: "To improve the under-privileged worker's performance, one must help him to learn *to want* . . . higher social goals for himself and his children. . . . The problem of changing the work habits and motivation of [lower class] people . . . is a problem of changing the goals, the ambitions, and the level of cultural and occupational aspiration of the underprivileged worker." (Emphasis in original.) Allison Davis, "The Motivation of the Underprivileged Worker," p. 90.

would have left with an empty truck. It is not even true of most of them, for most of the men he sees on the street this weekday morning do, in fact, have jobs. But since, at the moment, they are neither working nor sleeping, and since they hate the depressing room or apartment they live in, or because there is nothing to do there, or because they want to get away from their wives or anyone else living there, they are out on the street, indistinguishable from those who do not have jobs or do not want them. Some, like Boley, a member of a trash-collection crew in a suburban housing development, work Saturdays and are off on this weekday. Some, like Sweets, work nights cleaning up middle-class trash, dirt, dishes, and garbage, and mopping the floors of the office buildings, hotels, restaurants, toilets, and other public places dirtied during the day. Some men work for retail businesses such as liquor stores which do not begin the day until ten o'clock. Some laborers, like Tally, have already come back from the job because the ground was too wet for pick and shovel or because the weather was too cold for pouring concrete. Other employed men stayed off the job today for personal reasons: Clarence to go to a funeral at eleven this morning and Sea Cat to answer a subpoena as a witness in a criminal proceeding.

5   Also on the street, unwitting contributors to the impression taken away by the truck driver, are the halt and the lame. The man on the cast-iron steps strokes one gnarled arthritic hand with the other and says he doesn't know whether or not he'll live long enough to be eligible for Social Security. He pauses, then adds matter-of-factly, "Most times, I don't care whether I do or don't." Stoopy's left leg was polio-withered in childhood. Raymond, who looks as if he could tear out a fire hydrant, coughs up blood if he bends or moves suddenly. The quiet man who hangs out in front of the Saratoga apartments has a steel hook strapped onto his left elbow. And had the man in the truck been able to look into the wine-clouded eyes of the man in the green cap, he would have realized that the man did not even understand he was being offered a day's work.

6   Others, having had jobs and been laid off, are drawing unemployment compensation (up to $44 per week) and have nothing to gain by accepting work which pays little more than this and frequently less.

7   Still others, like Bumdoodle the numbers man, are working hard at illegal ways of making money, hustlers who are on the street to turn a dollar any way they can: buying and selling sex, liquor, narcotics, stolen goods, or anything else that turns up.

8   Only a handful remains unaccounted for. There is Tonk, who cannot bring himself to take a job away from the corner, because, according to the other men, he suspects his wife will be unfaithful if given the opportunity. There is Stanton, who has not reported to work for four days now, not since Bernice disappeared. He bought a brand new knife against her return. She had done this twice before, he said, but not for so long and not without warning, and he had forgiven her. But this time, "I ain't got it in me to forgive her again." His rage and shame are there for all to see

as he paces the Carry-out and the corner, day and night, hoping to catch a glimpse of her.

9   And finally, there are those like Arthur, able-bodied men who have no visible means of support, legal or illegal, who neither have jobs nor want them. The truck driver, among others, believes the Arthurs to be representative of all the men he sees idling on the street during his own working hours. They are not, but they cannot be dismissed simply because they are a small minority. It is not enough to explain them away as being lazy or irresponsible or both because an able-bodied man with responsibilities who refuses work is, by the truck driver's definition, lazy and irresponsible. Such an answer begs the question. It is descriptive of the facts; it does not explain them.

10 Moreover, despite their small numbers, the don't-work-and-don't-want-to-work minority is especially significant because they represent the strongest and clearest expression of those values and attitudes associated with making a living which, to varying degrees, are found throughout the streetcorner world. These men differ from the others in degree rather than in kind, the principal difference being that they are carrying out the implications of their values and experiences to their logical, inevitable conclusions. In this sense, the others have yet to come to terms with themselves and the world they live in.

11 Putting aside, for the moment, what the men say and feel, and looking at what they actually do and the choices they make, getting a job, keeping a job, and doing well at it is clearly of low priority. Arthur will not take a job at all. Leroy is supposed to be on his job at 4:00 P.M. but it is already 4:10 and he still cannot bring himself to leave the free games he has accumulated on the pinball machine in the Carry-out. Tonk started a construction job on Wednesday, worked Thursday and Friday, then didn't go back again. On the same kind of job, Sea Cat quit in the second week. Sweets had been working three months as a busboy in a restaurant, then quit without notice, not sure himself why he did so. A real estate agent, saying he was more interested in getting the job done than in the cost, asked Richard to give him an estimate on repairing and painting the inside of a house, but Richard, after looking over the job, somehow never got around to submitting an estimate. During one period, Tonk would not leave the corner to take a job because his wife might prove unfaithful; Stanton would not take a job because his woman had been unfaithful.

12 Thus, the man-job relationship is a tenuous one. At any given moment, a job may occupy a relatively low position on the streetcorner scale of real values. Getting a job may be subordinated to relations with women or to other non-job considerations; the commitment to a job one already has is frequently shallow and tentative.

13 The reasons are many. Some are objective and reside principally in the job; some are subjective and reside principally in the man. The line between them, however, is not a clear one. Behind the man's refusal to take a job or his decision to quit one is not a simple impulse or value

choice but a complex combination of assessments of objective reality on the one hand, and values, attitudes and beliefs drawn from different levels of his experience on the other.

14   Objective economic considerations are frequently a controlling factor in a man's refusal to take a job. How much the job pays is a crucial question but seldom asked. He knows how much it pays. Working as a stock clerk, a delivery boy, or even behind the counter of liquor stores, drug stores, and other retail businesses pays one dollar an hour. So, too, do most busboy, car-wash, janitorial, and other jobs available to him. Some jobs, such as dishwasher, may dip as low as eighty cents an hour and others, such as elevator operator or work in a junk yard, may offer $1.15 or $1.25. Take-home pay for jobs such as these ranges from $35 to $50 a week, but a take-home pay of over $45 for a five-day week is the exception rather than the rule.

15   One of the principal advantages of these kinds of jobs is that they offer fairly regular work. Most of them involve essential services and are therefore somewhat less responsive to business conditions than are some higher paying, less menial jobs. Most of them are also inside jobs not dependent on the weather, as are construction jobs and other higher-paying outside work.

16   Another seemingly important advantage of working in hotels, restaurants, office and apartment buildings, and retail establishments is that they frequently offer an opportunity for stealing on the job. But stealing can be a two-edged sword. Apart from increasing the cost of the goods or services to the general public, a less obvious result is that the practice usually acts as a depressant on the employee's own wage level. Owners of small retail establishments and other employers frequently anticipate employee stealing and adjust the wage rate accordingly. Tonk's employer explained why he was paying Tonk $35 for a 55–60 hour workweek. These men will all steal, he said. Although he keeps close watch on Tonk, he estimates that Tonk steals from $35 to $40 a week.[2] What he steals, when added to his regular earnings, brings his take-home pay to $70 or $75 per week. The employer said he did not mind this because Tonk is worth that much to the business. But if he were to pay Tonk outright the full value of his labor, Tonk would still be stealing $35–$40 per week and this, he said, the business simply would not support.

17   This wage arrangement, with stealing built-in, was satisfactory to both parties, with each one independently expressing his satisfaction. Such a wage-theft system, however, is not as balanced and equitable as it appears. Since the wage level rests on the premise that the employee will steal the unpaid value of his labor, the man who does not steal on the job is penalized. And furthermore, even if he does not steal, no one would be-

[2] Exactly the same estimate as the one made by Tonk himself. On the basis of personal knowledge of the stealing routine employed by Tonk, however, I suspect the actual amount is considerably smaller.

lieve him; the employer and others believe he steals because the system presumes it.

18   Nor is the man who steals, as he is expected to, as well off as he believes himself to be. The employer may occasionally close his eyes to the worker's stealing but not often and not for long. He is, after all, a businessman and cannot always find it within himself to let a man steal from him, even if the man is stealing his own wages. Moreover, it is only by keeping close watch on the worker that the employer can control how much is stolen and thereby protect himself against the employee's stealing more than he is worth. From this viewpoint, then, the employer is not in wage-theft collusion with the employee. In the case of Tonk, for instance, the employer was not actively abetting the theft. His estimate of how much Tonk was stealing was based on what he thought Tonk was able to steal despite his own best efforts to prevent him from stealing anything at all. Were he to have caught Tonk in the act of stealing, he would, of course, have fired him from the job and perhaps called the police as well. Thus, in an actual if not in a legal sense, all the elements of entrapment are present. The employer knowingly provides the conditions which entice (force) the employee to steal the unpaid value of his labor, but at the same time he punishes him for theft if he catches him doing so.

19   Other consequences of the wage-theft system are even more damaging to the employee. Let us, for argument's sake, say that Tonk is in no danger of entrapment; that his employer is willing to wink at the stealing and that Tonk, for his part, is perfectly willing to earn a little, steal a little. Let us say, too, that he is paid $35 a week and allowed to steal $35. His money income—as measured by the goods and services he can purchase with it—is, of course, $70. But not all of his income is available to him for all purposes. He cannot draw on what he steals to build his self-respect or to measure his self-worth. For this, he can draw only on his earnings— the amount given him publicly and voluntarily in exchange for his labor. His "respect" and "self-worth" income remains at $35—only half that of the man who also receives $70 but all of it in the form of wages. His earnings publicly measure the worth of his labor to his employer, and they are important to others and to himself in taking the measure of his worth as a man.

20   With or without stealing, and quite apart from any interior processes going on in the man who refuses such a job or quits it casually and without apparent reason, the objective fact is that menial jobs in retailing or in the service trades simply do not pay enough to support a man and his family. This is not to say that the worker is underpaid; this may or may not be true. Whether he is or not, the plain fact is that, in such a job, he cannot make a living. Nor can he take much comfort in the fact that these jobs tend to offer more regular, steadier work. If he cannot live on the $45 or $50 he makes in one week, the longer he works, the longer he cannot live on what he makes.

21   Construction work, even for unskilled laborers, usually pays better,

with the hourly rate ranging from $1.50 to $2.60 an hour.[3] Importantly, too, good references, a good driving record, a tenth grade (or any high school) education, previous experience, the ability to "bring police clearance with you" are not normally required of laborers as they frequently are for some of the jobs in retailing or in the service trades.

22   Construction work, however, has its own objective disadvantages. It is, first of all, seasonal work for the great bulk of the laborers, beginning early in the spring and tapering off as winter weather sets in. And even during the season the work is frequently irregular. Early or late in the season, snow or temperatures too low for concrete frequently sends the laborers back home, and during late spring or summer, a heavy rain on Tuesday or Wednesday, leaving a lot of water and mud behind it, can mean a two or three day workweek for the pick-and-shovel men and other unskilled laborers.[4]

23   The elements are not the only hazard. As the project moves from one construction stage to another, laborers—usually without warning—are laid off, sometimes permanently or sometimes for weeks at a time. The more fortunate or the better workers are told periodically to "take a walk for two, three days."

24   Both getting the construction job and getting to it are also relatively more difficult than is the case for the menial jobs in retailing and the service trades. Job competition is always fierce. In the city, the large construction projects are unionized. One has to have ready cash to get into the union to become eligible to work on these projects and, being eligible, one has to find an opening. Unless one "knows somebody," say a foreman or a laborer who knows the day before that they are going to take on new men in the morning, this can be a difficult and disheartening search.

25   Many of the nonunion jobs are in suburban Maryland or Virginia. The newspaper ads say, "Report ready to work to the trailer at the intersection of Rte. 11 and Old Bridge Rd., Bunston, Virginia (or Maryland)," but this location may be ten, fifteen, or even twenty-five miles from the Carry-out. Public transporation would require two or more hours to get there, if it services the area at all. Without access to a car or to a car-pool arrangement, it is not worthwhile reading the ad. So the men do not. Jobs such as these are usually filled by word of mouth information, beginning

3 The higher amount is 1962 union scale for building laborers. According to the Wage Agreement Contract for Heavy Construction Laborers (Washington, D.C., and vicinity) covering the period from May 1, 1963 to April 30, 1966, minimum hourly wage for heavy construction laborers was to go from $2.75 (May 1963) by annual increments to $2.92, effective November 1, 1965.

4 In a recent year, the crime rate in Washington for the month of August jumped 18 percent over the preceding month. A veteran police officer explained the increase to David L. Bazelon, Chief Judge, U.S. Court of Appeals for the District of Columbia. "It's quite simple. . . . You see, August was a very wet month. . . . These people wait on the street corner each morning around 6:00 or 6:30 for a truck to pick them up and take them to a construction site. If it's raining, that truck doesn't come, and the men are going to be idle that day. If the bad weather keeps up for three days . . . we know we are going to have trouble on our hands—and sure enough, there invariably follows a rash of purse-snatchings, housebreakings and the like. . . . These people have to eat like the rest of us, you know." David L. Bazelon, Address to the Federal Bar Association, p. 3.

with someone who knows someone or who is himself working there and looking for a paying rider. Furthermore, nonunion jobs in outlying areas tend to be smaller projects of relatively short duration and to pay somewhat less than scale.

26   Still another objective factor is the work itself. For some men, whether the job be digging, mixing mortar, pushing a wheelbarrow, unloading materials, carrying and placing steel rods for reinforcing concrete, or building or laying concrete forms, the work is simply too hard. Men such as Tally and Wee Tom can make such work look like child's play; some of the older work-hardened men, such as Budder and Stanton, can do it too, although not without showing unmistakable signs of strain and weariness at the end of the workday. But those who lack the robustness of a Tally or the time-inured immunity of a Budder must either forego jobs such as these or pay a heavy toll to keep them. For Leroy, in his early twenties, almost six feet tall but weighing under 140 pounds, it would be as difficult to push a loaded wheelbarrow, or to unload and stack 96-pound bags of cement all day long, as it would be for Stoopy with his withered leg. . . .

27   A healthy, sturdy, active man of good intelligence requires from two to four weeks to break in on a construction job.[5] Even if he is willing somehow to bull his way through the first few weeks, it frequently happens that his foreman or the craftsman he services with materials and general assistance is not willing to wait that long for him to get into condition or to learn at a glance the difference in size between a rough 2″ x 8″ and a finished 2″ x 10″. The foreman and the craftsman are themselves "under the gun" and cannot "carry" the man when other men, who are already used to the work and who know the tools and materials, are lined up to take the job.

28   Sea Cat was "healthy, sturdy, active and of good intelligence." When a judge gave him six weeks in which to pay his wife $200 in back child-support payments, he left his grocery-store job in order to take a higher-paying job as a laborer, arranged for him by a foreman friend. During the first week the weather was bad and he worked only Wednesday and Friday, cursing the elements all the while for cheating him out of the money he could have made. The second week, the weather was fair but he quit at the end of the fourth day, saying frankly that the work was too hard for him. He went back to his job at the grocery store and took a second job working nights as a dishwasher in a restaurant, earning little if any more at the two jobs than he would have earned as a laborer, and keeping at both of them until he had paid off his debts.

29   Tonk did not last as long as Sea Cat. No one made any predictions when he got a job in a parking lot, but when the men on the corner learned he was to start on a road construction job, estimates of how long

5 Estimate of Mr. Francis Greenfield, President of the International Hod Carriers, Building and Common Laborers' District Council of Washington, D.C., and Vicinity. I am indebted to Mr. Greenfield for several points in these paragraphs dealing with construction laborers.

he would last ranged from one to three weeks. Wednesday was his first day. He spent that evening and night at home. He did the same on Thursday. He worked Friday and spent Friday evening and part of Saturday draped over the mailbox on the corner. Sunday afternoon, Tonk decided he was not going to report on the job the next morning. He explained that after working three days, he knew enough about the job to know that it was too hard for him. He knew he wouldn't be able to keep up and he'd just as soon quit now as get fired later.

30   Logan was a tall, two-hundred-pound man in his late twenties. His back used to hurt him only on the job, he said, but now he can't straighten up for increasingly longer periods of time. He said he had traced this to the awkward walk he was forced to adopt by the loaded wheelbarrows which pull him down into a half-stoop. He's going to quit, he said, as soon as he can find another job. If he can't find one real soon, he guesses he'll quit anyway. It's not worth it, having to walk bent over and leaning to one side. . . .

31   In summary of objective job considerations, then, the most important fact is that a man who is able and willing to work cannot earn enough money to support himself, his wife, and one or more children. A man's chances for working regularly are good only if he is willing to work for less than he can live on, and sometimes not even then. On some jobs, the wage rate is deceptively higher than on others, but the higher the wage rate, the more difficult it is to get the job, and the less the job security. Higher-paying construction work tends to be seasonal and, during the season, the amount of work available is highly sensitive to business and weather conditions and to the changing requirements of individual projects. Moreover, high-paying construction jobs are frequently beyond the physical capacity of some of the men, and some of the low-paying jobs are scaled down even lower in accordance with the self-fulfilling assumption that the man will steal part of his wages on the job.

COMMENTARY

Liebow moves from a set of observations (the early-morning scene in the city as the pickup truck drives along the streets), to a hypothesis he rejects as incorrect ("these men wouldn't take a job if it were handed to them on a platter"), to a division and classification of the people who were observed (some have jobs but are not at work at the moment; some are off the job today for personal reasons; some are unable to work; some are currently drawing unemployment checks; some are working hard— but illegally; some, only a handful, "don't-work-and-don't-want-to-work"), to an exploration of the reasons why "the man-job relationship is a tenuous one." As he gives each of the reasons, Liebow provides two kinds of substantiation: examples from the lives of the men he came to know on the street corner and information (often precise financial data) from additional sources ranging from businessmen to professional publications in sociology.

What might have been either a dry exercise in economic analysis, on the one hand, or a sentimental apology on the other, becomes a lively, dramatic, and realistic essay of substantiation. It just might do what Liebow wants it to: change opinions about inner-city people who do not get or keep jobs. What helps the essay make an impression is its mixture of the two kinds of evidence. The details of people's personal lives prevent the discussion from seeming distant or abstract, while the "hard data" from other sources prevent the situation from being dismissed as unrepresentative.

OUTLINE

I. Introduction: street scene—paragraphs 1–3
II. Division and classification: those who have jobs, etc.—paragraphs 4–11
III. General principle: weakness of the man-job relationship—paragraph 12
IV. Reasons
    A. Service jobs: low pay, the assumption that workers will steal; example (Tonk)—paragraphs 13–20
    B. Construction work: its irregularity, the problem of getting to the job, the difficult physical labor involved; several examples (Sea Cat, Tonk, Logan)—paragraphs 21–30
V. Summary of the objective reasons for the low status accorded to work—paragraph 31

SUGGESTIONS FOR WRITING

1. Follow Liebow's logical procedure as you write about a subject with which you have some personal experience. First present a scene, then state what an outsider's mistaken judgment of that scene might be, then explain what's really going on, then explore why. For example: describe Thursday morning in the cafeteria (everyone is sitting around in various states of disrepair); state what a visiting parent thinks ("So this is college? Why aren't they in class learning something? A bunch of lazy bums"); explain that the students you don't see *are* in class, that some of the others had late-evening classes or have worked the night shift in a 24-hour doughnut shop. The general principle is that the students are busy on variable schedules, not that they're not busy. Explore the reasons why student life does not operate on the business world's nine-to-five schedule. Use as evidence your own personal experience plus information from published sources if you can find it.

2. Consider Liebow's subject, applying it to yourself: What is your attitude toward working, and why? The evidence for "why" will be your own personal experience with the world of work: whether the jobs that have been available to you have brought you significant amounts of money and satisfaction; whether other factors in your cultural environment (for instance "peer pressure," the pressure on you to do what the others are doing) have helped intensify or reduce the importance of the objective characteristics of the jobs themselves.

3. Apply Liebow's analysis to a different group of people, for example, farmers, people who play golf a lot, housewives, retirees, military personnel. What is the attitude of this group toward working, and why?

chalk

This selection presents two essays about chalk to show that even when people are discussing the same thing, the conclusions they reach will depend on the questions they start out asking. Huxley wants to know what a thing is and where it comes from. Chesterton wants to know what it means, what it represents. One works primarily by reasoning, the other by intuition. For Huxley, chalk poses a question: "What is this widespread component of the surface of the earth, and whence did it come?" (paragraph 4). For Chesterton, chalk becomes the answer to a human material and spiritual need; chalk comes to represent not only a color he needs to complete a picture, but also the "best quality" of his country (paragraph 3), "a tradition and a civilization" (paragraph 9) available to us all if we have only the insight to see it and use it.

Huxley also really has more on his mind than a piece of chalk. His investigation of chalk leads him to the foundation of physical science (paragraph 5) and suggests to him that the records of nature are more important than the records of humanity (paragraph 6). Moreover, it provides a proof that the Biblical version of creation lacks validity (paragraphs 28–29).

Huxley's paragraph 24 demonstrates how far apart he and Chesterton are. At this point, Huxley concedes that the mind naturally seeks "a knowledge of the remoter links in the chain of causation." But for Chesterton, the "remoter links" involve the imagination, which creates "devils and seraphim and blind old gods" (paragraph 4). Obviously these belong to the record of humanity, not the record of nature; and to Chesterton, who has no desire simply to imitate nature, it is the record of humanity which is by far the more valuable.

on a piece of chalk

THOMAS HENRY HUXLEY

1   **i**f a well were sunk at our feet in the midst of the city of Norwich, the diggers would very soon find themselves at work in that white substance almost too soft to be called rock, with which we are all familiar as "chalk."

2   Were the thin soil which covers it all washed away, a curved band of white chalk, here broader, and there narrower, might be followed diagonally across England from Lulworth in Dorset, to Flamborough Head in Yorkshire—a distance of over 280 miles as the crow flies. From this band to the North Sea, on the east, and the Channel, on the south, the chalk is largely hidden by other deposits; but, except in the Weald of Kent and Sussex, it enters into the very foundation of all the south-eastern counties.

3   Attaining, as it does in some places, a thickness of more than a thousand feet, the English chalk must be admitted to be a mass of considerable magnitude. Nevertheless, it covers but an insignificant portion of the whole area occupied by the chalk formation of the globe, much of which has the same general characters as ours, and is found in detached patches, some less, and others more extensive, than the English. Chalk occurs in northwest Ireland; it stretches over a large part of France,—the chalk which underlies Paris being, in fact, a continuation of that of the London basin; it runs through Denmark and Central Europe, and extends southward to North Africa; while eastward, it appears in the Crimea and in Syria, and may be traced as far as the shores of the Sea of Aral, in Central Asia. If all the points at which true chalk occurs were circumscribed, they would lie within an irregular oval about 3,000 miles in long diameter—the area of which would be as great as that of Europe, and would many times exceed that of the largest existing inland sea—the Mediterranean.

4   What is this wide-spread component of the surface of the earth? and whence did it come?

5   You may think this no very hopeful inquiry. You may not unnaturally suppose that the attempt to solve such problems as these can lead to no result, save that of entangling the inquirer in vague speculations, incapable of refutation and of verification. If such were really the case, I should have selected some other subject than a "piece of chalk" for my discourse. But, in truth, after much deliberation, I have been unable to think of any topic which would so well enable me to lead you to see how solid is the foundation upon which some of the most startling conclusions of physical science rest.

6   A great chapter of the history of the world is written in the chalk. Few passages in the history of man can be supported by such an over-

Source. Excerpted from Thomas Henry Huxley, *On a Piece of Chalk,* 1894.

whelming mass of direct and indirect evidence as that which testifies to the truth of the fragment of the history of the globe, which I hope to enable you to read, with your own eyes, to-night. Let me add, that few chapters of human history have a more profound significance for ourselves. I weigh my words well when I assert, that the man who should know the true history of the bit of chalk which every carpenter carries about in his breeches-pocket, though ignorant of all other history, is likely, if he will think his knowledge out to its ultimate results, to have a truer, and therefore a better, conception of this wonderful universe, and of man's relation to it, than the most learned student who is deep-read in the records of humanity and ignorant of those of Nature.

7   The language of the chalk is not hard to learn, not nearly so hard as Latin, if you only want to get at the broad features of the story it has to tell; and I propose that we now set to work to spell that story out together.

8   We all know that if we "burn" chalk the result is quicklime. Chalk, in fact, is a compound of carbonic acid gas, and lime, and when you make it very hot the carbonic acid flies away and the lime is left. By this method of procedure we see the lime, but we do not see the carbonic acid. If, on the other hand, you were to powder a little chalk and drop it into a good deal of strong vinegar, there would be a great bubbling and fizzing, and, finally, a clear liquid, in which no sign of chalk would appear. Here you see the carbonic acid in the bubbles; the lime, dissolved in the vinegar, vanishes from sight. There are a great many other ways of showing that chalk is essentially nothing but carbonic acid and quicklime. Chemists enunciate the result of all the experiments which prove this, by stating that chalk is almost wholly composed of "carbonate of lime."

9   It is desirable for us to start from the knowledge of this fact, though it may not seem to help us very far towards what we seek. For carbonate of lime is a widely-spread substance, and is met with under very various conditions. All sorts of limestones are composed of more or less pure carbonate of lime. The crust which is often deposited by waters which have drained through limestone rocks, in the form of what are called stalagmites and stalactites, is carbonate of lime. Or, to take a more familiar example, the fur on the inside of a tea-kettle is carbonate of lime; and, for anything chemistry tells us to the contrary, the chalk might be a kind of gigantic fur upon the bottom of the earth-kettle, which is kept pretty hot below.

10   Let us try another method of making the chalk tell us its own history. To the unassisted eye chalk looks simply like a very loose and open kind of stone. But it is possible to grind a slice of chalk down so thin that you can see through it—until it is thin enough, in fact, to be examined with any magnifying power that may be thought desirable. A thin slice of the fur of a kettle might be made in the same way. If it were examined microscopically, it would show itself to be a more or less distinctly laminated mineral substance, and nothing more.

11   But the slice of chalk presents a totally different appearance when

placed under the microscope. The general mass of it is made up of very minute granules; but, imbedded in this matrix, are innumerable bodies, some smaller and some larger, but, on a rough average, not more than a hundredth of an inch in diameter, having a well-defined shape and structure. A cubic inch of some specimens of chalk may contain hundreds of thousands of these bodies, compacted together with incalculable millions of the granules.

12   The examination of a transparent slice gives a good notion of the manner in which the components of the chalk are arranged, and of their relative proportions. But, by rubbing up some chalk with a brush in water and then pouring off the milky fluid, so as to obtain sediments of different degrees of fineness, the granules and the minute rounded bodies may be pretty well separated from one another, and submitted to microscopic examination, either as opaque or as transparent objects. By combining the views obtained in these various methods, each of the rounded bodies may be proved to be a beautifully-constructed calcareous fabric, made up of a number of chambers, communicating freely with one another. The chambered bodies are of various forms. One of the commonest is something like a badly-grown raspberry, being formed of a number of nearly globular chambers of different sizes congregated together. It is called *Globigerina,* and some specimens of chalk consist of little else than *Globigerinœ* and granules. Let us fix our attention upon the *Globigerina.* It is the spoor of the game we are tracking. If we can learn what it is and what are the conditions of its existence, we shall see our way to the origin and past history of the chalk.

13   A suggestion which may naturally enough present itself is, that these curious bodies are the result of some process of aggregation which has taken place in the carbonate of lime; that, just as in winter, the rime on our windows simulates the most delicate and elegantly arborescent foliage— proving that the mere mineral water may, under certain conditions, assume the outward form of organic bodies—so this mineral substance, carbonate of lime, hidden away in the bowels of the earth, has taken the shape of these chambered bodies. I am not raising a merely fanciful and unreal objection. Very learned men, in former days, have even entertained the notion that all the formed things found in rocks are of this nature; and if no such conception is at present held to be admissible, it is because long and varied experience has now shown that mineral matter never does assume the form and structure we find in fossils. If any one were to try to persuade you that an oyster-shell (which is also chiefly composed of carbonate of lime) had crystallized out of sea-water, I suppose you would laugh at the absurdity. Your laughter would be justified by the fact that all experience tends to show that oyster-shells are formed by the agency of oysters, and in no other way. And if there were no better reasons, we should be justified, on like grounds, in believing that *Globigerina* is not the product of anything but vital activity.

14   Happily, however, better evidence in proof of the organic nature of

the *Globigerinæ* than that of analogy is forthcoming. It so happens that calcareous skeletons, exactly similar to the *Globigerinæ* of the chalk, are being formed, at the present moment, by minute living creatures, which flourish in multitudes, literally more numerous than the sands of the sea-shore, over a large extent of that part of the earth's surface which is covered by the ocean.

15   *Globigerinæ* of every size, from the smallest to the largest, are associated together in the Atlantic mud, and the chambers of many are filled by a soft animal matter. This soft substance is, in fact, the remains of the creature to which the *Globigerina* shell, or rather skeleton, owes its existence—and which is an animal of the simplest imaginable description. It is, in fact, a mere particle of living jelly, without defined parts of any kind—without a mouth, nerves, muscles, or distinct organs, and only manifesting its vitality to ordinary observation by thrusting out and retracting from all parts of its surface, long filamentous processes, which serve for arms and legs. Yet this amorphous particle, devoid of everything which, in the higher animals, we call organs, is capable of feeding, growing, and multiplying; of separating from the ocean the small proportion of carbonate of lime which is dissolved in sea-water; and of building up that substance into a skeleton for itself, according to a pattern which can be imitated by no other known agency.

16   However, the important points for us are, that the living *Globigerinæ* are exclusively marine animals, the skeltons of which abound at the bottom of deep seas; and that there is not a shadow of reason for believing that the habits of the *Globigerinæ* of the chalk differed from those of the existing species. But if this be true, there is no escaping the conclusion that the chalk itself is the dried mud of an ancient deep sea.

17   [Not] only is it certain that the chalk is the mud of an ancient sea-bottom; but it is no less certain, that the chalk sea existed during an extremely long period, though we may not be prepared to give a precise estimate of the length of that period in years. The relative duration is clear, though the absolute duration may not be definable. The attempt to affix any precise date to the period at which the chalk sea began, or ended, its existence, is baffled by difficulties of the same kind. But the relative age of the cretaceous epoch may be determined with as great ease and certainty as the long duration of that epoch.

18   At one of the most charming spots on the coast of Norfolk, Cromer, you will see the boulder clay forming a vast mass, which lies upon the chalk, and must consequently have come into existence after it. Huge boulders of chalk are, in fact, included in the clay, and have evidently been brought to the position they now occupy by the same agency as that which has planted blocks of syenite from Norway side by side with them.

19   The chalk, then, is certainly older than the boulder clay. If you ask how much, I will again take you no further than the same spot upon your own coasts for evidence. I have spoken of the boulder clay and drift as resting upon the chalk. That is not strictly true. Interposed between the

chalk and the drift is a comparatively insignificant layer, containing vegetable matter. But that layer tells a wonderful history. It is full of stumps
of trees standing as they grew. Fir-trees are there with their cones, and
hazel-bushes with their nuts; there stand the stools of oak and yew trees,
beeches and alders. Hence this stratum is appropriately called the
"forest-bed."

20   It is obvious that the chalk must have been upheaved and converted
into dry land, before the timber trees could grow upon it. As the bolls of
some of these trees are from two to three feet in diameter, it is no less
clear that the dry land thus formed remained in the same condition for
long ages. And not only do the remains of stately oaks and well-grown
firs testify to the duration of this condition of things, but additional evidence to the same effect is afforded by the abundant remains of elephants,
rhinoceroses, hippopotamuses, and other great wild beasts, which it has
yielded to the zealous search of such men as the Rev. Mr. Gunn. When
you look at such a collection as he has formed, and bethink you that these
elephantine bones did veritably carry their owners about, and these great
grinders crunch, in the dark woods of which the forest-bed is now the
only trace, it is impossible not to feel that they are as good evidence of
the lapse of time as the annual rings of the tree stumps.

21   Thus there is a writing upon the wall of cliffs at Cromer, and whoso
runs may read it. It tells us, with an authority which cannot be impeached,
that the ancient sea-bed of the chalk sea was raised up, and remained dry
land, until it was covered with forest, stocked with the great game the
spoils of which have rejoiced your geologists. How long it remained in
that condition cannot be said; but "the whirligig of time brought its
revenges" in those days as in these. That dry land, with the bones and
teeth of generations of long-lived elephants, hidden away among the
gnarled roots and dry leaves of its ancient trees, sank gradually to the
bottom of the icy sea, which covered it with huge masses of drift and
boulder clay. Sea-beasts, such as the walrus, now restricted to the extreme
north, paddled about where birds had twittered among the topmost twigs
of the fir-trees. How long this state of things endured we know not, but
at length it came to an end. The upheaved glacial mud hardened into the
soil of modern Norfolk. Forests grew once more, the wolf and the beaver
replaced the reindeer and the elephant; and at length what we call the
history of England dawned.

22   Thus, evidence which cannot be rebutted, and which need not be
strengthened, though if time permitted I might indefinitely increase its
quantity, compels you to believe that the earth, from the time of the
chalk to the present day, has been the theatre of a series of changes as vast
in their amount, as they were slow in their progress. The area on which
we stand has been first sea and then land, for at least four alternations; and
has remained in each of these conditions for a period of great length.

23   But, great as is the magnitude of these physical changes of the world,
they have been accompanied by a no less striking series of modifications in

its living inhabitants. All the great classes of animals, beasts of the field, fowls of the air, creeping things, and things which dwell in the waters, flourished upon the globe long ages before the chalk was deposited. Very few, however, if any, of these ancient forms of animal life were identical with those which now live. Certainly not one of the higher animals was of the same species as any of those now in existence. The beasts of the field, in the days before the chalk, were not our beasts of the field, nor the fowls of the air such as those which the eye of man has seen flying, unless his antiquity dates infinitely further back than we at present surmise. If we could be carried back into those times, we should be as one suddenly set down in Australia before it was colonized. We should see mammals, birds, reptiles, fishes, insects, snails, and the like, clearly recognizable as such, and yet not one of them would be just the same as those with which we are familiar, and many would be extremely different.

24   Up to this moment I have stated, so far as I know, nothing but well-authenticated facts, and the immediate conclusions which they force upon the mind. But the mind is so constituted that it does not willingly rest in facts and immediate causes, but seeks always after a knowledge of the remoter links in the chain of causation.

25   Taking the many changes of any given spot of the earth's surface, from sea to land and from land to sea, as an established fact, we cannot refrain from asking ourselves how these changes have occurred. And when we have explained them—as they must be explained—by the alternate slow movements of elevation and depression which have affected the crust of the earth we go still further back, and ask, Why these movements?

26   I am not certain that any one can give you a satisfactory answer to that question. Assuredly I cannot. All that can be said, for certain, is, that such movements are part of the ordinary course of nature, inasmuch as they are going on at the present time. Direct proof may be given, that some parts of the land of the northern hemisphere are at this moment insensibly rising and others insensibly sinking; and there is indirect, but perfectly satisfactory, proof, that an enormous area now covered by the Pacific has been deepened thousands of feet, since the present inhabitants of that sea came into existence. Thus there is not a shadow of a reason for believing that the physical changes of the globe, in past times, have been effected by other than natural causes. Is there any more reason for believing that the concomitant modifications in the forms of the living inhabitants of the globe have been brought about in other ways?

27   Before attempting to answer this question, let us try to form a distinct mental picture of what has happened in some special case. The crocodiles are animals which, as a group, have a very vast antiquity. They abounded ages before the chalk was deposited; they throng the rivers in warm climates, at the present day. There is a difference in the form of the joints of the back-bone, and in some minor particulars, between the crocodiles of the present epoch and those which lived before the chalk; but, in the cretaceous epoch, the crocodiles had assumed the modern type of struc-

ture. Notwithstanding this, the crocodiles of the chalk are not identically the same as those which lived in the times called "older tertiary," which succeeded the cretaceous epoch; and the crocodiles of the older tertiaries are not identical with those of the newer tertiaries, nor are these identical with existing forms. I leave open the question whether particular species may have lived on from epoch to epoch. But each epoch has had its peculiar crocodiles; though all, since the chalk, have belonged to the modern type, and differ simply in their proportions, and in such structural particulars as are discernible only to trained eyes.

28   How is the existence of this long succession of different species of crocodiles to be accounted for? Only two suppositions seem to be open to us—Either each species of crocodile has been specially created, or it has arisen out of some pre-existing form by the operation of natural causes. Choose your hypothesis; I have chosen mine. I can find no warrant for believing in the distinct creation of a score of successive species of crocodiles in the course of countless ages of time. Science gives no countenance to such a wild fancy; nor can even the perverse ingenuity of a commentator pretend to discover this sense, in the simple words in which the writer of Genesis records the proceedings of the fifth and six days of the Creation.

29   On the other hand, I see no good reason for doubting the necessary alternative, that all these varied species have been evolved from pre-existing crocodilian forms, by the operation of causes as completely a part of the common order of nature as those which have effected the changes of the inorganic world. Few will venture to affirm that the reasoning which applies to crocodiles loses its force among other animals, or among plants. If one series of species has come into existence by the operation of natural causes, it seems folly to deny that all may have arisen in the same way.

30   A small beginning has led us to a great ending. If I were to put the bit of chalk with which we started into the hot but obscure flame of burning hydrogen, it would presently shine like the sun. It seems to me that this physical metamorphosis is no false image of what has been the result of our subjecting it to a jet of fervent, though no-wise brilliant, thought to-night. It has become luminous, and its clear rays, penetrating the abyss of the remote past, have brought within our ken some stages of the evolution of the earth. And in the shifting "without haste, but without rest" of the land and sea, as in the endless variation of the forms assumed by living beings, we have observed nothing but the natural product of the forces originally possessed by the substance of the universe.

a piece of chalk

G. K. CHESTERTON

1   I remember one splendid morning, all blue and silver, in the summer holidays, when I reluctantly tore myself away from the task of doing nothing in particular, and put on a hat of some sort and picked up a walking-stick, and put six very bright-coloured chalks in my pocket. I then went into the kitchen (which, along with the rest of the house, belonged to a very square and sensible old woman in a Sussex village), and asked the owner and occupant of the kitchen if she had any brown paper. She had a great deal; in fact, she had too much; and she mistook the purpose and the rationale of the existence of brown paper. She seemed to have an idea that if a person wanted brown paper he must be wanting to tie up parcels, which was the last thing I wanted to do; indeed, it is a thing which I have found to be beyond my mental capacity. Hence she dwelt very much on the varying qualities of toughness and endurance in the material. I explained to her that I only wanted to draw pictures on it, and that I did not want them to endure in the least; and that from my point of view, therefore, it was a question not of tough consistency, but of responsive surface, a thing comparatively irrelevant in a parcel. When she understood that I wanted to draw she offered to overwhelm me with note-paper, apparently supposing that I did my notes and correspondence on old brown paper wrappers from motives of economy.

2   I then tried to explain the rather delicate logical shade, that I not only liked brown paper, but liked the quality of brownness in paper, just as I liked the quality of brownness in October woods, or in beer, or in the peat-streams of the North. Brown paper represents the primal twilight of the first toil of creation, and with a bright-coloured chalk or two you can pick out points of fire in it, sparks of gold, and blood-red, and sea-green, like the first fierce stars that sprang out of divine darkness. All this I said (in an off-hand way) to the old woman; and I put the brown paper in my pocket along with the chalks, and possibly other things. I suppose every one must have reflected how primeval and how poetical are the things that one carries in one's pocket; the pocket-knife, for instance, the type of all human tools, the infant of the sword. Once I planned to write a book of poems entirely about the things in my pocket. But I found it would be too long; and the age of the great epics is past.

3   With my stick and my knife, my chalks and my brown paper, I went out on to the great downs. I crawled across those colossal contours that express the best quality of England, because they are at the same time soft and strong. The smoothness of them has the same meaning as the smoothness of great cart-horses, or the smoothness of the beech-tree; it

Source. From *Tremendous Trifles.* Copyright © 1926. Reprinted by permission of Miss D. E. Collins.

declares in the teeth of our timid and cruel theories that the mighty are merciful. As my eye swept the landscape, the landscape was as kindly as any of its cottages, but for power it was like an earthquake. The villages in the immense valley were safe, one could see, for centuries; yet the lifting of the whole land was like the lifting of one enormous wave to wash them all away.

4   I crossed one swell of living turf after another, looking for a place to sit down and draw. Do not, for heaven's sake, imagine I was going to sketch from Nature. I was going to draw devils and seraphim, and blind old gods that men worshipped before the dawn of right, and saints in robes of angry crimson, and seas of strange green, and all the sacred or mon-strous symbols that look so well in bright colours on brown paper. They are much better worth drawing than Nature; also they are much easier to draw. When a cow came slouching by in the field next to me, a mere artist might have drawn it; but I always get wrong in the hind legs of quadrupeds. So I drew the soul of the cow; which I saw there plainly walk-ing before me in the sunlight; and the soul was all purple and silver, and had seven horns and the mystery that belongs to all the beasts. But though I could not with a crayon get the best out of the landscape, it does not follow that the landscape was not getting the best out of me. And this, I think, is the mistake that people make about the old poets who lived before Wordsworth, and were supposed not to care very much about Nature because they did not describe it much.

5   They preferred writing about great men to writing about great hills; but they sat on the great hills to write it. They gave out much less about Nature, but they drank in, perhaps, much more. They painted the white robes of their holy virgins with the blinding snow, at which they had stared all day. They blazoned the shields of their paladins with the purple and gold of many heraldic sunsets. The greenness of a thousand green leaves clustered into the live green figure of Robin Hood. The blueness of a score of forgotten skies became the blue robes of the Virgin. The inspir-ation went in like sunbeams and came out like Apollo.

6   But as I sat scrawling these silly figures on the brown paper, it began to dawn on me, to my great disgust, that I had left one chalk, and that a most exquisite and essential chalk, behind. I searched all my pockets, but I could not find any white chalk. Now, those who are acquainted with all the philosophy (nay, religion) which is typified in the art of drawing on brown paper, know that white is positive and essential. I cannot avoid remarking here upon a moral significance. One of the wise and awful truths which this brown-paper art reveals, is this, that white is a colour. It is not a mere absence of colour; it is a shining and affirmative thing, as fierce as red, as definite as black. When (so to speak) your pencil grows red-hot, it draws roses; when it grows white-hot, it draws stars. And one of the two or three defiant verities of the best religious morality, of real Christianity for example, is exactly this same thing; the chief assertion of religious morality is that white is a colour. Virtue is not the absence of

vices or the avoidance of moral dangers; virtue is a vivid and separate thing, like pain or a particular smell. Mercy does not mean not being cruel or sparing people revenge or punishment; it means a plain and positive thing like the sun, which one has either seen or not seen. Chastity does not mean abstention from sexual wrong; it means something flaming, like Joan of Arc. In a word, God paints in many colours; but He never paints so gorgeously, I had almost said so gaudily, as when He paints in white. In a sense our age has realized this fact, and expressed it in our sullen costume. For if it were really true that white was a blank and colourless thing, negative and noncommittal, then white would be used instead of black and grey for the funeral dress of this pessimistic period. We should see city gentlemen in frock coats of spotless silver satin, with top hats as white as wonderful arum lilies. Which is not the case.

7   Meanwhile, I could not find my chalk.

8   I sat on the hill in a sort of despair. There was no town nearer than Chichester at which it was even remotely probable that there would be such a thing as an artist's colourman. And yet, without white, my absurd little pictures would be as pointless as the world would be if there were no good people in it. I stared stupidly round, racking my brain for expedients. Then I suddenly stood up and roared with laughter, again and again, so that the cows stared at me and called a committee. Imagine a man in the Sahara regretting that he had no sand for his hour-glass. Imagine a gentleman in mid-ocean wishing that he had brought some salt water with him for his chemical experiments. I was sitting on an immense warehouse of white chalk. The landscape was made entirely out of white chalk. White chalk was piled mere miles until it met the sky. I stooped and broke a piece off the rock I sat on: it did not mark so well as the shop chalks do; but it gave the effect. And I stood there in a trance of pleasure, realizing that this Southern England is not only a grand peninsula, and a tradition and a civilization; it is something even more admirable. It is a piece of chalk.

COMMENTARY

If Chesterton can be said to have a thesis, it is a mathematical proportion (or double metaphor): white chalk is to an artist what good people are to the world. Both are everywhere, easily available to respond to our needs, if we will only notice them. His attempt to substantiate this thesis bypasses common sense. (He disposes of the commonsensical old cook at once.) Instead, he proceeds poetically. Brown paper represents primeval twilight. Hills turn into cart-horses. Cows become purple and silver beasts with seven horns. Inspiration turns sunbeams into Apollo.

Huxley, on the other hand, works like a scientist. For 24 paragraphs he gives us nothing but "well-authenticated facts." (In its original form, his essay is twice as long as the version printed here.) He then concludes that life has proceeded, beyond any reasonable doubt, by natural causes rather than by special acts of creation.

Common sense tells us that Huxley is right. Most of us are like the old cook in Chesterton's essay, persuaded by and satisfied with logical substantiation. But what is one to say about those people who, by a special act of creative imagination, know that God punctuated the primal ooze of a crocodile world with chalk, with the moral worth that belongs peculiarly to mankind?

OUTLINES

Huxley

    I. Introduction: the geography of chalk—paragraphs 1–3

   II. The origins of chalk—paragraphs 4–21

      A. Introduction—paragraphs 5–7

      B. Its chemistry—paragraphs 8–9

      C. Its physiology—paragraphs 10–14

      D. Its history—paragraphs 15–21

  III. Evolution of organic life—paragraphs 22–23

  IV. Conclusion: life explained by nature's record, not man's (example of the crocodile, paragraphs 27–28)—paragraphs 24–30

Chesterton

    I. Introduction: personal experience (obtaining brown paper)—paragraphs 1–2

   II. Narration: journey to the downs, reflections on history—paragraphs—3–5

  III. Reflections on drawing and on morality—paragraphs 6–7

  IV. Discovery of the true meaning of chalk—paragraph 8

SUGGESTIONS FOR WRITING

1. Can both Huxley and Chesterton be right about what chalk is? State a thesis that answers this question and substantiate it.

2. The following explanation of "why leaves change their color" was prepared by the U.S. Forest Service. Its basic image links the leaves with factory machinery.

All during spring and summer the leaves have served as factories where most of the foods necessary for the trees' growth are manufactured. This food-making process takes place in the leaf in numerous cells containing the pigment chlorophyll, which gives the leaf its green color. This chlorophyll absorbs energy from sunlight and uses it in transforming carbon dioxide and water to carbohydrates, such as sugars and starch. Along with the green pigment leaves also contain yellow or orange carotenoids—which, for example, give the carrot its familiar color. Most of the year these yellowish colors are masked by the greater amount of green coloring. But in the fall, partly because of changes in the period of daylight and changes in temperature, the leaves stop their food-making process. The chlorophyll breaks down, the green color disappears, and the yellowish colors become visible and give the leaves part of their fall splendor.

At the same time other chemical changes may occur and cause the formation of additional pigments that vary from yellow to red to blue. Some of them give rise to the reddish and purplish fall colors of leaves of trees such as dogwoods and sumacs. Others give the sugar maple its brilliant orange or fiery red and yellow. The autumn foliage of some trees, such as quaking aspen, birch, and hickory, shows only yellow colors. Many oaks and others are mostly brownish, while beech turns golden bronze. These colors are due to the mixing of varying amounts of the chlorophyll and other pigments in the leaf during the fall season.*

Compare the Forest Service statement with Shakespeare's sonnet "That time of year" to answer this question: What information does each interpretation communicate to you? Or write your own "Chestertonian" explanation of why leaves change color.

THAT TIME OF YEAR—William Shakespeare

That time of year thou mayst in me behold
When yellow leaves, or none, or few, do hang
Upon those boughs which shake against the cold,
Bare ruined choirs where late the sweet birds sang.
In me thou see'st the twilight of such day
As after sunset fadeth in the west,
Which by and by black night doth take away,
Death's second self, that seals up all in rest.
In me thou see'st the glowing of such fire,
That on the ashes of his youth doth lie
As the deathbed whereon it must expire,
Consumed with that which it was nourished by.
This thou perceivest, which makes thy love more strong,
To love that well which thou must leave ere long.

3. In the paragraph below, Leslie White says that both science and art have the same purpose: "to render experience intelligible, i.e., to assist man to adjust himself to his environment."

Science is not merely a collection of facts and formulas. It is preeminently a way of dealing with experience. The word may be appropriately used as a verb: one *sciences,* i.e., deals with experience according to certain assumptions and with certain techniques. Science is one of two basic ways of dealing with experience. The other is art. And this word, too, may appropriately be used as a verb; one may *art* as well as science. The purpose of science and art is one: to render experience intelligible, i.e., to assist man to adjust himself to his environment in order that he may live. But although working toward the same goal, science and art approach it from opposite directions. Science deals with particulars in terms of universals: Uncle Tom disappears in the mass of Negro slaves. Art deals with universals in terms of particulars: the whole gamut of Negro slavery confronts us in the person of Uncle Tom. Art and science thus grasp a common experience, or reality, by opposite but inseparable poles.†

* Courtesy of the United States Department of Agriculture.
† Reprinted with the permission of Farrar, Straus & Giroux, Inc. from *The Science of Culture* by Leslie A. White, copyright © 1949 by Leslie A. White.

Support or refute this claim, using the Huxley and Chesterton essays on chalk as your evidence. Take Huxley's as representative of a scientific approach, Chesterton's an artistic. Do both of these writers assist us in adjusting to our environment? If so, in what ways? If not, where do they fall short of that purpose, and what other purpose might they have in mind?

series two

SUBSTANTIATION: READINGS WITHOUT COMMENTARY

a house
named hamerika

CORA DU BOIS

This brief and terrible story uses personal experience to substantiate the thesis that we cannot know in advance what the consequences of our actions will be. Everything we do involves other people in ways we cannot predict. Cora du Bois, an American scholar, went to the Indonesian island of Alor before World War II to study the people who lived there. They received her most kindly. In the village of Atimelang, they named a house "Hamerika" after the country from which their visitor said she came. A man named Malelaka and other islanders became her friends as well as her subjects for a social and psychological study.

The selection below, which deals with the consequences of du Bois' visit, appeared as a 1960 appendix to the original preface of her book (first published in 1944).

1   In the fifteen years that have elapsed since this first preface was written I have not returned to Alor. In that interim World War II swept over the area. In July, 1942, four months after the Dutch forces capitulated in Java, the Japanese garrisoned the island. The Dutch, having foreseen several years in advance the possibility of a Japanese invasion, are rumored to have had standing orders for the evacuation of their personnel from the outer islands of Indonesia. In any event, the Japanese took possession of Alor without opposition. . . .

Source. Reprinted by permission of the author and publishers from *The People of Alor,* vol. I, by Cora du Bois, Cambridge, Mass.: Harvard University Press, Copyright © 1944 by the University of Minnesota; © 1960, 1972 by Cora du Bois.

2   After the war I received a letter from a young controleur who was sent to Alor during the Dutch interregnum before Indonesia achieved independence. It was a jovial, almost a flippant, letter. I don't remember his name, but he offered me every hospitality if I wished to return and asked me for a copy of this book. He told quite casually the story of Atimelang and the house called Hamerika. The Japanese had used it as a patrol station, for the Japanese, like the Dutch, sent small groups of troops to crisscross the island at irregular intervals to maintain order and prevent uprisings. Word reached the Japanese command in Kalabahi that the village leaders of Atimelang were claiming that Hamerika would win the war. This could have been nothing but the most innocent fantasy to my friends in Atimelang since they had never even heard of the United States prior to my arrival. But to the Japanese, suffering from all the nervous apprehensions of any occupying power in a strange and therefore threatening environment, such talk could mean only rebellion. As the Dutch, years before, had sent a punitive expedition to the area after the murder of the radjah, as they had later imprisoned Malelaka because he had visions of the arrival of "good beings" (nala kang), so the Japanese sent troops to arrest five of my friends in Atimelang. I am not sure who all of them were from the young controleur's letter, but apparently Thomas, Malelaka, and the Chief of Dikimpe were among them. In Kalabahi they were publicly decapitated as a warning to the populace.

3   There is no end to the intricate chain of responsibility and guilt that the pursuit of even the most arcane social research involves. "No man is an island."

women drivers in
the trucking industry
ABIGAIL LAMBERT

The writer of this letter to the editor of *Ms.* magazine uses her personal experience to substantiate the thesis that the trucking industry discriminates against women drivers—women who want to be truck drivers, that is. The trucking companies' objections to women truck drivers show that the companies are reasoning in circles rather than in acceptable logical patterns.

Do you think that Lambert makes her case adequately? Or is she seeing only part of the picture?

Source. From *Ms.* magazine, June, 1974.

1 **a**lthough I am in perfect health, certified by a truck-driving training school, and in possession of a valid Class-One California driving license, I am running into problems getting employment in the trucking industry because I am female.

2 You may have heard that in recent years, more and more women have been entering the trucking profession. But here's the catch: in most cases, women are able to enter the trucking profession only as part of a husband-wife driving team. As for putting a single woman on with a male co-driver for long-distance hauling (where the best money in trucking is to be made), the companies that I've been to refuse, on the grounds that they could get into trouble for condoning fornication and adultery.

3 Even though two drivers sharing long-distance hauling are expected to alternate driving and sleeping shifts to keep running 20 or 22 hours a day, employers have told me they feel that inevitably I and a male co-driver would wind up spending all our time in the sleeper berth! In short, it's assumed that because I'm a woman, I'm incapable of behaving responsibly on the road, of enforcing any responsible attitude in my co-driver—who, of course, would be incapable of regarding me as anything other than a sex object, placed conveniently at his disposal by the firm while he's on the road. I've also been told that I could be hired by the company in question if only they had another woman driver to put me on with; but the company doesn't hire women anyway, so there's no woman driver to put me on with, so. . . .

4 There you have a nice circular argument trucking firms use to protect themselves against uppity women who dare to stay single, operate 35 tons of tractor-trailer assembly, and try to gross $14,000 to $50,000 income yearly, God forbid!

Abigail Lambert
San Jose, Calif.

---

a younger
sun, a colder earth?
CARL SAGAN

SWAG was a popular acronym some years ago. It stands for "scientific wild ass guess." When there is considerable evidence to support a thesis, but the evidence remains inconclusive, then all you can do is conjecture (guess). Eventually, new data may prove you right or wrong. Meanwhile your guess may provoke someone else to examine the problem and solve it.

Many advances in our knowledge of the world have begun with suggestive mistakes. Columbus, you will remember, was looking for Asia.

Only scientists could attempt to confirm or refute Sagan's "most likely resolution." The nonscientist can, however, appraise his logic. Is the analogy with Jupiter legitimate (how about the other planets)? Is the argument that ammonia would have retained heat, and therefore would have helped make life possible, adequate reason for believing that there *was* ammonia?

1   **S**tars, like people, do not live forever. But the lifetime of a person is measured in decades; the lifetime of a star in billions of years.

2   A star is born out of interstellar clouds of gas and dust. For a while, it stably converts hydrogen to helium in the thermonuclear furnaces of its deep interior. Then, in stellar old age, it encounters a set of minor or major catastrophes—a slow trickle or an explosive injection of star-stuff into space. During the more or less stable portion of the lifetime of the star, the hot interior region, converting hydrogen into helium, gradually eats its way outward from the very center. In the course of time, the star becomes slowly, almost imperceptibly, brighter.

3   After the flares and other impetuosities of its early adolescence, our sun settled down to a more or less constant radiation output. But four billion years ago it was about 30 percent dimmer than it is today. If we assume that the earth four billion years ago had the same distribution of land and water, clouds and polar ice, so that it absorbed the same relative amount of sunlight that it does today, and if we also assume that it had the same atmosphere it has today, we can calculate what its temperature would have been. The calculation reveals a temperature for the entire earth significantly below the freezing point of seawater. In fact, even two billion years ago, under these assumptions, the sun would not have been bright enough to keep the earth above the freezing point.

4   But we have a wide variety of evidence that this was not the case. There are in old mud deposits ripple marks caused by liquid water. There are pillow lavas produced by undersea volcanoes. There are enormous sedimentary deposits that can only be produced on ocean margins. There are biological products, called algal stromatolites, that can only be produced in water.

5   So what is wrong? Either our theory of the evolution of the sun is wrong or our assumption that the early earth was like the present earth is wrong. The theory of solar evolution seems to be in good shape. What uncertainties exist do not appear to affect the question of the sun's early luminosity.

6   The most likely resolution of this apparent paradox is that something was different on the early earth. After studying a wide range of possibilities, I conclude that what was different, two billion years ago and earlier, was

the presence of small quantities of ammonia in the earth's atmosphere. Ammonia is present on Jupiter today; it is the form of nitrogen expected under primitive conditions. It absorbs very strongly at the infrared wavelengths that the earth emits to space. Ammonia on the primitive earth would have held heat in, increasing the surface temperature through the greenhouse effect and keeping the global temperature of earth at congenial levels. Ammonia would have made possible the origin and early history of life and the abundance of liquid water early in the history of the planet. Ammonia is one of the atmospheric constituents needed for making the building blocks of life. The study of the sun's evolution leads us to information about the early history, chemical composition, and temperature of the earth, and therefore, to the circumstances of its habitability. Stellar and biological evolution are connected.

hands across the sea
ALEXANDER WOOLLCOTT

Woollcott uses personal experience, presented in narrative form, to substantiate two theses. One thesis (paragraph 1) is that it is "the small, unimportant days" we remember, not the events that might find their way into history books. To demonstrate this point, Woollcott, writing about World War I, tells a story not about a major battle but about an incident that has "no part in history at all," an incident depicting everyday characteristics of human nature: boredom, resentment at being ordered to "do this" or "do that," the tendency to take advantage of others.

Woollcott's second thesis is implied by the narrative itself, not openly stated. The sequence of events demonstrates that an apparently pointless everyday incident can contain a very dramatic meaning. You have to wait until later, until the whole story unfolds, to see what the meaning of apparently meaningless experiences will be.

THE night of the strange, swift inspection, held under a fitful light at all of the camps which American troops had pitched in the mud of Brittany.

1 **I**n the World War, when chance made me a spellbound witness of some great occasions, some part of me—the incorrigible journalist, I suppose— kept saying: "This will be something to remember. This will be something

Source. From *While Rome Burns* by Alexander Woollcott. Copyright 1934 by Alexander Woollcott. Reprinted by permission of The Viking Press, Inc.

to remember." Well, it seems I was wrong about that. I find I do not often think of the war at all, and when I do, it is the small, unimportant days that come drifting back, the ones that have no part in history at all. For example, of late my thoughts have taken unaccountably to jogging back along the road to Savenay, an ancient Breton village of steep, cobbled streets, and windmills that still, I suppose, turn sleepily against the sunset sky. And here I am, bent to the task of telling you about the evening of the strange inspection there.

2   It was at Savenay, in August of '17, that the base hospital recruited at the Post-Graduate in New York was established, with an enlisted personnel consisting, to an impressive extent, of bouncing undergraduates from Princeton and Rutgers who had enlisted early in May in order to escape the June exams. This frustrated group was part of a shipment of two thousand soldiers who sailed stealthily from Hoboken on a hot morning in July aboard the *Saratoga,* which aged transport got as far as Staten Island before being rammed and sunk. A week later, the same outfit tried again with another boat and got as far as Savenay. Then followed an interminable and corrupting wait through that bleak autumn of '17 when the war seemed to stretch ahead of us as a sterile condition of life of which we, at least, would never see the end. A time when only the real stalwarts were strong enough to keep from becoming silly or servile or both. A time of inaction and suspense and only the most sporadic and belated news from home. A time when no rumor could be too monstrous to be believed.

3   I emphasize this matter of rumors riding on every wind which came up the valley of the Loire only so that you may remember what tinder we all were for wild surmise, and what an outbreak of fantastic speculation there must have been one frosty December afternoon when, just after sundown, the bugles began blowing a summons which none of us, as we came tumbling out of quarters, could account for. "Line up, everybody! Line up! Line up!" This from the sergeants, all conscientiously gruff and authoritative, exhorting us and pushing us in any order into hastily formed queues which at once began shuffling docilely along in the quick-gathering darkness. Within sight, there were several such lines, each apparently working its way up to an appointed table, where there seemed to be muster-rolls spread out. We caught the gleam from officers' caps, bent in candle-lit conference. At the table, the line would pause for a moment, then move on and be swallowed up in the darkness. During this pause a light would flash on and off, on and off, like a winking beacon. What was up? It seemed to be some new kind of inspection. A curious hour for any kind. It was like a nightmare pay-day. But we had just *been* paid the week before. Perhaps the fool quartermaster wanted his francs back. Too late. Too late. There was smothered laughter, and a few foul but constructive suggestions as to what the quartermaster could do if he felt so inclined. A distant line had started up a song, and in a moment you could hear nothing else in the courtyard. It was that fine old pessimistic refrain to the tune of "Glory Hallelujah":

Every day we sign the pay-roll,
Every day we sign the pay-roll,
Every day we sign the pay-roll,
But we never get a
God-damned cent.

4   By this time my place in line was so far advanced that I could see something of what was going on. As each soldier reached the table, his name would be checked on the roll. Then he would be told to spread his hands on the table, palms down. An electric flash would spotlight them. The officers all bent low to examine them. Then palms up. Again the light. Again the close inspection. And that was all. No more than that. Well, for Christ's sake, was it leprosy they thought we had *this* time? The soldier would move on, bewildered. The next man would take his place. A moment later my own hands were spread out. By now the entire outfit was humming with surmise. It was a kind of off-stage hubbub with only the recurrent word "hands" distinguishable. Hands. Hands. Hands. Why did they want to see our hands? From the gossipy orderly in the adjutant's office we learned there had been a telephone call from the base and within half an hour, every hand in that outfit was being checked. Patients', orderlies', doctors', cooks', mechanics', everybody's. Except the nurses'.

5   We drifted out through the gate onto the road to Nantes. It lay hard as flint in the frost, white as snow in the light of the new-risen moon. Across the fields was a camp of the Seventeenth Engineers. There, too, the same puzzled line was forming, writhing. The same candle-lit table, the same winking flashlight. They were looking at all the American hands in Savenay. We later learned that, at that same moment, in Nantes, some thirty kilometers away, and in all the camps pitched in the frozen mud outside St. Nazaire, the same swift inspection was going on. Also, still later, we learned why. In a barn near the port that afternoon, a fourteen-year-old girl in a torn black smock had been found unconscious. She had been raped. They could learn from her only that she had been dragged there by a soldier in a brown uniform, and that, while she was struggling with him, she had caught his hand and bitten it. Bitten it until she tasted blood.

6   Well, that is the story. Not, as you see, an important one. It was unrelated to the major forces launched to make the world safe for democracy. But, every now and again, some sight of a line shuffling in the torch-lit darkness—a not altogether unfamiliar sight in *this* rescued democracy—some Proustian invocation of a bygone moment brings it all back to me.

7   And the end of the story? You want to know, perhaps, whether they found a man with a bitten hand. Yes, they did.

the decline and fill
of the american hot dog
STEFAN KANFER

Kanfer's question is whether the hot dog—no nutritional bargain—will survive. The way he deals with this question shows how wit and humor can be used to enliven essays of substantiation.

The pun has been called the lowest form of humor, something good writers avoid; but the hot dog is, by all accounts, a low form of food and seems to thrive on cheap jokes. Kanfer makes the most of his opportunity. "Fill" in the title, "frank companion" (paragraph 1), "chicken out" (paragraph 3), "beef it up" (paragraph 10) are a few examples. They might be called the salt, spices, and preservatives of a homely essay.

For the essay *is* homely—quite in harmony with the "fingershaped monster" it describes. Although he compares the hot dog to a ballistic missile, Kanfer avoids the kind of analysis that sophisticated readers might expect. He does not Freudianize the frank as a phallic symbol. He does not resort to innuendos about its German pedigree. Instead, he plays it straight: on the one hand, the frank's humble (some would say hideous) ingredients; on the other, its immense cultural clout. Whether or not it's here to stay, at the moment it's fit, if not for a king, for anyone who wants to capitalize on its all-American image. Insect parts, rodent hairs, and all.

1   **f**rankfurter can be found just below Frankenstein in the dictionary. It can also be found immediately beneath contempt in Ralph Nader's vast lexicon of villains. To Nader, the ABM and the smart bomb are scarcely more lethal than a chain of processed sausages. Hot dogs, insists the consumer advocate, are "among America's deadliest missiles." New York City's Consumer Affairs Commissioner Bess Myerson agrees: "After I found out what was in hot dogs, I stopped eating them." This people's entrée, this frank companion of alfresco meals and ball games—can it really be a finger-shaped monster? So it appears.

2   When a German-born restauranteur named Charles Feltman first popularized the frankfurter on a roll 100 years ago, the Coney Island Chamber of Commerce refused to endorse the sobriquet "hot dog." They thought it might evoke notions of processed mongrel. Today the public has less fanciful worries. According to the U.S. Department of Agriculture, since 1937 the frankfurter has gone from 19% fat and 19.6% protein to 28% fat and only 11.7% protein. (The rest is water, salt, spices and preservatives.) This deterioration is yet another of technology's ambiguous gifts.

3   Not long ago, for example, it was difficult to pulverize poultry cheaply; now hot-dog manufacturers enthusiastically chicken out, cramming up to

Source. Reprinted by permission from *Time, The Weekly Newsmagazine;* Copyright ©
Time Inc.

15% of their sausages with bird parts. Poultry is one of the more appetizing ingredients. Federal law allows hot dogs to contain such animal features as esophagi, ears, lips and snouts. In the words of Robert Benchley: "Ain't it offal?" And even these ingredients do not exhaust the bad news. Hot dogs are brimming with additives, including sodium nitrite, sodium acid pyrophosphate and glucona delta lactone. Without such chemicals, the hot dog would lose its pink blush and turn the color of unwashed sneakers. The wiener may also contain "binders," like dried milk, cereal or starchy vegetable flour. According to Consumers Union, there can also be occasional insect parts and rodent hairs. Moreover, frankfurters are no longer a bargain. There is little honest protein in even the purest of all-beef kosher franks. Discarding fat, water, etc., what protein remains comes to more than $10 per pound. For that you can get truffles. Or 4 lbs. of filet mignon. Or 8 lbs. of hamburger.

4   For all its critics, the hot dog, like any other American institution, does have its loyal defenders. "If I were an Oscar Mayer wiener," insists the jingle, "everyone would be in love with me." Edwin Anderson, president of the Zion Foods Corp., salutes the frankfurter with a serious mien. "Hot dogs," he maintains, "are still the American's favorite meat food. Let's compare apples with apples. The hot dog is a ready-to-eat product and should be compared with other similar products rather than with hamburger, which loses 30% to 40% of its weight in cooking." Adds Michael Levine of Continental Seasoning: "There are fewer chemicals in franks than in most of your cereals, mustard, mayonnaise or oleomargarine." Their logic does not stand grilling. Franks present should only be compared with franks past. As for mustard, it goes *on* those dubious wieners, adding its adulterates to theirs.

5   The frank still exerts appeal, but increasingly it has found succulent rivals in every U.S. city. McDonald's burgers (which are expressly forbidden by the franchiser to contain "hearts, lungs, tripe, suet, flavor boosters, preservatives, protein additives, fillers or cereals") have long passed the 6 billion mark in sales. The Near East may never solve its tensions, but American Arabs and Jews agree upon the merits of the felafel —Arabian bread stuffed with beans, salad, pickle, olives and sesame sauce. The gyro, a Greek concoction of lamb, tomato and onion, has pre-empted the frankfurter's place on many Eastern city streets. On both coasts, the Mexican taco has become a short-order staple. Soul food has gone national. Colonel Sanders' finger-lickin' Kentucky Fried Chicken outlets now number 3,500. The pizza, according to a Gallup Organization poll, is the No. 1 favorite snack of 21-to-34-year-olds. (Any of those foods may contain additives, too, but they have not yet been in the Nader pressure cooker.)

6   Few hot-dog manufacturers have bothered to read the entrails. For despite the tocsins from Washington, despite intruders from overseas, the maligned frankfurter has proved as irresistible in 1972 as it was in 1914 to a boy named Penrod. The hero of Booth Tarkington's Huckleberry novels thought the "winnywurst" was "all nectar and ambrosia . . . it was

rigidly forbidden by the home authorities." Like Penrod, contemporary Americans tend to ignore authorities; they consume 15 billion hot dogs every year—possibly even because of the warnings. Forbidden fruit tastes delicious; why not proscribed wieners?

7   There are other, better reasons for the hot dog to be top dog. Crackling tidily above briquettes, steaming under vendors' umbrellas and in short-order restaurants, the frank still emits a sharp democratic zonk, redolent of exotic spices and domestic meats. To most Americans, the hot dog is the equivalent of Proust's *madeleine;* it triggers memories of afternoons in the bleachers, and languorous Sundays spent lolling on picnic grounds. At 170 calories, it is modest enough to be included in a dietary lunch; yet the gourmet James Beard has wrapped a recipe around it: *choucroute à l'alsacienne.* (Translation: sauerkraut with local sausage. Beard prefers franks.)

8   Given these statistics and endorsements, even Ralph Nader would have to agree with Governor Nelson Rockefeller's dictum: "No candidate for any office can hope to get elected in this country without being photo-graphed eating a hot dog." (Indeed, F.D.R. went so far as to serve franks to King George VI.) One of those candidates, a consumer named Richard Nixon, once announced, "I come from humble origins. Why, we were raised on hot dogs and hamburgers. We've got to look after the hot dog."

9   Yet neither politicians nor preservatives can guarantee shelf life forever. Those who see the hot dog as an American symbol may be discomfited to learn that its very ethos is vanishing. Once, for example, franks were the staple of daytime World Series games. But this year, all weekday Series games will be played at night. Who wants a hot dog *after* dinner?

10   Europeans have customarily treated the wiener as a shaggy hot-dog story, absurdly amusing but not to be consumed too often or too seriously. It is quite possible that Whole Earth sensibilities, newly sophisticated palates and consumerism may yet do in the little sausage whose manufac-turers arrogantly refuse to beef it up—or pork it out. In that case, the great American hot dog will be only a memory. And, perhaps, many of the cherished institutions that seemed to go with it. Eventually, history judges a country as much by its cuisine as by its politics. As Lin Yutang rhetorically inquired: "What is patriotism but the love of the good things we ate in our childhood?"

the comics on the couch

GERALD CLARKE

Clarke's thesis is that even the comics have gone "relevant." They have left behind their traditional plots and characterizations and are concerning themselves with the real problems of life in the 1970s. With a few exceptions (*Blondie, Little Orphan Annie*), Clarke shows that the comics are now talking about poverty, race relations, politics, countercultures. Their heroes are becoming more like the rest of us. Superman, who isn't so super any more, has identity hang-ups and is tempted to seek the comfort of a psychiatrist's couch. Clarke's evidence is exactly what you would expect—illustrations from the comics themselves—and the nature of this evidence influences his tone. He keeps his sense of humor and avoids drawing ponderous conclusions. His purpose is limited to demonstrating that an important change has occurred in American popular culture.

1   **h**e was someone you could always count on, the savior of the helpless and oppressed, society's sword against the forces of evil and injustice. He could, among other things, "hurdle skyscrapers, leap an eighth of a mile, run faster than a streamline train—and nothing less than a bursting shell could penetrate his skin." He was, in short, a good buy for a dime. Even by today's hyped-up standards, Superman was quite a guy.

2   Yes, was. The man of steel that many Americans grew up with is not what he used to be. For one thing, his alter ego, Clark Kent, has given up the *Daily Planet* to become a newscaster for the Galaxy Broadcasting System, getting in and out of blue tights and red cape during commercial breaks. ("Personally, I still prefer Walter Cronkite," a mini-skirted Lois tells him. She, at least, is unchanged—as obnoxious as ever.) For another, Superman has succumbed to urban jitters; he obviously needs to spend some time on the couch. Just listen to some of his recent complaints: "I'm finished being anybody's Superman! . . . For years I've been dreaming of working and living as a plain man—without the responsibilities, the loneliness of Superman . . . I've a right to bitterness. No man has a better right. I've denied myself the comforts of home and family to continue helping these ingrates. I thought they admired me—for myself! I've lived in a fool's paradise!"

3   Superhang-ups for a superhero, but Superman is not the only hero hanging his cape outside Dr. Feelgood's door. Today almost all comic-book characters have problems. As in many fields, the word is relevance. The trend may have begun a decade ago, but in the socially aware '70s it has reached full blossom. The comics' caped crusaders have become as outraged about racial injustice as the congressional Black Caucus and as worried about pollution as the Sierra Club. Archfiends with memorable

Source. Reprinted by permission from *Time, The Weekly Newsmagazine;* Copyright ©
1971 Time Inc.

names like the Hulk and Dr. Doom are still around, but they are often pushed off the page by such new villains as air pollution and social injustice. Sometimes, indeed, the comics read like a *New York Times Illustrated.*

4   Recently the comics have discovered yet another field—a mixture of science fiction and the occult that lies somewhere beyond Consciousness III. In a comic book called *The New Gods,* for example, the forces of the good, the beautiful, under-30s, battle the forces of evil, the ugly militarists of Apokolips, in weird sequences that look and read like nightmares. Whatever they are doing, American comics, both the books and the strips, are full of life. In their 75th year, they are bursting—WUMP, BOMP, OOF! and ZAP!—from the page in a dozen new directions.

5   Along with responsibility has come respectability. One of the newest things about the new comics is that more than ever before they are being taken seriously as an art form by critics and as an authentic cultural expression by sociologists. Half a dozen or so learned histories have been written about them, and art galleries give them serious exhibitions. The comics have been included in courses at Brown University, and the creators of the new styles, particularly Marvel Comics' Stan Lee, who invented the idiom, are mobbed like rock stars on the campuses. So popular is Lee, in fact, that he will give a kind of sound and light show at Carnegie Hall next month.

6   Not all of the comics are trying to be with it, of course. *Blondie,* a strip that is syndicated in 1,164 newspapers and is one of the most widely read series in the world, still exists in a timeless never-never land of middle-class clichés where only Daisy the dog seems to have a spark of intelligence. Despite wrist TVs and spaceships, Dick Tracy continues to chase odd-looking crooks like Retsen Nester, a bald-domed, bespectacled type who hides heroin in volumes of Mother Goose. In the same old way, Little Orphan Annie and Sandy still fight the Red Menace and bleeding-heart liberals, and will probably continue to do so well into the 21st century. In a recent episode Annie was trying to find a poor but honest person who needed only Daddy Warbucks' "survival kit," $11,000, to make good. Daddy, a billionaire, is convinced that the "good old-fashioned pioneer spirit that made this country great is not dead" but "just kinda takin' a nap."

7   Many of the other oldtimers, however, have changed just about everything but their costumes. Evil, they are discovering, was much easier to spot when it had a funny name and wore an ugly mask. In a recent comic-book adventure, the Green Lantern collars a kid who has been beating up a fat man. But after being bombarded with garbage by the kid's ghetto neighbors, the Emerald Crusader learns that the man he has saved is a corrupt slumlord who is about to tear down the block for a parking lot. "I been readin' about you," says an old black who is soon to be evicted. "How you work for the blue skins and how on a planet someplace you helped out the orange skins, and you done considerable for the purple skins. Only there's skins you never bothered with—the black skins! I want to know: How come? Answer me that, Mr. Green Lantern!"

8   Now it's no good just to zap a few uglies either, as of yore. The Green
Lantern and his superhero colleagues are constantly being reminded these
days that the funny fiends are just front men for some very unfunny social
ills. The Green Lantern and his chum, the Green Arrow, are lectured by a
youthful victim: "Drugs are a symptom, and you, like the rest of society,
attack the symptom, not the disease." Another big change has been the
introduction of black characters, who now appear in such strips as *Peanuts,
Archie, Li'l Abner* and *Beetle Bailey; Friday Foster,* a swinging soul sister
from Harlem, has a strip all her own. Until a few years ago, the color barrier blocked all but a few Negro caricatures from the comics.

9   When it comes to politics, *Li'l Abner* and *Pogo,* which have satirized
it for years, are at least as up to date as the men in Washington. Two
characters that bear a remarkable resemblance to Senators Hubert Humphrey and Hugh Scott were recently dispatched to Li'l Abner's Dogpatch
to learn why it is the one pollution-free spot in the U.S. Reason: the Gob-
bleglops, which look like pigs with bunny tails, gobble up, in the words of
Mammy Yokum, "all glop, irregardless . . . They's natcheral-born incin-
erators. Thass why glop goes in 'em an' none comes out!!" *Pogo* has been
invaded in recent months by an odd beast, half Great Dane and half hyena,
that looks and alliterates like Spiro T. Agnew, by a bulldog that might be
taken for J. Edgar Hoover, and by a pipe-smoking, improbable baby eagle
that might fool even Martha Mitchell into thinking she had seen John.
This trio of animal crackers spends most of its time trying to decipher messages from an unseen chief who chooses to communicate by means of
undecipherable paper dolls. "Dashing deep-digging thought dominates his
delectable display," asserts the Spiroesque Great Dane-hyena, who wears
the uniform—or half the uniform—of a Greek colonel.

Source. Copyright © 1971 Walt Kelly. Courtesy Field Newspaper Syndicate.

10   While the political spectrum of the regular comic strips ranges from the
moderately liberal (*Pogo*) to the arch-conservative (*Little Orphan Annie*),
a relatively new phenomenon, underground comics, is pursuing radical political and sexual themes that their aboveground brothers would never dare
to touch. Begun in the mid-'60s, the undergrounds, or head comic books,

such as *Zap* and *Despair* and strips in papers like the Berkeley *Barb* and Manhattan's *East Village Other,* speak for the counterculture in a zany, raunchy and often obscene idiom. In one issue of the *East Village Other,* a strip depicts an Army company in Viet Nam. The sergeant's command "Present arms!" literally brings out the arms of the men in his company, heroin addicts all. Later, when all of the men are dead of overdoses—including the sergeant, whose name is, of course, Smack—it turns out that the CIA is the ultimate pusher. "Put it this way," says the agency's spook in charge, "we consider this something of an investment." . . .

11   With a few exceptions—*Wonder Woman* was into Women's Lib 20 years before Betty Friedan—the comics have always appealed to men more than women, to little boys more than little girls. One reason is the inevitable boy companion that the ten-year-old could identify with—*Batman's* Boy Wonder Robin, the Sandman's Sandy, the Shield's Rusty, to name only a few. Even when the ten-year-old identified too closely with that clever brat on paper as a rival, it was good for sales. Cartoonist Jules Feiffer, who has lately turned to writing for the theater and the movies (*Carnal Knowledge*), was both repelled and drawn to the Boy Wonder. "One need only look at him," Feiffer writes, "to see he could fight better, swing from a rope better, play ball better, eat better, and live better. For while I lived in the East Bronx, Robin lived in a mansion, and while I was trying somehow to please my mother—and getting it all wrong—Robin was rescuing Batman and getting the gold medals. You can imagine how pleased I was when, years later, I heard he was a fag."

12   Feiffer's was a love-hate relationship that the comic books lost for a while in the '50s and early '60s, when sales dropped and the industry appeared headed for extinction. In a world where almost anything was possible and usually visible on a 21-in. screen, outracing a locomotive or buzzing around like an ugly bug in drag seemed somehow tame and tedious. Young readers today, the comic men soon discovered, are more interested in their own problems and the problems they see around them. It is possi-

ble, indeed, to see the comics as an art of the people, offering clues to the national unconscious. Superman's enormous popularity might be looked upon as signaling the beginning of the end for the Horatio Alger myth of the self-made man. In the modern world, he seems to say, only the man with superpowers can survive and prosper. Still, though comics are indeed a popular art form, it is going a bit far to compare, as Critic Maurice Horn does, *Gasoline Alley* to Goethe's *Wilhelm Meister* and *Little Orphan Annie* to the works of Charles Dickens and Victor Hugo. As Mammy Yokum might say: "Some folks don't know when to stop."

13   Walt Kelly, still one of the best cartoonists, is a more solid expert on the genre. "A comic strip is like a dream," Turtle tells Bear in *Pogo*. "A tissue of paper reveries. It gloms an' glimmers its way thru unreality, fancy an' fantasy." To which Bear naturally responds: "Sho' 'nuff?" Sho' 'nuff.

who will do the
dirty work tomorrow?

EDMUND FALTERMAYER

To examine a question as broad as "Who will do the dirty work tomorrow?" in an essay of normal length isn't easy. Faltermayer must first demonstrate that we ought to worry about this problem. Usually we think of society's dirty work as little as possible. He must also present enough evidence for us to grasp several—if not all—facets of the problem, and he must refer to individual cases so that we can understand how the problem actually affects people's lives.

Faltermayer's prediction is that we will be unable to make machines do all of the dirty work for us. We will have to pay more to get it done by people, and we will have to find ways to get more of it done by *young* people.

1   In the computer age, millions of men and women still earn wages by carrying food trays, pushing brooms, shoveling dirt, and performing countless other menial tasks in ways that haven't changed much in centuries. Traditionally, these jobs have been taken by people with no choice: high-school dropouts, immigrants with language difficulties, members of racial minorities, women, and young people (as well as unemployed family heads in desperate straits and disproportionate numbers of ex-convicts, alcoholics,

Source. Reprinted from the January, 1974 issue of *Fortune* Magazine by special permission; Copyright © 1974 Time, Inc.

the mentally retarded, and people with personality disorders). But various currents of change—including egalitarianism, rising expectations, and ever-more-generous government programs of support for nonworkers—are tending to make it harder to fill such jobs as time goes by. Some observers, indeed, foresee an eventual drying up of the pool of labor available to do menial work.

2   Yet many of these "jobs of last resort," as they have been called, involve essential tasks that it would be difficult to dispense with or to mechanize. Under the pressure of rising wages, the U.S. has traveled far down the road of reducing menial labor, which currently engages somewhere between 10 and 15 percent of the working population. But we are approaching the limits of how far we can go, or wish to go.

3   On farms, for example, machines have replaced most manual toil. But a visit to California's Imperial Valley, one of the most efficient agricultural regions in the U.S., reveals that a surprising amount of "stoop" labor still survives. At construction sites, machines now do most of the heavy digging, but men with shovels still must work behind them. Much of the restaurant industry has shifted to self-service and throwaways, but growing numbers of Americans want to dine out in conventional fashion, with the food served on china plates.

4   In an effort to simplify cleaning, developers have modified the design of new office buildings, stores, and hotels, and industry now supplies improved chemicals and equipment. But Daniel Fraad, Jr., chairman of Allied Maintenance Corp., which cleans offices, factories, and passenger terminals across the U.S., sees few remaining breakthroughs in productivity. Years ago, he says, his company abandoned a mechanical wall-washing device after it was found to be less efficient than a man with a sponge. Says Fraad, himself a former window washer: "In the final analysis, cleaning is elbow grease."

5   All this helps explain why the century-long process in which Americans have been moving out of low-status jobs is decelerating and may even be reversing. Productivity in the remaining menial occupations is growing more slowly than in most other fields, and shorter working hours often necessitate larger working staffs even where the amount of work remains the same. According to the Department of Labor, the percentage of Americans who were either "nonfarm laborers" or "service workers" was higher in 1972 than in 1960.

6   Declines in some menial jobs, most notably maids and housekeepers, have been more than offset by increases in other occupations. The 1970 census showed 1,250,000 "janitors" at work in the U.S., up from 750,000 a decade earlier. In the same period the ranks of unskilled hospital workers, i.e., "nursing aides, orderlies and attendants," rose by nearly 80 percent to 720,000, and the number of "garbage collectors" doubled. And the trend seems likely to continue. Between now and 1985, the Bureau of Labor Statistics has predicted, openings in many low-status jobs will increase faster than total employment.

7   But who, in this era when the Army feels compelled to abolish K.P., will want to wait on tables, empty bedpans or, for that matter, bury the dead? In some cities it's already hard to keep menial jobs filled. In the booming Dallas region, with its unemployment rate of only 2.1 percent, jobs for waitresses, private guards, trash collectors, and busboys were recently going begging.

8   One restaurant owner who is short of "bus help" revealed that his current roster consists of an illiterate black man in his fifties, a white girl who is somewhat retarded, a divorced white man in his sixties with personality problems, and an unattached white man in his forties "who goes out and gets drunk each day after he finishes his shift."

9   In slack labor markets such as Boston, where the unemployment rate has been running above the recent national figure of 4.7 percent, employers are experiencing troubles of a different sort. There seem to be enough people to fill most menial jobs, but they just don't stay around.

10   At the popular Sheraton-Boston Hotel, the turnover among chambermaids is about 150 percent a year. On pleasant weekends, when absenteeism runs high, the hotel hurriedly telephones local college students on a standby list. Down in the kitchens, turnover among dishwashers on the night shift exceeds a phenomenal 400 percent a year. Sometimes, the hotel has to ask the local U.S.O. to send over Navy men on shore leave who want to earn some extra money by helping out in the kitchens.

11   In Boston, as in many other cities outside the South, liberal welfare benefits make it possible for a great many people to stay out of the labor market if they don't like the work and wages available. Stricter administration of welfare, currently being attempted in a number of states, may remove some cheaters and induce some other recipients to work. Under a 1971 provision of federal law, welfare mothers with no preschool children are required to register for work. But it would be unrealistic to expect a tightening effective enough to make any large number of welfare recipients take menial jobs.

12   A number of factors besides increasingly generous welfare have been eroding the supply of people available for menial work. Perhaps the leading expert on this subject is economist Harold Wool of the National Planning Association. Wool points out that during the Sixties society's efforts to keep young people in school reduced the number of dropouts entering the labor force. At the same time, he says, the U.S. drew down much of its remaining "reserve" of rural labor migrating to cities.

13   Most important of all, minority groups, especially blacks, began pushing in earnest toward equality in employment. According to Wool's reckoning, black young men with at least one year of college (but not teen-agers or young women) have actually achieved occupational parity with their white counterparts. This remarkable social achievement has been too little noticed.

14   Today a great many young black people refuse to take jobs they consider demeaning. Wool observes that while a decade ago 20 percent of the

black young women who had graduated from high school worked as domestics, only 3 percent were settling for that kind of work in 1970. "The service-type job," he says, "has become anathema to many blacks, even on a temporary basis." This helps explain why some service jobs are hard to fill even in cities where unemployment among young black people runs at dismayingly high rates.

15   It seems clear, then, that in years ahead the traditional supply of menial workers will not meet the demand. Some work will go undone. Many prosperous families whose counterparts even a decade ago would have employed household help now get along without any. Corners are clipped in services. Some restaurants, for example, have reduced the number of items on their menus, which among other things trims the customer's decision-making time and enables the waitress to move along faster.

16   But a lot of menial work will have to be done, one way or another. Society will have to respond to the tightening of the labor supply by improving pay and working conditions. Right now there are many places where the federal minimum wage of $1.60 an hour cannot buy work. In northern cities, even members of the so-called "secondary labor force"—women and young people whose pay supplements a family's principal source of income—are usually not willing to work for $1.60. For those groups, $2 to $2.50 is the real market "minimum" needed to balance supply and demand.

17   It may be a portent of things to come that New York City now pays its unionized sanitation men $12,886 a year (plus an ultraliberal pension). Hardly anybody ever quits, and thousands of men are on a waiting list for future job openings. At Chrysler Corp., unskilled "material handlers," whose job includes pushing carts around the plant floor by hand, get $4.90 an hour, which draws plenty of young married men, both white and black.

18   At Boston's Massachusetts General Hospital, the minimum starting pay for "dietary service aides" and "building service aides" is $2.78, more than local hotels pay busboys and chambermaids. But even so, few native Bostonians, black or white, are entering such jobs these days. Most of the hospital's recent hires for entry-level jobs are immigrants from Jamaica and other Caribbean Islands, or recent black arrivals from the rural South.

19   Higher pay, if it's high enough, clearly helps improve the status of menial work. Another way to improve its status is to raise the quality and complexity of the work itself. Some of the credit for a fairly low turnover rate at Massachusetts General Hospital goes to a training program begun in 1968 for those "building service aides," who previously had gone by the relatively servile titles of "maid" and "houseman."

20   The one-month program, which involves eighty hours in a classroom and a loose-leaf manual resembling one used by higher-skilled workers at the hospital, is not mere industrial-relations gimmickry. "Janitorial work in a hospital is different than in an office building," says Ruth MacRobert, the hospital's personnel director. "Here they need to learn aseptic techniques, and the fact that they can't use slippery compounds that might cause a

patient to trip and fall. If there's a spill, they can't leave broken glass lying around. It's a lot different than swabbing down a deserted office. Who cares if the John Hancock Building is wet and slippery after hours?"

21 A pleasanter work climate can also help make low-status work less lowly. Lack of amenity on the job is particularly noticeable in the clangorous kitchens where some of the country's 2,860,000 food service workers earn their living. Jan Lovell, president of the Dallas Restaurant Association, believes his industry is improving the work atmosphere but will have to do more in order to survive. In the most menial jobs, he says, "we used to have a tradition of taking the dregs of society off the street and working them twelve hours a day." This, he says, was bad for management as well as the worker.

22 "A few years ago it wasn't unusual for a restaurant to buy a $12,000 dishwashing machine and then hire two drunks or wetbacks at $75 a week who might forget to turn the water on. Today you pay one guy $150 a week who does the work of two. But maybe we also need to put in a radio and a rug on the floor. The restaurant business has been hot, dirty, and sweaty. Who needs it?"

23 Still another strategy is to make menial jobs a stepping-stone to something better. Texas Instruments, for example, offers a prospect of advancement to anyone who signs on to push a broom. Six years ago, in an effort to get better-quality work (and save money too), T.I. terminated contracts with outside cleaning firms and created a staff of its own to clean its factories and offices in the Dallas area. As in so many menial occupations, the staff has a nucleus of mature people who never aimed much higher in life, a majority of them black men in their fifties and sixties who in one supervisor's words are "a vanishing breed."

24 To lure younger replacements, the company offers a starting wage of $2.43 an hour, exactly the same as in production, and allows anyone to seek a transfer after six months. And like other T.I. employees, the sweepers are entitled to an exceptional fringe benefit: 90 percent of the cost of part-time education.

25 In a way, though, "promotability" makes it even harder to maintain a staff. Over the course of a year about 40 percent of T.I.'s "cleaning service attendants" move on to other jobs within the company, in addition to the 36 percent who quit or retire. One recently arrived janitor who is already looking around is Willie Gibson, a soft-spoken, twenty-year-old high-school graduate. Willie has been talking to "the head man in the machine shop" about the possibilities of a transfer. "There ain't nothing wrong with cleaning," he says. "It's got to be done. But me, I feel I can do better."

26 Texas Instruments is forced to search ceaselessly for replacements, who these days include Mexican-Americans and a few whites as well as blacks. Recruiting methods have included the announcement of janitorial vacancies from the pulpit of a black church.

27 Until the early 1920's, immigration provided an abundant supply of menial workers. And recent years have seen something of a resurgence.

Legal immigration has grown to 400,000 a year and now accounts for a fifth of the country's population growth. While many of the newcomers are professionals from the Philippines and India, the ranks also include a great many unskilled men and women from Mexico, the West Indies, and South America.

28   In addition, it is estimated that between one million and two million illegal aliens are at large in the U.S., mostly employed in low-status jobs. And the number of illegal aliens, whatever it may be, is undoubtedly growing. "Suddenly, in the last few months, there have been more of the illegals," says an official of the Texas Employment Commission in Dallas. The hiring of illegal immigrants is against the law in Texas, and the federal Immigration and Naturalization Service periodically rounds some of them up and deports them. But the very low unemployment rate in Dallas, the official says, acts as a magnet pulling in the illegals, who work in small enterprises that are not scrupulous about observing the law.

29   In northern cities, illegal immigration began to increase during the late 1960's. New York City alone may have as many as 250,000 illegals, including Chinese and Greeks as well as Haitians, Dominicans, and other Latin Americans. Such people can be an employer's dream. Often they have no welfare or unemployment compensation to fall back on, since applying for such assistance could reveal their existence to the authorities. In an era of liberal income-maintenance programs for the native population, says New York State Industrial Commissioner Louis Levine, such people "have a total incentive to work."

30   To rely on increasing numbers of immigrants to perform menial jobs, however, is to put off true long-range solutions to the problem. Sooner or later, every mature nation intent upon keeping its cultural identity will have to figure out a way to get most of the work done with its own native-born.

31   The U.S. cannot, and should not, close the door to all immigration, but a crackdown on illegal immigrants seems overdue. In addition to penalties against employers who hire illegal immigrants, an effective crackdown might require some device such as identity cards for all citizens. While repugnant to many Americans, such controls have long been a fact of life in France.

32   The U.S. is in a better position than most countries to move toward a state of "self-sufficiency in dirty work." Americans are generally free of Europe's ingrained class consciousness, and under certain conditions are rather flexible about the jobs they will take. And in recent years, in fact, white Americans have been moving into low-status jobs as black Americans move out. Most of these native-born recruits to menial work are women or young people.

33   In view of all the attention given to the women's liberation movement in recent years, it may seem paradoxical that many women have been moving into the lower end of the occupational scale. But there is not really any paradox. The desire of *some* women to pursue careers in managerial

and professional fields should certainly not preclude employment of a different kind of woman in a different kind of situation—the woman who is not a breadwinner and does not want a career, but who does want the freedom to divide her life between housekeeping and periods of work that entail no encumbering commitments between employer and employee.

34   A lot of these women are in jobs that are fairly pleasant, and whose "menialness" has more to do with society's prevailing view than with the nature of the work itself. Some restaurant work falls into this category. That is the opinion, for example, of Peggy Easter, a middle-aged white woman who waits on tables at Jan's Restaurant, a moderate-priced but clean and well-run establishment in a Dallas suburb. "Some people look down on this kind of work," she says. "But there's an art to this, and I like the hectic, fast pace because I have lots of nervous energy."

35   Like many waiters and waitresses, Mrs. Easter works only part time, coming in for three and a half hours each day during lunchtime. Her only child is married and her husband works full time as a diesel mechanic. With growing numbers of married women wanting to get out of the house, it is reasonable to expect that more Peggy Easters will turn up in the years ahead.

36   Young white people have moved into low-status jobs in even greater numbers than women. In 1960, according to census data, only 8 percent of the country's janitors were young whites under twenty-five. By 1970 that figure had jumped to 22 percent. Some of the movement of white young men *down* the occupational status scale (which partly accounts for that "parity" between blacks and whites who went to college) is a result of the postwar baby boom. Many of the young janitors, kitchen workers, and construction laborers are part-time workers from the ballooning population of high-school and college students. Others are full-time employees who, meeting heavy competition for jobs from their numerous contemporaries, have taken menial jobs until they can find something better. Another factor here is that many young whites live in the suburbs, where fast-food and other service jobs have grown more rapidly than in the cities.

37   Because the baby boom began waning in the late 1950's, the bulge in the number of employable young people will begin to recede during the middle and late 1970's. During the current decade as a whole, the sixteen to twenty-four age group will increase by 16 percent—somewhat less than the entire labor force, and far less than the phenomenal 48 percent growth during the Sixties.

38   To some extent, however, this demographic slowdown could be offset by a reduction in school hours, particularly in the high-school years. A growing number of educators and sociologists favor more part-time exposure of teen-agers to the working world, where they can benefit by rubbing shoulders with adults. One principal at a high school in the Northeast confided not long ago that all the basic material in his three-year curriculum, including the courses necessary for entering college, could be given in half the time. Not many principals, perhaps, would go that far, but cer-

tainly high-school education is now a very inefficient process. Any reduction in classroom time, of course, would make more teen-agers available for work, and much of that would be work generally considered menial.

39   In any event, it seems reasonable to expect that young people will be taking on more of those dirty jobs. According to a well-entrenched American tradition, almost unthinkable in much of Europe, it is healthy for sons and daughters of the middle class to wait on tables, scrub pots, and even clean toilets as part of their "rites of initiation" into the world of work. Late in the nineteenth century, the American author Edward Bellamy, in the Utopian novel *Looking Backward,* foresaw a day when all the onerous tasks of society would be performed by young people during a three-year period of obligatory service.

40   A formal period of "national youth service," a proposal that has been revived in recent years, runs against the American grain. But less extreme policies to encourage the employment of more young people would be a step in the right direction. Lots of young people might welcome earlier introduction to the world of work, especially high-school students, who these days seem increasingly inclined to work anyway.

41   Charles Muer, who operates a chain of restaurants headquartered in Detroit, employs young part-time workers extensively and considers it entirely feasible that they could take over most of the kitchen work. "You might have to pay them more," he says, "but productivity would be high. Kids are strong and enthusiastic, and dirty work can be fun, especially if you enjoy your co-workers and the management is nice."

42   Others are skeptical. "You've got to screen young people," says a hospital administrator, "and you can't leave them off by themselves where they'll goof off." Some tasks cannot and should not be performed by the young, particularly those involving nighttime shifts or long commuting distances. And some parents, of course, would object to their children's taking jobs they consider demeaning. John R. Coleman, the president of Haverford College whose experiences last year as an incognito ditchdigger and trash collector are described in his book *Time Out,* advises many of his students to get a taste of menial work. The parents most likely to be upset by such an idea, Coleman says, are "people unsure of their own status."

43   There's another and perhaps more formidable impediment. Until now the large number of young people bumping from one job to another as they slowly settle into careers has provided much of the labor pool for temporary dead-end work. (See "A Better Way to Deal With Unemployment," *Fortune,* June, 1973.) But some of the desirable education reforms now being tested are designed to enable high-school graduates to jump right into jobs with career ladders. If "career education" or something like it becomes widespread, it may become necessary to get that menial work out of students *before* they graduate. That would entail new social arrangements of some kind.

44   In an ideal world, all menial work would be a passing thing, whether for adults seeking a temporary change from their normal routine or for

young people who can count on better jobs later on. It won't turn out quite that way, of course. Some people, because of limited ability or sheer inclination, will mop floors or wait on tables throughout their working lives. If recent trends continue, however, their pay will rise and with it their self-esteem—and, of course, the costs of their labor, at a time when lots of other things are also getting costlier.

45   An indication of the direction things will move in can be seen in the way some airlines get their planes cleaned up between runs. The American Airlines system, for example, embodies nearly all of the features that society will probably have to incorporate into its low-status jobs. At New York's LaGuardia Airport a force of 185 "cabin service clerks" (an old designation rather than a recent euphemism) cleans floors, scrubs lavatories, and empties the ashtrays into which airline passengers grind their cigarettes. The men go about their work briskly, with no indication that they consider it demeaning. Two-thirds of them are white, the rest black and Puerto Rican. Their pay starts at $4.57 an hour, with a maximum of $5.15.

46   The job is not a dead end. Some recent hires are college graduates who, in the words of H. Lee Nichols, the staff's black manager, "get a foot in the door with an airline by taking a job like this." Most of these workers move on, replaced by a steady supply of new men attracted by the pay and the prospects for advancement. After all, Nichols says, "five years of cleaning ashtrays, if you have any drive, can get to you."

---

in pro football, they play best who play what they are

ARNOLD J. MANDELL

Football fans will agree that in recent years pro football has become increasingly mythologized. In this essay, it is psychoanalyzed. Mandell, a psychiatrist, tells us that personality traits are a sure index to playing positions: offensive players are orderly and conservative—establishment types; defensive players are sloppy and rebellious—anti-establishment types. Wide receivers are found to be vain, centers loquacious, defensive backs inhibited and possibly suicidal. All this analysis is delivered in proper psychiatric terminology.

Does Mandell's evidence adequately support his thesis? Or is his thesis perhaps not meant for serious consideration? How are we to take such claims as "my mother is an offensive lineman" (paragraph 31)?

1   **t**wo years ago Harland Svare, then head coach of the San Diego Chargers, asked me to lunch to talk about football. I was then, as I am now, chairman of the Department of Psychiatry at the University of California, San Diego. I had never paid much attention to football. During my five years of basic medical training, when we lived in the shadow of New Orleans's Sugar Bowl, I didn't attend a single game. I had been in San Diego as many years, and I still wasn't paying attention to football. The Chargers were a losing team, and Coach Svare, an imaginative man, wondered if my training might equip me to notice things about the attitudes and the behavior of his players that could help give the team what is often called "the winning edge."

2   Our lunch lasted three hours, and the result was that the Chargers retained me as a sort of psychiatrist-in-residence—the first, I believe, for a National Football League team. At Svare's invitation I began to hang around the team. I joined the members of the Charger squad in the locker room, at team lectures, at practice, on the plane to and from away games, and on the sidelines during the games. In all, I conducted over 200 hours of individual interviews with them. My function was to provide the coaches with a clearer understanding of the players and their positions and, more practically, to make actual personnel comments and recommendations.

3   When I first sat on the bench, I realized I was hearing the sounds of a Stone Age battleground. You can't pick them up on television or from a seat in the stadium. But on the bench you hear grunts, groans, hits—mankind's most fundamental sounds. I quickly learned what many Sunday widows already realized—that football is not a game but a religion, a metaphysical island of fundamental truth in a highly verbal, disguised society, a throwback of 30,000 generations of anthropological time.

4   When I was first around the team, the players thought I was spooky because I just stood there and watched. It was to take me more than a year to break down barriers and build trust between the players and me. But after only a few weeks, I rushed to Coach Svare with my first systematic insight. "Harland," I said, "I think I can tell whether a player is on offense or defense just by looking at his locker. The offensive players keep their lockers clean and orderly, but the lockers of the defensive men are a mess. In fact, the better the defensive player, the bigger the mess."

5   As I pored over scouting reports and interviewed players and coaches from numerous NFL teams, it became clear that offensive football players like structure and discipline. They want to maintain the status quo. They tend to be conservative as people, and as football players they take comfort in repetitive practice of well-planned and well-executed plays. The defensive players, just as clearly, can't stand structure; their attitudes, their be-

havior, and their lifestyles bear this out. They operate as though they've been put out of the tribe and are trying to show people that tribal structure is worthless anyway. Ostracism does not bother them; it serves as a source of fuel for their destructive energies. Rules or regulations put forward by anybody, anyplace, are to be challenged. Coaches find defensive players notably more difficult to control than their offensive teammates.

6   Offensive and defensive football players, I noticed, often had little or nothing to do with one another. There was one exception on the Chargers. Walt Sweeney, an all-pro offensive guard, had the personality of a defensive player, and his friends were all on the defensive team. (In fact, Sweeney wasn't that much of an exception. The Chargers drafted him to be a linebacker, and that was the position he himself preferred.)

7   When I mentioned my new "rule," Svare, a former linebacker, responded, "Sure, I never put it in words, but I'm basically a defensive player, and I find myself liking defensive players more than offensive players as people. I have very little patience with the rituals and repetition involved in the offense. We just don't look at the world the same way."

8   So I found that, despite the nomenclature, the offensive squad is made up of defenders of structure and the defensive squad is garrisoned with attack troops. I began to differentiate the personality profiles of these men independently of any prior knowledge about the specific requirements of their individual positions. Before long a personality classification in relation to position began to emerge. The consistency of the patterns seems explainable on the basis of the selection that occurs before any professional football player gains a regular starting position in the NFL.

9   Every year several thousand college football players are eligible; not more than 600 are seriously considered, and of those, 50 to 100 make it to the NFL. The selection goes on year after year. A player maintains his position by winning individual battles week after week on the field, where his performance is witnessed, filmed, and "graded." The crop of players is weeded systematically. The athletic difference between those who remain and those who are dropped is amazingly small. When it comes to making it in the NFL, practically every owner or coach with whom I've talked says, reverently and resignedly, "The game is in the mind." In addition to athletic ability, motivation, and commitment, the player needs a personality that meets the requirements of his position. This Darwinian process leaves each participant as an island of psychobiological organization in a circumstance that tests physical, psychological, intellectual, and spiritual strength—man-on-man—and in which psychological pressure from peers is even more potent a motivation than the challenge from the enemy. A suitable personality becomes the most significant and necessary component of survival. Making a proper match between player and position, then, is necessary for personal happiness, because players working in the wrong position are uneasy and attempt to correct for their uneasiness. Or, as aggressive and territorial individuals are very prone to do, they become depressed, turning their aggression inward. Like the rest of us, they become demoralized and

lose effectiveness when they aren't in the right place to function at their best.

10   It is important to realize that professional football players are, to mint a term, "homoclites." That is, they are extremely normal people—stable and anxiety-free, accustomed to handling pressures and performing extraordinarily and quickly. Many of them are also paranoid, but my use of that term—and of others from psychology—does not imply pathology; it implies a personality trait within normal limits.

11   The men who fill particular positions on the offensive team can be described by clusters of personality traits. The offensive linemen in general (centers, guards, tackles, and, to an extent, tight ends) are ambitious, tenacious, precise, attentive to detail. They manifest a kind of toughness that I would call stubborn rather than explosive. They work hard. Their traits clearly suit them for their work. As blocking assignments become ever more intricate, the linemen must practice like a ballet corps to coordinate perfectly the necessary spatial and temporal movements of blocking patterns. They also have to stand firm and cool when an opposing defensive line rushes their passer, no matter what verbal or physical abuse is thrown at them; they must care only about protecting their quarterback, not about proving their masculinity in an explosive way. A sacrificial attitude toward the welfare of the team is integral to the offensive linemen.

12   Within the offensive line itself, the typical personalities of centers, guards, tackles, and tight ends are readily distinguishable. The center, who often has to call signals, is usually the brightest. His loquaciousness in relation to other members of the line reflects his leadership. The guard may be bright, and he is quicker than the center. He may also be more aggressive—in the violent, rather than the stubborn, sense—because on sweeps he may be called upon to block downfield. His assertiveness is more persistent; the center's is more volatile. The tackle is slower, more patient, and even more persistent than the guard. He is not called on to be as mobile as the guard, and he doesn't have to get the middle linebacker with an explosive block, as the center does. He maintains and sustains. Stubborn tenacity is prototypical of the offensive tackle; his loyalty and commitment to the welfare of the team know no match.

13   The wide receiver is a very special human being. He shares many features with actors and movie stars. He is narcissistic and vain, and basically a loner.

14   Whereas the offensive linemen may hang around together (the center is particularly gregarious), the wide receiver often lives alone, dates alone, and remains a bit of a mystery. He is tactful in interpersonal encounters but elusive and hard to locate as a person. Like the track star, the good wide receiver is disciplined because the precision required to run intricate pass patterns and hold onto passes while he is getting clobbered requires discipline. Yet the courage of the wide receiver is more brittle than that of the other offensive linemen. His elusiveness may move beyond unpredictability to treachery. Typically, the wide receiver doesn't mind getting

hurt on the body, but he doesn't like his face to be touched—he's afraid of disfigurement. Essential, brilliant, vain, and not too friendly, he's rarely a popular member of the team. Disaffinity may be particularly acute between wide receivers and linebackers.

15   I have found two kinds of running backs. One is like the wide receiver: tough, treacherous, quick, lonely, and perhaps even paranoid, like the much-traveled Duane Thomas, perhaps the most gifted runner of all time. That paranoia is adaptive for a man whom everybody on defense is out to get. His particular unpredictability makes him even more difficult than a wide receiver to locate as a person. He's never where you expect him to be. In his days with the Chargers, Thomas was as difficult to locate off the field as on; if you made a date with him, he was likely not to be there. He is a good example of how a really great football player's personality is welded to his job.

16   The other kind of offensive back—the Larry Csonka kind—runs straight ahead. He's honest, tough, strong, disciplined, and if his toughness is a touch brutal, he may be great. He's not as quick, and he might not be as treacherous or paranoid as the flanking back. He will work long and hard; he has some offensive tackle in him.

17   Back to the line, to the tight end. It's difficult to find an ideal tight end because the chores he is required to do are virtually incompatible and therefore demand incompatible personality traits. The tight end must block like an offensive lineman or a fullback yet catch passes like a wide receiver. Blocking well requires bodily sacrifice for the welfare of others and does not gratify vanity; so the tight end can't have *too* much wide receiver in him. He does well to replace that with a bit of the distrust found in the Duane Thomas-type running back.

18   The most difficult of the offensive players to categorize are the quarterbacks. I have studied the scouting reports of a number of quarterbacks and talked about them with scouts, teammates, reporters, owners, and coaches. Given the physical ability, passing talent, and intelligence, the major determinant of success as a quarterback appears to be self-confidence—a self-confidence that is more akin to super-arrogance. The physical threat to a quarterback passing from the "pocket" is intolerable. To stand there to the last millisecond, waiting for your receiver to reach the place the ball is supposed to go while you are being rushed by mammoth defensive linemen —that takes sheer courage. A single mistake might negate all the efforts and sacrifices of your teammates—as well as lay you open to a fearful pounding.

19   To stand that kind of responsibility requires poise beyond that possessed by most men. How is the poise of the successful type of quarterback achieved? From my observations, there appear to be at least two routes. One is that of the naturally arrogant man who does not feel bound by the rules governing other men. He makes his own. He exploits the environment in a tough, tricky way and with very little compunction. Such men have run their talents and capacities to incredible self-advantage with no appar-

ent anxiety or guilt. And they win football games—yea, even champion-ships. The Joe Namaths and the Sonny Jurgensens fit well into this category.

20   The other way to turn in that kind of performance under those battle conditions is with assurance from On High. The Cowboys' Roger Staubach and the peerless John Unitas, who has finished his outstanding career, are in this group. So is Fran Tarkenton, the Vikings' renowned scrambler. We might call them and their comrades the religious quarterbacks. They attend church regularly, are active in such organizations as the Fellowship of Christian Athletes, and have a truly evangelical mission that they carry forward with the calm certitude of the believer, the chosen one. (In my two seasons with the Chargers, I got a chance to see Unitas up close and was struck by his religious commitment, as well as by his humility. These qualities helped insulate him from what was obviously a particularly stress-ful situation: the struggle of a player of his stature and past achievements to remain a first-stringer.)

21   The believer-quarterbacks win championships, too. But any quarter-back who leads with kindness and concern for others, who feels anxious about his responsibility to the 47 other men on the team and guilty over the outcome of his own actions, may collapse at critical moments—at the climax of a game or as his team moves closer to the playoffs. Students of the game point to John Hadl, the Rams' all-pro quarterback, whose pass-completion percentages dropped off drastically in the critical final games of last season.

22   The increasing use of computers to analyze the plays called by indi-vidual quarterbacks in various situations may change the personality re-quirements of successful quarterbacking. Except for audible signals (which can be employed in a significant percentage of the plays), computer-versus-computer may eventually lead to all plays being called from the bench. The defensive team may be able to guess what the opposing quarterback is going to do before he himself knows it—by a computer calculation of what he has done 77 percent of the time on "third and long" early in the fourth quarter when his team is behind by seven points.

23   Will this usurpation change the need for super-arrogance in quarter-backs? Maybe the super-arrogant will not obey readily. Many disciplined college quarterbacks who obeyed readily have not been able to make it in pro football; their opportunities may increase when plays are called from the bench.

24   The defensive team members are the renegades. They attack structure, and they feel that little is to be gained by identification with the establish-ment. They are basically angry and rebellious, primed to explode. The de-gree of inhibition controlling the trigger varies with the distance from the line of scrimmage. The defensive linemen, in contrast to offensive linemen, are restless, peevish, irritable, impatient, intolerant of detail, and barely under control. Usually, it is the defensive players (especially the linemen) who have committed the impulsive, flamboyant acts that make newspaper headlines. The defensive linemen have the least-well-organized inhibitory

systems. They are wild and free of conflict on the attack. The tackles may be reserved in some ways, but they, too, relish the hostilities. I remember one defensive tackle, a wonderful human being with his wife and family and friends, telling me gleefully in the heat of a game, "Look at that [a rookie quarterback entering the game for the opposing team]. It's like letting me into a candy store!"

25   Defensive ends have even more spleen, and they are quicker. They display swagger and showmanship. Defensive end Deacon Jones, the former Ram superstar now with the Chargers, demonstrated at least the spleen at last year's training camp. He parked his car in the same no-parking zone for 40 consecutive days, even though he got a ticket—and paid the fine— each day. The defensive lineman takes great joy in his unbridled assault on organization. Guilt or depression are not normally in his repertoire, although sometimes, as during the Monday blues, one can see vague hints. His temper, brutality, bluntness, and sarcastic sense of humor predict his success.

26   Linebackers experience more conflict about the aggression they manifest and by the same token achieve more precision of time and place in their attack. The linebacker in particular struggles with this balance of aggression and inhibition. Often he achieves a public image as a solid citizen; yet simultaneously he's a killer. When I asked a number of NFL scouts whom they would send behind the lines in wartime to assassinate an important enemy, they said a linebacker: his cleverness and air of legitimacy would get him into the country and let him pass as a good citizen, and his brutality would let him kill when the time came. The linebacker pays heavily for his control. Keeping so much hostility on short rein occasionally forces the aggression inward, and the linebacker typically has periods of depression. He needs a seventh sense and special visual capacities to diagnose plays and to go where he is needed. The defensive linemen either stay or charge, but the linebackers may need to stay, charge, or go back.

27   In linebackers I found two kinds of intelligence. Some have the capacity to memorize a sequence of rules of behavior for themselves. Following certain keys—movements by opposing centers, guards, or fullbacks—they behave according to that set of rules. Other linebackers achieve the same effectiveness without knowing the rules very well. They actually visualize the action of the entire field and have the capacity to follow the developing patterns of movement. These men often make brilliant plays; but, as in the case of all positions, if the opposing team knows their habits well, they can be badly fooled. The linebacker is a fascinating combination of control, brutality, and internal conflict. He does not lack vanity, but unlike the wide receiver, whose witnesses are his parents or the fans, the linebacker evaluates his own performance. He wants to look good to himself. When he fails, he can almost destroy himself in depression.

28   In the defensive backfield the aggression gets buried under more and more inhibition and discipline. These men are like long-distance runners:

they are loners, but they are nowhere near as hungry for glory as are the wide receivers. In place of the vanity and fantasies of the wide receivers, the defensive backs experience depression and rage. They have traits that can be found in offensive linemen, wide receivers, and linebackers. They are tenacious. They must learn zone and man-on-man pass-defense patterns that require incredible self-discipline in the furor of battle. They must not be led by their natural inclination, which is to follow receivers out of their zone before the quarterback releases the ball on a pass play. They must execute patterns precisely. To counter running plays, however, they must move up fast and, though lighter and weaker than the running backs they are trying to stop, hit very hard. So they need controlled and timed brutality and anger.

29   In my research team's recent study of more than 600 potential NFL draft choices, six men were found to be almost suicidally depressed; all of them were defensive backs. The depression of a corner back who has been "beaten" on a pass play may last for days, though the great ones shake it somehow. The depression resulting from the inhibition of so much aggression can put such men in constant danger of self-destruction.

30   Professional football, because there are objective criteria for performance, provides a model situation in which to observe an ultimate test of function. Given the same amount of athletic ability, why do some men fail and others succeed? Inevitably it is because the personality orientations of the latter better fit the tasks. No amount of coaching seems to alter these basic traits. Pragmatically, the NFL system quickly separates the misfits—even the athletically competent ones—from the team. My experiences with the men who play NFL football renewed my conviction that the psychobiological organization of personality, when it coincides with the appropriate role, is perhaps the most significant single determinant of personal success and happiness in life. De Gaulle was obviously a quarterback. Woody Allen is a defensive back. According to a recent profile in *The New Yorker,* Allen lives to "endlessly fend off guilt" with his continuous commitment to effort and performance. There is little or none of the vanity of the wide receiver in Woody Allen. Former President Nixon's stubbornly persistent and tenacious (not brilliant or explosive) management of his crises reminds me of the instincts of an offensive lineman. His attempts to be blunt, quick, and clever would have suited him to be an offensive guard.

31   My mother is an offensive lineman, a center-guard; my father, a classical wide receiver. My wife is a gifted center-guard. My medical school dean, John Moxely III, is a linebacker; my university chancellor, William McElroy, is a defensive personality, too, perhaps a linebacker. President Ford is a natural offensive lineman, which is in fact what he was at the University of Michigan. Truman Capote is a wide receiver. Kate Smith is a fullback, in more than size. Leonard Bernstein is a cross between a quarterback and a wide receiver.

32   I am often asked what I accomplished for the Chargers. The answer has to be: very little. The team's dismal record over the past two years—6

victories in 28 games—indicates that. So does my own professional observation. When attack troops hit the beach of the enemy's territory, some may benefit from benedictory reassurance, others from biochemical madness, few if any from a reminder that their current fear is reminiscent of the "castration anxiety" of their early childhood. Psychiatry and pro football, I conclude, probably don't mix. Or if they do, the blend is best left to the brewmaster, the head coach. The shrinks should stay with the rest of the armchair experts—in front of their television sets.

the macbeth murder mystery

JAMES THURBER

Thurber's thesis (unstated) is that different people, looking at precisely the same body of evidence, will come up with different conclusions. As Father Brown put it (p. 169), "Ten false philosophies will fit the universe." Thurber's evidence is a personal-experience narrative about a murder-mystery fan who thinks that everyone has missed the clues in Shakespeare's play *Macbeth*.

What assumptions does the "murder specialist" bring to bear in forming the theory that it wasn't Macbeth who killed the old king?

1 "**I**t was a stupid mistake to make," said the American woman I had met at my hotel in the English lake country, "but it was on the counter with the other Penguin books—the little sixpenny ones, you know, with the paper covers—and I supposed of course it was a detective story. All the others were detective stories. I'd read all the others, so I bought this one without really looking at it carefully. You can imagine how mad I was when I found it was Shakespeare." I murmured something sympathetically. "I don't see why the Penguin-books people had to get out Shakespeare plays in the same size and everything as the detective stories," went on my companion. "I think they have different-colored jackets," I said. "Well, I didn't notice that," she said. "Anyway, I got real comfy in bed that night and all ready to read a good mystery story and here I had 'The Tragedy of Macbeth'—a book for high-school students. Like 'Ivanhoe.' " "Or 'Lorna Doone,' " I said. "Exactly," said the American lady. "And I was

Source. Copyright © 1942 James Thurber. Copyright © 1970 Helen W. Thurber and Rosemary Thurber Sauers. From *My World—and Welcome to It,* published by Harcourt Brace Jovanovich. Originally printed in *The New Yorker.*

just crazy for a good Agatha Christie, or something. Hercule Poirot is my favorite detective." "Is he the rabbity one?" I asked. "Oh, no," said my crime-fiction expert. "He's the Belgian one. You're thinking of Mr. Pinkerton, the one that helps Inspector Bull. He's good, too."

2   Over her second cup of tea my companion began to tell the plot of a detective story that had fooled her completely—it seems it was the old family doctor all the time. But I cut in on her. "Tell me," I said. "Did you read 'Macbeth'?" "I *had* to read it," she said. "There wasn't a scrap of anything else to read in the whole room." "Did you like it?" I asked. "No, I did not," she said, decisively. "In the first place, I don't think for a moment that Macbeth did it." I looked at her blankly. "Did what?" I asked. "I don't think for a moment that he killed the King," she said. "I don't think the Macbeth woman was mixed up in it, either. You suspect them the most, of course, but those are the ones that are never guilty—or shouldn't be, anyway." "I'm afraid," I began, "that I—" "But don't you see?" said the American lady. "It would spoil everything if you could figure out right away who did it. Shakespeare was too smart for that. I've read that people never *have* figured out 'Hamlet,' so it isn't likely Shakespeare would have made 'Macbeth' as simple as it seems." I thought this over while I filled my pipe. "Who do you suspect?" I asked, suddenly. "Macduff," she said, promptly. "Good God!" I whispered, softly.

3   "Oh Macduff did it, all right," said the murder specialist. "Hercule Poirot would have got him easily." "How did you figure it out?" I demanded. "Well," she said, "I didn't right away. At first I suspected Banquo. And then, of course, he was the second person killed. That was good right in there, that part. The person you suspect of the first murder should always be the second victim." "Is that so?" I murmured. "Oh, yes," said my informant. "They have to keep surprising you. Well, after the second murder I didn't know *who* the killer was for a while." "How about Malcolm and Donalbain, the King's sons?" I asked. "As I remember it, they fled right after the first murder. That looks suspicious." "Too suspicious," said the American lady. "Much too suspicious. When they flee, they're never guilty. You can count on that." "I believe," I said, "I'll have a brandy," and I summoned the waiter. My companion leaned toward me, her eyes bright, her teacup quivering. "Do you know who discovered Duncan's body?" she demanded. I said I was sorry, but I had forgotten. "Macduff discovers it," she said, slipping into the historical present. "Then he comes running downstairs and shouts, 'Confusion has broke open the Lord's anointed temple' and 'Sacrilegious murder has made his masterpiece' and on and on like that." The good lady tapped me on the knee. "All that stuff was rehearsed," she said. "You wouldn't say a lot of stuff like that, offhand, would you—if you had found a body?" She fixed me with a glittering eye. "I—" I began. "You're right!" she said. "You wouldn't! Unless you had practiced it in advance. 'My God, there's a body in here!' is what an innocent man would say." She sat back with a confident glare.

4   I thought for a while. "But what do you make of the Third Murderer?"

I asked. "You know, the Third Murderer has puzzled 'Macbeth' scholars for three hundred years." "That's because they never thought of Macduff," said the American lady. "It was Macduff, I'm certain. You couldn't have one of the victims murdered by two ordinary thugs—the murderer always has to be somebody important." "But what about the banquet scene?" I asked, after a moment. "How do you account for Macbeth's guilty actions there, when Banquo's ghost came in and sat in his chair?" The lady leaned forward and tapped me on the knee again. "There wasn't any ghost," she said. "A big, strong man like that doesn't go around seeing ghosts—especially in a brightly lighted banquet hall with dozens of people around. Macbeth was *shielding somebody*!" "Who was he shielding?" I asked. "Mrs. Macbeth, of course," she said. "He thought she did it and he was going to take the rap himself. The husband always does that when the wife is suspected." "But what," I demanded, "about the sleepwalking scene, then?" "The same thing, only the other way around," said my companion. "That time *she* was shielding *him*. She wasn't asleep at all. Do you remember where it says, 'Enter Lady Macbeth with a taper'?" "Yes," I said. "Well, people who walk in their sleep *never carry lights*!" said my fellow-traveler. "They have a second sight. Did you ever hear of a sleepwalker carrying a light?" "No," I said, "I never did." "Well, then, she wasn't asleep. She was acting guilty to shield Macbeth." "I think," I said, "I'll have another brandy," and I called the waiter. When he brought it, I drank it rapidly and rose to go. "I believe," I said, "that you have got hold of something. Would you lend me that 'Macbeth'? I'd like to look it over tonight. I don't feel, somehow, as if I'd ever really read it." "I'll get it for you," she said. "But you'll find that I am right."

5 I read the play over carefully that night, and the next morning, after breakfast, I sought out the American woman. She was on the putting green, and I came up behind her silently and took her arm. She gave an exclamation. "Could I see you alone?" I asked, in a low voice. She nodded cautiously and followed me to a secluded spot. "You've found out something?" she breathed. "I've found out," I said, triumphantly, "the name of the murderer!" "You mean it wasn't Macduff?" she said. "Macduff is as innocent of those murders," I said, "as Macbeth and the Macbeth woman." I opened the copy of the play, which I had with me, and turned to Act II, Scene 2. "Here," I said, "you will see where Lady Macbeth says, 'I laid their daggers ready. He could not miss 'em. Had he not resembled my father as he slept, I had done it.' Do you see?" "No," said the American woman, bluntly, "I don't." "But it's simple!" I exclaimed. "I wonder I didn't see it years ago. The reason Duncan resembled Lady Macbeth's father as he slept is that *it actually was her father*!" "Good God!" breathed my companion, softly. "Lady Macbeth's father killed the King," I said, "and, hearing someone coming, thrust the body under the bed and crawled into the bed himself." "But," said the lady, "you can't have a murderer who only appears in the story once. You can't have that." "I know that," I said, and I turned to Act II, Scene 4. "It says here, 'Enter Ross with an

old Man.' Now, that old man is never identified and it is my contention he was old Mr. Macbeth, whose ambition it was to make his daughter Queen. There you have your motive." "But even then," cried the American lady, "he's still a minor character!" "Not," I said, gleefully, "when you realize that he was also *one of the weird sisters in disguise*!" "You mean one of the three witches?" "Precisely," I said. "Listen to this speech of the old man's. 'On Tuesday last, a falcon towering in her pride of place, was by a mousing owl hawk'd at and kill'd.' Who does that sound like?" "It sounds like the way the three witches talk," said my companion, reluctantly. "Precisely!" I said again. "Well," said the American woman, "maybe you're right, but—" "I'm sure I am," I said. "And do you know what I'm going to do now?" "No," she said. "What?" "Buy a copy of 'Hamlet,'" I said, "and solve *that*!" My companion's eye brightened. "Then," she said, "you don't think Hamlet did it?" "I am," I said, "absolutely positive he didn't." "But who," she demanded, "do you suspect?" I looked at her cryptically. "Everybody," I said, and disappeared into a small grove of trees as silently as I had come.

shakespeare in the bush
LAURA BOHANNAN

Bohannan's amusing account of her experiences in a West African community is an exercise in refutation. She once believed that "human nature is pretty much the same the whole world over" (paragraph 2); for example, anyone anywhere would get approximately the same meaning from Shakespeare's play *Hamlet*. But when she attempted to confirm this theory by discussing *Hamlet* with the elders of the Tiv tribe, she found that they interpreted the play very differently—although they too asserted that "people are the same everywhere" and that *Hamlet* has one universal meaning (paragraph 75). A thesis which had seemed valid as long as Bohannan was working within one culture turned out to be invalid when she gathered evidence from another culture (although the people there believed it also).

Bohannan's story also suggests that, while the universality of human nature cannot be substantiated in terms of a common understanding of *Hamlet,* perhaps it could be substantiated in terms of a common assumption that our own cultural values (whatever they happen to be) are the right ones. Perhaps what unites us all as human beings is, unfortunately, a spontaneous self-centeredness and ethnocentrism.

Source. From *Natural History* magazine. Copyright © 1966. Reprinted by permission of Laura Bohannan.

1 Just before I left Oxford for the Tiv in West Africa, conversation turned to the season at Stratford. "You Americans," said a friend, "often have difficulty with Shakespeare. He was, after all, a very English poet, and one can easily misinterpret the universal by misunderstanding the particular."

2 I protested that human nature is pretty much the same the whole world over; at least the general plot and motivation of the greater tragedies would always be clear—everywhere—although some details of custom might have to be explained and difficulties of translation might produce other slight changes. To end an argument we could not conclude, my friend gave me a copy of *Hamlet* to study in the African bush: it would, he hoped, lift my mind above its primitive surroundings, and possibly I might, by prolonged meditation, achieve the grace of correct interpretation.

3 It was my second field trip to that African tribe, and I thought myself ready to live in one of its remote sections—an area difficult to cross even on foot. I eventually settled on the hillock of a very knowledgeable old man, the head of a homestead of some hundred and forty people, all of whom were either his close relatives or their wives and children. Like the other elders of the vicinity, the old man spent most of his time performing ceremonies seldom seen these days in the more accessible parts of the tribe. I was delighted. Soon there would be three months of enforced isolation and leisure, between the harvest that takes place just before the rising of the swamps and the clearing of new farms when the water goes down. Then, I thought, they would have even more time to perform ceremonies and explain them to me.

4 I was quite mistaken. Most of the ceremonies demanded the presence of elders from several homesteads. As the swamps rose, the old men found it too difficult to walk from one homestead to the next, and the ceremonies gradually ceased. As the swamps rose even higher, all activities but one came to an end. The women brewed beer from maize and millet. Men, women, and children sat on their hillocks and drank it.

5 People began to drink at dawn. By midmorning the whole homestead was singing, dancing, and drumming. When it rained, people had to sit inside their huts: there they drank and sang or they drank and told stories. In any case, by noon or before, I either had to join the party or retire to my own hut and my books. "One does not discuss serious matters when there is beer. Come, drink with us." Since I lacked their capacity for the thick native beer, I spent more and more time with *Hamlet*. Before the end of the second month, grace descended on me. I was quite sure that *Hamlet* had only one possible interpretation, and that one universally obvious.

6 Early every morning, in the hope of having some serious talk before the beer party, I used to call on the old man at his reception hut—a circle of posts supporting a thatched roof above a low mud wall to keep out wind and rain. One day I crawled through the low doorway and found most of the men of the homestead sitting huddled in their ragged cloths on stools, low plank beds, and reclining chairs, warming themselves against the chill

of the rain around a smoky fire. In the center were three pots of beer. The party had started.

7   The old man greeted me cordially. "Sit down and drink." I accepted a large calabash full of beer, poured some into a small drinking gourd, and tossed it down. Then I poured some more into the same gourd for the man second in seniority to my host before I handed my calabash over to a young man for further distribution. Important people shouldn't ladle beer themselves.

8   "It is better like this," the old man said, looking at me approvingly and plucking at the thatch that had caught in my hair. "You should sit and drink with us more often. Your servants tell me that when you are not with us, you sit inside your hut looking at a paper."

9   The old man was acquainted with four kinds of "papers": tax receipts, bride price receipts, court fee receipts, and letters. The messenger who brought him letters from the chief used them mainly as a badge of office, for he always knew what was in them and told the old man. Personal letters for the few who had relatives in the government or mission stations were kept until someone went to a large market where there was a letter writer and reader. Since my arrival, letters were brought to me to be read. A few men also brought me bride price receipts, privately, with requests to change the figures to a higher sum. I found moral arguments were of no avail, since in-laws are fair game, and the technical hazards of forgery difficult to explain to an illiterate people. I did not wish them to think me silly enough to look at any such papers for days on end, and I hastily explained that my "paper" was one of the "things of long ago" of my country.

10   "Ah," said the old man. "Tell us."

11   I protested that I was not a storyteller. Storytelling is a skilled art among them; their standards are high, and the audiences critical—and vocal in their criticism. I protested in vain. This morning they wanted to hear a story while they drank. They threatened to tell me no more stories until I told them one of mine. Finally, the old man promised that no one would criticize my style "for we know you are struggling with our language." "But," put in one of the elders, "you must explain what we do not understand, as we do when we tell you our stories." Realizing that here was my chance to prove *Hamlet* universally intelligible, I agreed.

12   The old man handed me some more beer to help me on with my storytelling. Men filled their long wooden pipes and knocked coals from the fire to place in the pipe bowls; then, puffing contentedly, they sat back to listen. I began in the proper style, "Not yesterday, not yesterday, but long ago, a thing occurred. One night three men were keeping watch outside the homestead of the great chief, when suddenly they saw the former chief approach them."

13   "Why was he no longer their chief?"

14   "He was dead," I explained. "That is why they were troubled and afraid when they saw him."

15   "Impossible," began one of the elders, handing his pipe on to his neigh-

bor, who interrupted, "Of course it wasn't the dead chief. It was an omen sent by a witch. Go on."

16   Slightly shaken, I continued. "One of these three was a man who knew things"—the closest translation for scholar, but unfortunately it also meant witch. The second elder looked triumphantly at the first. "So he spoke to the dead chief saying, 'Tell us what we must do so you may rest in your grave,' but the dead chief did not answer. He vanished, and they could see him no more. Then the man who knew things—his name was Horatio—said this event was the affair of the dead chief's son, Hamlet."

17   There was a general shaking of heads round the circle. "Had the dead chief no living brothers? Or was this son the chief?"

18   "No," I replied. "That is, he had one living brother who became the chief when the elder brother died."

19   The old men muttered: such omens were matters for chiefs and elders, not for youngsters; no good could come of going behind a chief's back; clearly Horatio was not a man who knew things.

20   "Yes, he was," I insisted, shooing a chicken away from my beer. "In our country the son is next to the father. The dead chief's younger brother had become the great chief. He had also married his elder brother's widow only about a month after the funeral."

21   "He did well," the old man beamed and announced to the others, "I told you that if we knew more about Europeans, we would find they really were very like us. In our country also," he added to me, "the younger brother marries the elder brother's widow and becomes the father of his children. Now, if your uncle, who married your widowed mother, is your father's full brother, then he will be a real father to you. Did Hamlet's father and uncle have one mother?"

22   His question barely penetrated my mind; I was too upset and thrown too far off balance by having one of the most important elements of *Hamlet* knocked straight out of the picture. Rather uncertainly I said that I thought they had the same mother, but I wasn't sure—the story didn't say. The old man told me severely that these genealogical details made all the difference and that when I got home I must ask the elders about it. He shouted out the door to one of his younger wives to bring his goatskin bag.

23   Determined to save what I could of the mother motif, I took a deep breath and began again. "The son Hamlet was very sad because his mother had married again so quickly. There was no need for her to do so, and it is our custom for a widow not to go to her next husband until she has mourned for two years."

24   "Two years is too long," objected the wife, who had appeared with the old man's battered goatskin bag. "Who will hoe your farms for you while you have no husband?"

25   "Hamlet," I retorted without thinking, "was old enough to hoe his mother's farms himself. There was no need for her to remarry." No one looked convinced. I gave up. "His mother and the great chief told Hamlet not to be sad, for the great chief himself would be a father to Hamlet.

Furthermore, Hamlet would be the next chief: therefore he must stay to learn the things of a chief. Hamlet agreed to remain, and all the rest went off to drink beer."

26   While I paused, perplexed at how to render Hamlet's disgusted soliloquy to an audience convinced that Claudius and Gertrude had behaved in the best possible manner, one of the younger men asked me who had married the other wives of the dead chief.

27   "He had no other wives," I told him.

28   "But a chief must have many wives! How else can he brew beer and prepare food for all his guests?"

29   I said firmly that in our country even chiefs had only one wife, that they had servants to do their work, and that they paid them from tax money.

30   It was better, they returned, for a chief to have many wives and sons who would help him hoe his farms and feed his people; then everyone loved the chief who gave much and took nothing—taxes were a bad thing.

31   I agreed with the last comment, but for the rest fell back on their favorite way of fobbing off my questions: "That is the way it is done, so that is how we do it."

32   I decided to skip the soliloquy. Even if Claudius was here thought quite right to marry his brother's widow, there remained the poison motif, and I knew they would disapprove of fratricide. More hopefully I resumed, "That night Hamlet kept watch with the three who had seen his dead father. The dead chief again appeared, and although the others were afraid, Hamlet followed his dead father off to one side. When they were alone, Hamlet's dead father spoke."

33   "Omens can't talk!" The old man was emphatic.

34   "Hamlet's dead father wasn't an omen. Seeing him might have been an omen, but he was not." My audience looked as confused as I sounded. "It *was* Hamlet's dead father. It was a thing we call a 'ghost.'" I had to use the English word, for unlike many of the neighboring tribes, these people didn't believe in the survival after death of any individuating part of the personality.

35   "What is a 'ghost'? An omen?"

36   "No, a 'ghost' is someone who is dead but who walks around and can talk, and people can hear him and see him but not touch him."

37   They objected. "One can touch zombis."

38   "No, no! It was not a dead body the witches had animated to sacrifice and eat. No one else made Hamlet's dead father walk. He did it himself."

39   "Dead men can't walk," protested my audience as one man.

40   I was quite willing to compromise. "A 'ghost' is the dead man's shadow."

41   But again they objected. "Dead men cast no shadows."

42   "They do in my country," I snapped.

43   The old man quelled the babble of disbelief that arose immediately and told me with that insincere, but courteous, agreement one extends to the

fancies of the young, ignorant, and superstitious, "No doubt in your country the dead can also walk without being zombis." From the depths of his bag he produced a withered fragment of kola nut, bit off one end to show it wasn't poisoned, and handed me the rest as a peace offering.

44 "Anyhow," I resumed, "Hamlet's dead father said that his own brother, the one who became chief, had poisoned him. He wanted Hamlet to avenge him. Hamlet believed this in his heart, for he did not like his father's brother." I took another swallow of beer. "In the country of the great chief, living in the same homestead, for it was a very large one, was an important elder who was often with the chief to advise and help him. His name was Polonius. Hamlet was courting his daughter, but her father and her brother . . . [I cast hastily about for some tribal analogy] warned her not to let Hamlet visit her when she was alone on her farm, for he would be a great chief and so could not marry her."

45 "Why not?" asked the wife, who had settled down on the edge of the old man's chair. He frowned at her for asking stupid questions and growled, "They lived in the same homestead."

46 "That was not the reason," I informed them. "Polonius was a stranger who lived in the homestead because he helped the chief, not because he was a relative."

47 "Then why couldn't Hamlet marry her?"

48 "He could have," I explained, "but Polonius didn't think he would. After all, Hamlet was a man of great importance who ought to marry a chief's daughter, for in his country a man could have only one wife. Polonius was afraid that if Hamlet made love to his daughter, then no one else would give a high price for her."

49 "That might be true," remarked one of the shrewder elders, "but a chief's son would give his mistress's father enough presents and patronage to more than make up the difference. Polonius sounds like a fool to me."

50 "Many people think he was," I agreed. "Meanwhile Polonius sent his son Laertes off to Paris to learn the things of that country, for it was the homestead of a very great chief indeed. Because he was afraid that Laertes might waste a lot of money on beer and women and gambling, or get into trouble by fighting, he sent one of his servants to Paris secretly, to spy out what Laertes was doing. One day Hamlet came upon Polonius's daughter Ophelia. He behaved so oddly he frightened her. Indeed"—I was fumbling for words to express the dubious quality of Hamlet's madness—"the chief and many others had also noticed that when Hamlet talked one could understand the words but not what they meant. Many people thought that he had become mad." My audience suddenly became much more attentive. "The great chief wanted to know what was wrong with Hamlet, so he sent for two of Hamlet's age mates [school friends would have taken long explanation] to talk to Hamlet and find out what troubled his heart. Hamlet, seeing that they had been bribed by the chief to betray him, told them nothing. Polonius, however, insisted that Hamlet was mad because he had been forbidden to see Ophelia, whom he loved."

51   "Why," inquired a bewildered voice, "should anyone bewitch Hamlet on that account?"

52   "Bewitch him?"

53   "Yes, only witchcraft can make anyone mad, unless, of course, one sees the beings that lurk in the forest."

54   I stopped being a storyteller, took out my notebook and demanded to be told more about these two causes of madness. Even while they spoke and I jotted notes, I tried to calculate the effect of this new factor on the plot. Hamlet had not been exposed to the beings that lurk in the forests. Only his relatives in the male line could bewitch him. Barring relatives not mentioned by Shakespeare, it had to be Claudius who was attempting to harm him. And, of course, it was.

55   For the moment I staved off questions by saying that the great chief also refused to believe that Hamlet was mad for the love of Ophelia and nothing else. "He was sure that something much more important was troubling Hamlet's heart."

56   "Now Hamlet's age mates," I continued, "had brought with them a famous storyteller. Hamlet decided to have this man tell the chief and all his homestead a story about a man who had poisoned his brother because he desired his brother's wife and wished to be chief himself. Hamlet was sure the great chief could not hear the story without making a sign if he was indeed guilty, and then he would discover whether his dead father had told him the truth."

57   The old man interrupted, with deep cunning, "Why should a father lie to his son?" he asked.

58   I hedged: "Hamlet wasn't sure that it really was his dead father." It was impossible to say anything, in that language, about devil-inspired visions.

59   "You mean," he said, "it actually was an omen, and he knew witches sometimes send false ones. Hamlet was a fool not to go to one skilled in reading omens and divining the truth in the first place. A man-who-sees-the-truth could have told him how his father died, if he really had been poisoned, and if there was witchcraft in it; then Hamlet could have called the elders to settle the matter."

60   The shrewd elder ventured to disagree. "Because his father's brother was a great chief, one-who-sees-the-truth might therefore have been afraid to tell it. I think it was for that reason that a friend of Hamlet's father— a witch and an elder—sent an omen so his friend's son would know. Was the omen true?"

61   "Yes," I said, abandoning ghosts and the devil; a witch-sent omen it would have to be. "It was true, for when the storyteller was telling his tale before all the homestead, the great chief rose in fear. Afraid that Hamlet knew his secret he planned to have him killed."

62   The stage set of the next bit presented some difficulties of translation. I began cautiously. "The great chief told Hamlet's mother to find out from her son what he knew. But because a woman's children are always first in

her heart, he had the important elder Polonius hide behind a cloth that hung against the wall of Hamlet's mother's sleeping hut. Hamlet started to scold his mother for what she had done."

63 There was a shocked murmur from everyone. A man should never scold his mother.

64 "She called out in fear, and Polonius moved behind the cloth. Shouting, 'A rat!' Hamlet took his machete and slashed through the cloth." I paused for dramatic effect. "He had killed Polonius!"

65 The old men looked at each other in supreme disgust. "That Polonius truly was a fool and a man who knew nothing! What child would not know enough to shout, 'It's me!' " With a pang, I remembered that these people are ardent hunters, always armed with bow, arrow, and machete; at the first rustle in the grass an arrow is aimed and ready, and the hunter shouts "Game!" If no human voice answers immediately, the arrow speeds on its way. Like a good hunter Hamlet had shouted, "A rat!"

66 I rushed in to save Polonius's reputation. "Polonius did speak. Hamlet heard him. But he thought it was the chief and wished to kill him to avenge his father. He had meant to kill him earlier that evening. . . ." I broke down, unable to describe to these pagans, who had no belief in individual afterlife, the difference between dying at one's prayers and dying "unhousell'd, disappointed, unaneled."

67 This time I had shocked my audience seriously. "For a man to raise his hand against his father's brother and the one who has become his father—that is a terrible thing. The elders ought to let such a man be bewitched."

68 I nibbled at my kola nut in some perplexity, then pointed out that after all the man had killed Hamlet's father.

69 "No," pronounced the old man, speaking less to me than to the young men sitting behind the elders. "If your father's brother has killed your father, you must appeal to your father's age mates; *they* may avenge him. No man may use violence against his senior relatives." Another thought struck him. "But if his father's brother had indeed been wicked enough to bewitch Hamlet and make him mad that would be a good story indeed, for it would be his fault that Hamlet, being mad, no longer had any sense and thus was ready to kill his father's brother."

70 There was a murmur of applause. *Hamlet* was again a good story to them, but it no longer seemed quite the same story to me. As I thought over the coming complications of plot and motive, I lost courage and decided to skim over dangerous ground quickly.

71 "The great chief," I went on, "was not sorry that Hamlet had killed Polonius. It gave him a reason to send Hamlet away, with his two treacherous age mates, with letters to a chief of a far country, saying that Hamlet should be killed. But Hamlet changed the writing on their papers, so that the chief killed his age mates instead." I encountered a reproachful glare from one of the men whom I had told undetectable forgery was not merely immoral but beyond human skill. I looked the other way.

72   "Before Hamlet could return, Laertes came back for his father's funeral. The great chief told him Hamlet had killed Polonius. Laertes swore to kill Hamlet because of this, and because his sister Ophelia, hearing her father had been killed by the man she loved, went mad and drowned in the river."

73   "Have you already forgotten what we told you?" The old man was reproachful. "One cannot take vengeance on a madman; Hamlet killed Polonius in his madness. As for the girl, she not only went mad, she was drowned. Only witches can make people drown. Water itself can't hurt anything. It is merely something one drinks and bathes in."

74   I began to get cross. "If you don't like the story, I'll stop."

75   The old man made soothing noises and himself poured me some more beer. "You tell the story well, and we are listening. But it is clear that the elders of your country have never told you what the story really means. No, don't interrupt! We believe you when you say your marriage customs are different, or your clothes and weapons. But people are the same everywhere; therefore, there are always witches and it is we, the elders, who know how witches work. We told you it was the great chief who wished to kill Hamlet, and now your own words have proved us right. Who were Ophelia's male relatives?"

76   "There were only her father and her brother." Hamlet was clearly out of my hands.

77   "There must have been many more; this also you must ask of your elders when you get back to your country. From what you tell us, since Polonius was dead, it must have been Laertes who killed Ophelia, although I do not see the reason for it."

78   We had emptied one pot of beer, and the old men argued the point with slightly tipsy interest. Finally one of them demanded of me, "What did the servant of Polonius say on his return?"

79   With difficulty I recollected Reynaldo and his mission. "I don't think he did return before Polonius was killed."

80   "Listen," said the elder, "and I will tell you how it was and how your story will go, then you may tell me if I am right. Polonius knew his son would get into trouble, and so he did. He had many fines to pay for fighting, and debts from gambling. But he had only two ways of getting money quickly. One was to marry off his sister at once, but it is difficult to find a man who will marry a woman desired by the son of a chief. For if the chief's heir commits adultery with your wife, what can you do? Only a fool calls a case against a man who will someday be his judge. Therefore Laertes had to take the second way: he killed his sister by witchcraft, drowning her so he could secretly sell her body to the witches."

81   I raised an objection. "They found her body and buried it. Indeed Laertes jumped into the grave to see his sister once more—so, you see, the body was truly there. Hamlet, who had just come back, jumped in after him."

82   "What did I tell you?" The elder appealed to the others. "Laertes was

up to no good with his sister's body. Hamlet prevented him, because the chief's heir, like a chief, does not wish any other man to grow rich and powerful. Laertes would be angry, because he would have killed his sister without benefit to himself. In our country he would try to kill Hamlet for that reason. Is this not what happened?"

83   "More or less," I admitted. "When the great chief found Hamlet was still alive, he encouraged Laertes to try to kill Hamlet and arranged a fight with machetes between them. In the fight both the young men were wounded to death. Hamlet's mother drank the poisoned beer that the chief meant for Hamlet in case he won the fight. When he saw his mother die of poison, Hamlet, dying, managed to kill his father's brother with his machete."

84   "You see, I was right!" exclaimed the elder.

85   "That was a very good story," added the old man, "and you told it with very few mistakes. There was just one more error, at the very end. The poison Hamlet's mother drank was obviously meant for the survivor of the fight, whichever it was. If Laertes had won, the great chief would have poisoned him, for no one would know that he arranged Hamlet's death. Then, too, he need not fear Laertes' witchcraft; it takes a strong heart to kill one's only sister by witchcraft.

86   "Sometime," concluded the old man, gathering his ragged toga about him, "you must tell us some more stories of your country. We, who are elders, will instruct you in their true meaning, so that when you return to your own land your elders will see that you have not been sitting in the bush, but among those who know things and who have taught you wisdom."

eval uation

Evaluative writing intends to persuade us that *X*—whatever the subject may be—is good or bad, right or wrong, adequate or inadequate. When you say "that was a great game" or "chicken in pineapple sauce tastes lousy" or "cheap boots aren't really a good buy" or "there's nothing wrong with Harry," you are making an evaluation. When someone else puts a grade on a report you have written or says "sorry, you're not quite the right person for this job" or pays you $250 for one night's performance on the trombone, you are receiving an evaluation. We will be concerned here, naturally, with evaluations in the form of words on paper and with how you go about writing them.

One obligation of written evaluations is to clarify the meaning of such terms as "great" and "lousy" and "good" and "right" and "wrong." Two basic approaches are possible. The approach can be *utilitarian: X* is good, or not good, with reference to a job to be done. In this case, "good" and all other terms of approval mean "useful." Or the approach can be *moral: X* is good, or not good, with reference to ethical beliefs. In this case, "good" and all other terms of approval mean "inherently right." This distinction is important because the same thing can be good in one sense but not in the other. Machiavelli defends assassination and the breaking of promises as good for accomplishing certain political purposes, but most of us would regard these forms of behavior as bad.[1] Such conflicting evaluations of *X* can be reconciled if we agree on which basic approach to the meaning of "good" (or "bad") is more important to us. From a utilitarian viewpoint, assassination is good; from a moral viewpoint, it is bad. If we agree that morality is more important than expedience, we can conclude that assassination cannot be accepted as a means of accomplishing political ends.

There are more difficult instances. Abortion has been defended

---

[1] If a ruler wants to keep control of a newly conquered territory, Machiavelli advises, he should destroy the previous ruling family. And as for keeping one's word, Machiavelli explains that a ruler should honor his promises only as long as it is to his own advantage to do so. Niccolo Machiavelli, *The Prince* translated by N. H. Thomson, in *The Harvard Classics*, vol. 36 (New York: Collier, 1910), pp. 9, 60.

as "good" on practical, utilitarian grounds; it has also been condemned as "bad" on moral grounds. Similar conflicting evaluations have been made of the killing of animals (see Tennies, "In Defense of Deer Hunting and Killing," p. 404). It makes sense, from a practical viewpoint, to kill animals for people to eat, but is it morally right to do so? Which approach to the process of evaluation do you see as more important in such questions as these?

THE PROCESS OF EVALUATION

Whichever approach you take, the utilitarian or the moral, the logical process underlying evaluation is the same. You must first decide exactly what you are evaluating, and define it for your readers if necessary. This means limiting the topic to manageable proportions. You would not undertake to evaluate "the automobile" in a short essay, for example. But you might try evaluating standard-size cars manufactured by American companies between 1972 and 1975. (Or portable 19-inch black-and-white television sets, as in the *Consumer Reports* article, p. 318.) The first step in the process, then, is simply definition.

The next step will be the establishment of *criteria,* the standards against which X is to be judged good or bad or somewhere in between. The basic choice between the utilitarian and the moral approaches must now be made more precise. Let us assume that your approach to the subject of standard-size American cars manufactured between 1972 and 1975 will be the utilitarian one: are those cars good with reference to the job to be done? The inquiry is still inexact.

Choosing and Ranking the Criteria. There are many possible meanings of "good with reference to the job to be done." In evaluating the cars, that very general phrase suggests at least five different criteria. Are you trying to judge whether

1. the cars are inexpensive to operate and maintain;

2. the cars are reliable (do not have an excessive rate of mechanical failure);

3. the cars provide the passenger and luggage space needed by the average American family;

4. the cars are safe;

5. the cars are attractive to look at and comfortable to ride in; or what? In order for your evaluation to be responsible, you must know, and your reader must know, exactly what criteria you are applying.

If you decide to apply more than one criterion—to judge the cars, perhaps, in terms of expense, reliability, and safety—you will need to "rank the criteria," in other words to determine the order of priority among them. Is expense the most important factor, or is reliability, or is safety? Or are you interested in a concept of total performance, in which a high rating in one area could compensate for a low rating in another? When you are dealing with an evaluation that involves multiple X's (more than a dozen car models) and multiple criteria (expense, reliability, safety), thinking it through and writing it out may become quite complicated. If things get out of hand, you can reduce the scope of your inquiry. Perhaps the 1975 models alone will be enough to consider. You can also reduce the number of criteria. Perhaps it will be sufficient to rate the cars in terms of safety.

Whatever decisions you make about the scope of your X, and about the number and ranking of your criteria, should be evident to your readers also. Sometimes the criteria are obvious, in which case you don't need to state them. (Ossie Davis, p. 312, thinks of a "good" language as one that avoids racial prejudice, a "bad" language as one that involves it. These criteria are obvious from his attack on English for containing so many words that associate blackness with undesirable qualities.) But in case of doubt, write them out. If you have any suspicion that your readers will not be sure what criteria you are applying, tell them.

Making the Criteria Fair. It is pointless to apply a criterion that is unfair to whatever you are evaluating—a criterion intended for a different category of things or a criterion that unfairly emphasizes one part of the picture. It would be pointless to fault a standard-size passenger automobile for not being as speedy as a racing car, or for requiring more fuel than a subcompact. When Alice, on her way to Wonderland, complains that her older sister's book is useless because it has no pictures or conversations, she is applying criteria that are unfair because they do not fit the grown-up book that her sister is reading. (If it were a children's book, that would be a different story.) Similarly, to dismiss a film as "bad" because one bit part was inconsistently played, or to praise a dinner as "marvelous" because the olives were perfectly ripe, is unfair because a disproportionate emphasis is placed on one aspect of X. It's always possible to find one little thing to grumble at or glorify, but doing so proves only that you are being small.

Making the Criteria Precise. Let us assume that you have decided to evaluate cars only in terms of safety. That general criterion, which is certainly fair, now needs to be made more precise. What exactly does it mean to ask whether the cars are "safe"? Or what would it mean to ask whether they are "inexpensive"? Not much, because the terms are too vague. But you can assign to "safe" a maximum number of severe accidents sustained over a given period of time; you can assign to "inexpensive" a dollar value such as a maximum monthly cost for operation, maintenance, and repairs.

We often expect government agencies to establish the precise meanings of such terms as "safe" and "unsafe," "rich" and "poor" (or, as they are more likely to put it, "high income" and "low income"). Thus a Department of Agriculture publication, discussing the need to store food at "safe" temperatures so that it will not spoil and cause food poisoning, explains "Food may not be safe to eat if held for more than 3 or 4 hours at temperatures between 60° and 120°F., the zone where bacteria grow rapidly. This includes all time during preparation, storage, and serving." [2] A criterion this precise makes it possible for anyone to evaluate whether a cafeteria is keeping its food at safe temperatures. As for affluence and poverty, a government publication reports that in 1975 the federally defined "low income threshold" was $5050 in annual income for a non-farm family of four.[3] Equipped with this precise criterion, you can evaluate whether a scholarship program for poor students is successfully reaching the poor. (You might also want to evaluate the government's economists as unrealistic!)

Sometimes, as Truscott shows in trying to evaluate the Army (p. 364), it is extremely difficult to establish precise criteria. Sometimes the effort to do so occupies more of the finished piece of writing than does any other part of the evaluative process. Greeley spends the largest part of his evaluation of contemporary Christianity (p. 352) establishing his concept of what Jesus actually meant and intended, so that he can judge Christianity by that criterion.

Sometimes it is simply impossible to establish criteria as precise as "$5050 for a non-farm family of four" or "not more than 3 or 4 hours at temperatures between 60° and 120°F." Gutcheon praises soap operas for trying to educate us about ourselves and about alternative ways of life (p. 409). She does not attempt to specify exactly what proportion of its time on the air a given soap opera should spend on educational matters before deserving the evaluation "good, because educational."

The principle to remember: make your criteria as precise as you reasonably can. Somewhere between the extremes of a criterion so vague as to be useless—and a criterion so overprecise as to be idiotic—lies the right degree of precision for each piece of evaluative writing. The nature of your subject, the space and time you have to spend, the experience and degree of interest of your audience, and your own common sense will help you decide.

---

[2] *Handbook for the Home, the 1973 Yearbook of Agriculture* (Government Printing Office, Washington, D.C., 1973), p. 42, Carole A. Davis, "Safe Handling of Food, and Home Storage."

[3] *Federal Register*, vol. 40, #62 (March 31, 1975), p. 14318.

Justifying the Criteria. If your criteria are clearly identified, fair, and precise, most of your readers will accept them. But occasionally a criterion will need to be defended. If you want to evaluate a novel, for instance, and your criterion is that it should help you understand yourself, a reader could legitimately ask "Why?" Why should a novel be judged by that standard? Couldn't it deserve to be judged "good" if it helped you understand *other* people rather than yourself? Or if it provided an exciting and pleasurable experience that refreshed your spirits?

If you expect objections to your criteria, rethink them. Perhaps you should mention some other ways of evaluating the novel you have chosen, so that your reader will at least know that you're aware of them. Perhaps the issue is worth an open confrontation, in which case you might decide to spend three or four paragraphs explaining why you feel that a good novel is one that helps you understand yourself.

Whether the criteria will need to be justified depends, as so much else in writing does, on the audience for which you are writing. If you are evaluating your high school education and condemning it for not having taught you a marketable skill, do you need to justify that criterion? Probably not, if your audience consists of the other members of the Career Education in High School club; probably yes, if your audience consists of members of the Humanistic Education in High School club. The more unusual your criterion will seem to your audience, the more likely it becomes that you should take the time to defend it. If you want to evaluate spaghetti in terms of its tensile strength, you'd certainly better take the time to explain why.

Collecting Information. In order to see how well X measures up to your criteria—once the criteria have been chosen, ranked if there will be more than one, checked for fairness and precision, and justified if necessary—you will have to assemble information about X. Otherwise your judgment would be unsubstantiated. Except for whatever background information belongs in the introduction to your paper or in the section defining X, only information corresponding exactly to your chosen criteria should be kept in the final piece of writing. If you are evaluating three local drug stores in terms of their prices for brand-name vitamins and cold remedies, you would not include information about their check-cashing policies. If you are evaluating Levi and Wrangler jeans in terms of how long they last and what they cost (a "cost-effectiveness" analysis), you would not include information on where they are manufactured or what colors are available.

Sometimes the process of collecting the right information is made easier by the preparation of an outline, or a data sheet like this one for the drugstore evaluation:

	Prices		
	Bayer Aspirin, 100 tablets	Contac, 20 capsules	Sudafed decongestant syrup, 4 oz.
Store A			
Store B			
Store C			

The information on the data sheet can sometimes be presented as a chart in your evaluation paper or included at the end as an appendix (see *Consumer Reports* evaluation with appendix, p. 318). Or the data sheet may function only as a convenient way of making sure that you are gathering all the right information, and only the right information, as you prepare the paper. And you may not need one at all. If you are evaluating a film in terms of the usefulness of its social message, a data sheet is not likely to help. The important thing is to make sure, by any convenient system, that you have down on paper the information corresponding to your criteria before you proceed to the next logical step, drawing the judgment.

Drawing the Judgment. In the terminology of logic that we used in presenting substantiation (pp. 174–177), the process of drawing the judgment is a deductive argument. We can use the model of the syllogism.

1. An inexpensive car is a car that, on the average, gets at least 20 miles per gallon of gas and costs no more than $10 per month for maintenance and repairs, and has an initial purchase price of no more than $3500 (new, with standard equipment only, not including the interest expense for time payments). [Major premise.]

2. The 1975 Chevrolet model—— my father owns gets about 22 miles per gallon and costs him about $9 per month for maintenance and repairs. Its initial purchase price was $3420.46. [Minor premise.]

3. The 1975 Chevrolet model—— is, judging from the evidence available to me, an inexpensive car to purchase and to own. [Conclusion.]

The major premise in an evaluative syllogism is the criterion. If you are using more than one criterion, the major premise may be a rather long one.

It is wrong to permit someone to die when the means to prolong his or her life are available—unless the patient is suffering extreme pain, is elderly (65 years old or older), has physical and mental deterioration for which no reversal can be expected, is not known to hold any religious principles requiring the preservation of life to the utmost, and would require medical resources that are needed by somebody more likely to recover. If all those conditions exist, it is *not* wrong to permit the patient to die. If any one of those conditions is missing, it *is* wrong to permit the patient to die.

Similarly, you may well require more than one sentence to present the relevant information about *X* (the minor premise) or to state your judgment (the conclusion). Consider the following judgment:

We can see that bussing children to achieve school desegregation involves serious problems. The children who are bussed must spend time —in some school districts, up to two hours a day—in a way that usually contributes nothing to their educational development and in some cases may actually endanger their lives. The burden of being outsiders in a painful situation is placed upon them. The children of the receiving school feel invaded by strangers. Both groups of children are required to do what their parents and friends are not. It is surely a moral wrong to make our children do what we refuse to do ourselves. We are using them to atone for our sins.

On the other hand, we simply cannot tolerate segregated schools any longer. It is a greater moral wrong—given our criterion that the good of the community outweighs the good of individuals—to permit all of American society to be tainted by the shame of segregated schools, than it is to require some of our children to be in the front lines of a determined effort to integrate our schools *now*.

Nobody can pretend that bussing is a wholly good strategy. It is both good and bad. The balance, however, is tipped in its favor.

To summarize: the complete (or "full-form") process of evaluation we have been describing contains four elements.

1. Definition of the thing (*X*) to be evaluated;

2. Selection of criteria that are fair and adequately precise, and ranking and justifying of the criteria if necessary;

3. Collection of information about *X* so that it can be compared to the ideal established by the criteria;

4. Comparison of *X* to the criteria and statement of the judgment.

You can see all four elements most clearly in test reports of consumer goods or other evaluations of material items and objects. (See the *Consumer Reports* evaluation of 19-inch black-and-white TV sets, p. 318).

Abbreviated Evaluations. At times, however, only part of the full logical process of evaluation appears in the written report. What results is called an abbreviated (or "short-form") evaluation. The nature of *X*, if *X* is something familiar to most of us, may be left unspecified. The criteria may be implied—suggested by connotative language or by the inclusion and omission of certain subjects—rather than explicitly stated and ranked. If a writer discusses only the vitamin A content of different brands of frozen carrots, we can see that the standard of value is simply the amount of vitamin A (not the cost or the taste or the appearance of the carrots). Sometimes even the judgment may be left for the readers to infer and state in their own words.

An abbreviated evaluation is not necessarily an irresponsible one. Whatever can be taken for granted does not need to be spelled out. To tell people what they already know or what they can easily figure out for themselves is at best a waste of time, at worst an insult. But how much is it proper to omit?

The test of whether an abbreviated evaluation has been responsibly conducted is whether the reader can answer the following questions on the basis of material either stated or implied.

1. What are the limits of the subject (*X*)?
2. What criteria are being applied?
3. What information about *X* corresponds to those criteria?
4. What is the overall judgment?

Hungiville's essay "Groovin' in Academe" (p. 329) is an abbreviated evaluation but a responsible one—not one you will necessarily agree with, but one conducted so that you can see the logical process involved and the abundant evidence. The subject is the advertising campaign recently launched by American colleges. It is not essential that *X* be defined more exactly than that. The criteria are two: honesty and accuracy in advertising, and intellectual responsibility in education. These criteria are implied by Hungiville's criticisms of the colleges' publicity tactics rather than openly stated. The information about *X* consists of citation after citation from college catalogues, booklets, and posters. The judgment is not made explicit— the essay ends on a question, "Is anybody saluting?"—but we can infer it ourselves from the information we have been given. Hungiville, at least, is not saluting at all.

How responsible is this abbreviated evaluation?

The flour companies only will sell you what is known as an "all purpose flour." This is the flour that is available through grocery stores. This all purpose flour is a very, very poor quality soft wheat flour with very little strength. In their small flour bags such as five and ten pound sizes they pack a very, very, poor quality flour that will not even make good gravy thickening. In their 50 to 100 pound sacks of flour they pack another soft, poor quality flour that is entirely different from what they put in their 5 and 10 pound sacks. It will not make decent bread for rolls or pancakes or anything else for that matter.

Here are the flours that you must have in order to do good baking. All of these flours have been purposely made impossible to buy from your grocer.

1. Bread Flour. This is a high quality, strong patent flour. Without it, it is absolutely impossible to make a good loaf of bread or flaky pastry of any kind.

2. Pastry Flour. You must have this to make good rolls, muffins, pie crust, or even good pancakes.

3. Cake Flour. This must be an extremely fine high grade flour. You must have this very fine honest cake flour and a special emulsified shortening that will hold sugar well to make a really good cake. You cannot buy either.

4. High Glutin Flour. To make French, Vienna, Italian or Bohemian bread or applestrudel you must have this flour. It is absolutely impossible for the modern woman to make these items without these flours.

With these flours a child can bake beautifully; without them no one can.

Food editors of magazines, television, and newspapers, and cook book editors for the most part only know how to take pictures. They do not know how to cook and they have all been taken in by this flour and shortening racket. They keep printing recipes with beautiful pictures that will not work. The flour and shortening companies run enough advertisements in the magazines on television and newspapers to control anything that the food editors might print; in fact can actually pick the ones they want for the jobs. The flour companies even carefully get out cook books of their own with recipes that they know will discourage women from baking. The people that control the newspapers, magazines and television go right along on this racket and have cold bloodedly practically destroyed the woman's right to be a good woman and wife and do her own baking. This may seem like a small trifle but it is not. A woman is a natural housewife, cook and baker. Give her idle time from lack of being allowed to bake and even divorces can result.[4]

A SPECIAL TECHNIQUE OF EVALUATION: SATIRE

Satire is a technique of disapproval: it is a way of writing about X so that X looks ridiculous or offensive. It involves intentional dis-

---

[4] Courtesy, Herter's, Inc. from *Bull Cook and Authentic Historical Recipes and Practices*, vol. 1.

tortion. The writer chooses only the few characteristics of X that will make it look silly or ugly; he does not consider the whole picture. Or he does not attempt to describe the real X at all but instead creates an exaggerated verson of it, a "parody."

Consider the following evaluation of a book.

The new book which Mr. ———— has written about the Constitution is a very different kind of book. You can read it without thinking. If you have got tired trying to read the other kind of books, you will be glad of the nice restful book that Mr. ———— has written. It runs along like a story in a very interesting way. Most of the story is about how the Constitution got made. This is really history, but it is written in a very lively way like a novel, with a great many characters, almost all male, and plenty of conversation and a very exciting plot. Many of the chapters have names like those in a novel such as "The Opening of the Battle," "The Crisis," "The Dawn," "Nearing the End," "The Curtain Falls," and others. Besides the story there are many quotations from Shakespeare, Beethoven, Horace, Isaiah, Euripides, Beard, and other famous men. Many of these quotations are quite old, but some of them are fairly new. They help to make the book a real high-class book. There is not much more to say about the part of the book that tells how the Constitution got made, except that it is fun and easy to read and seems pretty true to life.[5]

This book review, which superficially praises X as "different," "lively," "fun," "easy to read," and so forth, actually mocks the book as simpleminded. The technique involved is to praise it as only a simpleminded person would praise it: in sentences that do not quite make sense, in a grammatical style that sounds like a ten-year-old's, in an idiom that suggests thoughtlessness ("a real high-class book," "true to life," and similar phrases are clichés a mature and critical writer would avoid). The implication is that you would have to be simpleminded to like this book—in other words that it is a very bad book indeed. The reviewer does not approve of a history book that tries to be a novel, "fun and easy to read," and that is decorated with quotations from "famous men" (a rather odd jumble of them). Therefore, he seizes upon these qualities, exaggerates them until they eclipse whatever other qualities the book may have and mocks them by pretending to be a simpleminded person who likes them.

Similarly, Thurber is annoyed with a relativity-theory example that strikes him as preposterous ("An Outline of Scientists," p. 333). The example is that if a man could travel faster than the speed of light, he would catch up with light rays representing events that happened in the past. Thurber, finding this nonsensical, takes it a step further and makes it downright ridiculous:

---

[5] From "Constitutional Metaphors," by Thomas Reed Powell, cited in Harold C. Martin and Richard M. Ohmann, *The Logic and Rhetoric of Exposition*, rev. ed., 1964.

I kept going over and over this section of the chapter on the Einstein theory. I even tried reading it backward, twice as fast as light, to see if I could capture Napoleon at Waterloo while he was still home in bed.

As this last example shows, satirical evaluations are not always fair. In fact, they do not try to be fair. They try to emphasize particular characteristics of X that seem, to their writers, so disqualifying that X does not deserve a standard evaluation. A cartoonist who draws a picture of a government official as all belly is suggesting that this person's greed so overwhelms all other characteristics that only the greed needs to be pointed out: we should take one look at that belly and vote "No." A *Mad* magazine-type feature portraying news commentators as speaking only in meaningless unconnected phrases ("Hello, here we are at . . . now we switch you to . . .on our left we have a . . . tune in again tomorrow!") is suggesting that the fragmentary nature of TV news presentations is so dominant a characteristic that it blots out all else.

Satirical evaluations are protests against aspects of our world that we may take for granted. The satirist asks, in effect, "Don't you see how greedy this politician is?" or "Don't you see how meaningless the TV news programs are?" The purpose of satirical evaluations is to make sure that we *do* see. They are useful not as replacements for standard evaluations, but as a means of waking people up when it is wrong—or dangerous—for them to be sleeping.

(Satirical evaluations are also fun to read and to write.)

THE VALUE OF EVALUATION

In full or abbreviated form, using a moral or a utilitarian approach, written in a straightforward or a satirical style, evaluations respond to the question "Is X good or bad?" Responsible evaluations do so in such a way that readers know whether the writer approves or disapproves and also understand the criteria and information on which the judgment is based.

Many of the most important questions we ask are questions of evaluation. Is it wrong to kill people in war? Is America a good country? Do I have a good relationship with the person I love most? Is there something wrong with me? Answering questions such as these often requires an evaluative process extending through a lifetime. One of the hardest tasks in life is to evaluate oneself accurately and realistically.

Some questions of evaluation need more urgent answers. You have probably decided whether your high school education was good or bad (or rather that it had some good and some bad characteristics). Probably you are now thinking about the value of a college education, perhaps even trying to decide by next term whether to stay in school and what to study if you do. Is college worth all this time, money, and effort? Will it increase your lifetime income? Will you derive more pleasure or meaning from life with a college education? You can answer these questions only by deciding upon criteria (what do you mean by "meaning," for instance?), gathering information, and drawing a judgment.

All of us want to believe that we can make the judgments that will improve our own lives. All of us want to back a winning horse. To choose a winner—to know which option is best—means to evaluate evidence accurately and to have clear, reasonable standards of measurement.

series one

EVALUATION: READINGS WITH COMMENTARY

the common stock of the coca-cola company

This selection comes from a booklet evaluating common stocks. (A share of stock represents part ownership of a business.) The booklet is written for people who might want to buy shares of stock as an investment. The company pays stockholders an annual dividend on each share, and the shares can often be sold later at a profit. The criterion for evaluating stock is the ability of the shares to make money for their owners.

After a two-sentence introduction to supply general information about the Coca-Cola Company, the writer discusses its recent growth in sales, earnings per share, and dividends. He then distinguishes between income from sales of soft drinks and income from sales of other products. The last paragraph offers a prediction of continued financial strength and the judgment that shares of Coca-Cola's common stock are "attractive" for people who want to see their money grow. "Attractive" clearly means, in this context, appealing not to the eye or the ear or the taste—but to the pocketbook.

1   **m**ore than 110-million times a day, someone, somewhere in the world, drinks a Coke—one of the most successful consumer products ever introduced. That success has made the Coca-Cola Company the dominant firm in the soft-drink industry, where it commands about 44% of the domestic market for bottled soft drinks and more than 85% of the market for trademarked fountain drinks. During the five years through 1968, Coca-

Source. Copyrighted 1969 Merrill Lynch, Pierce, Fenner & Smith, Inc., Reprinted by permission from Merrill Lynch, Pierce, Fenner & Smith, Inc.

Cola's sales grew at a compound annual rate of 13%, and earnings per share advanced at a 15% compound rate. The company has paid dividends each year since 1893 and has increased the dividend rate in each of the last seven years. The current annual dividend is $1.32 a share.

2   The company expects its sales of soft drinks in the United States to increase at an annual rate of 9-to-10% during the next three-to-five years, and it expects sales for the foreign division to grow even more rapidly, at a rate approaching 15%. Sales of soft drinks last year accounted for 75% of Coca-Cola's total revenues of $1.2 billion, to which domestic and foreign operations contributed equal amounts.

3   In addition to selling carbonated beverages, Coca-Cola is the world's largest processor of citrus concentrates and drinks and the largest producer of instant coffee and tea sold under private labels. We estimate that 1969 earnings, excluding unremitted foreign profits of about 11¢ a share, will be $2.15-to-2.20 a share compared with $1.93 a share in 1968.

4   In our opinion, Coca-Cola's sales and earnings will continue to expand in coming years. We base that expectation on the company's strong consumer franchise and on projections of increases in population, in standards of living, and in per-capita consumption of soft drinks throughout the world. Although Coca-Cola's outstanding record has not been overlooked by investors, we believe that the investment-grade shares remain attractive for growth.

COMMENTARY

This very short evaluation includes all parts of the full-form evaluation pattern except an explicit statement of the criteria. The important characteristics of X are defined in the first paragraph (Coca-Cola is "the dominant firm in the soft-drink industry," and so forth). The information most relevant to potential purchasers of the shares—information about the company's earnings (which govern its ability to pay dividends) and information about the dividends themselves—is provided in the next two paragraphs. The writer also includes predictions about the financial future to assure readers that if they buy Coca-Cola shares today, their investments will not be endangered tomorrow. The judgment is compressed into one word of approval: "attractive." And a reason is given to suggest why the approval is no stronger than that. Other investors have already bought Coca-Cola stock (the company's "outstanding record has not been overlooked"), so that its price may be fairly high.

This very efficient report functions quite satisfactorily without an explicit statement of criteria for two reasons. One is that, since it was written for a booklet issued by a stockbrokers' firm, it was unlikely to reach people who were not interested in making money. The other is that its own language indicates the standard of value being used. All of the financial terms ("sales," "market," "compound annual rate," "earnings per share," and so forth) give adequate evidence of this evaluation's orientation.

OUTLINE
   I.   Introduction: general information about *X*—paragraph 1
   II. Minor premise: information about *X* to correspond with criteria—paragraphs 2–3
   III. Conclusion: judgment that *X* is "attractive"—paragraph 4

SUGGESTIONS FOR WRITING

1. Write a short evaluation using a criterion that is obvious and can therefore remain unstated. For example, evaluate something you ate for lunch yesterday. You might begin with a one- or two-sentence definition (what you ate). Supply the important information ("it had a weird taste, as if somebody had taken cold farina and poured latex wall paint on it, hiding a few crumpled international postage stamps here and there for variety—I was aware of a distantly Italian spiciness in one lump, a Chinese crispness in another"). State your judgment at the end, compressing it into one word if possible.

2. Begin with the first sentence of the Coca-Cola evaluation: "More than 110-million times a day, someone, somewhere in the world, drinks a Coke— one of the most successful consumer products ever introduced." Write an evaluation for a different audience, perhaps the members of your class. Use a different criterion (flavor, nutritional value, pleasure), provide the appropriate information, and state your judgment at the end.

brown v. board of education of topeka
EARL WARREN

In this section of the famous 1954 Supreme Court decision banning segregation from public schools, Chief Justice Warren offers an evaluation. His criterion, based on the Fourteenth Amendment's guarantee of equal protection under the law, is that public education "must be made available to all on equal terms" (paragraph 1). His information consists of authoritative judgments that the so-called "separate but equal" schools do not, in fact, provide equal educational opportunities (paragraph 4). The judgment follows logically that segregated schools are unacceptable: they deny certain people their constitutional right to equal treatment under the law (paragraph 5). Thus he reverses the 1896 *Plessy* v. *Ferguson* decision that had accepted the concept of "separate but equal."

Notice that Justice Warren derives his criterion not from his personal

Source. United States Reports, vol. 347 (Washington, D.C.: Government Printing Office, 1954), pp. 483–96.

concepts of morality but from the Constitution he has been charged to uphold. Whether school segregation is right or wrong means, in this case, simply whether it is legal. Warren says no.

1   **I**n approaching this problem, we cannot turn the clock back to 1868 when the Amendment was adopted, or even to 1896 when *Plessy* v. *Ferguson* was written. We must consider public education in the light of its full development and its present place in American life throughout the Nation. Only in this way can it be determined if segregation in public schools deprives these plaintiffs of the equal protection of the laws.

2   Today, education is perhaps the most important function of state and local governments. Compulsory school attendance laws and the great expenditures for education both demonstrate our recognition of the importance of education to our democratic society. It is required in the performance of our most basic public responsibilities, even service in the armed forces. It is the very foundation of good citizenship. Today it is a principal instrument in awakening the child to cultural values, in preparing him for later professional training, and in helping him to adjust normally to his environment. In these days, it is doubtful that any child may reasonably be expected to succeed in life if he is denied the opportunity of an education. Such an opportunity, where the state has undertaken to provide it, is a right which must be made available to all on equal terms.

3   We come then to the question presented: Does segregation of children in public schools solely on the basis of race, even though the physical facilities and other "tangible" factors may be equal, deprive the children of the minority group of equal educational opportunities? We believe that it does.

4   In *Sweatt* v. *Painter, supra,* in finding that a segregated law school for Negroes could not provide them equal educational opportunities, this Court relied in large part on "those qualities which are incapable of objective measurement but which make for greatness in a law school." In *McLaurin* v. *Oklahoma State Regents, supra,* the Court, in requiring that a Negro admitted to a white graduate school be treated like all other students, again resorted to intangible considerations: ". . . his ability to study, to engage in discussions and exchange views with other students, and, in general, to learn his profession." Such considerations apply with added force to children in grade and high schools. To separate them from others of similar age and qualifications solely because of their race generates a feeling of inferiority as to their status in the community that may affect their hearts and minds in a way unlikely ever to be undone. The effect of this separation on their educational opportunities was well stated by a finding in the Kansas case by a court which nevertheless felt compelled to rule against the Negro plaintiffs:

Segregation of white and colored children in public schools has a detrimental effect upon the colored children. The impact is greater when it has the sanction of the law; for the policy of separating the races is usually interpreted as denoting the inferiority of the negro group. A sense of inferiority affects the motivation of a child to learn. Segregation with the sanction of law, therefore, has a tendency to retard the educational and mental development of negro children and to deprive them of some of the benefits they would receive in a racially integrated school system.

Whatever may have been the extent of psychological knowledge at the time of *Plessy* v. *Ferguson,* this finding is amply supported by modern authority. Any language in *Plessy* v. *Ferguson* contrary to this finding is rejected.

5   We conclude that in the field of public education the doctrine of "separate but equal" has no place. Separate educational facilities are inherently unequal. Therefore, we hold that the plaintiffs and others similarly situated for whom the actions have been brought are, by reason of the segregation complained of, deprived of the equal protection of the laws guaranteed by the Fourteenth Amendment.

COMMENTARY

Justice Warren's evaluation of segregated schools omits a definition of X, and sensibly so, since we already know what "segregation in public schools" (paragraph 1) means. A Supreme Court decision is expected to be to the point, not to waste time on the obvious. As for part 2 of the evaluative process (see p. 296), Warren uses the Constitution as the general criterion and an application of the Fourteenth Amendment as the precise criterion. In part 3, the presentation of information, Warren reports two opinions of experts and refers to modern psychological studies. He could be criticized for not collecting detailed information about the schools themselves instead. Do you see why he does not? Would it bog down his argument, or make it excessively long, or obscure its overall logical structure, if he were to examine a representative sample of segregated schools?

Part 4 of the evaluative process, the judgment, is stated briefly in paragraph 3, more fully in paragraph 5.

OUTLINE
I. Introduction: how to approach the issue—paragraphs 1–2
II. Major premise: the criterion—paragraph 2 (last sentence)
III. The issue restated, the criterion quickly summarized ("equal educational opportunities"), the judgment briefly given—paragraph 3
IV. Minor premise: information—paragraph 4
V. Conclusion: judgment—paragraph 5

SUGGESTIONS FOR WRITING

1. Write a short evaluation that follows Warren's evaluative process but applies it to a different subject. Choosing a well-known X will permit you to omit the definition section as he does. Examples: evaluate cigarette ads using a moral criterion (perhaps "it is wrong to urge people to do something harm-

ful"); evaluate nonreturnable soda or beer cans using a utilitarian criterion (perhaps convenience or low cost).

2. Briefly evaluate segregated schools (or neighborhoods or recreation facilities) on the basis of a criterion other than constitutionality. You may be familiar only with what is called *de facto* segregation, in other words segregation not required by local laws but occuring as a result of economic and social pressures. For example, the "ethnic neighborhood," once condemned as a form of *de facto* segregation of immigrants or poor people or members of religious sects, is now thought by some sociologists to be a good pattern for urban living. Does your experience lead you to judge it as good or bad? On the basis of what criteria?

3. The Fourteenth Amendment reads, in part, "No state shall . . . deny to any person within its jurisdiction the equal protection of the laws." Do you believe that abortion, or the imprisonment of lawbreakers, or the involuntary institutionalization of the mentally ill, or the existence of certain sex-segregated public facilities is wrong on the basis of that constitutional criterion?

the english language is my enemy!
OSSIE DAVIS

This selection shows very clearly how evaluation depends on substantiation. Davis begins by presenting us with evidence about the English language: a list of the favorable terms associated with "whiteness" and the unfavorable terms associated with "blackness." He identifies his source (a basic reference book, Roget's *Thesaurus)* so that we can check his evidence if we like. Having substantiated the thesis that a heritage of racial prejudice awaits any child born into an English-speaking culture (paragraph 3), Davis is ready to pass judgment. He does so in angry and vigorous language (paragraphs 3 and 4)—language that we might reject as mere hysteria if it were not preceded by the evidence that justifies it.

1   **a** superficial examination of Roget's Thesaurus Of The English Language reveals the following facts: the word WHITENESS has 134 synonyms; 44 of which are favorable and pleasing to contemplate, i.e. purity, cleanness, immaculateness, bright, shining, ivory, fair, blonde, stainless, clean, clear, chaste, unblemished, unsullied, innocent, honorable, upright, just, straight-forward, fair, genuine, trustworthy, (a white man-colloquialism). Only ten synonyms for WHITENESS appear to me to have negative

Source. Copyright © 1967 by The Association for the Study of Negro Life and History, Inc.

implications—and these only in the mildest sense: gloss over, whitewash, gray, wan, pale, ashen, etc.

2   The word BLACKNESS has 120 synonyms, 60 of which are distinctly unfavorable, and none of them even mildly positive. Among the offending 60 were such words as: blot, blotch, smut, smudge, sully, begrime, soot, becloud, obscure, dingy, murky, low-toned, threatening, frowning, foreboding, forbidden, sinister, baneful, dismal, thundery, evil, wicked, malignant, deadly, unclean, dirty, unwashed, foul, etc. . . . not to mention 20 synonyms directly related to race, such as: Negro, Negress, nigger, darky, blackamoor, etc.

3   When you consider the fact that *thinking* itself is sub-vocal speech—in other words, one must use *words* in order to think at all—you will appreciate the enormous heritage of racial prejudgement that lies in wait for any child born into the English Language. Any teacher good or bad, white or black, Jew or Gentile, who uses the English Language as a medium of communication is forced, willy-nilly, to teach the Negro child 60 ways to despise himself, and the white child 60 ways to aid and abet him in the crime.

4   Who speaks to me in my Mother Tongue damns me indeed! . . . the English Language—in which I cannot conceive my self as a black man without, at the same time, debasing myself . . . my enemy, with which to survive at all I must continually be at war.

COMMENTARY

Davis' logical precedure is simple. As the headnote points out, he moves from evidence (words) to a thesis based on that evidence (the English language is prejudiced against blacks) to a judgment based on that thesis (the English language is his enemy). He does not state the criterion that leads him to condemn his language, but it is easy enough to see that he believes a good language should be free from any "heritage of racial prejudgement." This criterion probably does not need to be openly stated and defended, because few people would oppose it. Davis' real work in this short evaluative essay is not in the development of the criterion, but in the demonstration that X does, in fact, fail to measure up.

    Would it help Davis' case if he referred to other people whom our language seems to describe unfavorably? Should he consider the ways in which our vocabulary seems prejudiced also against the aged (in favor of the young), the poor (in favor of the affluent), and so forth? Or would such an attempt to consider the whole picture become too sweeping, too impersonal, and so diminish this evaluation's dramatic power?

OUTLINE
    I. Presentation of evidence—paragraphs 1–2
    II. Thesis statement—paragraph 3
    III. Judgment: condemnation of the English language—paragraphs 3–4

SUGGESTIONS FOR WRITING

1. Davis uses a comparative technique: first he presents one member of a pair, then the other. Apply this technique to a pair of *X*'s: traveling by bus versus traveling by car, cooking your own food versus eating in the dorm, and so forth. Evaluate each aspect separately and then come to an overall judgment; for example, that food is likely to taste better and be less expensive if you prepare it yourself.

2. Following Davis' logical pattern, and using the same source (Roget's *Thesaurus*), write a similar evaluation of the English language's attitude toward some other group of people or toward any major factor in our culture (e.g. money, technology, religion). You will need a dictionary to establish the precise connotations of the words listed in the *Thesaurus,* because those are related terms, not exact synonyms.

You may want to review Hayakawa's distinction between "snarl" words and "purr" words (p. 141).

---

that country called woman: an artificial climate

DEBORAH AUSTIN

In this review of a book of poems, Deborah Austin, a poet herself, begins with praise for some of the poems but goes on to discuss "the kind of trouble this book runs into": the mistake of putting subject matter first, artistic merit second; in other words, a mistake in the ranking of priorities. Toward the end of the review, it becomes clear that this negative evaluation ("sisters, you're wrong," paragraph 4) depends directly on the reviewer's own definition of the way that artists work. "The first condition of achievement in any of the arts is to be able to bear solitude and make it blossom like the rose" (paragraph 9). Given that definition, art cannot be teamwork; the book of poems under review is necessarily at least a partial failure.

1 **t**here are many good poems in this collection.* Myra H. Messier's "She Said" deftly combines force and economy into what may be the best poem, *qua* poem, in the book. Barbara Friend's "Natasha" is strong and graceful,

Source. Copyright © 1975. Reprinted by permission of the *Journal of General Education.*

* *I, That Am Ever Stranger: Poems on Woman's Experience.* Nancy Esther James, editor, Mary Webber Balazs, Associate Editor. Published with the aid of grants from the Faculty Research Fund of Westminster College, New Wilmington, Pennsylvania, and the American Association of University Women Educational Foundation.

with a fine eye for the apt image. Other fine poems are Margaret Honton's "Out of the Depths," Adrienne Illah Harris's "mother went insane today," Kathryn Weldy's "For My Dad," Beth Baruch Joselow's trenchant "Ice Box," and Julie Kane's "The Good Women." Ann duCille's "Pickin' " is really alive and jivey, fully exploiting poetry's potentials for funmaking, rhythm, and surprises. There's also a neat surprise at the end of Edna Gerstner's "Priorities." Kathryn Martin's "House Mother" is a finely integrated poem; Nancy Esther James's "To Emily Dickinson" is a poem to think about for a long time. All this is cause for joy; there can never be enough good new poems—the demand will always exceed the supply. (I am not referring here to publishing; we all know the demand there is minimal. I'm talking about the shock of pleasure that comes to the reader who finds a good new poem.)

2   The subject of this anthology is Woman's Experience. It is by and about women, both particular and general, past, present, or future. Even at its angriest it is a book in celebration of being woman. Seventy-three women are its contributors, or seventy-four, if we include the designer of the cover. Their subjects are as various as the experiences women have, and the editors have taken fullest advantage of this variety by arranging the contents so that they run from birth through childhood, adolescence, young and mature adulthood, to old age. They have also avoided titling the categories, so that the arrangement gently and effectively forces itself on the reader's consciousness—a fine choice, which adds a good deal to the effect of the whole.

3   An anthology with so many contributors must run the risk of having a wide range of poetic competency displayed in its contents. No doubt many poets included here have written better poems, which were not suitable for this anthology and so could not appear in it. Perhaps some of the contributors, wishing to show that they were in sympathy with the editor's project, sent along poems they were not entirely satisfied with (for one rarely *is* entirely satisfied with a poem), yet which they felt might "do" for this book. And that seems to me to come close to defining the kind of trouble this book runs into—a kind of split in purpose which may not be a split at all, but a debatable decision. Is it better to publish a not-very-good poem about being woman in order to make the book a respectable size, or is it better to publish only the best poems? An anthology with a special subject-matter always runs into this problem. The editors of a dog-lovers' anthology, for instance, know that the dog-lovers who buy the book may or may not be poetry-lovers, but that if they buy the dog-lovers' anthology, they will be looking for something that will reinforce the way they feel about dogs. When I buy a book of poems, I want it to reinforce my feelings about poetry.

4   I am a woman myself, and I've always been glad I am, but it does not particularly reinforce my gladness to be a woman to see a whole book of poems by women about their gladness at, or frustration with, the state that we all share. I do not need to be reminded of my sisterhood in this way;

I have felt it all my life; it has been one of the deep joys of my life, as it has been one of the deep sorrows of my life that some of woman's central experiences (marriage, children) have not been shared by me. And because my feeling of sisterhood is strong, I need to say here: sisters, you're wrong. In the long run, where things really count for the serious artist, you're wrong.

5   Any woman who wants to write poetry about herself (or her mother, or her old-maid aunt, or a prostitute) as woman, *being* woman, is of course right to do so. Which of us has not? Which of us can write from any other place any more than a man can write "from" any other given than that of being man? Yet in any poet's life the number of poems *specifically* about being either woman or man must be outnumbered eventually by poems about being a human being in the world, reacting to the world, seeing, participating, and feeling in the world. No poet could long endure, boxed into the sole contemplation of his or her sexual self. After all, it is the oblique gaze, often, that results in the poem. A long, cold, head-on, eyeball-to-eyeball stare is apt to result in prose, and not very great prose at that.

6   From the point of view of poetry, there is only one serious reason for publishing a poetry anthology. And that is to give good poems a place where they can be found by people looking for them. Not people looking for good poems about women, or good poems about nature, or good poems about death, but *good poems,* which, thank God, may be about anything. To publish a poetry anthology for any other reason is to publish data for sociologists and professors of psychology, for superpatriots of that country called Woman, for students looking for material to write long papers on, for statisticians, for social historians, for jumpers-on-bandwagons, for lovers of the latest fashion. It does violence to the good poems in the book by confining them in an artificial climate, and inevitably it makes use of poems that are less than good to flesh out the basic skeleton of the book.

7   Poetry is an art. It is not a personal catharsis or a self-indulgence; it is a demanding discipline and a holy joy. The result of a lot of women getting together in a book because they have all written poetry about being woman is an embarrassment, because by its existence the book says that they have not considered their art first, but have considered getting together as women first. In doing so, they have betrayed their art by not putting it first.

8   Many times, in reading the work of a woman poet, or reading an anthology containing the work of both men and women, I have come across a poem on the subject of being woman, and have admired the poem as it isolated itself from the rest of the book in all its unique strength and individuality. But more than seventy-three poems on this subject leave me feeling claustrophobic and unhappy. Poetry doesn't need this. I wonder, even, if women need it—even now, when the eyes of history seem to be on us in so meaningful a way that it is almost impossible not to feel that now is the time to do something vigorous and special, having the floor as we do.

9   But "having the floor" may or may not be wholly a good thing in all instances. Like all potential goods, it carries in it the seeds of its own

destruction, and for woman artists those seeds are especially dangerous. For the artist must be both universal and particular, but timely only if and when timeliness suits the talent and the imagination of the individual. Above all, if we are poets, let's eschew togetherness *as poets.* Let's not be afraid of being ourselves, and alone. It is fallacious to argue that an anthology of women poets will give confidence to women writing, who will read it and be encouraged by it to persevere in their own work. The first condition of achievement in any of the arts is to be able to bear solitude and make it blossom like the rose. Nothing makes this easy, except the delight and compulsion of the work itself. If these are lacking, the knowledge that others are working is not going to change things. If these are present, nothing else is needed. And no flock ever sang so sweetly as one bird, alone on its bough.

COMMENTARY

Evaluations of literature are often subjective: different readers may want different things from a short story or novel or poem. One reader may want the excitement of a cliff-hanger plot, another the emotional release of a fantasy, another the pleasure of seeing everyday things in new ways. With so many possible meanings for the judgment "that's a good (or bad) book," the judgment would be almost meaningless—and the book review useless—unless the criteria are made clear. In Austin's review of *I, That Am Ever Stranger,* only the first two paragraphs are devoted to information about *X.* Most of the review is a discussion, in fact a defense, of the concept of artistic creation that makes Austin feel "claustrophobic and unhappy" about this book rather than delighted. The progress of the review, then, is from information about *X* (paragraphs 1 and 2), to a tentative negative judgment linking this book to others that have run into trouble (paragraph 3), to a definite negative judgment ("sisters, you're wrong," paragraph 4), and then to a full explanation of the criteria (paragraphs 5 to 9). This is a somewhat unusual organization. More commonly, the criteria are identified (and justified if necessary) before the judgment about *X* is made. Why do you think Austin arranged her material this way? Does the arrangement work?

Notice that in order to explain to her fellow poets the dangers of their togetherness, Austin first decides to "get together" with them herself. She takes care, in paragraph 4, to explain not only that she is a woman but also that her life has lacked some of the typical experiences of womanhood and that she has a strong feeling of "sisterhood" for other women. Superficially, a reader might criticize this information as irrelevant (it is not information about *X,* after all, since *X* is the poetry anthology, not poet Austin), but do you see why it is there?

OUTLINE

I. Information about *X*—paragraphs 1–2

II. Tentative negative judgment—paragraph 3

III. Definite negative judgment—paragraph 4
IV. Discussion of criteria—paragraphs 5–9
   A. The limited value of writing about one's sexual self—paragraph 5
   B. The proper criterion for choosing anthology selections—paragraph 6
   C. Poetry as an individual art—paragraphs 7–9

SUGGESTIONS FOR WRITING

1. Evaluate a work of literature (perhaps one of the poems included in this text). You might try Austin's structure: move from information about *X* to a judgment to a discussion of your criteria. Include information about yourself if you think it will help your evaluation gain acceptance.

2. Using negative criteria (*X* should *not* have certain characteristics), evaluate the dorm or apartment house you live in ("a dorm should not be noisy" might be one criterion); or evaluate a personal relationship ("marriage should not destroy each partner's individuality"); or evaluate one of your instructors ("a teacher should not . . ."). You may want to present your evaluation in the form of a letter. For instance, write to your landlord explaining that you do not plan to renew your lease because his apartment is not satisfactory.

19-inch black-and-white tv
CONSUMER REPORTS

This selection illustrates the full-form evaluation process. It applies utilitarian criteria to a product designed for consumer use: television sets. More narrowly, the items evaluated are 19-inch black-and-white TV sets. Thirteen such items are evaluated on the basis of several criteria, the most important of which ("overall picture quality") consists of five narrower criteria (paragraph 3). This assignment gives the writers an extremely large field to cover. Rather than plod through every characteristic of every *X*, they have chosen to highlight the most important characteristics of the most important *X*'s. The rest of the information is deposited in an appendix, where it is easily available for readers who want completeness, but where it will not present an obstacle for readers who want a concise and easily readable report.

Note that this *Consumer Reports* article stops short of recommenda-

Source. Copyright © 1973 by Consumers Union of United States, Inc., Mount Vernon, N.Y. 10550. Reprinted by permission from *Consumer Reports,* March 1973.

tion. The thesis is only that if you want a black-and-white TV in this age of color TV's, and if the criteria chosen by the *Consumer Reports* testers are the ones you too would choose, then one model in particular (see the "Key Findings" inset) should be your best buy. The writers are not trying to persuade you that you *should* buy a black-and-white TV rather than, say, a stereo set or a new mattress or an acre of land in Montana.

CU'S KEY FINDINGS

The check-rated *Sylvania MY2088WH,* we'd say, is your best bet. Its picture quality—crisp and correctly proportioned—was better than that of any other in this project. We judged the set easy to service. And, at $150 list, it is one of the least expensive, too.

---

1 **W**hy buy a black-and-white television set in the age of color TV? Well, black-and-white models are a good deal cheaper than color sets with screens of the same size. Repairs should be cheaper and less frequent, too, since black-and-white TVs have far fewer parts and less complex circuitry than color sets. For many people, a monochrome picture is altogether adequate; old-movie buffs especially can do nicely without color. In short, a black-and-white model has its virtues as a second set for a guest bedroom, den or playroom—or even as a first set for sporadic watchers or the budget-conscious.

2 Black-and-white sets with 19-inch screens have been particularly popular in recent years, so that's the kind we tested for this report: 13 models listing, by and large, from about $150 to about $170. Four of these models are totally solid-state, with transistors and integrated circuits throughout. Four are hybrids that incorporate tubes along with solid-state devices; the rest use only tubes. All are reasonably transportable; the *Zenith,* at 41 pounds, is the heaviest of the lot.

GETTING THE PICTURE

3 Besides evaluating overall picture quality, our chief criterion for rating a TV set's performance, we checked on a variety of factors that help to make a picture good. Those factors include crispness (sharpness of outlines), resolution (fineness of detail), focus (sharpness of horizontal scanning lines), interlace (even spacing of horizontal scanning lines, important to vertical detail), and geometric distortion (a warping or fattening of the transmitted image). We noted each set's ability to reproduce black as black, white as white and all the shades of gray in between. We made judgments of each set's tone quality. We assessed construction and design, paying special heed to features that would make a set convenient in operation and easy to service and repair.

4   The *Sylvania* offered picture quality we'd call good, overall; its picture helped that set earn check-rating. All of the rest managed to present a fair-to-good picture. Crispness left something to be desired with six models, as the Ratings note. Seven sets suffered from a slight lack of detail; with an eighth, the *JVC,* lack of detail was more apparent.

5   Nonuniform focus usually makes a picture's sides and corners blurry, though the center of the screen is sharp enough as a rule. Our electro-optical measurements confirmed that focus was rather nonuniform with the *Philco* and the *Wards.* None of the tested sets have a focus control you can adjust, as color sets usually do. A serviceman, however, can often improve focus by changing taps on a terminal inside the set (and that simple chore did indeed help the *Philco* and *Wards* models).

6   Geometric distortion of one kind or another was a problem with six sets. Such distortion often made straight lines seem curved and pulled outward at the corners, an effect known as pincushion distortion. Or it appeared as horizontal nonlinearity, making people and objects seem to increase in girth as they neared one side of the screen—usually the left.

7   When a set's interlace is stable, horizontal scanning lines remain evenly separated. One sign of stable interlace is a lack of tendency of scanning lines to pair with one another as the vertical-hold control is moved from its break-in to break-out point. (Those are the points at which a picture stops and starts rolling, respectively.) With the *RCA, Panasonic, Teledyne Packard Bell* and *GE* models, those scanning lines paired at three, four and even five positions within the range of the vertical-hold control, to the detriment of vertical detail; you could expect their pictures to be often out of interlace, and consequently coarse-looking.

8   The better its brightness, the easier a set is to view in brightly lit rooms. Brightness was especially high with the *RCA* and the *Panasonic,* and adequate with all the other tested models.

9   If a set enjoys perfect d-c restoration, its screen shows the same variations in average brightness that the TV camera sees. As the camera pans, say, from a sunlit lawn to a shady porch, or cuts from a brightly lit interior to an outdoor shot at night, the brightness of the picture changes accordingly. (Without d-c restoration the dark shot would appear as gray.) Similarly, your set is able to do justice to special lighting effects and fades. Although d-c restoration is not an absolute necessity, it's a nicety well worth having. The *Sylvania* was unique among these models in having d-c restoration; and laboratory tests showed its restoration was, for all practical purposes, perfect.

10   The Federal Communications Commission doesn't assign adjacent broadcasting frequencies to any one area (channels 4 and 5 are not neighbors in frequency—just in number). That's to prevent interference between adjacent channels that could afflict the picture with annoying lines and curlicues. Such interference could occur, however, in locations where a set can pull in stations from more than one area or city. In those areas you'd want a set that can reject adjacent-channel reception well. Adjacent-channel

rejection was unusually high with the *Motorola,* the *Teledyne Packard Bell* and the *GE,* and satisfactory with the other tested units.

11   As we've come to expect with all but console models, the tone quality of these TV sets was uniformly mediocre: no better than about poor-to-fair, in the judgment of our experienced listeners. Technically, though, there's no justification for that. Some small portable AM radios actually sound better than the FM audio of these TV sets, which are hard even on the spoken word—let alone music.

GETTING IN TUNE

12   A set's front panel is the logical place for controls that may need frequent adjustment: those for brightness, contrast and vertical hold. Horizontal hold, too, should be reasonably accessible, though not necessarily on the front panel (you probably won't need to adjust it as often as the others). The *Sylvania* and the *Motorola* are the only sets to have all those controls where CU thinks they should be. The Ratings note controls that, in our view, are inconveniently located.

13   You get picture and sound about half a minute after switching on the *Zenith, Philco* and *Wards* models. After switching on the others, you get picture and sound almost instantly, thanks to their "quick warm-up" feature. That convenience keeps sets continuously warm and ready for action by providing them with a low voltage even when the on-off switch is off. Quick warm-up may even prolong a set's life by sparing tubes (in solid-state sets, only the picture tube) the shock of high current rushes as they warm up. True, the feature boosts household bills a little: With electricity billed at 3¢ per kilowatt hour, you might pay about $6 a year extra for quick warm-up if daily viewing time is six hours (a span a national polling organization contends is the national average). A handy vacation switch lets you flick off the quick warm-up of the *Sylvania* and the *GE* should you take a trip; with the other models that offer the feature, you have to unplug the line cord.

14   The *Motorola* has a single-button "Quick-Set" picture control that's meant to eliminate the need for adjusting certain separate controls by hand. Pressing the button shifts the set from its front-panel controls to an alternate group of factory-set controls, automatically delivering a picture whose brightness, contrast and vertical hold have been preset. Our *Motorola's* vertical-hold control was preset in the middle of its fairly wide range—midway between points where rolling begins and ends, and just about where it should be. Brightness and contrast are a matter of taste; if you didn't like the factory settings, you could have a serviceman readjust the recessed controls for them. When you use *Motorola's* one-button tuning, you can't make adjustments to compensate for any differences in picture contrast from program to program or to correct faults in an aging set's picture. But in such cases, you can always return to manual tuning with the front-panel controls.

15   Unless the manufacturer aligns a set properly in the factory, the set many be incapable of giving you its best picture when you fine-tune. In that event, you actually "detune" to improve the picture, thereby making the set susceptible to various kinds of interference. Obvious clues to misalignment are herringbone patterns that come and go in step with sound rhythms, or a hum that changes as the scene changes, and neither can be removed without a sacrifice in picture sharpness. Misalignment may be the culprit if areas of your picture persist in wiggling ("worming"), be it ever so slightly. To learn whether these sets could in fact be fine-tuned to deliver their best picture, we used a radio-frequency spectrum analyzer; the analyzer told us when fine-tuning was set at exactly the right frequency for optimal reception from CU's laboratory transmitter. Two samples of the *Panasonic,* one of the *JVC* and one of the *Philco* proved to be misaligned. That kind of deficiency should be corrected under the terms of a set's guarantee.

16   With most of these sets, you need to fine-tune a given VHF channel (numbers 2 to 13) just once; thereafter a preset fine-tuning feature "remembers" the tuning point for that channel, even if you move the fine-tuning control to bring in another channel clearly. Since that convenience has been standard on all but some small-screen sets for many years now, we downrated three of the sets that lack it: the *Teledyne Packard Bell,* the *GE* and the *Admiral.* The lack of preset fine-tuning for individual channels is a real nuisance, we think, since it may force you to fiddle with the fine-tuning control whenever you change channels.

17   When you preset a channel's fine-tuning point, let the set warm up for 15 minutes or so first, whether it has quick warm-up or not. Tuning drift, which could occur during that time, might slightly impair a picture fine-tuned immediately after switch-on. We observed varying degrees of drift with some of these sets, though we didn't make it a Ratings factor since no clear-cut pattern emerged.

18   To comply with a recent ruling by the FCC, click-stop or detent tuning will eventually be standard for UHF, as it is at present for VHF stations. The *Sylvania, Magnavox, JVC* and *Philco* models have click-stop tuners preset for all 70 UHF channels; with those units, switching stations would be equally convenient on either VHF or UHF band. UHF tuners on the *Sears* and the *Panasonic* have six and 10 click-stops, respectively, that you can easily preset to points near the channels you use most often. With the other sets you must do the continuous dial-twirling that used to be the only way of tuning in UHF stations. None of the new UHF click-tuners, be it noted, have preset fine-tuning; you still have to fine-tune every time you switch channels.

19   Unless the light in your room is right, you have to guess which channel you've tuned to with the *Wards,* the *Teledyne Packard Bell* and the *Admiral,* units that lack channel-selector lights. The small VHF and UHF channel numbers of the *JVC* were hard to read even though illuminated.

20   Miscellaneous features? Each of these sets, being more-or-less portable,

has a carrying handle; we judged the handles of the *Sylvania* and the *GE* to be uncomfortable. And every model lets you store the line cord neatly out of the way. Six models have an earphone jack, and with five of those an earphone is supplied; you'd have to get your own earphone for the *Sears*. A cart comes with five models, noted in the Ratings. The *JVC* has a built-in, three-hour timer; you can adjust the timer to switch the set off automatically if you fall asleep while viewing. Many of these units come with a dark-tinted, detachable screen as an aid to outdoor viewing under a bright sky—on a porch or terrace, say.

21   As TV sets age, the picture tends to shrink horizontally. To correct that, all the sets but the *Sears,* the *RCA,* the *JVC* and the *Admiral* have some provision to adjust the picture's horizontal size. But, in most cases, you should leave that adjustment to a serviceman. It can be hazardous to meddle with a TV's innards—and the adjustment requires just that. Either a screwdriver must be poked from outside the cabinet into a recessed control or the back cover of the set must be taken off to reconnect wires. A novelty: You can safely adjust the *Motorola's* control yourself; the control is easy to operate by hand, it's clearly labeled and it sticks conveniently out of the back of the set.

ANTENNAS, REPAIRS

22   All the tested sets come with a built-in rabbit-ear antenna for VHF and a separate antenna for attachment to their UHF terminals. But unless reception in your area is unusually good, those indoor antennas are unlikely to give good results. For best viewing, you should tie sets like these to an outdoor antenna. Check your 1973 Buying Guide Issue—page 254 for some pointers on TV roof antennas and, if you already have an antenna with a TV set hooked up to it, page 258 for a discussion of TV-set couplers.

23   For fringe signals—the weak signals you might get in areas where reception is very difficult—a good roof antenna is mandatory. We fed our sets the equivalent of a fringe signal and compared their performance on both VHF and UHF bands. If you live in a weak-signal area, or if you're obliged to make do with indoor antennas, check the box on p. 324 to see which models offered the best fringe reception. (Note that misalignment, from which some of our sets suffered, can be of critical importance in fringe-area reception.)

24   You can usually expect to pay more for repairs that entail carting a set off to the shop than for servicing a repairman can do in the home. On-the-spot service on solid-state sets should be easy when their circuitry is on plug-in modules or circuit boards, since the repairman need only substitute a good module for an ailing one. The *RCA* consists primarily of modules. The solid-state *Teledyne Packard Bell* and the *GE* have only one module; most of their circuitry is on the main chassis.

25   Most of these units have a well laid-out chassis that offers easy access to the repairman, and inside the cabinet there's generally a tube- or compo-

nent-layout diagram. Only one set impressed us as being somewhat inconvenient to service: the *Admiral*. Removing the *Admiral's* tuner for cleaning, a commonplace need, would be tough since the tuner-shield is solidly soldered in place. Repairs to tuners, power-supply sections and other circuitry these sets have in common with color models won't cost you less than they would for a color TV—but you can forget about bills for repairing color circuits for demodulation, convergence and the like.

A CLEAR CHOICE

26 In our view, the check-rated *Sylvania* is clearly preferable to the other tested sets. Its picture, crisp and correctly proportioned, with the added attraction of d-c restoration, was the best. The set should be easy to service. And at $150, the *Sylvania* was among the least expensive of the tested models. Some other models with preset tuning might be attractive if impressively discounted—and if you're willing to settle for picture quality that's only fair-to-good.

27 Most of the guarantees don't cover service or repairs unless you actually bring the set into an authorized service shop. That's not much of a chore—these black-and-white units are less bulky than the typical 19-inch

FRINGE-SIGNAL RECEPTION

For those who live in fringe (weak-signal) reception areas, the tested models are listed below by groups for weak-signal viewing with VHF and with UHF. Within each quality group, listing is alphabetical.

VHF	UHF
GOOD	GOOD
Admiral 19P639C	Admiral 19P639C
General Electric UA4110WD	JVC 2865
Motorola BP535HW	FAIR-TO-GOOD
Philco B734BWA	General Electric UA4110WD
Wards 13442	Panasonic TR539
FAIR-TO-GOOD	RCA AR193
JVC 2865	Teledyne Packard Bell
Panasonic TR539	2M623WL
RCA AR193	Wards 13442
Sears 5133	Zenith D2009W
Zenith D2009W	FAIR
FAIR	Motorola BP535HW
Magnavox 5056	POOR
Sylvania MY2088WH	Magnavox 5056
Teledyne Packard Bell	Philco B734BWA
2M623WL	Sears 5133
	Sylvania MY2088WH

color set and not overly hefty. As a rule, guarantees run one year for the picture tube and other parts and 90 days for labor; the Ratings note exceptions.

RATINGS OF 19-INCH BLACK-AND-WHITE TV SETS

Listed in order of estimated overall quality for use in strong- and medium-signal areas when using a good roof antenna. Dimensions are in order of height, width and depth. Prices, except as noted, are manufacturer's suggested retail, rounded to the nearest dollar; discounts are generally available.

All have a built-in rabbit-ear VHF antenna and a separate indoor UHF antenna, carrying handle and cord-storage provision; and all were judged poor-to-fair in tone quality. Except as noted, all were judged adequate in adjacent-channel rejection and at least adequate in brightness and interlace; have individual-channel fine-tuning, quick warmup, lighted VHF and UHF channel numbers, continuous UHF tuning and provision for serviceman to adjust horizontal picture size; and were judged convenient to service. And unless otherwise indicated, all come with a guarantee of 1 yr. on picture tube, 1 yr. on other parts and 90 days on labor if the set is taken to authorized dealer for service.

ACCEPTABLE

✔**Sylvania MY2088WH** (GTE Sylvania, Inc., Batavia, N.Y.), $150. 17x22x 14½ in. 38 lb. Overall picture quality, good. Only tested set with d-c restoration (see story). Hybrid design (mostly tubes). Carrying handle on cabinet judged uncomfortable. Has 70-channel-detent UHF switching. Quick warm-up has vacation switch. Has detachable tinted screen.

Sears Cat. No. 5133 (Sears, Roebuck), $148 plus shipping. 17x22½x13¼ in. 37 lb. Overall picture quality, fair-to-good: slight lack of crispness. Hybrid design (mostly tubes). Control for vertical hold in rear, and controls for contrast and brightness at top rear of set; locations judged inconvenient. Has 6-position-detent UHF switching. No horizontal-size control. Has earphone jack; earphone not supplied. Has detachable tinted screen.

Motorola BP535HW (Motorola, Inc., Franklin Park, Ill.) $150 including cart. 16½x22½x13½ in. 39 lb. Overall picture quality, fair-to-good: slight lack of crispness. Adjacent-channel rejection, better than most. Tube design. Single button actuates a second set of factory-preset controls for brightness, contrast and vertical hold (see story). Horizontal-size control may be adjusted by owner, an advantage. Has earphone jack; earphone supplied.

Magnavox 5056 (The Magnavox Co., Fort Wayne, Ind.), $150 including cart. 18x24x13 in. 38 lb. Overall picture quality, fair-to-good: slight lack of detail, moderate geometric distortion. Hybrid design (mostly solid-state) with modules. Control for vertical hold in rear; location judged inconvenient. Has 70-channel-detent UHF switching. According to the manufacturer, the following model has essentially the same chassis: *5058.*

RCA AR193 (RCA Consumer Electronics, Indianapolis), $170. 16½x22¾x13 in. 38 lb. Overall picture quality, fair-to-good. Interlace not stable; scanning lines had considerable tendency to pair. Among the brightest sets tested. Solid-state design with modules. Controls for vertical hold and contrast in rear; location judged inconvenient. No horizontal-size control. Guarantee: 1 yr. on labor.

Panasonic TR539 (Matsushita Electric Corp. of America, NYC), $190 including cart. 16⅛x22½x14 in. 40 lb. Overall picture quality, fair-to-good: slight lack of crispness, slight geometric distortion. Interlace not stable; scanning lines had considerable tendency to pair. Both of CU's samples were improperly aligned at the factory (see story). Among the brightest sets tested. Solid-state design. Controls for vertical hold and horizontal hold on side; location judged possibly inconvenient. Has 10-position-detent UHF switching. Has earphone jack; earphone supplied. Has detachable tinted screen. Guarantee: 1 yr. on labor.

Zenith D2009W (Zenith Radio Corp., Chicago), no suggested price, $150 to $160. 16½x23½x13½ in. 41 lb. Overall picture quality, fair-to-good: slight lack of detail, moderate geometric distortion. Tube design. Controls for contrast, brightness and vertical hold on side; location judged possibly inconvenient. No quick warm-up. Guarantee: 90 days on parts. According to the manufacturer, the following models have essentially the same chassis: *D2004W, D2005W.*

JVC 2865 (JVC America, Inc., Maspeth, N.Y.), $160. 16¼x22¾x13½ in. 39 lb. Overall picture quality, fair-to-good: slight lack of crispness, moderate lack of detail. One of CU's samples was improperly aligned at the factory (see story). Tube design. Vertical-hold control in rear; location judged inconvenient. Has 70-channel-detent UHF switching. No horizontal-size control. Has earphone jack; earphone supplied. Has detachable tinted screen. Has 3-hr. timer that can be adjusted to switch set off automatically. VHF and UHF dial numbers judged somewhat hard to read.

Philco B734BWA (Philco-Ford Corp., Blue Bell, Pa.), $165 including cart. 17x22¼x13¼ in. 38 lb. Overall picture quality, fair-to-good: slight lack of detail, focus rather nonuniform, moderate geometric distortion. One of CU's samples was improperly aligned at the factory (see story). Hybrid design (mostly solid-state). Control for contrast in rear; location judged inconvenient. Has 70-channel-detent UHF switching. No quick warm-up. Has earphone jack; earphone supplied. Has detachable tinted screen. Guarantee: 90 days on parts.

Wards Cat. No. 13442 (Montgomery Ward), $148 plus shipping. 16x22x14 in. 39 lb. Overall picture quality, fair-to-good; slight lack of crispness and detail, focus rather nonuniform, moderate geometric distortion. Tube design. Controls for contrast and vertical hold in rear; location judged inconvenient. No channel-selector light. No quick warm-up. Has detachable tinted screen. Guarantee: 5 yr. on transistors. According to the manufacturer, the following model has essentially the same chassis: *13493.*

The following sets were downrated because they lack individual-channel VHF fine-tuning (see story).

Teledyne Packard Bell 2M623WL (Teledyne Packard Bell, West Los Angeles), no suggested price, about $170. 16¼x23x13½ in. 37 lb. Overall picture quality, fair-to-good: slight lack of detail, slight geometric distortion. Interlace **not**

stable; scanning lines had considerable tendency to pair. Adjacent-channel rejection, better than most. Solid-state design with 1 module. Control for vertical hold in rear; location judged inconvenient. No channel-selector light. Has detachable tinted screen. Guarantee: 2 yr. on picture tube, 1 yr. on labor. According to the manufacturer, the following model has essentially the same chassis: *2M621BG*.

General Electric UA4110WD (General Electric Co., Portsmouth, Va.), $170. 16¾x23x14 in. 35 lb. Overall picture quality, fair-to-good: slight lack of crispness and detail. Interlace not stable; scanning lines had moderate tendency to pair. Adjacent-channel rejection, better than most. Solid-state design with 1 module. Control for vertical hold in rear; location judged inconvenient. Carrying handle on cabinet judged uncomfortable. Quick warm-up has vacation switch. Has earphone jack; earphone supplied. Has detachable tinted screen. Guarantee: 1 yr. on labor. According to the manufacturer, the following models have essentially the same chassis: *UA4104WD, UA4108WD*.

Admiral 19P639C (Admiral Corp., Chicago), $150 including cart. 17½x23x14 in. 35 lb. Overall picture quality, fair-to-good: slight lack of detail. Tube design. Set judged somewhat inconvenient to service (see story). Control for vertical hold in rear; location judged inconvenient. No channel-selector light. VHF and UHF dial numbers judged hard to read. No horizontal-size control. Guarantee: 90 days on parts, 1 yr. on picture tube but prorated next 4 yr. According to the manufacturer, the following model has essentially the same chassis: *19P647C*.

COMMENTARY

To some extent, the *Consumer Reports* writers can assume a nearly captive audience. Most people who would read this article in the magazine would already have an interest in buying a television set. Nevertheless, this is an age in which many people think color when they think TV, so that the introductory paragraph here is devoted to a "justification," an explanation of why the writers think that *X* is a worthwhile subject to discuss. The next obligation is definition, first a definition of precisely what category is included in the report (black-and-white sets, with 19-inch screens, costing from about $150 to about $170), and then a definition of the criteria that will be used.

The process of evaluation itself begins in paragraph 4. The organization is by criteria rather than by television set (the appendix will offer set-by-set data). The writers begin with overall picture quality because this is, in their opinion, the most important criterion. Then they discuss tuning, "miscellaneous features," antennas and reception, and repairs. The judgment summarizes all of these separate evaluations by pointing to one model as "clearly preferable to the other tested sets" (paragraph 26). An alternative set of ratings is included in the box labeled "Fringe-Signal Reception" for readers who feel that a different criterion (the ability to pull in weak signals) should receive top priority.

The final paragraph of the report functions in two ways. It reminds potential purchasers of the limitations of guarantees and calls their attention to the "Ratings" section which follows as an appendix.

You may have noticed that the writers are evaluating TV sets from only one point of view, that of the individual consumer who wants reliable and relatively inexpensive home entertainment. They ignore other perspectives—the cost to society of each individual's desire for consumer goods, the cost to all of us of spending many hours being entertained by a metal and glass and plastic box rather than going outdoors to grow vegetables in the backyard or walking around the neighborhood to discover other human beings. To be sure, this article was designed for *Consumer Reports*; it has apparently chosen the right point of view for its own audience. No evaluation can look at anything from every conceivable perspective. But before accepting any evaluative conclusion, we ought to ask whether we accept the initial decision about values on which the conclusion depends.

OUTLINE
I. Introduction: justification—paragraph 1
II. Definitions of the sample being tested, and of the criteria—paragraphs 2–3
III. The evaluation—paragraphs 4–25
  A. Picture quality—paragraphs 4–11
  B. Tuning—paragraphs 12–19
  C. Miscellaneous features—paragraphs 20–21
  D. Antennas and reception—paragraphs 22–23
  E. Repairs—paragraphs 24–25
IV. Conclusion: Sylvania as the choice—paragraph 26
V. Transition to "Ratings" section—paragraph 27

SUGGESTIONS FOR WRITING

1. Evaluate some object designed for consumer use. You will probably deal with only one example of the type (not, as the *Consumer Reports* writers do, with 13 models), and you may not have access to all the kinds of information they use. But your personal-experience evaluation will correspond to the way that most of us decide whether a product we buy once will appear on our shopping list again.

2. Evaluate some item (perhaps TV sets) from a perspective other than that of the consumer seeking the most performance for his money.

groovin' in academe

MAURICE HUNGIVILLE

Hungiville is evaluating an advertising campaign—the one recently launched by American colleges.

If you chose your college because it was in your neighborhood or it was the cheapest school available, then you may not have been influenced by the public relations campaigns that many colleges have adopted in the 1970s. But you were probably aware of college sales pressure in your high school counselors' offices or in newspaper or TV appeals.

This essay records one person's amusement and indignation at the excesses of college propaganda. The implication is that if the colleges actually deliver what they are promising, true education has come to a halt. Either way, the advertising campaign is a bad thing: if the colleges don't deliver, that's fraud; if they do, that's a poor substitute for an education.

1 **a**merican colleges did not lack for students in the lush 1960s. A plentiful supply of war babies had come of age, determined to avoid their own war in Vietnam. Given the choice between carrying a book on campus or an M-16 rifle in a far-off jungle, most young men decided to go to college and make grades, not war.

2 Colleges in the 1970s, however, are frequently confronted with steadily shrinking enrollments, sparsely populated classrooms, and half-filled but fully mortgaged dormitories. Many colleges, as a result, have been compelled to sell themselves with all the slogans that we normally associate with odorless underarms or slip-proof dentures. The better (i.e., larger and more generously endowed) colleges may be relatively immune to this kind of hard-sell sales promotion; there is not—yet—any advertising that asks, "Wouldn't you rather have a Harvard?" But the smaller schools, which are only No. 2 or 2,000, must indeed try harder. Their advertisements constitute a curious composite portrait of the college as a commodity and the student as a customer.

INDIVIDUALITY COMES FIRST

3 What follows, then, is an unvarnished, unscientific, unqualified, admittedly impressionistic survey of some prevailing themes in academic advertising. Most of this material is probably presented in fuller more dignified detail in the college catalogs, but it is available in all its gaudy commercial simplicity only in the booklets and brochures that are sent to students.

4 Throughout these brochures certain expressions appear often enough to suggest a significance beyond their banality. Among them the word "individual" thrusts itself forward with all the mechanical predictability of a

Source. Reprinted with permission from *The National Observer*, copyright © Dow Jones & Company, Inc. 1974.

neon sign. Students at every college are assured that they are "individuals," "unique persons," or "somebodies." The smaller colleges often use these words as incantations to call up terrifying, Kafkaesque visions of impersonality at larger colleges and universities, where a student is merely a "number on a computer card" or an anonymous "face in the crowd."

5   The psychedelic poster put out by Suomi College in Hancock, Mich., is fairly typical in its emphasis on the individual. Featuring a busty girl wearing an "I'm somebody" T-shirt, the poster promises that Suomi College is "a people place," a "place where you can be the center of a successful educational experience." Additional information about Suomi College—and an affirmation of self—can be had by signing a postcard titled, "Yes, I'm Somebody Too."

"A PIECE OF THE ACTION"

6   The concern for the personal and the individual that prevails throughout these academic advertisements is invariably combined with assurances that a dazzling array of impersonal technology is also available. Widener College in Chester, Pa., quite typically features both personalized "mini-courses" along with "full-equipped, multimedia classrooms" and a learning center that provides "access to instant replays of lectures, dial access to film, video tape and recorded information in controlled acoustics and air-conditioned rooms."

7   In addition to the latest in learning technology, higher education—at least the 1974 model—features student power above all else. What was wrung so slowly from college administrators in the 1960s is now a standard built-in feature of most colleges. Entering freshmen at Macalester College in Minnesota are invited to "voice their opinions at regular monthly meetings of the faculty," while students at Rockford College in Illinois are offered "a piece of the action." At Tarkio College in Missouri, students are urged to "vote with management" on the board of directors. Hood College in Maryland is even more specific in its invitation to "learn governance by governing, by sitting on policy-making college committees, by administering $30,000 in student-activity fees, by helping the college evaluate itself and what it is doing."

8   Throughout these brochures there is a general acceptance of the notion that the student is the best judge of his educational needs. The curriculum, as a result, is often described as a plastic, polymorphously perverse substance that is easily shaped to accommodate itself to shifting student interests. Students at Hood College—and nearly everywhere else—are promised that "we not only listen when you express what you want from life, but we shape our curriculum to your individual needs." At Union College in Schenectady, N.Y., students are assured that they may "initiate independent courses, interdepartmental and interdisciplinary offerings."

9   If these student-initiated courses prove too constricting, it is also possible for the Union student to undertake "innovative academic options out-

side the usual class structure" or to pursue "many academically accredited programs away from campus." Elsewhere, students are invited to "create your own major," "design your own curriculum," and "build your own image." The emphasis everywhere is on "free-choice curriculum," or as Carroll College in Wisconsin so succinctly puts it, "courses that are desired rather than required."

AMBUSH AT PODIUM GAP

10   Some concrete effects of such a "free-choice curriculum" are evident in particular courses. At Western Michigan University the general-education requirements are offered under the tantalizing title of "Getting It Together " The "Getting It Together," or GIT, program includes such courses as "In Pursuit of Awareness," "Beyond Survival," "The Many Faces of Nature," and "Mystic and Creative Mythology." At other colleges students are enticed with new or "recycled" courses on "Death," "Silence," "Futurism," and "Me-ology," the study of the self.

11   One might expect that the promotion of Cedar Rapids, Iowa, as "a swinging place" would be the campus copy writer's greatest challenge, but many of the brochures seem to have little difficulty in depicting desolate Midwestern prairies as desirable, muggerless, smog-free Edens. Many colleges also have exotic branches in such places as London, Paris, Vienna, and Alexandria, Egypt. Students who tire of Evansville, Ind., for example, can shuttle over to the University of Evansville's overseas campus in Grantham, England. Here they can pursue their studies at the Harlaxton Study Centre, "a stone mansion in Gothic style standing in 55 acres of garden and park lands."

12   It is the faculty, far more than the locality, that seems to pose the greatest promotional problems. Like the undeniable tar in the filter cigaret or the taste of the most unpleasant mouthwash, the faculty is the part of the product that seems to arouse the greatest consumer resistance. Most schools face this problem by featuring a few photographs of professors smiling benignly at undergraduates or occasionally lecturing with manic passion. Several schools boast of the number of Ph.D.s on their staff, and one or two even boast about their lack of them.

13   Many colleges are, however, reluctant to suggest that their professors might be excessively learned or interested in anything but teaching. Coe College, for example, announces that all its professors are "hung up on teaching undergraduates" and that Coe occasionally prefers an M.A. "who can communicate to a Ph.D. who can't bridge the podium gap." Professors at Coe, when they are not bridging the podium gap, are poised to engage in "spontaneous and personal dialog with students."

14   Seton College in Yonkers, N.Y., seems to be most reassuring about faculty. In a full-page ad in the New York Times, Seton features several group photographs of students and faculty idling about in joyful intimacy and challenges the reader to guess, "Which one is the professor?" The pro-

fessor inevitably turns out to be the most garishly dressed, the most fashionably hirsute, and even the most youthful of the group.

15   The promises of power, individuality, and freedom from organized knowledge that dominate the selling of the academy suggest that the radical slogans of the 1960s have been easily assimilated by the advertising of the 1970s. These advertisements may not, of course, be a reliable guide to what is actually happening on campus, but they do reflect student expectations as perceived—and promoted—by the college account executives and the marketing-research specialist. If nothing else, this is what's being run up the flagpole. Is anybody saluting?

COMMENTARY

Superficially, Hungiville seems simply to describe the methods used in the 1970s to attract students to colleges in the face of shrinking enrollment. (An outline of the essay shows this neutral quality and nothing more, because outlines indicate what is being discussed rather than how.) At no point does he say "These methods are good" or "These methods are bad." Yet we know that he rejects the entire advertising procedure. His essay is an indictment, a negative evaluation, of the colleges' attempts to sell themselves to students.

How does he succeed in conveying his judgment without openly stating it? Largely by the use of connotative language (see Altick, p. 000). Often he exaggerates the inflated claims of the colleges in words that make them sound absurd. For example, "the word 'individual' thrusts itself forward with all the mechanical predictability of a neon sign" (paragraph 4). The comparison to a neon sign highlights the commercialism of the enterprise, while "mechanical predictability" makes the pretense of individuality seem ridiculous. The description of the curriculum as "a plastic, polymorphously perverse substance" (paragraph 8) makes it resemble Silly Putty or modeling clay and so achieves the same purpose of conveying Hungiville's opinion that this is greasy kids' stuff at best.

Second, his images and diction not only exaggerate but also become ironic. When he gives the "tantalizing title" of general requirements at one school (paragraph 10) or refers to the "muggerless, smog-free Edens" (paragraph 11) of the Midwest, we recognize that these characteristics are nonsensical. Only silly people would find "GIT" or a course in "Me-ology" tantalizing, and the small towns of Iowa hardly qualify as "Edens."

These techniques of style are designed to produce a resounding "No!" in answer to Hungiville's rhetorical question at the end. Rather than stating his evaluation, he is trying to produce it in us.

OUTLINE

   I. Colleges' quests for students in the 1970s—paragraphs 1–2
  II. Promotional devices—paragraphs 3–14
      A. Guaranteed individualism—paragraphs 3–5

B. Participation in governance—paragraphs 6–7
C. Self-selected curricula—paragraphs 8–10
D. Attractive campuses—paragraph 11
E. Attractive faculty—paragraphs 12–14
III. Summary—paragraph 15

SUGGESTIONS FOR WRITING

1. Evaluate the publicity your college uses for recruiting new students: get a packet of the materials mailed to prospective students (probably from the Admissions Office) and examine the "sales pitch" used. Do you approve of it?

2. Imitate Hungiville's technique of letting the style do the job. Write an evaluation of any commercial product (tomato soup, paper kites, plastic Christmas trees, etc.) without openly stating your opinion. Let your choice of words make it clear that you approve or disapprove.

an outline of scientists

JAMES THURBER

In our time it has become fashionable to analyze and evaluate everything— including amusing things—in a serious way. Cowboy movies, comic strips, games, the sex life of baboons and baronets all receive earnest attention from our social investigators. (See Clarke, p. 261.) Occasionally, however, a humorist turns the tables on us and provides a funny evaluation of something serious. And one good joke can sometimes tell us more about a person or an event than volumes of sober analysis.

Thurber's evaluation of scientists is a good example. His eight paragraphs of humor balance (perhaps neutralize) the entire four volumes of the *Outline of Science* edited by J. Arthur Thomson, Regius Professor of Natural History at the University of Aberdeen.

1 **h**aving been laid up by a bumblebee for a couple of weeks, I ran through the few old novels there were in the cottage I had rented in Bermuda and finally was reduced to reading "The Outline of Science, a Plain Story Simply Told," in four volumes. These books were published by Putnam's fifteen years ago and were edited by J. Arthur Thomson, Regius

Source. Copyright © 1937 James Thurber. Copyright © 1965 Helen W. Thurber and Rosemary Thurber Sauers. From *Let Your Mind Alone!*, published by Harper & Row. Originally printed in *The New Yorker*.

Professor of Natural History at the University of Aberdeen. The volumes contained hundreds of articles written by various scientists and over eight hundred illustrations, forty of which, the editor bragged on the flyleaf, were in color. A plain story simply told with a lot of illustrations, many of them in color, seemed just about the right mental fare for a man who had been laid up by a bee. Human nature being what it is, I suppose the morbid reader is more interested in how I happened to be laid up by a bee than in what I found in my scientific research, so I will dismiss that unfortunate matter in a few words. The bee stung me in the foot and I got an infection (staphylococcus, for short). It was the first time in my life that anything smaller than a turtle had ever got the best of me, and naturally I don't like to dwell on it. I prefer to go on to my studies in "The Outline of Science," if everybody is satisfied.

2   I happened to pick up Volume IV first and was presently in the midst of a plain and simple explanation of the Einstein theory, a theory about which in my time I have done as much talking as the next man, although I admit now that I never understood it very clearly. I understood it even less clearly after I had tackled a little problem about a man running a hundred-yard dash and an aviator in a plane above him. Everything, from the roundness of the earth to the immortality of the soul, has been demonstrated by the figures of men in action, but here was a new proposition. It seems that if the aviator were travelling as fast as light, the stop watch held by the track judge would not, from the aviator's viewpoint, move at all. (You've got to make believe that the aviator could see the watch, which is going to be just as hard for you as it was for me.) You might think that this phenomenon of the unmoving watch hand would enable the runner to make a hundred yards in nothing flat, but, if so, you are living in a fool's paradise. To an aviator going as fast as light, the hundred-yard track would shrink to nothing at all. If the aviator were going *twice* as fast as light, the report of the track judge's gun would wake up the track judge, who would still be in bed in his pajamas, not yet having got up to go to the track meet. This last is my own private extension of the general theory, but it seems to me as sound as the rest of it.

3   I finally gave up the stop watch and the airplane, and went deeper into the chapter till I came to the author's summary of a scientific romance called "Lumen," by the celebrated French astronomer, M. Flammarion (in my youth, the Hearst Sunday feature sections leaned heavily on M. Flammarion's discoveries). The great man's lurid little romance deals, it seems, with a man who died in 1864 and whose soul flew with the speed of thought to one of the stars in the constellation Capella. This star was so far from the earth that it took light rays seventy-two years to get there, hence the man's soul kept catching up with light rays from old historical events and passing them. Thus the man's soul was able to see the battle of Waterloo, fought backward. First the man's soul—oh, let's call him Mr. Lumen—first Mr. Lumen saw a lot of dead soldiers and then he saw them get up and start fighting. "Two hundred thousand corpses, come to

life, marched off the field in perfect order," wrote M. Flammarion. Perfect order, I should think, only backward.

4 I kept going over and over this section of the chapter on the Einstein theory. I even tried reading it backward, twice as fast as light, to see if I could capture Napoleon at Waterloo while he was still home in bed. If you are interested in the profound mathematical theory of the distinguished German scientist, you may care to glance at a diagram I drew for my own guidance, as follows:

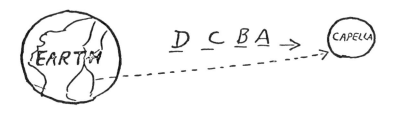

Now, A represents Napoleon entering the field at Waterloo and B represents his defeat there. The dotted line is, of course, Mr. Lumen, going hell-for-leather. C and D you need pay no particular attention to; the first represents the birth of Mr. George L. Snively, an obscure American engineer, in 1819, and the second the founding of the New England Glass Company, in 1826. I put them in to give the thing roundness and verisimilitude and to suggest that Mr. Lumen passed a lot of other events besides Waterloo.

5 In spite of my diagram and my careful reading and rereading of the chapter on the Einstein theory, I left it in the end with a feeling that my old grip on it, as weak as it may have been, was stronger than my new grip on it, and simpler, since it had not been mixed up with aviators, stop watches, Mr. Lumen, and Napoleon. The discouraging conviction crept over me that science was too much for me, that these brooding scientists, with their bewildering problems, many of which work backward, live on an intellectual level which I, who think of a hundred-yard dash as a hundred-dash, could never attain to. It was with relief that I drifted on to Chapter XXXVI, "The Story of Domesticated Animals." There wouldn't be anything in that going as fast as light or faster, and it was more the kind of thing that a man who has been put to bed by a bee should read for the alleviation of his humiliation. I picked out the section on dogs, and very shortly I came to this: "There are few dogs which do not inspire affection; many crave it. But there are some which seem to repel us, like the bloodhound. True, man has made him what he is. Terrible to look at and terrible to encounter, man has raised him up to hunt down his fellowman." Accompanying the article was a picture of a dignified and mournful-looking bloodhound, about as terrible to look at as Abraham Lincoln, about as terrible to encounter as Jimmy Durante.

6   Poor, frightened little scientist! I wondered who he was, this man whom Mr. J. Arthur Thomson, Regius Professor of Natural History at the University of Aberdeen, had selected to inform the world about dogs. Some of the chapters were signed, but this one wasn't, and neither was the one on the Einstein theory (you were given to understand that they had all been written by eminent scientists, however). I had the strange feeling that both of these articles had been written by the same man. I had the strange feeling that *all* scientists are the same man. Could it be possible that I had isolated here, as under a microscope, the true nature of the scientist? It pleased me to think so; it still pleases me to think so. I have never liked or trusted scientists very much, and I think now that I know why: they are afraid of bloodhounds. They must, therefore, be afraid of frogs, jack rabbits, and the larger pussycats. This must be the reason that most of them withdraw from the world and devote themselves to the study of the inanimate and the impalpable. Out of my analysis of those few sentences on the bloodhound, one of the gentlest of all breeds of dogs, I have arrived at what I call Thurber's Law, which is that scientists don't really know anything about anything. I doubt everything they have ever discovered. I don't think light has a speed of 7,000,000 miles per second at all (or whatever the legendary speed is). Scientists just think light is going that fast, because they are afraid of it. It's so terrible to look at. I have always suspected that light just plodded along, and now I am positive of it.

7   I can understand how that big baby dropped the subject of bloodhounds with those few shuddering sentences, but I propose to scare him and his fellow-scientists a little more about the huge and feral creatures. Bloodhounds are sometimes put on the trail of old lost ladies or little children who have wandered away from home. When a bloodhound finds an old lady or a little child, he instantly swallows the old lady or the little child whole, clothes and all. This is probably what happened to Charlie Ross, Judge Crater, Agnes Tufverson, and a man named Colonel Appel, who disappeared at the battle of Shiloh. God only knows how many thousands of people bloodhounds have swallowed, but it is probably twice as many as the Saint Bernards have swallowed. As everybody knows, the Saint

Bernards, when they find travellers fainting in the snow, finish them off. Monks have notoriously little to eat and it stands to reason they couldn't feed a lot of big, full-grown Saint Bernards; hence they sick them on the lost travellers, who would never get anywhere, anyway. The brandy in the little kegs the dogs wear around their necks is used by the Saint Bernards in drunken orgies that follow the killings.

8   I guess that's all I have to say to the scientists right now, except *boo!*

COMMENTARY

Thurber's way of organizing his essay is to begin familiarly with a disclosure about himself: "Having been laid up by a bumblebee . . ." (paragraph 1). Then he gives us a description of his reading in Thomson's *Outline* (paragraphs 2 to 5). He concludes with an evaluation, which he converts into a whimsical "Law."

The trick in this essay is that he leads us to one judgment in paragraph 5: scientists live on a higher intellectual level than ordinary people like himself—presumably like us also—who can't understand their theories even with the aid of illustrations about aviators, stop watches, and so forth. This judgment is then reversed in paragraph 6: "scientists don't really know anything about anything." The joke is that the two judgments are not really inconsistent, for if your intellectual life is too "high," you lose touch with reality and don't understand anything about it. The scientist who abandons reality is no better than a child giving expression to his own fears and fantasies.

Thurber's irritation with such people leads to his ironic paragraph 7 on man-eating bloodhounds and drunken St. Bernards. He exaggerates a scientist's erroneous description to the point of hilarious absurdity. A serious point has been made, however. Science can be only as good as its practitioners. An *Outline of Science* deserves our attention only if the people who write it seem to be reasonable and realistic.

OUTLINE

    I. Introduction: brief account of a personal experience to explain how he happened to read the *Outline*—paragraph 1

    II. The *Outline*: relativity theory, dogs—paragraphs 2–5

    III. Judgment: "Thurber's Law" that scientists are afraid of reality—paragraph 6

    IV. Epilogue: Thurber's teasing scientists with an absurd story about dogs and a parting shot, "Boo!"—paragraphs 7–8

SUGGESTIONS FOR WRITING

1. Evaluate one of your textbooks by describing a short section (as Thurber does with the chapter on the Einstein theory and the comments on dogs) and recording your response. Quote from the book if that helps.

2. Serious people tell us that the sun will shortly burn out, that mankind will starve if women have more than 2.1 babies each, that you'll die an ugly death if you don't buckle your seatbelt, that America is economically depressed and full of undernourished, homeless people. Choose any general claim such as these and write a personal account that invalidates it by making it funny.

3. Write an article, parallel to Thurber's, evaluating the social scientist or humanist instead of the scientist. Psychology or sociology or literature or history professors might furnish you with examples.

4. On the basis of Thurber's essay, would you call him an anti-intellectual? How fair is his attack?

education
ROGER PRICE

The essays in this section are evaluations. The following essay, a selection from a book, is an overt *de*valuation. The author is angry about America's pretension to education without the performance to back it up. He underlines his anger by deliberately insulting his readers when, in a footnote, he answers the question "$8 \times 8 = ?$" (paragraph 7). He repeatedly uses the word "Roob," which he has earlier defined as the urban Mass Man, "the eternal plebeian" who thrives on mediocrity and makes it a national goal. The reader, Price hints, may well be a Roob.

Why would an author attack his reader? How does he keep you reading even while he calls you names? Or do you want to stop? (In that case his strategy has backfired.) But the most important question to ask about sweeping indictments such as this one is whether the evidence adequately supports the author's judgment.

1 **t**o estimate the extent to which the attitudes of the New People will affect our future, we must examine, with a modest amount of cynicism, the Educational Process, for it is there, in the school as an environment, that they are gestating.

2 We tell ourselves, of course, that American Education is superior because there is so much of it, confusing, as we invariably do, quantity with quality. But is it superior? Are we, in fact, really educated at all?

3 We can be justifiably proud of the fact that the number of people in the United States who cannot read or write is negligible, but no matter

Source. From *The Great Roob Revolution,* by Roger Price. Copyright © 1970 by Roger Price. Reprinted by permission of Random House, Inc.

where we locate ourselves on the cultural spectrum, how many of us can read or write or even *talk* with a degree of competence, much less skill?

4   With no trouble I could quote statistics to "prove" that we are even *relatively* uneducated; that we are less literate than the Japanese; that we have fewer bookstores than Sweden; that twenty percent of our citizens are officially designated as "functionally illiterate," meaning that they do not have the equivalent of an eighth-grade education, etc.

5   But that is not my premise.

6   My premise, which is not amenable to statistics, is that we are all, as a whole, as a nation, dumb. We simply don't know very much. We are educated only in the way that a chimpanzee who sits at a table and drinks from a saucer is educated compared to a baboon. Our schools have trained us in the techniques of modern living, they have turned out excellent technologists, engineers, professional people, but they have not educated us.

7   Except for the fragmentary and specialized knowledge associated with our work, we have only the most superficial information about the world. We do not read well[1] and we do not read books. Except for a few childish folk tales, we know nothing whatever about history, and being ignorant of the past, we have no realistic idea of the future. We are surrounded by, and entirely dependent on, a technology which we cannot understand. We are intellectually *passive,* watching and listening but never understanding or remembering. Our memories are so weak that the introduction of a simple zip code causes a near panic and evokes angry howls of "I don't like it." We remember only that we are Americans, so we must therefore be educated. But can you identify, even vaguely, Charlemagne? Can you extract a simple square root? Do you know what a square root *is*? What is the capital of Illinois? Who were, in order, the last six Presidents of the United States? How much is eight times eight?[2]

8   Not only do we have no data,[3] but we have only the most tenuous grip on the basis of all intelligence: language. We have a recognition, or reading, vocabulary of only a few thousand words and often only a hazy idea of their exact meaning. We have no respect for language and accept common (i.e., Roob) usage as a criterion for correctness. We believe fatuously that language is merely another convenience, like the electric toaster, which is here to serve us. We don't realize that words, words arranged in the proper sequence, are what lead men to war, are what connect us with the past, are what brought the electric toaster into being. Without words we are not even barbarians, or even apes; we once again are what deep in our hearts we know we are anyway—wolves. Without words we cannot think, and to the extent that we neglect language, to that extent are we becoming Roobs, accepting ourselves as members of the mass, capable only of emotionalism.

---

1 As we identify quality with quantity, we also equate speed with proficiency. Hence the ridiculous "speed-reading" courses.
2 Sixty-four!
3 The culture abounds with data, but it's all processed and stored in machines.

The mass, let us not forget, has its own identity, its own consciousness, but it is always motivated by emotion, never by intellect.

9   Alas, we have forgotten, as a nation and as individuals, how to Think.[4] And this mass dumbness is not, as it was in past times, counterbalanced by a small but truly educated minority, an intelligentsia, an educated upper class. We are all there is—and we are dumb.

10   What then is happening in the gigantic and complex school system that we are so proud of?

11   Well. . . .

12   Education, like Pet Food, Sports, Sex, Pimples and Fun, has become Big Business. It is, in fact the *biggest* business, employing more people and paying more salaries than any other specific national enterprise.

13   In every section of the country we see brand-new teaching "plants," their classrooms equipped with the latest pastel-colored plastic seats, each with a patented E-Z-Swing writing arm, arranged on terraces around an electronically amplified lectern. Each plant comes complete with a poured-concrete library, a student union, a science building and a parking problem. To approach any of these new, improved schools during class time, one must struggle across an ugly tundra of parked cars which stretches in all directions much farther than any eye cares to see.[5]

14   Many of these new facilities are junior or community colleges which are little more than extension high schools, filled with tacky students wiping their noses on their Dacron sleeves and looking upon the Learning Experience exactly as they look upon anything that takes them away from the telephone and the Box—as a drag. They go, have done with it, and rush back to the parking lot. They are passing their time. They aren't waiting. Just passing time.

15   On the other hand, the huge universities with fifteen thousand or more undergraduates have the appearance of the Ford River Rouge Plant. Their new federally funded buildings are often, due to space limitations, jammed in between the older museum-type structures, giving the campus the look of a 1939 World's Fair.

16   These huge factories, however, hum night and day, turning out graduates as efficiently as the Campbell Company turns out soup, except that unlike the soup company the university has no Quality Control. But they, the universities, are not really responsible for their product. Their students' conditioning began much earlier, in primary and nursery schools, where for twenty years they have been standardized by Avant Roob mysticism and a succession of scientific theories. And strangely, this standardization of the pupil is at every level justified in the name of its opposite, Individualism.

---

[4] "One of the frightening things about our time is the number of people who think it is a sign of intellectual audacity to be stupid. A whole generation seems to be taking on an easy distrust of thought . . . it is as though information and reason itself were a form of pedantry."—Renata Adler (*The New York Times,* March, 1968)
[5] For the past two years I've been making forays into the scholastic world to give lectures at various colleges, and wherever I go, I find the Big Problem is always parking. The secondary problem is the auditorium, which will hold only four percent of the student body.

17   At exactly this point in this manuscript, I went into the kitchen for my 6:30 coffee break (when writing, I get up at 4:30 A.M.) and turned on the Box, and there in front of the NBC cameras was a clutch of three college teachers discussing education. I'd heard it all before, but they saved me the trouble of reconstructing it. Compressed, this is their message:

The aim of the educator is to develop the complete child so that he becomes an integrated individual in a democratic society. Old-fashioned schooling forced students to learn rote answers to uninteresting problems and to strive for grades. Grades are definitely not the answer. Bad grades discourage the student. Rote learning inhibits his creativity. Modern teaching techniques, however, structure a learning situation in which the student finds excitement in discovering social and scholastic skills. Once the student does not feel threatened by a fear of criticism, he is able to evaluate his own progress and create his own planning situation. In this way he can express himself and realize his potential as an individual.

18   Spokesmen for the humanities, and particularly pedagogues, seem to have not only a fondness but a talent for the spectral abstraction and the cryptic theory, and to be totally uninterested in empirical results. Means, to them, are everything and lead only to more complex Means—never to an End. They are often in the position of a lecturer who, standing beside a pan of boiling water, explains his theory that water freezes when its temperature is raised. "You will notice," he says confidently, "that when I turn the heat up under this pan, the water freezes even more rapidly." And beside him the water continues to boil.

19   Their dedication to the holy cause of Education as Panacea leads many teachers to speak of it as if it were a theology, designed to save the student's soul rather than a discipline meant to improve his mind. The widespread resistance to giving the student data, to "rote learning," seems to me very strange because what really is education if not the acquiring of information and data? An example of pure Roobthink is the student who says, "I can't learn because the subject is not taught in a way that interests me. It is boring." In other words, he "doesn't like it," and when he does not learn, it is the *teacher's* fault. This student often seems to feel that if he does learn anything, it is a favor to someone—his teacher, his parents, someone. How interesting can learning the multiplication table or analytical calculus be if there is no interest within the student for learning itself? Or if there is no capacity for learning? Do they want Raquel Welch to teach them the atomic numbers and weights of the 103 elements? And how can one begin to understand English history until one memorizes the cluttered sequence of the reigns of the various rulers? How can one make a decision about anything without data related to the subject? The answer obviously is that without information one can only make an emotional, or Roob, decision based on "I like it" or "I don't like it."

20   Or if, as has been claimed, the purpose of education is to build Character, how can one have Character without discipline? Any organism can only recognize its characteristics, discover what it is able to do, when it is

challenged. If I don't challenge myself by trying to play the piano or second base, how can I know whether or not I have the ability to be a pianist or a second baseman?

21   Unfortunately a real challenge involves Competition either with one's peers or with an abstract criterion of excellence; and "competition" is the Number One Bad Word in the pedagogical lexicon. Increasingly, colleges today are doing away with competitive examinations[6] and many refuse to compile or release class standings. Competition is considered undemocratic, and with it the idea that anyone is smarter, quicker or more industrious than anyone else.

22   In place of Competition, the pedagogues have substituted Individualism. Webster defines Individualism as "the living of one's own life without regard for others," and for twenty years young people have been brought up in the shadow of this asocial idea. It is no wonder that today they are able to submerge all of their confusions into the one need for Self-Gratification.

23   There are certainly many excellent schools in the United States, tough schools which have no time for the numbskull or the goof-off. Schools which encourage thought and respect, originality and accomplishment. But more and more these good schools are being subjected to the pressures of rising enrollment, undergraduate turbulence and right-wing political power, and Roobism is insidiously gaining a foothold. At Harvard, Columbia, Berkeley, Cornell, Princeton—in all of our greatest universities—mob boorishness is the order of the day. And the examples set in these institutions and widely and constantly publicized by TV are reflected in upheavals in lesser colleges and even in many high schools. Extracurricular activity has taken the form of a South American revolution. Shots are fired; buildings are stormed; "hostages" are taken; bricks, blows and invective are exchanged, and the word "confrontation" is knocked about like a badminton bird. And on almost all large campuses these days, heroin addiction (the *reductio ad absurdum* of Fun to the ultimate vulgarity) is openly discussed as a school problem.

24   In the larger state universities the students have been aware of the Roob Power inherent in their mass for some time, and each semester sees more of them organizing and "demanding" greater control of the universities—the right to judge teachers and vote on their tenure, the right to decide what shall be taught and who shall be admitted. Although these ad hoc gangs exhibit all the characteristics of a lynch mob and seldom reflect the majority attitude of the student body, they are often supported by the Avant Faculty (who probably have visions of a Guillotine being erected on the Mall at any moment). And more often than not, school administrators bow to the "demands" made by the mob, and we find the anonymous mass student, the burgeoning Roob, arrogantly imposing his brute standards of "I like," "I don't like" upon the entire educational framework.

[6] Tests are given incessantly, but tests which "evaluate" the student's personality, adjustment, sex life and attitude toward tests.

Soon he will control the schools as completely as he controls the mass media and industry. Soon Quality Education will be confined to a few private and parochial schools. The rest will become giant Play Pens. Fun Places.

COMMENTARY

Many people imagine that essay writing is a pretty tame business and that only fiction writers elicit powerful feelings. In the hands of a skillful writer, however, an essay can become equally powerful. Price's attack on American education is a good example. He uses many rhetorical devices for heightening emotion: short paragraphs (5 and 11); short sentences, including emphatic and deliberate "fragments" (paragraph 23); unusual capitalization (e.g. Educational Process, Box, Means, Ends, Character); and striking diction (an ugly tundra of parked cars, Roobthink, ad hoc gangs). Hungiville (p. 329) uses similar devices.

While Price is substantiating his thesis that American education does not educate, he is at the same time implying the criteria by which he will evaluate it. Education itself he defines as "the acquiring of information and data" (paragraph 19). He shows that Americans are "dumb" by claiming that we can't do mathematics and that we know nothing about history or language (paragraphs 7 and 8). He does not support these allegations with facts but invites us to supply the facts for him by admitting that we are guilty. *We* are dumb. We become Exhibit A in his prosecution of the case, and we are thus engaged in the argument whether we want to be or not. Then Price points the finger of blame at our educational institutions because they have not, by and large, taught us mathematics, history, and language. This is appealing because each reader can say to himself: "I may be dumb, but it's not my fault."

Price's denunciation is so passionate that we may neglect to ask for evidence. Are American students "dumber" than those of other nations? How can this be measured? Are Price's conclusions adequately validated? Also, we may neglect to consider the fairness and acceptability of his criteria. Should education really be measured by students' ability to solve math problems and to recall facts?

OUTLINE

I. Americans are "dumb"—paragraphs 1–9
II. What's wrong with American education?—paragraphs 9–23
    A. Junior college education achieves nothing—paragraph 14
    B. Large universities robotize students—paragraphs 15–16
    C. Educators misconceive their purpose—paragraphs 17–20
    D. Discipline and competition are absent—paragraphs 21–23
III. Outside a few quality schools, "Roob Power" rules—paragraphs 23–24

SUGGESTIONS FOR WRITING

1. Evaluate a specific aspect of high school or college in terms of Price's criteria. Present information, for instance, about your high school's history courses. Did they give you what Price would consider a quality education in history?

2. If your concept of education is different from Price's, evaluate the same *X* as in Suggestion 1, using your own criteria.

3. According to Price, there are a few "quality schools" and many bad ones. All two-year schools and large universities are bad. Interview a graduate of a good school and a bad one (by Price's criteria) and evaluate the accuracy of Price's distinction. Does your evidence show that the education given by a two-year school or a large university corresponds to Price's assessment of what goes on there?

4. If you know a student educated outside the United States (don't forget Canada and Mexico), compare his knowledge with yours and decide who is "dumber."

future schlock

ROBERT CLAIBORNE

We have been bombarded with "futuristics" in recent years. Science fiction, TV programs such as "Star Trek," and a flood of books and articles that predict our future have accustomed us to accept change uncritically. Claiborne calls us up short for this habit of mind. His article is a review of Alvin Toffler's book *Future Shock;* but in addition to evaluating the book, he evaluates the frame of mind that has become common as a result of what he calls "schlock sociology" (paragraph 2). The criteria for measuring "schlockiness" are numerous. The list runs for seven paragraphs (3–9). Claiborne then illustrates a number of "schlock" tests, ploys, and capers (e.g., Evasive We, Plausible Passive, Gold Brick Generality, and Semantic Fast Shuffle).

Claiborne exaggerates "schlock" into parody: he makes fun of it by practicing it himself. His own "lively literary style" joins "gussie" colloquialism with antique formality ("Deponent sayeth not," in paragraph 22). The last paragraph makes a recommendation ("we must confront . . ."), but this seems to be an afterthought. Claiborne's main thrust is to discredit (devalue) a popular way of thinking.

schlock, *n. slang:* Merchandise of meretricious or obviously inferior quality . . .
AMERICAN HERITAGE DICTIONARY

1   **a**merica, which leads the world in almost every economic category, leads it above all in the production of schlock. Christmas toys broken before New Year's, wash-n-wear suits that neither wash well nor wear well, appliances that expire a month after the guarantee, Barbie dolls, frozen pizza—these are but a few of the shoddy goods whose main contribution to our civilization, apart from a momentary satisfaction to the purchaser, is to swell the sanitary-fill schlock heaps that are the feces of our Gross (and how!) National Product.

2   America's schlock output is not limited to material goods, of course. Schlock novels, movies and TV programs are an old story, and the spread of higher education has more recently begotten a new division of schlock software: intellectual schlock. We have schlock anthropology (Ardrey, Morris); schlock psychology (Franzblau, Brothers, many more); and schlock criticism (you name 'em). President Nixon has obviously been relying on schlock economics, even as the Pentagon has long dealt in schlock geopolitics. Most omnipresent of all is the subject of the present essay: schlock sociology.

3   Sociological schlock, like any other variety, is designed to exploit a human need—in this case, the craving to make some sort of sense out of an increasingly demented society. Since the market is assured, and virtually limitless, the production of schlock sociology for fun and profit is not particularly difficult, given a reasonable amount of imagination and a firm grasp of the major requirements. An important ingredient is a lively literary style; the ideal product should read like *The Decline of the West* rewritten by Vance Packard (who would himself qualify as a schlock sociologist if he were a bit more pretentious). But even a lumpy style can sometimes be adequately leavened by some trendy chapter headings.

4   The absolutely essential ingredient, however, is an Insight—a phrase that sums up, aphoristically or antithetically, some current—and usually alarming—social tendency and thereby strikes a nerve in the body politic. Representative Insights include "the lonely crowd," "the true believer," "the end of ideology," "organization man," "repressive tolerance" and—the probable granddaddy of them all—"the managerial revolution."

5   As will be seen from these examples, an Insight need not necessarily be false and in fact is usually true—though a really virtuoso performer can make do with one that is merely catchy ("the medium is the message"). It is not by the validity of his Insight that one identifies the schlock sociologist, but by how he develops it: the fulsomeness of his documentation, the plausible superficiality of his analysis, and the evasiveness of his conclusion.

6   There is, to be sure, a much simpler test for schlockiness: time. Within five years (and often by the time the book is out in paperback) events will have made clear whether the acuteness of the author's Insight is matched by his understanding of its genesis and future development. Thus it was

not many years after Daniel Bell's funeral oration over the grave of ideology that ideological movements dislodged an American President and brought France close to civil war. The reader interested in quicker methods of intellectual quality control, however, may care to consider the following diagnostic traits, any one of which should create a suspicion of schlock, while together they can be taken as conclusive.

7   *Documentation:* This will be voluminous, multi-disciplinary and preferably multilingual; the effect will be to overwhelm the reader with "facts" so that he has little opportunity to reflect on whether they are true, let alone whether they fit together. The longer the bibliography and the more obscure or inaccessible its constituents, moreover, the more certain that— whether or not the author has read all the items—no reader will be familiar, now or ever, with more than a small fraction of them. Often, however, the reader can apply the simple touchstone of the "I Was There" test: locate in the index some person, institution or field of knowledge of which he happens to have detailed personal knowledge and then check to see how the author handles it. My own disenchantment with *The Lonely Crowd* began when I read in it a number of statements which I knew to be nonsense—because they dealt with a magazine I happened to be working for.

8   *Analysis:* The most conspicuous giveaway is an explicit rejection or an implicit abandonment of logic, but this is dangerously obvious unless the author possesses the bravura of a McLuhan, or is addressing the ill-educated young. Most schlock sociologists, therefore, prefer to rely primarily on obfuscation by means of various identifiable rhetorical ploys, some of which I shall describe in detail in a moment.

9   *Conclusion:* However ominous the world that the schlock sociologist portrays, he will invariably conclude that either (a) nothing *can* be done about it (e.g., *The Organization Man*) or (b) nothing *need* be done about it (e.g., *The Greening of America*) or (c) nothing *much* need be done about it—i.e., the difficulty can be resolved without seriously discommoding the reader or anyone else. An author who tells you that dealing with the problem he poses will cost you time, trouble and conceivably your life, your fortune and your sacred honor may be a nut, a commie or an ignoramus, but he is assuredly not a schlock merchant.

10   Analyzed by these techniques, Alvin Toffler's *Future Shock* assays as unmistakable schlock, albeit of superior quality. His style is lively and readable—his chapter and section headings, in particular, glitter with such gems as "The Paper Wedding Gown," "The Modular Man," "Communes and Homosexual Daddies" and (my favorite) "Twiggy and the K-Mesons." And, to do him full justice, he has come up with an absolute dilly of an Insight: Future Shock, "the shattering stress and disorientation that we induce in individuals by subjecting them to too much change in too short a time." Future shock is in effect a subdivision of cultural shock—"what happens when the familiar psychological cues that help an individual to function in society are suddenly withdrawn and replaced by new ones that

are strange or incomprehensible." Toffler deserves our gratitude for having the wit to see that culture shock can occur not only in space but also in time.

11 Thus, he writes, "the increased rate at which situations flow past us vastly complicates the entire structure of life, multiplying the number of roles we must play and the number of choices we are forced to make. . . . The speeded-up flow-through of situations demands much more work from the complex focusing mechanisms by which we shift our attention from one situation to another. There is more switching back and forth, less time for extended, peaceful attention to one problem or situation at a time. . . ." Moreover, "rising rates of change . . . compel us not merely to cope with a faster flow, but with more and more situations to which previous personal experience does not apply."

12 Given an Insight of this potency, it doesn't much matter that Toffler's account of its origins is overlong and exaggerated, or that his discussion of the physical and psychological ills it entrains is overshort and scientifically inconclusive. Future shock is a reality that most of us can feel in our guts. Change implies uncertainty—and there is a limit to the amount of uncertainty a man can cope with before freaking out; coping with change requires energy—and there is a limit to the amount of energy a man can expend in a given time without succumbing to nervous and/or physical exhaustion. Almost everyone has experienced this sort of overstress at least occasionally; the accelerating rate of innovation in our world and the multiplying choices we must make among innovations now threaten to make it chronic.

13 Yet for all that, the book, by the tests cited above, still comes out schlock. As regards documentation, we note that Toffler's bibliography includes no less than 358 books, plus seven "consulted" periodicals, in half a dozen languages including the Scandinavian. They range from *A Social Psychological Interpretation of the Udall, Kansas, Tornado* to John Barth's *The Floating Opera*. Less than half of them are listed in the footnotes, engendering the suspicion that at least some of the remainder are padding. Suspicion is strengthened when we notice a tendency common among schlock sociologists: citation of other schlock or quasi-schlock authorities. As a rule of thumb, suspicion of mutual schlock-scratching exists when an author cites more than six works by Vance Packard, Buckminster Fuller, David Riesman, Marshall McLuhan, B. F. Skinner and Margaret Mead, singly or in combination. Toffler cites fourteen. (I should add that my characterization of Miss Mead's sociological efforts obviously does not apply to her anthropological contributions.)

14 The book also fails to pass a simple "I Was There" test. Toffler, seeking a metaphor for the wracking social transition we are now undergoing, comes up with the "traumatic" period in which our vertebrate ancestors were evolving from fish to amphibians: "Eons ago, the shrinking seas cast millions of unwilling aquatic creatures onto the newly created beaches. Deprived of their familiar environment, they died, gasping and clawing for

each additional instant of eternity. . . ." Now, I Was There, in the sense that, having written three books and part of a fourth dealing in one way or another with evolution, I have considerable expertise in the field. I can therefore say flatly that there is not the slightest evidence that during the period in question the seas were shrinking—especially not with such suddenness as to strand millions of aquatic creatures. There is, moreover, much evidence that the evolutionary transition from fish to amphibian occurred, not upon ocean beaches, "newly created" or otherwise, but in freshwater swamps. Finally, there is no reason to suppose that the transition was especially "traumatic" for any of the organisms involved. Toffler's affecting narrative is pure hokum. Admittedly, *hokum in unum, hokum in omnium* is by no means an absolute principle, but in schlock testing it is a useful working hypothesis.

15   It is when we examine Toffler's analytic methods, however, that the suspicion of schlockiness becomes certainty, for he consistently uses most of the half-dozen ploys by which the schlock sociologist obfuscates the problem he is ostensibly elucidating. To begin with, the Evasive We, invaluable for shifting the responsibility for a social problem from somebody to nobody. Thus (my emphasis) "*We* have created the disposable person: Modular Man"; "*We* are forcing people to adapt to a new life pace"; "*We* have not merely extended the scope and scale of change, *we* have radically altered its pace"—*und so weiter*. To make certain that an author is employing the Evasive We, replace "we" with "I and my friends"; if the result is gibberish, you are being conned.

16   Sometimes, however, the Evasive We won't do; only a fool would expect to get away with saying that "*We* are making new scientific discoveries every day and *we* are putting them to work more quickly than ever before." Toffler therefore adopts the Plausible Passive: "New scientific discoveries are being made every day. . . . These new ideas are being put to work more quickly. . . ."—thereby rather neatly obscuring the fact that scientists and engineers (mostly paid by industry) are making the discoveries and industrialists (often with the aid of public funds) are putting them to work. An alternative to the Plausible Passive is the Elusive Impersonal: "Buildings in New York literally disappear overnight." What Toffler is trying to avoid saying is that contractors and real estate speculators *destroy* buildings overnight.

17   But if not industrialists and speculators, *something* is surely causing social change, and Toffler is too expert a schlockmeister to ignore this fact. He therefore resorts to yet another ploy, Rampant Reification, in which conceptual abstractions are transformed into causal realities. Thus he speaks of "the roaring current of change" as " an elemental force" and of "that great, growling engine of change—technology." Which of course completely begs the question of what fuels the engine and whose hand is on the throttle. One does not cross-examine an elemental force, let alone suggest that it may have been engendered by monopoly profits (especially in defense and aerospace) or accelerated by government incentives (e.g.,

open or concealed subsidies, low capital gains tax, accelerated depreciation —which Nixon is now seeking to reinstitute).

18 Space does not allow a detailed discussion of all Toffler's schlock ploys. There is the "Now I Say It, Now I Don't" maneuver, especially useful for trapping critics who, in pouncing on some particularly silly statement, may well overlook the author's own refutation of it some chapters away. There is the Goldbrick Generality, in which a plating of generalized truth conceals the leaden absence of specifics within. ("We would do well to hasten the controlled—selective—arrival of tomorrow's technologies" seems reasonable until you realize that nothing is said about who is to do the controlling, by what social mechanisms, and to what ends.) In fact about the only important ploy *not* present is that favorite of McLuhan's, the Semantic Fast Shuffle, where a word means one thing going into a paragraph and something else coming out. Two devices, however, must be singled out for special attention because they bear on the substance—if that is the word—of Toffler's argument.

19 The first is the Things Are Usually What They Seem caper. Toffler gets into this because, while deploring the headlong pace of change in general (Goldbrick Generality), he fights shy of attacking specific kinds of changes, and in fact seems to feel that in most areas change is a pretty Good Thing. Thus he finds traditional bureaucracy changing to a looser-structured (and presumably less dehumanizing) arrangement that he calls Ad-hocracy. This is obviously a Good Thing—so long as one ignores the fact that the new Ad-hocracies somehow end up doing the same manipulative, self-serving and often stupid things as the old bureaucracies (for documentation, see under PENTAGON, LOCKHEED, BOEING, PENN CENTRAL, etc.).

20 Again, he sees modern technology as by and large a Good Thing; it does not (as suggested by some) lock us into a rigid, dehumanized existence but rather enormously expands the choices open to us. As an example of these choices, he quotes McLuhan (who else?) on the various "combinations of styles, options and colors available on a certain new family sports car"; the total works out at some 25 million "choices." Unfortunately, every goddamn one of the 25 million pollutes the atmosphere, dents if you lean on it too hard and is unsafe at any speed. As most thoughtful consumers have become aware, the choices open to them are governed by the Law of Minimal Differences: the degree of substantive difference among functionally similar products varies inversely with the number of such products—i.e., as the number approaches infinity, the difference approaches zero. Schlock sociology, like schlock everything else, focuses on the package, not the contents.

21 Yet despite his evident reluctance to indict any specific changes as dispensable, Toffler has made too powerful a case against future shock to drop the matter there. Indeed, he concedes that both future shock and most of our other problems "stem not from implacable natural forces but from man-made processes that are at least potentially subject to our control." Taken together with his previous citation of the "elemental force"

of change, this is of course a Now I Say It Now I Don't, and simultaneously a Goldbrick Generality, since it leaves hanging the central question of what men are in fact making these man-made processes.

22   Insofar as he makes a stab at answering the question, in passages scattered throughout the book, Toffler resorts to perhaps the most basic maneuver of all liberal schlock sociology: All Men Are Guilty—and So What? Manufacturers are guilty—"many of the annual model changes . . . are not technologically substantive." Well then, should we—meaning I and my friends—try to force manufacturers to dispense with trivial changes? Deponent sayeth not. Manufacturers are guilty—and so what?

23   Advertising is also not blameless: "Madison Avenue frequently exaggerates the importance of new features and encourages consumers to dispose of partially worn-out goods to make way for the new." Should we perhaps do something about Madison Avenue—say, a truth in advertising law, or a limit on the amount of advertising that can be charged off as tax-deductible? Toffler doesn't tell us.

24   Consumers, too, are guilty: often the consumer "has a vague feeling that he wants a change." This statement is undocumented and, in my own case, untrue; if anything, I have a by-no-means-vague feeling that change is what I *don't* want. This derives from repeated experiences with a new marketing principle: if it works, change it—whereby products that I know and like disappear, to be replaced by other, inferior versions. But assuming that it *is* true of some consumers—so what should we do about it? So nothing!

25   Obviously, tackling the problem of unnecessary change from any of these directions, let alone all three together, would involve a long, hard and dubious battle. Toffler, as a partisan of the "nothing much need be done about it" school, wants none of this. What he proposes is not struggle but a series of Mad Tea Parties. Thus he recommends "the construction of highly intricate models, games and simulations, the preparation of detailed speculative scenarios" to descry the alternative futures open to us. We must, in other words, consult those clever people who gave us Vietnam—which, as one very knowledgeable commentator has noted, was the most thoroughly "gamed" and "scenarioed" war in history. We need to construct "utopia factories" which can experiment with new models of society. We need, God help us, to "convene . . . democratic constituent assemblies charged with social stock-taking . . . with defining and assigning priorities to specific social goals. . . ." National priorities . . . social goals. . . . Oy! Having told us that we are being psychologically raped by change, Toffler finally concludes that with just a bit of painless social tinkering we can relax and enjoy it.

26   A meaningful, non-schlock analysis of the future-shock problem would have to begin with Toffler's own unexceptionable conclusion: "Change rampant, change unguided and unrestrained, accelerated change, overwhelming not only man's physical defenses but his decisional processes—such change is the enemy of life." It would continue with the recognition

that most changes in our society—at a guess, something like 80 per cent —are unnecessary (in the sense that they make no contribution toward meeting human needs or improving the human condition) and often actively inimical. At best, they are feats of packaging which are not "technologically substantive," which gussie up schlock products—or institutions —for the benefit of their proprietors; at worst, they are substantively antihuman, enforced by top corporate and governmental bureaucrats (or Adhocrats) for their own power or profit. (Toffler cites the case of an executive compelled to change his residence twenty-eight times in twenty-three years of married life!)

27   We do not have to put up with these changes. We do not have to have an SST or an Everglades jetport; we do not have to have the annual spate of new, "improved" models in everything from automobiles to skirts; we do not have to have conglomerates, nonreturnable bottles, paper wedding gowns or any of the other innovations which simultaneously foul up our natural, our social and (as Toffler has made clear) our psychological environments. We do not have to have schlock.

28   But to set bounds to these changes, be they inimical or merely spurious, involves facing up to the nature of their source. Toffler himself, in one of his few non-schlock passages, says of technological change what could equally be said of change in general: "In the West, the basic criterion for filtering out certain . . . innovations and applying others remains economic profitability." If we are to seize control of our own future, we must confront the long, difficult problem of restructuring social institutions so that they march to a different drummer, making man, not Mammon, the measure of all things. And if, bemused by the agile evasions and trendy catchwords of schlock sociology, we fail to do this, then we—meaning I and my friends and all the rest of us—will deserve what we get: both future shock and a schlock future.

COMMENTARY

Mockery is a favorite way to attack anything that becomes exaggerated. Claiborne's target is our exaggerated and (to him) irresponsible preoccupation with the future. He takes a typical example of this preoccupation, Alvin Toffler's *Future Shock,* and turns it inside out by showing that it is a symptom of the disease it was intended to diagnose.

Claiborne lists the assumptions and procedures that "futurologists" use and shows how they lead to invalid conclusions. His essay works like a little encyclopedia of logical fallacies and phony rhetorical devices. By capitalizing words and phrases that we usually accept without question ("Insight," "Now I Say It, Now I Don't"), he alerts us to the shoddy thinking that clever language often conceals. For example, we are often guilty of the "Evasive We" and the "All Men Are Guilty" ploys—by which we imply "I'm really okay, but all those other people are at fault."

The strength of Claiborne's evaluation derives partly from his ingenuity in singling out the stock devices of bad (schlocky) thinking and partly from sheer quantity. Anything that fits so many criteria for "bad" *must* be inferior. But Claiborne is not saying that *all* preoccupation with the future is foolish. His last paragraphs point out that because the future is so threatening, we must resist cheap and easy solutions. Future shock/ schlock demands more serious and clearer thought than it has received.

OUTLINE
    I. The prevalence of schlock—paragraphs 1–2
    II. Definition of sociological schlock by division into parts—paragraphs 3–9
    III. Application to Toffler's *Future Shock*—paragraphs 10–26
    IV. Preferable alternatives—paragraphs 26–28

SUGGESTIONS FOR WRITING

1. Evaluate any popular fad or movement by using Claiborne's technique of parodying its assumptions and methods. For example, the science fiction fad, women's lib, campus fashions, professional sports, antique collecting, hunting or fishing or camping.

2. What happens to serious issues (ecology, various religious movements, the "counterculture" revolution in music or art, the search for ethnic identity, etc.) once they are commercialized? Examine familiar terms, slogans, and claims popularly associated with the issue you choose.

a christmas biography

ANDREW M. GREELEY

Greeley's "Christmas Biography" is, as you might expect from its title and its date of publication (December 23), an article about the life of Jesus. But beyond that, it is an evaluation of modern Christianity on the basis of Jesus's own standards. If Jesus were to return today, Greeley says, he would not find much to win his approval in the modern "Christian" world.

Greeley has chosen to use a set of criteria about which there is much disagreement: principles derived from Jesus's own experiences and teachings. To prevent confusion, Greeley spends much of his essay on defining the particular version of those criteria that he wants to use. He devotes ten paragraphs to the historical Jesus and another eight to summarizing Jesus's message. Then he returns to the evaluative question: Was Jesus (so defined) right? If so, our "Christian" world, a world so insensitive to Jesus's ideals that it would recrucify him, is terribly wrong. Greeley, who believes that Jesus *was* right, is forced to a sharply negative evaluation of contemporary Christianity because it falls short of its founder's message.

1   **t**here is good news, we are told, and bad news.

2   The good news? Jesus has come back to the world! The bad news? He's really ticked off!

3   The joke in its unmodified original form is undoubtedly vulgar. To some, it may seem to skirt the edge of blasphemy. In fact, however, it conveys a profound historical and theological truth. The rabbi from Nazareth would scarcely be pleased with his followers at any time since his departure. Should he reappear on the scene today, he might respond to the current attempts to make him an entertainment culture hero in about the same way he responded to the money-changers in the temple.

4   Jesus would not like the picture created by some Catholics portraying him as a gun-toting revolutionary. He would scarcely be edified by the argument of some conservative Protestants that he is an American super-patriot. He would not be excited by the news that he made the cover of Time magazine not once but twice as a hippie hero. As a man who never sought anything for himself, Jesus would be acutely embarrassed by the attempt of the fundamentalist "Key 73" campaign to "win America for Christ." What they could win, he wouldn't want. "Godspell" and "Superstar" would repel him, and he would be made faintly ill by Leonard Bernstein's pseudo-significant "Mass." Doubtless, he would not be particularly happy that the Danish Government was funding a pornographic film about his loves, and that some Christian enthusiasts were throwing Molotov cocktails at Danish embassies in reprisals.

5   He would not be pleased by the plea of the Catholic Church that nothing besides periodic continence can be done about the world's population problems. But then, he wouldn't like much the propensity of Protestant clergymen in solemn assembly convened to pass a lengthy set of resolutions providing detailed answers to all existing political and social problems. He would not, I suspect, enjoy a tourist trip through the Vatican museums and the Sistine Chapel, but then neither would he be impressed by the endless committee meetings of the World Council of Churches. He might very well be permitted to attend the annual meeting of the National Council of Catholic Bishops, but he scarcely would be entitled to vote.

6   Fundamentalist, revolutionary, ecclesiastical bureaucrat, counterculture hippie, porno film maker—all are busily engaged in making Jesus into their own images and likenesses. He didn't go for that sort of thing once, and there is no reason to think he'd go for it now. What's more, contemporary historical scholarship tells us enough about the person and message of Jesus to make it certain that those who are serving up their own models of Jesus don't know what they're talking about. He was not a

bureaucrat enforcing canon law, nor a freaked-out hippie, nor a political agitator, nor a confused liberal, nor an effeminate pietist. Indeed, if one wants a picture of Jesus most in keeping with what we know about him, one might turn to the Pantocrator of the Monreale mosaic which portrays Jesus as a strong, fierce, vigorously attractive male—an appealing but very tough customer indeed; certainly no one to mess with.

7   The debate about the "historical Jesus" has been a lengthy and complex one with the water muddied by the obscure historical philosophies of German scholarship. Still, there is a reasonably broad consensus at the present time that while we may not be able to write a biography of Jesus the way we could write a biography of Napoleon or Franklin Roosevelt, it is still possible to have a reasonably clear picture of what sort of person he was and what kind of message he was preaching. This scholarly consensus, incidentally, cuts across denominational lines and would probably be subscribed to, at least in broad terms, by Jewish and agnostic scholars as well as by representatives of the various Christian denominations. There are two areas of scholarly research that have provided a special payoff in this search to find the "real" Jesus.

8   The first is the critical study of the New Testament. The patient Scripture researchers have been able to trace the various levels and layers in the New Testament stories and block out a substantial number of sections that, if they do not represent verbatim quotations from Jesus, at least represent what was the core of his teaching and the basic style of his behavior. (It is interesting, incidentally, to note how some of the layers of Christian tradition which began to be added even a couple of decades after Jesus's departure made perhaps unconscious attempts to tone down the sometimes scandalous vigor of his pronouncements.)

9   While the New Testament critics probe back toward the basic message and behavior of Jesus, the "intertestamental"—or "second temple"—historians have made considerable progress toward understanding the fantastically creative religious era of which Jesus was a part. Judaism during the last century B.C. and the first A.D. was a vigorously heterogeneous, diversified phenomenon.

10   There is little "debunking" involved in this scholarly research. New Testament criticism and New Testament history once may have had a strong flavor of agnostic rationalism about them, and even now each new "discovery" as reported briefly in the daily papers may be taken by some traditional believers as an attack on their faith. In fact, however, most of the scholars are simply interested in understanding better Jesus and his time.

11   What, then, can be said about Jesus of Nazareth?

12   The New Testament can be treated neither as legend nor scientific history. It is not all fabrication, but it is not a journalistic account. No scholar doubts that Jesus actually existed, that he preached, that he had followers and that he was executed by the Romans. Yet, we do not know what he looked like, we do not know exactly what year he was born, we

know almost nothing about his family life. It seems safe to assume that he began his preaching in the wake of a powerful religious experience. But we do not know what he did before that—his friends, his interests, his education if any. We know that he had a profound knowledge of the Jewish religious tradition and religio-poetic abilities of the highest order but we cannot be sure where he acquired his knowledge or what his religious activities were before his preaching began, or even exactly how old he was when he started to preach. That he was dragged before the Romans by a group of his own people is certain enough, but the precise nature of the charges and the process of the trial are much less clear.

13   But because we do not know his height, or his weight, or the house in which he lived or who his childhood friends were, it does not follow that we are ignorant about him. We can put him into a historical context, see what he was in that context, and recapture the essence of his message out of that context. Such knowledge may be of less interest to our fiction-loving modern literary tastes, but it is of decisive historical and religious importance.

14   First of all, he was a Jew; his preaching, his teaching, his vocabulary, his rhetoric, his style were solidly in the Jewish tradition. A visitor from another planet, not knowing the history of the ensuing 2,000 years, would read the teachings of Jesus and be astonished at the thought that they represented a different religion from that which was presented in the Jewish Scriptures. The outer-space scholar might acknowledge considerable development in the teachings of Jesus, but if he could read the intertestamental literature, he would agree that this development was a logical extension of the Scriptures and was a product of the whole religious environment of which Jesus was a part. Jesus defined himself as a Jew, was highly conscious of the Jewishness of his message and would have found it impossible to conceive of himself as anything but Jewish.

15   Does this mean that he did not intend to found a church distinct from Judaism? To phrase the question that way would be to put back into the time of Jesus questions that, however pertinent they may be for us, were irrelevant to the context in which he found himself. He surely did not set up the code of canon law or the papal diplomatic service or the World Council of Churches. On the other hand, he was aware that a community of followers was gathering around him, and he did provide this band of followers with simple organizational principles and profound religious challenges. Did he contemplate an organizational break with Judaism? Again, such a question would not have been relevant in the context in which Jesus found himself. Until the final failure of the Jewish revolutionaries at the end of the first century, there was such a wide and amorphous pluralism within the Jewish religious tradition that rigid organizational structures were not necessary.

16   Some Jewish and Christian scholars are beginning to say very tentatively that the late first-century and early second-century split between church and synagogue was a historical mistake and tragedy not intended

by the best and most sensitive people on either side. Indeed, a couple of Jewish scholars have admitted to me—off the record, of course—that there may well be some elements of intertestamental Judaism that would have been better preserved by Christianity than they have been by the rabbinic Judaism that was codified at the end of the first and the beginning of the second century. Be that as it may, there is reasonable historical ground for saying that Christianity is a Jewish sect which emerged within the fluid context of first-century Jewish pluralism and became separated from the other strains of testamental Judaism by reason of a series of historical accidents.

17   The teaching of Jesus, then, must be placed squarely in the Jewish religious context of the time. Moreover, applying the terminology of a later era, there is no way to escape the conclusion that Jesus was not merely a Jew, but a left-wing Jew. He was not a member of the politically fanatic Zealots, though occasionally he used some of their rhetoric. He was surely not part of the Establishment temple priesthood. Nor was he a "counterculture" Essene seeking purity and integrity in isolated desert monasteries. Indeed, one might just as well use immediately the troublesome word: Jesus was a Pharisee, part of a religious revival movement which began in Palestine after the end of Jewish political power. He may not have been a card-carrying Pharisee in the sense of being affiliated with any particular Pharisaic group. (Such groups were far more fluid in his day than comparable movements would be in our day—after all, the Xerox machine hadn't been invented.) But he was a Pharisee—and a left-wing Pharisee, at that.

18   The Pharisees get a bad press in the New Testament. They are portrayed as implacable enemies of Jesus—righteous, rigid, legalistic hypocrites. But scholars say that such a view reflects in part the conflicts and concerns of several decades after Jesus's departure, and in part the plurality within the Pharisaic movement. There are, according to the Talmud, seven kinds of Pharisees, and Jesus apparently must be identified with the "Pharisees of Love." His opponents in the New Testament dialogues represented other aspects of the Pharisaic movement.

19   It is hard for most Christians, schooled to believe that the Pharisees were the bad guys, to adjust themselves to the notion that the Pharisaic movement was an extraordinary religious phenomenon. And the personalization and humanization of the Jewish religious tradition accomplished by the Pharisees—in a logical development of such late prophetic writers as Ezekiel and Jeremiah—was one of the most extraordinary religious revolutions in human history, one to which the later Christian development is in very deep debt.

20   Jesus was also a rabbi, the lay preacher interpreting the meaning of religious law, and his conflict, more or less open, with the temple priesthood was a familiar phenomenon of the era. The rabbi was not exactly a prophet: it was assumed in this era that the voice of prophesy was dead. But he was closer to the role and function of the prophet than he was to

any of the other forms of religious leadership that coexisted with him—the temple priests, the political revolutionaries, the leaders of the separatist monastic sects. The rabbi preached about human problems and human relationships and attempted to interpret these problems in light of the religious heritage and tradition. Jesus's interpretation was sweeping and radical. Yet his contempt for legalism was to be found in other such wandering teachers of his day. He may have been willing to push the Pharisaic insight about love further than any of the other rabbis, but it was not an insight that was uniquely his.

21 He was also—though one hesitates to use the word because it has become so flabby—a revolutionary. One might quickly add that he was a "religious" and not a "political" revolutionary save that that distinction may have more meaning for our time than it did for his. He was certainly not a political activist in the sense of organizing a mass movement to overthrow the Roman Empire, and it ought to be clear—though it may not have been so to the Romans—that he did not advocate violence as a political tactic. To try to sort it out in our own terms, he was a religious revolutionary in the sense that all great religious thinkers are revolutionary: he offered a profound challenge to the way human beings lived their lives and organized their societies.

22 He was also a mystical visionary. We have in the New Testament accounts of two such experiences, one at the time of his baptism by John and another with three of his followers on the side of a mountain. Most scholars are agreed that these accounts do reflect, though surely not in precise journalistic detail, events that actually happened. Moreover, these two ecstatic experiences represent high points of a life that was characterized throughout by an intense awareness of the "nearness" of God.

23 When we begin to speak of this nearness, this intimacy which Jesus claimed with God, we approach the core of his person and his message and also the core of the puzzle and bafflement he has left in his wake ever since. Many of his followers interpreted this "nearness" as chronological: God was about to re-enter human history in a dramatic way and begin a new era. There appears to have been some chronological element in Jesus's own expression of his sense of the nearness of God, but the chronological component seems to be of relatively minor importance. God is near not merely, or not even principally, in the sense that He may come tomorrow or next week or next year; He is near to us now, this day, this minute, in loving intimacy.

24 These, then, are the things that can be said about Jesus with a considerable amount of confidence. He was a Jew, a Pharisee, a religious radical, a rabbi, something of a prophet and a religious visionary. He also seems to have been an extraordinarily attractive and charming human being. The crowds flocked after him, and the gentleness and wisdom and the poetic insight of the traditions that can be traced directly to him are impressive and appealing even to those who reject all the developments in Christianity since the time of Jesus.

25   The problem, then, is not so much the man as the message. But what was the message, what did Jesus really preach, what did he really reveal, what did he really mean?

26   There are really two questions. The first is: What is his message?—and the second is: Was he right? About the second, there will be endless debate as long as the human race persists, but about the first, there ought not to be really much doubt.

27   Like all religious visionaries, Jesus proposed to speak of God. By speaking of God, of course, he was speaking of the nature of the universe and the meaning and the purpose of human life. For the category "God" is a symbol into which we pour and onto which we attach our convictions about the nature of the universe and of life.

28   Contemporary scholars tell us that if we wish to be most confident that we are in contact with the original message of Jesus, we should turn to his parables—quick, decisive stories used to illustrate and make clear the fundamental points of his teaching. For our present purposes two will suffice: the parable of the crazy farmer and the parable of the prodigal son (which might more appropriately be retitled the parable of the loving father).

29   It was harvest time and the work was plentiful. The owner of the farm went repeatedly into the marketplace—the hiring hall of his day—to recruit workers for his fields. Given the time of the year and the amount of work, those who were still idling the day with small talk at the 11th hour must have been a lazy and shiftless lot. Still, the farmer needed workers and even they were called into the field. One presumes they took their time getting there, shuffled about and did a little bit of work. They were awarded a full day's pay. For those who heard Jesus tell the story, the end represented a sharp twist. In the familiar rabbinic parable, those who arrived at the 11th hour earned the whole day's pay because they worked so hard. In the version of Jesus, the emphasis is not on the diligence of the workers but on the gratuitous generosity of the farmer: presumably the families of these idlers depended on the income for their nightly meal. It was a mad, crazy, insanely generous act. No human farmer or businessman could behave that way and remain in business for very long. Even today, we are affronted by the farmer's overpayment of loafers. The point of the parable: God's love for us is so passionate that if humans behaved toward one another the way He behaves toward us, they would be written off as lunatics. What is the universe all about? The reality with which Jesus felt so intimate was passionate love, so passionate as to appear by human standards to be insane.

30   Similarly, the prodigal son walks down the road rehearsing the speech he will give. The father (sitting on a porch in a rocking chair?) sees him coming and dashes off to meet him. The young man gets only the first sentence of his speech out before the father embraces him, puts a new robe on him and proclaims a celebration. Hardly an appropriate way to deal with an aberrant son. The boy had been spoiled in the first place, and if

the father spoils him again, he'll never change. By human standards, crazy behavior.

31   But it is a craziness that demands joy. The farmer is upset with those who work the whole day because they are not willing to celebrate his generosity. The father proclaims a celebration for the returning son and is appalled when the other son will not join it. Reality, Jesus tells us, is passionately loving and demands a joyous response from us.

32   The evidence, of course, is to the contrary. Reality, the universe, the cosmos, life, call it what we will, seems most of the time to be absurd, capricious, random—and occasionally downright ugly and vindictive. We are tempted to write it all off as senseless folly. And yet, we cannot quite eliminate our hope. Human beings are born with two diseases: life, from which we die; hope, which says that the first disease is not futile. Hopefulness is built into the structure of our personalities, into the depths of our unconscious, it plagues us to the very moment of our death. The critical question is whether hopefulness is self-deception, the ultimate cruelty of a cruel and tricky universe, or whether it is just possibly the hint of an explanation. The preaching of Jesus in its essence responded to that question. In effect, Jesus said, hope your wildest hopes, dream your maddest dreams, imagine your most fantastic fantasies. Where your hopes and your dreams and your imagination leave off, the love of my heavenly Father only begins. "For eye has not seen nor has ear heard nor is it entered into the heart of man the things that God has prepared for those who love Him."

33   That is the message. One may quibble about some of the details, but there would not be, I think, much debate among contemporary scholars about such being the essence of the message of Jesus. It is a beautiful, attractive, moving message.

34   But was he right? That is the final, critical and, indeed, only relevant question about Jesus. Did he see things the way they really are more clearly than anyone else in human history, or were his self-deceptions more profound and pervasive than those of anyone else in human history? Was he right or was he wrong? In the final analysis, it has to be either one or the other.

35   Most reasonable people since then have thought he was wrong. Some say as much explicitly. Others (including most professed Christians) hedge their bets. They profess to believe what Jesus said, but live daily lives in which joyous response to a message of passionate love is quite invisible. All the controversies, the theological debates, the holy wars, the vast volumes of scholarly research, the huge organizational structures, the endless factional feuds, the horrendous persecutions of those who seem to disagree—all of these, when they are not ways of escaping from the challenge of the message, are ultimately irrelevant to the basic question: Was he right? That question must be answered by each person who has encountered, in some fashion or another, the message of Jesus, and it must be answered in the cold loneliness of existential doubt. Much better to think of Jesus as

superstar or as a hero of pornographic films than as somebody laying down that kind of challenge.

36 He was too much for his own contemporaries. He was arrested and executed, and that was that. Much blood has been shed and many debates have raged over who was responsible for his arrest and execution. It was only after considerable debate (and some brilliant lobbying by the American Jewish Committee) that the fathers of the Vatican Council were willing to follow the example of Jesus and end the shameful history of accusing the Jewish people—past and present—of responsibility for the death of Jesus. The notion that a given people (be they Romans or be they Jews) have some sort of collective responsibility that reaches even into our own era for what happened to Jesus is absurd psychologically, ethically, historically and theologically. The whole point of the story of Jesus, of course, is that the same thing would have happened to him at any time, in any place.

37 And so he was buried, and that should have been the end of that. An itinerant Galilean rabbi, with a ragtag band of followers, living in the midst of immense religious ferment on the fringes of the Roman Empire—hardly worth noticing. The stone was rolled across the entrance of the tomb, and he ought to have been promptly forgotten.

38 But he wasn't. For something strange happened. The consensus of most scholars at present is that the strange event actually occurred. It was not something made up by the New Testament writers. There is absolutely no explanation for the development of the Christian impulse after the death of Jesus unless this strange event actually occurred. Most of the scholars are willing to add that the event was not the result of plot, not some sort of deliberate deception, not even a psychologically superficial exercise in self-deception. If it was self-deception, it was something that occurred at very profound levels of the personalities of those involved. Beyond that, the historians are able to say little. They cannot describe the event either historically or psychologically.

39 What actually occurred will probably never be known in any detail. How it occurred becomes a subject for theological interpretation and debate—and there's been much of that—but the critical religious question is what the strange event meant. Those who experienced it claimed that Jesus was still alive and his persistence in life was a validation of his message. The continued life of Jesus, and the validity of his message, are ultimately the same issue, but they are issues not of history or psychology or literary analysis, but of religious faith. Actually, it may be easier to believe that one man lives than to believe that love is at the core of the universe.

40 The early Christians were quite convinced that he was a man like themselves—a Jew, a Pharisee, a rabbi, a religious visionary—but there was also something (or, if one prefers, Something) different about him. Trying to balance the "just like everyone else" and the "something different" has been one of the key theological dilemmas of Christian history. By and large, the followers of Jesus have not done a very good job of

maintaining the balance. Curiously enough, at most times in human history the "man just like us" component has suffered at the expense of the "Something Else," or, to use the names of ancient heresies, Monophysitism is usually more popular than Nestorianism (though rarely has Nestorianism been pushed to the limits of state-subsidized pornography as in contemporary Denmark). But of course it is much easier to argue about how one balances the two experiences of Jesus than it is to devote one's principal energies to responding to his message.

41   No one can write about Jesus and pretend to be dispassionate, but the passion ought most appropriately be reserved for whether he was right or wrong and not for any relatively less important issues. I tentatively and hesitantly (more than that no one can claim) believe that he was right. Most of the time, alas, I don't live that way, which makes me not all that different from those readers who believe he was wrong—and infinitely inferior to those who reject what they take to be the message of Jesus, and yet live lives which assume that reality is as lovingly gracious as Jesus claimed.

42   In effect, Jesus said little more than that which we barely and dimly hope to be true. It is a message that is powerfully disconcerting both in its simplicity and in the totality of its demands for loving, joyous, and enthusiastic response. But who wants or needs or can stand such simplicity, such urgency, such insistent demands for love and joy? Better to argue about trivia, to write articles for obscure journals, to engage in holy wars and to create cultural Jesuses who reflect and reinforce our own prejudices.

43   If Jesus came back today, would he be crucified again?

44   You better believe he would.

COMMENTARY

Greeley's opening paragraphs are intended as a direct challenge to most of his readers. Almost everyone who has thought at all about Jesus finds himself in one of the categories that Greeley condemns. Greeley must now justify his attack on contemporary Christianity by presenting us with Jesus's own standards—and convincing us that this version of Jesus is the one we should accept as a yardstick by which to measure ourselves.

Greeley begins this section by describing his sources of information (paragraphs 8 and 9) so that we know he is not simply expressing personal opinions. Next he authenticates, as well as he can with this controversial subject, Jesus's historical roles (paragraphs 11 to 24). The purpose of this discussion is to give us an image of Jesus as a person. If we use this image as a standard, we will have to reject many modern interpretations of his character.

Greeley now turns to Jesus's message, singling out one idea as fundamental: the doctrine of love (paragraphs 28 to 31). He recounts the parables expressing this doctrine, explains its significance, and then bears personal witness to its truth. This is a difficult section because Greeley seems unwilling to say flatly that Jesus *is* God. That fact (if it is fact) establishes the truth of Jesus's message beyond doubt. But Greeley avoids such a statement, perhaps because he knows that many readers would find it unpalatable. Instead, he alludes to the "strange event" (i.e., the resurrection) and to "something different" about Jesus (i.e., his immortality).

Having presented his view of the historical Jesus and the doctrines he preached, Greeley can now evaluate Christianity from Jesus's vantage point. His judgment is that most of us ("most reasonable people" since Jesus's time, paragraph 35) do not live in ways that would confirm his teaching (paragraph 44).

Do you find this harsh indictment valid? Is Greeley (a priest) presumptuous in trying, in effect, to speak for Jesus in evaluating modern Christianity? By what criteria should a religion be judged?

OUTLINE

I. Introduction: Jesus would not condone the current versions of Jesus —paragraphs 1–6

II. The historical Jesus—paragraphs 7–24
   A. Sources of information
      1. Scriptural study—paragraph 8
      2. "Intertestamental" study—paragraph 9
   B. Aspects of Jesus's personality—paragraphs 11–24
      1. His Jewish heritage—paragraph 14
      2. Identity as Pharisee—paragraphs 17–19
      3. Identity as rabbi—paragraph 20
      4. Identity as revolutionary—paragraph 21
      5. Identity as visionary—paragraph 22
   C. Summary—paragraph 24

III. Assessment of Jesus's message—paragraphs 25–40
   A. The doctrine of love—paragraphs 28–33
      1. Illustrative parable of the crazy farmer—paragraph 29
      2. Illustrative parable of the prodigal son—paragraph 30
   B. Discussion of the doctrine of love—paragraphs 34–42
      1. Controversy—paragraphs 35–36
      2. Importance of resurrection—paragraphs 37–40

IV. Judgment of our response to Jesus—paragraphs 43–44

SUGGESTIONS FOR WRITING

1. Greeley lists many activities and slogans that have been associated in our time with Jesus (paragraphs 4–6). Write an essay on one of them with which you are familiar. Using Greeley's criteria, evaluate it: does that slogan or activity promote a valid Christian ideal?

2. Evaluate the role of religious faith in the life of someone you know. Has being "religious" made that person good? By what criteria?

3. On the next page is a short account, by Eldridge Cleaver, of an experi-

ence in a religious context. Notice how Cleaver evaluates as he tells his story. After reading this personal-experience evaluation, write your own evaluative account of a religious experience.

A RELIGIOUS CONVERSION, MORE OR LESS*—Eldridge Cleaver

Folsom Prison
September 10, 1965

1   Once I was a Catholic. I was baptized, made my first Communion, my Confirmation, and I wore a Cross with Jesus on it around my neck. I prayed at night, said my Rosary, went to Confession, and said all the Hail Marys and Our Fathers to which I was sentenced by the priest. Hopelessly enamored of sin myself, yet appalled by the sins of others, I longed for Judgment Day and a trial before a jury of my peers—this was my only chance to escape the flames which I could feel already licking at my feet. I was in a California Youth Authority institution at the time, having transgressed the laws of man —God did not indict me that time; if He did, it was a secret indictment, for I was never informed of any charges brought against me. The reason I became a Catholic was that the rule of the institution held that every Sunday each inmate had to attend the church of his choice. I chose the Catholic Church because all the Negroes and Mexicans went there. The whites went to the Protestant Chapel. Had I been a fool enough to go to the Protestant chapel, one black face in a sea of white, and with guerilla warfare going on between us, I might have ended up a Christian martyr—St. Eldridge the Stupe.

2   It all ended one day when, at a catechism class, the priest asked if anyone present understood the mystery of the Holy Trinity. I had been studying my lessons diligently and knew by heart what I'd been taught. Up shot my hand, my heart throbbing with piety (pride) for this chance to demonstrate my knowledge of the Word. To my great shock and embarrassment, the Father announced, and it sounded like a thunderclap, that I was lying, that no one, not even the Pope, understood the Godhead, and why else did I think they called it the *mystery* of the Holy Trinity? I saw in a flash, stung to the quick by the jeers of my fellow catechumens, that I had been used, that the Father had been lying in wait for the chance to drop that thunderbolt, in order to drive home the point that the Holy Trinity was not to be taken lightly.

3   I had intended to explain the Trinity with an analogy to 3-in-1 oil, so it was probably just as well.

notes on a broken promise

LUCIAN K. TRUSCOTT IV

Truscott's purpose is to assess the problems of today's volunteer army. He could do this by identifying its problems (definition), and then amassing data about them and drawing inferences from the data (substantiation) to arrive at a judgment. He complicates the process for himself and his readers by introducing a strong autobiographical element. He is himself a product and a victim of what he is evaluating. This gives him the advantage of firsthand experience. But it poses a dilemma: the criteria by which he makes value judgments are both subjective and objective. For better or worse, he shares the military value system even though he has separated himself from the military establishment. For Truscott, the result is painful, but this emotional involvement enhances the dramatic impact of his essay.

1   **t**he faces of soldiers always got to me when I was an infantry platoon leader five years ago at Fort Carson, Colorado. Less than a year out of West Point, as green as a young lieutenant could be, I found myself at the mercy of the faces of my men. Words were unnecessary, for no matter how smoothly things might go on the surface, the men's judgment always appeared in their eyes, watching and measuring.

2   Soldiers have an unnervingly keen feeling for each other, for their leaders, for the spirit of the Army itself. This was not something we were taught at the Military Academy. Nor was it something I learned from my father, an infantry colonel, or from my grandfather, a general and a World War II division, corps, and Army commander. No, the secrets of the ways men live and work together were left for us to discover from one another. This uncanny facility—to read men the way one reads a book—has marked great military leaders for centuries.

3   As we shall see, I never quite made it as a lieutenant. The feeling between me and my men was, at best, a fleeting and temporary thing; finally it disappeared altogether. I felt a sickness of the spirit as an officer in the United States Army, and I have always asked myself, was the sickness my own, or was it the Army's? When I accepted a magazine assignment to assess the new "volunteer Army," I also turned that assessment into a search for an answer to that old question. I went looking for the keen-eyed judgment of the men. I wanted their instinctive feeling about the health of the Army. At the same time, I would accept that judgment as a criticism of myself.

4   I began at Fort Ord, California, just north of the Monterey Peninsula. The combination of the climate, the ocean, and its closeness to San Francisco would make Ord a fat duty assignment except that Ord also is the locus of a major Army training center, and training is the most harrowing duty known to man. I went to Fort Ord to spend some time with new volunteers in the first few weeks of their training, but I ended up spending more time with their officers. This was partly due to circumstance, and partly because I admired the extraordinary quality of Capt. Carlos Boswell, a basic-training company commander. But first, the new troops.

5   The profile of the volunteer entering the Army today is quite different from the profile of the draftee of several years ago. This is how he differs: he is younger—eighteen or nineteen years old, as opposed to the average draftee's age of twenty or twenty-one; he is less likely to be married; he has less education—about 50 percent of today's volunteers have not completed high school; he is, by 3 to 5 percentage points, more likely to be black or brown.

6   But statistics don't say much about the Army volunteer. The question that must be asked and answered affirmatively if the no-draft system is to survive is this: can the new Army volunteer become a good soldier, despite many apparent deficiencies in his background? Practically everyone has an opinion on this matter, but nobody claims to have the answer. Few of the officers I spoke with at Fort Ord were optimistic.

7   Maj. J. D. Coleman, information officer for Fort Ord: "How do you teach a guy to fight, to be a goddamn soldier, when the whole emphasis now is on learning a specialized trade? Fully one-half of each crop of citizens that becomes eligible for military service each year has attitudes which are directly opposed, hostile, to the military. The Army advertisements claim, 'We can teach you this, and we can teach you that.' But what we've really got to teach these guys is how to kill somebody." Capt. Glen Meyers, company commander of B/1/1 Basic Training Company: "This company has seventy non-high-school grads out of 190. Forty blacks, six Indians, seventeen Spanish. A lot of these guys are young kids who never finished anything they started. Many of the non-grads don't intend to use the Army to get a trade, or to get their high-school equivalency diploma, qualify for the GI bill, and eventually go to college. For half of them, this is just one more place they've drifted to.

8   "I've talked at some length to eight of the nine I've considered recommending for discharge. Every one of them was just knocking around, living off the land, and a couple of them were literally hungry the day they enlisted. They wanted a meal, a roof, a shirt on their backs. Most of them said something like this: 'Here I am, locked up for three years, and I never thought about it. The most I've ever thought ahead in my life is two days, and when those days came, I never looked back.' This also applies to some of the jobless young marrieds, who were looking for a way to feed a wife and kids. I'd say there's a whole generation out there right now, the new drifters, almost like the bums during the Depression, except they're

younger, they've got long hair. But they're just as uneducated, just as broke, just as hungry."

9 Capt. Carlos Boswell, company commander, B/1/3 Basic Training Company: "This is my second tour as a basic training CO. I was here in 1968, during the Vietnam buildup, when they were drafting pretty much anybody. How do these guys compare? We had the same number of problems in '68—it's just that now they're a different kind. We've got more young soldier problems, especially homesickness.

10 "When I heard the Army was going all volunteer, I was halfway panicky. Now I've cycled through several companies of volunteers, and I think its going to work out okay. We've had to change some of our training methods to reach the guy who just plain isn't as smart as the average draftee, but these guys will make good troops. All they need is somebody as good as they are to lead them."

11 There was something indefinable about Captain Boswell that marked him as a leader of men and set him apart from most other officers I had ever met. He was thirty-one years old, short in stature, his face prematurely lined. He had served seven years as an enlisted man, gone through Officer Candidate School, and served eight more as an officer. I spent an afternoon with him while his company completed bayonet training. As the captain wandered around the training area, he smiled and talked about the company. The men were his for only two weeks, but he knew all their names, and they responded to him, not warmly, not affectionately, but directly, like men who appreciated a good CO. He recognized one man, discussed an injured hand; spoke with another about a problem with his parents; urged yet another to attack an obstacle in the bayonet course with more enthusiasm. "Like this," said Captain Boswell, and he showed how he wanted it done. The man gave out a savage yell and vaulted over a four-foot wall.

12 In an earlier time Captain Boswell would have been a professional fighting man—a Spartan, a crusader, a cossack. Not that he is some unthinking robot, barely able to control a violent urge to kill. Quite the contrary, Boswell possesses the very different qualities that a truly great warrior must have: the ability to give more of himself than he asks from his men; the peculiar attraction that makes men want to follow him; a precise feeling for their mood, their spirit, their limits, and just how far he can push them. Taken together, all these qualities enable a leader to transfer his power to his men, to give them strength they don't know they have.

13 Much of this may sound romantic and silly. But it is not. Those are simply the qualities Boswell has, and he displays them as naturally as he breathes. The Army used to have many men like Boswell. I remember my father and other officers, friends of his, when I was growing up in the Army. They were men you could look up to, men who made you want to be like them.

14 Fort Ord gave me hope that there was really something afoot in the new volunteer Army. The commanding General, Maj. Gen. Robert Gard,

is a fine, hardworking man who appears to know and care for his men. Almost everywhere I went on the post, someone would say, "General Gard came through, and he wanted it done *this* way, and that's the way we do it." It's a great feeling knowing one has a commander like Gard—a man who knows what he wants done and how he wants it done. The men I spoke to had a real sense of security and togetherness, and they liked it.

15 So I had a hope that what I would next find at Fort Carson, in my old battalion, would confirm the progress and esprit I had seen at Fort Ord. My first day at Fort Carson was gray and cold. Outside the window of my old company mess hall, troops moved with shoulders hunched and heads bent against the wind, just as they had four years before. Across the table from me sat ten soldiers, most of them eighteen or nineteen, only one a twenty-two-year-old veteran of Vietnam. All were volunteers; only the veteran had entered the Army under the draft. The faces looked familiar: black, brown, chalk white; one face pockmarked by acne, drawn and hard from the Kentucky hills. On my left an American Indian, his skin the color of fine mahogany, smiled with pearly teeth.

16 I identified myself as a former lieutenant from the same battalion, but before I could tell the troops in the mess hall exactly what I was looking for, a PFC spoke up. His first words were shocking.

17 "The Army's changed a lot since you been in, sir," he said, picking his words slowly. The others nodded in agreement. "There's no discipline anymore. This Army is shit. They come out with this VOLAR [the acronym for the Army's "volunteer Army" program of a few years back]. First they give you freedom, then they turn around and take it away. No explanations. No nothing.

18 "Privates like us are telling sergeants and lieutenants where to get off. Nothing happens. They just take it. Nobody does anything about it. Nobody cares.

19 "You were a platoon leader, sir? Well, there's no such thing as a platoon leader anymore. It's just a guy who stands out in front of a formation, then disappears. We never see them. They don't know who's here and who's not. Hell, on my floor alone we got four guys AWOL. Half the time they're carried present for duty on the morning report so the unit can pass the strength reports. The officers don't go into the barracks to check up on us anymore. There's just no discipline. It's all falling apart."

20 I was thunderstruck at the idea of a nineteen-year-old private, just beginning to sprout a fuzzy moustache, telling me about the need for discipline. I expected to hear that from an aging sergeant, longing for the days when an order was an order, no questions asked. But here was a group of young soldiers, all of them volunteers, only one old enough to have been drafted, complaining that no one cared anymore about waxed floors and clean barracks and accurate morning reports. What they were saying was that no one cared enough to lead them. "How would you explain this behavior?" I asked no one in particular. There was a silence; the men looked at one another, and then the same soldier spoke again.

21   "Most of your combat-experienced officers are the better ones, but even that doesn't always hold true. Some are assholes who still wander around talking about blowing away gooks. Crazies. Other guys, the new lieutenants, they come in and do things strictly by the book. But it just doesn't work that way. The book is fine. It's dandy. Like Communism looks good on paper, but it doesn't work in the real world."

22   How do you explain officers and noncoms who don't give a damn? The Vietnam vet, who had remained silent and expressionless, spoke.

23   "VOLAR did it. When they brought in that volunteer Army shit. They think they're gonna get an Army by paying more money. They tell a guy he's gonna get a $2,500 bonus for going combat arms, and he says, 'Where do I sign? Yeah, man.' But you've got to have guys who want to soldier for other reasons than money.

24   In my old platoon's barracks, I talked to a sergeant E-5 with five years in, and two tours of duty in Vietnam under his belt.

25   "We need a better goddamn Army, sir. Look at this place. There ain't nothing right here." Indeed, what was once a platoon bay with neat rows of bunk beds and stacked foot lockers had become a *Life* magazine vision of the new, volunteer Army. The bay had been divided into four-man rooms with a narrow aisle down the middle. The rooms were comfortable, hung with curtains and posters. Had it still been my platoon, I would have been proud of the layout, and glad for the new comforts that eased the enlisted man's hard life.

26   But the barracks stank. The latrine was slimy with a week's growth of old razor blades and toothpaste droppings. Several toilets didn't work. The hallway was muddy. The rooms were a mess. There was no pride in the barracks, something my platoon had had, even if only in small amounts. And the lack of pride, the filth, all of it hurt.

27   "See what I mean?" the sergeant asked. There was sadness in his eyes. "I'm going to join the Australian army when I get out. I already got my paperwork in. I seen them when I was over in the Nam. I'm getting out of this Army. There's nothing here for anybody who wants to be a soldier."

28   "Everybody's talking about professionalism now," said another man. "But that's all it is, talk. You check out C Company commander, and *then* tell me about professionalism."

29   "We had a dud CO in 1970," I said. "What's so special about this guy?"

30   "Downrange on a field exercise somebody tried to do him in. Picked up an entrenching tool, and a bunch of them chased him off in the boonies one night and hit him in the mouth. Beat the shit out of him. He's had to grow a moustache to hide the scar. You think anybody did anything? Hell, no. He's afraid of his own men. Afraid to court-martial the ones who beat him up. Afraid to even go in his own barracks. The whole company hates him."

31   "And he's still company commander, after all that?"

32   "He just slinks in and out of his office each day, signs his name a bunch of times. Some army, huh?"

33   When I got my introduction to the Army of the 1970s, I was living in a rented trailer off post in Columbus, Georgia, while I attended the Infantry Officer Basic Course. I made a phone call one night from a booth across the road from the trailer. A car carrying four men pulled up, blocking the door. I turned around. The door opened. A white T-shirt moved, a fist wearing a large gold ring crashed into my face. I was beaten down to the floor of the booth. I was pulled out by the legs. All four of them fell on me, kicking and pounding my face and chest. I curled up and tried to protect myself, screaming at them to stop. All I heard was, "You white motherfucker. You white motherfucker."

34   Suddenly, car headlights appeared down the road, and someone yelled. Three of the men ran back to the car, but the biggest one, the one with the ring, continued to beat me as I tried to get away. Finally he, too, ran for the car, and they were gone. Both my eyes were swollen shut, and I was bruised and bloody to the waist.

35   They were four GIs from an engineer battalion on the post. Later that night, they picked up a white hitchhiker, a fellow GI, pulled him into an empty parking lot and completely disfigured him, nearly killing him. They were caught by the local police in the process of beating yet another victim late that night. The next morning, by prying one eye open with my fingers, I was able to identify the guy with the ring, whom I had seen up close. I made a statement. They were charged with assault with intent to kill. Apparently, the police had been trying to catch them for several weeks.

36   No one at Fort Benning was particularly surprised. My battalion commander said it was too bad, but it was just one of those things that happened these days. No one ever spoke to me about the beating, except in the abstract. It was blamed on the "race problem." And the "race problem" was dealt with in the abstract.

37   In 1970, first at Fort Carson, then on an Armywide basis, the brass ordered "racial seminars," "race councils," classes in "race relations." Meanwhile, down in the units, the problem persisted. Blacks beat up whites. Whites beat up blacks. There was racial separatism within units. There were arrests on both sides, on post and off post. The lives of young men were scarred and ruined. And attitudes, which policy was supposed to change, continued to be set in the concrete of hatred and revenge. There were, too, the makings of a serious drug problem, which the Army refused to face until it became a scandal, not just a problem. An entire galaxy of problems faced the returning Vietnam veteran, and at Fort Carson in 1970 they had combined to produce an atmosphere as volatile as coal dust.

38   On my recent visits to Fort Carson and Fort Ord, I was glad to see that all these problems had been reduced. One measure of the change is that a green recruit in the volunteer Army earns more than my base pay as a second lieutenant in the draft Army. In my platoon in 1969, I had

men with three years' service and three rows of combat ribbons who could not adequately support their families. They lived on food stamps (for which 50 percent of the platoon was eligible) or stole excess food from the mess hall. Sheer necessity forced me to supervise such theft—to ensure equal distribution of the excess food—rather than prosecute it as a crime.

39 How did a lieutenant tell a man who could not afford to feed his family that he had a duty to his country? How did a lieutenant tell the same man that the "computer screwed up" when he was incorrectly paid for the third month in a row, and arrangements could not be made to correct the error in time for his car payment, which meant that his car would be repossessed?

40 It was no accident that good men turned to booze or drugs or both, or went AWOL, or waded into melees in downtown bars and ended up in jail, or walked into the office of the company commander in a blind rage and told him to get fucked. But these everyday problems were symptoms of a deeper infection. In the faces of my men I saw a more profound problem, one that depressed all of us like endless rain on a tin roof.

41 It was a problem I cannot remember talking about with anyone but my best friend. Even today I have difficulty expressing myself, which is probably why I have shied away from writing about the Army. But I have always known that I would have to confront this formless feeling of loss and emptiness.

42 That feeling surely underlay the confusion of my battalion. Marijuana usage was conservatively put at greater than 80 percent by anyone who knew what he was talking about. (Battalion, brigade, or division headquarters would have called it negligible.) In fact, nearly everyone smoked grass, which made for an us/them situation that produced two distinct side effects.

43 The first was a feeling of esprit that previously had been lacking. Once the liaison of potheads was firmly established, that feeling seeped through the company like laughing gas. We devised ways of working around the company commander (one of "them"). Fraternization among officers, noncoms, and enlisted men became commonplace. One platoon leader's apartment became a sort of crash pad for men in the company who needed a place to stay on weekends, or who might be having problems with the old lady, or who just wanted to drink, hang out, and smoke some dope in what the men laughingly called "the new action Army."

44 The other side effect was a yearning for the comforting predictability of Army life: the regularity of receiving orders, carrying them out, and being rewarded. We longed, secretly, for the "good old days" we had never experienced.

45 The problems not only persisted, they got worse. They had their roots, of course, in the society from which all of us entered the Army. That was a fine, easy excuse which neatly explained race problems, drugs, drinking, crime—the whole mess. It was often cited by commanders who were bewildered at the state of their units.

46 What was wrong with the Army, though, was precisely the confusion

of those commanders. At West Point, we were drilled in the axiom, "As a leader, you are responsible for everything your unit does or fails to do." *Everything.* But in practice—in the real world, as the saying went—nobody ended up being directly responsible for anything.

47   All problems were sloughed off into the abstract area of problems with a capital *P.* There was official Concern, Analysis, and Study—all of which eventually resulted in Policy. Meanwhile, a platoon leader was not held responsible for racial tension among his men, for drug use within the platoon, or even for his AWOLs. And this failure to take responsibility was true on up the line, from platoon leaders to division commanders.

48   One morning at reveille, one of my sergeants asked me if I had seen the division commander on television the night before. I said no. "Well, they asked him what was the biggest problem he had at Fort Carson, and he thought for a minute and said, 'Haircuts.' "

49   "Haircuts? You're kidding me."

50   "No sir, I'm not. Haircuts. Guess that means we're in pretty good shape, huh?"

51   These were the facts: AWOL rates were juggled so they didn't look as bad as they really were. Strength and readiness reports (which established the unit's overall readiness category—a critical matter in a war emergency) were falsified, too. Drug usage was simply ignored.

52   The war in Vietnam produced a generation of commanders weaned on the infamous "body count," and by 1970 lying in the Army had become standard operating procedure. Covering up deficiencies, falsifying reports, falsely certifying inspections, stealing, cheating, and deceiving to pass command maintenance inspections—all of it went on as a matter of course. The West Point motto, "Duty, Honor, Country," had become a shell game at a two-bit carnival, and one never knew which shell the pea was under, or if it was there at all. Before we had been lieutenants a year, most of us had been forced to redefine honor as it was practiced in the Army. A major asked one of my classmates to take a college validation test for him so the major could be exempted from a Bachelor of Science requirement for four years of math. When my classmate declined, he was ordered. When he refused the order, the major said: "You can be sure this disloyalty will be reflected on your efficiency report."

53   The My Lai massacre and coverup were imprinted on the collective military psyche much more indelibly than was popularly supposed. Their resolution convinced many that anything was allowed, so long as you got away with it. Adding to the My Lai effect were the other scandals that embarrassed the military command: the case of Maj. Gen. Carl C. Turner, the Army's chief law-enforcement officer, who unlawfully obtained surplus weapons from the Chicago Police Department (the Army refused to try him, but he eventually pleaded guilty to a thirteen-count federal indictment); the case of Sgt. Maj. of the Army William O. Woodridge, who was involved in the service club scandal; and, more recently, the Lavelle secret bombing and the Pentagon spy ring in the National Security Council, in-

volving Adm. Thomas H. Moorer, Chairman of the Joint Chiefs of Staff, the highest-ranking military man in America. Each of these scandals was a fist in the gut of the Army, and each developed the old idea that rank has its privileges into something far more ominous and dispiriting. *The brass is beyond the law.* The conclusion was inescapable, and it filtered down through the ranks like a thick fog.

54   I fell victim to that fog, and I looked for means to fight my way out of it, for things to rebel against: moral wrongs, superiors I didn't respect, the war in Vietnam—it really didn't matter. When I found them, my way of rebelling was to write articles in *The Village Voice,* mimeographed fliers and newsletters, anything that could be held in one's hands and read. All of it infuriated the brass. Here was this lieutenant, the scion of a great Army family running amok. They were enraged and I was delighted.

55   Over a short period of time, however, I fell apart as a leader and as a man. I began drinking heavily and eating huge quantities of mescaline and methamphetamine. I guess I had problems with authority figures all my life, and in the Army, the problems got worse, not better. At twenty-two, it was beyond my means to understand what was happening to me. The examples of my father and grandfather hung over me like a great cloud, a stifling weirdness I could feel but not see.

56   I didn't make it. I just wasn't cut out to be the leader Captain Boswell is, that my father and my grandfather were. In April 1970, less than a year after I had graduated from West Point, administrative discharge procedures were initiated against me, and in July I was discharged. I waived all my rights to hearings and appeals.

57   But many others I knew at West Point and elsewhere in the Army were cut from the Boswell mold, and it is with these men my concern lies. Let us accept, for the sake of argument, Boswell's idea that "a troop is a troop," and, further, that "all they need is somebody as good as they are to lead them." If we accept these premises, what becomes most important about a volunteer Army is not the volunteer but his leaders.

58   My concern has this at its heart: the best men I knew in the Army have resigned, are in the process of resigning, or will resign sometime in the near future. The despair that I felt in 1969 and 1970, which only served to add to my personal problems, apparently continues in more subtle forms.

59   When I was at Fort Carson last fall, I spoke with two officers who had been classmates at West Point. I had known one of them when we were kids. His father was an officer, too. The other man and I had been in the same company at West Point for two years. Both resigned in June.

60   "The guys who are getting out," one of them explained, "are the men you would want to serve with if you were going to stay in." Then he recited a familiar litany. "Remember Jones? He's getting out. Smith, too. Everyone I can think of who's worth a damn—they're all resigning in June. If not this year, next year. And you can just imagine who's staying in."

61   "Remember Thomas?" he asked. (The names are changed here on his request.) "He was in an air-defense unit in Germany. Remember how gung

ho he was? Well, that's changed. It started out slow with him. Falsify this little arms-room check sheet, that little report. Then they were telling him to take the total amount of money donated to the United Fund and divide it by the number of guys in his battery, so it would come to 100 percent participation. Then it was monkeying with strength and readiness reports. Finally Thomas said he wasn't going to have any more of it, and refused to falsify any more documents. He found himself in one big heap of trouble —got moved around from job to job. He isn't gung ho anymore. He'll be getting out this year, too."

62   The man he described was one of the four regimental commanders in my class at West Point and was expected to make General one day. I can think of a list of men as long as the rest of this page who were top-notch military men, each in his own way, but who have resigned from the Army: Josiah Bunting III, major, Rhodes scholar, author, former first captain at Virginia Military Institute; Bob Gardner, first lieutenant, platoon leader, one of the finest Army officers I ever knew; Gary Israelson, captain, West Point 1966; Martin Cassidy, captain, number two in West Point 1967; Gary Moyer and Rich Hubshman, captains, also West Point 1967; Jim Hedrick, captain, sixteen years in the Army, ten of them enlisted, a grass-roots, from-the-gut soldier like Boswell, and one of a dying breed.

63   We have broken a promise, those of us who have left an Army in disrepair. I have broken it perhaps most profoundly, but the promise was the same. Ours was the promise of leadership. Ours was the promise of command with understanding and a sense of responsibility and purpose. Ours was the promise of discipline tempered with justice, a sense of evenness and fairness. Ours was the promise of patriotism measured with care.

64   It turns out that ours was an imperfect promise, and nothing shows that more clearly than our desertion of the Army. We broke a promise to the country, but more than this, we broke our promise to the men who served with us, and to the men who would serve in the future. To match their obligation with our obligation, their dedication with our dedication, their loyalty with our loyalty, their honor with our honor. We let them down, and, worse, none of all this seems possible anymore. Why?

65   Despite my rebellion against authority, despite the sense of doom I felt following in the footsteps of my father and my grandfather, despite the terrible feeling of loving and respecting them yet all the time living in their shadow and hating them for it—despite all of this, I could have served out my time. If I did not exactly serve with distinction, at least I would not have let my men down. I could have done it somehow. It would have meant pulling punches, compromising a little too close for comfort, fighting in a war that turned my stomach politically and morally. Yet inexorably 1974 would have come along, and I, too, would now be a civilian.

66   Consider these statistics: 36 percent of the West Point class of 1965 are now in civilian life; so are 31 percent of the class of 1966 and 33 percent of the class of 1967. (Figures on the class of 1968 are not yet complete.) I suspect that over a third of my classmates will have resigned by

a year from now. Among them will be four conscientious objectors and several who were discharged for political reasons, but the great majority will be men who couldn't take it any longer. They will be men who have a bad taste in their mouths after having served their country as officers in the United States Army.

67   Why? Why must we go on breaking the promise of leadership that West Point has traditionally held out to the rest of the Army? Why must this promise be broken by other young leaders, just as able, just as dedicated, and just as disgusted as the West Pointers? I've asked myself this question for years, and I'm damned if I have an answer. I've spoken to many of those who have resigned, including my father and others of his generation who have left the Army in disgust. And they don't have any answer. There is a sickness somewhere, a corruption eating away at the guts of the Army, as my father once put it. For this, no one yet has a cure.

COMMENTARY

As the outline shows, Truscott alternates between objective data about the army and confessional disclosures about himself. Aware that much of his analysis is personal, he supplements his experience by citing the parallel experiences of other people. He wants the reader to see his own case as representative so that his final judgment will carry conviction.

To show that he is not seeing only one side of the picture, Truscott includes Captain Boswell, whose character and role run wholly counter to the author's. Boswell succeeds. He is a good soldier and a good leader. Since in Truscott's opinion this good man is a dying breed, he does not damage the basic judgment that there is a "sickness of the spirit" in the military. Boswell's function is to provide the moral fulcrum for the entire article—to show us an image of health that will make the prevailing sickness all the more apparent.

What are the criteria by which Truscott judges the army? Do you believe that his evaluation is fair? Or is he expecting things of the army that no segment of our society now provides?

OUTLINE

I. Author's army background—paragraphs 1–4
II. Profile of new volunteers—paragraphs 5–32
   A. Reports of others, emphasizing Captain Boswell—paragraphs 7–14
   B. Firsthand impressions—paragraphs 15–32
III. Author's personal narrative of his military experiences—paragraphs 33–44
IV. Analysis of army problems—paragraphs 45–53
V. Author's own culpability—paragraphs 54–62
VI. Identification of the army's "sickness"—paragraphs 63–67

SUGGESTIONS FOR WRITING

1. All evaluations depend on establishing criteria. Establish your own criteria for what a military man or woman—or the military services as a whole—should be.

2. Describe an occupation or profession with which you have had firsthand experience. Emphasize two or three "case histories" that enable you to evaluate the general health (or lack of it) of the enterprise. For example, you have now been "discharged" from your four-year service as a high school student. How healthy was that enterprise? (You may need to concentrate on only one or two aspects.)

3. One of the problems with the army, Truscott thinks, is the absence of capable leaders. What are the criteria for a successful leader?

Evaluate the leadership performance of someone under whose direction you participated in a group activity: a scout leader, youth-group organizer, bandmaster, the kid in your neighborhood whom all the others imitated and obeyed. Or if you have been in a leadership role yourself, evaluate your own performance.

presidential voices

This pair of selections offers two evaluations of major presidential speeches —and shows that good writing breeds good writing.

What qualities makes us remember the great speeches of American history? Lincoln's collected writings fill several volumes, but only a few short pieces are remembered as great writing. Most contemporary political rhetoric will not deserve to be remembered at all.

Part of the importance of a speech derives from its subject and occasion, of course. Nobody would expect a routine tax message to be of widespread and permanent interest. But among the many speeches devoted to important subjects and significant occasions, those with literary excellence are the ones most likely to survive.

Gilbert Highet's analysis of Lincoln's Gettysburg Address judges it as "a work of art," specifically as a successful illustration of certain techniques of classical oratory. The *New Yorker* editorial applies similar criteria to John F. Kennedy's 1961 Inaugural Address. Both evaluations assume that the style of political addresses is at least as important as their substance. Would you agree?

(We reprint the two speeches along with the essays that evaluate them.)

the gettysburg address
GILBERT HIGHET

1   Fourscore and seven years ago our fathers brought forth on this continent, a new nation, conceived in Liberty, and dedicated to the proposition that all men are created equal.

2   Now we are engaged in a great civil war, testing whether that nation or any nation so conceived and so dedicated, can long endure. We are met on a great battle-field of that war. We have come to dedicate a portion of that field, as a final resting place for those who here gave their lives that that nation might live. It is altogether fitting and proper that we should do this.

3   But, in a larger sense, we can not dedicate—we can not consecrate—we can not hallow—this ground. The brave men, living and dead, who struggled here, have consecrated it, far above our poor power to add or detract. The world will little note, nor long remember, what we say here, but it can never forget what they did here. It is for us the living, rather, to be dedicated here to the unfinished work which they who fought here have thus far so nobly advanced. It is rather for us to be here dedicated to the great task remaining before us—that from these honored dead we take increased devotion to that cause for which they gave the last full measure of devotion—that we here highly resolve that these dead shall not have died in vain—that this nation, under God, shall have a new birth of freedom—and that government of the people, by the people, for the people, shall not perish from the earth.

1   **f**ourscore *and seven years ago . . .*

2   These five words stand at the entrance to the best-known monument of American prose, one of the finest utterances in the entire language and surely one of the greatest speeches in all history. Greatness is like granite: it is molded in fire, and it lasts for many centuries.

3   Fourscore and seven years ago . . . . It is strange to think that President Lincoln was looking back to the 4th of July 1776, and that he and his speech are now further removed from us than he himself was from George Washington and the Declaration of Independence. Fourscore and seven years before the Gettysburg Address, a small group of patriots signed the Declaration. Fourscore and seven years after the Gettysburg Address, it was the year 1950,[1] and that date is already receding rapidly into our troubled, adventurous, and valiant past.

4   Inadequately prepared and at first scarcely realized in its full importance, the dedication of the graveyard at Gettysburg was one of the supreme moments of American history. The battle itself had been a turning point of the war. On the 4th of July 1863, General Meade repelled Lee's invasion of Pennsylvania. Although he did not follow up his victory, he had broken one of the most formidable aggressive enterprises of the Confederate armies. Losses were heavy on both sides. Thousands of dead were

Source. From *A Clerk of Oxenford: Essays on Literature and Life* by Gilbert Highet. Copyright © 1954 by Gilbert Highet. Reprinted by permission of Oxford University Press, Inc.

[1] In November 1950 the Chinese had just entered the war in Korea.

left on the field, and thousands of wounded died in the hot days following the battle. At first, their burial was more or less haphazard; but thoughtful men gradually came to feel that an adequate burying place and memorial were required. These were established by an interstate commission that autumn, and the finest speaker in the North was invited to dedicate them. This was the scholar and statesman Edward Everett of Harvard. He made a good speech—which is still extant: not at all academic, it is full of close strategic analysis and deep historical understanding.

5   Lincoln was not invited to speak, at first. Although people knew him as an effective debater, they were not sure whether he was capable of making a serious speech on such a solemn occasion. But one of the impressive things about Lincoln's career is that he constantly strove to *grow*. He was anxious to appear on that occasion and to say something worthy of it. (Also, it has been suggested, he was anxious to remove the impression that he did not know how to behave properly—an impression which had been strengthened by a shocking story about his clowning on the battlefield of Antietam the previous year). Therefore when he was invited he took considerable care with his speech. He drafted rather more than half of it in the White House before leaving, finished it in the hotel at Gettysburg the night before the ceremony (not in the train, as sometimes reported), and wrote out a fair copy next morning.

6   There are many accounts of the day itself, 19 November 1863. There are many descriptions of Lincoln, all showing the same curious blend of grandeur and awkwardness, or lack of dignity, or—it would be best to call it humility. In the procession he rode horseback: a tall lean man in a high plug hat, straddling a short horse, with his feet too near the ground. He arrived before the chief speaker, and had to wait patiently for half an hour or more. His own speech came right at the end of a long and exhausting ceremony, lasted less than three minutes, and made little impression on the audience. In part this was because they were tired, in part because (as eye-witnesses said) he ended almost before they knew he had begun, and in part because he did not speak the Address, but read it, very slowly, in a thin high voice, with a marked Kentucky accent, pronouncing "to" as "toe" and dropping his final R's.

7   Some people of course were alert enough to be impressed. Everett congratulated him at once. But most of the newspapers paid little attention to the speech, and some sneered at it. The *Patriot and Union* of Harrisburg wrote, "We pass over the silly remarks of the President; for the credit of the nation we are willing . . . that they shall no more be repeated or thought of"; and the London *Times* said, "The ceremony was rendered ludicrous by some of the sallies of that poor President Lincoln," calling his remarks "dull and commonplace." The first commendation of the Address came in a single sentence of the Chicago *Tribune,* and the first discriminating and detailed praise of it appeared in the Springfield *Republican,* the Providence *Journal,* and the Philadelphia *Bulletin.* However, three weeks

after the ceremony and then again the following spring, the editor of *Harper's Weekly* published a sincere and thorough eulogy of the Address, and soon it was attaining recognition as a masterpiece.

8   At the time, Lincoln could not care much about the reception of his words. He was exhausted and ill. In the train back to Washington, he lay down with a wet towel on his head. He had caught smallpox. At that moment he was incubating it, and he was stricken down soon after he re-entered the White House. Fortunately it was a mild attack, and it evoked one of his best jokes: he told his visitors, "At last I have something I can give to everybody."

9   He had more than that to give to everybody. He was a unique person, far greater than most people realize until they read his life with care. The wisdom of his policy, the sources of his statesmanship—these were things too complex to be discussed in a brief essay. But we can say something about the Gettysburg Address as a work of art.

10   A work of art. Yes: for Lincoln was a literary artist, trained both by others and by himself. The textbooks he used as a boy were full of difficult exercises and skillful devices in formal rhetoric, stressing the qualities he practiced in his own speaking: antithesis, parallelism, and verbal harmony. Then he read and reread many admirable models of thought and expression: the King James Bible, the essays of Bacon, the best plays of Shakepeare. His favorites were *Hamlet, Lear, Macbeth, Richard III,* and *Henry VIII,* which he had read dozens of times. He loved reading aloud, too, and spent hours reading poetry to his friends. (He told his partner Herndon that he preferred getting the sense of any document by reading it aloud.) Therefore his serious speeches are important parts of the long and noble classical tradition of oratory which begins in Greece, runs through Rome to the modern world, and is still capable (if we do not neglect it) of producing masterpieces.

11   The first proof of this is that the Gettysburg Address is full of quotations—or rather of adaptations—which give it strength. It is partly religious, partly (in the highest sense) political: therefore it is interwoven with memories of the Bible and memories of American history. The first and the last words are Biblical cadences. Normally Lincoln did not say "fourscore" when he meant eighty; but on this solemn occasion he recalled the important dates in the Bible—such as the age of Abram when his first son was born to him, and he was "fourscore and six years old." [2] Similarly he did not say there was a chance that democracy might die out: he recalled the somber phrasing of the Book of Job—where Bildad speaks of the destruction of one who shall vanish without a trace, and says that "his branch shall be cut off; his remembrance shall perish from the earth." [3] Then again, the famous description of our State as "government of the

---

[2] Gen. 16.16; cf. Exod. 7.7.
[3] Job 18.16—17; cf. Jer. 10.11, Micah 7.2.

people, by the people, for the people" was adumbrated by Daniel Webster in 1830 (he spoke of "the people's government, made for the people, made by the people, and answerable to the people") and then elaborated in 1854 by the abolitionist Theodore Parker (as "government of all the people, by all the people, for all the people"). There is good reason to think that Lincoln took the important phrase "under God" (which he interpolated at the last moment) from Weems, the biographer of Washington; and we know that it had been used at least once by Washington himself.

12   Analyzing the Address further, we find that it is based on a highly imaginative theme, or group of themes. The subject is—how can we put it so as not to disfigure it?—the subject is the kinship of life and death, that mysterious linkage which we see sometimes as the physical succession of birth and death in our world, sometimes as the contrast, which is perhaps a unity, between death and immortality. The first sentence is concerned with birth:

> Our *fathers brought forth* a *new* nation, *conceived* in liberty.

The final phrase but one expresses the hope that

> this nation, under God, shall have a *new birth* of freedom.

And the last phrase of all speaks of continuing life as the triumph over death. Again and again throughout the speech, this mystical contrast and kinship reappear: "those who *gave their lives* that that nation might *live,*" "the brave men *living* and *dead,*" and so in the central assertion that the dead have already consecrated their own burial place, while "it is for us, the *living,* rather to be dedicated . . . to the great task remaining." The Gettysburg Address is a prose poem; it belongs to the same world as the great elegies, and the adagios of Beethoven.

13   Its structure, however, is that of a skillfully contrived speech. The oratorical pattern is perfectly clear. Lincoln describes the occasion, dedicates the ground, and then draws a larger conclusion by calling on his hearers to dedicate themselves to the preservation of the Union. But within that, we can trace his constant use of at least two important rhetorical devices.

14   The first of these is *antithesis:* opposition, contrast. The speech is full of it. Listen:

> The world will little *note*
> nor long *remember*   what *we say* here
> but   it can never *forget*   what *they did* here.

And so in nearly every sentence: "brave men, *living* and *dead*"; "to *add* or *detract.*" There is the antithesis of the Founding Fathers and the men of Lincoln's own time:

> Our *fathers brought forth* a new nation . . .
> now *we* are testing whether that nation . . . can *long endure.*

And there is the more terrible antithesis of those who have already died and those who still live to do their duty. Now, antithesis is the figure of contrast and conflict. Lincoln was speaking in the midst of a great civil war.

15   The other important pattern is different. It is technically called *tricolon* —the division of an idea into three harmonious parts, usually of increasing power. The most famous phrase of the Address is a tricolon:

> government of the people
>   by the people
>   and   for the people.

The most solemn sentence is a tricolon:

> we cannot dedicate
> we cannot consecrate
> we cannot hallow this ground.

And above all, the last sentence (which has sometimes been criticized as too complex) is essentially two parallel phrases, with a tricolon growing out of the second and then producing another tricolon: a trunk, three branches, and a cluster of flowers. Lincoln says that it is for his hearers to be dedicated to the great task remaining before them. Then he goes on,

> that from these honored dead

—apparently he means "in such a way that from these honored dead"—

> we take increased devotion to that cause.

Next, he restates this more briefly:

> that we here highly resolve . . .

And now the actual resolution follows, in three parts of growing intensity:

> that these dead shall not have died in vain
> that this nation, under God, shall have a new birth of freedom

and that (one more tricolon)

> government of the people
>   by the people
>   and   for the people
> shall not perish from the earth.

Now, the tricolon is the figure which, through division, emphasizes basic harmony and unity. Lincoln used antithesis because he was speaking to a people at war. He used the tricolon because he was hoping, planning, praying for peace.

16   No one thinks that when he was drafting the Gettysburg Address, Lincoln deliberately looked up these quotations and consciously chose these particular patterns of thought. No, he chose the theme. From its development and from the emotional tone of the entire occasion, all the rest followed, or grew—by that marvelous process of choice and rejection which is essential to artistic creation. It does not spoil such a work of art to analyze it as closely as we have done; it is altogether fitting and proper

that we should do this: for it helps us to penetrate more deeply into the rich meaning of the Gettysburg Address, and it allows us the very rare privilege of watching the workings of a great man's mind.

W. E. Barton, *Lincoln at Gettysburg* (Bobbs-Merrill, 1930).
R. P. Basler, "Abraham Lincoln's Rhetoric," *American Literature* 11 (1939–40), 167–82.
L. E. Robinson, *Abraham Lincoln as a Man of Letters* (Chicago, 1918).

the rhetoric of
the kennedy address

THE NEW YORKER

VICE-PRESIDENT JOHNSON, MR. SPEAKER, MR. CHIEF JUSTICE, PRESIDENT EISENHOWER, VICE-PRESIDENT NIXON, PRESIDENT TRUMAN, REVEREND CLERGY, FELLOW CITIZENS:

1   We observe today not a victory of party but a celebration of freedom—symbolizing an end as well as a beginning—signifying renewal as well as change. For I have sworn before you and Almighty God the same solemn oath our forebearers prescribed nearly a century and three-quarters ago.

2   The world is very different now. For man holds in his mortal hands the power to abolish all forms of human poverty and all forms of human life. And yet the same revolutionary beliefs for which our forebearers fought are still at issue around the globe—the belief that the rights of man come not from the generosity of the state but from the hand of God.

3   We dare not forget today that we are the heirs of that first revolution. Let the word go forth from this time and place, to friend and foe alike, that the torch has been passed to a new generation of Americans—born in this century, tempered by war, disciplined by a hard and bitter peace, proud of our ancient heritage—and unwilling to witness or permit the slow undoing of those human rights to which this nation has always been committed, and to which we are committed today at home and around the world.

4   Let every nation know, whether it wishes us well or ill, that we shall pay any price, bear any burden, meet any hardship, support any friend, oppose any foe to assure the survival and the success of liberty.

5   This much we pledge—and more.

6   To those old allies whose cultural and spiritual origins we share, we pledge the loyalty of faithful friends. United, there is little we cannot do in a host of co-operative ventures. Divided, there is little we can do—for we dare not meet a powerful challenge at odds and split asunder.

7   To those new states whom we welcome to the ranks of the free, we pledge our word that one form of colonial control shall not have passed away merely to be replaced by a far more iron tyranny. We shall not always expect to find them supporting our view. But we shall always hope to find them strongly supporting their own freedom—and to remember that, in the past, those who foolishly sought power by riding the back of the tiger ended up inside.

8   To those people in the huts and villages of half the globe struggling to break the bonds of mass misery, we pledge our best efforts to help them help themselves, for whatever period is required—not because the Communists may be doing it, not because we seek their votes, but because it is right. If a free society cannot help the many who are poor, it cannot save the few who are rich.

9   To our sister republics south of our border, we offer a special pledge—to convert our good words into good deeds—in a new alliance for progress—to assist free men and free governments in casting off the chains of poverty. But this peaceful revolution of hope cannot become the prey of hostile powers. Let all our neighbors know that we shall join with them to oppose aggression or subversion anywhere in the Americas. And let every other power know that this hemisphere intends to remain the master of its own house.

10   To that world assembly of sovereign states, the United Nations, our last best hope in an age where the instruments of war have far outpaced the instruments of peace, we renew our pledge of support—to prevent it from becoming merely a forum for invective—to strengthen its shield of the new and the weak —and to enlarge the area in which its writ may run.

11   Finally, to those nations who would make themselves our adversary, we offer not a pledge but a request: that both sides begin anew the quest for peace, before the dark powers of destruction unleashed by science engulf all humanity in planned or accidental self-destruction.

12   We dare not tempt them with weakness. For only when our arms are sufficient beyond doubt can we be certain beyond doubt that they will never be employed.

13   But neither can two great and powerful groups of nations take comfort from our present course—both sides overburdened by the cost of modern weapons, both rightly alarmed by the steady spread of the deadly atom, yet both racing to alter that uncertain balance of terror that stays the hand of mankind's final war.

14   So let us begin anew—remembering on both sides that civility is not a sign of weakness, and sincerity is always subject to proof. Let us never negotiate out of fear. But let us never fear to negotiate.

15   Let both sides explore what problems unite us instead of belaboring those problems which divide us.

16   Let both sides, for the first time, formulate serious and precise proposals for the inspection and control of arms—and bring the absolute power to destroy other nations under the absolute control of all nations.

17   Let both sides seek to invoke the wonders of science instead of its terrors. Together let us explore the stars, conquer the deserts, eradicate disease, tap the ocean depths, and encourage the arts and commerce.

18   Let both sides unite to heed in all corners of the earth the command of Isaiah—to "undo the heavy burdens . . . [and] let the oppressed go free."

19   And if a beachhead of co-operation may push back the jungle of suspicion, let both sides join in creating a new endeavor, not a new balance of power, but

a new world of law, where the strong are just and the weak secure and the peace preserved.

20   All this will not be finished in the first one hundred days. Nor will it be finished in the first one thousand days, nor in the life of this administration, nor even perhaps in our lifetime on this planet. But let us begin.

21   In your hands, my fellow citizens, more than mine, will rest the final success or failure of our course. Since this country was founded, each generation of Americans has been summoned to give testimony to its national loyalty. The graves of young Americans who answered the call to service surround the globe.

22   Now the trumpet summons us again—not as a call to bear arms, though arms we need—not as a call to battle, though embattled we are—but a call to bear the burden of a long twilight struggle, year in and year out, "rejoicing in hope, patient in tribulation"—a struggle against the common enemies of man: tyranny, poverty, disease, and war itself.

23   Can we forge against these enemies a grand and global alliance, North and South, East and West, that can assure a more fruitful life for all mankind? Will you join in that historic effort?

24   In the long history of the world, only a few generations have been granted the role of defending freedom in its hour of maximum danger. I do not shrink from this responsibility—I welcome it. I do not believe that any of us would exchange places with any other people or any other generation. The energy, the faith, the devotion which we bring to this endeavor will light our country and all who serve it—and the glow from that fire can truly light the world.

25   And so, my fellow Americans: ask not what your country can do for you —ask what you can do for your country.

26   My fellow citizens of the world: ask not what America will do for you, but what together we can do for the freedom of man.

27   Finally, whether you are citizens of America or citizens of the world, ask of us here the same high standards of strength and sacrifice which we ask of you. With a good conscience our only sure reward, with history the final judge of our deeds, let us go forth to lead the land we love, asking His blessing and His help, but knowing that here on earth God's work must truly be our own.

1   **a**s rhetoric has become an increasingly dispensable member of the liberal arts, people have abandoned the idea, held so firmly by the ancient Greeks and Romans, that eloquence is indispensable to politics. Perhaps President Kennedy's achievements in both spheres will revive a taste for good oratory —a taste that has been alternately frustrated by inarticulateness and dulled by bombast. There have been a few notable orators in our day—most recently, Adlai Stevenson—but they have been the exceptions, and it has taken Mr. Kennedy's success as a politician to suggest that the power to "enchant souls through words" (Socrates) may soon be at a premium once more. Whatever the impact of the Inaugural Address on contemporary New Frontiersmen, we find it hard to believe that an Athenian or Roman citizen could have listened to it unmoved, or that Cicero, however jealous of his own reputation, would have found reason to object to it.

2   We are all familiar by now with the generally high praise the President received for his first speech, but before the responsibility for a final judg-

ment is yielded to Time it would be a shame not to seek the opinion of a couple of true professionals. Both Aristotle and Cicero, the one a theorist and the other a theorizing orator, believed that rhetoric could be an art to the extent that the orator was, first, a logician, and, second, a psychologist with an appreciation and understanding of words. Cicero felt, further, that the ideal orator was the thoroughly educated man. (He would be pleased by Mr. Kennedy's background with its strong emphasis on affairs of state: the philosopher-orator-statesman.) Of the three types of oratory defined by the ancients—political, forensic, and display (in which audience participation was limited to a judgment of style)—the political was esteemed most highly, because it dealt with the loftiest of issues: namely, the fate of peoples, rather than of individuals. ("Now the trumpet summons us again . . . against the common enemies of man. . . .") The ideal speech was thought to be one in which three kinds of persuasion were used by the speaker: logical, to present the facts of the case and construct an argument based on them; emotional, to reach the audience psychologically; and "ethical," to appeal to the audience by establishing one's own integrity and sincerity. The Inaugural Address, being a variation on the single theme of man's rights and obligations, is not primarily logical, although it contains no illogic; it is an appeal to men's souls rather than to their minds. During the Presidential campaign, Mr. Kennedy tested and patented an exercise in American psychology that proved to be all the emotional appeal he required for the inaugural speech: "And so, my fellow Americans, ask not what your country can do for you, ask what you can do for your country." His ethical persuasion, or indication of his personal probity, consisted of an extension of that appeal: ". . . ask of us here the same high standards of strength and sacrifice which we ask of you."

3   Aristotle recognized only one (good) style, while Cicero thought that there were three styles—the plain, the middle, and the grand. To Aristotle, who considered it sufficient for a style to be clear and appropriate, avoiding undue elevation (whence bombast) and excessive lowliness, it would have seemed that Mr. Kennedy had achieved the Golden Mean. The formality of the Inaugural Address ("To that world assembly of sovereign states, the United Nations . . .") is appropriate to the subject; the language ("In your hands, my fellow citizens, more than mine, will rest the final success or failure of our course") is clear and direct. Cicero's ideal orator was able to speak in all three styles, in accordance with the demands of his subject, and in that respect Mr. Kennedy filled the role by speaking plainly on the practical ("All this will not be finished in the first one hundred days"), by speaking formally but directly on the purpose of national defense ("For only when our arms are sufficient beyond doubt can we be certain beyond doubt that they will never be employed"), and by speaking grandly on the potential accomplishments of the movement toward the New Frontier ("The energy, the faith, the devotion which we bring to this endeavor will light our country and all who serve it—and the glow from that fire can truly light the world").

4   The address, however, is largely in the grand style, which is characterized by Cicero as the ultimate source of emotional persuasion, through
figures of speech and a certain degree of dignified periodic rhythm, not
iambic ("The world is very different now. For man holds in his mortal
hands the power to abolish all forms of human poverty and all forms of
human life"). The oration is so rich in figures of speech—the many metaphors include a torch, a beachhead, jungles, a trumpet, a tiger—that we
can imagine students of the future studying it for examples of antithesis
("If a free society cannot help the many who are poor, it cannot save the
few who are rich"), personification (". . . the hand of mankind's final
war"), and anaphora ("Not as a call to bear arms, though arms we need;
not as a call to battle, though embattled we are . . ."). "Battle" and "embattled"—an excellent example of paronomasia.*

5   And so we leave the speech to the students of rhetoric, having invoked
for Mr. Kennedy the blessings of Aristotle and Cicero, and for ourself the
hope that he has reestablished the tradition of political eloquence.

COMMENTARY

Highet spends his first eight paragraphs identifying his subject and establishing historical background. Although a great deal of information is
skillfully compressed into these paragraphs, they are a rather long introduction if his purpose is to demonstrate that the Gettysburg Address is
"one of the greatest speeches in all history" (paragraph 2). Is this introductory section justified? What purposes does it serve?

Paragraphs 9 to 14 examine in detail Lincoln's "art": the content and
the stylistic devices of the address. To Highet, who believes in the value
of tradition, it is high praise to say that Lincoln's speech belongs in "the
long and noble classical tradition of oratory." He divides this general
principle of literary excellence into several specific qualities: adaptations
of earlier writings (paragraph 11); a theme of permanent importance
(paragraph 12); a clear oratorical pattern (paragraph 13); the devices of
antithesis and tricolon (paragraphs 13 and 14). Highet believes that the
tricolon is such a valuable device that he uses it himself (at the end of
paragraph 14, in describing how Lincoln used it).

The *New Yorker's* considerably shorter evaluation of Kennedy's speech
omits the historical introduction (why?). It begins instead with an assertion
of value: rhetorical excellence is becoming important again (paragraph 1).
Like Highet, the *New Yorker* critic divides his material. Here the rhetorical
theories of two classical writers serve as the principle of division. We are
introduced to Aristotle and Cicero and then told what each of them would

---

* Antithesis: balanced opposition of ideas and words ("many . . . poor," "few . . . rich");
personification: presentation of something that is not human as if it were human ("war"
as if it had a hand); anaphora: repetition of words used to introduce sentences or clauses
("not as . . . ," "not as . . . ."); paronomasia: repetition of a word with a change in sound
or meaning. These are "figures of speech" discussed by the classical rhetoricians.—Eds.

think of Kennedy's address (paragraphs 2 to 4). Criteria appear throughout these paragraphs (for example, "the ideal speech was thought to be. . . ," (paragraph 2). Each criterion is immediately applied to the speech. This technique could become tiresome, but the entire review is only five paragraphs long, and we can therefore tolerate the repeated judgments: Kennedy's speech is good this way, this way, this way, and this way.

The *New Yorker* critic says nothing at all about the *content* of Kennedy's address (Highet thought that Lincoln's derived part of its power from its theme). Do you find this kind of evaluation sufficient? Has the favorable judgment in the *New Yorker* article's last paragraph been adequately defended? Or is it inappropriate to assess political speeches in terms of their style only?

Some rhetoricians have claimed that we should not teach people how to write or speak movingly unless we also teach them a sense of responsibility so that they will not use the power of words for evil purposes. Eloquence can be a dangerous weapon, they point out, and we should not put dangerous weapons in the hands of everybody. If you agree with this position, you will probably evaluate the *New Yorker* article, and to some extent Highet's also, as incomplete because they do not try to demonstrate the excellence of the speeches' ideas.

Should our criteria for evaluating political rhetoric be utilitarian (does a speech work?) or moral (does it propose good ideas?) or both?

OUTLINE: HIGHET

    I. Introduction: the power and permanence of the address—paragraph 1
   II. Historical background—paragraphs 4–8
      A. Occasion of the address—paragraphs 4–6
      B. Its impact—paragraph 7
  III. The "art" of the address—paragraphs 9–14
      A. Lincoln's training and sources—paragraphs 10–11
      B. Themes—paragraph 12
      C. Devices of style—paragraphs 13–14
  IV. Summary of the value of the address and assertion that analyzing it increases its meaning—paragraph 15

OUTLINE: *NEW YORKER* EDITORIAL

    I. Introduction: the revival of oratory—paragraph 1
   II. Evaluation of Kennedy's address, using criteria of Aristotle and Cicero—paragraphs 2–4
  III. Conclusion: summary of Aristotle's and Cicero's evaluation (they would give the Kennedy speech their "blessing"); reassertion of hope that we will see a revival of oratory—paragraph 5

SUGGESTIONS FOR WRITING

1. The criteria used by Highet and by the *New Yorker* editor are similar but not identical. Reverse them: evaluate Lincoln's speech using some of the *New Yorker*'s criteria or Kennedy's using some of Highet's. For example, evaluate the Gettysburg Address on the basis of these criteria from Cicero (*New Yorker* article, paragraph 2): "The ideal speech was thought to be one in which three kinds of persuasion were used by the speaker: logical, to present the facts of the case and construct an argument based on them; emotional, to reach the audience psychologically; and 'ethical,' to appeal to the audience by establishing one's own integrity and sincerity." Does Lincoln use all three kinds of persuasion?

2. Lincoln once said that a nation must hear "mystic chords of memory stretching from every battlefield and patriot grave to every living heart and hearthstone." Many Americans apparently no longer hear those chords.

What would the Gettysburg Address mean to a person who does not recognize its sources or accept its patriotic themes?

Reevaluate Lincoln's speech (or Kennedy's), using not criteria drawn from classical rhetoric but whatever contemporary criteria you think it is appropriate to apply.

series two

EVALUATION: READINGS WITHOUT COMMENTARY

---

the squirrel memo

THE WALL STREET JOURNAL

The subject of this short evaluation is bureaucratic red tape, specifically the endless and senseless forms and questionnaires that government agencies ask people to fill out. An HEW (Department of Health, Education, and Welfare) application form is made to seem ridiculous when someone answers it in terms of squirrels.

The *Wall Street Journal* writer uses the evaluative technique known as "damning with faint praise": he finds something to approve of, but it is so minor a characteristic, and his praise is so lukewarm, that the overall evaluation is clearly negative. Thus the last paragraph finds that it is "nice" (a trivial term) to see a sense of humor in a government agency that has "an occupational devotion to red tape." We are meant to remain annoyed with HEW for its red tape. The sense of humor belongs mostly to the university staff member who had the bright idea of sending those nuts a few squirrels.

1   **m**any releases and handouts that cross newspaper desks each day could be offered as prime exhibits for hiking the postal rates on unsolicited mail. But occasionally there's gold in them thar hills, and we offer as evidence a recent item from the news bureau of Washington and Lee University in Lexington, Va.

2   It seems that one Frank Parsons, assistant to the university president, was struggling with a lengthy application for federal funds to be used in

building the university's proposed new library. Among other things, HEW wanted to know how the proposed project "may affect energy sources by introducing or deleting electro-magnetic wave sources which may alter man-made or natural structures or the physiology, behavior patterns, and/ or activities of 10% of a human, animal or plant population." The questions go on and on, but you get the idea.

3   Assistant Parsons plugged away, dutifully answering as best he could. And then he came to the section on animal populations, where he was asked to list the extent to which the proposed library would "create or precipitate an identifiable long-term change in the diversity of species within its natural habitat."

4   "There are some 10 to 20 squirrels living, or appearing to live, in the site proposed for the new library," he wrote. "Some trees that now provide either homes or exercise areas for the squirrels will be removed, but there appear to be ample other trees to serve either or both of these purposes. No major food source for the squirrels will be affected. It is likely that the squirrels will find no difficulty in adjusting to this intrusion. . . . They have had no apparent difficulty in adjusting to relocations brought on by non-federally supported projects."

5   To the question of whether the proposal will "create or precipitate an identifiable change in the behavior patterns of an animal population," he assured HEW the squirrels and such would have to make some adjustments but "it will be difficult to tell if they're unhappy about having to find new trees to live in and sport about."

6   Eventually the application was shipped off to Washington, and lo and behold before long HEW official Richard R. Holden actually wrote the president of the school. He said: "Perhaps bureaucracy will tremble, but I salute Washington and Lee University . . . . The mountain of paperwork which confronts me daily somehow seemed much smaller the day I read about the squirrels in Lexington. May they and your great university co-exist in harmony for many, many years." As copies of the correspondence zipped throughout federal agencies, with all the speed of a confidential memo destined for Jack Anderson, bureaucrats from all over telephoned their congratulations to the "squirrel memo man."

7   We're still not sure exactly what lesson is to be drawn from all this. Our initial reaction was surprise that anyone actually reads these exhaustive applications, and even now we're undecided whether that's cause for comfort or dismay. Yet while we never doubted that HEW possessed a sense of humor—indeed, we've gotten some of our biggest laughs from proposals emanating from the vicinity of 330 Independence Ave., S.W.—it's nice to know that an occupational devotion to red tape has not completely eroded the agency's ability to laugh at itself.

the 1974 world series

JOE GARAGIOLA

This short evaluation—a five-minute radio commentary—discusses the problem of choosing the "most valuable player" in the 1974 Series. Sportscaster Garagiola mentions several criteria: overall performance, batting average, outstanding pitching measured by "earned run averages," and so forth. The basic conclusion, however, is that this Series did not produce any player clearly worthy of that honor. Garagiola's commentary ends, therefore, with two facetious nominations for the honor: the weatherman and ex-Series-player Garagiola himself.

1   **I**t's difficult now to figure how this past World Series will be remembered. It was close, certainly, with four of the five games ending in scores of three to two. But even closer was the race for picking the most valuable player in the Series. Traditionally, the player chosen for that honor got a car, and the winner this year, by vote of the press, was Rollie Fingers, Oakland relief pitcher.

2   The selection was not unanimous. There was support for Joe Rudi, who hit .333, batted in four runs, and hit the home run that won the final game. There were those who thought Bert Campaneris should have gotten it, because he had the highest batting average of the Oakland regulars, and because he was, in the opinion of many, cheated out of the honor last year.

3   But the simple fact is that this World Series didn't have that dominant player that usually pops up. Brooks Robinson did it one year, so did Lew Burdette, and Dusty Rhodes. These men completely overshadowed the rest. But in this year's Series there was no performance like that. Dick Green, Oakland second baseman, had an outstanding defensive World Series. But it would be tough to pick him as the top player when he didn't get a base hit. Of all the regulars in the Series, Steve Garvey, Dodgers first baseman, had the highest batting average, .381. But he batted in only one run. The pitching was not really outstanding. There were no shutouts in the Series, and, in fact, there were no complete games. If you want to use earned run averages as a yardstick for pitchers, Fingers had an E.R.A. under two, but his teammates, Ken Holtzman and Catfish Hunter, had E.R.A.'s lower than Fingers did.

4   If there was one guy who had an outstanding World Series, it was the weatherman. You come to expect real good baseball weather in southern California, but the Bay Area in October can get a little damp. Twelve years ago, when the Giants played the Yankees, we ran into a stretch of San Francisco weather that made us wonder if the two clubs would have to travel by ark.

5   Did you realize that in one World Series game I got as many hits as

Source. Courtesy of Joe Garagiola and the National Broadcasting Company.

Sal Bando, Billy North, and Joe Ferguson, put together, got in this whole World Series? Why do I mention it? If I don't, who will?

6   This is Joe Garagiola on the NBC Radio Network.

bombing the paragraph
HENRY SEIDEL CANBY

Canby's article on the paragraph makes its evaluation clear in the very first sentence: he thinks that the paragraph is in bad shape. To be sure, he exaggerates. To save the paragraph, we do not need one major "act of national recovery" but rather thousands of little acts by writers to make each paragraph do its job. Having defined his term in paragraphs 3 and 4, he deplores the deterioration of paragraph composition and blames the mass press. Since we don't want to be thought of as "feebleminded," we are prepared to join Canby in his campaign of reconstruction. (For a different view, see Ogilvy, p. 456.)

Note his use of familiar images: a paragraph is like a bombed building that requires reconstruction; it is a ship, a fan, and a nut (paragraph 2); it is food that can be made fit for eating by a skillful cook (paragraph 3). Might we say that Canby is guilty of writing some "flashy" journalism himself? Or does this kind of writing support his judgment that logical organization and ample evidence are essential?

1   **S**ome act of national recovery is needed if the English paragraph is to be saved. Let us recall to the memories of those who were once accustomed to good English what the paragraph was supposed to be before it ran upon the rocks of mass production and was splintered into incoherent sentences.

2   The paragraph was a trim little vessel in the days when journalists still wrote for minds trained to hold more than one thought at a time. Rhetoricians spoke of it as one full step in the development of an idea, and might have compared it with a fan which spreads without losing its unity, increasing its usefulness without changing its control. An idea stated in a single sentence (topic, they used to call it) is self-sufficient only for the very wise or the very simple. Emerson and Thoreau, among Americans, wrote self-sufficient sentences for the wise, and the race of columnists (who call themselves paragraphers) have carried on this tradition of apothegm all the way

Source. From Seven Years' Harvest: Notes on Contemporary Literature by Henry Seidel Canby. Copyright © 1936 by Henry Seidel Canby. Copyright © 1964 by Marion Ponsonby Gauss Canby. Reprinted by permission of Holt, Rinehart and Winston, Publishers.

into wisecrack—a sentence paragraph which is a nut that a sharp mind can bite into.

3   But this is specialists' work. The general utility paragraph led off (in the days of coherence) with a sentence that said simply and definitely what the writer thought. But thought is never so simple as that. It must be qualified, developed, explained, if it is to satisfy the sophisticated. Only the naïve will swallow a generalization without chewing on it. The English paragraph in its prime was raw material made fit for eating by a skillful cook. If the writer began "Democracy depends upon intelligence," he could not leave it at that. Simple minds might be content, but in those days readers were not that simple. They asked why and were prepared to reserve judgment until, item after item, the explanation or argument unrolled to a Q.E.D. at the end of the paragraph. Macaulay, whose diminishing reputation as a historian still leaves him one of the world's great journalists, could fling out a reverberating paragraph as organized and emphatic and lucid as the simplest sentence, which prepared, held, and satisfied the attentive reader by a structure which had all the advantages of a formula without its dangerous simplicity. Frank Cobb of the old *World* could drop his sequent sentences one after another in perfect harmony for a column before the packed theme with which he began had been unpacked and become an organism of thought.

4   The paragraph, like many other good things, was wrecked by mass production. When newspapers, and then magazines, began to be published for the millions, writers soon found that their readers were short-winded. They would hold their brains together for three or four sentences, not more. News was rewritten for them in short paragraphs, the ramp of the story broken up into little steps; and that was good, especially when the sentences took on the color of contemporary impressionism, for in the reporting of successive incidents, the successive topics are facts which need no logical development. Paragraphs are relatively unimportant in narrative. Not so with editorials and articles. When the writers whose duty it was to exhort or explain discarded the paragraph (the Hearst newspapers began it) and wrote series of short, sharp sentences, each set apart so that it might be easily assimilated by the dumbest readers, they scored at first a great journalistic success. Strong writing, it seemed to be, punches from the shoulder, very persuasive to the man who must have a thought knocked into him, well calculated indeed for a nation of quick readers who seldom read books and lacked the patience (and often the ability) to follow the testing of an idea through a paragraph. And thousands of writers, noting the success with the masses of these disintegrated paragraphs, imitated them, until even when an idea had to be tested, explained, in order to mean anything at all, their paragraphs were still split into groups of pointed sentences, one statement at a time, so that even the feebleminded could read.

5   That is where we are today in the bulk of English writing outside of books and the better magazines. Unfortunately, however, the immense ma-

jority of readers, even among the masses, are not feebleminded. They are, one suspects, beginning to react by not reading at all, or by taking the first punch and dodging all the rest. After all, this method of writing was first devised, not for journalism, but for children's reading-books, where not only paragraphs but long words were split for immature minds. Our journalists have treated their readers like children and they are getting a child's reactions, violent, brief, and oversimplified. They have violated the natural order of thinking and, as a result, give no training and get no response in thought. Like the advertisers and the politicians, they have been playing upon the unformed mass mind for profits, consistently making thought easy in the hope of speedier results. It is a phase of exploitation, and will produce its reactions in both reader and writer, like every other attempt to debase the currency of human intercourse.

a wasp stings back
ROBERT CLAIBORNE

This is an evaluation of a cultural group, the WASPs (White Anglo-Saxon Protestants), a group that has become a new collective antihero condemned by virtually every other segment of American society and often by itself. The writer asserts that WASPs deserve our approval for at least one contribution to American culture: the concept of limited government. Beyond that, he says, they are no worse than the rest of us. Thus, he points out that the Catholics, who are among the critics of the WASPs, "ripped off" his ancestor's farm and that the persecution of minorities exists also in Third World countries, despite their criticism of WASP persecution of minorities.

Do you think that Claiborne's defense of WASP values is adequate? What seem to be his criteria for judging people?

1   **O**ver the past few years, American pop culture has acquired a new folk antihero: the Wasp. One slick magazine tells us that the White Anglo-Saxon Protestants rule New York City, while other media gurus credit (or discredit) them with ruling the country—and, by inference, ruining it. A Polish-American declares in a leading newspaper that Wasps have "no sense of honor." *Newsweek* patronizingly describes Chautauqua as a citadel of "Wasp values," while other folklorists characterize these values more explicitly as a compulsive commitment to the work ethic, emotional up-

Source. Copyright © *Newsweek*, Inc., 1974. Reprinted by permission.

tightness and sexual inhibition. The Wasps, in fact, are rapidly becoming the one minority that every other ethnic group—blacks, Italians, chicanos, Jews, Poles and all the rest—feels absolutely free to dump on. I have not yet had a friend greet me with "Did you hear the one about the two Wasps who . . .?"—but any day now!

2   I come of a long line of Wasps; if you disregard my French great-great-grandmother and a couple of putatively Irish ancestors of the same vintage, a rather pure line. My mother has long been one of the Colonial Dames, an organization some of whose members consider the Daughters of the American Revolution rather parvenu. My umpty-umpth Wasp great-grand-father, William Claiborne, founded the first European settlement in what is now Maryland (his farm and trading post were later ripped off by the Catholic Lord Baltimore, Maryland politics being much the same then as now).

THE STEREOTYPE

3   As a Wasp, the mildest thing I can say about the stereotype emerging from the current wave of anti-Wasp chic is that I don't recognize myself. As regards emotional uptightness and sexual inhibition, modesty forbids comment—though I dare say various friends and lovers of mine could testify on these points if they cared to. I will admit to enjoying work—because I am lucky enough to be able to work at what I enjoy—but not, I think, to the point of compulsiveness. And so far as ruling America, or even New York, is concerned, I can say flatly that (a) it's a damn lie because (b) if I *did* rule them, both would be in better shape than they are. Indeed I and all my Wasp relatives, taken in a lump, have far less clout with the powers that run this country than any one of the Buckleys or Kennedys (Irish Catholic), the Sulzbergers or Guggenheims (Jewish), or the late A. P. Giannini (Italian) of the Bank of America.

4   Admittedly, both corporate and (to a lesser extent) political America are dominated by Wasps—just as (let us say) the garment industry is dominated by Jews, and organized crime by Italians. But to conclude from this that The Wasps are the American elite is as silly as to say that The Jews are cloak-and-suiters or The Italians are gangsters. Wasps, like other ethnics, come in all varieties, including criminals—political, corporate and otherwise.

THE VALUES

5   More seriously, I would like to say a word for the maligned "Wasp values," one of them in particular. As a matter of historical fact, it was we Wasps—by which I mean here the English-speaking peoples—who invented the idea of *limited governments:* that there are some things that no king, President or other official is allowed to do. It began more than seven centuries ago, with Magna Carta, and continued (to cite only the high spots) through the wrangles between Parliament and the Stuart kings, the Puritan

Revolution of 1640, the English Bill of Rights of 1688, the American Revolution and our own Bill of Rights and Constitution.

6   The Wasp principle of limited government emerged through protracted struggle with the much older principle of unlimited government. This latter was never more cogently expressed than at the trial of Charles I, when the hapless monarch informed his judges that, as an anointed king, he was not accountable to any court in the land. A not dissimilar position was taken more recently by another Wasp head of state—and with no more success; executive privilege went over no better in 1974 than divine right did in 1649. The notion that a king, a President, or any other official can do as he damn well pleases has never played in Peoria—or Liverpool or Glasgow, Melbourne or Toronto. For more than 300 years, no Wasp nation has endured an absolute monarchy, dictatorship or any other form of unlimited government—which is something no Frenchman, Italian, German, Pole, Russian or Hispanic can say.

7   It is perfectly true, of course, that we Wasps have on occasion imposed unlimited governments on other (usually darker) peoples. We have, that is, acted in much the same way as have most other nations that possessed the requisite power and opportunity—including many Third World nations whose leaders delight in lecturing us on political morality (for recent information on this point, consult the files on Biafra, Bangladesh and Brazil, Indian tribes of). Yet even here, Wasp values have played an honorable part. When you start with the idea that Englishmen are entitled to self-government, you end by conceding the same right to Africans and Indians. If you begin by declaring that all (white) men are created equal, you must sooner or later face up to the fact that blacks are also men—and conform your conduct, however reluctantly, to your values.

THE FAITH

8   Keeping the Wasp faith hasn't always been easy. We Wasps, like other people, don't always live up to our own principles, and those of us who don't, if occupying positions of power, can pose formidable problems to the rest of us. Time after time, in the name of anti-Communism, peace with honor or some other slippery shibboleth, we have been conned or bullied into tolerating government interference with our liberties and privacy in all sorts of covert—and sometimes overt—ways; time after time we have had to relearn the lesson that eternal vigilance is the price of liberty.

9   It was a Wasp who uttered that last thought. And it was a congress of Wasps who, about the same time, denounced the executive privileges of George III and committed to the cause of liberty their lives, their fortunes and—*pace* my Polish-American compatriot—their sacred honor.

chicanos and american literature

PHILIP O. ORTEGO
AND JOSE A. CARRASCO

This selection demonstrates that an evaluation sometimes needs an extensive substantiation section. The authors provide example after example to substantiate their assertion that Mexican-Americans are "inaccurately and superficially" depicted in our literature—either falsely romanticized as "hot-blooded, sexually animated creatures" or falsely degraded into "passive, humble servants." In all, the presentation of Mexican-Americans in our literature has been "deplorable."

This selection also demonstrates how evaluation is influenced by each writer's assumptions, his overall viewpoint toward the world. If we looked at other segments of the evidence or looked at the evidence differently, we might come up with a less negative evaluation of the Mexican-American's literary image. And a wider examination of literatures would show that virtually every minority group and every section of the majority group has at some time received similar treatment. It might also be pointed out that, while Ortego and Carrasco attack American literature for a variety of unrealistic images of Mexican-Americans, many people do not feel that this criterion of value—"realism"—is the right one to apply to fiction. Nevertheless, we should not accept more comforting evaluations without considering this condemnation too.

1   **W**hat passes for Mexican-American literature and culture at times tends to be material that puts the Mexican-American and his Mexican kinsmen in a bad literary light, as Professor Cecil Robinson pointed out in his work *With the Ears of Strangers*. For like other minority groups, Mexican-Americans were and continue to be inaccurately and superficially represented in literature, movies, television, and other mass media.[1] This situation sometimes has been caused by prejudice, but it has also been caused by those well-meaning romanticists who have seriously distorted the image of the Mexican-American for the sake of their art.

2   Mexican-Americans have been characterized at both ends of the spectrum of human behavior (seldom in the middle) as untrustworthy, villainous, ruthless, tequila-drinking, and philandering *machos* or else as courteous, devout, and fatalistic peasants who are to be treated more as pets than as people. More often than not Mexican-Americans have been cast either as bandits or as lovable rogues; as hot-blooded, sexually animated creatures or as passive, humble servants.

[1] Philip D. Ortego, "Chicago Odyssey," *Transaction* (April 1970), p. 82.

3   The result has usually been that Mexican-American youngsters are taught about the cruelty of their Spanish forebears and the savagery of their Mexican-Indian forebears; they have been taught about the Spanish greed for gold, of the infamous Spanish Inquisition, of Aztec human sacrifices, of Mexican bandits, and of the massacre at the Alamo. They seldom, if ever, learn of the other men at the Alamo, their Mexican forebears—unknown and unsung in American history—who were killed fighting on the Texas side. American children probably have never heard of such men as Juan Abamillo, Juan Badillo, Carlos Espalier, Gregorio Esparza, Antonio Fuentes, Jose Maria Guerrero, Toribio Losoya, Andres Nava, and other Texas Mexicans at the Alamo.

4   Information about the literary accomplishments of Mexican-Americans during the period from the end of the Mexican-American War to the turn of the century, for example, has been negligible. As Américo Paredes has pointed out, "With few exceptions, documents available for study of the region are in English, being for the most part reports made by officials who were, to put it mildly, prejudiced against the people they were trying to pacify."[2] In short, editors of American literary texts have tended to minimize the literary achievement of Mexican-Americans for reasons ranging from jingoism to ignorance.

5   It should be noted, however, that no sooner had the Spanish established their hold on Mexico than they started a printing press in Mexico City in 1529, more than a century earlier than any established in the British colonies of North America. Indeed, there was a substantial Spanish-reading public in New Spain and Mexico, including the North American states, both before and after the lands were ceded to the United States in 1848. Spanish literature was read and written in both the Spanish peninsula and in the New World. Such Spanish playwrights as Pedro Calderon de la Barca and Lope de Vega extended their literary influence to Spanish America just as the Mexican-born playright Juan Ruiz de Alarcon extended his literary influence to Spain. By the time of the Mexican-American War, the Mexican Southwest had been thoroughly nurtured on drama, poetry, and folktales of a literary tradition of several hundred years. Mexicans who became Americans continued the Indo-Hispanic literary tradition, not only by preserving the old literary materials but also by creating new ones in the superimposed American political ambiance.

6   Nevertheless, Mexican-Americans were poorly regarded by the vast majority of Anglo-Americans who came in contact with them, and many of the literary portraits of Mexican-Americans by Anglo-American writers exerted undue influence on generations of Americans down to our time. The disparaging images of Mexican-Americans were drawn by such American writers as Richard Henry Dana, who, in *Two Years Before the Mast,* described Mexican-Americans as "an idle, thriftless people" who could

2 Américo Paredes, "Folklore and History," *Singers and Storytellers,* ed. Mody C. Boatwright, Wilson M. Hudson, and Allen Maxwell (Dallas: Southern Methodist University Press, 1961), pp. 162–163.

"make nothing for themselves."[3] In 1852 Col. John Monroe reported to Washington:

The New Mexicans are thoroughly debased and totally incapable of self-government, and there is no latent quality about them that can ever make them respectable. They have more Indian blood than Spanish, and in some respects are below the Pueblo Indians, for they are not as honest or as industrious.[4]

7   In 1868, *The Overland Monthly* published an article by William V. Wells, "The French in Mexico," in which he wrote that "in the open field, a charge of disciplined troops usually sufficed to put to flight the collection of frowzy-headed mestizos, leperos, mulattoes, Indians, Samboes, and other mongrels now, as in the time of our war with them, composing a Mexican Army."[5] In our own time Walter Prescott Webb characterized the Mexicans as possessing "a cruel streak" that he believes was inherited partly from the Spanish of the Inquisition and partly from their Indian forebears. Webb asserts:

On the whole, the Mexican warrior . . . was inferior to the Comanche and wholly unequal to Texans, the whine of the leaden slugs stirred in him an irresistible impulse to travel with, rather than against, the music. He won more victories over the Texans partly by parley than by force of arms. For making promises and for breaking them he had no peer.[6]

The glamour and appeal of such noted writers has of course proven destructive to the Mexican in general, but more so to the Mexican-Americans who continue to be victimized by this spurious body of literature.

8   The early works of Bert Harte, Gertrude Atherton, Jack London, and others popularized the romantic notions of the California of the Dons, the days of the noble land-grant *gachupin* indulging in elaborate Spanish-European festivities and rodeos, of the Spanish *caballero* mounted upon his excellent steed while señoritas in their silk and embroidered gowns, proud and seemingly uninterested, awaited breathlessly the outcome of horse races. At the same time, some Anglo-American writers took great pains to alert their readers not to mistake the *caballero* for the "greaser," the Mexican male who was undisciplined, uncultured, still savage, and constantly in need of a firm hand and direction. Nor was the "Spanish" señorita to be confused with the "Mexican" wench who was fiery, free-loving, and easily accessible, and who always dressed simply and colorfully to complement her carefree life style.

9   In her short story "The Pearls of Loreto," Gertrude Atherton[7] glorifies and romanticizes the California days of the Dons out of focus for the times. While she makes no distinctions between the *criollo* (New World

3 Richard Henry Dana, *Two Years Before the Mast* (1840. Various eds.).
4 United States Congress, *Congressional Globe,* 32nd Congress, 2nd Session, 10 Jan. 1953, Appendix, p. 104.
5 William V. Wells, "The French in Mexico," *The Overland Monthly* (Sept. 1868), p. 232.
6 Walter Prescott Webb, *The Texas Rangers: A Century of Frontier Defense* (Austin: University of Texas Press, revised ed., 1965), p. 14.
7 Gertrude Atherton, "The Pearls of Loreto," *An Anthology of Famous American Stories,* ed. Angus Burrell and Bennett Cerf (New York: Modern Library 1953).

Spaniard) and the *Californio* of mixed blood, the subtlety of her remarks about the latter leaves little room for equivocation about her attitudes toward the people she professed to care about. For example, her quick, fleeting references to "heavy-lips" in her descriptions of Mexican men may be read matter-of-factly by Anglo readers, but her mind-set is exposed. Her attitude toward "color" filters through when she describes a strange *caballero* from the south who is fair and with dark-blue eyes. So different is this *caballero* from the local *vaqueros* that all the women are totally enamored by his majestic demeanor: "But the Stranger is so handsome!" "Dios de mi vida! his eyes are like dark blue stars."

10   The young *caballero* proceeds to fall in love with Ysabel, the rose of California, who, as it turns out, is also light-skinned and green-eyed. We learn from Atherton that when Ysabel looked up as the *caballero* rode past, "his bold profile and thin face were full of power. Such a face was *rare* among the *languid shallow* men of her *race.*" (Emphasis added.)

11   The denigrated character of the Mexican and Mexican-American in American literature changed little toward the end of the nineteenth century and in the first half of the twentieth century. In fact, strengthened by a plethora of studies by social scientists, the profile of the Mexican-American and Mexican became a motley enumeration of characteristics that have debilitated Mexican-Americans even further. The tragedy (perhaps "crime" is the better word) is that Anglo writers of fiction have shamelessly depicted Mexican-Americans in terms of these utterly pernicious characteristics. For example, in his short story "The Gambler, the Nun, and the Radio" Ernest Hemingway[8] details the derogation of Mexicans in the dialogue of his characters. And like Atherton, Hemingway resorts to a sterotypical English linguistic construction in order to create the aura of a Spanish-speaking environment. What really happens is that the Mexican characters all sound like Puritans speaking Elizabethan English. At one point in the story, Frazer responds to one of the Mexican characters: "I thought marijuana was the opium of the poor." Afterwards he refers to the smaller of the three Mexicans as "that dyspeptic little joint keeper." And later, Hemingway writes:

The last time [the Mexicans] played Mr. Frazer lay in his room with his door open and listened to the noisy, bad music and could not keep from thinking. When they wanted to know what he wished played, he asked for the Cucaracha, which has the *sinister* lightness and *deftness* of so many of the tunes men have gone to die to. They played noisily and with emotion. (Emphasis ours.)

Frazer is always referred to by name, but Cayetano is most often referred to as "the Mexican."

12   The perversion and dehumanization of the image of the "Mexican" in American literature has become almost an Anglo-American tradition practiced by the "best" of American writers. In John Steinbeck's story

---

8 Ernest Hemingway, "The Gambler, the Nun, and the Radio," *An Anthology of Famous American Stories,* ed. Burrell and Cerf.

"Flight," [9] the Mexican-American youth, Pepe, is characterized as a naive, knife-wielding farm boy who on his first trip to town kills a man who calls him names. In the end he is hunted down like an animal and killed. Anglo-Americans might argue that the story is a sympathetic portrayal of the Mexican-American experience. That's what Anglo-Americans said about William Styron's *Nat Turner.* "Flight" is one of those gratuitous stories that reaches pretentious heights only because of the fame of its author, not because Steinbeck knew what the Mexican-American experience was all about.

13   So too Katherine Anne Porter wrote about Mexicans from the perspective that since she was a Texan she knew all about them. Her preferred setting was Mexico, and in her stories she always had a "white Christian intellectual" present to interpret the folkways and mores of the "natives." In "María Concepción," [10] for example, Porter created Given as the American "observer" in Mexico who felt a fatherly indulgence for the "primitive and childish ways" of the Mexicans. Porter attempted to portray the elusive and fictive dynamics of *"machismo"* in "María Concepción," a characteristic all too commonly ascribed to the Mexican male, caricaturizing him as lusty and passionate and philandering. Essentially, *machismo* is defined or depicted as that behavior which is meant to project or defend the *utter* masculinity of the Mexican male. Thus, as a consequence of *machismo,* Pedro Villegas, María Concepción's husband, emerges as a prototypical lovable bastard of the first rank. But what does this do to Mexican-Americans who are regarded via the image of Pedro Villegas?

14   The pejorations and generalizations about Mexican-Americans are to be deplored, and Mexican-Americans today are beginning to rise up against the perpetuation of such racial clichés. Mexican-Americans have been struggling within the predominately Anglo-American culture of the United States for over 122 years. Although Mexican-Americans have been writing all that time, the realization of Mexican-American literature as the *élan vital* in the life styles of the people themselves has come about only within recent years. In the fall of 1967 a cohort of Mexican-American writers at Berkeley, California, formed Quinto Sol Publications in a tiny office over a candy store. Their purpose was "to provide a forum for Mexican-American self-definition and expression on . . . issues of relevance to Mexican-Americans in American society today."

15   Alternatives is the key word in what has blossomed into the Chicano Renaissance. Mexican-Americans had been completely disenchanted with the plethora of writings about them, writings that depicted them in a variety of literary contexts resorting to the most blatant stereotypes and racial clichés, all of them by "intellectual mercenaries," as the Quinto Sol group called them in the first issue of their literary quarterly magazine,

9 John Steinbeck, "Flight," *The Literature of the United States: From World War 1 to the Present,* bk. 2, 3rd ed., ed. Walter Blair et al. (Glenview, Ill.: Scott, Foresman and Company, 1969).
10 Katherine Anne Porter, "María Concepción," *An Anthology of Famous American Stories,* ed. Burrell and Cerf.

El Grito: A Journal of Contemporary Mexican American Thought. The promise of *El Grito* was that it would be the forum for Mexican-Americans to articulate their own sense of identity, a promise which continues to be fulfilled. Even more important in the Chicano Renaissance, the printed word was seen as a very important medium in the Chicano struggle for equality. Hundreds of Chicano literary outlets sprang up after 1967 as Chicanos became increasingly aware of the power of the pen and the persuasiveness of print. And, importantly, in the process Chicanos have discovered their Indian roots and that they were of the Americas before the conquistadores and before the Puritans, and that essentially—despite the overlay of Spanish culture—they are descendants of the great Indian civilizations of Mexico, and they are Montezuma's children more than Coronado's.

baby machos
PAULINE KAEL

Machos is a Spanish word meaning men. Thus the title of this film evaluation means "baby men." Kael uses the term ironically: *machos* connotes masculinity—adult male power—which would not apply to the "virginal" youngsters of the film she is reviewing, *The Cowboys*. The irony of the title continues throughout the article and establishes a tone that itself judges the film.

What are Kael's criteria? In the first sentence, she calls *The Cowboys* an "index to the confusion of values" in Hollywood. She includes specific examples of this confusion throughout the article: lack of preparation for the killings at the end of the movie (paragraph 4); obscene complacency over the boys' sadism (paragraph 5); sexual and racial hypocrisy (paragraphs 3 and 7). These are signs not only of confusion; Kael suggests they are signs also of cynical commercialism. *The Cowboys* panders to the public's taste for violence and exhibits a warped moral attitude toward children.

This evaluation of a film thus functions as an evaluation (negative) of Hollywood filmmakers as well.

"The Cowboys," which features one of the most torpid cattle drives since the invention of motion pictures, is an incomparable index to the confusion of values in the movie business right now. This Western epic, shaped for the family trade, is set in cattle country in 1877. John Wayne is a rancher whose hired hands desert him when there's a gold strike; unable to find men to help drive his cattle to market, he takes on eleven local schoolboys—aged nine to fifteen—and trains them during the four-hundred-mile drive. *Cow-boys*—get it? The movie, which minds its language and is sexually clean as a eunuch's whistle, is sufficiently sanctimonious to have earned a GP ("Contains material which may not be suitable for pre-teenagers") rating. It is playing at Radio City Music Hall, which was graced with an appearance by Wayne himself, who then lunched with five hundred newsboys and winners of "Cowboys" contests. It is being touted as the biggest family picture since "The Sound of Music." One could easily think that Warner Brothers and the director, Mark Rydell, and the writers, Irving Ravetch and his wife, Harriet Frank, Jr., and William Dale Jennings (who also wrote the original novel), were in the business of corrupting minors, because this movie is about how these schoolboys become men through learning the old-fashioned virtues of killing.

2   It's a no-nonsense view of growing up; the *macho* cadets are well-mannered, obedient, good-boy killers. The whole world knows that Wayne is not a man to put up with any guff. Almost in passing, he cures a boy of stuttering by telling him that if he wanted to speak clearly he could, and the boy cries "Son of a bitch!" over and over with perfect articulation. Is Warners getting ready to sell holy water under the Warner Brothers-Lourdes label?

3   At one point along the trail, there is an encounter with a madam (Colleen Dewhurst) and her girls, and you may guess that the plot logic requires the boys to be sexually initiated as part of their transition to manhood. A look at the book on which the movie is based confirms your guess, but in the movie the whores (starlets in exquisitely laundered petticoats) are introduced and then left with nothing to do. The boys can kill and the movie gets its GP and is booked into the Music Hall, but if they had been sexually initiated the picture would have been restricted. *One* boy getting initiated—and so tactfully that you might have thought he was taking the veil—was sufficient to get "Summer of '42" restricted; the mothers of America may not go to the movies anymore, but they are still the watchdogs of movie morality when it comes to their sons' purity. So the boys must be virginal killers; sex would make them bad, dirty boys.

4   In the first half of the picture, the actors seem to be planted where they speak, and there's an awesome interval before anyone replies. It feels like a long wait before overlapping dialogue will be invented. Wayne is presented as an idealized Western father figure, and his screen career as the archetypal good guy gives weight to the homely, reactionary platitudes that make this a family picture. Even when he works himself up for an oath, the final words are always genteel. He pontificates to his gruff, understanding wife—played by Sarah Cunningham, who is in the Leora Dana-Anne Revere mold: the strong women who turn understanding into a form of doughy piousness. They're *boring;* that's no service to women—and their

dreary goodness certainly doesn't light up the screen. And this movie needs lighting up, because the eleven boys don't do much for it. They're Disney choirboys—clean, scrubbed nothings—so there's no dramatic or psychological preparation for the explosion of killing. The director doesn't care about the characters; he is just marking time until the mayhem. The only preparation for the explosions is in Wayne's code of honor.

5   Wayne's teaching is that there are good men and there are bad men; there are no crossovers and nothing in between. People don't get a second chance around him; to err once is to be doomed. Most of the bloodshed seems to be caused by his pigheadedness, but that is definitely not the movie's point of view. The boys learn their lessons so well that when Wayne is killed by rustlers they know better than to waste effort trying to bring the rustlers to justice. The movie is set up so that *they* are justice. Their faces are strong and clear-eyed as they slaughter some seventeen men; they appear to have an almost mystic union as they act in concert, infallibly, and without a glimmer of doubt or of pity. When the ex-convict villain (Bruce Dern) is trapped under his horse and pleads for help, a boy cuts one strap loose and fires a gun to frighten the horse, and the whole troupe watches with manly impassivity as the horse runs, dragging the man screaming to his death. The obscenely complacent movie invites us to identify with these good little men and to be proud of them.

6   There are things going on in this movie for kids that shouldn't escape notice. Some of these things—like the way that people don't die in clean kills but writhe in slow torture—may be among the reasons that this movie is expected to make money. In its way, it's innovative: the sensual pleasures of violence haven't been packaged with eternal verities before. Blood and homilies.

7   The confusion of values in the seedy folklore is glaringly obvious in matters of race. The Negro cook on the drive is played with peerless urbanity by Roscoe Lee Browne; with his reserves of charm to call upon, and with that deep voice rising from his great chest, Browne acts Wayne right off the screen, and without raising a bead of sweat. Not only does Browne come across as the only real actor in the movie but the cook is by far the verbal and intellectual superior of everyone else. He's wickedly, incongruously suave, like a Shakespearean ham lost in the sticks but dressing for dinner every night. If you retain any sense of humor, you may ask yourself why the *cook* isn't the father figure for the boys, particularly since it is he who devises the strategies that enable them to kill all the rustlers without loss of a boy. Parading their own lack of prejudice, the moviemakers have turned the cook into a super-black and then let Browne do his number. He's entertaining—which is better than the moviemakers deserve. And, still trying to save face, they toss in a bit of dialogue in which one of the boys informs Wayne that he is fighting-Jewish—which enables Wayne to show his patriarchal tolerance. (Another boy is an Indian— distrusted at first, but he proves himself.) As long as the movie isn't anti-Semitic or anti-Negro, the Hollywood liberals who worked on it can prob-

ably convince themselves that they have retained their image. The villains are—natch—all nondenominational whites, and they are such vipers that you hear rattles on the sound track when they are lurking nearby. Bruce Dern gives the kind of wheedling, cringing-cur ex-convict performance that disappeared for decades but is now renascent. Pro-violence, pro-revenge movies like "Dirty Harry" and "The Cowboys" require the unredeemably vicious villains of primitive melodrama. But these movies are not inconsequential melodramas; they thump for a simplistic right-wing ideology at a time when people may be ready to buy it.

8   Wayne says, "It's a hard life," and that's supposed to be the truth that explains why boys must learn to be killers. It's not such a hard life for the Hollywood moviemakers who are peddling this line. "The Cowboys" cost five million dollars, and most of us will never earn in a lifetime what an anxious hack director makes on a five-million-dollar movie. Mark Rydell hasn't mastered much film technique—just enough of the old show-biz one-two to raise lumps in some throats—and the violence is bloody-banal. The Hollywood hills are full of educated liberals who will make a movie glorifying the tortures at the Dacca race course and try to get it to come out right by working in a Puerto Rican love interest or a black rabbi.

in defense of
deer hunting and killing
ARTHUR C. TENNIES

Tennies uses a straight chronological organization to recount the events of a day spent deer hunting (paragraphs 3, 8, 18 to 44). But by word count, only about one-fourth of the article tells the story of hunting. The rest is commentary about the author and about game management and its relationship to the management of human life. The narrative, therefore, is mainly an occasion for evaluating the deer hunter. Tennies shows that deer populations, like human populations, can grow beyond the ability of their environment to feed them. Therefore the hunter performs a valuable service —and derives a psychological reward from it as well.

Is Tennies' "defense" successful, or does he leave some questions unanswered?

1 **"Y**ou hunt deer?" When I nodded, my shocked colleague went on to say, "Why my whole image of you has been shattered. How can you kill such beautiful creatures?"

2 And so would many others who view the deliberate killing of deer as brutal and senseless. Such people look upon the hunter as a barbaric hangover from the distant past of the human race. To my colleague, the incongruity between the barbarism of hunting and normal civilized conduct was made more intense because I was a minister. How could I as a minister do such a thing?

3 I thought about that as I drove through the early morning darkness toward the southeastern part of Chenango County. It was a little after 5 a.m. I had gotten up at 4, something I do only in the case of an emergency or when I am going deer hunting. It was cold, the temperature in the 20s. With the ground frozen, it would be too noisy for still hunting until the sun had had a chance to thaw the frost. So it would be wait and freeze. My first thoughts about why I would hunt deer had nothing to do with the supposed barbarism of it. I thought of the foolishness of it. Wait hour after hour in the cold, feet numb, hands numb, and small chance of getting a deer.

4 I was going to hunt on Schlafer Hill on the farm of Pershing Schlafer. My choice of a place to hunt had been determined by the party permit that three of us had, which allowed us to kill one other deer of either sex besides the three bucks that we were allowed.

5 I thought about the party system in New York, the way the state controlled the size of the deer herd. The state is divided into about 40 deer-management areas. The state biologists know how many deer each area can handle, how many deer can feed on the browse available without destroying it. If there are too many deer, they will kill the plants and bushes upon which they depend. The next step is starvation for large numbers. Since the deer's natural predators were wiped out by the first settlers, the only control over their numbers now is starvation or hunting. Thus, so many deer must be killed in a deer-management area. A certain number will be killed by motor vehicles. The biologists can estimate how many will be killed on the highways and also the number of bucks that will be killed. The surplus is taken care of by issuing a set number of party permits.

6 I have often marveled at the state biologists, their skill and knowledge in managing the deer herd. As I have pondered the problems of people—poverty, starvation, injustice, and all the others—and our frantic and often futile efforts to solve these problems, I have thought, "If only we could manage the problems of people as well as we can manage a deer herd."

7 Then I realize the great difference between the two. People are not for being managed. We manage people only by robbing them of the right to choose—and the most brutal attempts to manage are ultimately frustrated by the obstinacy of human nature, its refusal to be managed. A handful of biologists may manage a deer herd and a handful of scientists may be able to put a man on the moon, but no handful of planners will ever manage

the human race. And so I thought again, as the car rushed through the dark, that all of our modern management techniques would fail to come up with quick and perfect solutions to the problems of people.

8   While the darkness was still on the land, I reached the bottom of the hill. I parked the car, put on my hunting shirts, took my gun, and began the long climb up the hill. For a few minutes, I could hardly see the old road. Slowly my eyes adjusted to the dark. The trees in the woods on my right took shape and the road became clearly visible. I walked with greater confidence. As I climbed, the sun climbed toward the horizon to drive away the night. By the time I reached the top of the hill, the half-light of dawn had arrived.

9   Off to my left in the valley were lights and people, but on the hill I was alone. It had not always been that way. Once long ago the hilltop had been filled with people. Following the Revolution, white settlers came into Chenango County, and some had chosen that hilltop. I stopped and tried to picture in my mind their struggles to turn the forest into farms. I looked at the stone fence off to my right and wondered how many days it had taken to clear the stones from the fields and pile them into a fence. The fence ran into the woods. Woods again where there had been fields or pasture.

10   I looked on down the road. I could not see the old barn down farther on the left, the only structure from the past still standing. All of the others were gone. I had seen before the crumbling stone foundations where once houses had stood. A half century or more ago, if I had stood there, I could have seen a half-dozen houses. Smoke would have been rolling out of chimneys as fires were started to chase away the cold. Men and boys would have been outside and in the barns getting the chores done. Women and girls would have been busy in the kitchen getting breakfast. The hill would have been full of people and empty of deer. Now it was empty of people and full of deer.

11   On that hill and on many others, like Bucktooth Run, is a story of the hand of man upon the land. Before the settlers came, only a few deer lived on that hill, far fewer than there are now, because the forests provided little food for the deer. The few were soon killed off. While the disappearance of the deer was the fault of the early hunters, there was more to it than that. There was no room for deer on the hill. As my Dad, who was born on Bucktooth Run, has pointed out:

12   *These farms were worked over morning and evening by the farmers and their sons and their dogs going after the cattle. The wood lots were worked over during the winter for wood. The larger tracts of woodland were worked over by the lumbermen.*

13   *Then came World War I and the years following. Large areas of land were abandoned. Where once the woods resounded to the call of "Come, boss!" and in the winter the woods echoed the ring of the ax and whine of the saw, the sylvan stillness, for months on end, was unbroken by the human voice. Where once the deer had no place to rest from the constant activity of the busy*

farmer and lumberman, there was now a chance for the deer to carry on its life in solitude.

14 *In 1900 there were no deer in much of New York. The state did some stocking shortly after that, and deer came across the border from Pennsylvania. The abandoned land provided a perfect setting for the deer and there were no natural enemies to stay their march. By the late 1930s, most of the state had a deer season.*

15 So as the farmers retreated from the hill, the deer returned. Now the hill is perfect for deer . . . some fields used by farmers, like Pershing, for pasture and hay, good feed for deer for most of the year . . . brush for browse during the winter . . . woods, old and new, mixed with evergreen for cover. And most of the year, except during the hunting season, only a few people make their way to the top of the hill.

16 Let nature have her way and in another century nature's hospitality to the deer will be withdrawn as large trees again cover the hill as they did before the first white settlers came.

17 I started to walk again and felt like I had left one world, the world of technology, and entered another one, the world of nature. The rush to get things done had to give way to waiting and patience, for nature does not live at our frantic pace. The noise had to give way to quietness, for only in silence can one get close to a deer.

18 But the ground crunched beneath my feet, so I walked to a likely spot and waited. Two hours and nothing, except a few small birds. Finally the cold forced me to move. I walked and found some fresh tracks in the snow. I followed them for an hour, trying to get close enough to the deer wandering in the woods ahead of me. But I was too noisy. All I saw was the flash of brown bodies and white tails too far ahead. I waited some more. No luck. I walked to another spot where deer cross.

19 I waited another hour. It was warmer now. Finally a deer appeared, a head above a rise. It started to come nearer. Then it stopped. Something was wrong. It decided to leave. As it turned, my gun came up and I shot. It lurched sideways, kicking and thrashing, disappearing under a pine tree. I walked to the spot. No deer. I went around the tree and there it lay. In a second it was dead.

20 I looked down at the deer, a button buck, and I thought: This is the way of nature, one creature feeding on another. Thousands of years ago our forebearers survived in just this way. They killed, gutted, butchered, and ate. Now we buy in a supermarket or order in a restaurant.

21 The first task was to gut the deer, kind of a messy process. I got my knife out, turned the deer on his back, and slit him open. I spilled the guts out on the ground. I saved the liver and heart, even though the heart had been mangled by the bullet. I cut through the diaphragm and pulled the lungs out.

22 Then I was ready to pull the deer back to the car. It was 3 p.m. when I got to the car. Time yet to hunt for a buck, so I dumped the deer into the

trunk. Back up the hill, but no luck. As night came on, I got back to the car. I tied the deer on the top of the trunk and started for home.

23   As I drove toward home, I had a sense of satisfaction. I had fitted myself to nature's way and had been successful. For a few short hours, I had marched to the beat of nature's drum, not that of our modern world. At least for me, the barrier that we had built between nature and us could still be breached.

24   Back in suburbia, I parked the car in the driveway and went into the house. Jan and the kids were eating supper.

25   "Any luck?" Jan asked.

26   "Not much."

27   "Did you get a deer?" one of the kids asked.

28   "Yup, a button buck."

29   Then the excited rush to see the deer, and the thrill of shared success.

30   After that there was the tedious job of butchering. I hung the deer in the garage. Then I began the task of skinning it. Once skinned, I cut the deer in half, then in quarters. Jan washed the blood and hair off of each quarter. I then cut the quarters into smaller pieces, and then Jan sliced it up into roasts, steaks, and stew meat.

31   "Can you get the brains out?" Jan wanted to know.

32   "I can try, but why the brains?"

33   "We always had brains when we butchered."

34   So I went to work to cut the skull open and get the brains out.

35   When I got back into the kitchen, Jan had a skillet on.

36   "Let's have some venison," she said.

37   "At this hour?"

38   "Sure."

39   So she had some brains and I had some liver. As I sat there weary, eating the liver, I thought, "This meat is on the table because I put it there." By our efforts, and ours alone, it had gone from field to table.

40   "Don't you want some brains?" Jan asked.

41   "No."

42   "But they are a delicacy."

43   "That may be, but I'll stick to the liver."

44   As I went to sleep that night I thought: "I suppose that no matter what I say, a lot of people will still never understand why I hunt deer. Well, they don't have to, but let only vegetarians condemn me."

there isn't anything wishy-washy about soaps

BETH GUTCHEON

Gutcheon defends a much-attacked form of popular culture, the TV soap opera. Her favorable evaluation of the "soaps" is based on two qualities she finds in recent productions: the attempt to educate audiences about contemporary problems and the attempt to make people question their own way of life. The evidence that the "soaps" are fulfilling these goals consists of plot summaries of a number of recent programs and information drawn from Gutcheon's interviews with soap-opera writers, television executives, and other people who control what we see when we turn on our television sets. Gutcheon avoids making an exaggerated claim for the virtues of her subject. As she summarizes (paragraph 17), "I'm not suggesting that soaps are great art; just that they are often good television, and that there are legitimate uses (as well as abuses) of television."

Would you agree that "good television" means television programs with an educational or social purpose?

1   **I**n case you haven't tuned in since the days of "Mary Noble, Backstage Wife" (or Mary, Noble Backstage Wife), soap operas have come a long way. The organ music, the convoluted and bathetic plots persist—but with a twist. Soap writers are increasingly using the serial form—as Charles Dickens once did—to educate audiences or lead them to question their insular attitudes in ways that little else in their lives may do.

2   Consider the way some soaps have come to handle members of the groups my upstairs neighbor refers to as "those people." CBS's "Search for Tomorrow," for example, introduced a black orderly, developed him as all jive and sass, and established a polarity between him and a wealthy respectable bigot out to get him fired. But after the writers have set us up for weeks the orderly is revealed to be a talented Vietnam-trained paramedic who saves the bigot's life while all the doctors are at lunch. Similarly, NBC's "Somerset" gave us a hippie wanderer with long hair and no history; after arousing our suspicion and dislike, he turned out to be a shell-shocked war hero with amnesia and a chestful of medals. CBS's "As the World Turns" uses its access to some 8 million viewers daily to investigate prejudice against white lawyers with beards and bad manners: hirsute attorney Grant Colman offended almost everybody when he came to town, and glamorous oft-married widow Lisa Miller Hughes Shea didn't like him one little bit. But the better she knows him . . . .

Source. From *Ms.,* Copyright © 1974. Reprinted by permission of *Ms.* Magazine Corporation.

3   Some soaps use this familiar "hero-disguised" device more creatively. For instance, "Search for Tomorrow" evolved a long romantic plot line featuring a mysterious character who was deaf and unable to speak (played by Linda Bove, who is also deaf). When the suds settled, viewers had learned a good deal of sign language; they were also exposed in considerable depth to the ways in which families, schools, communities, and society at large discriminate against the handicapped. The heroine's elegant wealthy parents, preoccupied with their own pain, had sent her to special schools that tried to teach her to "talk" rather than those that would encourage her family and community to learn her language. Her parents responded with such shock and embarrassment to the awkward lowing sounds she made that she ran away. It was not until they found her months later, betrothed to a fine young doctor and chattering gaily with her hands to her new neighbors, that they began to see that she could be accepted as she was by a "normal" community.

4   "Search for Tomorrow," still doing business with the same old characters at the same old stand for 23 years, has somehow become the most forthrightly feminist soap on the air. In the past year, husband and wife writers Ralph Ellis and Eugenie Hunt have developed a woman lawyer who chooses not to have children because she prefers her career (and her husband encourages her). At the office, she does research and legwork while her husband, whose credentials are the same as hers, is given important briefs and litigation to handle. She quits (again applauded by her husband). A black woman, denied a bank loan because she is a woman (*not* because she is black), is successfully defended by the woman lawyer— the bank unsuccessfully defended by her ex-boss, Doug Martin, who has for umpteen years been one of the sympathetic stalwarts of the show. Then Doug Martin's nice little wife Eunice takes up part-time free-lance writing (she works at home, doesn't neglect the baby, and still has dinner ready at six every night). Nice old Doug erupts into a fever of *macho* pigginess that ends with mayhem, murder, adultery, and divorce; all clearly established as caused by, not justifying, his irrational behavior. Incidentally, "Search" has the largest proportion of male viewers—16 percent, or nearly one million—of any on the air.

5   When I asked Agnes Nixon, queen of the soap writers, how she—and others—got off the nonstop, pro-marriage, baby-boom go-round popular for so long, she took the novel view that the best way to entertain people is to make them think. She holds what may be a unique record in the industry for entertaining people. Nixon created "Search for Tomorrow," the longest continuously running program of any kind on television. With the legendary late Irna Phillips she co-created "As the World Turns," which, after 18 years, still has one of the highest ratings.

6   Nixon likes to beef up the suds with high-protein filler. Soap operas are considered audio entertainment; it is assumed that the viewer is looking at the enzyme presoak most of the time and not at the screen. So whatever the actors are doing, it's up to the writer to keep the dialogue continuous,

which explains all that homey chitchat about meat loaf and slipcovers. Agnes Nixon, however, drops in one-liners about pollution or zero population growth. As long as the ratings are up and the sponsors happy, she can even elevate a public service conversation to a subplot. On "One Life To Live" (ABC), she had young Cathy Craig, ace reporter, bend everyone's ear about a story she was writing on the VD epidemic. The article was then offered free to the viewers, and 10,000 of them requested copies.

7   Earlier, when Cathy Craig was found to be "experimenting with drugs," Nixon arranged with drug therapist Dr. Judianne Densen-Gerber to have "Cathy" participate in a group therapy program at New York's Odyssey House. Taped segments of the real thing were integrated into the soap. ABC and Odyssey House were swamped with calls from people who don't watch documentaries, or read the New York *Times,* and perhaps could not have been reached any other way.

8   Nixon respects her audience to a certain extent; enough, for example, not to offer to them a staged drug-rehabilitation therapy group when she could get them the real thing. But by far the more telling motive for her innovations has been respect for her own power. Nixon's position is unique because after many years of reviving slumped ratings for CBS and NBC, she moved to ABC on her own terms: she owns the soaps she writes. She created "One Life To Live," but recently sold it to the network to give herself time to act as consultant for their made-for-women afternoon movies, called "Afternoon Playbreaks." She still owns and head-writes "All My Children."

9   On "All My Children," Nixon's popular bitch goddess Erica Martin had television's first legal abortion. The network went nuts ("You're teaching our daughters and wives how to get abortions we don't want them to have"), but network rage doesn't bother Nixon much. She's the one soap writer who cannot be fired (the rest are replaced about yearly). And viewer rage bothers her not at all: "An angry viewer is a hooked viewer." Robert Cenedella, another long-running soap writer, tells of the viewer who wrote him: "If Rachel ["Another World," NBC] isn't punished by next week, I am going to stop watching." She wrote him the same letter, twice a month, for four years.

10   The question of content on soaps depends on ratings first, with morals, taste, audience response, and responsibility running a distant second. Content is proposed by head writers, then approved, abridged, or vetoed by the network or sponsors, or both. (Even Nixon must submit to this sort of review, but as a soap owner, she has the last word.) Murders, marriages, organized crime, diseases, and psychoses are soap staples, as they are on prime time. Race and class issues are rarely met head-on—a fairly suspicious circumstance since demographics indicate that a sizable proportion of the audience is blue collar or black, or both. Except for a janitor on "General Hospital" and a waitress on "One Life To Live" (both ABC) and a woman who works in a factory on "The Young and the Restless" (CBS), the social scale ranges from absurdly prosperous nurses, doctors,

lawyers, and executives right on up to the congenitally wealthy. Only "One Life To Live" has ever evolved a major plot line focusing on (rather than pointedly ignoring) race. With actress Ellen Holly, Agnes Nixon created a black woman who passed for white because as a light-skinned black she had been rejected by both white and black communities. The point was to examine the motivations and consequences of denying race and heritage: the woman, established as white, fell in love with a black man. Throughout the romance only the writers knew she was going to turn out to be black, and the moment the couple first kissed, every TV set below the Mason-Dixon line went blank.

11   Genuine social issues are high-risk material—not at all what the networks had in mind when they brought soaps to TV back in the fifties. In those days, Irna Phillips (creator of "The Guiding Light," "Young Doctor Malone," "Love Is a Many Splendored Thing," and "As the World Turns") ruled the roost.

12   Phillips had a dream, or more precisely a magic formula: a folksy American vision of a vast community of nice, wholesome middle-class people, all of whom care deeply and without malice about the most trivial details of each others' lives. Everyone works who wants to, but the need to earn money never features as a motive for anything. A dream you can see functioning to this day on "As the World Turns" without the slightest reference to contemporary, or any, reality. I am sorry to report that, with a 33 percent audience share, it is one of the most popular soaps on the air and has been since 1961. I personally find it salacious, depressing, and rather offensive. After all, if you expunge all consciousness of war, racism, sexism, inflation, unemployment, poverty, or politics, you are pretty much left with pregnancy, crime, and illness. The children have heart conditions, the women are all pregnant, mostly by men other than their husbands, and the death rate is simply terrific. Which is probably a good thing, since no one has heard of contraception or abortion yet, and the place is a one-town population explosion.

13   Nevertheless, I sometimes watch it. I started in the last months of my pregnancy, and I still tune in, even though the writers have so little regard for my sense of probability that they allowed one character (who was a loathsome, wet, sentimental specimen) to kill herself, on the morning after her wedding, by falling *up* the stairs. (I think it likely that I watch because of incidents like that. Months later, when I entered a lonely, diaper-ridden period of my life, I needed a good laugh.)

14   On the other hand, I turn off the sound before I answer the phone, lest anyone know I'm watching. Now why is that? My husband watches the World Series and has to wade through such lard as a pregame interview on the subject of what Yogi Berra had for breakfast (answer—a western omelet), and he doesn't feel personally threatened. It doesn't affect anyone's opinion of his general intelligence. Why should I feel responsible for the occasional flotsam on soap operas? It hasn't rotted my brain. If any-

thing, it has sharpened my sense of satire. Yet the fact that you're watching soaps isn't the sort of thing you want to get around.

15   I think that people are contemptuous not of the serial form, nor of the content, but of the audience. Women. Women who stay home. Women who "don't work." Housewives. One CBS daytime executive, for example, volunteered the information that he had defended a fine, sensitive plot line for "The Young and the Restless," involving a young woman who is raped. He added, however, that he killed writer William Bell's suggestion of a plot in which the same character, although highly qualified, is denied a job simply because she is a woman. He told me that his audience doesn't know from jobs; they stay home, they're not interested. Viewers are hooked on all those women doctors and lawyers because of their personal struggles, not their professional ones.

16   If he asked me—and he didn't—I would have said that people don't get addicted to soap operas or anything else because they are smug and satisfied. Certainly for the time in my own life when I was most wired on soaps, when, all kidding aside, I really *needed* to tune in tomorrow, the reason was precisely that I was dying to work. I had chosen to take a year out of my life to spend with my infant son, yes, but in terms of daily reality, I had One Life To Live and I appeared to be spending it peeling carrots. If I had allowed myself to focus on carrots completely, I'd have been a candidate for a straitjacket. Why shouldn't I listen to soap operas? At the same time in my life, I developed a temporary passion for mystery novels, which no one thought at all funny, though most of them were not as well written as the soaps.

17   I'm not suggesting that soaps are great art; just that they are often good television, and that there are legitimate uses (as well as abuses) of television. Soaps, regardless of their plots, consistently deal with aspects of women's physical and emotional health that one certainly finds nowhere else on television: On "Love Is a Many Splendored Thing" (CBS), a young mother faced advanced cervical cancer because she neglected to have a Pap test. On "The Guiding Light" (CBS), Janet Norris's (woman) doctor tells her firmly that her self-effacing absorption with her home and baby is not noble but neurotic, that it indicates an unwillingness to face something basically painful in her life situation. (Janet has also had trouble "responding" to her husband since the birth of her daughter. Apparently that's not uncommon, but I wouldn't have known it if they hadn't told me.) On "The Edge of Night" (CBS), a menopausal woman is suffering "empty nest syndrome." On "The Secret Storm" (CBS), shortly before its cancellation last February, the neighborhood shrink gently explained to Laurie Reddin that her growing obsession with fantasy was also a symptom of something in her life that she was afraid to face (her husband, the ex-priest, is angry and drinks).

18   I like soaps because they are about women and because they occasionally have ideas in them; further, I prefer the serial form to the episodic

because I am interested in the details of life as well as the climaxes. "All My Children" may be sentimental, but currently it's unfolding a plot about the causes and consequences of child abuse. As a daughter and a mother I'm interested in the ways parents damage children—so when it's my turn to wash the dishes I'll probably do them at one o'clock while I listen— maybe I'll find out why I sometimes feel like slugging my son. Maybe I'll find out why my mother slugged me. (No, Dr. Welby, it has nothing to do with being adopted or illegitimate—it has to do with my looking exactly like her.) And NBC recently introduced a new soap called "How To Survive a Marriage." Hampered as it sometimes is by pseudo-hip dialogue, it is at least founded squarely on the proposition, may Irna Phillips rest in peace, that marriage can be damaging.

19   Soaps may be melodramatic and predictable, but they are never as devoid of intellectual content as "Cannon" or "Mannix" or the Daddy-figure prime-time doctor/lawyer things. Soaps are better than those and watching them hasn't made me any more ridiculous than I was before. Soaps are a phenomenon touching the lives of an estimated 30 million women daily—no laughing matter. I'm tired of seeing soaps treated as a joke—partly because the writers and actors honestly deserve better, and partly because the joke is really aimed at me.

---

custer died for your sins
VINE DELORIA, JR.

Deloria, an American Indian, writes a vehemently negative evaluation of the anthropologists who stream into Indian territory every summer to analyze, teach, give advice, and develop leadership among the Indians. Deloria's disgust with the tribe of "anthros" is based on their tendency to concentrate on "great abstractions," to encourage young Indians to turn away from "the world of real problems to the lands of make-believe." His criterion of value, then, is utilitarian: Indians need help that is directly useful, especially money. This evaluation becomes a recommendation at the end, since Deloria offers two specific proposals (that anthropologists be permitted to study Indians only if they bring money into the Indian communities; and that Congress give directly to the tribes the money now spent on government-regulated Indian services). The emphasis of the article, however, is not on persuading us to adopt these proposals in particular, but on persuading us that the current approach to the "Indian problem" is a bad one.

Source. Copyright © 1969 by Vine Deloria, Jr. Originally appeared in *Playboy* Magazine.

1   **I**nto each life, it is said, some rain must fall. Some people have bad horoscopes; others take tips on the stock market. McNamara created the TFX and the Edsel. American politics has George Wallace. But Indians have been cursed above all other people in history. Indians have anthropologists.

2   Every summer when school is out, a stream of immigrants heads into Indian country. The Oregon Trail was never as heavily populated as Route 66 and Highway 18 in the summertime. From every rock and cranny in the East, *they* emerge, as if responding to some primeval migratory longing, and flock to the reservations. They are the anthropologists—the most prominent members of the scholarly community that infests the land of the free and the homes of the braves. Their origin is a mystery hidden in the historical mists. Indians are certain that all ancient societies of the Near East had anthropologists at one time, because all those societies are now defunct. They are equally certain that Columbus brought anthropologists on his ships when he came to the New World. How else could he have made so many wrong deductions about where he was? While their origins are uncertain, anthropologists can readily be identified on the reservations. Go into any crowd of people. Pick out a tall, gaunt white man wearing Bermuda shorts, a World War Two Army Air Corps flying jacket, an Australian bush hat and tennis shoes and packing a large knapsack incorrectly strapped on his back. He will invariably have a thin, sexy wife with stringy hair, an IQ of 191 and a vocabularly in which even the prepositions have 11 syllables. And he usually has a camera, tape recorder, telescope, and life jacket all hanging from his elongated frame.

3   This odd creature comes to Indian reservations to make *observations*. During the winter, these observations will become books by which future anthropologists will be trained, so that they can come out to reservations years from now and verify the observations in more books, summaries of which then appear in the scholarly journals and serve as a catalyst to inspire yet other anthropologists to make the great pilgrimage the following summer. And so on.

4   The summaries, meanwhile, are condensed. Some condensations are sent to Government agencies as reports justifying the previous summer's research. Others are sent to foundations, in an effort to finance the following summer's expedition West. The reports are spread through the Government agencies and foundations all winter. The only problem is that no one has time to read them. So $5000-a-year secretaries are assigned to decode them. Since these secretaries cannot comprehend complex theories, they reduce the reports to the best slogans possible. The slogans become conference themes in the early spring, when the anthropological expeditions are being planned. They then turn into battle cries of opposing groups of anthropologists who chance to meet on the reservations the following summer.

5   Each summer there is a new battle cry, which inspires new insights into the nature of the "Indian problem." One summer Indians will be greeted with the joyful cry "Indians are bilingual!" The following summer this

great truth will be expanded to "Indians are not only bilingual, they are *bicultural!*" Biculturality creates great problems for the opposing anthropological camp. For two summers, they have been bested in sloganeering and their funds are running low. So the opposing school of thought breaks into the clear faster than Gale Sayers. "Indians," the losing anthros cry, "are a *folk* people!" The tide of battle turns and a balance, so dearly sought by Mother Nature, is finally achieved. Thus go the anthropological wars, testing whether this school or that school can long endure. The battlefields, unfortunately, are the lives of Indian people.

6   The anthro is usually devoted to *pure research.* A 1969 thesis restating a proposition of 1773, complete with footnotes to all material published between 1773 and 1969, is pure research. There are, however, anthropologists who are not clever at collecting footnotes. They depend on their field observations and write long, adventurous narratives in which their personal observations are used to verify their suspicions. Their reports, books and articles are called *applied research.* The difference, then, between pure and applied research is primarily one of footnotes. Pure has many footnotes, applied has few footnotes. Relevancy to subject matter is not discussed in polite company.

7   Anthropologists came to Indian country only after the tribes had agreed to live on reservations and had given up their warlike ways. Had the tribes been given a choice of fighting the cavalry or the anthropologists, there is little doubt as to whom they would have chosen. In a crisis situation, men always attack the biggest threat to their existence. A warrior killed in battle could always go to the happy hunting grounds. But where does an Indian laid low by an anthro go? To the library?

8   The fundamental thesis of the anthropologist is that people are objects for observation. It then follows that people are considered objects for experimentation, for manipulation, and for eventual extinction. The anthropologist thus furnishes the justification for treating Indian people like so many chessmen, available for anyone to play with. The mass production of useless knowledge by anthropologists attempting to capture real Indians in a network of theories has contributed substantially to the invisibility of Indian people today. After all, who can believe in the actual existence of a food-gathering, berrypicking, semi-nomadic, fire-worshiping, high-plains-and-mountain-dwelling, horse-riding, canoe-toting, bead-using, pottery-making, ribbon-coveting, wickiup-sheltered people who began flourishing when Alfred Frump mentioned them in 1803 in *Our Feathered Friends?*

9   Not even Indians can see themselves as this type of creature—who, to anthropologists, is the "real" Indian. Indian people begin to feel that they are merely shadows of a mythical super-Indian. Many Indians, in fact, have come to parrot the ideas of anthropologists, because it appears that they know everything about Indian communities. Thus, many ideas that pass for Indian thinking are in reality theories originally advanced by anthropologists and echoed by Indian people in an attempt to communicate the

real situation. Many anthros reinforce this sense of inadequacy in order to further influence the Indian people.

10 Since 1955, there have been a number of workshops conducted in Indian country as a device for training "young Indian leaders." Churches, white Indian-interest groups, colleges, and, finally, poverty programs have each gone the workshop route as the most feasible means for introducing new ideas to younger Indians, so as to create leaders. The tragic nature of the workshops is apparent when one examines their history. One core group of anthropologists has institutionalized the workshop and the courses taught in it. Trudging valiantly from workshop to workshop, from state to state, college to college, tribe to tribe, these noble spirits have served as the catalyst for the creation of workshops that are identical in purpose and content and often in the student-body itself.

11 The anthropological message to young Indians has not varied a jot or a tittle in ten years. It is the same message these anthros learned as fuzzy-cheeked graduate students in the post-War years—Indians are a folk people, whites are an urban people, and never the twain shall meet. Derived from this basic premise are all the other sterling insights: Indians are between two cultures, Indians are bicultural, Indians have lost their identity, and Indians are warriors. These theories, propounded every year with deadening regularity and an overtone of Sinaitic authority, have become a major mental block in the development of young Indian people. For these slogans have come to be excuses for Indian failures. They are crutches by which young Indians have avoided the arduous task of thinking out the implications of the status of Indian people in the modern world.

12 If there is one single cause that has importance today for Indian people, it is tribalism. Against all odds, Indians have retained title to some 53,000,000 acres of land, worth about three and half billion dollars. Approximately half of the country's 1,000,000 Indians relate meaningfully to this land, either by living and working on it or by frequently visiting it. If Indians fully recaptured the idea that they are tribes communally in possession of this land, they would realize that they are not truly impoverished. But the creation of modern tribalism has been stifled by a ready acceptance of the Indians-are-a-folk-people premise of the anthropologists. This premise implies a drastic split between folk and urban cultures, in which the folk peoples have two prime characteristics: They dance and they are desperately poor. Creative thought in Indian affairs has not, therefore, come from the younger Indians who have grown up reading and talking to anthropologists. Rather, it has come from the older generation that believes in tribalism—and that the youngsters mistakenly insist has been brainwashed by Government schools.

13 Because other groups have been spurred on by their younger generations, Indians have come to believe that, through education, a new generation of leaders will arise to solve the pressing contemporary problems. Tribal leaders have been taught to accept this thesis by the scholarly com-

munity in its annual invasion of the reservations. Bureau of Indian Affairs educators harp continuously on this theme. Wherever authority raises its head in Indian country, this thesis is its message. The facts prove the opposite, however. Relatively untouched by anthropologists, educators, and scholars are the Apache tribes of the Southwest. The Mescalero, San Carlos, White Mountain, and Jicarilla Apaches have very few young people in college, compared with other tribes. They have even fewer people in the annual workshop orgy during the summers. If ever there was a distinction between folk and urban, this group of Indians characterizes it.

14   The Apaches see themselves, however, as neither folk nor urban but *tribal*. There is little sense of a lost identity. Apaches could not care less about the anthropological dilemmas that worry other tribes. Instead, they continue to work on massive plans for development that they themselves have created. Tribal identity is assumed, not defined, by these reservation people. Freedom to choose from a wide variety of paths of progress is a characteristic of the Apaches; they don't worry about what type of Indianism is real. Above all, they cannot be ego-fed by abstract theories and, hence, unwittingly manipulated.

15   . . . Abstract theories create abstract action. Lumping together the variety of tribal problems and seeking the demonic principle at work that is destroying Indian people may be intellectually satisfying, but it does not change the situation. By concentrating on great abstractions, anthropologists have unintentionally removed many young Indians from the world of real problems to the lands of make-believe.

16   As an example of a real problem, the Pyramid Lake Paiutes and the Gila River Pima and Maricopa are poor because they have been systematically cheated out of their water rights, and on desert reservations, water is the single most important factor in life. No matter how many worlds Indians straddle, the Plains Indians have an inadequate land base that continues to shrink because of land sales. Straddling worlds is irrelevant to straddling small pieces of land and trying to earn a living.

17   Along the Missouri River, the Sioux used to live in comparative peace and harmony. Although land allotments were small, families were able to achieve a fair standard of living through a combination of gardening and livestock raising and supplemental work. Little cash income was required, because the basic necessities of food, shelter, and community life were provided. After World War Two, anthropologists came to call. They were horrified that the Indians didn't carry on their old customs, such as dancing, feasts, and giveaways. In fact, the people did keep up a substantial number of customs, but they had been transposed into church gatherings, participation in the county fairs, and tribal celebrations, particularly fairs and rodeos. The people did Indian dances. But they didn't do them all the time.

18   Suddenly, the Sioux were presented with an authority figure who bemoaned the fact that whenever he visited the reservations, the Sioux were not out dancing in the manner of their ancestors. Today, the summers are

taken up with one great orgy of dancing and celebrating, as each small community of Indians sponsors a weekend powwow for the people in the surrounding communities. Gone are the little gardens that used to provide fresh vegetables in the summer and canned goods in the winter. Gone are the chickens that provided eggs and Sunday dinners. In the winter, the situation becomes critical for families who spent the summer dancing. While the poverty programs have done much to counteract the situation, few Indians recognize that the condition was artificial from start to finish. The people were innocently led astray, and even the anthropologists did not realize what had happened.

19 One example: The Oglala Sioux are perhaps the most well known of the Sioux bands. Among their past leaders were Red Cloud, the only Indian who ever defeated the United States in a war, and Crazy Horse, most revered of the Sioux war chiefs. The Oglala were, and perhaps still are, the meanest group of Indians ever assembled. They would take after a cavalry troop just to see if their bowstrings were taut enough. When they had settled on the reservation, the Oglala made a fairly smooth transition to the new life. They had good herds of cattle, they settled along the numerous creeks that cross the reservation, and they created a very strong community spirit. The Episcopalians and the Roman Catholics had the missionary franchise on the reservation and the tribe was pretty evenly split between the two. In the Episcopal Church, at least, the congregations were fairly self-governing and stable.

20 But over the years, the Oglala Sioux have had a number of problems. Their population has grown faster than their means of support. The Government allowed white farmers to come into the eastern part of the reservation and create a county, with the best farmlands owned or operated by whites. The reservation was allotted—taken out of the collective hands of the tribe and parceled out to individuals—and when ownership became too complicated, control of the land passed out of Indian hands. The Government displaced a number of families during World War Two by taking a part of the reservation for use as a bombing range to train crews for combat. Only last year was this land returned to tribal and individual use.

21 The tribe became a favorite subject for anthropological study quite early, because of its romantic past. Theories arose attempting to explain the apparent lack of progress of the Oglala Sioux. The true issue—white control of the reservation—was overlooked completely. Instead, every conceivable intangible cultural distinction was used to explain the lack of economic, social, and educational progress of a people who were, to all intents and purposes, absentee landlords because of the Government policy of leasing their lands to whites.

22 One study advanced the startling proposition that Indians with many cattle were, on the average, better off than Indians without cattle. Cattle Indians, it seems, had more capital and income than did noncattle Indians. Surprise! The study had innumerable charts and graphs that demonstrated this great truth beyond the doubt of a reasonably prudent man. Studies of

this type were common but unexciting. They lacked that certain flair of insight so beloved by anthropologists. Then one day a famous anthropologist advanced the theory, probably valid at the time and in the manner in which he advanced it, that the Oglala were "warriors without weapons."

23   The chase was on. Before the ink had dried on the scholarly journals, anthropologists from every library stack in the nation converged on the Oglala Sioux to test this new theory. Outfitting anthropological expeditions became the number-one industry of the small off-reservation Nebraska towns south of Pine Ridge. Surely, supplying the Third Crusade to the Holy Land was a minor feat compared with the task of keeping the anthropologists at Pine Ridge.

24   Every conceivable difference between the Oglala Sioux and the folks at Bar Harbor was attributed to the quaint warrior tradition of the Oglala Sioux. From lack of roads to unshined shoes, Sioux problems were generated, so the anthros discovered, by the refusal of the white man to recognize the great desire of the Oglala to go to war. Why expect an Oglala to become a small businessman, when he was only waiting for that wagon train to come around the bend? The very real and human problems of the reservation were considered to be merely by-products of the failure of a warrior people to become domesticated. The fairly respectable thesis of past exploits in war, perhaps romanticized for morale purposes, became a spiritual force all its own. Some Indians, in a tongue-in-cheek manner for which Indans are justly famous, suggested that a subsidized wagon train be run through the reservation each morning at nine o'clock and the reservation people paid a minimum wage for attacking it.

25   By outlining this problem, I am not deriding the Sioux. I lived on that reservation for 18 years and know many of the problems from which it suffers. How, I ask, can the Oglala Sioux make any headway in education when their lack of education is ascribed to a desire to go to war? Would not, perhaps, an incredibly low per-capita income, virtually nonexistent housing, extremely inadequate roads, and domination by white farmers and ranchers make some difference? If the little Sioux boy or girl had no breakfast, had to walk miles to a small school, and had no decent clothes nor place to study in a one-room log cabin, should the level of education be comparable with that of Scarsdale High?

26   What use would roads, houses, schools, businesses, and income be to a people who, everyone expected, would soon depart on the warpath? I would submit that a great deal of the lack of progress at Pine Ridge is occasioned by people who believe they are helping the Oglala when they insist on seeing, in the life of the people of that reservation, only those things they want to see. Real problems and real people become invisible before the great romantic and nonsensical notion that the Sioux yearn for the days of Crazy Horse and Red Cloud and will do nothing until those days return.

27   The question of the Oglala Sioux is one that plagues every Indian tribe in the nation, if it will closely examine itself. Tribes have been defined;

the definition has been completely explored; test scores have been advanced promoting and deriding the thesis; and, finally, the conclusion has been reached: Indians must be redefined in terms that white men will accept, even if that means re-Indianizing them according to the white man's idea of what they were like in the past and should logically become in the future.

28 What, I ask, would a school board in Moline, Illinois—or Skokie, even—do if the scholarly community tried to reorient its educational system to conform with outmoded ideas of Sweden in the glory days of Gustavus Adolphus? Would they be expected to sing *"Ein' feste Burg"* and charge out of the mists at the Roman Catholics to save the Reformation every morning as school began? Or the Irish—would they submit to a group of Indians coming to Boston and telling them to dress in green and hunt leprechauns?

29 Consider the implications of theories put forward to solve the problem of poverty among the blacks. Several years ago, the word went forth that black poverty was due to the disintegration of the black family, that the black father no longer had a prominent place in the home. How incredibly shortsighted that thesis was. How typically Anglo-Saxon! How in the world could there have been a black family if people were sold like cattle for 200 years, if there were large plantations that served merely as farms to breed more slaves, if white owners systematically ravaged black women? When did the black family unit ever become integrated? Herein lies a trap into which many Americans have fallen: Once a problem is defined and understood by a significant number of people who have some relation to it, the fallacy goes, the problem ceases to exist. The rest of America had better beware of having quaint mores that attract anthropologists, or it will soon become a victim of the conceptual prison into which blacks and Indians, among others, have been thrown. One day you may find yourself cataloged—perhaps as a credit-card-carrying, turnpike-commuting, condominium-dwelling, fraternity-joining, church-going, sports-watching, time-purchase-buying, television-watching, magazine-subscribing, politically inert transmigrated urbanite who, through the phenomenon of the second car and the shopping center, has become a golf-playing, wife-swapping, etc., etc., etc., suburbanite. Or have you already been characterized—and caricatured—in ways that struck you as absurd? If so, you will understand what has been happening to Indians for a long, long time.

30 In defense of the anthropologists, it must be recognized that those who do not publish perish. Those who do not bring in a substantial sum of research money soon slide down the scale of university approval. What university is not equally balanced between the actual education of its students and a multitude of small bureaus, projects, institutes, and programs that are designed to harvest grants for the university?

31 The effect of anthropologists on Indians should be clear. Compilation of useless knowledge for knowledge's sake should be utterly rejected by the Indian people. We should not be objects of observation for those who do nothing to help us. During the critical days of 1954, when the Senate was

pushing for termination of all Indian rights, not one scholar, anthropologist, sociologist, historian, or economist came forward to support the tribes against the detrimental policy. Why didn't the academic community march to the side of the tribes? Certainly the past few years have shown how much influence academe can exert when it feels compelled to enlist in a cause. Is Vietnam any more crucial to the moral stance of America than the great debt owed to the Indian tribes?

32 Perhaps we should suspect the motives of members of the academic community. They have the Indian field well defined and under control. Their concern is not the ultimate policy that will affect the Indian people, but merely the creation of new slogans and doctrines by which they can climb the university totem pole. Reduction of people to statistics for purposes of observation appears to be inconsequential to the anthropologist when compared with the immediate benefits he can derive—the acquisition of further prestige and the chance to appear as the high priest of American society, orienting and manipulating to his heart's desire.

33 Roger Jourdain, chairman of the Red Lake Chippewa tribe of Minnesota, casually had the anthropologists escorted from his reservation a couple of years ago. This was the tip of the iceberg. If only more Indians had the insight of Jourdain. Why should we continue to provide private zoos for anthropologists? Why should tribes have to compete with scholars for funds, when their scholarly productions are so useless and irrelevant to life?

34 Several years ago, an anthropologist stated that over a period of some 20 years he had spent, from all sources, close to $10,000,000 studying a tribe of fewer than 1000 people. Imagine what that amount of money would have meant to that group of people had it been invested in buildings and businesses. There would have been no problems to study.

35 I sometimes think that Indian tribes could improve relations between themselves and the anthropologists by adopting the following policy: Each anthro desiring to study a tribe should be made to apply to the tribal council for permission to do his study. He would be given such permission only if he raised as a contribution to the tribal budget an amount of money equal to the amount he proposed to spend on his study. Anthropologists would thus become productive members of Indian society, instead of ideological vultures.

36 This proposal was discussed at one time in Indian circles. It blew no small number of anthro minds. Irrational shrieks of "academic freedom" rose like rockets from launching pads. The very idea of putting a tax on useless information was intolerable to the anthropologists we talked with. But the question is very simple. Are the anthros concerned about freedom —or license? Academic freedom certainly does not imply that one group of people has to become chessmen for another group of people. Why should Indian communities be subjected to prying non-Indians any more than other communities? Should any group have a franchise to stick its nose into someone else's business?

37 I don't think my proposal ever will be accepted. It contradicts the anthropologists' self-image much too strongly. What is more likely is that Indians will continue to allow their communities to be turned inside out until they come to realize the damage that is being done to them. Then they will seal up the reservations and no further knowledge—useless or otherwise—will be created. This may be the best course. Once, at a Congressional hearing, someone asked Alex Chasing Hawk, a council member of the Cheyenne Sioux for 30 years, "Just what do you Indians want?" Alex replied, "A leave-us-alone law."

38 The primary goal and need of Indians today is not for someone to study us, feel sorry for us, identify with us, or claim descent from Pocahontas to make us feel better. Nor do we need to be classified as semiwhite and have programs made to bleach us further. Nor do we need further studies to see if we are "feasible." We need, instead, a new policy from Congress that acknowledges our intelligence, and our dignity.

39 In its simplest form, such a policy would give a tribe the amount of money now being spent in the area on Federal schools and other services. With this block grant, the tribe itself would communally establish and run its own schools and hospital and police and fire departments—and, in time, its own income-producing endeavors, whether in industry or agriculture. The tribe would not be taxed until enough capital had accumulated so that individual Indians were getting fat dividends.

40 Many tribes are beginning to acquire the skills necessary for this sort of independence, but the odds are long: An Indian district at Pine Ridge was excited recently about the possibility of running its own schools, and a bond issue was put before them that would have made it possible for them to do so. In the meantime, however, anthropologists visiting the community convinced its people that they were culturally unprepared to assume this sort of responsibility; so the tribe voted down the bond issue. Three universities have sent teams to the area to discover why the issue was defeated. The teams are planning to spend more on their studies than the bond issue would have cost.

41 I would expect an instant rebuttal by the anthros. They will say that my sentiments do not represent the views of all Indians—and they are right, they have brainwashed many of my brothers. But a new day is coming. Until then, it would be wise for anthropologists to climb down from their thrones of authority and pure research and begin helping Indian tribes instead of preying on them. For the wheel of karma grinds slowly, but it does grind fine. And it makes a complete circle.

recommendation

Speak roughly to your little boy,
And beat him when he sneezes
He only does it to annoy
Because he knows it teases.

This curious bit of advice is given to a wondering Alice by a thoroughly insane Duchess and is not one we are expected to follow.[1] There are many times, however, when one person wants to tell another what to do, what to say, what to think, or where to get off— in other words, to make a recommendation—and to have it taken seriously.

You have already examined ways to define a subject, to substantiate a thesis made about it, to evaluate it as good or bad. You may now be ready to persuade people to do something about it. This final step is not always necessary. If your purpose is to describe a roadrunner or to evaluate the new volunteer army, there is no need to do anything further. But if your purpose is to save Alaskan fur seals or to convince citizens to be more (or less) patriotic, then your writing task will not be complete until you persuasively advocate a course of action or the adoption of a new attitude. Many of our most urgent questions ask, What should we do? The essays that answer such questions are called recommendations.

Jefferson in the Declaration of Independence, Paine in *Common Sense,* and Kennedy in his Inaugural Address intended to stimulate action. These recommendations have great visibility for historical reasons and because they are well written. But the methods of these writers are not very different from those of the ordinary citizen who writes a letter to his local newspaper in support of a zoning ordinance

[1]Lewis Carroll [Charles L. Dodgson], *Alice's Adventures in Wonderland,* in *The Complete Works of Lewis Carroll,* introduction by Alexander Woollcott (New York: Modern Library, n.d., p. 68).

or the student who writes a proposal to undertake a special project. Even a letter home asking for money is an exercise in persuasion: you are recommending a course of action that you hope your parents will accept.

From political manifestos to proposals of marriage, recommendations affect us throughout our lives. The ability to make recommendations effectively, as well as to evaluate the recommendations made by others, helps us get what we want out of life—and avoid being sold what we don't want.

Recommendations are also particularly satisfying to write. Sometimes, having completed a piece of writing of another kind, you may suspect that your readers will think, "Okay, but so what?" In a recommendation, you have the opportunity to make the "so what" perfectly clear: you want people to behave or believe in a certain way, and you tell them so.

The most primitive form of recommendation, in fact, does no more than flatly state what ought to be done. This primitive form is the command: "Stop" or "Stop or I'll shoot!" When the word "Stop" appears on a red-and-white road sign, it is a recommendation with the authority of the law behind it; when "Stop or I'll shoot!" is shouted by a person taking aim with a revolver, it is a recommendation with the authority of force behind it. In such circumstances, few people need to know anything more. Other commands, like the signs to "Eat here" along the highway, function as invitations rather than orders. Still others, like the advice to "Insert Tab A into Slot B," function as instructions. All commands, however, are recommendations with an implicit "or else": stop or you'll be sorry, eat here or you'll miss a good meal, insert Tab A into Slot B or the gadget won't work. In a formal recommendation essay, as we shall see below, the "or else"—the reason why something ought to be done, the type of loss we will suffer if we don't do it—is fully spelled out.

A more complex form of recommendation than the simple command is the advertisement. Americans spend billions of dollars a year following the advice of advertisements that tell them what to buy. The term "Madison Avenue" has become a household word because of the remarkable influence exerted by the advertising agencies on that New York City street—and they sell not only bleaching compounds and breakfast cereals but also politicians and philosophies. Studying the techniques of advertising (should we call it propaganda?) is one way to approach the subject of preparing recommendations—and avoid being convinced by recommendations that do not deserve acceptance.

Ogilvy (p. 460), one of the most successful writers in the advertising business, prepared a list of rules for writing advertising "copy," in other words the text below the headline. His list includes these recommendations: (1) don't beat around the bush; (2) avoid superlatives, generalizations, and platitudes—be specific and factual; (3) include endorsements from satisfied users; (4) avoid "fine writing," writing that calls attention to itself and therefore distracts attention from the subject. And we ought to pile "one fascinating fact on another," Ogilvy says, recognizing that information properly presented is dramatic.

Ads usually rely on emotional associations rather than logical argument. They may use no words at all; sometimes a photograph of a gorgeous landscape through which two beautiful young people walk, carrying a bottle of Somebody's Scotch or proffering each other a Somebody's cigarette, is all that is needed. Or a five-word slogan appealing to hunger, sex drives, or snobbery may suffice to sell candy or engine oil. You have probably seen pictures of happy people—young and old, hardhat and hippie—guzzling a beverage, and no more needs to be said than that you too can "join the Pepsi generation." Gasoline additives are inseparable from sexy girls; virile and successful men use spray-on underarm deodorant. However untrue such associations may be, they seem to work—at least on people who don't think.

Essays of recommendation are based on the assumption that people can and do think.

THE FORMAL RECOMMENDATION

Formal recommendations, sometimes called proposals, often follow a pattern composed of four elements.

Establishing the Need to Do Something. Whether the issue is "I need a new car" or "something must be done to increase our energy supply," recommendations always assume that there is a problem requiring a solution: we need to do something about X. It may not be obvious to everyone else, however, that something needs to be done. Most people would rather ignore problems—especially somebody else's—and therefore the first obligation of a formal recommendation is to explain exactly what the problem is and why it requires attention *now*. As a writer, if you want to move your audience off dead center, you will have to show that a failure to move will cause harm to someone or everyone. As a reader, before you make a move toward any commitment, you should know that a failure to move will cause harm to yourself or to other people who matter to you.

A charitable organization recently ran a fund-raising campaign using the slogan "Give to Birth Defects!" A wealthy and usually generous old man, when approached for his contribution, snapped "Why should I? Birth defects are doing well enough without my help." The people who planned the campaign failed twice. They failed to define the problem and were thus thought to be claiming that birth defects needed support. And they failed to prove that the problem was serious enough to make that skeptical old man reach for his checkbook. The example is an extreme one, but the reaction of the old man is not. Most people, when told to do something, are going to ask (or think) "Why should I?" and it is risky to fail to answer that perfectly legitimate question.

The Declaration of Independence (p. 449) is the most famous recommendation written in America and one of the most effective. It won widespread endorsement for a radical change. It begins with a discussion of the problem: "When . . . it becomes necessary to dissolve the political bands. . . ." The audience's immediate response was probably to ask *why* it was necessary, and the Declaration answers this question by providing an extensive list of reasons: the "long train of abuses," over a lengthy historical period, that proved the king's intention to establish an absolute tyranny over the American colonies.

Considering the Alternatives. If the first section of a formal recommendation has done its job, the reader should now agree: "Yes, we'd better do something about *X*. Things can't go on this way any longer." The next step is to define the types of "something" that we might do, in other words to set forth the alternative solutions to the problem. If there is a shortage of electricity in Dutchess County, New York, the alternatives might be to build a dam on the Hudson River, or to construct an atomic power plant or a plant powered by coal or solar energy. Another alternative would be to buy or borrow electricity from a nearby area with a surplus. Still another alternative would be to cut power consumption and learn to live within our electrical means.

Unless you consider all reasonable alternatives, the reader will suspect you of being ill-informed or of having an ulterior motive in concealing some of the solutions and expressing others. When an official in the state government recommends that federal welfare funds be channeled through his office and doesn't seem aware that the money could instead be sent directly from Washington to the local schools and hospitals and individuals for whom it is meant, we should suspect that there's a reason for this failure to discuss the alternatives.

The writers of the Declaration of Independence wanted people to know not only what grievances existed but also what solutions less drastic than revolution had already been tried. "In every stage of these oppressions we have petitioned for redress," they wrote. They explained that they had sought satisfaction by nonviolent means so that readers should not think they were militarists who agitated for war at the drop of a hat (or hike of a tax).

Choosing the Best Solution. The second section of the recommendation essay has identified the alternative solutions. The next step is to determine which of those possible solutions would be the best one to enact. At this point an evaluation is to be made, and it will be necessary to choose, and probably state, the criteria. If the only criterion in solving a power shortage is money, then the cheapest source of energy will be best; if the only criterion is immediacy, then the solution that can deliver electricity soonest will be best. But perhaps the cheapest or fastest solution to the energy shortage would destroy the beauty of a river and the habitats of wildlife, and such ecological effects are important to the residents of Dutchess County. As in every evaluation, choosing what is best becomes harder when multiple—and conflicting—criteria must be met. Often the best solution is a compromise: a power-generating source not as cheap as some but not as damaging to the environment as others.

Sometimes all that must be done to determine the best solution is to point out that the others have been given a chance and have failed. The most famous passage in the Declaration is the one beginning "We hold these truths to be self-evident." This section, which states the "unalienable rights" of all men, served as the standard by which the writers evaluated governments. It was clear, from the list of the British government's "abuses," that the colonial system had failed to provide the kind of government the colonists wanted. And it was clear, from the statement that petitions and other traditional means of adjusting differences had been useless, that the colonial system had been given every chance.

Demonstrating Feasibility. Once the best solution has been chosen, it is still necessary to show that it is "feasible," in other words that no insurmountable obstacle stands in the way of its enactment. It would be possible to build a dam across the Hudson, but if Congress has passed a bill prohibiting further damming of rivers used by large population centers, it will not be feasible to do so. You shouldn't recommend this solution to Dutchess County's energy shortage, then, unless you are prepared to recommend repealing the law also (and to demonstrate the feasibility of that!).

You can usually demonstrate feasibility by showing that money is available for your project, that a majority of the people affected by it approve of it, or that any legal or moral objections can be overcome. You can tell exactly what sort of feasibility demonstration your recommendation needs by asking, "What will it take to get this done?" and then checking to see that none of the necessary ingredients is beyond your reach. If you are uncertain, be honest about your uncertainty. "If we can find a large enough room in any building near the center of campus," you may have to write, "we can have an African Studies Center since everything else we need is available."

Sometimes you may discover, as you try to demonstrate feasibility, that the best solution—the one that comes nearest to meeting the criteria—is simply not feasible and must be discarded in favor of a next-best solution. Solar energy is preferable because it is clean, but Dutchess County has no funds to build a solar-energy plant, and only a few months ago the voters turned down a bond issue that would have provided such funds. Damming the river is an excellent compromise solution, and dams receive federal funds—but this solution is not feasible either since it is now illegal to dam the Hudson. The next-best solution on the list, however, does turn out to be feasible: Dutchess County can buy electricity from a Canadian power cooperative. Nobody is delighted at this recommendation, but finding a solution that will keep the wires humming is much more useful than proposing pipe dreams.

No doubt some signers of the Declaration of Independence would have preferred to remain British subjects. (Many Americans did.) But their experience had shown that it was impossible to reconcile their belief in their "unalienable rights" with the British government. Only one course of action remained open to them: to declare their separation. The document itself demonstrates the feasibility of making such a declaration. As for the feasibility of a revolution, however, the signers were intelligent enough to realize that while it was easy enough to declare a war, it wasn't going to be easy to win one. Rather than itemize their resources, which might have given too much information to the enemy, they simply pledged whatever they themselves had to offer: "our lives, our fortunes, and our sacred honor." If other colonists did the same, the war could be won. History shows that their assessment of the Revolution's feasibility was correct.

A formal recommendation, then, defines the problem and establishes the need to do something about it, considers the alternative solutions, chooses the best solution, and demonstrates that the solution it recommends is feasible. The ingredients need not be presented in this order—although the order is a logical one for both writer and reader to follow.

You will notice that this model for making recommendations involves the other kinds of writing you have studied. It involves definition: both the problem and the solutions need to be defined. And substantiation: a number of theses may need to be substantiated, for example, the thesis that the problem needs attention or the thesis that the solution is feasible. And evaluation: competing solutions need to be evaluated on the basis of criteria in order to single out the best one.

What is new here is the open call to action, the movement from "this is best" to "let's get it done, and now." Sometimes the call to action is not so urgent—tomorrow or next year will do; and sometimes the call is not for action but for a change in our thoughts or attitudes. But the overall intention is the same. The writer wants to move the readers off dead center toward a new goal.

THE ABBREVIATED RECOMMENDATION

Some recommendations, like some evaluations, omit part of the full logical model. There are two legitimate reasons for doing so. First, the principle that what is obvious does not need to be said applies here, as well as in other types of essays. Someone writing to recommend a particular form of cancer research does not need to spend time demonstrating that cancer is a problem we should care about; we are already familiar with its importance as a major cause of death in industrialized societies. Someone writing to recommend that Americans get more exercise does not need to consider a long list of alternatives to exercise: there's really no substitute (except to die sooner). Someone writing to recommend that we turn the lights off when we don't need them on does not need to explain why this course of action is better than the alternative. It's obvious that using electricity sensibly is better than wasting it. In this example, the writer wouldn't need to demonstrate feasibility either. Just flick the switch as you go out the door.

There is another reason for omitting part of the formal model. Sometimes the writer cannot complete all parts of the model because the information is not available, or because no single course of action can be endorsed, or because his intention is only to explore the problem and leave the decision up to us. Raymond Carroll's article "How to Ease the Hunger Pangs" (p. 442) discusses seven alternatives but stops short of a "Do this" recommendation because each of the alternatives involves a serious feasibility problem. (The best alternative, in fact, involves the greatest feasibility problem.) In this case, the writer could make a strong "Do this" recommendation only by being dishonest, by pretending that the obstacles didn't exist.

The Negative Recommendation. A special form of abbreviated recommendation is the negative recommendation, which says *"Don't do this"* or *"Stop* doing this." Its purpose is only to persuade us that a certain course of action, or way of thinking, does not deserve our endorsement. It usually does not tell us what to do or think instead. Clubb's short article "And God Created Person" (p. 439) recommends that we *not* try to solve problems of sex discrimination by replacing the word "man" with "person."

A negative recommendation can back up its thesis, *"Don't do this,"* by attacking any part of the standard recommendation model. If your thesis is "Let's not have separate men's and women's sex-education classes," you can show that there is no problem (step 1) with the current mixed classes; or that separating the classes by sex would be irrelevant to whatever problem exists—not a reasonable alternative to consider (step 2); or that this is not the best alternative (step 3); or that it isn't feasible (step 4) because of the scheduling complications, not to mention federal laws prohibiting sex discrimination and eliminating "separate but equal" schooling.

The negative recommendation is often a useful and even necessary step in solving complex problems. We need to guard against wasting our energies on pseudo-solutions, solutions that look as if they will work but really won't. The negative recommendation acts like a warning flag to protect us from such pitfalls.

Unless a negative recommendation can provoke us to think toward a new positive solution, however, it runs the risk of accomplishing next to nothing. If we merely agree not to act, the problem (if one exists) is likely to remain unsolved. We will avoid making things worse, and that, to be sure, is a gain; but we will not succeed in making things better.

The Mock Recommendation. Sometimes a writer will begin by recommending a course of action that seems extreme, even a little absurd. The more we read the more absurd it seems, until we reject it altogether. This is exactly the effect the writer wants: the real purpose in saying "Let's do this" while making the proposal sound ridiculous is to say "Let's *not* do this—it's ridiculous." The mock or satiric recommendation is thus one type of negative recommendation.

The most famous mock recommendation in the English language is Jonathan Swift's "A Modest Proposal" (p. 504). Swift pretends that he is a politician telling the British Parliament about the perfect solution to the problem of poverty and starvation in Ireland. His solution is that since there are too many poor and hungry people in Ireland, some of them ought to eat the others. Then there wouldn't be so many people, and the ones left wouldn't be so hungry. With a very self-satisfied air, the politician explains the economic and nutritional advantages of his solution, even providing various recipes for roast baby, until we are filled with disgust and contempt for his entire attitude. He fails to realize that he is talking about people, suffering human beings, not about an abstract economic issue or domesticated animals. Swift's intention in writing "A Modest Proposal" was to produce in his readers a rejection of all dehumanizing solutions.

For a mock recommendation to be effective, it must somehow "tip us off" that the superficial thesis, the initial "Do this," is not to be taken seriously. This can be accomplished by exaggerating the recommendation until it is clearly inane or unfeasible or morally unacceptable, or by making the *persona* (the apparent personality of the writer) seem unattractive so that we begin to dislike the idea because we dislike the person advocating it. Swift uses both of these techniques. He includes details about the cooking of babies to dramatize the process and make its moral unacceptability perfectly clear. And he makes his *persona*—the politician delivering the speech— a stuffy, pompous, self-serving character whom we come to detest.

Mock recommendations are fun, but risky. If the audience fails to sense the satiric purpose and takes the mock advice for real advice, one of two undesirable results will occur. People will act on the mock advice, which is just the opposite of what the writer intends. Or people will reject the writer (not seeing the difference between him and his fictitious *persona*) as an inhuman or a stupid person. If you write a mock recommendation, then, be sure that something in your essay—an utterly fantastic setting, a wildly improbable detail of the proposal, a thoroughly repulsive *persona*—will let the audience know that this one isn't for real.

RECOMMENDATIONS AND THE WRITER'S INVOLVEMENT

Once there was a student who wrote one failing paper after another. Nothing he put down on paper was ever any good, and both he and his teacher knew it. Finally he quit school, and as he packed his bags he wrote a long note to the dean. He explained that he had wanted to be an auto mechanic, not a college student, but that social pressure and his sense of duty to his family had forced him to go to school. It just wasn't working out, and his composition course was the worst course of all. He recommended that composition teachers give students more realistic and practical assignments and encourage them to write what they *need* to write.

The remarkable thing about this farewell note to the dean was that it was itself an outstanding example of good writing. There were no errors in grammar or punctuation or spelling. The prose flowed when it should have flowed, was crisp when it should have been crisp. It was full of the right information, in the right place, at the right time —in other words, full of dramatic power. Despite a series of failing compositions, this student knew how to write—but only when he felt he had something important to say and someone to say it to.

Writing recommendations is an invitation to have something important to say to somebody. You have every incentive to get the facts right as you define the problem and substantiate the thesis that we must do something about it; you have every incentive to consider the alternative solutions, evaluate them honestly to identify the best one, and demonstrate that the solution you recommend is feasible. If you do these things well, something much more important than a good grade on a paper might result: you might be on your way to changing your corner of the world.

Language is power, as the poets have said. At least some of the time, the pen is mightier than the sword. And language is the civilized way to bring about change, to remake the world so that it conforms a little more to the image of the world we want.

That last word, "want," points out a critical element of good writing: writing is most likely to be good when the writer *wants* it to be, when the degree of involvement in the subject is high, when the feeling behind the sentences is genuine. When you write a recommendation—or any other type of essay—say what you *want* to, in such a way that your readers will be persuaded to accept your goals as theirs also. Writing is a way of bringing people together.

series one

RECOMMENDATION: READINGS WITH COMMENTARY

the intellectual taxicab company

PETER CARLSON

Carlson, a college student majoring in journalism, is about to have a personal confrontation with a widespread problem: getting a job. He and other educated people are finding that there is a very small market for the intellectual skills they have learned and enjoy practicing. The only alternatives for the liberal-arts graduate seem to be to go to graduate school or drive a taxicab.

Carlson proposes a "simple answer" to this problem. Why not combine the intellectual training of young people with their ability to drive cars? As drivers for "The Intellectual Taxicab Company," college students could "bring adult education to the streets" by providing, simultaneously, a ride and a quick summary of the latest news in psychology, economics, or English literature.

Do you think that Carlson is serious?

1   **m**y friend Danny hung his Boston University diploma below the hack license in his cab.

2   After seventeen years of education in the finest schools in America, Danny, at 22, couldn't fix his stopped sink, repair a burnt connection in his fuse box, replace a pane of glass in his kitchen or locate the carburetor in his car.

435

3   Danny is an educated man. He is a master of writing research papers, taking tests, talking and filling out forms. He can rattle off his social-security number as easily as he can his name because it was also his student identification number. He can analyze Freud from a Marxian viewpoint and he can analyze Marx from a Freudian viewpoint.

4   In short, Danny is an unskilled worker and he has a sociology degree to prove it. He is of very little use to American industry.

5   This is nothing new. Colleges have been turning out unskilled workers for decades. Until five years ago, most of these unskilled workers took their degrees in sociology, philosophy, political science or history and marched right into the American middle class. Some filled executive positions in business and government but many, if not most, went into education, which is the only thing they knew anything about. Once there, they taught another generation the skills necessary to take tests and write papers.

6   But that cycle broke down. Teachers are overabundant these days, college applications are down, plumbers are making $12 an hour and liberal-arts graduates are faced with a choice—graduate school or the taxicab.

7   Danny chose the taxicab because driving was about the only marketable skill he possessed. Danny refers to his job as "Real World 101." He has been shot at, punched, sideswiped and propositioned. But he has also acquired some practical skills—he can get his tickets fixed; he knows how to cheat the company out of a few extra dollars a week; he found his carburetor and he can fix it.

8   Soon, I will be in the same position. I'll graduate from Boston University with a B.S. in journalism. Whatever skills that degree symbolizes are not currently in demand. I suppose I could go to graduate school, but, Christ, I've been doing the same thing for seventeen years and I'm getting a little tired of it. Besides, there are a lot of grad-school graduates who are driving cabs, too.

9   And that brings me to the Intellectual Taxicab Company.

10   Danny and I were discussing the hack business recently and we came up with the idea. It is the simple answer to a simple question: why should all that college education go to waste reading road signs when masses of people are looking for knowledge and riding in cabs?

11   What America needs is a system to bring together all the knowledgeable cabbies and the undereducated rest of the country. The system we propose is the Intellectual Taxicab Company.

12   The Intellectual Taxicab Company would consist of a dispatcher and a fleet of cabs driven by recent college graduates. When you need a ride, you call the company and say something like: "I'd like to go from Wall Street over to East 83rd and I'd like to discuss the world monetary situation."

13   "All right, sir, we'll have an NYU economics graduate over in five minutes."

14   Or: "Hello, I'm in Central Square and I'd like to go to Brookline and discuss whether or not there is a God."

15   "You're in luck, madame, we have a Harvard philosophy graduate who minored in Comparative Religions right in the neighborhood."

16   The educational possibilities of this plan are staggering. English and Drama graduates could take the after-theater run, explaining the literary ramifications of the shows. Political Science graduates could hack around Capitol Hill or City Hall. Regular bus runs could be set up to conduct seminars on popular topics.

17   The Intellectual Taxicab Company would bring adult education to the streets. It would also give all those alienated college graduates a feeling that they didn't waste four years and all that tuition money. And it would elevate the snotty cabdriver to an art form: cabbies would quote Voltaire while they rant about how bad the mayor is.

18   Surely there must be some foundation money or unimpounded Federal funds available to begin such a noble experiment in education. If there is, Danny and I are ready to start immediately. In fact, Danny is licking his lips in anticipation. "Just think how much my tips will go up," he said.

COMMENTARY

Carlson begins with the story of his friend Danny to capture our interest. Danny, we find, represents a whole generation of young people with a problem (paragraphs 1 to 7). The writer belongs to this group too. (Why do you think he decided to describe Danny in the first paragraphs rather than himself?) Nearly half of this short article is spent acquainting us with the problem.

In paragraphs 9 and 10 we are introduced to Carlson's "simple answer to a simple question," the Intellectual Taxicab Company. Then we are told exactly how this multipurpose operation would work so that we can accept it as feasible. At the end of the article, Carlson summarizes the benefits of his proposal, suggests that somebody offer him an initial stake to get the business under way, and conveys his desire to get something done *now* by remarking that he and his friend are "ready to start immediately."

This short recommendation moves from a definition of the problem, to a brief mention of two alternatives to be rejected (graduate school and ordinary taxi-driving), to a presentation of the alternative the writer prefers, to a demonstration of its feasibility, to an evaluation of its usefulness, and finally to a summarizing call for action. It corresponds almost exactly to to the model for recommendations discussed in the introduction to this section.

But how is this proposal intended? Carlson's exaggerated language leads us to suspect that he is half in jest. We get suspicious when he calls the employment problem "simple" (paragraph 10). We get more suspicious when he introduces his solution with the grandiloquent phrase "What

America needs is a system . . ." (paragraph 11). We have seen so many systems come and go that we are doubtful whether America needs one more. Similarly, when Carlson calls the educational possibilities of his idea "staggering" (paragraph 16), he is not quite credible.

What, on the whole, do you think his recommendation is? Does he really want to start an Intellectual Taxicab Company? Perhaps he is proposing "Let's do *something*. If you think my idea is silly, think of a better one."

OUTLINE

    I. The problem—paragraphs 1–6

   II. The alternatives

       A. Alternatives rejected: standard taxi-driving, graduate school—paragraphs 7–8

       B. Alternative recommended: Intellectual Taxicab Company—paragraphs 9–16

          1. This alternative is *preferable*—paragraph 11

          2. This alternative is *feasible*—paragraphs 12–16

  III. Summary: benefits of proposal, call to action—paragraphs 17–18

SUGGESTIONS FOR WRITING

1. Write a recommendation suggesting a "simple answer to a simple question." You may be fully serious or only partly so. For example, given the problem of the high cost of sugar, propose that we simply do without sugar; given the problem of highway deaths—some 60,000 a year—propose that we simply close all the highways; given the problem of racial discrimination, propose that we all wear paper bags over our heads and mittens on our hands so that nobody could see our skins.

2. Carlson says (paragraph 4) that Danny, educated in sociology, is "of very little use to American industry." But maybe Carlson is wrong. Write a letter of recommendation for Danny or someone else like him: a person educated not in a production-oriented skill but in a liberal-arts subject (history, philosophy, social science, literature, etc.) that has trained him to think clearly, to express himself well, and to see the human side of problems. Recommend this person for a job in some part of "American industry." For example, recommend him for a job as an encyclopedia salesman, a loan officer in a bank, a department-store purchaser of furniture, a caseworker in a government welfare office, an on-the-job counselor for "unemployables" being employed in an auto factory.

and god created person

MERREL D. CLUBB, JR.

"In the beginning was the word," as the Bible says, recognizing the immense power of language. Clubb's essay (actually a letter to an editor) is a vehement negative recommendation about words. His thesis is that we should not replace the word "man" by the word "person." This might seem harmless enough—except that his recommendation occurs in the context of a national controversy about the liberation of women and the way that language influences our perceptions of one another.

Clubb defends "man" as the preferable alternative by appealing to the history of words and by citing term after term, phrase after phrase, in which the "person" suffix sounds awkward or silly. He seems to be suggesting that our new sensitivity to the sexual connotations of ordinary words is silly. Do you agree, or do you think that he is behaving too much like a *maleperson?*

To the Editor:

The women's liberation movement has, of course, given birth to many worthwhile improvements, but it has also spawned at least one linguistic monstrosity. One can, with some ease, accept the new form *Ms* as filling an empty slot in our language; but is *chairperson,* or even *chairwoman* really necessary? *Chairperson* is fast infiltrating our newspapers and magazines, but when it begins to appear in the publications of our most august Modern Language Association of America, it is time for those concerned with the "purity" of our language to cry forth. If we go the route of *chairperson* we may just as well start talking about *clergyperson, churchperson, countryperson, journeyperson, kinsperson, longshoreperson, foreperson, postperson, brakeperson, milkperson, Redperson, Peking person, inner person,* and *freshperson; personhour, personhunt, personservant, personslaughter, personhole, personmade, personkind, personhood, personly,* and *personliness; person of the world, person in the street, person of God, person of straw, person of war,* and *person o'war bird.* We may even talk about *personing the ship* and *personing the production lines.* And finally, *Persons' Room.* Now surely, we would want to be able to tell what is behind the door labeled "Persons' Room," wouldn't we? So, we will have to start talking about *Persons' Room* in contrast to *Wopersons' Room.* This will lead to *flagperson* and *flagwoperson, policeperson* and *policewoperson, salesperson* and *saleswoperson, personish* and *wopersonish, person of the house* and *woperson of the house,* and—*chairperson* and *chairwoperson.* Most surely, wopersons—or fepersons—would wish to distinguish *woperson power* from *person power, woperson suffrage* from *person suffrage,* and most of all, *wopersons' lib* from *persons' lib!*

Source. Copyright © 1974. Reprinted by permission of the Modern Language Association of America from the *MLA Newsletter.*

2   The insistence on such forms as *chairperson, cochairperson,* and *chairpersonship* only goes to show how uninformed avid wopersons and their campfollowers can be. What does the form *man* mean in its various contexts? The modern *man* comes from Old English *man* (in various spellings, as early as 971 A.D.). The meaning of Old English *man* along with its cognates in all the Germanic languages was twofold: (1) "an adult male human being" and (2) "a human being of either sex." Moreover, the more common meaning of *man* in Old English was the latter—"human being or person" without reference to age or sex—and the distinctive sex terms were *wer,* "man, adult male" and *wif,* "woman, adult female." The forerunner of modern *woman,* Old English *wifman,* meant literally "female human being" or "female person." The dual meaning of *man* has continued in English down to the present day, although the meaning "human being" has become somewhat more constricted in that it occurs now only in general or indefinite applications. In many words such as *swordsman, penman, policeman, chairman,* etc., the unstressed form *man* is no longer even a word, but, in effect, a derivational suffix with meanings of, roughly, "one who is skilled in the use of something" (a sword, a pen) or "one who is connected with some act" (policing, chairing). In short, why bring in a relative Johnny-come-lately *person* (originally from Old French) to replace a perfectly good English form *man?* Do we really want to talk about Shakespeare's *Two Gentlepersons of Verona,* Pope's *An Essay on Person,* Shaw's *Person and Superperson,* O'Neill's *The Iceperson Cometh?* Must we open Milton's *Paradise Lost* and read: "Of Person's First Disobedience, and the Fruit/Of that Forbidden tree . . ."?

Merrel D. Clubb, Jr.
Univ. of Montana

COMMENTARY

A recommendation logically involves all the forms of writing previously examined in this text: definition, substantiation, and evaluation. And this can be accomplished within a very short space, as Clubb's two-paragraph recommendation shows—with room to spare for a good amount of specific data supporting the writer's proposal. This letter to an editor shows how effective a "high compression" technique can be.

The first sentence supplies background, functioning as a definition of the situation; the second sentence provides a thesis in the form of a question: Is the word *chairperson* necessary? The third sentence presents the author's recommendation to "cry forth" against this "monstrosity," and those words themselves indicate his evaluation: negative. The remainder of the first paragraph shows that if you consistently substitute "person" for "man," you create absurdities. (This tactic is called *reductio ad absurdum,* reducing something to absurdity.) Paragraph two argues that "man" hasn't historically meant "male" in any case, and therefore it doesn't need to be replaced to be fair to women (*wopersons*). The final sentence provides a slightly different kind of argument: to require "person" would destroy some of the poetry of our language.

OUTLINE
  I. Introduction: women's lib has created a context—paragraph 1 (first sentences)
  II. Statement of recommendation: let's not adopt *chairperson*—paragraph 1
  III. Defense of the chosen alternative: *-person* formations are silly—paragraph 1
  IV. Defense of the chosen alternative: *man* doesn't mean "male" anyway—paragraph 2
  V. Defense of the chosen alternative: we have some fine poetry using *man*—paragraph 2

SUGGESTIONS FOR WRITING

1. Not long ago, leaders of the Black Liberation Movement endorsed calling one another "man" as a symbol of defiance against whites who referred condescendingly to adult blacks as "boys." You may still hear people sprinkle their conversation with the word "man" as a way of asserting their status. Like cool, man! Write an essay recommending that this functional use of "man" be encouraged and paralleled by a similar use of "woman": Like cool, woman! Or write an essay recommending the opposite.

2. Write an essay recommending the retention or expulsion of another controversial word. For example, should the indefinite pronoun "he" be replaced by the phrase "he or she," or perhaps by a new indefinite pronoun altogether, such as " 'e"? (This last was the proposal of a two-year-old child who was unsure which adults were male and which were female anyway, and hit upon " 'e" as a way of never being definitely wrong about the pronoun.) Other sexless pronouns that have been proposed are "hesh" (he/she), "hirs" (his/hers), and "herm" (him/her).

3. Clubb attacks "chairperson" and similar words on linguistic grounds: they sound awkward or foolish as words. Defend or attack the use of "chairperson" on other grounds, for example, its social, psychological, or political implications.

4. Language is not the only element of our culture open to criticism for the attitudes it implies. Write an essay recommending, or recommending against, a change in the conventions of dress (for instance, some restaurants require that a man wear a jacket and tie, and many local ordinances require that a woman—but not a man—wear upper-body clothing) or sports (most sports are sex-segregated). Should there be a Persons' Football Team?

how to ease the hunger pangs

RAYMOND CARROLL

This article from *Newsweek* presents seven proposals for narrowing the gap between the food available around the world and the people who need it. The problem of food shortages is very complex. Every proposed solution stumbles over a feasibility obstacle. Attempting to deal honestly with this situation, the article refrains from concluding with a strong "Do this" recommendation. Instead, it intends to make us aware of the many different things that might be done and of the obstacles that have so far prevented these solutions from having much effect.

1   **a**t the Rome food conference this week, the experts are certain to peer into their crystal balls and, like a chorus of latter-day Malthusians, predict that the future simply won't work. Not, at least, if something isn't done about the global food crisis—and soon. The technology to feed the world adequately already exists. Agronomists are confident that in the next few years, for example, it will be possible for an American farmer to harvest his crop with an amazing hay baler that can wrap 20 tons per hour in polypropylene, a plastic that cattle can eat, which is fortified with vitamins and minerals. And other scientists are equally hopeful that even India's problems can be overcome with what they call "the four F's"—more food, foreign exchange, fuel and fertilizer.

2   But as might be expected, the medicine to cure the world's hunger pangs is easier to prescribe than to administer. For one thing, it will take a lot of money—perhaps hundreds of billions of dollars a year for many years. For another, it will require a great deal of sacrifice in living standards on the part of the more fortunate one-third of the world's population to help the other two-thirds become self-sufficient in food. And that may be hard to achieve. "The man in the street," warns one expert of the Food and Agriculture Organization, "may become so inured to the food crisis and the likelihood of starvation that he may start thinking of mass starvation as something that is inevitable." The rich nations, in short, may simply cease to care.

3   Even if the affluent and well-fed can be persuaded to make the commitment to help feed their fellow men, the problem will not be easily solved. The transfer of capital is so massive, the political implications so immense, the technology so complex that a variety of efforts will have to be made. Below, some of the most often talked about approaches:

1 NEW FARMLANDS

4   At present, only 11 per cent of the world's total land surface—or about 3.5 billion acres—is under cultivation. And there are agronomists who believe that enormous areas of the globe amounting to another 6.6 billion acres could be converted into farmland. They are not talking about Asia, where an estimated 85 per cent of the arable land is already under the plow. For the most part, they look to such remote jungles as the Amazon River basin and parts of tsetse-ridden West Africa. Such an expansion of cultivated land is not out of the question—technically.

5   The problem, however, is cost. Most of the land that is tillable at feasible prices is already being farmed. It would take about $4 billion a year to add 20 million acres to the world's farmland by 1985. And at the estimated rate of $2,000 per acre, it would cost a staggering $13.2 trillion to bring all 6.6 billion acres under cultivation. "The people who are talking about adding more land," comments Lester Brown, a leading authority on world food problems, "are not considering the cost. If you are willing to pay the price, you can farm the slope of Mt. Everest."

2 BETTER YIELDS

6   Thanks to the "Green Revolution," world production of such vital foods as wheat and rice rose dramatically during the 1960s. New "miracle" seeds, expanded irrigation systems and the application of chemical fertilizers enabled farmers—particularly in food-short parts of Asia—to bring in record harvests. And yet, discouragingly, the unprecedented increases in crop yields have barely enabled the world to keep pace with the skyrocketing growth of population.

7   Optimists believe that modern technology can produce substantially greater yields per acre. And, indeed, the scientists have come up with still newer and even more productive seeds. One experiment envisions grafting wheat to soybean roots, since wheat requires nitrogen and soybeans generate their own nitrogen. But many such developments will require large supplies of water to make them effective. Ambitious plans like desalination of the ocean waters on a large scale would be exorbitantly expensive and are unlikely to be a major factor in improving the global water supply. Similarly, weather-control schemes such as cloud seeding have so far proved to be of dubious value climatically; rather, they have been a source of potential political mischief. Rhodesia, which initiated a cloud-seeding operation in 1973, has already been accused by its African neighbors of undertaking what they termed "meteorological aggression."

8   The key to increased food production in the developing nations is cheap energy. It takes enormous amounts of oil to operate farm machinery, run irrigation pumps and produce fertilizer. The fivefold increase in oil prices over the past two years has had a devastating impact on the farmlands of the poorer nations. Suggestions have been made that Americans cut back on the use of fertilizer for lawns, golf courses and house plants in

order to send massive shipments abroad for agricultural purposes—but neither the U.S. nor any other affluent country in the world seems ready for this kind of sacrifice.

3 POPULATION CONTROL

9   All food experts agree that the world will never be able to feed its people properly unless the exploding population growth rate of 2.4 per cent a year is cut to practically zero. The $250 million currently being spent by public and private sources each year to spread the message of family planning is clearly inadequate, and many demographers believe it will take $1 billion annually to have any significant impact. Others are so despairing that they think it may be necessary for governments to adopt coercive population control—including forced sterilization—to head off disaster.

10   It is not likely that such draconian methods will be adopted. Two months ago at the world population conference in Bucharest, many developing nations made it plain that they viewed population-control proposals as a racist plot by the rich countries of North America and West Europe to keep them weak and powerless.

4 NEW FOOD

11   Over the years, the food scientists have emerged time and again from their laboratories to announce new discoveries—the production of food from oil, the creation of protein food from leaves, the use of fish meal as a food. Algae have been advanced as a nutritious food, and laboratory-created mixes such as Incaparina—a blend of corn, cottonseed flour, soy flour and amino acids—have been marketed in Central America. But so far, at least, human taste and the high cost of the alternative foods have prevented them from displacing more conventional edibles. Similarly, food experts have long dreamed of "farming the sea" so as to vastly increase the supply of fish for human consumption. But given the high costs and an apparent lack of international will, there is no reason to believe that the sea will provide substantially more of man's food in the years ahead. Indeed, due to pollution and overfishing, statistics show the world catch actually has been in a steady decline.

5 EATING LESS

12   Some experts believe a more practical way of getting food to the world's hungry would be a cutdown on the intake of animal protein in the affluent world. It takes 7 pounds of grain to produce a pound of beef. "If Americans would decrease the meat they eat by 10 per cent," contends Harvard nutritionist Jean Mayer, "it would release enough grain to feed 60 million people."

13   In addition, it is estimated that Americans waste up to 25 per cent of the food they buy. And if the amount of food that contributes to obesity is taken into account, that figure goes as high as 50 per cent. Yet all proposals to get Americans to cut down on their food consumption inevitably run into opposition from the food lobby. When Sen. Hubert Humphrey suggested that Americans eat one less hamburger a week to make more grain available for consumption by the world's hungry, he was criticized by Agriculture Secretary Earl Butz as "a fuzzy-thinking do-gooder." As for mandatory food rationing, one Agriculture Department official remarks: "I think we would have food riots on our hands."

6 LAND REFORM

14   After World War II, the U.S. occupation in Japan put an end to the ownership of farms by absentee landlords and placed land in the hands of the tillers. As a result, though Japanese farms are small (averaging one one-hundredth the size in the U.S.), the incentive derived from private ownership and a native industriousness have made Japanese farmers four times as productive as other Asians. Similar reform measures in Taiwan, Egypt and Mexico have also led to substantial increases in production.

15   Vast areas of farmland in Asia and Latin America, however, are still in the hands of absentee owners, and the poor sharecroppers who actually work the fields have little incentive to improve the land. In parts of Africa, arbitrary control over land parcels by tribal chiefs also tends to discourage individual initiative and long-term investment in the land.

16   Whether in small farms or vast collectives such as are used in China, it has proven true that farmers need incentives—a share of the profits, ownership of the land or a sense of contributing to the general welfare of their nation. "After all," says Demetrios Christodoulou, a specialist on agricultural reform at the Food and Agriculture Organization, "a man is just more likely to have the will to work his own land."

7 GLOBAL COOPERATION

17   Most food experts believe that a vast program of international cooperation is necessary to solve the current crisis. And they hope that the Arabs will join that program by throwing some of their extra petrodollars into a special agricultural fund, which would provide loans on easy terms for the poorer countries. There is also talk of setting up a worldwide system to give early warning of conditions that could cause famine.

18   More controversial are proposals for the establishment of a strategic grain reserve. Once the hungry of the world could rely on vast surpluses in the major grainaries of the world—chiefly in the U.S. But worldwide demand—and the free-market policies of the Nixon and Ford administrations—have depleted the once-swollen stores. "We will have to come up with some kind of a system in which between 10 million and 50 million

metric tons of grain are held in reserve to meet the sort of emergencies we have now," argues Earl D. Kellogg, an agricultural economist at the University of Illinois. But the more conservative interests among the American farm bloc are deeply suspicious of the possible price-depressing consequences of a food reserve plan—and are determined to keep it in private hands if one has to be set up. "The Farm Bureau people," says one food analyst, "believe that if there are hungry people in the world, they should have to pay the high going rate to the private sector in order to eat."

19   Because there seems to be a general lack of enthusiasm to spend the money and make the necessary sacrifices, Dr. Norman Borlaug, usually acknowledged as the "father of the Green Revolution" for his pioneering work on miracle seeds, sounded a distinctly somber note last week on the eve of the Rome food meeting. "I think the conference may be a forewarning of disaster," he told *Newsweek,* "but there will be no coming together of minds until a major famine brings people together."

20   There is general agreement that the time has long passed when the world's food problems can be solved by mammoth overseas shipments of surplus U.S. grain. The bitter lesson of the give-away program was that it was not good either for the U.S. or for the recipient nation to remain on the American food dole indefinitely. Unquestionably, emergency aid will have to be continued—even in the face of economic and political difficulties. But at the same time, the emphasis must now fall on assistance that will enable deficit countries to put their own agricultural houses in order. As many food experts note, China has managed to overcome its age-old problem of famine. Few Westerners would advocate the regimentation involved in Peking's approach to agriculture, but many of them do applaud the Chinese concentration on self-sufficiency.

21   Clearly the world is faced with hard choices, and many of the experts take an uncharacteristically apocalyptic approach. Prof. Richard Gardner of Columbia believes the situation is so critical that the developed and developing countries must make a "mutual survival pact." The raw-materials-producing countries would have to be guaranteed access to the markets, management skills and capital of the industrialized world in return for an agreement to keep their prices within reason. Under such an agreement, the poor would have to abide by certain expected norms of behavior. For instance, the U.S. would not give vast amounts of food aid to India if that country cut its budget for family planning and invested scarce resources in the testing of nuclear weapons. Says Don Paarlberg, the chief economist of the Agriculture Department: "There can only be solutions to these world problems if there is world cooperation."

22   But if there is a growing realization in the latter third of the twentieth century that the nations of the globe are essentially interdependent, the will to act that way is not always there. Severe inflation, a wide range of domestic problems and resurging nationalism have caused many countries to turn inward. And when they do look abroad, their view is still ruled by

national self-interest and balance-of-power politics. Under these circumstances, global cooperation may prove to be the most difficult solution of all.

COMMENTARY

This *Newsweek* article begins by establishing the problem, "the global food crisis." It then states a general principle that applies to all specific proposals: the technology is available now but the money and the determination are not. We expect, then, that the article will explain the financial and political obstacles that stand in the way of each proposal, and this is exactly what it does. With the first alternative, for example—the proposal that additional land areas be used for growing food—the problem is cost. With the second alternative, the problem is cost and "potential political mischief"; with the third, the fear of racism—and so forth.

The intention of the *Newsweek* writers is not, however, to say "There's nothing we can do; let's forget about it and let two-thirds of the world starve if it must." Each alternative is presented not as hopeless but as difficult, requiring further commitment on our part if it is to be made feasible. The hope behind this strategy is that each reader will respond to at least one of the seven proposals and do whatever an individual can to reduce the size of its obstacle. Since in combatting hunger it is not necessary to endorse one solution only (all of them together would help), if everyone will work at something, the aim of this recommendation could be accomplished.

Is the problem presented dramatically enough to make you care about it? Do you see a way in which you could become involved in any of the solutions discussed?

OUTLINE

    I. Introduction: identification of the problem and the occasion (the food conference at Rome); general principle that the technology exists but the money or desire does not—paragraphs 1–3

   II. The alternatives (each is defined and its feasibility considered)—paragraphs 4–22

      A. New farmlands—paragraphs 4–5

      B. Better yields—paragraphs 6–8

      C. Population control—paragraphs 9–10

      D. New kinds of food—paragraph 11

      E. Eating less in prosperous countries—paragraphs 12–13

      F. Land reform—paragraphs 14–16

      G. Global cooperation—paragraphs 17–22

SUGGESTIONS FOR WRITING

    1. Write an essay recommending positive action on one of the *Newsweek* article's seven alternatives. Show what you and other people like yourself can

do. How, for instance, should we go about persuading minority groups that population control is necessary (see alternative 3)? Or how can we encourage the use of America's backyards as vegetable gardens (alternative 1)? What can you, as an individual, do to promote global cooperation (alternative 7)? For example, you might study foreign languages or Far Eastern history, so that you can comprehend the countries with which cooperation is necessary. Try to confront, rather than to avoid, whatever problem interferes with feasibility.

2. One of the obstacles to many proposals to ease food shortages is that people in the prosperous countries don't care enough. To put it frankly, we are selfish; and our communications media encourage this selfishness by carrying advertisements for expensive and unnecessary luxury foods.

Write a letter to the Federal Communications Commission or to your local TV station recommending a ban on ads for luxury foods for American people —or for their pets.

TO MY FAMILY, MY PHYSICIAN, MY LAWYER, MY CLERGYMAN
TO ANY MEDICAL FACILITY IN WHOSE CARE I HAPPEN TO BE
TO ANY INDIVIDUAL WHO MAY BECOME RESPONSIBLE FOR MY HEALTH, WELFARE OR
AFFAIRS

Death is as much a reality as birth, growth, maturity and old age—it is the one certainty of life. If the time comes when I, _____ can no longer take part in decisions for my own future, let this statement stand as an expression of my wishes, while I am still of sound mind.

If the situation should arise in which there is no reasonable expectation of my recovery from physical or mental disability, I request that I be allowed to die and not be kept alive by artificial means or "heroic measures". I do not fear death itself as much as the indignities of deterioration, dependence and hopeless pain. I, therefore, ask that medication be mercifully administered to me to alleviate suffering even though this may hasten the moment of death.

This request is made after careful consideration. I hope you who care for me will feel morally bound to follow its mandate. I recognize that this appears to place a heavy responsibility upon you, but it is with the intention of relieving you of such responsibility and of placing it upon myself in accordance with my strong convictions, that this statement is made.

Signed _____

Date _____

Witness _____

Witness _____

Copies of this request have been given to _____

_____

_____

_____

Source. Courtesy of the Euthanasia Educational Council.

3. Write a recommendation essay using the pattern followed by the *News-week* article. Identify a complex problem and present a number of alternative solutions, each involving an obstacle of feasibility or desirability. Your purpose is not to say "Let's not do anything," but instead to make people see the problem realistically so that they can develop a solution that will work.

For example, consider the complex problem of dying in modern America. The process of dying, especially for the elderly, is often lengthy and lonely. Among the solutions that have been suggested are that we keep elderly people at home, where they can die in familiar surroundings; that we make nursing homes and hospitals (where about two-thirds of the elderly die) more pleasant places by increasing their staffs and improving their facilities; that we ease the loneliness of dying people and provide wages for women whose children keep them at home by government-sponsored programs to place slowly dying people in individual family settings; and that we encourage people to die promptly, and doctors to let them die, if they so choose. The "Living Will" reproduced on facing page (prepared by Euthanasia Educational Council) shows how the last alternative might be specified by someone who chooses what is called "Death with Dignity," a person's right to die when it seems that medical care will not restore him to a normal condition.

In your essay, discuss these alternatives and any others you may be familiar with; admit the obstacles to each alternative; suggest what you think is the best course of action, despite the obstacles, if you can.

the declaration of independence
THOMAS JEFFERSON and others

A "declaration" or "manifesto" is not simply an announcement that somebody is going to do something. It is also a call to action—a recommendation, even an impassioned plea—to other people to contribute their energies and if necessary their lives. The writers of a declaration must therefore not only explain their program (definition) but also demonstrate that a problem exists (substantiation), show that what they want to do is right (evaluation), and ask us to support them (recommendation).

Jefferson and the delegates of the Continental Congress accomplish all these functions in the Declaration of Independence. They appeal to our subjective beliefs by stating the philosophical principles they live by and are willing, if need be, to die by. But they also invite an objective assessment by carefully rehearsing "the facts" as proof of the reasonableness of their action.

IN CONGRESS, JULY 4, 1776

THE UNANIMOUS DECLARATION OF THE THIRTEEN UNITED
STATES OF AMERICA,

1   **W**hen in the Course of human events, it becomes necessary for one people to dissolve the political bands which have connected them with another, and to assume among the powers of the earth, the separate and equal station to which the Laws of Nature and of Nature's God entitle them, a decent respect to the opinions of mankind requires that they should declare the causes which impel them to the separation.

2   We hold these truths to be self-evident, that all men are created equal, that they are endowed by their Creator with certain unalienable Rights, that among these are Life, Liberty and the pursuit of Happiness. That to secure these rights, Governments are instituted among Men, deriving their just powers from the consent of the governed. That whenever any Form of Government becomes destructive of these ends, it is the Right of the People to alter or to abolish it, and to institute a new Government, laying its foundation on such principles, and organizing its powers in such form, as to them shall seem most likely to effect their Safety and Happiness. Prudence, indeed, will dictate that Governments long established should not be changed for light and transient causes; and accordingly all experience hath shewn, that mankind are more disposed to suffer, while evils are sufferable, than to right themselves by abolishing the forms to which they are accustomed. But when a long train of abuses and usurpations, pursuing invariably the same Object, evinces a design to reduce them under absolute Despotism, it is their right, it is their duty, to throw off such Government, and to provide new Guards for their future security. Such has been the patient sufferance of these Colonies; and such is now the necessity which constrains them to alter their former Systems of Government. The history of the present King of Great Britain is a history of repeated injuries and usurpations, all having in direct object the establishment of an absolute Tyranny over these States. To prove this, let Facts be submitted to a candid world:

3   He has refused his Assent to Laws, the most wholesome and necessary for the public good.

4   He has forbidden his Governors to pass Laws of immediate and pressing importance, unless suspended in their operation till his Assent should be obtained; and when so suspended, he has utterly neglected to attend to them.

5   He has refused to pass other Laws for the accommodation of large districts of people, unless those people would relinquish the right of Representation in the Legislature, a right inestimable to them and formidable to tyrants only.

6   He has called together legislative bodies at places unusual, uncom-

fortable, and distant from the depository of their public Records, for the sole purpose of fatiguing them into compliance with his measures.

7   He has dissolved Representative Houses repeatedly, for opposing with manly firmness his invasions on the rights of the people.

8   He has refused for a long time, after such dissolutions, to cause others to be elected; whereby the Legislative powers, incapable of Annihilation, have returned to the People at large for their exercise; the State remaining in the mean time exposed to all the dangers of invasion from without, and convulsions within.

9   He has endeavoured to prevent the population of these States; for that purpose obstructing the Laws for Naturalization of Foreigners; refusing to pass others to encourage their migrations hither, and raising the conditions of new Appropriations of Lands.

10   He has obstructed the Administration of Justice, by refusing his Assent to Laws for establishing Judiciary powers.

11   He has made Judges dependent on his Will alone, for the tenure of their offices, and the amount and payment of their salaries.

12   He has erected a multitude of New Offices, and sent hither swarms of Officers to harass our people, and eat out their substance.

13   He has kept among us, in times of peace, Standing Armies, without the Consent of our legislatures.

14   He has affected to render the Military independent of and superior to the Civil power.

15   He has combined with others to subject us to a jurisdiction foreign to our constitution, and unacknowledged by our laws; giving his Assent to their Acts of pretended Legislation:

16   For quartering large bodies of armed troops among us:

17   For protecting them, by a mock Trial, from punishment for any Murders which they should commit on the Inhabitants of these States:

18   For cutting off our Trade with all parts of the world:

19   For imposing Taxes on us without our Consent:

20   For depriving us in many cases of the benefits of Trial by Jury:

21   For transporting us beyond Seas to be tried for pretended offences:

22   For abolishing the free System of English Laws in a neighbouring Province, establishing therein an Arbitrary government, and enlarging its Boundaries so as to render it at once an example and fit instrument for introducing the same absolute rule into these Colonies:

23   For taking away our Charters, abolishing our most valuable Laws and altering fundamentally the Forms of our Governments:

24   For suspending our own Legislatures, and declaring themselves invested with power to legislate for us in all cases whatsoever.

25   He has abdicated Government here by declaring us out of his Protection and waging War against us.

26   He has plundered our seas, ravaged our Coasts, burnt our towns, and destroyed the lives of our people.

27   He is at this time transporting large Armies of foreign Mercenaries to

compleat the works of death, desolation and tyranny, already begun with circumstances of Cruelty & perfidy scarcely paralleled in the most barbarous ages, and totally unworthy the Head of a civilized nation.

28   He has constrained our fellow Citizens taken Captive on the high Seas to bear Arms against their Country, to become the executioners of their friends and Brethren, or to fall themselves by their Hands.

29   He has excited domestic insurrections amongst us, and has endeavoured to bring on the inhabitants of our frontiers, the merciless Indian Savages, whose known rule of warfare is an undistinguished destruction of all ages, sexes and conditions.

30   In every stage of these Oppressions We have Petitioned for Redress in the most humble terms. Our repeated Petitions have been answered only by repeated injury. A Prince, whose character is thus marked by every act which may define a Tyrant, is unfit to be the ruler of a free people.

31   Nor have We been wanting in attentions to our British brethren. We have warned them from time to time of attempts by their legislature to extend an unwarrantable jurisdiction over us. We have reminded them of the circumstances of our emigration and settlement here. We have appealed to their native justice and magnanimity, and we have conjured them by the ties of our common kindred to disavow these usurpations, which would inevitably interrupt our connections and correspondence. They too have been deaf to the voice of justice and of consanguinity. We must, therefore, acquiesce in the necessity, which denounces our Separation, and hold them, as we hold the rest of mankind, Enemies in War, in Peace Friends.

32   WE THEREFORE the Representatives of the UNITED STATES OF AMER-ICA, in General Congress, Assembled, appealing to the Supreme Judge of the world for the rectitude of our intentions, do, in the Name and by Authority of the good People of these Colonies, solemnly publish and declare, That these United Colonies are and of Right ought to be FREE AND INDEPENDENT STATES; that they are Absolved from all Allegiance to the British Crown, and that all political connection between them and the State of Great Britain, is and ought to be totally dissolved; and that as FREE AND INDEPENDENT STATES, they have full Power to levy War, conclude Peace, contract Alliances, establish Commerce, and to do all other Acts and Things which INDEPENDENT states may of right do. AND for the support of this Declaration, with a firm reliance on the protection of divine Providence, we mutually pledge to each other our Lives, our Fortunes and our sacred Honor.

COMMENTARY

The Declaration begins by announcing what its signers intend to do. It then proceeds to explain the beliefs they hold—standards that serve as the basis for judging King George's government. It is only because the signers believe that governments exist to secure the inherent rights of "life, liberty, and the pursuit of happiness" that they can condemn the British rule. (If you believe, for instance, that governments exist to secure their own prosperity, you might find that the British rule was admirably trying to perform its job.) The explanation of concepts of government (paragraph 2) is appropriate here, therefore, because it functions as the statement of criteria for an evaluation. The writers of the Declaration are not simply sounding off.

Similarly, the rehearsal of the colonists' grievances against the king (paragraphs 3 to 29) is appropriate because it provides evidence. The largest part of the Declaration consists of this list of grievances. The decision on the part of Jefferson and his comrades to devote so much of their document to presenting "the facts" shows the very high value they put on the rational abilities of the human mind. (Their era is sometimes called the Age of Reason and they themselves Rationalists.) Without this section, the Declaration would sound merely like the angry protest of an unreasoning loser or the tantrum of a child. The colonists do not want to be mistaken for children.

After the presentation of evidence, the Declaration asserts that the preferable alternative to war—peaceful redress of grievances—has been tried and found ineffective. This claim justifies (note the transitional "therefore," paragraph 32) the conclusion that the colonists now have no alternative except independence.

There is very little discussion of feasibility here. To present details about the resources available for war might have divulged too much information to the enemy. To demonstrate the feasibility of the endeavor, the writers simply assert that they will rely upon God and upon their own willingness to sacrifice everything for this cause. The eloquent last phrases are a summons to everyone else who shares their beliefs and has suffered from the same injustices to do the same.

OUTLINE

    I. Introduction: statement of the problem—paragraph 1
   II. Demonstration that something must be done: that British rule has repeatedly violated the basic principles of true government—paragraphs 2–29
      A. Principles of government—paragraph 2
      B. British violations of those principles—paragraphs 3–29
  III. Consideration of the alternatives: peaceful negotiation has failed—paragraphs 30–31
  IV. Choice of the remaining best (only) alternative, brief demonstration of feasibility, and call to action—paragraph 32

SUGGESTIONS FOR WRITING

    1. Following the pattern of the Declaration of Independence, write a manifesto of your own. Show that a problem exists because someone or something does not conform to your criteria and that other alternatives have been tried

but have not worked. Conclude with an invitation to others to join you. Use some of the language of the Declaration if that seems appropriate. You might find the "Declaration of Sentiments" of the Woman's Suffrage Movement, modeled precisely upon the Declaration of Independence, useful.

DECLARATION OF SENTIMENTS—
Elizabeth Cady Stanton and Others

1   When, in the course of human events, it becomes necessary for one portion of the family of man to assume among the people of the earth a position different from that which they have hitherto occupied, but one to which the laws of nature and of nature's God entitle them, a decent respect to the opinions of mankind requires that they should declare the causes that impel them to such a course.

2   We hold these truths to be self-evident: that all men and women are created equal; that they are endowed by their Creator with certain inalienable rights; that among these are life, liberty, and the pursuit of happiness; that to secure these rights governments are instituted, deriving their just powers from the consent of the governed. Whenever any form of government becomes destructive of these ends, it is the right of those who suffer from it to refuse allegiance to it, and to insist upon the institution of a new government, laying its foundation on such principles, and organizing its powers in such form, as to them shall seem most likely to effect their safety and happiness. Prudence indeed, will dictate that governments long established should not be changed for light and transient causes; and accordingly all experience hath shown that mankind are more disposed to suffer, while evils are sufferable, than to right themselves by abolishing the forms to which they were accustomed. But when a long train of abuses and usurpations, pursuing invariably the same object evinces a design to reduce them under absolute despotism, it is their duty to throw off such government, and to provide new guards for their future security. Such has been the patient sufferance of the women under this government, and such is now the necessity which constrains them to demand the equal station to which they are entitled.

3   The history of mankind is a history of repeated injuries and usurpations on the part of man toward woman, having in direct object the establishment of an absolute tyranny over her. To prove this, let facts be submitted to a candid world.

4   He has never permitted her to exercise her inalienable right to the elective franchise.

5   He has compelled her to submit to laws, in the formation of which she had no voice.

6   He has withheld from her rights which are given to the most ignorant and degraded men—both natives and foreigners.

7   Having deprived her of this first right of a citizen, the elective franchise, thereby leaving her without representation in the halls of legislation, he has oppressed her on all sides.

8   He has made her, if married, in the eye of the law, civilly dead.

9   He has taken from her all right in property, even to the wages she earns.

10   He has made her, morally, an irresponsible being, as she can commit many crimes with impunity, provided they be done in the presence of her husband. In the covenant of marriage, she is compelled to promise obedience to her husband, he becoming, to all intents and purposes, her master—the law giving him power to deprive her of her liberty, and to administer chastisement.

Source. History of Woman Suffrage, ed. Elizabeth Cady Stanton, Susan B. Anthony, and Matilda Joslyn Gage, Vol I, 1848–1861 (New York: Fowler, 1881).

11   He has so framed the laws of divorce, as to what shall be the proper causes, and in case of separation, to whom the guardianship of the children shall be given, as to be wholly regardless of the happiness of women—the law, in all cases, going upon a false supposition of the supremacy of man, and giving all power into his hands.

12   After depriving her of all rights as a married woman, if single, and the owner of property, he has taxed her to support a government which recognizes her only when her property can be made profitable to it.

13   He has monopolized nearly all the profitable employments, and from those she is permitted to follow, she receives but a scanty remuneration. He closes against her all the avenues to wealth and distinction which he considers most honorable to himself. As a teacher of theology, medicine, or law, she is not known.

14   He has denied her the facilities for obtaining a thorough education, all colleges being closed against her.

15   He allows her in Church, as well as State, but a subordinate position, claiming Apostolic authority for her exclusion from the ministry, and, with some exceptions, from any public participation in the affairs of the Church.

16   He has created a false public sentiment by giving to the world a different code of morals for men and women, by which moral delinquencies which exclude women from society, are not only tolerated, but deemed of little account in man.

17   He has usurped the prerogative of Jehovah himself, claiming it as his right to assign for her a sphere of action, when that belongs to her conscience and to her God.

18   He has endeavored, in every way that he could, to destroy her confidence in her own powers, to lessen her self-respect, and to make her willing to lead a dependent and abject life.

19   Now, in view of this entire disfranchisement of one-half the people of this country, their social and religious degradation—in view of the unjust laws above mentioned, and because women do feel themselves aggrieved, oppressed, and fraudulently deprived of their most sacred rights, we insist that they have immediate admission to all the rights and privileges which belong to them as citizens of the United States.

20   In entering upon the great work before us, we anticipate no small amount of misconception, misrepresentation, and ridicule; but we shall use every instrumentality within our power to effect our object. We shall employ agents, circulate tracts, petition the State and National legislatures, and endeavor to enlist the pulpit and the press in our behalf. We hope this Convention will be followed by a series of Conventions embracing every part of the country.

2. Write a declaration in reply to either of the ones printed above. Pretend that you are King George or an official of the British government, or that you are a man defending the traditional concept of male dominance. The "facts," as well as the principles, will look rather different from this perspective. Every writer chooses the evidence and the governing generalizations that are appropriate to his purpose, so that it is possible to have two opposing manifestos without either of them telling lies: each simply reports a different segment of the truth. (How then does a reader know which to accept?)

science and
the sanctity of life

P. B. MEDAWAR

In this selection, Nobel Prize winner Medawar discusses a question of
eugenics (the improvement of the human species by scientifically planned
matings). Medawar proposes that we identify the people who are carriers
of certain genetic disorders and discourage them from marrying one
another. In this way we can prevent the birth of defective children. Medawar first defines the problem, taking care to explain the technical terms
his argument involves. He then describes one of the options, providing a
special environment for defective children once they are born, but rejects
it in favor of another, preventing their birth in the first place.

A moral problem is involved in this proposal: is it right to interfere
with people's private lives—to use scientific evidence to identify disease
carriers and then bring pressure upon them not to marry one another?
Rather than avoid this problem, Medawar confronts it openly, arguing that
we accept other limitations on our right to marry and should accept this
limitation too.

1   **S**ome "inborn" defects—some defects that are the direct consequence of
an individual's genetic make-up as it was fixed at the moment of conception
—are said to be of *recessive* determination. By a recessive defect is meant
one that is caused by, to put it crudely, a "bad" gene that must be present
in both the gametes that unite to form a fertilised egg, i.e., in both sperma-
tozoon and egg cell, not just in one or the other. If the bad gene is present
in only one of the gametes, the individual that grows out of its fusion with
the other is said to be a *carrier* (technically, a heterozygote).

2   Recessive defects are individually rather rare—their frequency is of the
order of one in ten thousand—but collectively they are most important.
Among them are, for example, phenylketonuria, a congenital inability to
handle a certain dietary constituent, the amino acid phenylalanine, a constituent of many proteins; galactosaemia, another inborn biochemical deficiency, the victims of which cannot cope metabolically with galactose, an
immediate derivative of milk sugar; and, more common than either, fibro-
cystic disease of the pancreas, believed to be the symptom of a generalised
disorder of mucus-secreting cells. All three are caused by particular single
genetic defects; but their secondary consequences are manifold and deep-
seated. The phenylketonuric baby is on the way to becoming an imbecile.
The victim of galactosaemia may become blind through cataract and be
mentally retarded.

3   Contrary to popular superstition, many congenital ailments can be pre-

Source. From *Encounter,* Copyright © 1966. Reprinted by permission of *Encounter,* Ltd.
(London).

vented or, if not prevented, cured. But in this context prevention and cure have very special meanings.

4 The phenylketonuric or galactosaemic child may be protected from the consequences of his genetic lesion by keeping him on a diet free from phenylalanine in the one case or lactose in the other. This is a most unnatural proceeding, and much easier said than done, but I take it no one would be prepared to argue that it was an unwarrantable interference with the workings of providence. It is not a cure in the usual medical sense because it neither removes nor repairs the underlying congenital deficiency. What it does is to create around the patient a special little world, a microcosm free from phenylalanine or galactose as the case may be, in which the genetic deficiency cannot express itself outwardly.

5 Now consider the underlying morality of prevention.

6 We can prevent phenylketonuria by preventing the genetic conjunction responsible for it in the first instance, i.e., by preventing the coming together of an egg cell and a sperm each carrying that same one harmful recessive gene. All but a very small proportion of overt phenylketonurics are the children of parents who are both carriers—carriers, you remember, being the people who inherited the gene from one only of the two gametes that fused at their conception. Carriers greatly outnumber the overtly afflicted. When two carriers of the same gene marry and bear children, one quarter of their children (on the average) will be normal, one quarter will be afflicted, and one half will be carriers like themselves. We shall accomplish our purpose, therefore, if, having identified the carriers—another thing easier said than done, but it *can* be done, and in an increasing number of recessive disorders—we try to discourage them *from marrying each other* by pointing out the likely consequences if they do so. The arithmetic of this is not very alarming. In a typical recessive disease, about one marriage in every five or ten thousand would be discouraged or warned against, and each disappointed party would have between fifty and a hundred other mates to choose from.

7 If this policy were to be carried out, the overt incidence of diseases like phenylketonuria, in which carriers can be identified, would fall almost to zero between one generation and the next.

8 Nevertheless the first reaction to such a proposal may be one of outrage. Here is medical officiousness planning yet another insult to human dignity, yet another deprivation of the rights of man. First it was vaccination and then fluoride; if now people are not to be allowed to marry whom they please, why not make a clean job of it and overthrow the Crown or the U.S. Constitution?

9 But reflect for a moment. What is being suggested is that a certain small proportion of marriages should be discouraged for genetic reasons, to do our best to avoid bringing into the world children who are biochemically crippled. In all cultures marriages are already prohibited for genetic reasons—the prohibition, for example, of certain degrees of inbreeding (the

exact degree varies from one culture or religion to another). It is difficult to see why the prohibition should have arisen to some extent independently in different cultures unless it grew out of the common observation that abnormalities are more common in the children of marriages between close relatives than in children generally. Thus the prohibition of marriage for genetic reasons has an immemorial authority behind it. As to the violation of human dignity entailed by performing tests on engaged couples that are no more complex or offensive than blood tests, let me say only this: if anyone thinks or has ever thought that religion, wealth, or colour are matters that may properly be taken into account when deciding whether or not a certain marriage is a suitable one, then let him not dare to suggest that the genetic welfare of human beings should not be given equal weight.

10   I think myself that engaged couples should themselves decide, and I am pretty certain they would be guided by the thought of the welfare of their future children. When it came to be learned about twenty years ago that marriages between Rhesus-positive men and Rhesus-negative women might lead to the birth of children afflicted by haemolytic disease, a number of young couples are said to have ended their engagements—needlessly, in most cases, because the dangers were over-estimated through not being understood. But that is evidence enough that young people marrying today are not likely to take a stand upon some hypothetical right to give birth to defective children if, by taking thought, they can do otherwise.

COMMENTARY

One of Medawar's major tasks is to explain scientific concepts so that we can follow his discussion. Defining the problem, usually a rather brief part of a recommendation, here requires two substantial paragraphs tightly packed with information. In considering the alternatives, Medawar must clarify even such common terms as "prevention" and "cure" because they involve unusual meanings in this specialized context. Notice, however, that he is not trying to impress us with his technical vocabulary. He uses it only when he really needs it. It virtually disappears from the last part of the essay where he defends the morality of his proposal. In discussing morality, he and we are equals, and his language can become less formal (consider such conversational phrases as "let me say only this" or "I am pretty certain").

The difficult part of this recommendation, aside from the need for careful definition, is the evaluation of the alternatives. Medawar does not bother to say that on utilitarian criteria of efficiency or expense, it is better to prevent the birth of defective children than to provide special care for them throughout their lives. From the utilitarian viewpoint, prevention is obviously better, and the obvious does not need to be stated. It is from the moral viewpoint that Medawar's proposal is questionable. His argument is that since we already accept prohibitions against marrying our near relatives, we should accept further eugenic limitations on our potential mates.

Do you agree with that? Are you persuaded by his reference to "a number of young couples" who apparently agreed not to marry when they thought their marriages would produce damaged babies? Do you think that most young people would or should be "guided by the thought of the welfare of their future children," as Medawar does—or are young people guided by other kinds of thoughts? Finally, does Medawar seem aware of all the alternatives? (The date of his article is 1966.) What else might be done about "biochemically crippled" children?

OUTLINE

I. Introduction: the definition of a recessive defect, two examples—paragraphs 1–2

II. The alternatives: "cure" or prevention—paragraphs 3–7
   A. What "cure" means—paragraph 4
   B. What "prevention" means—paragraphs 5–7

III. Evaluation of the policy of prevention—paragraphs 8–10
   A. A hostile reaction, outrage—paragraph 8
   B. Defense of the policy—paragraphs 9–10

SUGGESTIONS FOR WRITING

1. Write an essay recommending a different solution to the problem Medawar describes; show why your alternative is preferable to his.

2. Medawar is interested in recommending an overall policy, not in developing it in detail. Most people, however, want to know how a policy will work before they accept it. Write an essay recommending a way to implement the policy of "trying to discourage" carriers of genetic disorders from marrying one another. What kinds of pressure would it be right to bring upon such people? What group would be responsible for doing the discouraging (doctors, professional family counselors, lawyers, "peers" defined in some specific way, etc.)?

3. Medawar's subject of eugenics belongs to the larger subject of medical ethics: the decisions about human values that science permits or forces us to confront. Other problems in medical ethics are abortion, organ transplantation (see Ritchie-Calder, p. 559), and euthanasia. Recommend a solution, or recommend that we *not* adopt a proposed solution, to some problem involving both science and values. Follow Medawar's overall procedure—explain the problem carefully, consider alternatives, and defend the one you prefer. (Discuss feasibility also, if necessary.)

how to
write potent copy

DAVID OGILVY

This chapter from Ogilvy's book *Confessions of an Advertising Man* is a "how to": a recommendation that something be done in a certain way. It uses lists and short paragraphs to present a set of basic instructions or general principles, each supported by detailed advice and by examples.

Assuming that you want to write advertising copy, Ogilvy tells you how. His proof that his way is preferable to others and is feasible is confined to brief explanatory paragraphs after each major item of his recommendation. He quotes authorities (paragraphs 29 and 32) and provides numerous examples and anecdotes; but most of all, he relies on his own reputation. These are techniques that worked for Ogilvy himself—and made him a wealthy man.

Do the ads you see in current magazines confirm or contradict his policy?

I. HEADLINES

1   **t**he headline is the most important element in most advertisements. It is the telegram which decides the reader whether to read the copy.

2   On the average, five times as many people read the headline as read the body copy. When you have written your headline, you have spent eighty cents out of your dollar.

3   If you haven't done some selling in your headline, you have wasted 80 per cent of your client's money. The wickedest of all sins is to run an advertisement *without* a headline. Such headless wonders are still to be found; I don't envy the copywriter who submits one to me.

4   A change of headline can make a difference of ten to one in sales. I never write fewer than sixteen headlines for a single advertisement, and I observe certain guides in writing them:

5   (1) The headline is the "ticket on the meat." Use it to flag down the readers who are prospects for the kind of product you are advertising. If you are selling a remedy for bladder weakness, display the words BLADDER WEAKNESS in your headline; they catch the eye of everyone who suffers from this inconvenience. If you want *mothers* to read your advertisement, display MOTHERS in your headline. And so on.

6   Conversely, do not say anything in your headline which is likely to *exclude* any readers who might be prospects for your product. Thus, if you are advertising a product which can be used equally well by men and

women, don't slant your headline at women alone; it would frighten men away.

7   (2) Every headline should appeal to the reader's *self-interest*. It should promise her a benefit, as in my headline for Helena Rubinstein's Hormone Cream: HOW WOMEN OVER 35 CAN LOOK YOUNGER.

8   (3) Always try to inject *news* into your headlines, because the consumer is always on the lookout for new products, or new ways to use an old product, or new improvements in an old product.

9   The two most powerful words you can use in a headline are FREE and NEW. You can seldom use FREE, but you can almost always use NEW— if you try hard enough.

10   (4) Other words and phrases which work wonders are HOW TO SUDDENLY, NOW, ANNOUNCING, INTRODUCING, IT'S HERE, JUST ARRIVED, IMPORTANT DEVELOPMENT, IMPROVEMENT, AMAZING, SENSATIONAL, REMARKABLE, REVOLUTIONARY, STARTLING, MIRACLE, MAGIC, OFFER, QUICK, EASY, WANTED, CHALLENGE, ADVICE TO, THE TRUTH ABOUT, COMPARE, BARGAIN, HURRY, LAST CHANCE.

11   Don't turn up your nose at these clichés. They may be shopworn, but they work. That is why you see them turn up so often in the headlines of mail-order advertisers and others who can measure the results of their advertisements.

12   Headlines can be strengthened by the inclusion of *emotional* words, like DARLING, LOVE, FEAR, PROUD, FRIEND, and BABY. One of the most provocative advertisements which has come out of our agency showed a girl in a bathtub, talking to her lover on the telephone. The headline: *Darling, I'm having the most extraordinary experience . . . I'm head over heels in* DOVE.

13   (5) Five times as many people read the headline as read the body copy, so it is important that these glancers should at least be told what brand is being advertised. That is why you should always include the brand name in your headlines.

14   (6) Include your selling promise in your headline. This requires long headlines. When the New York University School of Retailing ran head-line tests with the cooperation of a big department store, they found that headlines of ten words or longer, containing news and information, con-sistently sold more merchandise than short headlines.

15   Headlines containing six to twelve words pull more coupon returns than short headlines, and there is no significant difference between the readership of twelve-word headlines and the readership of three-word headlines. The best headline I ever wrote contained *eighteen* words: *At Sixty Miles an Hour the Loudest Noise in the New Rolls-Royce comes from the electric clock.*[1]

---

[1] When the chief engineer at the Rolls-Royce factory read this, he shook his head sadly and said, "It is time we did something about that damned clock."

16 (7) People are more likely to read your body copy if your headline arouses their curiosity; so you should end your headline with a lure to read on.

17 (8) Some copywriters write *tricky* headlines—puns, literary allusions, and other obscurities. This is a sin.

18 In the average newspaper your headline has to compete for attention with 350 others. Research has shown that readers travel so fast through this jungle that they don't stop to decipher the meaning of obscure headlines. Your headline must *telegraph* what you want to say, and it must telegraph it in plain language. Don't play games with the reader.

19 In 1960 the *Times Literary Supplement* attacked the whimsical tradition in British advertising, calling it "self-indulgent—a kind of middle-class private joke, apparently designed to amuse the advertiser and his client." Amen.

20 (9) Research shows that it is dangerous to use *negatives* in headlines. If, for example, you write OUR SALT CONTAINS NO ARSENIC, many readers will miss the negative and go away with the impression that you wrote OUR SALT CONTAINS ARSENIC.

21 (10) Avoid *blind* headlines—the kind which mean nothing unless you read the body copy underneath them; most people *don't*.

II. BODY COPY

22 When you sit down to write your body copy, pretend that you are talking to the woman on your right at a dinner party. She has asked you, "I am thinking of buying a new car. Which would you recommend?" Write your copy as if you were answering that question.

23 (1) Don't beat about the bush—go straight to the point. Avoid analogies of the "just as, so too" variety. Dr. Gallup has demonstrated that these two-stage arguments are generally misunderstood.

24 (2) Avoid superlatives, generalizations, and platitudes. Be specific and factual. Be enthusiastic, friendly, and memorable. Don't be a bore. Tell the truth, but make the truth fascinating.

25 How long should your copy be? It depends on the product. If you are advertising chewing gum, there isn't much to tell, so make your copy short. If, on the other hand, you are advertising a product which has a great many different qualities to recommend it, write long copy: the more you tell, the more you sell.

26 There is a universal belief in lay circles that people won't read long copy. Nothing could be farther from the truth. Claude Hopkins once wrote five pages of solid text for Schlitz beer. In a few months, Schlitz moved up from fifth place to first. I once wrote a page of solid text for Good Luck Margarine, with most gratifying results.

27   Research shows that readership falls off rapidly up to fifty words of copy, but drops very little between fifty and 500 words. In my first Rolls-Royce advertisement I used 719 words—piling one fascinating fact on another. In the last paragraph I wrote, "People who feel diffident about driving a Rolls-Royce can buy a Bentley." Judging from the number of motorists who picked up the word "diffident" and bandied it about, I concluded that the advertisement was thoroughly read. In the next one I used 1400 words.

28   Every advertisement should be a *complete* sales pitch for your product. It is unrealistic to assume that consumers will read a *series* of advertisements for the same product. You should shoot the works in every advertisement, on the assumption that it is the only chance you will ever have to sell your product to the reader—*now or never.*

29   Says Dr. Charles Edwards of the graduate School of Retailing at New York University, "The more facts you tell, the more you sell. An advertisement's chance for success invariably increases as the number of pertinent merchandise facts included in the advertisement increases."

30   In my first advertisement for Puerto Rico's Operation Bootstrap, I used 961 words, and persuaded Beardsley Ruml to sign them. Fourteen thousand readers clipped the coupon from this advertisement, and scores of them later established factories in Puerto Rico. The greatest professional satisfaction I have yet had is to see the prosperity in Puerto Rican communities which had lived on the edge of starvation for four hundred years before I wrote my advertisement. If I had confined myself to a few vacuous generalities, nothing would have happened.

31   We have even been able to get people to read long copy about gasoline. One of our Shell advertisements contained 617 words, and 22 per cent of male readers read more than half of them.

32   Vic Schwab tells the story of Max Hart (of Hart, Schaffner & Marx) and his advertising manager, George L. Dyer, arguing about long copy. Dyer said, "I'll bet you ten dollars I can write a newspaper page of solid type and you'd read every word of it."

33   Hart scoffed at the idea. "I don't have to write a line of it to prove my point," Dyer replied. "I'll only tell you the headline: THIS PAGE IS ALL ABOUT MAX HART."

34   Advertisers who put coupons in their advertisements *know* that short copy doesn't sell. In split-run tests, long copy invariably outsells short copy.

35   Do I hear someone say that no copywriter can write long advertisements unless his media department gives him big spaces to work with? This question should not arise, because the copywriter should be consulted before planning the media schedule.

36   (3) You should always include testimonials in your copy. The reader finds it easier to believe the endorsement of a fellow consumer than the puffery of an anonymous copywriter. Says Jim Young, one of the best copywriters alive today, "Every type of advertiser has the same problem:

namely to be believed. The mail-order man knows nothing so potent for this purpose as the testimonial, yet the general advertiser seldom uses it."

37   Testimonials from celebrities get remarkably high readership, and if they are honestly written they still do not seem to provoke incredulity. The better known the celebrity, the more readers you will attract. We have featured Queen Elizabeth and Winston Churchill in "Come to Britain" advertisements, and we were able to persuade Mrs. Roosevelt to make television commercials for Good Luck Margarine. When we advertised charge accounts for Sears, Roebuck, we reproduced the credit card of Ted Williams, "recently traded by Boston to Sears."

38   Sometimes you can cast your entire copy in the form of a testimonial. My first advertisement for Austin cars took the form of a letter from an "anonymous diplomat" who was sending his son to Groton with money he had saved driving an Austin—a well-aimed combination of snobbery and economy. Alas, a perspicacious *Time* editor guessed that I was the anonymous diplomat, and asked the headmaster of Groton to comment. Dr. Crocker was so cross that I decided to send my son to Hotchkiss.

39   (4) Another profitable gambit is to give the reader helpful advice, or service. It hooks about 75 per cent more readers than copy which deals entirely with the product.

40   One of our Rinso advertisements told housewives how to remove stains. It was better read (Starch) and better remembered (Gallup) than any detergent advertisement in history. Unfortunately, however, it forgot to feature Rinso's main selling promise—that Rinso washes whiter; for this reason it should never have run.[2]

41   (5) I have never admired the *belles lettres* school of advertising, which reached its pompous peak in Theodore F. MacManus' famous advertisement for Cadillac, "The Penalty of Leadership," and Ned Jordan's classic, "Somewhere West of Laramie." Forty years ago the business community seems to have been impressed by these pieces of purple prose, but I have always thought them absurd; they did not give the reader a single *fact*. I share Claude Hopkins' view that "fine writing is a distinct disadvantage. So is unique literary style. They take attention away from the subject."

42   (6) Avoid bombast. Raymond Rubicam's famous slogan for Squibb, "The priceless ingredient of every product is the honor and integrity of its maker," reminds me of my father's advice: when a company boasts about its integrity, or a woman about her virtue, avoid the former and cultivate the latter.

---

2 The photograph showed several different kinds of stain—lipstick, coffee, shoe-polish, blood and so forth. The blood was my own; I am the only copywriter who has ever *bled* for his client.

43 (7) Unless you have some special reason to be solemn and pretentious, write your copy in the colloquial language which your customers use in everyday conversation. I have never acquired a sufficiently good ear for vernacular American to write it, but I admire copywriters who can pull it off, as in this unpublished pearl from a dairy farmer:

> Carnation Milk is the best in the land,
> Here I sit with a can in my hand.
> No tits to pull, no hay to pitch,
> Just punch a hole in the son-of-a-bitch.

44 It is a mistake to use highfalutin language when you advertise to uneducated people. I once used the word OBSOLETE in a headline, only to discover that 43 per cent of housewives had no idea what it meant. In another headline, I used the word INEFFABLE, only to discover that I didn't know what it meant myself.

45 However, many copywriters of my vintage err on the side of underestimating the educational level of the population. Philip Hauser, head of the Sociology Department at the University of Chicago, draws attention to the changes which are taking place:

> The increasing exposure of the population to formal schooling . . . can be expected to effect important changes in . . . the style of advertising. . . . Messages aimed at the "average" American on the assumption that he has had less than a grade school education are likely to find themselves with a declining or disappearing clientele.[3]

46 Meanwhile, all copywriters should read Dr. Rudolph Flesch's *Art of Plain Talk*. It will persuade them to use short words, short sentences, short paragraphs, and highly *personal* copy.

47 Aldous Huxley, who once tried his hand at writing advertisements, concluded that "any trace of literariness in an advertisement is fatal to its success. Advertisement writers may not be lyrical, or obscure, or in any way esoteric. They must be universally intelligible. A good advertisement has this in common with drama and oratory, that it must be immediately comprehensible and directly moving."[4]

48 (8) Resist the temptation to write the kind of copy which wins awards. I am always gratified when I win an award, but most of the campaigns which produce *results* never win awards, because they don't draw attention to themselves.

49 The juries that bestow awards are never given enough information about the *results* of the advertisements they are called upon to judge. In the absence of such information, they rely on their opinions, which are always warped toward the highbrow.

---

[3] *Scientific American* (October 1962).
[4] *Essays Old And New* (Harper & Brothers, 1927). Charles Lamb and Byron also wrote advertisements. So did Bernard Shaw, Hemingway, Marquand, Sherwood Anderson, and Faulkner—none of them with any degree of success.

50 (9) Good copywriters have always resisted the temptation to *entertain*. Their achievement lies in the number of new products they get off to a flying start. In a class by himself stands Claude Hopkins, who is to advertising what Escoffier is to cooking. By today's standards, Hopkins was an unscrupulous barbarian, but technically he was the supreme master. Next I would place Raymond Rubicam, George Cecil, and James Webb Young, all of whom lacked Hopkins' ruthless salesmanship, but made up for it by their honesty, by the broader range of their work, and by their ability to write civilized copy when the occasion required it. Next I would place John Caples, the mail-order specialist from whom I have learned much.

51 These giants wrote their advertisements for newspapers and magazines. It is still too early to identify the best writers for television.

COMMENTARY

Canby (p. 391) complains about the fragmentation of substantial and coherent paragraphs into short and unconnected sentence sequences. He blames this change on journalists who treat readers as if they are "feeble-minded" people who cannot digest evidence in support of a thesis sentence.

In advertisements, the paragraph is often reduced to a skeletal sentence, sometimes accompanied by a photograph ("Marlboro country") or embedded in a tune (the "Pepsi generation"). The aim of such multimedia appeals is clearly to the senses, not the mind. Ogilvy's essay could serve as an example of Canby's point about the deterioration of paragraphs. (Also note Gerstenberg, p. 532) Ogilvy writes no paragraph with more than five sentences. Most of the time he is satisfied with two or three, sometimes with one. Does his brevity invite a thoughtless acceptance of his ideas? If so, it is not a characteristic to be admired. Or is it a style appropriate to an adman, whose intention is not the same as that of an essayist trying to describe or prove or evaluate something completely?

However we may judge him, Ogilvy is an extremely effective writer. He has probably had more influence on human behavior than many better-known writers of our time (see paragraph 30). And he practices what he preaches: simple diction, short sentences, colloquial usage, lots of eye-catching italics and capital letters.

OUTLINE

SUGGESTIONS FOR WRITING

1. Starting with Ogilvy's comments on the virtues and defects of the two automobile advertisements, write a "how to" recommending ways to improve a current advertisement or promotional campaign. For example, if you always hurry past the Salvation Army's Christmas bell-ringing appeals (trying your best to look busy and penniless), you know what *doesn't* work, at least for you, in that appeal. What advice can you offer to make people like yourself contribute their loose change?

2. Compare two or three essays of recommendation in this text. Do they appeal more to our senses and sentiments or to our reasoning abilities?

3. Write a "how to" for writing recommendation essays, concentrating on one aspect of the process. For example, write a "how to write introductions to recommendations" (which introductions worked best for you?). Or write a "how to use emotional language in recommendations: how to succeed without really crying."

4. The article on Franklin's legacy printed below appeared in the annual report of a company that manages people's savings. Its purpose, evidently, is to encourage readers to save money at interest. It is a recommendation based on an account of something that happened. The sequence of events illustrates the truth of the Franklin proverbs that appear at the beginning of the article. Proverbs are often compressed recommendations.

Choose some proverb that makes a recommendation and illustrate it with a story.

A BEN FRANKLIN LEGACY

A penny saved is two pence clear. A pin a-day is a groat a-year. Save and have.

Little strokes fell great oaks.

He that can have patience can have what he will.

1   These familiar words remind us of Ben Franklin's preoccupation with the virtues of Thrift, Industry, and well-spent Time.

2   Time, Franklin knew, could be an ally or a foe. But, fortunately for the city of Boston, he knew how to use Time as an ally in the accumulation of wealth.

Source. Courtesy of the Research Equity Fund, Inc.

3   In 1791, Mr. Franklin gave 1,000 pounds ($5,000) to the Town of Boston, saying: "The said sum of one thousand pounds sterling if accepted by the Inhabitants of the Town of Boston, shall be managed under the direction of the Selectmen, who are to let out the same upon Interest at 5% per annum to such married artificers under the age of twenty-five years, as have served an Apprenticeship in said Town," the money not to be touched for one hundred years. Franklin projected that the 1,000 pounds would then be 131 thousand pounds of "which I would have the Managers . . . lay out 100,000 pounds in Public Works. The remaining thirty-one thousand pounds to be let out at interest in the manner above directed for another hundred years. . . . At the end of this second Term if no unfortunate accident has prevented the operation, the sum will be four millions and sixty-one thousand Pounds."

4   By 1893, the original $5,000 had grown to $424,945. The managers of the fund then divided this sum into two parts: $322,490 for Public Works; and $102,455 to be reinvested for another hundred years.

5   By 1973, that part of the money set aside for loans ($102,455) had grown to $2,809,305. That money is now being lent (at interest) to third and fourth year students at the Schools of Medicine of Boston, Harvard and Tufts University.

6   By 1905, the $322,490 set aside for Public Works had grown to $408,000. At this point Andrew Carnegie matched the fund's value, bringing the total to $916,000. This money was then used to establish and support the Franklin Technical Institute which trains its students in applied engineering. In 1973, the Institute Building was appraised for $3,231,000 with $379,360 outstanding for additional expansion.

7   Times were trying for this young country in 1791. There have been trying times since. But witness the results of Ben Franklin's faith in his country's Industry . . . plus Interest . . . plus Time. The original $5,000 plus the $408,000 added by Mr. Carnegie has an estimated value of $6,419,665 today!

life between
two racial worlds
KATHLEEN TAMAGAWA (ELDRIDGE)

Tamagawa, who recommends against interracial marriage, is herself a product of it. In fact, her story puts one in mind of a sort of marital yo-yo. Her mother was an Adams, and her son is an Eldridge—standard Anglo-American names. She, however, is "an ultimate, international, legal absurdity," a "prize freak" (paragraph 89), an outsider wherever she goes. The unhappiness of her personal experience leads to her negative recommendation: "I do not approve of Eurasian marriages. I do not approve of international marriages." Marriage against racial and ethnic boundaries is only a pseudo-solution to social problems, she believes, not a real one.

(This article is a condensation of Tamagawa's 250-page autobiography. Obviously many details have been sacrificed in order to compress her story into a short narrative that is both coherent and convincing.)

1   **t**he trouble with me is my ancestry. I really should not have been born. No, I am not illegitimate, but just an outlawed product of a legal marriage. Illegitimacy is often inconspicuous and easily concealed and sometimes it is even paraded for purposes of publicity. My problem goes deeper than that, for no law can change, no later ceremony right it—the problem of ancestry will remain.

2   My parents came from two small islands on opposite sides of the Earth. My mother was "North of Ireland," my father is Japanese, and I have faced the traditions of two worlds, so to speak: an Occidental and an Oriental. Ireland and Japan! Even an instant's consideration of that combination will convey the thought that such a field of battle for life needs be a "scene of tragedy and intense gaiety."

3   My father came to America when he was a little boy of eleven. In those days when Japan was first opened, it was progressive for young Japan to accept gracefully and completely the new world. So Father was sent here as a child to enter our Chicago public schools and study our strange barbaric customs.

4   He must have been a likeable chap, for in my long and intimate dealings with him as a parent, he has always won my total admiration. It was in high school that he met my uncle Frank, who became his best friend. Uncle Frank was not an ordinary person; in fact, none of the Adamses were ordinary.

5   Some one sent me a newspaper clipping just the other day headed, "The Adams Still Survive." Most of it spoke of the American branch, but toward the end it said, "As a family they have been inclined to advocate unpopular causes, to speak out in meeting and sometimes to make themselves obnoxious. But no one has ever questioned their ability, their patriotism, their honesty of purpose, or their integrity of character." I can't resist the temptation to quote this, because it so typically describes my mother. I don't know whether she included my father among her early advocacy of unpopular causes, but when Uncle Frank brought him home she promptly fell in love with him.

6   Grandmother disapproved. She disapproved all over the map, so much so, in fact, that when her husband's sisters sent for one of the children to "finish" in Europe, at the time of my grandfather's death, it was Mother who was chosen. I'm sure my grandmother must have recognized all the danger my father was to her daughter, who was a real Adams—"inclined to advocate unpopular causes, to speak out in meeting and to make them-

selves obnoxious." I can see her now, in that old Chicago house, settling that "outlandish affair of Kate's"—packing Mother off to Europe to "get her senses."

7   My mother stayed six years in Europe, yet all the while was answering Father's missives. Perhaps words are nothing, nothing but pleasant little tinkling symbols blown upon white fields of blank paper, unless they might be judged by their effectiveness upon the reader. Father's words brought Mother home from Europe, brought her home against the wishes of the Adams aunts, of my inflexible grandmother and her own better judgment, and were, in a way, responsible for my very being.

8   Her marriage to Father was the result of so many causes that one might almost believe it to have been fate. Besides my father's love for her there was this lack of sympathy at home and her own desire for the extraordinary. Someone called her a woman with a "flair." She revelled in adventure and daring; after all, she was the daughter of "Dare-Devil-Dick-Adams," who had been arrested time and again for driving six horses tandem through the streets of Londonderry. Then, too, my father was very much in the position of an "unpopular cause."

9   They eloped.

10   For Mother an elopement seems quite in season, but for my father it seems too fantastic to be true. Young men in Japan still marry according to the dictates of their family . . . and these two eloped in eighteen eighty something. For him to marry anyone of a different race was astonishing enough, for he came of good family, but for him to marry without his family's consent and against the wishes of hers is, indeed, inconceivable from a Japanese standpoint.

11   Grandmother was essentially cold, but when she heard the news, she simply froze. This blue white glacier in her soul remained intact until I unconsciously began thawing it at the age of three. During the interim Kate's name was nonexistent in that household and woe to any reference to Japan. It was Uncle Frank who, making a trip east, went a little out of his way to see the banished Kate. He begged Mother to forget, forgive and take Father and me home to Chicago, to Grandmother. . . .

12   I don't know the exact details of the war which he must have fought with Grandmother on his return to Chicago, but the result was that my earliest memories are all of that rather grim household with its ultra polished floors and its slippery Turkish rugs.

13   It's well that tonsils and appendixes had not become the rage then, or I should undoubtedly have lost mine. Everything was "done," everything that could possibly improve me, but the thing they could not change and which I did not escape, was my heritage—the "Japanese," this thought-stimulating, imagination-firing label which inevitably leads to complications.

14   To the friends who visited us in those days, I felt myself to be a comicality, a toy; I was often spoken of as a "Japanese doll," or worse still as the "cute," little Japanese. My mother's guests found in me what Pierre Loti found in all Japan, "qui n'a pas l'air sérieux, qui fait l'effet d'une

chose pour rire."* I felt this more keenly than I understood it. I had never been to Japan; I was as innocent of any real knowledge of the Japanese as those who visited us, but whatever I did, of good or of bad, was sure to be because I was Japanese.

15   These mental pit-falls surprised me, and alienated me from all the rest of the world, even from old, fat Nan, the colored wash woman.

16   One lovely summer's afternoon when I was about six, I was down in the basement, where I spent much of my time. Our cat had had kittens and while Nan was busy with the family washing, I watched the antics of the sprawling kittens over their languid mother. Suddenly it occurred to me that the large collie dog across the street might also be interested in the new kittens. Mother was in the attic when she heard my voice in the side yard, "Come along, Friskey, I want to show you our nice, new kittens. . . ."

17   She rushed down three long flights of stairs only to find a revolving mass of cat and dog among the furnace pipes. Nan's wig had been snatched from her head in the mix-up and every movable article in the laundry room displaced.

18   "Oh, Mother," I cried, choking on my tears, "I didn't know they would do that!"

19   I shall never forget how funny Nan looked without her wig or how thought-inspiring her words. "Maybe cats and dogs don't have no fights in Japan, but they sure do in the U-u-nited States."

20   Strange, distant and delightful Japan, land of childhood dreams, where anything might be! But all of my encounters with this mythical Japan were not so fascinating. There was the dirty-faced boy who sat on the back fence calling, "Chink! Chink!" whenever I ventured into his presence in search of a playmate.

21   Hurrying back to my mother and weeping real tears brought small comfort, for she only said, "Why didn't you tell him you were not a Chink?" She did not seem to understand my problem, for she never, even to her dying day, admitted that there was, or could be, a problem.

22   "But, Mother," I parried, on that first occasion, "you told me never to contradict."

23   This sent the family into peals of mirth.

24   But I see it as an early tragedy, however funny, for what could I have told the young warrior on the back fence? That I was not a "Chink"— only a "Jap"? My childish instinct had but introduced me to the polite withdrawal as one of the few possible responses to other people's little phantasms concerning me. True, I have long since reached the saturation point, and now frequently view with intense gaiety the mental gyrations of my critics.

25   At that time I was attending John Dewey's School of Education, but there I was the very conspicuous Japanese. This was exactly what they strove to avoid, but their constant reassurance made one doubt. There was

---

* "Who takes nothing seriously and seems like something to laugh at."

Barr, a Mexican girl who came each day with her swarthy Mexican nurse, there was a Dutch boy with a peculiarly blurred accent, there was a French Miss whose dresses were always copied by sewing mothers, there was Aie Fujita, a real Japanese child, the consul's little girl, and there were still a good majority of thorough Anglo-Saxons for contrast. Our teachers constantly reiterated that "All nations are the same. Though the little Dutch boys wear wooden shoes and the little Chinese ladies pinch their feet and the little Eskimos wear fur boots, we are all the same, we are just alike. One human family." Dear teachers, kind, well meaning souls who so earnestly fought to blanket the word "human." But this little polyglot community of my early school days was "human" enough to make us feel our differences. We were a collection of freaks, of children with race contrasts or faddist mothers and we never doubted it for an instant. How many internationalists make this same mistake! Do they ever convince?

26   Every summer, Mother and I made a pilgrimage to Forest Hall. The long summer months spent there brought me a fulfillment of love for America which can never be broken. Slowly and secretly this country came my native land. Secretly, because at the time my mother had taught me to say, "Grandmother, Mother and Uncle Frank are British, but Father and I are Japanese," and to look forward to a time when I should find my real home in that remote, unknown Japan.

27   But the peace and security of these early days were all shattered and broken by the death of my Uncle Frank. My grandmother, for the only time in my remembrance of her, seemed crushed. But strangest of all my mother and father seemed to have lost something vital from their relationship. All the pleasant chatter and intimacy were gone. As for myself, I buried all of my happiest childhood in his grave. And then, one day, I was thirteen at the time, my mother announced that we were going to Japan as Father was being sent out by the Corticelli Silk Company as a silk buyer.

28   I dreaded leaving my grandmother, for I could not readjust myself so suddenly to the new order, and my cousins became doubly dear. Now that I was actually going, I lost my curiosity about Japan, I was not at all sure that I wanted to see Japan after all. I began to understand that what was for my mother a flaring adventure, and for my father a turning homeward, was for me only the tragedy of tearing away all my early roots of home and homeland.

29   My only consoling thought was that at last I would cease to be "une chose pour rire"—"the little Japanese"—a toy for the passing whim of the public mind. In other words, I was at last to become ordinary, inconspicuous. I was to feel a oneness with a people. I should no longer be "different." It is only when one can understand my utter faith in my Orientalism that one can glimpse the extent of my disappointment and disillusionment.

30   Disillusionment can be a comedy and a tragedy all rolled into one! I had believed that I was Japanese and that Japan was my home. Why

should I have doubted this when no one had ever suggested otherwise, when everyone, in fact, had assured me that it was so?

31   Fear is said to be man's greatest emotion and with fear I greeted Japan. And with every step I took after alighting from our ship at Yokohama, my original fear increased. Nothing I had been taught, told or imagined was in the least like Japan, and, this much being true, what was I to expect? Such disillusionment gave me an uncertainty as to everything in the world. No kitten ever put in a cage with wild cats had more instincts for self-preservation than I and to me Japan was even worse than wild cats—it was gargoyles and disenchantment.

32   In Chicago I had been merely conspicuous in what now appeared to have been a limited social group. In Yokohama I was something far worse than conspicuous; I was a regular show for the entire city! I was not even going to be able to walk down the street without a crowd forming. This was demolition of illusion with a vengeance. My only alternative was not to care and this I could not quite do, for I was half Japanese.

33   "What does the word *ijin san* mean?" I asked at last of my father.

34   His look was full of sympathy as he answered quietly, "It means foreigner."

35   The facts were these—in America I was Japanese. In Japan I was an American. I had an Oriental father who wished to live like an Occidental and an Irish mother who wished to live like a Japanese. I had a series of eccentric traditions on my Western side and a thousand unknown, silent Tamagawas, buried in their own family cemetery, on the other.

36   My mother's friends had thought of me as a decoration, or a gimcrack; and my father's friends now thought of me as a barbarism and a blemish. I had had an uncle in America who had played doll's store on the ironing board for my amusement, and I now had an uncle in Japan who sat on a cushion, in the mysterious dimness of an inner temple, and "thought he was God"—was this to be for my amusement also?

37   Somewhere in between all this, I existed. I was neither American, nor Irish, nor Japanese. I had no race, nationality or home. Everybody who seriously considered me at all immediately focused upon me an eye glued to a microscope or monocle. I was a curiosity, of that I was certain, and I could see little concealment or delicacy in it all. What I wanted to know was whether I was a pleasing or an unpleasing curiosity, for I could not spend my life chasing other people's trains of thought and missing one train after another. That was annoying even to an Irish-Japanese of thirteen years.

38   There was something vitally wrong with the logic of the whole situation. I was as far from being what I now recognized as the "Japanese doll" as a monkey is from being a jelly fish. But on the other hand, could I be as completely crude and boorish as my father's friends evidently thought me? My thinking resulted in chaos. There were no answers to these questions. They were all perplexing whirlpools of thought to me, aged thirteen,

and instead of becoming quiet lakes of reflections, some of them have become regular maelstroms, now that I am thirty-six. I began to see that
people thought in groups, in societies, in nations and in whole races, and
they all thought differently. The unaccepted, the unexpected, like myself,
must remain forever outside of it all, but nature fortunately left such exceptions with a sense of humor.

39   I lived on in Japan and yet never as a Japanese would live, and I was
Japanese and I was not Japanese. For no one who had even the most su-
perficial knowledge of Japan considered that I was Japanese, and the
Japanese themselves considered me as a foreigner, and yet was I a real
American? Would I ever be completely anything? Or must I always be the
exception? Unanswerable questions.

40   Meanwhile I grew up in the foreign community of Yokohama, and
reached at last the leisurely years of 1910–12. I made my debut and was
"popular" as all we girls bred in the foreign community were. It was an
October evening in 1911 that I first met Frank Eldridge, "one of the boys
from the American Consulate," at one of the most festive of consular parties. I fell in love with him immediately because I thought him divinely
ordinary.

41   If there was one thing I longed for above all others at that point of my
existence, it was the ordinary. To be simple—insignificant—and to melt
inconspicuously into some environment—seemed to me worth the ambition
of a lifetime. This was quite understandable, for I had found my seat on
the bucking bronco of internationalism anything but restful. . . . Try as I
would I could never find the charm in being raceless, countryless, and now
to all intents and purposes practically relativeless as well—though Mother
said it was charming and many agreed with her. Like the old song from
the opera *Pinafore,* I "might have been a Roosian or a French or Turk or
Proosian, or perhaps Itali-an." For by the time I was introduced to my
prince of the proletariat, I had had the opportunity of dismissing a number
of worldly and attractive men of different nationalities. But I had had my
practical lessons in trying to be native in two countries and I lacked any
curiosity for a third splicing of my nationality.

42   We were married a year later. I was nineteen at the time and Frank
was twenty-three. Of course, I was to find that the most actually extraordinary man of the lot was my husband. But I did not discover this until
I was so firmly rooted in the character of the conservative Mrs. Eldridge
that I had forgotten I had ever been considered, or had considered myself,
a freak, and from that safe viewpoint could even admire his unexpectedness.

43   In the spring of 1914 Frank sailed for America to enter private business. The plan was for me to stay on in Japan and await the success of his
business affairs before following him, and so it was not till the next spring
that he sent for me.

44   There were many, many things that entered into my feeling about my
homegoing. I wanted to go. I had never really loved Japan, though I had

been deeply interested. Nevertheless the language, the habits, the Bushido had made a stranger of me; to Japan I was always a foreigner.

45 I sailed on the *S. S. China*. My destination in the United States was the South. That meant only a place "where Frank was" to me then, but it turned out to be a place where a lot of other people were as well.

46 To live in a small southern town, to do my own work and be Mrs. Eldridge—a nice, insignificant, every-day sort of person, was just what I had most wished to do. I had never discussed the matter with my husband. Needless to say I had not stressed the fact that I especially admired what I considered his "divine ordinariness" and it never occurred to me that he might have admired me for any of my unusualness. This I had always believed to be but an illusion in other people's minds. But Frank had been a whole year in that southern town and he had been enthusiastically expecting me for months. He met me filled with desire to present me to his new-found friends, and attentions were heaped upon me by everyone.

47 It is of these attentions that I wish to speak. They are the "prayers in the horse's ear." They came to me in that southern town and they come to me still from the majority of the people I meet. They surprise me. They seem to me to be vague utterances of a mystic Western philosophy, which my horse's ear refuses to understand. They are definite schools of thought with which people here in the United States make their friendly onslaughts upon me.

48 As a little girl when I went to Japan I had thought I was to be Japanese, but the Japanese themselves had gaped at me and decided differently. Now that I had returned to America, the problem was something complex and at first confusing to me in that quiet southern town.

49 People did a great deal more than gape at me. They had "ideas" about me, theories, preconceptions—*beliefs!*

50 One type thought of me as "cute." I remember once being taken to an Arts Club by one of these persons, and being introduced as the "little Japanese lady."

51 Then there are the people who insist that I am an Oriental and when I even meekly suggest that I have certain doubts on the subject, they assume the attitude that I am posing as an Occidental but that they are too clever and have discovered me. They usually end by getting very sentimental over Oriental art and religion, and find in my reticence all sorts of mysterious and beautiful philosophies which I, being an Oriental, do not reveal.

52 There are the moderns who analyze my sentences as I talk, "Ah, now that's your Irish," "Ah, now—that's your Japanese." These are usually the most annoying, for they consistently refuse to be human. They generally close their ears to what I am saying in their efforts to have me properly assorted and psychologically tabulated.

53 There are the anthropological hounds. They are not half bad, because in their intellectual peregrinations they have discovered that mixed races

have existed since the world began. Their examinations are limited to the shape of my nose and the quality of my hair.

54   There are the dramatists who are interested in what they call my "racial pulls." What am I feeling? In America, do I long for Japan? In Japan, do I long for America? Or do my feelings explode when they clash somewhere in the middle of the Pacific as they rush violently in both directions?

55   The educationalists (and not all of them are confined to the schools and colleges) have a keen desire to make something out of me. Meanwhile they consider me a sort of Oriental information bureau. "Are the Japanese becoming a Christian Nation?" "It is true that the Chinese are more honest than the Japanese?"—and so on.

56   There are the people who are actually afraid of me. I am a menace! I find them in all classes of society from the most charming of Californians to my colored scrub-woman, whom I found one night sitting on the front door-step.

57   "Lucy, what are you doing out here?"

58   "Oh, Miss Eldridge, I'se afeared. I never did like to work with them idols in the house nohow, and money ain't gwine to hire me to stay in thar after it gits dark."

59   Fortunately for the welfare of my soul, however, there is a great middle class who, after they have discovered my heredity, do accept the "is" where they find it. They start by asking me, "Just when did you learn to eat with a knife and fork?" "How long did it take your feet to grow?" Then they urge me to "say something in Japanese so I can hear what it's like," and by that time they are feeling almost as foolish as they care to feel and begin to be human by "say, which do you think is better to lead from, a sneak or just follow the fourth-highest-of-your-longest-suit rule?"

60   Frank introduced me to all these varieties of thought in that southern town. After several months of their attention and consideration, I began to wonder seriously if I was actually as phenomenal as without a doubt I was supposed to be.

61   My eldest son, Francis, was expected in July 1916. It was decided that I was to go to the hospital to receive him. At the time I was miserable and depressed. I was very happy with my husband, but I had not found myself living the nice sequestered life I had pictured. Though I had been supplied with all the materials, a good husband, a small salary; a quiet town, life's most conventional domestic situation; a coming baby . . . and so far as I could see, it should have been the most ordinary of all American situations and I the most average and usual of all American girls—but I was not.

62   As soon as I reached the hospital, I was greeted by a young nurse who ushered me into the stifling hot little room where my son was to be born, and when I gave my name, she grinned a knowing assurance, "Oh, we all know *all* about you. We are all so interested."

63   I think most women feel when they enter the hospital on these occa-

sions that they are victims of one of Nature's dreadful traps, but I suddenly felt, as I looked at my neat uniformed attendant, that I was trapped by Humanity as well. I had not crawled into some impersonal hole where I could have my baby in peace. Instead, I had been heralded by Heaven alone knew what mysterious beliefs about me. Was I a Japanese doll, or a menace? Her sickly sweet smile informed me that in her case at least it was the Japanese doll.

64   After a while another nurse whisked into the room. She was cold and formal, but I soon felt that she too "knew all about me." She dismissed the first with a quiet stare and jammed a thermometer into my mouth with a do-or-die attitude that was provoking. To this one I was a menace, but at least I could hope to count on her impersonal service.

65   Then a long animal-like cry shattered my thoughts.

66   "What's that?"

67   "That?" She dismissed it with a sniff. "One of those half-nigger girls in the ward. It is her first baby. She has been going on like that for hours. You can hear her all over the place every time the door is opened."

68   "Poor, poor thing. Can't something be done for her?"

69   "Oh, she's alright. These niggers make an awful 'to-do' about nothing."

70   "Oh—" the pain had wrenched my back. But I must not let this woman say that about me. I must be silent. This place wasn't a hospital. No. It was a sort of moral testing ground. Whatever happened, I would be "decent." No one would ever say, "It's that Jap girl in room 31, making an awful 'to-do' about nothing."

71   Hour after hour the pains grew more terrible. But I was silent. With each new racking attack of horror I drew on every atom of my will power not to cry out, not to betray my mother, my father and husband who believed me to be decent.

72   The room, the doctor and the nurses all faded away from my sight into a blazing world of pain. Then suddenly, as if suffering were only an asbestos curtain at the theatre, it lifted and I was conscious of the room and the people and my coral-colored son who was being held up by his heels and shaken by the doctor.

73   I must admit that just for a second or so I felt heroic. Everyone in the room seemed to be feeling that emotional relief that can but be called happiness. But all this feeling of ecstasy lasted for only five or ten minutes. It was the youngest nurse who smashed it all with, "Isn't the baby too cute! It's not often that the Stork brings us a little Japanese baby!"

74   Next morning the old nurse was as ungracious as ever. My heroism of the night before had not melted her.

75   I dared to question her, "Was there anything unusual about the birth?"

76   "No, absolutely normal."

77   That was something to be glad about. I could at least have an average birth to my credit. I was not unusual or extraordinary in that.

78   But half an hour later the younger nurse had destroyed my illusions.

79   "The doctor says it's a perfectly *marvelous* case. Of course these things

have been known to be true in the Orient. But to have it happen right here in our own hospital!"

80   "What happened?"—"What is it?"

81   "A *painless* birth!"

82   Nineteen seventeen—the war, and we were off to Washington, Frank accepting the post of assistant Chief of the Far Eastern Division, Department of Commerce. In Washington I found that I was no longer an Adams or a Tamagawa—I was Mrs. Eldridge. I baked and scrubbed and attended functions and played bridge with the other wives of the Department officials. Most of the other Department officials' wives were doing the same things. I was not sequestered, nor even rooted, but, at least, I was ordinary.

83   I belonged completely and absolutely to this international group of roving diplomats and cruising Trade Commissioners and Attachés and their families. I felt and knew their esprit de corps and was one with them as I never have been one with any other group. These people were filled with too many other interests to bother about whether I was Japanese or not. Who-is-who and why was a far more interesting question than whether or not I was a little Japanese lady, or a menace.

84   The years went on in Washington, happy, satisfying years. Although our Washington friends still arrived and departed, we ourselves had now begun to feel like old residents. In fact, never before had I felt such delusions of a rooted security. Day followed day without the tremor of a change —nothing seemed to indicate the slightest disturbance of my happily dull and calm existence. . . .

85   And then a shattering event took place on the other side of the world which was to vitally affect our lives—September 1st, 1923, the great earthquake of Japan. This tremendous cataclysm changed the destinies of almost all those who had even the remotest connections over there, however far they were scattered over the world. It shook us out of our smugness of mind, scattered our peace, demolished our illusions of security. It brought Mother back to America, shaken in spirit, in faith and in her ability to "flair."

86   My mother's presence in our household made us face facts that might otherwise have been buried in our busy lives. When she came to us she brought Japan with her and renewed my own mental confusion regarding my ancestry without meaning to do so. In fact, her intention was just the opposite, to make me forget my Japanese. Her expressed position was that there was no problem in an Eurasian marriage and she retained her viewpoint until the day she died.

87   However, I do not approve of Eurasian marriages. I do not approve of international marriages. Because this world is full of uncertainties, confusions and insecurities for all of us, Occidental and Oriental alike are afraid to climb down from the psychological horses they are riding, however many prayers our priests of philosophy, science, economy and travel may be muttering. We must stick to our horses or fall, because we have not

yet learned to unhorse gracefully. I disapprove of Eurasian marriages because there are so few among the many in Europe, in Asia or in America who have the wit and ability, or the moral and spiritual stamina and determination, or the keen, blind, deaf and dumb intellect that will allow them to drive their psychological horse in triumph to its goal.

88   And now, with my mother gone and my father in Japan, the problem of their marriage should have ended. But I now find that it has only just seriously begun, for the Japanese Government now tells me that I do not exist, that I never have existed, as far as they are concerned, because I was never registered as a Japanese. Here, then, is an official refusal to accept the "is" of the thing. Legally I am not and never was; therefore, I cannot be the lineal descendant of my parents or an inheritor of my mother's estate.

89   My lawyers say that I am "an ultimate, international, legal absurdity." As a citizen of Nowhere, I don't know whether it's better to be a born Oriental, or a born Occidental. I don't know whether Japan is the delightful fairyland of Lafcadio Hearn, or the dangerous yellow peril of the Californians. I don't know whether I have had the ideal home and the perfectly mated parents that my mother said I had, or whether I was the victim of one of the most horrible marital combinations ever perpetrated. I'm not even sure that I'm not the world's prize freak, though I believe myself to be addicted to the conventional life. Who can say whether it's better to dance on your heels with your toes turned in, or on your toes with your heels turned in?

90   Perhaps it's wise to be foolish and foolish to be wise. But it's safer, much safer, to ride a nice, still, conventional wooden horse secured to a merry-go-round than a wild, untrained and untamed international steed.

91   For only the nonexistent can stand on their feet in mid-Pacific!

COMMENTARY

It is said that truth is stranger than fiction. Life itself often contains patterns that would seem contrived in a novel. To have Ireland and Japan form a union in Chicago and produce "Kathleen Tamagawa" may be extraordinary, but it is believable. The surprise occurs when extraordinary Kathleen insists on being an ordinary American (or Japanese) girl. Most ordinary people try to be "different." Here is a "different" girl who longs to be ordinary because her uniqueness deprives her of a personal, cultural, or legal identity. But try as she will, life plays tricks on her. She marries a man named Frank, like Uncle Frank who brought her parents together. Disillusioned with her "Oriental" character, she returns to America—on a ship called S. S. China.

The writer's racial dilemma determines the structure of her narrative. She begins with a prologue about her parents (paragraphs 1 to 12) to introduce the issue of dual identity. Then she recounts her life, first as an American (paragraphs 13 to 30) and then as a Japanese (paragraphs 31 to

45). Uncle Frank dies at the end of the first phase; husband Frank returns to America at the end of the second. In the third phase of her life, she tries to live as an ordinary "Mrs. Eldridge," but the people around her insist on seeing her as either a cute little doll or a threat (paragraphs 46 to 81). Only in the unique social group of Washington diplomats has she ever been treated as a person, not a curiosity (paragraphs 82 to 84); but this brief period of emotional security ends with the arrival of her mother (paragraphs 85 and 86).

In the final paragraphs, Tamagawa evaluates her experience as "a citizen of Nowhere" and explains that until human behavior changes, until group identity ceases to be important, she recommends that people not marry across visible identity lines. The burden on their children is too great.

OUTLINE

I. Introduction: identification of the problem—paragraph 1
II. Background: her parents—paragraphs 2–12
III. Her American childhood—paragraphs 12–27
IV. Her Japanese childhood and growing-up years—paragraphs 28–44
V. Her life in a town in the American South—paragraphs 45–81
VI. Her life in a Washington international community—paragraphs 82–86
VII. Evaluation and recommendation: it's safer to stay within conventional boundaries —paragraphs 87–91

SUGGESTIONS FOR WRITING

1. Using Tamagawa's narrative structure as a model, present a recommendation based on the history of your life so far. Introduce a problem in the first paragraph; tell your story, choosing the incidents and people related to the problem; evaluate and recommend at the end. For example, if your family moved frequently while you were a child, do you recommend—or recommend against—that way of life? If both of your parents worked full-time while you were a child, do you recommend—or recommend against—that way of life?

2. To what extent does Tamagawa's recommendation depend on the precise circumstances in which she grew up? Do you think that the increase in international and interracial marriage since World War II would make her feel less negative about her experience if she could repeat it today? Would a child of unusual ancestry still suffer from the loss of identity she describes?

Write a letter to a friend who is considering an interracial marriage and has asked your advice. Tell your friend about Tamagawa's experience, and then, putting Tamagawa's case in proper perspective, make your recommendation.

3. Tamagawa concludes by recommending that people stay within conventional boundaries. Describe some episode in an international, interfaith, or interracial relationship in which you participated; evaluate it and make a rec-

ommendation: Should we stay within conventional boundaries? Or does your experience show that it is better to cross them?

4. Tamagawa's experience taught her a lesson. But what are the limits of the proverb "Experience is the best teacher"? When people's experiences differ, how do we decide which lesson to follow?

patriotism—but how?
HOWARD MUMFORD JONES

This essay may be difficult to read for two reasons. First, it was written during a time of national alarm prior to World War II. Americans wondered whether the nation could survive a military challenge. Many citizens had lost faith in democracy. Some embraced alien ideologies such as fascism and communism. Thus, Jones refers to National Socialism as an immediate threat, but now young people scarcely remember it. The specific context in which Jones writes is unfamiliar to us.

Second, Jones is a historian and believes that national survival requires a lively sense of history. He fills his essays with historical facts, names, and the legends that he calls the American mythology. But most of us know a good deal less about America's past than did the people for whom Jones was writing. In paragraph 7, he tells students "No fair looking in a reference book." In the 1970s, most teachers as well as most students need a reference book to pass the little quiz and to understand many of his allusions.

But the essay is worth the trouble. The problems it dramatizes are probably more acute now than they were in the 1930s. At the nation's 200th birthday, we are still aware that we need genuine patriotism. Jones offers two useful recommendations: one, that we recapture a sense of the excitement of our history; two, that we guard against false patriots who would do us more harm than good.

Like Jones, we recognize the need for affectionate respect for our home. And like Jones, we may have to conclude not with a specific proposal for the creation of genuine patriots, but with his question, "How?"

I

1   While discussion clubs incline a serious ear to speeches on "Can Democracy Survive?" and our better correspondents smuggle dispatches out

Source. Copyright © 1938, ® 1966, by *The Atlantic Monthly* Company, Boston, Mass. Reprinted with permission of Howard Mumford Jones and the publisher.

of Europe showing that the dictator countries are committing economic suicide, few people seem to inquire why, if the fascist and communistic nations are economically insane, they constitute so serious a menace to political democracy. At this distance it looks as if they had something democracy does not possess, or rather something American democracy has lost during the dolorous twentieth century. That something is not state regulation of business, nor holidays for workingmen, nor concentration camps, nor a well-oiled bureaucracy, nor even the capacity to make trains run on time. We can show American precedents for all these. What the dictator countries have succeeded in doing is to make patriotism glamorous. Among higher liberal circles in the United States patriotism seems nowadays to be regarded as the last refuge of a scoundrel.

2   Glamour has turned the trick. The technical name for this sort of trick is propaganda, but it is not ideational propaganda I am talking about. What I refer to is the prompt and efficient creation by the dictators of glamorous mythological images. These images please their downtrodden subjects, make them feel swell, and send them off to the army or a labor camp singing mistaken patriotic songs. We used to have Glamour in this country, but during the rush of intellection to the head in the twenties we rubbed it all off.

3   It is, of course, commonplace that Mussolini is a semi-divine Duce and Hitler a sacrosanct Führer. It is also commonplace that you can't turn around in Berlin or Rome or Moscow without seeing a swastika, the Roman fasces, or a sickle and hammer. Everybody knows about the parades, the "spontaneous" cheering, the farcical elections, the uniforms, and the perpetual celebrations. Naziism has its martyrs—the "Horst Wessel" song commemorates one of them—fascism its saints, and communism its heroes. It is true that the official history of these countries, which obedient citizens are required to swallow, would not delude even a weakminded freshman in the United States, but that is not the point: the point is that the official history is full of heroism, chivalry, romance. It takes the form of the rescuing of the helpless maiden Germania or Italia or Russia by knights-errant against overwhelming odds. It is a modern version of the King Arthur story, the American Revolution, and freeing the slaves, all in one. The result is that the communist or fascist citizen, at least in his public moments, has an exhilarating sense of living in a vast grand opera.

4   Why is there no American grand opera to correspond? Why has American democracy mislaid its mythology and lost its glamour? The answer is in part that we had our own grand opera until, under the combined attacks of "progressive" educators, the debunking biographers, and social historians, we grew shamefaced about it. Take, for example, the matter of the musical score. "The Star-Spangled Banner," though unsingable, is just as vigorous a tune as "Giovinezza," but we don't know the words. "Columbia, the Gem of the Ocean" tingles with vitality, but try to get it sung at a ball park! "The Battle Hymn of the Republic" (peace to the South!) is a superb song —we can sing the chorus, some of us chanting "Glory, glory, hallelujah"

and others "John Brown's body lies a-mouldering in the grave." I do not care for "America," with its mouldy flavor of commencement programmes, but "Yankee Doodle" is a good fighting song, which we can't even burble. Everybody shouts when the band plays "Dixie," but will some kind Rotarian recite the verses? The sorrowful fact that well-intentiond citizens mistake Sousa's "Stars and Stripes Forever" for the national anthem is not the sort of error that Mussolini or Hitler or Stalin permits.

5   Grand opera, however, is more than a musical score; it supposes characters and a plot. Let us have an examination in the plot of the American story.* Can any little boy or girl earn a dime by telling me the anecdote which gave birth to each of the following sentences? "Damn the torpedoes —full speed ahead!" "You may fire when ready, Gridley." We have met the enemy and they are ours." "Don't cheer, boys—the poor devils are dying." "Don't give up the ship." "Millions for defence, but not one cent for tribute." "I would rather be right than be President" (No, Sammy, this does *not* refer to George M. Cohan). "I only regret that I have but one life to lose for my country." "Our Federal Union: it must be preserved."

6   The class will next recite from memory, thus rivaling good communists, (1) Patrick Henry's oration; (2) the Declaration of Independence as far as the bill of particulars; (3) the peroration of Webster's "Reply to Hayne"; (4) Senator Thurston on Cuban affairs; (5) Lincoln's Second Inaugural Address. Next, the boys and girls will tell teacher the facts in the case of (*a*) Molly Pitcher; (*b*) Johnny Appleseed; (*c*) Kit Carson; (*d*) Davy Crockett; (*e*) R. P. Hobson; (*f*) Stephen Decatur; (*g*) Marcus Whitman; and (*h*) General Stark. The examination will conclude by having the scholars identify the author and name the poem in which each of the following phrases occurs: "When Freedom from her mountain height"; "Ay, tear her tattered ensign down"; "The Turk lay dreaming of the hour"; "All quiet along the Potomac"; "Out of the focal and foremost fire"; "By the flow of the inland river Whence the fleets of iron have fled"; "John P. Robinson, he sez he wunt vote fer Guvener B."; "When faith is lost, when honor dies, The man is dead"; "Blindness we may forgive, but baseness we will smite." (Southern children will be placed under a slight handicap concerning one of these items.)

7   If this is too hard, the C students may identify any five of the following: (1) Old Fuss and Feathers; (2) the Swamp Fox; (3) the Mill Boy of the Slashes; (4) The Pathfinder (*not* Natty Bumppo); (5) the Rock of Chickamauga; (6) The American Farmer; (7) Me Too Platt; (8) Hosea Biglow; (9) Old Rough-and-Ready; (10) Tippecanoe and Tyler too. No fair looking in a reference book. A grade of fifty will be considered passing.

8   I realize, of course, that a number of these items have a regrettable military flavor, which World Peaceways, Inc., would not approve. I can only say that the heroic moments of history seem to be commonly associated with the danger of death. In fact, I shall dare the scorn of advanced

---

* Answers to Jones' "tests" are given after Suggestions for Writing.

intellectuals by citing a quotation guaranteed to make the ghost of Hart Crane wince:

> And how can man die better
> Than facing fearful odds,
> For the ashes of his fathers
> And the temples of his gods?

No, this is not an American poem, and it is banned from our better school readers because its author has passed out of fashion. Its sentiment, however, seems to be powerful in an important Mediterranean kingdom, somewhat to the present embarrassment of the nation which produced the poet.

9   I likewise freely admit that under the searchlight of historical science some of the sentences I have quoted have been proved apocryphal, and some of the heroes whose sobriquets are given above have been conclusively shown up by modern writers. I also know that Washington did not pray at Valley Forge, that the Boston Massacre was not a massacre, that John Hancock made a good thing out of violating the revenue laws, that Sheridan's ride never occurred, and that the charge on San Juan Hill, was from every sensible point of view, an hilarious absurdity. I have, however, one advantage over the rising generation: I knew my American mythology before I knew its historical corrective; and inasmuch as the vaunted conflict among ideologies threatens to be won by the nation with the greatest belief in its own mythology, I wonder, now that scientific historians have destroyed most of the American myth, what it is that American democrats are to believe in during the coming struggle. To quote from another frayed classic, also scorned in intellectual circles, Harvard men who died in the Civil War were men who, in Lowell's opinion,

> . . . followed [Truth] and found her
> Where all may hope to find,
> Not in the ashes of the burnt-out mind,
> But beautiful, with danger's sweetness round her.

If democracy should have to fight, will it be emotionally inspired by the sound historic fact that the Lincoln administration is supposed to have favored the high-tariff crowd?

II

10   In the nineteenth century, Americans were simple-minded enough to have a mythology. The facts of American history were widely known. Rising generations learned them in school. On Friday afternoon classes were adjourned while perspiring victims declaimed fragments of nationally known orations, patriotic poetry, and sound rhetorical pieces describing a blind preacher, narrating a thrilling climb up the Natural Bridge, or excoriating Benedict Arnold. No child of the Iodine State who toiled through William Gilmore Simms's history of South Carolina, written for schools, could be

ignorant of the exploits of Francis Marion or General Nathanael Greene. No schoolboy put through *Appleton's Fifth Reader* failed to discover that Daniel Webster was the greatest man who ever lived. No boy who learned both text and gestures from the immortal McGuffey but was thoroughly grounded in the dramatic moments of the history of freedom:

"Make way for liberty," he cried,
Made way for liberty, and died.

Breathes there the man with soul so dead
Who never to himself hath said,
This is my own, my native land!

The boy stood on the burning deck,
Whence all but him had fled.

The fact that a perverse and adulterate generation continues this last quotation by an apocryphal reference to goobers is simply a tribute to the thoroughness with which the nation was once taught to admire Mrs. Hemans's hero. But if you did not care for the immortal youth you could hang out the old flag with Barbara Frietchie or ride twenty miles with Phil Sheridan and Thomas Buchanan Read.

11   The patriotic reader met an immense and genuine demand. Throughout most of the nineteenth century every American knew that this nation was the greatest thing that had ever happened in the history of the human race. Every Fourth of July some rising young lawyer read aloud the Declaration on the village green. At every county fair an itinerant Congressman pulled the lion's tail and made the eagle scream. All good Americans abhorred the effete monarchies of Europe. All good Americans understood that the immediate purpose of any British duke was to place his heel on the neck of freeborn republicans. The image of Washington or Jackson or Lincoln or Lee held precisely the same place in the esteem of the people as Mussolini or Hitler or Stalin wants to hold in the esteem of his own nation. In those times we made the welkin ring, painted the firmament red, white, and blue, and annnounced to an amused universe that Columbia was bounded on the north by the Aurora Borealis, on the east by the Garden of Eden, on the west by the Fortunate Isles, and on the south by the Day of Judgment. We made ourselves supremely ridiculous and supremely happy. Observers like Dickens, Mrs. Trollope, Miss Martineau, and others satirized our effervescence and envied our simplicity. We had our mythology, and we believed in it.

12   To-day Washington is a figure on a postage stamp, we are not quite sure whether Andy or Stonewall Jackson beat the British at New Orleans, and purple passages about the American eagle are no longer heard, even in Congress. We are all for social justice or the Townsend plan, but neither programme has yet produced its demigod. When economic analysis comes in at the door, patriotic figures of speech fly out at the window. It is im-

possible to twist the lion's tail with one hand and make a graph of the wages of coal miners with the other. In all the argument over minimum-wage laws, nobody has referred to the full dinner pail, the pauper millions of Europe, or pressing a crown of thorns upon the brow of labor. Statistics are valuable, but a little old-fashioned Fourth-of-July oratory is the tonic we really need.

13   The fervor has gone out of our sublime and ridiculous enthusiasm in the twentieth century for a variety of reasons—economic determinism, sociological analysis, the radio (which killed off the string-tie orator), realism on the stage and in fiction, which forbids romantic gestures and heroic thought. One cause worth discussing is professional enthusiasm for a new sort of education supposed to develop the free personality of the child.

14   The fact that the child was to develop in the United States of America and not in a gray abstraction called the modern world has not troubled educators who look down on Jean Jacques Rousseau as an unscientific generalizer. The child is to remain a child as long as possible, and consequently he is not to be given adult stuff to read until the latest possible moment. The child is supposed to be brought up to love his fellow man, and therefore stories like the fight of the *Serapis* and the *Bonhomme Richard* have been quietly dropped from school. Instead, he learns to love the kindly Indians, who built tepees. The child is nevertheless supposed to develop into a little voter, and in place of learning to hate Benedict Arnold he is instructed in the mysteries of the local waterworks. It is not yet clear, after a quarter of a century of advanced education, that the results, as shown in municipal politics, have justified the erasure of romantic drama from the American school.

15   Think of the comment of sturdy Mr. McGuffey upon the book from which a friend of mine, aged six, is learning to read. I quote from the incredible preface:

> The purpose of *Our Animal Books* is to motivate in the growing citizen, from his pre-school days to junior high school, an intelligent regard for his own pets and for the animals of his city, state, and country. He, however, rather than the animal, is the chief factor [sic] in the book. . . .
> The primer, *Fuzzy Tail*, is devoted to the kitten, telling in story form just how a kitten should be fed, handled, and properly played with [!].

16   I have no doubt that school superintendents who adopt this series look down on Maria Edgeworth (if they have ever heard of her) as a didactic old woman bent on ruining the lives of children, though the precise difference between this sort of pedagogy and eighteenth-century didacticism is not evident. But let us return to *Our Animal Books*. After *Fuzzy Tail*, we rise through *Sniff*, which "gives youthful owners similar instruction in the feeding, housing, exercising, and general upbringing of a puppy, again through story medium" (why medium?), to *Paths to Conservation*, which "points toward participation in the protection and conservation of the vanishing bird and mammal life of our country." (As the little boy said, mammals are apparently not as extinct as they used to be.) I read likewise that

"all information pertaining to the care and treatment of animals has been checked carefully by respective [*sic*] authorities."

17   Let us not make fun of McGuffey's rhetoric. McGuffey never dreamed that a child had to be "motivated" as a "factor," knew not the word "correlation," more blessed than the waters of Abana and Pharpar, and failed to consult "respective" authorities. Nevertheless, I ever and again meet aging Americans who can with honest pride recite piece after piece from McGuffey or Appleton, but in the course of teaching several thousand undergraduates over a period of years I do not find that they can recite anything at all, and their ignorance of American history is so immense that Harvard University has just instituted a system of competitive prizes to get them to read some of it.

18   The history books have gone the way of the school readers. I admire Professor Charles A. Beard, like all who have to do with American history; but, from the point of view of keeping alive a necessary patriotic glow in the juvenile breast, he has had an unfortunate influence. The school of social historians has substituted movements for personalities, conflicts of economic interest for dramatic events, sociology for the romance of personal endeavor, and "citizenship" for hairbreadth escapes by sea and land. Some stories, it is true, have been spared. General Lee still rides sadly through the Confederate Army on Traveller, and Lincoln is still assassinated by the cowardly Booth. I have no doubt the school histories are sounder, better, and more intelligent books than Simms's parochial *History of South Carolina* or Ridpath's *History of the World*. I do not deny that to learn how the Puritans grew corn or what early railways were like is exciting. But I cannot picture a younger generation going into Armageddon, should that be tragically necessary, inspired by memories of railroad grants or aglow with accounts of the rise of sectionalism in the Deep South.

19   We debunked too much. During the iconoclastic twenties spirited biographers laid about them with a mighty modern hand. They told us that Lincoln was a small-town politician, Washington a land grabber, Grant a stubborn and conceited mule, and Bryan an amusing idiot. We learned that there was something to be said for Aaron Burr, but not very much for Sam Adams, Longfellow, or Harriet Beecher Stowe. In place of being American vikings, the pioneers turned out to be neurotic, dissatisfied fellows unpopular in their home towns, and Columbia, the gem of the ocean, was described as a sort of kept woman in the pay of millionaires. Apparently the only Americans who ever died to make the world safe for democracy died in 1917–1918, and made a mistake in doing so. I do not deny either the truth or the necessity of many of these modern biographies. I am no more comfortable than the next man in a room full of plaster saints. But, when the biographers got through, all the heroes had disappeared.

20   Meanwhile in Germany, Italy, and Russia the manufacture of heroes has gone steadily forward. There is no use in saying they are fake heroes. The only way to conquer an alien mythology is to have a better mythology of your own.

III

21   What we need is a patriotic renaissance, but we need not shut our eyes to the dangerous fact that a patriotic renaissance is exactly what a number of interested pressure groups are playing for. Advanced liberals are perfectly right in assuming that every patriot is guilty until he is proved innocent. Too many selfish interests have adopted the star-spangled manner. In fact, one of the difficulties of rehabilitating our mythology is that all the stirring phrases have been appropriated by organizations of the right or organizations of the left. The Liberty League, the American Legion, the Constitution Society, the American Minute Men, the Daughters of the American Revolution, the International League for Peace and Freedom, the United Daughters of the Confederacy, the Colonial Dames—the trouble is that most of these bodies have an axe to grind. They want to call somebody else un-American.

22   Patriotism may not always be the last refuge of a scoundrel, but it is too often a convenient disguise for a one-hundred-per-center who wants somebody else to go back home. Nor are radicals without guile. If the La Follette committee has turned the spotlight on reactionaries whose favorite reading matter is the Constitution whenever they import plug-uglies to break a strike, I have noted a wonderful interest in the Bill of Rights among communists in danger of arrest and deportation. The devil can cite Scripture for his purpose. There is scarcely a pressure group in the country that cannot cite Jefferson or Lincoln, Washington or Wilson, in support of a quiet little programme of its own.

23   It is not thus that a patriotic renaissance is to come about. Because the dictator countries have cleverly manipulated a patriotic mythology for sinister ends it does not follow, because we are not yet a dictator country, that patriotic mythology cannot be manipulated for sinister ends in the United States. We regard ourselves as a free and enlightened people, but so do patriotic Italians, Germans, and Russians regard themselves. If we think they are deceived, they have a right to retort the argument on us. I do not wish to be so deceived. I do not want any scientifically manipulated propaganda. I regret that Americans cannot sing their own national anthem, but if it comes to a choice between singing it under compulsion or remaining silent in a concentration camp I trust I shall not be too old to go to the concentration camp. If, as the overzealous believe, there is a red network over the land, God forbid that we should now create a red-white-and-blue network. I have no desire to echo Madame Roland's pathetic cry: "O Liberty! Liberty! how many crimes are committed in thy name!"

24   Neither do we want any unhistorical history. Official persons who suppress school texts in the interests of "Americanism" because some honest historian has tried to tell the truth as he sees it are not only thoroughly un-American, but doing in a small way precisely what Messrs. Mussolini, Hitler, and Stalin are doing on a larger scale. If the "Aryan" version of

history is funny, or would be if it were not so deplorable, an "American" version of history would be just as comic and just as disastrous. We want no legends marked: "Approved by the Bureau of Propaganda, Washington, D. C." I do not propose that on a given date all good Americans shall devoutly believe that Washington cut down the cherry tree, cheerfully remarking, "Father, I cannot tell a lie." But what seems to have happened is that in our enthusiasm for social forces we have omitted most of the thrilling anecdotes. We have modernized American history so thoroughly that it is everywhere up to date, and as a result John Smith, Thomas Jefferson, and Buffalo Bill are made to behave as if they were members of the Kiwanis Club looking for better business sites.

25   It would be idle to deny the economic motive which sent adventurers to the New World, but it seems to me equal folly to omit for that reason the tale of the lonely and heroic exploits which they wrought. I have no doubt that the Massachusetts Bay Colony was intended as a profitable commercial enterprise, but the Pilgrims and the Puritans both wanted to worship God in their own way. General Oglethorpe was really a noble soul, and Roger Williams is still a great man. The debtor classes and hardboiled merchants undoubtedly egged on the American Revolution; nevertheless Tom Paine was not writing nonsense when he exclaimed: "These are the times that try men's souls!" Does the fact that Vergennes wanted to increase French prestige lessen the romantic gallantry of Lafayette? Washington did not cross the Delaware in the fatuous manner of the celebrated painting; nevertheless he crossed it, and it was full of floating ice. I may add that he and his ragged Continentals were likewise extremely uncomfortable at Valley Forge.

26   A whole regiment of researchers looking for sectionalism cannot rob the little American navy of glorious episodes during the Tripolitan campaign or the War of 1812. Such, however, is our zeal for sociology and economic determinism that Mr. Stephen Vincent Benét seems to be the only American to realize that Daniel Webster was a great and thrilling man. If it was wrong for Jared Sparks to correct the erratic spelling of the Father of his Country, what shall we say of historical works which dismiss the Lewis and Clark expedition in a single phrase, send the Mormons to Utah in a sentence, and mention Custer's Last Stand in a footnote? We have a picturesque and romantic past, which we seem bent on making as dull and modern as we can.

IV

27   If we really want to believe that political democracy is worth fighting for, we need to be told over and over again what pain and suffering it has cost. Wiser than we, the nineteenth century kept its eye on that issue. Scientific historians we have in abundance; what we lack is a Macaulay, sure that the Whigs were right and the Tories wrong, and heartily concerned lest political liberty might suffer. We need to be told about Magna Carta

and Arnold von Winkelried and John Huss and Savonarola and Pym and Hampden and the Gray Champion and Sergeant Moultrie and the burning zeal of Calhoun and the fervid faith of William Lloyd Garrison and the quiet heroism of Grant's last years and the career of Fighting Bob La Follette. We need to know about the Watauga settlement and Boonesboro and Fort Bridger and the Oregon trail. We need to know these things, not as the products of economic forces, but as human drama. Men are but children of a larger growth. They will listen to a tale of D'Artagnan and Richelieu when a dissertation on the economic policy of Colbert leaves them cold.

28   Mr. Bernard DeVoto is a novelist and critic for whom I have a vast respect. Recently he argued that the historical novel came to its full flower in the works of Mr. James Boyd, the theory being that Mr. Boyd is the first person to picture adequately the experiences and emotions of an average, inarticulate man participating in great events. This is what may be called the realistic theory of historical fiction, and there is a great deal to be said for it. But there is also a great deal to be said on the other side of the argument. There is such a thing as historical romance. Any practising novelist can write rings around Thomas Nelson Page and George W. Cable, but the practical result of the romantic school of Southern historical novelists was to make Southern history a living tradition in that region. What I should like to see is a school of writers and dramatists trying to make the history of liberty a living tradition.

29   Such a literature will fail, however, if it confines its interests to the Colonial Society of Massachusetts and the F. F. V.'s. "Old Americans" (hateful phrase!) tend to take the point of view that American history is their private possession because they were here first. Aside from the fact that the only persons entitled to the benefit of this silly argument are the Indians, the assumption is not even true. In New England the French Canadians have a better claim, or at least as good a one; and as for the South, your proud first families will have to mingle with the Mexican descendants of Spaniards who pushed their frontier up into North Carolina if they are consistent.

30   It is unfortunate that neither the *Mayflower* nor Captain Smith's little fleet carried anybody by the name of Shimultowski, Cohen, Paladopolous, Tokanyan, Lauria, McGillicuddy, Swenson, or Schimmelpfennig on their rolls, because it is precisely the children and grandchildren of the millions who "came over" some centuries after these earlier immigrations who need to have their imaginations kindled by American mythology. The gulf between the Boston Brahmins and the Boston Irish, old Detroiters and the swarming thousands of automobile workers, the first families of Cleveland and the Poles, the Armenians, the Czechs, the Ruthenians, and other racial groups, is not, however, going to be bridged by a bright recital of the French and Indian Wars.

31   No race or religion or group or nationality can be permitted to assume that it has a monopoly of American history, and no race or religion or

group or nationality can be permitted to feel it is excluded, if political democracy is to survive. The founding fathers did not, unfortunately, include race-ism among the elements to be combated in the Bill of Rights; for in the eighteenth century men were men, not herds of stock for breeding purposes. Consequently, if democracy is to revive its living legend, it cannot confine that legend to the exploits of a favored few. We shall somehow have to include the drama of human liberty in our renaissance, no less than the drama of American democracy.

32   As the letter paper of the National Rededication Movement remarks: "America is unbelievably undersold to its own citizens." True, but who are the Americans? How shall we revive patriotism without chauvinism, economic self-interest, or racial snobbery? And if we do not revive the history of liberty as a living faith, how shall we combat an alien mythology of race, militarism, and an uncomfortable version of the heroic in history?

COMMENTARY

Jones' subject is a basic American paradox: the nation has committed some indefensible acts in defense of its ideals or in forgetfulness of them. Modern historical research has pointed out America's faults so thoroughly that we no longer believe in the old mythology of democracy or the old heroes of the Republic. Historical honesty, to be sure, is good, but the price we are paying is that we no longer believe in America at all. And if we do not believe in her, we will not fight for her. The totalitarian countries, by contrast, have extremely effective mythologies. Their citizens will fight because they have something to believe they are fighting for.

What can we do? Having established that there is a problem (paragraphs 1 to 9), Jones glances backward to the nineteenth century, when schoolbooks taught the American myths (paragraphs 10 and 11) rather than the uninspiring stuff they teach now (paragraphs 12 to 19). This comparison produces a recommendation: "The only way to conquer an alien mythology is to have a better mythology of your own" (paragraph 20). The rest of the essay confronts the question of *how* we are to achieve "a patriotic renaissance." Jones rejects one alternative, the narrow-minded activities of pressure groups (paragraphs 21 and 22). He rejects another alternative, "scientifically manipulated propaganda" (paragraph 23), and another, historical lying (paragraph 24). However, we are advised to put back into the history books the thrilling anecdotes, the "lonely and heroic exploits" of the American past (paragraphs 24 to 26). We are also advised to emphasize the dramatic story of the sufferings of America—an America including all of its peoples (paragraphs 27 to 31). Americans of every origin must learn the myths of the nation so they can share a common memory. It is shared memory that preserves nations just as it preserves families.

Jones recognizes the incompleteness of his recommendations. We will have to recover our mythology "somehow," he says (paragraph 31)—but he does not see exactly how. Perhaps the frustration at the difficulty of the task explains the sarcasm of his tone: "No, Sammy, this does *not* refer to George M. Cohan" (paragraph 5); "We are all for social justice or the Townsend Plan" (paragraph 12); the schoolboy "learns to love the kindly Indians, who built teepees" (paragraph 15). To endorse a revival of mythology—a grand opera approach to history—without sentimentalizing or falsifying is almost impossible during a period of widespread cynicism about national values. This is why Jones urges upon his readers veritable catalogs (paragraph 27, for example) of dynamic people and dramatic events. He hopes to re-excite us about our national past.

OUTLINE

    I. Introduction: the status of patriotism in America and in the totalitarian countries—paragraphs 1–3

   II. The problem and its cause (our "grand opera" has been lost)—paragraphs 4–9

  III. Schoolbooks, past and present—paragraphs 10–19

  IV. Recommendation: create a better mythology—paragraph 20

   V. The feasibility problem: "How?"—paragraphs 21–31

       A. Alternatives to be rejected—paragraphs 21–24

       B. Alternatives to be accepted—paragraphs 24–31

  VI. Summary: appeal for a solution—paragraph 32

SUGGESTIONS FOR WRITING

1. National events generate catch phrases. World War II produced General McArthur's "I shall return" and the song "Praise the Lord and Pass the Ammunition." (What phrases did Vietnam produce?) Identify a slogan currently popular in the nation or in your community or school. Explain its effect: How does it produce the sense of solidarity among those who accept it? Then evaluate its effect as good or bad, and recommend that we do or do not continue to use it.

2. Which single event in American history best represents for you the spirit of the nation? Would you recommend that this event be emphasized in grade school history books?

3. Jones recommends that a renewed American mythology concern itself more with the contributions of America's various ethnic groups than the old mythology did (paragraph 31). Write a letter to your high school principal recommending an American history unit designed so that "no race or religion or group or nationality" will feel excluded, as Jones puts it (paragraph 31). Among the alternatives would be special sections of the course devoted to the exploits and legends of minority groups, or the inclusion of minority-group material in all sections of the course. Which of those alternatives would be better?

Or recommend an American literature reading list for junior high school students, or an American mythology series for educational TV.

You are trying to provide a partial answer to Jones' question, "How?" By what means or programs can a genuine patriotism be achieved?

ANSWERS TO JONES' "TESTS"

Paragraph 5

"Damn the torpedoes—full speed ahead!" David G. Farragut at the Battle of Mobile Bay, August 5, 1864.

"You may fire when ready, Gridley." George Dewey to the flagship captain at the Battle of Manila Bay, May 1, 1898.

"We have met the enemy and they are ours." Oliver H. Perry dispatch to General William H. Harrison announcing victory at the Battle of Lake Erie, September 10, 1813.

"Don't cheer, boys—the poor devils are dying." John W. Philip of the battleship *Texas* as she swept past the burning Spanish ship *Vizcaya* at the Battle of Santiago, July 4, 1898.

"Don't give up the ship." More accurately, "Tell the men to fire faster and not to give up the ship; fight her till she sinks." James Lawrence's final order as he was carried below fatally wounded before his ship the U. S. frigate *Chesapeake*, was captured by the British frigate *Shannon*, June 1, 1813.

"Millions for defense, but not one cent for tribute." Robert G. Harper, a toast at a banquet for Justice John Marshall, June 18, 1798, referring to ransom demands made by Tripoli pirates for the return of captured U.S. ships.

"I would rather be right than be president." Henry Clay, speech, 1850.

"I only regret that I have but one life to lose for my country." Nathan Hale: last words before the British hanged him as a spy, September 22, 1776.

"Our Federal Union: it must be preserved." Andrew Jackson, a toast at the Jefferson Birthday Celebration, 1830.

Paragraph 6

"When Freedom from her mountain height," Joseph Brodman Drake (1795–1820), "The American Flag," 1819.

"Ay, tear her tattered ensign down," Oliver Wendell Holmes (1809–1894), *Old Ironsides*, 1830.

"The Turk lay dreaming of the hour," Fitz-Greene Halleck (1790–1867), *Marco Bozzaris*, 1825.

"All quiet along the Potomac," General George B. McClellan (1826–1885), frequent report from his Union Headquarters, 1861.

"Out of the focal and foremost fire," Francis O. Ticknor (1822–1874), "Little Griffen," 1879.

"By the flow of the inland river Whence the fleets of iron have fled," Francis M. Finch (1827–1907), "The Blue and the Gray," 1867.

"John P. Robinson, he sez he wunt vote fer Guvener B.," James Russell Lowell (1819–1891), *Bigelow Papers*, Series I, 1848.

"When faith is lost, when honor dies, The man is dead," John Greenleaf Whittier (1807–1892), *Ichabod*, 1850.

"Blindness we may forgive, but baseness we will smite," William Vaughn Moody (1869–1910), *An Ode in Time of Hesitation,* 1901.

Paragraph 7

1. Old Fuss and Feathers—General Winfield Scott (1786–1866)
2. The Swamp Fox—General Francis Marion (1732–1795)
3. The Mill Boy of the Slashes—Henry Clay (1777–1852)
4. The Pathfinder—John Charles Fremont (1813–1890)
5. The Rock of Chickamauga—General George H. Thomas (1816–1870)
6. The American Farmer—J. Hector St. John de Crevecoeur (1735–1813)
7. Me Too Platt—Thomas C. Platt (1833–1910)
8. Hosea Biglow—James Russell Lowell (1819–1891)
9. Old Rough-and-Ready—General Zachary Taylor (1784–1850)
10. Tippecanoe and Tyler too—William Henry Harrison (1773–1841)

how to lie with statistics
DARRELL HUFF

This selection is a mock recommendation. The superficial proposal, as suggested by the title, is that we should use statistics dishonestly. The real proposal, stated in the last paragraph, is that we should become familiar with the dishonest uses of statistics in order to avoid being deceived by them. Unless we learn the con game, we will become its victims.

Do you think that Huff's real purpose—to tell us "Don't be deceived by statistical lies"—is adequately served by this presentation? Or does the tactic of explaining the con game run the risk that some people will learn it only too well? What other ways are there to convince readers that statistics can lie and that they must know how to protect themselves?

1   "The average Yaleman, Class of '24," *Time* magazine reported last year after reading something in the New York *Sun,* a newspaper published in those days, "makes $25,111 a year."

2   Well, good for him!

3   But, come to think of it, what does this improbably precise and salubrius figure mean? Is it, as it appears to be, evidence that if you send your boy to Yale you won't have to work in your old age and neither will he? Is this average a mean or is it a median? What kind of sample is it based on? You could lump one Texas oilman with two hundred hungry free-

lance writers and report *their* average income as $25,000-odd a year. The arithmetic is impeccable, the figure is convincingly precise, and the amount of meaning there is in it you could put in your eye.

4   In just such ways is the secret language of statistics, so appealing in a fact-minded culture, being used to sensationalize, inflate, confuse, and oversimplify. Statistical terms are necessary in reporting the mass data of social and economic trends, business conditions, "opinion" polls, this year's census. But without writers who use the words with honesty and understanding and readers who know what they mean, the result can only be semantic nonsense.

5   In popular writing on scientific research, the abused statistic is almost crowding out the picture of the white-jacketed hero laboring overtime without time-and-a-half in an ill-lit laboratory. Like the "little dash of powder, little pot of paint," statistics are making many an important fact "look like what she ain't." Here are some of the ways it is done.

6   *The sample with the built-in bias.* Our Yale men—or Yalemen, as they say in the Time-Life building—belong to this flourishing group. The exaggerated estimate of their income is not based on all members of the class nor on a random or representative sample of them. At least two interesting categories of 1924-model Yale men have been excluded.

7   First there are those whose present addresses are unknown to their classmates. Wouldn't you bet that these lost sheep are earning less than the boys from prominent families and the others who can be handily reached from a Wall Street office?

8   There are those who chucked the questionnaire into the nearest wastebasket. Maybe they didn't answer because they were not making enough money to brag about. Like the fellow who found a note clipped to his first pay check suggesting that he consider the amount of his salary confidential: "Don't worry," he told the boss. "I'm just as ashamed of it as you are."

9   Omitted from our sample then are just the two groups most likely to depress the average. The $25,111 figure is beginning to account for itself. It may indeed be a true figure for those of the Class of '24 whose addresses are known and who are willing to stand up and tell how much they earn. But even that requires a possibly dangerous assumption that the gentlemen are telling the truth.

10   To be dependable to any useful degree at all, a sampling study must use a representative sample (which can lead to trouble too) or a truly random one. If *all* the Class of '24 is included, that's all right. If every tenth name on a complete list is used, that is all right too, and so is drawing an adequate number of names out of a hat. The test is this: Does every name in the group have an equal chance to be in the sample?

11   You'll recall that ignoring this requirement was what produced the *Literary Digest's* famed fiasco. When names for polling were taken only from telephone books and subscription lists, people who did not have telephones or *Literary Digest* subscriptions had no chance to be in the sample.

They possibly did not mind this underprivilege a bit, but their absence was in the end very hard on the magazine that relied on the figures.

12   This leads to a moral: You can prove about anything you want to by letting your sample bias itself. As a consumer of statistical data—a reader, for example, of a news magazine—remember that no statistical conclusion can rise above the quality of the sample it is based upon. In the absence of information about the procedures behind it, you are not warranted in giving any credence at all to the result.

13   *The truncated, or gee-whiz, graph.* If you want to show some statistical information quickly and clearly, draw a picture of it. Graphic presentation is the thing today. If you don't mind misleading the hasty looker, or if you quite clearly *want* to deceive him, you can save some space by chopping the bottom off many kinds of graphs.

14   Suppose you are showing the upward trend of national income month by month for a year. The total rise, as in one recent year, is 7 per cent. It looks like this:

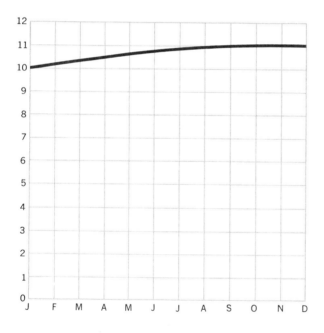

That is clear enough. Anybody can see that the trend is slightly upward. You are showing a 7 per cent increase and that is exactly what it looks like.

15   But it lacks schmaltz. So you chop off the bottom, this way:

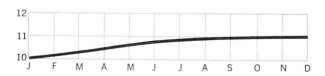

The figures are the same. It is the same graph and nothing has been falsified—except the impression that it gives. Anyone looking at it can just feel prosperity throbbing in the arteries of the country. It is a subtler equivalent of editing "National income rose 7 per cent" into ". . . climbed a whopping 7 per cent."

16   It is vastly more effective, however, because of that illusion of objectivity.

17   *The souped-up graph.* Sometimes truncating is not enough. The trifling rise in something or other still looks almost as insignificant as it is. You can make that 7 per cent look livelier than 100 per cent ordinarily does. Simply change the proportion between the ordinate and the abscissa. There's no rule against it, and it does give your graph a prettier shape.

18   But it exaggerates, to say the least, something awful:

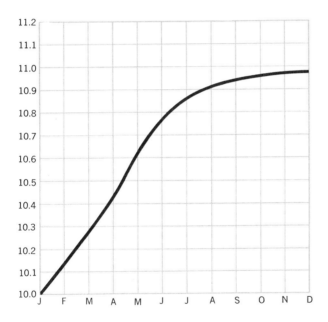

19   *The well-chosen average.* I live near a country neighborhood for which I can report an average income of $15,000. I could also report it as $3,500.

20   If I should want to sell real estate hereabouts to people having a high snobbery content, the first figure would be handy. The second figure, however, is the one to use in an argument against raising taxes, or the local bus fare.

21   Both are legitimate averages, legally arrived at. Yet it is obvious that at least one of them must be as misleading as an out-and-out lie. The $15,000-figure is a mean, the arithmetic average of the incomes of all the families in the community. The smaller figure is a median; it might be called the income of the average family in the group. It indicates that half the families have less than $3,500 a year and half have more.

22   Here is where some of the confusion about averages comes from. Many human characteristics have the grace to fall into what is called the "normal" distribution. If you draw a picture of it, you get a curve that is shaped like a bell. Mean and median fall at about the same point, so it doesn't make very much difference which you use.

23   But some things refuse to follow this neat curve. Income is one of them. Incomes for most large areas will range from under $1,000 a year to upward of $50,000. Almost everybody will be under $10,000, way over on the left-hand side of that curve.

24   One of the things that made the income figure for the "average Yale-man" meaningless is that we are not told whether it is a mean or a median. It is not that one type of average is invariably better than the other; it depends upon what you are talking about. But neither gives you any real information—and either may be highly misleading—unless you know which of those two kinds of average it is.

25   In the country neighborhood I mentioned, almost everyone has less than the average—the mean, that is—of $10,500. These people are all small farmers, except for a trio of millionaire week-enders who bring up the mean enormously.

26   You can be pretty sure that when an income average is given in the form of a mean nearly everybody has less than that.

27   *The insignificant difference or the elusive error.* Your two children Peter and Linda (we might as well give them modish names while we're about it) take intelligence tests. Peter's IQ, you learn, is 98 and Linda's is 101. Aha! Linda is your brighter child.

28   Is she? An intelligence test is, or purports to be, a sampling of intellect. An IQ, like other products of sampling, is a figure with a statistical error, which expresses the precision or reliability of the figure. The size of this probable error can be calculated. For their test the makers of the much-used Revised Stanford-Binet have found it to be about 3 per cent. So Peter's indicated IQ of 98 really means only that there is an even chance that it falls between 95 and 101. There is an equal probability that it falls somewhere else—below 95 or above 101. Similarly, Linda's has no better than a fifty-fifty chance of being within the fairly sizeable range of 98 to 104.

29   You can work out some comparisons from that. One is that there is rather better than one chance in four that Peter, with his lower IQ rating, is really at least three points smarter than Linda. A statistician doesn't like to consider a difference significant unless you can hand him odds a lot longer than that.

30   Ignoring the error in a sampling study leads to all kinds of silly conclusions. There are magazine editors to whom readership surveys are gospel; with a 40 per cent readership reported for one article and a 35 per cent for another, they demand more like the first. I've seen even smaller differences given tremendous weight, because statistics are a mystery and

numbers are impressive. The same thing goes for market surveys and so-called public-opinion polls. The rule is that you cannot make a valid comparison between two such figures unless you know the deviations. And unless the difference between the figures is many times greater than the probable error of each, you have only a guess that the one appearing greater really is.

31   Otherwise you are like the man choosing a camp site from a report of mean temperature alone. One place in California with a mean annual temperature of 61 is San Nicolas Island on the south coast, where it always stays in the comfortable range between 47 and 87. Another with a mean of 61 is in the inland desert, where the thermometer hops around from 15 to 104. The deviation from the mean marks the difference, and you can freeze or roast if you ignore it.

32   *The one-dimensional picture.* Suppose you have just two or three figures to compare—say the average weekly wage of carpenters in the United States and another country. The sums might be $60 and $30. An ordinary bar chart makes the difference graphic.

That is an honest picture. It looks good for American carpenters, but perhaps it does not have quite the oomph you are after. Can't you make that difference appear overwhelming and at the same time give it what I am afraid is known as eye-appeal? Of course you can. Following tradition, you represent these sums by pictures of money bags. If the $30 bag is one inch high, you draw the $60 bag two inches high. That's in proportion, isn't it? The catch is, of course, that the American's money bag, being twice as tall as that of the $30 man, covers an area on your page four times as great. And since your two-dimensional picture represents an object that would in fact have three dimensions, the money bags actually would differ much

more than that. The volumes of any two similar solids vary as the cubes of their heights. If the unfortunate foreigner's bag holds $30 worth of dimes, the American's would hold not $60 but a neat $240.

33   You didn't say that, though, did you? And you can't be blamed, you're only doing it the way practically everybody else does.

34   *The ever-impressive decimal.* For a spurious air of precision that will lend all kinds of weight to the most disreputable statistics, consider the decimal.

35   Ask a hundred citizens how many hours they slept last night. Come out with a total of, say, 781.3. Your data are far from precise to begin with. Most people will miss their guess by fifteen minutes or more and some will recall five sleepless minutes as half a night of tossing insomnia.

36   But go ahead, do your arithmetic, announce that people sleep an average of 7.813 hours a night. You will sound as if you knew precisely what you are talking about. If you were foolish enough to say 7.8 (or "almost 8") hours it would sound like what it was—an approximation.

37   *The semi-attached figure.* If you can't prove what you want to prove, demonstrate something else and pretend that they are the same thing. In the daze that follows the collision of statistics with the human mind, hardly anybody will notice the difference. The semi-attached figure is a durable device guaranteed to stand you in good stead. It always has.

38   If you can't prove that your nostrum cures colds, publish a sworn laboratory report that the stuff killed 31,108 germs in a test tube in eleven seconds. There may be no connection at all between assorted germs in a test tube and the whatever-it-is that produces colds, but people aren't going to reason that sharply, especially while sniffling.

39   Maybe that one is too obvious and people are beginning to catch on. Here is a trickier version.

40   Let us say that in a period when race prejudice is growing it is to

your advantage to "prove" otherwise. You will not find it a difficult assignment.

41 Ask that usual cross section of the population if they think Negroes have as good a chance as white people to get jobs. Ask again a few months later. As Princeton's Office of Public Opinion Research has found out, people who are most unsympathetic to Negroes are the ones most likely to answer yes to this question.

42 As prejudice increases in a country, the percentage of affirmative answers you will get to this question will become larger. What looks on the face of it like growing opportunity for Negroes actually is mounting prejudice and nothing else. You have achieved something rather remarkable: the worse things get, the better your survey makes them look.

43 *The unwarranted assumption, or* post hoc *rides again.* The interrelation of cause and effect, so often obscure anyway, can be most neatly hidden in statistical data.

44 Somebody once went to a good deal of trouble to find out if cigarette smokers make lower college grades than non-smokers. They did. This naturally pleased many people, and they made much of it.

45 The unwarranted assumption, of course, was that smoking had produced dull minds. It seemed vaguely reasonable on the face of it, so it was quite widely accepted. But it really proved nothing of the sort, any more than it proved that poor grades drive students to the solace of tobacco. Maybe the relationship worked in one direction, maybe in the other. And maybe all this is only an indication that the sociable sort of fellow who is likely to take his books less than seriously is also likely to sit around and smoke many cigarettes.

46 Permitting statistical treatment to befog causal relationships is little better than superstition. It is like the conviction among the people of the Hebrides that body lice produce good health. Observation over the centuries had taught them that people in good health had lice and sick people often did not. *Ergo,* lice made a man healthy. Everybody should have them.

47 Scantier evidence, treated statistically at the expense of common sense, has made many a medical fortune and many a medical article in magazines, including professional ones. More sophisticated observers finally got things straightened out in the Hebrides. As it turned out, almost everybody in those circles had lice most of the time. But when a man took a fever (quite possibly carried to him by those same lice) and his body became hot, the lice left.

48 Here you have cause and effect not only reversed, but intermingled.

49 There you have a primer in some ways to use statistics to deceive. A well-wrapped statistic is better than Hitler's "big lie": it misleads, yet it can't be pinned onto you.

50 Is this little list altogether too much like a manual for swindlers? Perhaps I can justify it in the manner of the retired burglar whose published reminiscences amounted to a graduate course in how to pick a lock and

muffle a footfall: The crooks already know these tricks. Honest men must learn them in self-defense.

COMMENTARY

This recommendation spends almost all of its effort on a definition of the problem, on translating "the secret language of statistics" into terms that all of us can understand—and see through. Once we have seen how statistics can lie, two alternatives are open to us, and Huff confronts them in his final paragraphs. We can join in the swindle, or we can resist that temptation and instead help to defeat the swindle by not letting it get us. Huff does not bother to present a detailed explanation of which alternative is better. He simply says "The crooks already know these tricks. Honest men must learn them in self-defense" (paragraph 50). Those of us who want to be honest, at least, have received the message. But those of us who want to be crooked might have received one too!

Huff's procedure uses the "division and classification" technique discussed earlier in this book (p. 30). He divides the statistical con game into what he thinks are its major parts, classifies them (on what principle?), and explains each one by an illustration. He tries to keep his tone conversational and nontechnical because he wants us to accept him as one of us, an "honest" common man unmasking the games-players who indulge in verbal razzle-dazzle to prevent us from seeing what they're doing. At least once, however, Huff himself uses technical language and fails to explain it. (In paragraph 28, he refers to "probable error," which identifies the range where 50 percent of the tested subjects will be. Thus a "probable error" of 3—really plus or minus 3—for Peter's score means that 50 percent of the children who receive scores of 98 actually have IQs between 95, or 98 minus 3; and 101, or 98 plus 3. Without this definition, we don't see why Peter's score is as likely to fall outside the range as within it).

Does Huff's recommendation work? Do you know how to avoid being lied to by statistics? And do you *want* to? Is he safe in assuming that all he needs to do to prove the superiority of his choice is remind us of honesty? Perhaps people are so easily fooled by statistical (and other) con games because they want to be fooled. In that case, if they learn Huff's lessons, it will not be in the "self-defense" of their integrity, but in defense of their conviction that everyone is out to win whatever he can anyway, so they might as well play along. A reader with this orientation will take Huff's mock title as his real one.

OUTLINE

C. The souped-up graph—paragraphs 17–18
D. The well-chosen average—paragraphs 19–26
E. The insignificant difference—paragraphs 27–31
F. The one-dimensional picture—paragraphs 32–33
G. The ever-impressive decimal—paragraphs 34–36
H. The semi-attached figure—paragraphs 37–42
I. The unwarranted assumption—paragraphs 43–48
III. The alternatives, evaluation, recommendation: honest men must learn these tricks in self-defense—paragraphs 49–50

SUGGESTIONS FOR WRITING

1. Huff's recommendation relies on the general principle that we ought to acquaint ourselves with evil in order to conquer it. If you don't know what it's like to be drunk, the argument goes, you can't know how to help people avoid excessive drinking; if you don't know what it's like to steal, you can't understand the mentality of criminals, and you won't know what to do about crime. Write a recommendation essay based on your personal experience in dealing with wrongdoing. Would you recommend that we try it to understand it? Is it worth the risk that if we try it, we'll like it?

2. Huff explains how simple statistical information can be used to suggest different, even contradictory, meanings. Assume that you are a public relations official of a corporation being criticized for its large profits. Some information about the company's finances is given below. Write a short recommendation report to the president of the company indicating how he should use this information at a press conference. (If you adopt this "suggestion for writing," what would Huff think of your integrity?)

INFORMATION ABOUT AMSTAR CORPORATION[1]

In 1974, the company received an estimated $1,046,900,000 in income.
In 1974, the company's net income (after expenses were subtracted), before taxes, was an estimated $58,440,000.
In 1974, the company's net income after paying taxes was an estimated $31,410,000.
In 1974, the company paid out a large amount of its net income to its shareholders: $1.725 per share on 3,722,274 shares. These shares are owned by 13,864 shareholders.
In 1974, the company employed 6568 people. Sugar and sugar products accounted for about 90 percent of its income; about 70 percent of the sugar was sold to food processors (not directly to retail customers). The company was estimated to be worth about $138,900,000; it was the largest domestic manufacturer of sugar and sugar products.

Additional information: during 1974, retail sugar prices increased some 300 percent. Amstar reported that its profits rose by 250 percent for one three-

[1] Data from Standard and Poor's Standard N.Y.S.E. Stock Reports: "Amstar Corp.," vol. 41, no. 169 (September 3, 1974).

month period [i.e. its profits for that quarter-year were two-and-a-half times what they had been for that quarter in the preceding year].[2]

3. Write a mock "how-to"—how to get an unsafe car through inspection (and be a successful highway suicide); how to spend a full week's grocery money on fancy foods that will feed you for a mere day-and-a-half; how to do all the schoolwork for your midterm exams the night before (and get a rapid-transit ticket out of college). Explain in detail, as Huff does, exactly how the system works, in order to recommend that your readers *not* let the system work on them.

2 *Newsweek,* November 11, 1974, p. 94.

a modest proposal
JONATHAN SWIFT

When a person unknowingly says something contrary to fact, he is simply wrong, perhaps foolish. When he says something that he *knows* is contrary to fact, he is lying. But when both speaker and audience know the superficial meaning is not the real one, speaker and audience share a trick, and we call this irony. Some taint of its kinship to the lie makes irony more or less harsh, often cruel.

Such is the case with Swift's essay, which is one of the most famous instances of irony in the English language. Written in 1729, it records Swift's indignation against the English government's inhumane treatment of the Irish people. Some readers have mistaken the serious tone and precise detail as signs that Swift really meant to endorse cannibalism, as the essay superficially proposes. Careful readers do not make this mistake, but they often find it difficult to explain why.

A MODEST PROPOSAL
FOR PREVENTING THE CHILDREN OF POOR PEOPLE IN IRELAND
FROM BEING A BURDEN TO THEIR PARENTS OR COUNTRY,
AND FOR MAKING THEM BENEFICIAL TO THE PUBLIC

1   It is a melancholy object to those who walk through this great town or travel in the country, when they see the streets, the roads, and cabin doors, crowded with beggars of the female-sex, followed by three, four, or six children, all in rags and importuning every passenger for an alms. These mothers, instead of being able to work for their honest livelihood, are forced to employ all their time in strolling to beg sustenance for their help-

less infants, who, as they grow up, either turn thieves for want of work, or leave their dear native country to fight for the Pretender in Spain, or sell themselves to the Barbadoes.[1]

2   I think it is agreed by all parties that this prodigious number of children in the arms, or on the backs, or at the heels of their mothers, and frequently of their fathers, is in the present deplorable state of the kingdom a very great additional grievance; and therefore whoever could find out a fair, cheap, and easy method of making these children sound, useful members of the commonwealth would deserve so well of the public as to have his statue set up for a preserver of the nation.

3   But my intention is very far from being confined to provide only for the children of professed beggars; it is of a much greater extent, and shall take in the whole number of infants at a certain age who are born of parents in effect as little able to support them as those who demand our charity in the streets.

4   As to my own part, having turned my thoughts for many years upon this important subject, and maturely weighed the several schemes of other projectors, I have always found them grossly mistaken in their computation. It is true, a child just dropped from its dam may be supported by her milk for a solar year, with little other nourishment; at most not above the value of two shillings, which the mother may certainly get, or the value in scraps, by her lawful occupation of begging; and it is exactly at one year old that I propose to provide for them in such a manner as instead of being a charge upon their parents or the parish, or wanting food and raiment for the rest of their lives, they shall on the contrary contribute to the feeding, and partly to the clothing, of many thousands.

5   There is likewise another great advantage in my scheme, that it will prevent those voluntary abortions, and that horrid practice of women murdering their bastard children, alas, too frequent among us, sacrificing the poor innocent babes, I doubt, more to avoid the expense than the shame, which would move tears and pity in the most savage and inhuman breast.

6   The number of souls in this kingdom being usually reckoned one million and a half, of these I calculate there may be about two hundred thousand couples whose wives are breeders; from which number I subtract thirty thousand couples who are able to maintain their own children, although I apprehend there cannot be so many under the present distresses of the kingdom; but this being granted, there will remain an hundred and seventy thousand breeders. I again subtract fifty thousand for those women who miscarry, or whose children die by accident or disease within the year. There only remain an hundred and twenty thousand children of poor parents annually born. The question therefore is, how this number shall be reared and provided for, which, as I have already said, under the present situation of affairs, is utterly impossible by all the methods hitherto proposed. For we can neither employ them in handicraft nor agriculture; we

---

1 That is, contract themselves to work in order to pay the cost of transportation to a colony.

neither build houses (I mean in the country) nor cultivate land. They can very seldom pick up a livelihood by stealing till they arrive at six years old, except where they are of towardly parts; although I confess they learn the rudiments much earlier, during which time they can however be looked upon only as probationers, as I have been informed by a principal gentleman in the county of Cavan, who protested to me that he never knew above one or two instances under the age of six, even in a part of the kingdom so renowned for the quickest proficiency in that art.

7   I am assured by our merchants that a boy or a girl before twelve years old is no salable commodity; and even when they come to this age they will not yield above three pounds, or three pounds and half a crown at most on the Exchange; which cannot turn to account either to the parents or the kingdom, the charge of nutriment and rags having been at least four times that value.

8   I shall now therefore humbly propose my own thoughts, which I hope will not be liable to the least objection.

9   I have been assured by a very knowing American of my acquaintance in London, that a young healthy child well nursed is at a year old a most delicious, nourishing, and wholesome food, whether stewed, roasted, baked, or boiled; and I make no doubt that it will equally serve in a fricassee or a ragout.

10   I do therefore humbly offer it to public consideration that of the hundred and twenty thousand children, already computed, twenty thousand may be reserved for breed, whereof only one fourth part to be males, which is more than we allow to sheep, black cattle, or swine; and my reason is that these children are seldom the fruits of marriage, a circumstance not much regarded by our savages, therefore one male will be sufficient to serve four females. That the remaining hundred thousand may at a year old be offered in sale to the persons of quality and fortune through the kingdom, always advising the mother to let them suck plentifully in the last month, so as to render them plump and fat for a good table. A child will make two dishes at an entertainment for friends; and when the family dines alone, the fore or hind quarter will make a reasonable dish, and seasoned with a little pepper or salt will be very good boiled on the fourth day, especially in winter.

11   I have reckoned upon a medium that a child just born will weigh twelve pounds, and in a solar year if tolerably nursed increaseth to twenty-eight pounds.

12   I grant this food will be somewhat dear, and therefore very proper for landlords, who, as they have already devoured most of the parents, seem to have the best title to the children.

13   Infant's flesh will be in season throughout the year, but more plentiful in March, and a little before and after. For we are told by a grave author, an eminent French physician,[2] that fish being a prolific diet, there are more

---

2 Rabelais.

children born in Roman Catholic countries about nine months after Lent than at any other season; therefore, reckoning a year after Lent, the markets will be more glutted than usual, because the number of popish infants is at least three to one in this kingdom; and therefore it will have one other collateral advantage, by lessening the number of Papists among us.

14   I have already computed the charge of nursing a beggar's child (in which list I reckon all cottagers, laborers, and four fifths of the farmers) to be about two shillings per annum, rags included; and I believe no gentleman would repine to give ten shillings for the carcass of a good fat child, which, as I have said, will make four dishes of excellent nutritive meat, when he hath only some particular friend or his own family to dine with him. Thus the squire will learn to be a good landlord, and grow popular among the tenants; the mother will have eight shillings net profit, and be fit for work till she produces another child.

15   Those who are more thrifty (as I must confess the times require) may flay the carcass; the skin of which artificially dressed will make admirable gloves for ladies, and summer boots for fine gentlemen.

16   As to our city of Dublin, shambles may be appointed for this purpose in the most convenient parts of it, and butchers we may be assured will not be wanting; although I rather recommend buying the children alive, and dressing them hot from the knife as we do roasting pigs.

17   A very worthy person, a true lover of his country, and whose virtues I highly esteem, was lately pleased in discoursing on this matter to offer a refinement upon my scheme. He said that many gentlemen of this kingdom having of late destroyed their deer, he conceived that the want of venison might be well supplied by the bodies of young lads and maidens, not exceeding fourteen years of age nor under twelve, so great a number of both sexes in every county being now ready to starve for want of work and service; and these to be disposed of by their parents, if alive, or otherwise by their nearest relations. But with due deference to so excellent a friend and so deserving a patriot, I cannot be altogether in his sentiments; for as to the males, my American acquaintance assured me from frequent experience that their flesh was generally tough and lean, like that of our schoolboys, by continual exercise, and their taste disagreeable; and to fatten them would not answer the charge. Then as to the females, it would, I think with humble submission, be a loss to the public, because they soon would become breeders themselves: and besides, it is not improbable that some scrupulous people might be apt to censure such a practice (although indeed very unjustly) as a little bordering upon cruelty; which, I confess, hath always been with me the strongest objection against any project, how well soever intended.

18   But in order to justify my friend, he confessed that this expedient was put into his head by the famous Psalmanazar, a native of the island Formosa, who came from thence to London above twenty years ago, and in conversation told my friend that in his country when any young person happened to be put to death, the executioner sold the carcass to persons

of quality as a prime dainty; and that in his time the body of a plump girl of fifteen, who was crucified for an attempt to poison the emperor, was sold to his Imperial Majesty's prime minister of state, and other great mandarins of the court, in joints from the gibbet, at four hundred crowns. Neither indeed can I deny that if the same use were made of several plump young girls in this town, who without one single groat to their fortunes cannot stir abroad without a chair, and appear at the playhouse and assemblies in foreign fineries which they never will pay for, the kingdom would not be the worse.

19   Some persons of a desponding spirit are in great concern about that vast number of poor people who are aged, diseased, or maimed, and I have been desired to employ my thoughts what course may be taken to ease the nation of so grievous an encumbrance. But I am not in the least pain upon that matter, because it is very well known that they are every day dying and rotting by cold and famine, and filth and vermin, as fast as can be reasonably expected. And as to the younger laborers, they are now in almost as hopeful a condition. They cannot get work, and consequently pine away for want of nourishment to a degree that if at any time they are accidentally hired to common labor, they have not strength to perform it; and thus the country and themselves are happily delivered from the evils to come.

20   I have too long digressed, and therefore shall return to my subject. I think the advantages by the proposal which I have made are obvious and many, as well as of the highest importance.

21   For first, as I have already observed, it would greatly lessen the number of Papists, with whom we are yearly overrun, being the principal breeders of the nation as well as our most dangerous enemies; and who stay at home on purpose to deliver the kingdom to the Pretender, hoping to take their advantage by the absence of so many good Protestants, who have chosen rather to leave their country than to stay at home and pay tithes against their conscience to an Episcopal curate.

22   Secondly, the poorer tenants will have something valuable of their own, which by law may be made liable to distress, and help to pay their landlord's rent, their corn and cattle being already seized and money a thing unknown.

23   Thirdly, whereas the maintenance of an hundred thousand children, from two years old and upwards, cannot be computed at less than ten shillings a piece per annum, the nation's stock will be thereby increased fifty thousand pounds per annum, besides the profit of a new dish introduced to the tables of all gentlemen of fortune in the kingdom who have any refinement in taste. And the money will circulate among ourselves, the goods being entirely of our own growth and maufacture.

24   Fourthly, the constant breeders, besides the gain of eight shillings sterling per annum by the sale of their children, will be rid of the charge of maintaining them after the first year.

25   Fifthly, this food would likewise bring great custom to taverns, where

the vintners will certainly be so prudent as to procure the best receipts for dressing it to perfection, and consequently have their houses frequented by all the fine gentlemen, who justly value themselves upon their knowledge in good eating; and a skillful cook, who understands how to oblige his guests, will contrive to make it as expensive as they please.

26   Sixthly, this would be a great inducement to marriage, which all wise nations have either encouraged by rewards or enforced by laws and penalties. It would increase the care and tenderness of mothers toward their children, when they were sure of a settlement for life to the poor babes, provided in some sort by the public, to their annual profit instead of expense. We should see an honest emulation among the married women, which of them could bring the fattest child to the market. Men would become as fond of their wives during the time of their pregnancy as they are now of their mares in foal, their cows in calf, or sows when they are ready to farrow; nor offer to beat or kick them (as is too frequent a practice) for fear of a miscarriage.

27   Many other advantages might be enumerated. For instance, the addition of some thousand carcasses in our exportation of barreled beef, the propagation of swine's flesh, and improvement in the art of making good bacon, so much wanted among us by the great destruction of pigs, too frequent at our tables, which are no way comparable in taste or magnificence to a well-grown, fat, yearling child, which roasted whole will make a considerable figure at a lord mayor's feast or any other public entertainment. But this and many others I omit, being studious of brevity.

28   Supposing that one thousand families in this city would be constant customers for infants' flesh, besides others who might have it at merry meetings, particularly weddings and christenings, I compute that Dublin would take off annually about twenty thousand carcasses, and the rest of the kingdom (where probably they will be sold somewhat cheaper) the remaining eighty thousand.

29   I can think of no one objection that will possibly be raised against this proposal, unless it should be urged that the number of people will be thereby much lessened in the kingdom. This I freely own, and it was indeed one principal design in offering it to the world. I desire the reader will observe, that I calculate my remedy for this one individual kingdom of Ireland and for no other that ever was, is, or I think ever can be upon earth. Therefore let no man talk to me of other expedients: of taxing our absentees at five shillings a pound: of using neither clothes nor household furniture except what is of our own growth and manufacture: of utterly rejecting the materials and instruments that promote foreign luxury: of curing the expensiveness of pride, vanity, idleness, and gaming in our women: of introducing a vein of parsimony, prudence, and temperance: of learning to love our country, in the want of which we differ even from Laplanders and the inhabitants of Topinamboo[3]: of quitting our animosities

3 A district in Brazil.

and factions, nor acting any longer like the Jews, who were murdering one another at the very moment their city was taken: of being a little cautious not to sell our country and conscience for nothing: of teaching landlords to have at least one degree of mercy toward their tenants: lastly, of putting a spirit of honesty, industry, and skill into our shopkeepers; who, if a resolution could now be taken to buy only our native goods, would immediately unite to cheat and exact upon us in the price, the measure, and the goodness, nor could ever yet be brought to make one fair proposal of just dealing, though often and earnestly invited to it.[4]

30 Therefore I repeat, let no man talk to me of these and the like expedients, till he hath at least some glimpse of hope that there will ever be some hearty and sincere attempt to put them in practice.

31 But as to myself, having been wearied out for many years with offering vain, idle, visionary thoughts, and at length utterly despairing of success, I fortunately fell upon this proposal, which, as it is wholly new, so it hath something solid and real, of no expense and little trouble, full in our own power, and whereby we can incur no danger in disobliging England. For this kind of commodity will not bear exportation, the flesh being of too tender a consistence to admit a long continuance in salt, although perhaps I could name a country which would be glad to eat up our whole nation without it.

32 After all, I am not so violently bent upon my own opinion as to reject any offer proposed by wise men, which shall be found equally innocent, cheap, easy, and effectual. But before something of that kind shall be advanced in contradiction to my scheme, and offering a better, I desire the author or authors will be pleased maturely to consider two points. First, as things now stand, how they will be able to find food and raiment for an hundred thousand useless mouths and backs. And secondly, there being a round million of creatures in human figure throughout this kingdom, whose sole subsistence put into a common stock would leave them in debt two millions of pounds sterling, adding those who are beggars by profession to the bulk of farmers, cottagers, and laborers, with their wives and children who are beggars in effect; I desire those politicians who dislike my overture, and may perhaps be so bold to attempt an answer, that they will first ask the parents of these mortals whether they would not at this day think it a great happiness to have been sold for food at a year old in the manner I prescribe, and thereby have avoided such a perpetual scene of misfortunes as they have since gone through by the oppression of landlords, the impossibility of paying rent without money or trade, the want of common sustenance, with neither house nor clothes to cover them from the inclemencies of the weather, and the most inevitable prospect of entailing the like or greater miseries upon their breed forever.

33 I profess, in the sincerity of my heart, that I have not the least personal interest in endeavoring to promote this necessary work, having no

---

[4] Swift himself made these proposals in his own earlier works.

other motive than the public good of my country, by advancing our trade, providing for infants, relieving the poor, and giving some pleasure to the rich. I have no children by which I can propose to get a single penny; the youngest being nine years old, and my wife past childbearing.

COMMENTARY

The main problem with irony is that people often "don't get it." Explaining irony to someone is like explaining a joke. The effect is lost, and the person who needs an explanation may even get angry at the "trick" that has been played on him. A skillful ironic writer exaggerates just enough to let perceptive readers know he does not mean what he says, but not enough to make his technique blatantly obvious. If it is too obvious, our pleasure at being part of the trick (a pleasure similar to the feeling produced by being part of an "in-joke") will disappear.

It is easier to speak ironically than to write ironically because so much can be suggested by the tone of voice. This is why a writer frequently uses the first-person pronoun "I" to convey an ironic message: it sounds like a person speaking. We call the character who seems to be speaking the *persona*. Swift's *persona* in "A Modest Proposal" is a pompous and smug politician.

You may begin to question the *persona* here when he refers to "a child just dropped from its dam" (paragraph 4) or to wives as "breeders" (paragraph 6) or to a population "whereof only one fourth part [are] to be males, which is more than we allow" to animals (paragraph 10). The casual way in which Swift's politician equates people to sheep or pigs should make you dislike him. By paragraph 12, the trick becomes more obvious when Swift has the speaker compare the landlords' figurative "devouring" of parents by exhorbitant rents to the literal eating of children. This comparison gives us a glimpse of Swift's real target. What the heartless politician accepts, we reject. The politician regards both forms of exploitation of suffering people as reasonable; therefore we regard both as *un*reasonable. Swift himself believes that the rich should not be allowed to prey upon the poor.

Notice that this mock recommendation includes the standard ingredients of a serious recommendation. Swift's *persona* identifies the problem, presents his proposal, evaluates it favorably because of the benefits it would produce, and rejects alternatives. (These alternatives are, of course, the proposals that Swift himself would really recommend to us. By now we always want the opposite of what the *persona* wants, so when he rejects them, we accept them.) At the end of his speech, the *persona* summarizes the problem and offers assurances of his sincerity and objectivity—his credentials, in effect.

A vital element in any recommendation is the presence of dramatic information. (This recommendation, being ironic, advocates the opposite of what the *persona* says.) The writer must present facts to appeal to his audience's reasoning abilities and vivid details to appeal to his audience's emotions. Swift accomplishes these aims. His "Modest Proposal" is credited with convincing the English officials to improve conditions in Ireland.

OUTLINE

    I. Definition of the problem—paragraphs 1–7
    II. Presentation of the proposal—paragraphs 8–18
    (digression on the aged)—paragraph 19
    III. Evaluation of the proposal—paragraphs 20–28
    IV. Objections and alternatives refuted—paragraphs 29–30
    V. Summary of the problem, praise of the proposal, presentation of the speaker's credentials—paragraphs 31–33

SUGGESTIONS FOR WRITING

1. Draw up a preamble for the constitution of (a) a Society for the Restitution of American Lands (or Australian or South African) to the Aborigines, or (b) a Society for the Elevation (or Reduction) of Sea Level by 1000 feet, or (c) a Society for the Propagation of Elves or Cockroaches or People with Six Toes, etc. Make sure that your real (opposite) proposal is perceptible: perhaps "Let's have no more organizations."

2. Students and teachers often discover bodies of knowledge, or new attitudes toward old bodies of knowledge, that they think should be included in programs of study. Draw up a course proposal for Introduction to Contemporary Costume or Introduction to Body Language in Ethnic Groups. Your proposal might emphasize racist, sexist, or religious overtones implicit in the subject—and thus suggest your real thesis: "Let's have no more faintly disguised courses in prejudice."

3. Write a mock proposal requesting funds for some project. Write a letter to your local United Fund chapter asking for money to hold a Happy Tuesday Parade every Tuesday (the real recommendation is that there be fewer silly celebrations of nothing). Or write a newspaper advertisement asking people to contribute $10 each to buy the local high school a $16,000 escalator so that the students won't have to walk up one flight of stairs (the real recommendation is that we stop buying expensive gadgetry to pamper American teen-agers). The following "serious proposal" may give you some suggestions. It appears to be a recommendation that we build pyramids in Minnesota; but the real recommendation is that we stop building meaningless, useless, and unimaginative monuments—and stop forming volunteer corps for fatuous purposes.

PYRAMIDS FOR MINNESOTA: A SERIOUS PROPOSAL—THOMAS M. DISCH

1   Q. Does Minnesota need pyramids?

2   A. No. Pyramids transcend the notion of "utility." This, indeed, is their special merit. If they could be put to any use whatever, people would not be interested in them. Why do people go to Europe? Not to see its magnificent grain elevators and factories, but to climb the ramparts of indefensible forts

churches—hundreds of churches, thousands of churches, ever more and more churches!

3   Q. Why not build churches, then?

4   A. It would confuse too many people. They would want the church to belong to a religion or express a style; they would complain of the expense, insisting that so much money and effort were better spent feeding poor children or searching for a cure for leukemia. Pyramids elude such controversies. They stand outside the flow of History. It is the very inexpressiveness of a pyramid, like that of a corpse or a crystal, that is so awesome.

5   Q. Why Minnesota, then? Why not in a desert?

6   A. There too, by all means. But, really, why *not* Minnesota?

7   Q. Should they all be the same size?

8   A. Yes. Especially if there are to be several in one area.

9   Q. And of the same degree of steepness?

10   A. Yes—45°. As there will not be steps, this will dispel any lingering doubts as to their usefulness. One should never be prompted to climb a pyramid for the sake of a view. This is principally what is wrong with mountains.

11   Q. Passageways?

12   A. Absolutely not! No time capsules either. Rock-solid throughout. If they are to be vandalized, it should be from motives as disinterested as those that led to their formation.

13   Q. Who will build them?

14   A. All of us who want to. Volunteers must enlist for at least one year, but for no longer than three, thus steering a course between the Scylla of amateurism and the Charybdis of expertise. All volunteers must spend at least half their workweek in the actual labor of construction. Those who have clearly shirked or malingered must forfeit the bond they posted upon enlisting.

15   Q. Why would anyone volunteer?

16   A. For the reason one does anything—the experience promises to be congenial to one's temperament. Undoubtedly the slaves who hewed and moved and fit in place the blocks of the first pyramids felt a secret gratification at taking part in the erection of such great monuments. Who can read of the building of Chartres without a smart of envy? By enlisting in the Pyramid Corps, one becomes part of a community devoted to a high and selfless goal, and yet there is no danger, in this case, of unwittingly furthering less worthy aims while pursuing one's own enlightenment. The CIA will have as little patience with pyramids as the church of Rome, but no great animus against them either. Pyramids, being all alike, do not excite the imagination, and so even the least competent of painters, architects, or interior decorators should be able to view their construction with equanimity. What other undertaking could be at once so strenuous and so little self-deluding? This is an even purer form than working for an insurance company of modern, secular monasticism.

17   Q. Where will they be located?

18   A. Outside the towns of Fairmont, Pipestone, Moorhead, Bemidji, and Aurora. Anyone who wants to see them should have to make a special effort.

19   Q. How can I help *now*?

20   A. Send your name and address to PYRAMIDS, c/o this magazine, indicating whether your interest is in contributing funds or your own labor. When sufficient interest has been demonstrated, a nonprofit Pyramid Foudation will be established, and you will be notified.

Source. Disch.

the impact of language

These selections offer a pair of proposals. They share the same thesis: we should make our language tell us what's really happening, not be satisfied with fuzzy phrases that tell us nothing. Orwell presents this thesis in the standard recommendation form. Royko presents it as a mock recommendation.

Orwell's essay, which has been popular for 25 years, urges us to save our language from vagueness and pretentiousness. Orwell begins by asserting the political importance of language: if we use words more carefully, we will be able to think more clearly, and by thinking more clearly we may be able to regenerate our society. He then cites examples to prove that our language is being abused, analyzes the ingredients of bad style, and clarifies its relationship to such qualities of bad thinking as insincerity and hypocrisy. He concludes by recommending six rules for the improvement of style.

Royko's mock recommendation at first appears to urge us to write nonsense, and it shows us how. Its real thesis is that we should *not* write nonsense, and we should not be impressed by people who do. Royko's ironic technique is to make nonsense-language look silly by presenting it in an oversimplified "Chinese menu" format: all we have to do is pick one from Column A, one from Column B, and so forth. "Try it," says Royko, but he has made it look so much like child's play that we'd feel childish playing the game. This is exactly what the essay's purpose is—to make us reject nonsensical prose as unworthy of our adult minds.

Which essay do you find more effective? Which approach (standard recommendation, mock recommendation) seems better suited to this subject?

politics and the english language

GEORGE ORWELL

1 **m**ost people who bother with the matter at all would admit that the English language is in a bad way, but it is generally assumed that we cannot by conscious action do anything about it. Our civilization is decadent and our language—so the argument runs—must inevitably share in the general collapse. It follows that any struggle against the abuse of language is a sentimental archaism, like preferring candles to electric light or hansom cabs to aeroplanes. Underneath this lies the half-conscious belief that language is a natural growth and not an instrument which we shape for our own purposes.

2 Now, it is clear that the decline of a language must ultimately have political and economic causes: it is not due simply to the bad influence of this or that individual writer. But an effect can become a cause, reinforcing the original cause and producing the same effect in an intensified form, and so on indefinitely. A man may take to drink because he feels himself to be a failure, and then fail all the more completely because he drinks. It is rather the same thing that is happening to the English language. It becomes ugly and inaccurate because our thoughts are foolish, but the slovenliness of our language makes it easier for us to have foolish thoughts. The point is that the process is reversible. Modern English, especially written English, is full of bad habits which spread by imitation and which can be avoided if one is willing to take the necessary trouble. If one gets rid of these habits one can think more clearly, and to think clearly is a necessary first step towards political regeneration: so that the fight against bad English is not frivolous and is not the exclusive concern of professional writers. I will come back to this presently, and I hope that by that time the meaning of what I have said here will have become clearer. Meanwhile, here are five specimens of the English language as it is now habitually written.

3 These five passages have not been picked out because they are especially bad—I could have quoted far worse if I had chosen—but because they illustrate various of the mental vices from which we now suffer. They are a little below the average, but are fairly representative samples. I number them so that I can refer back to them when necessary:

(1) I am not, indeed, sure whether it is not true to say that the Milton who once seemed not unlike a seventeenth-century Shelley had not become,

Source. From *Shooting an Elephant and Other Essays* by George Orwell, copyright © 1945, 1946, 1949, 1950, by Sonia Brownell Orwell, copyright © 1973, 1974 by Sonia Orwell. Reprinted by permission of Harcourt Brace Jovanovich, Inc.

out of an experience ever more bitter in each year, more alien [*sic*] to the founder of that Jesuit sect which nothing could induce him to tolerate.

Professor Harold Laski
(Essay in *Freedom of Expression*).

(2) Above all, we cannot play ducks and drakes with a native battery of idioms which prescribes such egregious collocations of vocables as the Basic *put up with* for *tolerate* or *put at a loss* for *bewilder*.

Professor Lancelot Hogben (*Interglossa*).

(3) On the one side we have the free personality: by definition it is not neurotic, for it has neither conflict nor dream. Its desires, such as they are, are transparent, for they are just what institutional approval keeps in the forefront of consciousness; another institutional pattern would alter their number and intensity; there is little in them that is natural, irreducible, or culturally dangerous. But *on the other side,* the social bond itself is nothing but the mutual reflection of these self-secure integrities. Recall the definition of love. Is not this the very picture of a small academic? Where is there a place in this hall of mirrors for either personality or fraternity?

Essay on psychology in *Politics* (New York).

(4) All the "best people" from the gentlemen's clubs, and all the frantic fascist captains, united in common hatred of Socialism and bestial horror of the rising tide of the mass revolutionary movement, have turned to acts of provocation, to foul incendiarism, to medieval legends of poisoned wells, to legalize their own destruction of proletarian organizations, and rouse the agitated petty-bourgeoisie to chauvinistic fervor on behalf of the fight against the revolutionary way out of the crisis.

Communist pamphlet.

(5) If a new spirit *is* to be infused into this old country, there is one thorny and contentious reform which must be tackled, and that is the humanization and galvanization of the B.B.C. Timidity here will bespeak canker and atrophy of the soul. The heart of Britain may be sound and of strong beat, for instance, but the British lion's roar at present is like that of Bottom in Shakespeare's *Midsummer Night's Dream*—as gentle as any sucking dove. A virile new Britain cannot continue indefinitely to be traduced in the eyes or rather ears, of the world by the effete languors of Langham Place, brazenly masquerading as "standard English." When the Voice of Britain is heard at nine o'clock, better far and infinitely less ludicrous to hear aitches honestly dropped than the present priggish, inflated, inhibited, school-ma'amish arch braying of blameless bashful mewing maidens!

Letter in *Tribune*

4   Each of these passages has faults of its own, but, quite apart from avoidable ugliness, two qualities are common to all of them. The first is staleness of imagery; the other is lack of precision. The writer either has a meaning and cannot express it, or he inadvertently says something else, or he is almost indifferent as to whether his words mean anything or not. This mixture of vagueness and sheer incompetence is the most marked characteristic of modern English prose, and especially of any kind of political writing. As soon as certain topics are raised, the concrete melts into the abstract and no one seems able to think of turns of speech that are

not hackneyed: prose consists less and less of *words* chosen for the sake of their meaning, and more and more of *phrases* tacked together like the sections of a prefabricated hen-house. I list below, with notes and examples, various of the tricks by means of which the work of prose-construction is habitually dodged:

5   *Dying metaphors.* A newly invented metaphor assists thought by evoking a visual image, while on the other hand a metaphor which is technically "dead" (e.g. *iron resolution)* has in effect reverted to being an ordinary word and can generally be used without loss of vividness. But in between these two classes there is a huge dump of worn-out metaphors which have lost all evocative power and are merely used because they save people the trouble of inventing phrases for themselves. Examples are: *Ring the changes on, take up the cudgels for, toe the line, ride roughshod over, stand shoulder to shoulder with, play into the hands of, no axe to grind, grist to the mill, fishing in troubled waters, on the order of the day, Achilles' heel, swan song, hotbed.* Many of these are used without knowledge of their meaning (what is a "rift," for instance?), and incompatible metaphors are frequently mixed, a sure sign that the writer is not interested in what he is saying. Some metaphors now current have been twisted out of their original meaning without those who use them even being aware of the fact. For example, *toe the line* is sometimes written *tow the line.* Another example is *the hammer and the anvil,* now always used with the implication that the anvil gets the worst of it. In real life it is always the anvil that breaks the hammer, never the other way about: a writer who stopped to think what he was saying would be aware of this, and would avoid perverting the original phrase.

6   *Operators* or *verbal false limbs.* These save the trouble of picking out appropriate verbs and nouns, and at the same time pad each sentence with extra syllables which give it an appearance of symmetry. Characteristic phrases are *render inoperative, militate against, make contact with, be subjected to, give rise to, give grounds for, have the effect of, play a leading part (role) in, make itself felt, take effect, exhibit a tendency to, serve the purpose of, etc., etc.* The keynote is the elimination of simple verbs. Instead of being a single word, such as *break, stop, spoil, mend, kill,* a verb becomes a *phrase,* made up of a noun or adjective tacked on to some general-purpose verb such as *prove, serve, form, play, render.* In addition, the passive voice is wherever possible used in preference to the active, and noun constructions are used instead of gerunds (*by examination of* instead of *by examining).* The range of verbs is further cut down by means of the *-ize* and *de-* formations, and the banal statements are given an appearance of profundity by means of the *not un-* formation. Simple conjunctions and prepositions are replaced by such phrases as *with respect to, having regard to, the fact that, by dint of, in view of, in the interests of, on the hypothesis that;* and the ends of sentences are saved from anticlimax by such resound-

ing common-places as *greatly to be desired, cannot be left out of account, a development to be expected in the near future, deserving of serious consideration, brought to a satisfactory conclusion,* and so on and so forth.

7   *Pretentious diction.* Words like *phenomenon, element, individual* (as noun), *objective, categorical, effective, virtual, basic, primary, promote, constitute, exhibit, exploit, utilize, eliminate, liquidate,* are used to dress up simple statements and give an air of scientific impartiality to biased judgments. Adjectives like *epoch-making, epic, historic, unforgettable, triumphant, age-old, inevitable, inexorable, veritable,* are used to dignify the sordid processes of international politics, while writing that aims at glorifying war usually takes on an archaic color, its characteristic words being: *realm, throne, chariot, mailed fist, trident, sword, shield, buckler, banner, jackboot, clarion.* Foreign words and expressions such as *cul de sac, ancien régime, deus ex machina, mutatis mutandis, status quo, gleichschaltung, weltanschauung,* are used to give an air of culture and elegance. Except for the useful abbreviations *i.e., e.g.,* and *etc.,* there is no real need for any of the hundreds of foreign phrases now current in English. Bad writers, and especially scientific, political and sociological writers, are nearly always haunted by the notion that Latin or Greek words are grander than Saxon ones, and unnecessary words like *expedite, ameliorate, predict, extraneous, deracinated, clandestine, subaqueous* and hundreds of others constantly gain ground from their Anglo-Saxon opposite numbers.[1] The jargon peculiar to Marxist writing (*hyena, hangman, cannibal, petty bourgeois, these gentry, lacquey, flunkey, mad dog, White Guard,* etc.) consists largely of words and phrases translated from Russian, German or French; but the normal way of coining a new word is to use a Latin or Greek root with the appropriate affix and, where necessary, the *-ize* formation. It is often easier to make up words of this kind (*deregionalize, impermissible, extramarital, non-fragmentary* and so forth) than to think up the English words that will cover one's meaning. The result, in general, is an increase in slovenliness and vagueness.

8   *Meaningless words.* In certain kinds of writing, particularly in art criticism and literary criticism, it is normal to come across long passages which are almost completely lacking in meaning.[2] Words like *romantic, plastic, values, human, dead, sentimental, natural, vitality,* as used in art criticism, are strictly meaningless, in the sense that they not only do not point to any

[1] An interesting illustration of this is the way in which the English flower names which were in use till very recently are being ousted by Greek ones, *snapdragon* becoming *antirrhinum, forget-me-not* becoming *myosotis,* etc. It is hard to see any practical reason for this change of fashion: it is probably due to an instinctive turning-away from the more homely word and a vague feeling that the Greek word is scientific.

[2] Example: "Comfort's catholicity of perception and image, strangely Whitmanesque in range, almost the exact opposite in aesthetic compulsion, continues to evoke that trembling atmospheric accumulative hinting at a cruel, an inexorably serene timelessness. . . . When Gardiner scores by aiming at simple bull's-eyes with precision. Only they are not so simple, and through this contented sadness runs more than the surface bitter-sweet of resignation." (*Poetry Quarterly.*)

discoverable object, but are hardly ever expected to do so by the reader. When one critic writes, "The outstanding feature of Mr. X's work is its living quality," while another writes, "The immediately striking thing about Mr. X's work is its peculiar deadness," the reader accepts this as a simple difference of opinion. If words like *black* and *white* were involved, instead of the jargon words *dead* and *living,* he would see at once that language was being used in an improper way. Many political words are similarly abused. The word *Fascism* has now no meaning except in so far as it signifies "something not desirable." The words *democracy, socialism, freedom, patriotic, realistic, justice,* have each of them several different meanings which cannot be reconciled with one another. In the case of a word like *democracy,* not only is there no agreed definition, but the attempt to make one is resisted from all sides. It is almost universally felt that when we call a country democratic we are praising it: consequently the defenders of every kind of régime claim that it is a democracy, and fear that they might have to stop using the word if it were tied down to any one meaning. Words of this kind are often used in a consciously dishonest way. That is, the person who uses them has his own private definition, but allows his hearer to think he means something quite different. Statements like *Marshal Pétain was a true patriot, The Soviet Press is the freest in the world, The Catholic Church is opposed to persecution,* are almost always made with intent to deceive. Other words used in variable meanings, in most cases more or less dishonestly, are: *class, totalitarian, science, progressive, reactionary, bourgeois, equality.*

9   Now that I have made this catalogue of swindles and perversions, let me give another example of the kind of writing that they lead to. This time it must of its nature be an imaginary one. I am going to translate a passage of good English into modern English of the worst sort. Here is a well-known verse from *Ecclesiastes:*

"I returned and saw under the sun, that the race is not to the swift, nor the battle to the strong, neither yet bread to the wise, nor yet riches to men of understanding, nor yet favour to men of skill; but time and chance happeneth to them all."

10   Here it is in modern English:

"Objective considerations of contemporary phenomena compels the conclusion that success or failure in competitive activities exhibits no tendency to be commensurate with innate capacity, but that a considerable element of the unpredictable must invariably be taken into account."

11   This is a parody, but not a very gross one. Exhibit (3), above, for instance, contains several patches of the same kind of English. It will be seen that I have not made a full translation. The beginning and ending of the sentence follow the original meaning fairly closely, but in the middle the concrete illustrations—race, battle, bread—dissolve into the vague phrase "success or failure in competitive activities." This had to be so, because no modern writer of the kind I am discussing—no one capable

of using phrases like "objective consideration of contemporary phenomena" —would ever tabulate his thoughts in that precise and detailed way. The whole tendency of modern prose is away from concreteness. Now analyse these two sentences a little more closely. The first contains forty-nine words but only sixty syllables, and all its words are those of everyday life. The second contains thirty-eight words of ninety syllables: eighteen of its words are from Latin roots, and one from Greek. The first sentence contains six vivid images, and only one phrase ("time and chance") that could be called vague. The second contains not a single fresh, arresting phrase, and in spite of its ninety syllables it gives only a shortened version of the meaning contained in the first. Yet without a doubt it is the second kind of sentence that is gaining ground in modern English. I do not want to exaggerate. This kind of writing is not yet universal, and outcrops of simplicity will occur here and there in the worst-written page. Still, if you or I were told to write a few lines on the uncertainty of human fortunes, we should probably come much nearer to my imaginary sentence than to the one from *Ecclesiastes*.

12   As I have tried to show, modern writing at its worst does not consist in picking out words for the sake of their meaning and inventing images in order to make the meaning clearer. It consists in gumming together long strips of words which have already been set in order by someone else, and making the results presentable by sheer humbug. The attraction of this way of writing is that it is easy. It is easier—even quicker, once you have the habit—to say *In my opinion it is not an unjustifiable assumption that* than to say *I think*. If you use ready-made phrases, you not only don't have to hunt about for words; you also don't have to bother with the rhythms of your sentences, since these phrases are generally so arranged as to be more or less euphonious. When you are composing in a hurry—when you are dictating to a stenographer, for instance, or making a public speech— it is natural to fall into a pretentious, Latinized style. Tags like a *consideration which we should do well to bear in mind* or *a conclusion to which all of us would readily assent* will save many a sentence from coming down with a bump. By using stale metaphors, similes and idioms, you save much mental effort, at the cost of leaving your meaning vague, not only for your reader but for yourself. This is the significance of mixed metaphors. The sole aim of a metaphor is to call up a visual image. When these images clash—as in *The Fascist octopus has sung its swan song, the jackboot is thrown into the melting pot*—it can be taken as certain that the writer is not seeing a mental image of the objects he is naming; in other words he is not really thinking. Look again at the examples I gave at the beginning of this essay. Professor Laski (1) uses five negatives in fifty-three words. One of these is superfluous, making nonsense of the whole passage, and in addition there is the slip *alien* for akin, making futher nonsense, and several avoidable pieces of clumsiness which increase the general vagueness. Professor Hogben (2) plays ducks and drakes with a battery which is able to write prescriptions, and, while disapproving of the everyday phrase *put*

up with, is unwilling to look *egregious* up in the dictionary and see what it means; (3), if one takes an uncharitable attitude towards it, is simply meaningless: probably one could work out its intended meaning by reading the whole of the article in which it occurs. In (4), the writer knows more or less what he wants to say, but an accumulation of stale phrases chokes him like tea leaves blocking a sink. In (5), words and meaning have almost parted company. People who write in this manner usually have a general emotional meaning—they dislike one thing and want to express solidarity with another—but they are not interested in the detail of what they are saying. A scrupulous writer, in every sentence that he writes, will ask himself at least four questions, thus: What am I trying to say? What words will express it? What image or idiom will make it clearer? Is this image fresh enough to have an effect? And he will probably ask himself two more: Could I put it more shortly? Have I said anything that is avoidably ugly? But you are not obliged to go to all this trouble. You can shirk it by simply throwing your mind open and letting the ready-made phrases come crowding in. They will construct your sentences for you—even think your thoughts for you, to a certain extent—and at need they will perform the important service of partially concealing your meaning even from yourself. It is at this point that the special connection between politics and the debasement of language becomes clear.

13   In our time it is broadly true that political writing is bad writing. Where it is not true, it will generally be found that the writer is some kind of rebel, expressing his private opinions and not a "party line." Orthodoxy, of whatever color, seems to demand a lifeless, imitative style. The political dialects to be found in pamphlets, leading articles, manifestos, White Papers and the speeches of under-secretaries do, of course, vary from party to party, but they are all alike in that one almost never finds in them a fresh, vivid, home-made turn of speech. When one watches some tired hack on the platform mechanically repeating the familiar phrases—*bestial atrocities, iron heel, bloodstained tyranny, free peoples of the world, stand shoulder to shoulder*—one often has a curious feeling that one is not watching a live human being but some kind of dummy: a feeling which suddenly becomes stronger at moments when the light catches the speaker's spectacles and turns them into blank discs which seem to have no eyes behind them. And this is not altogether fanciful. A speaker who uses that kind of phraseology has gone some distance towards turning himself into a machine. The appropriate noises are coming out of his larynx, but his brain is not involved as it would be if he were choosing his words for himself. If the speech he is making is one that he is accustomed to make over and over again, he may be almost unconscious of what he is saying, as one is when one utters the responses in church. And this reduced state of consciousness, if not indispensable, is at any rate favorable to political conformity.

14   In our time, political speech and writing are largely the defence of the indefensible. Things like the continuance of British rule in India, the Russian purges and deportations, the dropping of the atom bombs on

Japan, can indeed be defended, but only by arguments which are too brutal for most people to face, and which do not square with the professed aims of political parties. Thus political language has to consist largely of euphemism, question-begging and sheer cloudy vagueness. Defenceless villages are bombarded from the air, the inhabitants driven out into the countryside, the cattle machine-gunned, the huts set on fire with incendiary bullets: this is called *pacification*. Millions of peasants are robbed of their farms and sent trudging along the roads with no more than they can carry: this is called *transfer of population* or *rectification of frontiers*. People are imprisoned for years without trial, or shot in the back of the neck or sent to die of scurvy in Arctic lumber camps: this is called *elimination of unreliable elements*. Such phraseology is needed if one wants to name things without calling up mental pictures of them. Consider for instance some comfortable English professor defending Russian totalitarianism. He cannot say outright, "I believe in killing off your opponents when you can get good results by doing so." Probably, therefore, he will say something like this:

"While freely conceding that the Soviet régime exhibits certain features which the humanitarian may be inclined to deplore, we must, I think, agree that a certain curtailment of the right to political opposition is an unavoidable concomitant of transitional periods, and that the rigors which the Russian people have been called upon to undergo have been amply justified in the sphere of concrete achievement."

15   The inflated style is itself a kind of euphemism. A mass of Latin words falls upon the facts like soft snow, blurring the outlines and covering up all the details. The great enemy of clear language is insincerity. When there is a gap between one's real and one's declared aims, one turns as it were instinctively to long words and exhausted idioms, like a cuttlefish squirting out ink. In our age there is no such thing as "keeping out of politics." All issues are political issues, and politics itself is a mass of lies, evasions, folly, hatred and schizophrenia. When the general atmosphere is bad, language must suffer. I should expect to find—this is a guess which I have not sufficient knowledge to verify—that the German, Russian and Italian languages have all deteriorated in the last ten or fifteen years, as a result of dictatorship.

16   But if thought corrupts language, language can also corrupt thought. A bad usage can spread by tradition and imitation, even among people who should and do know better. The debased language that I have been discussing is in some ways very convenient. Phrases like *a not unjustifiable assumption, leaves much to be desired, would serve no good purpose, a consideration which we should do well to bear in mind,* are a continuous temptation, a packet of aspirins always at one's elbow. Look back through this essay, and for certain you will find that I have again and again committed the very faults I am protesting against. By this morning's post I have received a pamphlet dealing with conditions in Germany. The author tells me that he "felt impelled" to write it. I open it at random, and here is almost the

first sentence that I see: "[The Allies] have an opportunity not only of achieving a radical transformation of Germany's social and political structure in such a way as to avoid a nationalistic reaction in Germany itself, but at the same time of laying the foundations of a co-operative and unified Europe." You see, he "feels impelled" to write—feels, presumably, that he has something new to say—and yet his words, like cavalry horses answering the bugle, group themselves automatically into the familiar dreary pattern. This invasion of one's mind by ready-made phrases (*lay the foundations, achieve a radical transformation*) can only be prevented if one is constantly on guard against them, and every such phrase anaesthetizes a portion of one's brain.

17   I said earlier that the decadence of our language is probably curable. Those who deny this would argue, if they produced an argument at all, that language merely reflects existing social conditions, and that we cannot influence its development by any direct tinkering with words and constructions. So far as the general tone or spirit of a language goes, this may be true, but it is not true in detail. Silly words and expressions have often disappeared, not through any evolutionary process but owing to the conscious action of a minority. Two recent examples were *explore every avenue* and *leave no stone unturned,* which were killed by the jeers of a few journalists. There is a long list of flyblown metaphors which could similarly be got rid of if enough people would interest themselves in the job; and it should also be possible to laugh the *not un-* formation out of existence,[3] to reduce the amount of Latin and Greek in the average sentence, to drive out foreign phrases and strayed scientific words, and, in general, to make pretentiousness unfashionable. But all these are minor points. The defence of the English language implies more than this, and perhaps it is best to start by saying what it does *not* imply.

18   To begin with it has nothing to do with archaism, with the salvaging of obsolete words and turns of speech, or with the setting up of a "standard English" which must never be departed from. On the contrary, it is especially concerned with the scrapping of every word or idiom which has outworn its usefulness. It has nothing to do with correct grammar and syntax, which are of no importance so long as one makes one's meaning clear, or with the avoidance of Americanisms, or with having what is called a "good prose style." On the other hand it is not concerned with fake simplicity and the attempt to make written English colloquial. Nor does it even imply in every case preferring the Saxon word to the Latin one, though it does imply using the fewest and shortest words that will cover one's meaning. What is above all needed is to let the meaning choose the word, and not the other way about. In prose, the worst thing one can do with words is to surrender to them. When you think of a concrete object, you think wordlessly, and then, if you want to describe the thing you have been

---

[3] One can cure oneself of the *not un-* formation by memorizing this sentence: *A not unblack dog was chasing a not unsmall rabbit across a not ungreen field.*

visualizing you probably hunt about till you find the exact words that seem to fit it. When you think of something abstract you are more inclined to use words from the start, and unless you make a conscious effort to prevent it, the existing dialect will come rushing in and do the job for you, at the expense of blurring or even changing your meaning. Probably it is better to put off using words as long as possible and get one's meaning as clear as one can through pictures or sensations. Afterwards one can choose —not simply *accept*—the phrases that will best cover the meaning, and then switch round and decide what impression one's words are likely to make on another person. This last effort of the mind cuts out all stale or mixed images, all prefabricated phrases, needless repetitions, and humbug and vagueness generally. But one can often be in doubt about the effect of a word or a phrase, and one needs rules that one can rely on when instinct fails. I think the following rules will cover most cases:

(i) Never use a metaphor, simile or other figure of speech which you are used to seeing in print.

(ii) Never use a long word where a short one will do.

(iii) If it is possible to cut a word out, always cut it out.

(iv) Never use the passive where you can use the active.

(v) Never use a foreign phrase, a scientific word or a jargon word if you can think of an everyday English equivalent.

(vi) Break any of these rules sooner than say anything outright barbarous.

These rules sound elementary, and so they are, but they demand a deep change of attitude in anyone who has grown used to writing in the style now fashionable. One could keep all of them and still write bad English, but one could not write the kind of stuff that I quoted in those five specimens at the beginning of this article.

19   I have not here been considering the literary use of language, but merely language as an instrument for expressing and not for concealing or preventing thought. Stuart Chase and others have come near to claiming that all abstract words are meaningless, and have used this as a pretext for advocating a kind of political quietism. Since you don't know what Fascism is, how can you struggle against Fascism? One need not swallow such absurdities as this, but one ought to recognize that the present political chaos is connected with the decay of language, and that one can probably bring about some improvement by starting at the verbal end. If you simplify your English, you are freed from the worst follies of orthodoxy. You cannot speak any of the necessary dialects, and when you make a stupid remark its stupidity will be obvious, even to yourself. Political language— and with variations this is true of all political parties, from Conservatives to Anarchists—is designed to make lies sound truthful and murder respectable, and to give an appearance of solidity to pure wind. One cannot

change this all in a moment, but one can at least change one's own habits, and from time to time one can even, if one jeers loudly enough, send some worn-out and useless phrase—some *jackboot, Achilles' heel, hotbed, melting pot, acid test, veritable inferno* or other lump of verbal refuse—into the dustbin where it belongs.

talking smart
like educators do
MIKE ROYKO

1   **U**ntil now, only professional educators knew how to speak educatorese, that mysterious language with which they befuddle the rest of us.

2   But now, for the first time, anyone can learn to speak it.

3   All you need is the new guide: "How to speak like an Educator without being educated."

4   And as a public service, the guide is being printed in its entirety below.

5   In a moment, I'll provide instructions on its use. But first, a word of credit to its creators.

6   The guide is the work of two Rhetoric and speech teachers at Danville (Ill.) Junior College, Barbara Stover and Ilva Walker. They compiled it after years of wading through administrative circulars.

7   They did it for fun, but some of their students have found the phrases are useful in preparing papers for sociology classes.

8   The guide is simple to use.

9   Take one word from each of the five columns. It doesn't matter which word. Take them in any order, or in no order.

10   For instance, if you take the second word of column "A," the fourth word from column "B," the sixth word from column "C," and the eighth and tenth words from the last two columns, you will have:

Flexible ontological productivity implement control group and experimental group.

11   That doesn't make sense, does it? But now add a few connecting words, and we have:

Flexible and ontological productivity will implement the control group and experimental group.

Source. Reprinted with permission from the *Chicago Daily News.*

12   That still doesn't make any sense. But it sounds like it does. Which means it is perfect Educatorese.

13   You can do it with any combination of the words. As an example, use the first five digits of my office phone: 321-21. . . . This works out to:

Adaptable reciprocal nucleii terminate total modular exchange.

14   Add a few little words and you have a splendid sentence, worthy of at least an assistant superintendent:

"Adaptable and reciprocal nucleii will terminate in total modular exchange." And you can quote me on that.

15   Go to it, with this guide you can say things like:

"The interdisciplinary or supportive input will encapsulate vertical team structure."

16   Or "Optimal ethnic accountability should facilitate post-secondary education enrichment."

17   Try it yourself. Once you get the hang of it—who knows?—You might wind up with Supt. Redmond's job.

-A-	-B-
Comprehensive	Cognitive
Flexible	Reciprocal
Adaptable	Stylistic
Culturally	Ontological
Perceptual	Prime
Evaluative	Supportive
Innovative	Workable
Interdisciplinary	Resultant
Conceptual	Behavioral
Ideological	Judgmental
Optimal	Ethnic
Minimal	Attitudinal
Categorically	Multicultural
Unequivocally	Encounter
Intrapersonal	Counterproductive
Interpersonal	Generative
	Cognate

-C-

Nucleii
Interaction
Focus
Balance
Chain of command
Productivity
Conformance
Panacea
Rationale
Input
Throughput
Accountability
Feedback
Objective
Resources
Perspective
Curricula
Priorities
Diversity
Environment
Overview
Strategies
Posture
Methodologies
Introversion
Posits
Concept
Gestalt

-D-

Indicates
Terminate
Geared
Compile
Articulate
Verbalize
Facilitate
Implement
Incur
Sensitize
Synthesize
Integrate
Fragment
Maximize
Minimize
Energize
Individualize
Encapsulate
Orientate

-E-

Total modular exchange
In-depth discussion
Multipurpose framework and goals
Serial communication
Serial transmission of applicable cable tools and instrumentation
Post-secondary education enrichment
Changing needs of society
Motivational serial communications
High potential for assessing failure
Control group and experimental group
Student-faculty relationships
Identifiable decision-making process
Sophisticated resource systems analyses
Vertical team structure
Translation in depth
Classroom context
Individual horizons

COMMENTARY

Orwell's first task is to prove that the problem he has noticed ("the English language is in a bad way," paragraph 1) ought to matter to the rest of us. Many people simply do not care very much about how they write and speak, or how other people write and speak to them. Orwell cares passionately. He believes that we cannot be a free people politically—we cannot preserve democracy—unless we know what's really going on in the world; and we can't know what's going on unless the language we use is frank and honest. Thus the English language is a political tool. Orwell suggests this function for language in his title, spends his first two paragraphs explaining it, and returns to it again and again. "All issues are political issues," he says (paragraph 16). Unless he can make us believe that language is politically important, his cause is lost. Does he convince you of this point?

Much of his essay is spent on definition, a detailed clarification of what he means by saying that English "is in a bad way." He provides samples of meaningless paragraphs, a classification of linguistic sins, a comparison between a vivid statement and a vague one. He suggests a cause for bad writing: it is easier. Lazy people find it easier to stitch ready-made phrases into a patchwork quilt than to find the individual words that correspond to what they really want to say.

We cannot be permitted to go away in despair, however. People who despair feel too defeated to do anything. Therefore, Orwell ends his essay on an optimistic note. He shows us what we can do to save the language and ourselves.

Royko satisfies himself with one part of the recommendation process: the proposal itself, in the form of a "how-to" guide. The proposal is so exaggerated, however, that it defeats itself. Royko has signaled this intention in his first paragraph by referring to "the mysterious language" in which educators "befuddle" the rest of us. He shows that writing the "smart" language is really very simple. You don't need to have the slightest idea of what you're saying: just pick one item from each group. Royko even provides the groups so that anyone can sound "smart."

The pattern behind the groups is that column A consists of adjectives and adverbs, column B of adjectives, column C of words that will function as nouns, column D of verbs, and column E of those complicated phrases that are used to function as anything at all. Thus by any set of choices, we can construct a sentence with a superficial resemblance to English. In fact, we can construct whole paragraphs, or term papers, or college textbooks—or lives. But they will all be meaningless, Royko reminds us. Their only possible function is to "befuddle." He is angry at people who use language to befuddle, particularly at educators. (Orwell is angry particularly at politicians.)

The limitation of Royko's presentation is that it does not show us what we should do. Like all negative recommendations, it shows us only what we should *not* do. But perhaps its brevity and its ironic manner would appeal to people who would not respond to Orwell's longer and more serious presentation. The decision about whether to write a standard recommendation or a mock recommendation is based partly on the type of audience it is intended to reach.

OUTLINE: ORWELL
    I. Introduction: the problem ("English is in a bad way") and why it matters—paragraphs 1–2
   II. Detailed definition of the problem—paragraphs 3–11
      A. Definition by example—paragraphs 3–4
      B. Division and classification: the ingredients of bad style
         1. Dying metaphors—paragraph 5
         2. False limbs—paragraph 6
         3. Pretentious diction—paragraph 7
         4. Meaningless words—paragraph 8
         5. Abstract words for concrete—paragraphs 9–11
  III. The causes of the problem—paragraphs 12–16
      A. Stereotyped thought—paragraph 12
      B. Political orthodoxy—paragraph 13
      C. Defending the indefensible—paragraph 14
      D. Insincerity—paragraph 15
      E. Self-perpetuation of bad style—paragraph 16
  IV. Recommendations for a cure—paragraphs 17–19
      A. Rules—paragraph 18
      B. Simplify—paragraph 19

OUTLINE: ROYKO
    I. Introduction: the problem—paragraph 1
   II. Recommendations for a cure—paragraphs 2–17
      A. Background information about the "guide"—paragraphs 2–7
      B. Instructions for using the "guide"—paragraphs 3–16
      C. Summarizing call to action—paragraph 17

SUGGESTIONS FOR WRITING

1. The English (or Communications) Department in your school is considering new textbooks to use in a course called Modern Communications. The course, intended for freshmen, is an introduction to the major communications media—newspapers, magazines, radio, television. Among the textbooks being considered is *Communication Science and Technology*, by Patrick R. Penland. You and a group of other students are asked to evaluate the book, specifically its writing style. You vote against it. Somehow Mr. Penland learns of your negative opinion and wants to know what's wrong with his English and how he ought to improve it.

On the basis of the following excerpt, write a letter to Mr. Penland, recommending ways for him to improve his writing style. (The excerpt is from the book's introduction; the number in parenthesis in paragraph 2 refers to a bibliography entry.)

INTRODUCTION

The new social bases of message design and usage have meant a revolution in the distribution of information and in popular culture. Information has become a social resource to be exploited for the betterment of all men. The institutions of communication have created publics and have cultivated common tastes across boundaries of time, space, status, and culture. New patterns of information flow stimulate social development and machine control, and cybernetically shape the referential terms of our negotiations with one another and the real world.

Any change in the process of information stimuli and in the negotiation of mutual intentions alters both the individual personality and the nature of human society. Society is today in the midst of revolutionary transformations. Communications science consequently has had to encounter major change both in technology and in the societal enterprise based on symbol production and use. New media alter form, content, and context. New modes of communication change ways of selecting, composing, and sharing messages and perspectives. The message and the medium tend to become reciprocal as McLuhan (111) has dramatized so remarkably.

The technology exists for the almost unlimited collection, storage, and organization of the data of scholarship as well as the nonverbal and audiovisual message space of the people. The infrastructure networks that have been developed by media, library, and information science are available for the wide geographic deployment of data resources. These two recent developments are the more remarkable when it is realized to what a limited extent the data of scholarship have been permitted to enter the social acculturation and diffusion process.

To move from the milieu of the communications elite to that of the communications have-nots is often to experience a serious mental dislocation. The urban disorder of our time may largely be a revolutionary demand for conditions wherein information surprise can be engendered in a rapidly widening range of the communications have-nots.

The specter that has always plagued civilization continues to haunt society: how to so transmit scholarship to the masses in sufficient time to avoid the disorderly transformations of violent revolution. Technological and network deployment alone do not constitute a social method sufficiently compelling to meet the imperative of rapid cultural diffusion. The conditions necessary for engendering the surprise value of those data in the minds of a wide range of people remain primitive, particularly in the urban community, despite the fact that a plethora of data infrastructures exist.

The profession associated with communications systems and technology such as that which include media, library, and information specialists is a general social method accountable to society. Society expects leadership to emerge from the professional cohort for the development of social policy as well as community and individual decision making. The social collective expects help from such communications leaders in the articulation of social and individual concerns and in the creation of situations and systems wherein meaning can be engendered in the minds of people.

2. Present a recommendation in two ways. Write a short essay presenting your idea as a standard recommendation; write a second short essay presenting it as a mock recommendation (i.e., superficially recommend the opposite). Design the two essays for different audiences. For example, assume that your proposal is to cut down on Christmas extravagance. Write (1) a standard essay to be published in a popular magazine. (If it's good enough, send it to *Reader's Digest*, which pays for contributions.) Then write (2) an ironic editorial to be published in a local newspaper, perhaps a campus newspaper.

3. Royko's technique was anticipated about a century ago by Lewis Carroll, who included a nonsense-poem, "Jabberwocky," in *Through the Looking-Glass*. Like Royko's Educatorese sentences, its lines seem to include adjectives and nouns and verbs in the right places, but it doesn't mean anything. Here is the first stanza:

> 'Twas brillig, and the slithy toves
> Did gyre and gimble in the wabe:
> All mimsy were the borogoves,
> And the mome raths outgrabe.*

Write a mock recommendation urging people to write meaningless advertisements ("Buy Arfies! They will amplify your hargles"), or meaningless thank-you letters ("Dear Aunt Wilhelmina, I really loved your socks, I ate them up right away"), or some other form of noncommunication. Your real thesis is that if we are going to write at all, we should say something that makes sense. Include examples. In fact, prepare a complete "how-to" guide like Royko's if you like.

---

* Lewis Carroll, *Through the Looking-Glass* in *The Complete Works of Lewis Carroll*, introduction by Alexander Woollcott (New York: Modern Library, n.d.), p. 153.

series two

RECOMMENDATION: READINGS WITHOUT COMMENTARY

a message to america's car buyers

R. C. GERSTENBERG,
CHAIRMAN, GENERAL MOTORS

This selection demonstrates the very close relationship between advertisements and recommendations. It appeared as an ad in a newspaper read by middle-class and well-educated people. To attract this audience, the copy-writer decided to rely on arguments rather than emotional associations or a pretty picture. The ad that resulted includes most of the elements of a formal recommendation. It identifies the problem ("inflation-weakened America"), considers alternatives ("common-sense conservation" versus "empty austerity"), uses an example (a chilly house) to persuade us that conservation is better than austerity, and concludes by recommending that we enact a policy of conservation by buying new cars: buying cars will benefit the economy. The only thing missing is the demonstration of feasibility, and even this is hinted at: if you "see your dealer," the ad implies, you'll be able to make a deal.

Like many ads, this one uses repetition to drive its car home. Having said "no growth makes no sense," the ad says it again ("not for America") and a third time ("not for anyone")—and, in case the message might have been missed by a really dim-witted reader, summarizes with a blunt "Right now is the time to buy a new car." Our impulse is directed toward General Motors showrooms specifically by the advice under the company's name: "See your Chevrolet, Pontiac, Oldsmobile, Buick or Cadillac dealer today."

Are you likely to act on this recommendation?

Source. Reprinted by courtesy of *Barron's National Business and Financial Weekly.* Copyright © 1974.

A message to America's car buyers...

Inflation-weakened America needs common-sense conservation, not empty austerity. Conservation is insulating the attic and saving fuel; austerity is shivering in your living room.

In a similar way, when new cars replace old, the nation's primary means of transportation gains efficiency. Our new 1975 cars conserve gasoline, even as they emit less pollution, provide more safety features, and cost less to operate and maintain than earlier models.

The purchasing of new cars is the common-sense conservation we need. It keeps the wheel of progress rolling. It means growth and investment. This means more jobs for our people, more revenue for our government, more value for our customers, and more dividends for our stockholders.

No growth makes no sense; not for America, not for anyone.

Right now is the time to buy a new car.

R.C. Gerstenberg

R.C. Gerstenberg
Chairman
General Motors Corporation

General Motors

See your Chevrolet, Pontiac, Oldsmobile, Buick or Cadillac dealer today.

forget the rat hair, the body protein's there

KATEY LEHMAN

Lehman's subject is tuna fish. Should we eat it or not, given the reports that it is contaminated by everything from mercury to rat hair? Yes we should, she decides. In fact, she proposes to have some for supper. She also offers a more general recommendation: "cheer up" (paragraph 5). We should make the best of things as they are rather than be perfectionists.

Notice the essay's neat pro-and-con structure. Paragraph 1 presents an argument against eating tuna, paragraphs 2 and 3 an argument for, paragraph 4 against, paragraph 5 for, paragraph 6 against, paragraphs 7 and 8 for. The essay comes to rest on the positive side of the argument. You might contrast it with Kanfer's on the hotdog (p. 258).

1   Several years ago I set out platters of small sandwiches for some guests who dropped in after a gymnastics meet. When I told one of them that one platter held tuna fish sandwiches, he refused to eat any because there were reports that tuna fish was contaminated by mercury.

2   Since then, however, most people have learned that the tolerance level set by the FDA is an arbitrary criterion, set without any basis in tests on animals or humans. That's what I read in the latest issue of *Consumer Reports,* which tested all brands of canned tuna and found that out of 104 samples, only 2 exceeded the 0.5 parts per million mercury tolerance, and not by very much.

3   The article states, "Too little is known about mercury poisoning, we believe, for anyone to feel wholly comfortable with arbitrary limits on mercury content in foods." Okay, we may now eat canned tuna, which I am about to fix for supper, without worrying about mercury.

4   The article on tuna then goes on to list some of the contaminants that made people shy away from hot dogs a few years ago (although I've noticed that they're still selling well at ball games). There were no parasites in CU's samples of fish, but there were "a disturbing number of rodent hairs, other animal hairs, fragments of feathers, moth scales, and insect and maggot parts."

5   Oh, cheer up. I'm still planning to make a tuna casserole.

6   "The FDA's usual excuse," continues the article, "for its lax standards on filth in food is that the filth originated in nature and couldn't be readily removed. Well, rats don't live in or around tuna fish in the ocean. Nor do birds or maggots, moths, or other insects. It is therefore safe to conclude that the filth we found in canned tuna was introduced after catching."

7   Even so, *Consumer Reports* wouldn't go to all the trouble of testing the various brands if its editors thought tuna should be avoided. Actually,

Source. Reprinted from *The Centre Daily Times,* State College, Pa. Oct. 28, 1974.

as they say, it "provides sound nutritional value. It's so rich in essential amino acids, the building blocks of body protein, that a single seven-ounce can contains the average U.S. Recommended Daily Allowance for protein. It's also high in vitamins, iodine, fluorine, and phosphorus."

8   If I drop any of my own hair into the casserole, I'll merely inform the family that it's a sterilized rat hair which will not interfere with their building blocks of body protein.

---

stop the juggernaut —auto safety is hurtling toward a dead end

ROBERT M. BLEIBERG

This short recommendation proposes that to save lives on the highways we concern ourselves with the driver, not with the vehicle. Bleiberg begins by discussing the government's attempts to "tinker with the automobile." He asserts that safety equipment is expensive and ineffective and that reduced driving speeds, necessitated by the fuel shortages of the 1970s, yield a much more significant saving in lives. The last two sentences summarize his recommendation that we discard one way of doing something and try another.

1   **d**espite mounting financial costs and conflicting scientific evidence—the air bag, claims much of Detroit, is of doubtful efficacy, while a plaintiff has just won a multi-million-dollar damage suit which blames a highway death upon a faulty federally mandated headrest—the U.S. government persists in tinkering with the automobile. Yet as we have said before, and as the latest spate of evidence overwhelmingly indicates, in this matter of life and death, what counts is the man behind the wheel.

2   In 1966, however, Congress, through passage of the National Motor Vehicle and Traffic Safety Act, made a distressingly wrong turn. Under a series of directors, some of whom have felt free, so to speak, to ride their hobby horses, the National Highway Traffic Safety Administration over the years has promulgated two score and more motor vehicle standards. Thanks to its zeal, automobiles today come equipped with energy-absorbing steering columns, high-penetration-resistant window glass, improved instrument

Source. Reprinted by courtesy of *Barron's National Business and Financial Weekly.* Copyright © 1974.

panels, reinforced door structures, headrests, seat belts and interlocking systems that won't permit the car to start unless the belts are on. Down the road, if NHTSA and Nader have their way, loom further marvels of technology: fuel tank integrity, radar braking, air bags.

3   From a cost standpoint, such innovations have had a ponderable impact. For one thing, motorists' long-simmering wrath at the inconvenience and expense has begun to boil over. According to those who are pushing for air bags and other so-called passive restraints (no action is required of drivers or passengers), at least two out of five seat belts lie idle. Repair shops which specialize in ridding new cars of anti-pollution and safety devices, legally or otherwise, do a thriving business; in Detroit, a car can be completely "debugged" for ten dollars, in an age of inflation a modest sum and one which indicates heavy traffic. Weight-wise and in dollars-and-cents, rough estimates are available, too. Depending on the make and model, safety equipment has added 300-odd pounds to gross vehicle weight, and, with respect to the '74s, $300 to the price (over $500 by 1976). All told, including the extra gas needed to move the added weight, safety is costing the not-so-happy motorist a sum approaching $5 billion per year, and the end is nowhere in sight.

4   Like the federal bulldozer, the safety juggernaut is no economy model. For its huge outlay, the motoring public has precious little to show. By government decree, all '73s had to be equipped with bumpers that could meet low speed barrier tests, thereby reducing the frequency of front and rear damage. While the latter has fallen off, savings have been wholly offset by the higher cost of repairing the new bumpers. Volkswagen has just served notice on owners of Beetles made between 1968 and 1972 that seat and shoulder belts, improperly stowed, may be weakened by an accumulation of battery acid on the floor. Consumers Union has found four out of seven federally approved auto seats for children faulty. In December, 1972, a U.S. Circuit Court of Appeals delayed imposition of mandated passive restraints because the official test dummies (why should they be any different) failed to work right.

5   According to the Department of Transportation, the effectiveness of head restraints "has been very low"; in at least one case, they allegedly have proven lethal. Josephine B. Hubbell, widow of a psychiatrist who died after striking a headrest in his Chevy Nova during a rear-end collision, has just won $2 million in damages from GM (which has filed an appeal). And the safety statistics furnished cold comfort. As we wrote last fall, deaths per million vehicle miles were down, but the decline "barely matched that of the 'Fifties, when Detroit was allegedly selling razzle-dazzle and Ralph Nader was still in school."

6   Thanks to the gasoline shortage, however, the free world lately has turned into a safety laboratory, with what can only be viewed as astonishing results. According to the National Safety Council, U.S. vehicle-miles driven in November and December lagged the year-earlier total by perhaps 2%. Yet, as speed limits throughout the country were lowered to 55 miles

an hour, the number of highway fatalities in the two months dropped 9% and 19%, respectively. In January, with driving off perhaps 5–10% (Safety Council figures aren't available yet), U.S. highway deaths plunged 25%. (In Germany, a 62 m.p.h. limit cut the number of fatalities and injuries by three-fifths.) Even the National Highway Traffic Safety Administration seems impressed. It reports that 16 states with lowered speed limits in November showed a 15%–20% drop in the number of highway deaths, those which left them unchanged only 2%. NHTSA may not fully grasp the significance of such statistics, or may not want to, but the meaning is clear. In automotive safety, the U.S., by over-emphasizing the car and virtually ignoring the driver, has been hurtling toward a dead end. It's time to slam on the brakes and back up.

the special joys of super-slow reading

SYDNEY PIDDINGTON

There is a story about a young man who completed a "speed-reading" course and boasted that he had just read Tolstoy's *War and Peace* in 47 minutes flat. "What's it about?" someone asked. "Russians," he replied.

Piddington recommends reading not for speed but for "delight." He offers no statistics and no testimonials, only an account of how slow reading functioned as therapy for him in times of trouble: during the frustration of a day when everything went wrong on the job and during the fearful boredom of three and a half years as a prisoner of war.

1   **e**ven for the pressure-cooker world of advertising, it had been a frustrating, tension-building day. I took home a briefcase full of troubles. A major contract was in danger of being lost at the last minute, two executives of a company with whom we hoped to clinch a deal were being elusive, and a strike threatened the opening of a business that held my money and my future.

2   As I sat down on that hot and humid evening, there seemed to be no solutions to the problems thrashing around in my brain. So I picked up a book, settled into a comfortable chair and applied my own special therapy —super-slow reading.

3   I spent three hours on two short chapters of *Personal History* by Vin-

Source. Reprinted with permission from the June 1973 *Reader's Digest.* Copyright 1973 by The Reader's Digest Assn., Inc.

cent Sheean—savoring each paragraph, lingering over a sentence, a phrase, or even a single word, building a detailed mental picture of the scene. No longer was I in Sydney, Australia, on a sticky heatwave night. Relishing every word, I joined foreign correspondent Sheean on a mission to China and another to Russia. I lost myself in the author's world, *living* his book. And when finally I put it down, my mind was totally refreshed.

4   Next morning, four words from the book—"take the long view"—were still in my mind. At my desk, I had a long-view look at my problems. I concluded that the strike would end sooner or later, so I made positive plans about what to do then. The two executives would see me eventually; if not, I would find other customers. That left me free to concentrate on the main thing, saving the contract. Once more, super-slow reading had given me not only pleasure but perspective, and helped me in my everyday affairs.

5   I discovered its worth years ago, in the infamous Changi prisoner-of-war camp in Singapore. I was 19, an artillery sergeant, when the city fell to the Japanese on February 15, 1942. Waiting with other Australian POWs to be marched off, I tried to decide what I should take in the single pack permitted. The only limit was what a weary man could carry the 17 miles to Changi. Our officer thoughtfully suggested, "Each man should find room for a book."

6   So I stuffed into my pack a copy of Lin Yutang's *The Importance of Living*—a title of almost macabre appropriateness—and began a reading habit that was to keep me sane for the next three and a half years. Previously, if I had been really interested in a book, I would race from page to page, eager to know what came next. Now, I decided, I had to become a miser with words and stretch every sentence like a poor man spending his last dollar.

7   During the first few days at Changi, I took Lin Yutang out of my pack three or four times, just gazing at the cover, the binding and the illustrated inside cover. Finally, as the sun went down one evening, I walked out into the prison yard, sat down on a pile of wood and, under the glare of prison lights, slowly opened the book to the title page and frontispiece. I spent three sessions on the preface, then two whole evenings on the contents pages—three and a half pages of chapter headings with fascinating subtitles—before I even reached page one. Night after night I sat there with my treasure. Fellow prisoners argued, played cards and walked about all around me. I was oblivious. I disappeared so completely into my book that sometimes my closest friends thought I had gone bonkers.

8   I had started with the practical object of making my book last. But by the end of the second week, still only on page ten, I began to realize how much I was getting from super-slow reading itself. Sometimes just a particular phrase caught my attention, sometimes a sentence. I would read it slowly, analyze it, read it again—perhaps changing down into an even lower gear—and then sit for 20 minutes thinking about it before moving

on. I was like a pianist studying a piece of music, phrase by phrase, rehearsing it, trying to discover and recreate exactly what the composer was trying to convey.

9   It is difficult to do justice to the intensity of the relationship. When Lin Yutang wrote of preparations for a tea party, I could see the charcoal fire, hear the tinkle of tiny teacups, almost taste the delicate flavor of the tea. I read myself in so thoroughly that it became not a mass of words but a living experience.

10   It took me something like two months to read Lin Yutang's book. By then, his philosophy on tea-making had become my philosophy on reading: You can do it fast, but it's a whole lot better done slowly. I held to the method, even after we had persuaded the Japanese to give us several hundred books from the famous Raffles library in Singapore.

11   The realization dawned on me that, although my body was captive, my mind was free to roam the world. From Changi, I sailed with William Albert Robinson, through his book *Deep Water and Shoal*. In my crowded cell at night, lying on a concrete floor, I felt myself dropping off to sleep in a warm cabin, the boat pitching under me. Next day, I'd be on deck again, in a storm, and after two or three graphic paragraphs I'd be gripping the helm myself, with the roar of the wind in my ears, my hair thick with salt. I wouldn't let go of the helm until we sailed into the calmer waters of a new chapter. If I had read with my old momentum, it would have been like viewing Sydney Harbor from a speedboat, instead of experiencing it from the deck of my own yacht.

12   My voyage took me just short of eight weeks. Had I raced through the book at my former speed, I could never have experienced the blessed release of Robinson's reality becoming so vividly mine.

13   Sitting on a woodpile in the prison yard or crouched on my haunches in any unoccupied corner, I slow-read biographies, philosophy, encyclopedias, even the *Concise Oxford Dictionary*. One favorite was W. Somerset Maugham's *The Summing Up*. I was no longer on a rough prison woodpile, wasting away from hunger; I was in an elegant drawing room on the French Riviera, a decanter of old port at hand, listening to a great writer talking just to me about his journey through life, passing on the wisdom he had gained.

14   An average speed reader might dispose of *The Summing Up* in 50 minutes. But he wouldn't be living that book with the writer, as I did during the nine weeks I took to read its 379 pages. (A slow reader himself, Maugham wrote scathingly of those who "read with their eyes and not with their sensibility. It is a mechanical exercise like the Tibetans' turning of a prayer wheel.") I handled *The Summing Up* so much that it fell to pieces in the tropical heat. Then I carefully rebound it with dried banana leaves and rubber gum. I still have it, the most treasured volume in my bookcase.

15   I developed the habit in Changi of copying passages that especially ap-

pealed to me. One of these, from Aldous Huxley's *Ends and Means,* told how training is needed before one can fully savor anything—even alcohol and tobacco:

"First whiskies seem revolting, first pipes turn even the strongest of boyish stomachs. . . . First Shakespeare sonnets seem meaningless; first Bach fugues a bore, first differential equations sheer torture. But in due course, contact with an obscurely beautiful poem, an elaborate piece of counterpoint, or of mathematical reasoning, causes us to feel direct intuitions of beauty and significance."

16   I defy anyone to pick anything really significant out of a book like that by speed reading. It would be like playing a Beethoven record at the wrong speed!

17   Once, something I copied proved useful in camp. Our own commander had ordered us to give any spare clothing to our officers so they could appear immaculately dressed before the Japanese. The order incensed everybody. I pinned over my bunk some words from T. E. Lawrence's *Seven Pillars of Wisdom:*

18   "Among the Arabs there were no distinctions, traditional or natural, except the unconscious power given a famous sheik by virtue of his accomplishment, and they taught me that no man could be their leader except that he ate the ranks' food, wore their clothes, lived level with them, and yet appeared better in himself."

19   That night hundreds of slips of paper bearing these words were pinned up all over Changi, a possible nasty conflict averted.

20   Beyond giving me the will to survive in Changi, slow reading helps me today. Of course, super-slow reading is not for the man clearing out his briefcase or dealing with the Niagara of paper flowing across his desk. I can skim an inter-office memo as fast as the next person. But when faced with a real problem, to clear my mind of everyday clutter I will sit down quietly at home and slowly read myself into another world.

21   As Lin Yutang wrote: "There are two kinds of reading, reading out of business necessity, and reading as a luxury. The second kind partakes of the nature of a secret delight. It is like a walk in the woods, instead of a trip to the market. One brings home, not packages of canned tomatoes, but a brightened face and lungs filled with good clear air."

22   That is what super-slow reading is all about. Try it. As I read somewhere, a man is poor only when he doesn't know where his next book is coming from. And if he can get out of a book everything the author put into it, he is rich indeed.

the negro artist and the racial mountain

LANGSTON HUGHES

Published in 1926, this article expresses attitudes that have now become commonplace: that "black is beautiful" and that true art arises from folk roots, not from the top branches of society.

Hughes begins with the story of a black poet alienated from his own origins. He generalizes the story into a racial problem typical among black artists (substantiation—paragraphs 2 and 3), and condemns them for isolating themselves from their own people (evaluation—paragraphs 6 and 13). A large portion of the essay demonstrates that art can and does emerge from native roots (e.g., paragraphs 4, 11 and 12). Though the path is hard, though an obstacle as huge as a mountain stands in the way, black artists should prefer that path because it alone will lead to a true Negro art. That is Hughes' recommendation.

Half a century later, there is a black literature indicating that many writers have followed Hughes' advice. Wright, Ellison, Baldwin, and Jones provide examples. Other groups also have accepted Hughes' typically modern idea that art comes from the folk regions of society. We have seen many kinds of "ethnic" art develop. One result, some people say, has been an increase in tensions as each group asserts its superiority.

Do new recommendations seem to be called for and feasible in the 1970s to improve the arts and to strengthen American culture?

1 One of the most promising of the young Negro poets said to me once, "I want to be a poet—not a Negro poet," meaning, I believe, "I want to write like a white poet"; meaning subconsciously, "I would like to be a white poet"; meaning behind that, "I would like to be white." And I was sorry the young man said that, for no great poet has ever been afraid of being himself. And I doubted then that, with his desire to run away spiritually from his race, this boy would ever be a great poet. But this is the mountain standing in the way of any true Negro art in America—this urge within the race toward whiteness, the desire to pour racial individuality into the mold of American standardization, and to be as little Negro and as much American as possible.

2 But let us look at the immediate background of this young poet. His family is of what I suppose one would call the Negro middle class: people who are by no means rich yet never uncomfortable nor hungry—smug, contented, respectable folk, members of the Baptist church. The father goes to work every morning. He is a chief steward at a large white club. The mother sometimes does fancy sewing or supervises parties for the rich families of the town. The children go to a mixed school. In the home they

read white papers and magazines. And the mother often says "Don't be like niggers" when the children are bad. A frequent phrase from the father is, "Look how well a white man does things." And so the word white comes to be unconsciously a symbol of all the virtues. It holds for the children beauty, morality, and money. The whisper of "I want to be white" runs silently through their minds. This young poet's home is, I believe, a fairly typical home of the colored middle class. One sees immediately how difficult it would be for an artist born in such a home to interest himself in interpreting the beauty of his own people. He is never taught to see that beauty. He is taught rather not to see it, or if he does, to be ashamed of it when it is not according to Caucasian patterns.

3   For racial culture the home of a self-styled "high-class" Negro has nothing better to offer. Instead there will perhaps be more aping of things white than in a less cultured or less wealthy home. The father is perhaps a doctor, lawyer, landowner, or politician. The mother may be a social worker, or a teacher, or she may do nothing and have a maid. Father is often dark but he has usually married the lightest woman he could find. The family attend a fashionable church where few really colored faces are to be found. And they themselves draw a color line. In the North they go to white theaters and white movies. And in the South they have at least two cars and a house "like white folks." Nordic manners, Nordic faces, Nordic hair, Nordic art (if any), and an Episcopal heaven. A very high mountain indeed for the would-be racial artist to climb in order to discover himself and his people.

4   But then there are the low-down folks, the so-called common element, and they are the majority—may the Lord be praised! The people who have their nip of gin on Saturday nights and are not too important to themselves or the community, or too well fed, or too learned to watch the lazy world go round. They live on Seventh Street in Washington or State Street in Chicago and they do not particularly care whether they are like white folks or anybody else. Their joy runs, bang! into ecstasy. Their religion soars to a shout. Work maybe a little today, rest a little tomorrow. Play awhile. Sing awhile. O, let's dance! These common people are not afraid of spirituals, as for a long time their more intellectual brethren were, and jazz is their child. They furnish a wealth of colorful, distinctive material for any artist because they still hold their own individuality in the face of American standardizations. And perhaps these common people will give to the world its truly great Negro artist, the one who is not afraid to be himself. Whereas the better-class Negro would tell the artist what to do, the people at least let him alone when he does appear. And they are not ashamed of him— if they know he exists at all. And they accept what beauty is their own without question.

5   Certainly there is, for the American Negro artist who can escape the restrictions the more advanced among his own group would put upon him, a great field of unused material ready for his art. Without going outside his race, and even among the better classes with their "white" culture and con-

scious American manners, but still Negro enough to be different, there is sufficient matter to furnish a black artist with a lifetime of creative work. And when he chooses to touch on the relations between Negroes and whites in this country with their innumerable overtones and undertones, surely, and especially for literature and the drama, there is an inexaustible supply of themes at hand. To these the Negro artist can give his racial individuality, his heritage of rhythm and warmth, and his incongruous humor that so often, as in the Blues, becomes ironic laughter mixed with tears. But let us look again at the mountain.

6   A prominent Negro clubwoman in Philadelphia paid eleven dollars to hear Raquel Meller sing Andalusian popular songs. But she told me a few weeks before she would not think of going to hear "that woman," Clara Smith, a great black artist, sing Negro folksongs. And many an upper-class Negro church, even now, would not dream of employing a spiritual in its services. The drab melodies in white folks' hymnbooks are much to be preferred. "We want to worship the Lord correctly and quietly. We don't believe in 'shouting.' Let's be dull like the Nordics," they say, in effect.

7   The road for the serious black artist, then, who would produce a racial art is most certainly rocky and the mountain is high. Until recently he received almost no encouragement for his work from either white or colored people. The fine novels of Chestnutt go out of print with neither race noticing their passing. The quaint charm and humor of Dunbar's dialect verse brought to him, in his day, largely the same kind of encouragement one would give a side-show freak (A colored man writing poetry! How odd!) or a clown (How amusing!).

8   The present vogue in things Negro, although it may do as much harm as good for the budding colored artist, has at least done this: it has brought him forcibly to the attention of his own people among whom for so long, unless the other race had noticed him beforehand, he was a prophet with little honor. I understand that Charles Gilpin acted for years in Negro theaters without any special acclaim from his own, but when Broadway gave him eight curtain calls, Negroes, too, began to beat a tin pan in his honor. I know a young colored writer, a manual worker by day, who had been writing well for the colored magazines for some years, but it was not until he recently broke into the white publications and his first book was accepted by a prominent New York publisher that the "best" Negroes in his city took the trouble to discover that he lived there. Then almost immediately they decided to give a grand dinner for him. But the society ladies were careful to whisper to his mother that perhaps she'd better not come. They were not sure she would have an evening gown.

9   The Negro artist works against an undertow of sharp criticism and misunderstanding from his own group and unintentional bribes from the whites. "O, be respectable, write about nice people, show how good we are," say the Negroes. "Be stereotyped, don't go too far, don't shatter our illusions about you, don't amuse us too seriously. We will pay you," say the whites. Both would have told Jean Toomer not to write "Cane." The

colored people did not praise it. The white people did not buy it. Most of the colored people who did read "Cane" hated it. They are afraid of it. Although the critics gave it good reviews the public remained indifferent. Yet (excepting the work of DuBois) "Cane" contains the finest prose written by a Negro in America. And like the singing of Robeson, it is truly racial.

10   But in spite of the Nordicized Negro intelligentsia and the desires of some white editors we have an honest American Negro literature already with us. Now I await the rise of the Negro theater. Our folk music, having achieved world-wide fame, offers itself to the genius of the great individual American Negro composer who is to come. And within the next decade I expect to see the work of a growing school of colored artists who paint and model the beauty of dark faces and create with new technique the expressions of their own soul-world. And the Negro dancers who will dance like flame and the singers who will continue to carry our songs to all who listen—they will be with us in even greater numbers tomorrow.

11   Most of my own poems are racial in theme and treatment, derived from the life I know. In many of them I try to grasp and hold some of the meanings and rhythms of jazz. I am as sincere as I know how to be in these poems and yet after every reading I answer questions like these from my own people: Do you think Negroes should always write about Negroes? I wish you wouldn't read some of your poems to white folks. How do you find anything interesting in a place like a cabaret? Why do you write about black people? You aren't black. What makes you do so many jazz poems?

12   But jazz to me is one of the inherent expressions of Negro life in America: the eternal tom-tom beating in the Negro soul—the tom-tom of revolt against weariness in a white world, a world of subway trains, and work, work, work; the tom-tom of joy and laughter, and pain swallowed in a smile. Yet the Philadelphia clubwoman is ashamed to say that her race created it and she does not like me to write about it. The old subconscious "white is best" runs through her mind. Years of study under white teachers, a lifetime of white books, pictures, and papers, and white manners, morals, and Puritan standards made her dislike the spirituals. And now she turns up her nose at jazz and all its manifestations—likewise almost everything else distinctly racial. She doesn't care for the Winold Reiss portraits of Negroes because they are "too Negro." She does not want a true picture of herself from anybody. She wants the artist to flatter her, to make the white world believe that all Negroes are as smug and as near white in soul as she wants to be. But, to my mind, it is the duty of the younger Negro artist, if he accepts any duties at all from outsiders, to change through the force of his art that old whispering "I want to be white," hidden in the aspirations of his people, to "Why should I want to be white? I am a Negro—and beautiful!"

13   So I am ashamed for the black poet who says, "I want to be a poet, not a Negro poet," as though his own racial world were not as interesting as any other world. I am ashamed, too, for the colored artist who runs

from the painting of Negro faces to the painting of sunsets after the manner of the academicians because he fears the strange un-whiteness of his own features. An artist must be free to choose what he does, certainly, but he must also never be afraid to do what he might choose.

14   Let the blare of Negro jazz bands and the bellowing voice of Bessie Smith singing Blues penetrate the closed ears of the colored near-intellectuals until they listen and perhaps understand. Let Paul Robeson singing Water Boy, and Rudolph Fisher writing about the streets of Harlem, and Jean Toomer holding the heart of Georgia in his hands, and Aaron Douglas drawing strange black fantasies cause the smug Negro middle class to turn from their white, respectable, ordinary books and papers to catch a glimmer of their own beauty. We younger Negro artists who create now intend to express our individual dark-skinned selves without fear or shame. If white people are pleased we are glad. If they are not, it doesn't matter. We know we are beautiful. And ugly too. The tom-tom cries and the tom-tom laughs. If colored people are pleased we are glad. If they are not, their displeasure doesn't matter either. We build our temples for tomorrow, strong as we know how, and we stand on top of the mountain, free within ourselves.

the god that failed
RICHARD WRIGHT

During the 1930s, Richard Wright was an enthusiastic supporter of the Communist Party. Black, poor, and living in a Chicago slum, he believed that communism could provide a solution to racial problems as well as to other varieties of human injustice. The selection below reports part of his gradual disillusionment with the Party. The time is 1936; the scene, a Party parade for May Day. Wright's essay moves from a narrative showing that one course of action does not work, at least for him, to an analysis in which he formulates a new alternative: no longer able to endorse the Party, he resolves to speak as a person "really alone now" (paragraph 34).

We are not explicitly asked or told to do anything, but the concept Wright recommends is clear. We should work for progress not by joining mass protest movements but by trying, as individuals, to understand how to live a genuinely "human" life (paragraph 33).

Source: From *The God That Failed,* edited by Richard Crossman. Copyright © 1944 by Richard Wright. Reprinted by permission of Harper & Row, Publishers.

1   **a**s May Day of 1936 approached, it was voted by the union membership that we should march in the public procession. On the morning of May Day I received printed instructions as to the time and place where our union contingent would assemble to join the parade. At noon, I hurried to the spot and found that the parade was already in progress. In vain I searched for the banners of my union local. Where were they? I went up and down the streets, asking for the location of my local.

2   "Oh, that local's gone fifteen minutes ago," a Negro told me. "If you're going to march, you'd better fall in somewhere."

3   I thanked him and walked through the milling crowds. Suddenly I heard my name called. I turned. To my left was the Communist Party's South Side section, lined up and ready to march.

4   "Come here!" an old Party friend called to me.

5   I walked over to him.

6   "Aren't you marching today?" he asked me.

7   "I missed my union local," I told him.

8   "What the hell," he said. "March with us."

9   "I don't know," I said, remembering my last visit to the headquarters of the Party, and my status as an "enemy."

10   "This is May Day," he said. "Get into the ranks."

11   "You know the trouble I've had," I said.

12   "That's nothing," he said. "Everybody's marching today."

13   "I don't think I'd better," I said, shaking my head.

14   "Are you scared?" he asked. "This is *May Day*."

15   He caught my right arm and pulled me into line beside him. I stood talking to him, asking about his work, about common friends.

16   "Get out of our ranks!" a voice barked.

17   I turned. A white Communist, a leader of the district of the Communist Party, Cy Perry, a slender, close-cropped fellow, stood glaring at me.

18   "I—It's May Day and I want to march," I said.

19   "Get out!" he shouted.

20   "I was invited here," I said.

21   I turned to the Negro Communist who had invited me into the ranks. I did not want public violence. I looked at my friend. He turned his eyes away. He was afraid. I did not know what to do.

22   "You asked me to march here," I said to him.

23   He did not answer.

24   "Tell him that you did invite me," I said, pulling his sleeve.

25   "I'm asking you for the last time to get out of our ranks!" Cy Perry shouted.

26   I did not move. I had intended to, but I was beset by so many impulses that I could not act. Another white Communist came to assist Perry. Perry caught hold of my collar and pulled at me. I resisted. They held me fast. I struggled to free myself.

27   "Turn me loose!" I said.

28   Hands lifted me bodily from the sidewalk; I felt myself being pitched

headlong through the air. I saved myself from landing on my head by clutching a curbstone with my hands. Slowly I rose and stood. Perry and his assistant were glaring at me. The rows of white and black Communists were looking at me with cold eyes of nonrecognition. I could not quite believe what had happened, even though my hands were smarting and bleeding. I had suffered a public, physical assault by two white Communists with black Communists looking on. I could not move from the spot. I was empty of any idea about what to do. But I did not feel belligerent. I had outgrown my childhood.

29   Suddenly, the vast ranks of the Communist Party began to move. Scarlet banners with the hammer and sickle emblem of world revolution were lifted, and they fluttered in the May breeze. Drums beat. Voices were chanting. The tramp of many feet shook the earth. A long line of set-faced men and women, white and black, flowed past me.

30   I followed the procession to the Loop and went into Grant Park Plaza and sat upon a bench. I was not thinking; I could not think. But an objectivity of vision was being born within me. A surging sweep of many odds and ends came together and formed an attitude, a perspective. "They're blind," I said to myself. "Their enemies have blinded them with too much oppression." I lit a cigarette and I heard a song floating over the sunlit air:

Arise, you pris'ners of starvation!

31   I remembered the stories I had written, the stories in which I had assigned a role of honor and glory to the Communist Party, and I was glad that they were down in black and white, were finished. For I knew in my heart that I should never be able to write that way again, should never be able to feel with that simple sharpness about life, should never again express such passionate hope, should never again make so total a commitment of faith.

A better world's in birth. . . .

32   The procession still passed. Banners still floated. Voices of hope still chanted.

33   I headed toward home alone, really alone now, telling myself that in all the sprawling immensity of our mighty continent the least-known factor of living was the human heart, the least-sought goal of being was a way to live a human life. Perhaps, I thought, out of my tortured feelings I could fling a spark into this darkness. I would try, not because I wanted to, but because I felt that I had to if I were to live at all.

34   I would hurl words into this darkness and wait for an echo; and if an echo sounded, no matter how faintly, I would send other words to tell, to march, to fight, to create a sense of the hunger for life that gnaws in us all, to keep alive in our hearts a sense of the inexpressibly human.

the seal killing controversy

VICTOR B. SCHEFFER

This article recommends a course of action based not only on factual evidence but also on the moral evaluation of evidence. Scheffer tries to resolve a characteristic modern dilemma: what responsibilities does man have to the other creatures with which he shares the earth? To what extent should he "harvest the resources of the world" (paragraph 4) for his own benefit?

Whether Scheffer succeeds in resolving this dilemma will depend partly on your own moral principles. When he describes the two kinds of seals and the two methods of killing them, he is providing objective information. But when he confronts the moral issue (paragraph 21), he becomes personal and subjective. The transition is not easy. You may want clearer definitions of "kindness" (paragraph 24) or of "the sensitive person" (paragraph 25) before you are prepared to accept Scheffer's recommendation.

1   You pause for a moment in a shop where a sealskin coat is on display. You admire its rich and perfect texture. Expensive, yes; but oh, so handsome.

2   Then a troubling thought: Is it right to want such luxury at the cost of wildlife? You remember the ads and articles and television shows that deplore the killing of seals. You hesitate—then drift on. Maybe you'll return, but for the moment, you're overwhelmed by an odd sense of guilt.

3   For thirty years I have studied the seals and their secret ways on land and sea. I have seen myself mirrored in their dark eyes. And I have thought of their tragic past as individuals and as species.

4   Now a sound and fury are rising from two opposing camps: those who would continue to harvest the seal resources of the world for the benefit (they say) of mankind, and those who would not. I feel a commitment to step in. But my experience calls me to discuss facts, not philosophy. And I write only in the hope that my knowledge can help illuminate the issues— so that you, the reader, may make your own choice.

5   Commercial sealing is a Jack London story that never ends. It tells of ships crushed in the ice and fog, and of men who lie, cheat, and gamble for the possession of furs. It tells of the shame of America in 1868 when the beaches of the Pribilof Islands ran red with the blood of 300,000 animals. And it tells of the pride of America today in the conservation of the great Alaska fur seal herd.

6   The debate over sealing is fraught with emotion. In Canada and Europe, movies were shown of baby harp seals skinned alive on the sea-ice

Source. Copyright © 1973 by the National Wildlife Federation. Reprinted from the June-July issue of *National Wildlife* Magazine.

of Newfoundland. In waves of protest, letters poured into the capitals of Canada and Norway, those nations with the greatest stake in the harp seal business. In one week alone, the Canadian Government received over 5,000 letters. The sealskin market plummeted. But the Government says the pictures were untrue. A commercial company made a film purporting to show a regular seal hunt; yet it hired novices to play the hunters.

7   Pickets march in Washington, D.C., angered to learn that the Alaska fur seal herd will again be cropped under Federal care, as it has been cropped every year for a century. And a national news magazine insists that "a campaign of vilification is afoot against the fur trade."

8   The seal controversy has two distinct issues, one of *conservation,* or the effect of killing upon the animal population; and one of *morality,* or the effect of killing upon the human spirit. The consumer of fur coats seldom knows or cares about the conservation elements involved in the seal resource, trusting that the wildlife agency in charge is a true and faithful steward. On the point of morality—when people must decide in private whether to wear a coat at the cost of wildlife—the consumer is alone in the little room of his or her own conscience.

9   Let the harp seals and Alaska fur seals illustrate the issues. Of the twenty main kinds of seals in the world, these two are the most valuable. Both feed along the coasts of North America.

10   Harp seals visit the sea-ice of eastern Canada to give birth in March. Some congregate in the Gulf of St. Lawrence (the so-called "Gulf" seal herd which produces 200,000 pups a year) and some off Newfoundland (the "Front" seals, with 100,000 pups). The two stocks probably intermix. The products of the harp seal industry are pelts, blubber, and leather valued at about $3 million a year.

11   The Alaska fur seal herd visits the Pribilof Islands in the Bering Sea and gives birth in mid-summer to approximately 300,000 pups. The main products of the industry which harvests these seals are the rich pelts of the half-grown males. Also, a thousand tons of dark red "sealburger" are processed each year for animal feed, primarily pet food. The value of this fur seal crop is about $5 million.

12   Are seal populations threatened at present levels of harvesting? The answer is no—and yes.

13   With respect to the harp seals, a recent report of the International Commission for the Northwest Atlantic Fisheries says "the combined (Gulf seal and Front seal) sustainable yield at present is estimated to be no more than 125,000 young harp seals. Present annual catches average 218,000 young, and the effort is increasing." Control of overkill has been hard to achieve because more than one nation's sealers are involved. However, Canada and Norway are now working through treaties to reduce the combined kill to a conservative figure.

14   Meanwhile in the Pribilof Islands, records carefully maintained over 100 years plainly show that the annual harvest of about 50,000 bachelor fur seals, or one-third of the male pups born, can be sustained. Hence, the

Alaska fur seal is not easily lumped into the sealing controversy, simply because the regular harvesting of this species has nothing to do with a "conservation crisis."

15   But what about the moral issue? It has two parts: Are the methods of sealing humane? And why should *any* seals have to be killed?

16   Because humaneness is indefinable, all I can do is describe the killing methods. The tools used in harvesting harp seals are the club, the "hakapik" (a Norwegian tool resembling an ice axe), and the rifle. Elizabeth Simpson, English veterinarian, believes that the best way to judge, postmortem, whether a seal was unconscious at the time of skinning is to examine the skull. In 1968 she wrote that "It would be pleasant to say that cruelty had been reduced to an acceptable minimum, but this, unfortunately, is not the case." Seventeen percent of the skulls she examined had *not* been fractured by the sealer's club.

17   As a result of pressure from humane societies, the Canadian and Norwegian Governments tightened the harp sealing laws in 1970. The killing season was delayed until late March and early April, giving the pups time to shed their white birthcoats, to be weaned, and to teach themselves to swim. Other laws now protect the adult seals on the breeding patches, forbid the use of aircraft (except for locating the patches), specify the weapons, and so on.

18   The method of cropping fur seals in Alaska is different. Here the animals are killed by natives born and trained on the seal islands. In June and July they drive the seals from the beaches to grassy meadows, where they select the three- and four-year males. These they kill with a blow on the head from a club and follow with a knife puncture through the heart. When Dr. Simpson visited the Pribilofs, she found fewer than two percent of intact skulls on the killing field, a figure which she thought was at an "acceptably humane level."

19   Government, university, and humane societies officials also visited the Pribilofs. Working as a task force, they tested new ways of killing seals: by suffocation, by electrocution, and by shooting. All methods were impractical. The task force could recommend no quicker, cleaner way of killing a seal than by bashing it in the head with a heavy club. Commenting later on this group's report, and reflecting on the ways seals ordinarily die in the wild, the President of the Humane Society of the United States wondered whether "death is any nicer by starvation, trampling, or disease, than by a quick blow on the head."

20   At any rate, killing Alaska fur seals on land is more humane than killing them at sea. The famous Fur Seal Treaty of 1911 put an end to the bloody days of open sea hunting. Before then, the animals—many of them females bulging with unborn young—were shot indiscriminately, and many sank before they could be recovered.

21   But the ultimate question of the moral issue still needs be faced: Should seals be killed under any circumstances? If you believe in a man-centered

world you will probably answer "yes," and if you believe in a man-shared world you will say, "perhaps," or "no."

22 My own attitude toward animals is partitioned. My "kill-reluctance" is graduated on a scale, lowest for the crawling creatures, highest for the warm-blooded mammals like myself, especially their females and young. I don't apologize for my feelings, though I admit that they come from the heart rather than the head.

23 In an old trunk I find a faded "Band of Mercy" pledge that I signed in a school campaign in 1914. I promised then that I would "try to be kind to all harmless living creatures and to protect them from cruel usage." Thus, early in my career as a biologist, I was put in the hard position of having to decide which animals were "harmless" and therefore, to be treated with "kindness."

24 Kindness is a lovely word. It means recognizing others of one's kind without asking where the limits of other-kindness should be drawn. The morality issue is really asking the question: Shall seals be killed to satisfy not only our *needs* but our *wants*? Few would deny an Alaskan native the right to kill a seal for food, though many have questioned the right of a government to provide pelts for a luxury trade. Satisfying hunger is not the same as satisfying vanity, or even gratifying a universal fondness for beautiful clothing.

25 The sensitive person will not buy the time-worn argument: Sealing may be a bloody business, but it does employ a lot of people. But let's be honest; the number employed in *any* business is a poor index of its character.

26 On the other hand, the flames of the seal debate have attracted an extremist familiar to all wildlife conservationists, the professional savior— usually well-meaning, but often inept, unfair, or inaccurate. I quote from an illustrated ad of such a savior organization. My own comments are in parentheses:

27 "The seal . . . is crying out to the man because he has just skinned her little one alive. (Indeed, she is threatening him with bared teeth; she believes her pup is *still* alive!) . . . Hundreds of thousands of baby seals are butchered this way every year." (And billions of domestic sheep, cattle, pigs, goats, rabbits, horses, and in the Orient, dogs, are slaughtered annually to satisfy the public's hunger.)

28 Part of the sealing problem is that we do not like to think of the actual suffering or death of any animal—wild or domestic—though we are quite willing to use its products in our economy. "Human kind," wrote T.S. Eliot, "cannot bear very much reality."

29 Have I left you wondering what I believe about killing seals? I know that the harp seals and the Alaska fur seals will continue to be killed as long as world opinion assigns a high priority to their commercial use. But I hope that world opinion will change; that present values and goals will increasingly be questioned; and that living seals will one day be valued

above dead ones. A six-man committee on seals and sealing appointed by the Canadian Government recommended in 1972 "a phasing out of the Canadian and Norwegian harp and hood seal hunt." (The hood seal is a North Atlantic species taken in small numbers.) I would be pleased if the northern nations would agree to stop the killing of seals altogether. The beautiful Pribilof Islands would be conserved as a great international park of education and wildlife study. The seals would suddenly appear in the spring, glistening wet in the May sun, and after their summer ashore, disappear into the sea fogs of November. They would mate and give birth, some would fight to the death, and pups would be trampled in the mire of the rookeries. As in any national park, the whole splendid cycle of life, death, and regeneration would be played continuously before the eyes of visitors.

30   In the meanwhile, I believe that the American, Canadian, and Norwegian sealing agencies should discuss and interpret their programs more openly than they have in the past. When I first began to study the Alaska fur seal in 1940, no one was allowed to set foot on the Pribilofs without permission of the Interior Department in faraway Washington, D.C. And no one was allowed to photograph the killing scenes. Now tourists arrive weekly from Anchorage, most of them carrying cameras. This is a start. Yet the full story of sealing is still unknown to the public at large.

31   I strongly believe that completely independent citizen advisory councils should periodically review all agency programs. Much has already been accomplished by concerned men and women to reduce the carelessness and unintentional cruelty of the sealing business. Yet still more needs to be done.

street girls of the '70s
CELESTE MacLEOD

A useful essay-writing technique is the presentation of "case histories." To prove a point (substantiate a thesis), you can present a series of short "true stories" that dramatize the issue and lead to a generalization. MacLeod tells us about Peggy, Wilma, Mia, and Shirley; and we readily accept the generalization that "street girls" are victims not only of unfortunate backgrounds but also of obsolete laws and useless correctional institutions.

This analysis of the problem leads to a recommendation: we need to revise the delinquency laws and provide homeless girls with something better than jails or reform schools. MacLeod summarizes the recommendations of several specialists—Barmack and Zimmerman (paragraph 3), Blum and Smith (paragraph 15), Richette (paragraph 16), and others. She herself endorses the concept of group homes. To show that they are feasible, she tells us that legislation to establish such facilities has been introduced in Congress (paragraph 17).

The only question that remains is how to keep parents from creating new Peggy's and Wilma's. MacLeod doesn't answer that.

1   **P**eggy will not sleep in a doorway tonight. She will stand on the street until some man decides to take her home for dinner and bed in exchange for sex. Peggy is 15 and has been living on the streets of Berkeley for more than a year. Her counterparts haunt certain sections of dozens of American cities. Is she a special problem of the sour 1970s? No, she is a variation on a very old one.

2   Girls like Peggy used to be called wayward—some people still use the term. Peggy hasn't had much in life, but she is rich in labels. Doctors may have labeled her a battered child, if they saw her at all as an infant. Her parents and others who raised her began by calling her nuisance, brat and slut, and ended by declaring her incorrigible, petitioning the courts to dispose of her. Newspapers called her a juvenile delinquent; some gentle souls called her a strayed lamb and prescribed Bible verses; while the labels that psychiatrists and social workers put on her could run for pages. Judges called her whatever they saw fit and sent her off to reform school. They had little choice, because few options exist for these girls whom nobody wants.

3   In the past we heard little about the Peggy's in our society because they were locked away in state institutions. They could be kept there until they turned 21, even if they had done nothing that would be considered a crime if committed by an adult. They were imprisoned for their own protection, the law said, to keep them from the danger of leading "an idle, dissolute, lewd, or immoral life." The emergence of a street scene in this country has given some of these girls an alternative to spending their teens behind bars. It has also given people a chance to know these girls outside an institutional setting and to evolve new ways of helping them. Beth Barmack and Elaine Zimmerman, young women involved in community action, have been working with street girls of Berkeley for three years. In 1971, while students at the University of California, they volunteered to teach English at East Campus (the Berkeley continuation high school, a loosely structured, half-day program for students who can't function well in the regular setting).

4   They found that girls in their classes (many of them former street people who had been in and out of foster homes and juvenile halls) had a strong need to share their experiences and explore alternative means of survival. To fill this need, Zimmerman and Barmack started a Women's Program. They covered topics such as jobs for women, single mothers,

rape, prostitution and sexism, using current articles and speakers to evoke group discussions. The strong response to their program led them to set up additional problem-solving sessions, where girls could discuss their lives and crises. They also talked with dozens of street girls on Telegraph Avenue, after their students had introduced them as "safe" (meaning that they wouldn't turn in runaways). [See MacLeod: "Street People: The New Migrants," *The Nation,* October 22, 1973.]

5   In a resulting paper by Elaine Zimmerman, "Berkeley's Juvenile Girls in Conflict," a vivid picture emerges. Girls on the street come from "alarmingly difficult family backgrounds," she found. From infancy on they have been tossed from parents to grandparents, friends, foster homes and juvenile halls. Only one in ten grew up with both biological parents. With little education and virtually no salable skill except sex, they "have low self-images, base their identities on possession of a man, do not trust women, have no respect or faith in authority, are lonely and bored, and have no one to confide in." But they are eager to be loved and cared for.

6   Wilma is still looking for love. She spent her first five years with family friends in Oklahoma, until her mother remarried and took back Wilma and her brother. Wilma never saw her real father. Her mother, herself a runaway, was determined that her daughter would not go astray. To that end, she beat her continually, using "whatever was handy, a bullwhip or a yardstick"; as punishment she burned her daughter's hand over the electric stove. When Wilma was 9, her mother split her head open with a belt buckle and rushed her to the hospital, telling the doctors she had fallen out of a tree house. Then the mother's marriage broke up, Wilma was sent to friends, put into foster homes, reclaimed by her mother, who kept her one day and sent her back to friends. When Wilma was 12, her mother phoned: "Wilma, please come home. I love you. I need you." Wilma rushed back. A few months later her mother beat her senseless. During the next years she was in and out of reform schools, mental hospitals and the street. At 13 she escaped from a reformatory and went to New York's East Village. She lived with a succession of men and for a time came under the protection of the Hells Angels, but she often went hungry, was raped many times, and turned to drugs. Eventually she came out to California and settled down on the streets of Berkeley.

7   Many of Wilma's problems stem from her status. The runaway girl is a fugitive, forced to live like an escaped convict, even if her parents have thrown her out and she has been on her own for years. Legally she must be under the supervision of a parent, guardian, husband or the state until the day she turns 18. (Age laws may vary from state to state; boys are generally free at 16.) In a few states she can apply at 16 to become an emancipated minor, but as a runaway with a record, she has little chance of being granted that status. She cannot take a job to support herself. She cannot enroll in school and finish her education. She cannot take part in any activity where her identity may be recognized, or she will be thrown into jail. Most girls survive by the only means open to them—panhandling,

subsistence prostitution and sometimes petty theft. Meanwhile, they search for "the" man, who they dream will give them all the love they never had.

8   In practice the runaway laws have generated a strange irony. A man who gives a ride to a female runaway may be more likely to get into trouble if he tries to help her (he may be arrested for contributing to the delinquency of a minor) than if he rapes her and leaves her stranded on the highway. Police are unlikely to believe such a story from a distraught girl who has obviously "been around." Last year Mia, a 17-year-old girl who lived with her boy friend with parental consent, was kidnapped and raped by another man. When she reported it to the police, they arrested her as a runaway and shipped her off to Juvenile Hall, instead of going after the rapist. Wilma had a similar experience on the East Coast at 16, when she went back for a visit. Raped and dumped by a man who gave her a ride, she made her way to the nearest police station, where she was promptly arrested. The judge, seeing her past record, said he would sentence her to the state reformatory until she was 21, unless the social worker put her on a plane to California (and out of his state's way) within twenty-four hours. Miraculously, the social worker came up with the fare.

9   Not all girls who run away fit the "discard" category. During the Flower Children era of 1967, it became fashionable to run, and masses of middle-class children turned up on the streets, fresh from home. Runaway centers, such as Huckleberry House in San Francisco and Runaway House in Washington, D.C., gradually opened in many cities, to help both runaways and their parents. The need for more such facilities led to the proposed Runaway Youth Act, introduced in 1971 by Sen. Birch Bayh. (It passed the Senate in 1972 and 1973 and is now in committee in the House.) The bill allocates grants, through H.E.W., for small runaway centers to provide "temporary shelter and counseling services" for runaways. It keeps such centers ". . . whenever possible . . . outside the law-enforcement structure and juvenile justice system." At hearings held early in 1972 Brian Slatterly of Huckleberry House said that, judging from his conversations with them, "Police patrolmen almost unanimously think that runaways should not be a police problem, that having police arrest and detain them . . . doesn't help either the runaways, their families, or the police."

10   Several witnesses pointed out that the majority of runaways in America are girls. Girls are also arrested more often than boys for status offenses—runaway, truancy and the MINS, PINS and CINS statute (minors, persons and children in need of supervision). Girls are jailed for status offenses longer than boys (or girls) are jailed for felonies such as theft or assault. Such treatment is legal, because their incarceration is labeled prevention instead of punishment. Thus when a 17-year-old girl was sentenced to four years at the Connecticut State Farm for Women, because she was "in manifest danger of falling into habits of vice" (*Mattielo* v. *Conn.* 154 Conn. 737) the Supreme Court, in 1969, refused to review the case. Preventive detention, a practice we deplore in Communist and Fascist countries, is all right in our own, as long as it is applied only to children.

11   The landmark 1967 *Gault* decision, which gives children arrested for a crime the right to a lawyer, is not always extended to girls held on status offenses—because they have committed no crime. Appeal after conviction is rare, since the girls usually come from poor families, and there are no jailhouse lawyers or law books in juvenile institutions. Once girls are committed, the only way they can get out, it seems, is over the wall, and many girls who were sentenced to institutions after they ran away from home have managed to escape. No matter how difficult and depressing their life on the street, every girl interviewed prefers this homeless existence to incarceration in an institution. "At least you're free." Yet they are not happy with street life. As one girl put it, "I'd like a place to crash where you don't have to ball all the time." Passage of the Runaway Youth Act can give more such girls a place, outside the feared juvenile justice system, where they can go for help.

12   For Shirley, the support she received from the Women's Program at East Campus may have been the rock that anchored her. When she was a baby, her mother (who had run away from her own punitive father) worked as a prostitute to put her husband through college. Often she received her customers in the same room with Shirley. After graduating, the father left them, and Shirley's mother had a nervous breakdown. She was never the same, says Shirley. When she was 12, her mother urged her to have affairs "for experience." At 14, Shirley was kidnapped by two couples: she was beaten, raped, and had her hair shaved off. The police would not believe her story; they advised Shirley's mother to send her out of town for a while, which she did. When it was time to return, her mother would not send the bus fare. Shirley hitchhiked back and, finding herself unwelcome at home, went to the streets of nearby Berkeley. She slept in a school warehouse, panhandled, lived with a series of men, and had two abortions. During this same period she enrolled at East Campus (theoretically, she was under parental guidance and not a runaway); she was graduated from high school and joined the Women's Program. "It came at the right time for me," says Shirley, who today at 18 is in better shape than many girls emerging from "rehabilitative" institutions. She found a job in a bookstore, has developed a strong sense of self, and plans to enter college.

13   Shirley and Wilma are both white, but patterns similar to their lives occur in every racial background. Foster homes, the traditional placement for these girls, are rarely successful. The girls have been in and out of so many foster homes already that they have lost faith in the parental role, no matter who plays it. "It's too late for them to put on ribbons and be sweet little girls in a nuclear family," says Zimmerman. Teen-aged girls are also the hardest to place, she adds, because they spell sex and trouble to foster parents, just as they did to their own. Zimmerman and Barmack favor the new concept of small group homes in a community setting. They are in the process of setting up such a home in Berkeley.

14   Ten juvenile girls will live cooperatively in the group home, attending

Berkeley's continuation high school. A staff member will be on hand around the clock, aided by part-time therapists. By exchanging experiences in group sessions and in everyday life, says Barmack, the girls will find that their problems are not unique and that they can learn from one another. No longer dependent on a male for survival as they were on the street, they can make friends with other girls, instead of viewing them as hated rivals. They will have a voice in shaping house policies, as well as being responsible for their share of the work. But it will be *their* house, says Barmack, a different situation from the authoritarian atmosphere they knew in homes and institutions.

15   Staff members at Sanctuary, a runaway center in Boston, share Barmack's and Zimmerman's belief that large juvenile institutions are destructive. In *Nothing Left to Lose* Jeffrey Blum and Judith Smith tell how difficult it is to reach juveniles who come out of state institutions. These young people, they find, "do not come out unscathed. They adapt to survive: they become cynical, manipulative, amoral." Massachusetts closed all of its juvenile institutions in 1972. In the past three years New York City has closed three of its four secure juvenile facilities, diverting children into foster or group homes instead. The National Association of Sheriffs has condemned the practice of jailing juveniles. Nevertheless, incarceration remains the major way of dealing with troubled children in this country.

16   In *The Throwaway Children* Judge Lisa Aversa Richette of Philadelphia poignantly describes the tragedies that engulf children who are brought before the juvenile court, and the frustration of court personnel who have no effective way to help them under present laws and programs. "There are no houses—nice or otherwise—for children who are rejected by everyone and literally thrown away into the streets like litter," she wrote in 1969. "Not in Philadelphia, nor in any American city. Jails, detention centers, correctional institutions, yes. But a quiet loving home where a boy or girl can live, study, and be understood, that is quite another thing." Judge Richette believes that "due process of law—one of society's most profoundly civilized values—may mean more in the life of all children than all the rhetoric of the therapists." Some of the changes in juvenile law which she advocates in her writings are contained in federal legislation now pending.

17   In 1972, after many hearings, the Subcommittee to Investigate Juvenile Delinquency of the Senate Judiciary Committee developed the Juvenile Justice and Delinquency Prevention Act. It was introduced by Senator Bayh, chairman of the subcommittee, and Sen. Marlow Cook of Kentucky. The bill would provide resources (both money and consultant help) for states and communities that set up new programs for juvenile offenders, emphasizing small community-based facilities such as group homes, halfway houses, foster care and shelter-care facilities. "There's a real need for federal leadership in this area," says John C. Rector, staff director and

chief counsel of the subcommittee. In President Nixon's 25,000-word State of the Union message, Rector points out, "There was . . . not one word that would reflect a concern for young people in trouble."

18 The bill (now in committee) is preventive, Rector adds. It sets up a series of Youth Service Bureaus from which children with problems can be referred to appropriate agencies for help. The aim is to keep young people from ever becoming entangled in the juvenile justice system. Other features of the bill include increased constitutional rights for arrested juveniles, more effective sealings of juvenile records, prohibiting the jailing of juveniles with adults, and an office in H.E.W.

19 No changes in age limitations are included in the present bill. Wilma is angry that the court would not let her be on her own at 15 or 16, so she could have looked for work without being arrested. Bob Walker, an attorney at the Youth Law Center in San Francisco, says a minor status is an advantage for some, because it requires their parents or the state to support them. For girls like Wilma, who in fact have been on their own since 12 or 13, Walker thinks the law should offer a way for them to become emancipated long before 18.

20 Tom Jennings, another attorney at the Youth Law Center, says lawyers are making gradual headway in challenging statutes that allow juveniles to be jailed on virtually any pretext. In *Gonzales* v. *Maillard* (ND Calif. 1971) a three-judge panel ruled that the statute phrase "in danger of leading an immoral life" is "unconstitutionally vague." But statutes designating persons in need of supervision are still on the books in most states. A Puritan strain permeates our laws pertaining to juvenile girls. Their morals are considered more important than their rights or welfare. Girls, but not boys, are locked up for having sexual relations at an early age.

21 This same attitude extends into the home. Parents often regard their adolescent daughters as potentially dangerous sex machines, which must be strictly regulated to perform as directed. Girls have been declared incorrigible by their parents, and jailed for many years, for offenses such as having friends the parents don't like, staying out late one night, or talking back.

22 Group homes may not be the answer for all such girls, but they are a hopeful alternative to penal dumping grounds. Zimmerman and Barmack in Berkeley believe that the confidence and self-reliance which girls can develop in a group-home setting will keep them from becoming tomorrow's adult throwaways. As Judge Richette puts it: "We generally underestimate just how much young people can do for themselves, if adults will let them."

the doctor's dilemma
LORD RITCHIE-CALDER

The dilemma Ritchie-Calder describes is the conflict between biological experimentation and its moral consequences. His sense of moral urgency makes his language constantly suggest value judgments. He concludes by recommending that we establish an "international tribunal of ethics" to help resolve the dilemma. If that is not feasible, he would apparently settle for "a new personal ethic" to guide doctors, but he seems to have no specific procedure for developing one.

The mysteries of scientific experimentation are often beyond the grasp of laymen, but they now threaten to have drastic effects on human life. It is therefore crucial that Ritchie-Calder translate his personal alarm as a scientist into terms that most readers can understand. The success of his recommendation will depend on them. If laymen do not support his tribunal and if doctors do not adopt a new personal ethic, nothing will improve; the bio-engineers will go on with business as usual.

1   In the brief lifetime of the protesting youth of today, we have had four major epochs—the atomic age, the computer age, the space age, and the bio-engineering, or DNA, age. Each of them is as significant as the Bronze Age, the Iron Age, the Renaissance, or the Industrial Revolution, and all have been telescoped into the postwar years. The first has given Man the capacity to veto the further evolution of his own species by bringing on a nuclear holocaust. The second has given the machine the ultimate capacity to replace human labor and ape the logical faculties of the human brain. The third has broken the gravitational fences of our planet and at the cost of forty billion dollars has put man on the moon. The fourth is more portentous, for it is ignorance masquerading as knowledge.

2   Thirty-five years ago, a wise man, Sir Frederick Gowland Hopkins, Nobel Prize-winning scientist, said to me, "A vitamin is a unit of our ignorance. Every new vitamin that is discovered is the reminder of the food factors we have not discovered." Which is another way of putting Claude Bernard's aphorism, "True science teaches us to doubt and in ignorance to refrain." He was not calling for a halt to research. He was calling for sure footing. I would call it "going into an uncharted minefield with a mine detector."

3   We know what we did with the secret of matter; we exploded it as a cataclysmic bomb. And we have not caught up with the moral, military, or political consequences yet. In 1945, the safebreakers forced the lock of the nucleus before the locksmiths knew how it worked. Since 1945, we have spent billions of dollars providing high-voltage accelerators for nuclear

Source. Reprinted from the September/October, 1971, issue of *The Center Magazine,* a publication of the Center for the Study of Democratic Institutions, Santa Barbara, California.

physicists to find out what the fundamental particles, the wards of the lock, really are.

4   What we are playing about with now is the secret of life. We know the DNA code and we know that the genetic specifications thus encoded for the production of a person from a fertilized ovum, if spelled out in English, would fill five hundred volumes the size of the Encyclopaedia Britannica. And any misprint—a slip in the sequence, a mutation—will repeat itself through successive generations. We certainly do not know the code for "will," "judgment," "inspiration," "morality," "evil," "kindness," "brutality."

5   Even the crude changes which are now possible are fraught with incalculable dangers. It is possible to modify germs. A British scientist died of the germ he "invented." An eminent colleague said, "Thank God he did not sneeze. He could have started a world epidemic against which there would have been no natural immunity."

6   This capacity to manipulate the genes of living things certainly represents an ethical crisis. It is only a matter of time (and with the intensification of research the interval gets shorter and shorter) until we shall be able to transpose or dispose the DNA groupings so that we can determine artificially how cells will behave. We shall correct the misbehavior of cells that we call cancer. We shall modify hereditary defects and then we shall provide prescriptions for better specimens. But who are "we"? The Nazis had the idea of Aryan supermen and they aimed to "purify" the genetic code by eliminating unwanted genes by means of the gas chambers and the biological experiments in the concentration camps.

7   No doubt the computer could produce a better model. Falling in love may be a corny way to dispense random genes but somehow I feel that it is preferable to computer-selected characteristics to be chemically converted into the DNA code and transmitted to posterity. There would be garbled versions, like a printer's cliché, repeating themselves generation after generation.

8   The ethical crisis is felt and expressed by the scientists responsible. The Nobel Prize for the double helix of DNA was shared by Francis Crick, James Watson, and Maurice Wilkins. Crick, in expressing his concern, hopefully suggested that common sense will prevail and that the wilder genetic possibilities will not happen because "people simply will not stand for them." Watson appeared before a congressional subcommittee to urge that restrictions should be imposed on human-cell manipulation. Wilkins has become the president of the British Society for the Social Responsibility of Science.

9   George Beadle, who received a subsequent Nobel Prize for his DNA work, urged his colleagues not to embark on genetic manipulation because the effects would be irreversible. And, anyway, he pointed out that we had not done nearly enough in the cultural improvement of the species. "Especially after birth," he said at the Guildhall in London, "the information that is fed into the nervous system in massive amounts plays a large and

important role in determining what we are. It includes a large input of cultural inheritance." Salvador Luria, another Nobel Prize winner, has said, "geneticists are not yet ready to conquer the earth, either for good or for evil," and he called for some sort of body, national or preferably international, to apply ethical constraints. Short of tampering with the DNA code there is much to be done in correcting genetic aberrations. There is an obvious need for more genetic clinics where couples can have tests and advice if there is any reason to suspect that they may have genetically handicapped children, that is, with serious hereditary effects. They should be discouraged from having children or should have the condition corrected by well-confirmed methods.

10 But we are already shuffling and redealing the cards of posterity. Artificial insemination, by which the infertile father consents to being the before-conception foster-father of his wife's child by an anonymous donor, is now regular practice. In animals, it is a practical proposition to have an ovum which has been fertilized in the womb of a mother transferred to the womb of another whose genes have no part of the offspring but who will carry it through gestation to delivery. This is one way film stars might produce children without risk to their figures or shooting schedule. It is only the obstetrical version of the lady of the manor, before the days of feeding bottles, putting her baby out to the village wet-nurse. This would be the prenatal foster-mother.

11 Artificial insemination can be carried a step further. Just as we have sperm banks with the male genes kept on ice, so there can be ova banks. This suggests fascinating possibilities of anachronous matings. H. J. Muller suggested in *Out of the Night* in 1935 that the frozen sperm of Stalin might have been used to fertilize generations of Soviet women, but imagine Shakespeare's genes artificially mated with those of Mrs. Siddons and parturated by a Hollywood starlet. Imagine what would happen to the hereditary peerage if the freeze-packed thirteenth earl was begotten after the fifteenth.

12 We have antisterility pills producing four, five, and six babies. Sex determination is an imminent likelihood and that will produce problems for the demographers if we have fashions in babies as we have fashions in clothes and some biological Dior decides that the vogue should be male babies.

13 It is urgent that we should consider what is happening in that other form of bio-engineering—organ transplanting. There would not, at first sight, seem to be much ethical difference between having a nose straightened or a face lifted by plastic surgery and having an organ replacement. Indeed, one could maintain that the internal organ was more humanly necessary than superficial cosmetics. The ethical dilemma, however, is of a different order.

14 Before kidney transplants people had an ethical unease about renal dialysis—the artificial kidney machine. Unquestionably it was a great technical advance making it possible to treat kidney dysfunctions from which

thousands die. But the machine was, and is, expensive and involves intensive care of the patient by doctors and nurses. For whom the machine? In the United States the dilemma was evaded but not solved by having lay panels, like juries, making life-or-death choices. In Britain, where the National Health Service entitles everyone, rich or poor, to have access to any necessary treatment, the responsibility rests on the medical staff. It was (and still is) a difficult decision.

15   Assume that some V.I.P., a famous man of advanced years, and a boy of fifteen both require the available machine, to whom would it be allocated? The living museum piece whose obituary would be thus postponed or the boy who might live to be a Nobel Prize winner or a criminal? Nor must we forget the doctors and nurses who have died of infectious hepatitis, the occupational hazard of renal dialysis.

16   With the discovery of chemical means of counteracting immunological rejection it became possible to transplant actual organs. The natural defensive system by which the body can repel germs or reject alien tissue, genetically incompatible, could be repressed so that the graft would "take." Thus a stranger's kidney could be transferred to a patient (again, to whom the suitable kidney?). That led to heart transplants and heart-and-lung transplants. An essential condition is that the organ must be "fresh."

17   To the point of scandal we have had a near Burke-and-Hare situation. (Burke and Hare were the Edinburgh grave-robbers who supplied Knox, the anatomist, with cadavers for dissection and finished up by providing warm corpses.) Doctors, collaborating with the heart surgeons, would remove the heart at the moment of death and rush it to the operating theater. But what is the "moment of death"? The old method of holding a mirror to the mouth to get the mist of breathing has been long discarded. The pulse or the beating of the heart is no longer the test. The test is the encephalograph to detect brain waves. If there is no signal the patient is dead. Thus the seat of life has become the brain. If it was hopelessly damaged or ceased to function, the instant removal of the heart was considered justified.

18   Apart from the ethic of the decision, this raises the question, what is the ultimate object of the entire exercise? Assume (and it is a safe assumption) that any and every organ is capable of being transplanted and that a human artifact could be reconstituted out of "spare parts." To what end? Presumably to service the brain, the vestigial remains of life. But the brain, however marvelous, is a biological computer. One can debate whether it is even the "mind." It is certainly not the human personality *in se*. Our personality is compounded from the chemistry and the responses of the whole body—not just the endocrines but our lymph glands and our gastric propensities as well. We are remaking not only a machine of cells and tissues, we are remaking a personality. The question arises as to the identity of the person modified by surgical plumbing. What is the legal, moral, or psychiatric identity of a human so altered by medical manipulation that he has become an artifact?

19   There is another severely practical but profoundly important question. What is the cost in money but also in human sacrifice of the diversion of scarce facilities and scarcer medical manpower to the intensive care of those "interesting cases"? Even those who get it are a tiny fraction of those who may need it. Thousands, tens of thousands, hundreds of thousands and, in the wider world, millions of useful lives are being wasted and an immense amount of suffering is being endured because of the lack of conventional treatment.

20   There is another dilemma. With all this "doing over": with plutonium pacemakers being implanted and attached to the heart; with the promise of miniature computers being connected to our brain to compensate our failing memories; with electronic stimulators promised to enliven our "pleasure centers"; with all the advances in biochemistry and geriatric care; and with the protection against and treatment of infectious disease; we can expand the span of life. We can keep people alive indefinitely. This is a social problem of first magnitude. It is also a personal problem for all of us: it involves a basic human right—the right to live or die with dignity.

21   There is a need for a consensus of conscience; an international tribunal of ethics; a surveillance, which need not be suppression, of the kind of things which are happening and which, irresponsibly, can endanger mankind; for a new personal ethic for doctors and medical scientists. The Hippocratic Oath, noble in its intention, no longer serves. It has been overtaken by events. The "judgment" which innovation imposes on the doctor exceeds the professional common sense which the "good doctor" could apply in good conscience. In the phrase of the biophysicist Leroy Augenstein, "he is being asked to play God."

22   I have, as consultant to the human rights division of the United Nations concerned with the technological threat to those rights, suggested that we bring together a body of wise men from all over the world and from diverse cultures to consider the inventory of opportunities but also of mischief, actual and potential. They must give us a basis for a working philosophy. They must produce instruments and institutions, legal and professional, which can apply ethical restraints. They must, for the individual scientist and doctor, produce a new Hippocratic Oath.

23   The poet Clough wrote, "Thou shalt not kill; but needst not strive officiously to keep alive." While I personally am grateful for the time I have borrowed through medical science, I have no desire to be a zombie, nor a vegetable, nor an interesting specimen of bio-engineering. As a parliamentarian I have been considering the possibility of a bill which is simple in intent but, in legal terms, difficult to draft. I want any individual in full possession of his faculties to say, and make binding on others, the conditions under which he would not be kept artificially alive.

24   The operative phrase in any such bill would be "in full possession of his faculties," because when the time comes and his earnest doctors and his devoted family are, with the best intentions, conspiring to keep him

alive, he will not be in any position to decide. This is not a question of birth certificates, nor senility; the circumstances can arise at any age through accident or, indeed, through delayed resuscitation on the operating table, when the higher cells of the brain are deprived of oxygen. In the compassion of true medicine, respect for human dignity cannot accept the living dead, the bio-artifact, the non-person.

articles from experience
ROLLIE HOCHSTEIN

This how-to-do-it recommendation begins with an example of the finished product, an essay written about Hochstein's personal experience. The first five paragraphs function, then, like a baseball player who shows you how to hit by saying "Do it this way" and sending the ball into the bleachers. But since most people need a set of instructions as well as an example, Hochstein goes on to analyze how her introductory example works and to offer five specific recommendations, each clarified by a discussion of the principle involved and further examples. She concludes with a call to action, a quick "pep talk" urging her audience to write from experience because, as she puts it, "Nobody else can write the personal essay that you can write."

1 **W**hen I began writing magazine humor—it cannot be more than eight years ago!—I had a miniature ax that wanted grinding. I was, at the time, the mother of two very young children and had recently taken up residence in the suburbs. I think I was having an Identity Crisis. In those days it was not enough to live impromptu: I felt somehow that I needed to know exactly who and what I was. Experience in both areas has taught me that labeling is utterly irrelevant; but at that raw, unsettled time of my life, it seemed crucial for me to decide whether I was a housewife who wrote or a writer who kept house.

2 The chief antagonists in my battle for identity were The Sociologists, who continually showed up in mass media authoritatively lumping The American Housewife into one great, sticky glob. The glob was oppressed by a male-dominated culture. The glob emasculated its husbands. The glob was spoiled, child-centered, over-educated, under-emancipated. There I was, having an Identity Crisis, and there they were—those snide Sociologists—trying to agglutinate my Identity!

Source. From A. S. Burack, *The Writer's Handbook,* Copyright © 1974. Reprinted by permission of The Writer, Inc.

3   My method of protest was to burn them with a searingly satirical article, which was to begin: "The sociologists make me feel about as individual as a stick of spaghetti." I really liked that phrase. I clearly remember the demonic relish with which I typed it. And I also remember the reluctance with which I crossed it out when, after many rereadings of the first draft, I had to admit that it didn't go. It was a "pre-peat" of the second sentence, and the second sentence was more germane to the rest of the piece. The final version—called "I'm a Method Wife"—was published in the old *Coronet.* It began: "Whenever I pick up a magazine or tune in a panel discussion, some sociologist is lecturing me about my role in life."

4   Publication made me feel much better: with one shot, I'd got something off my chest and something into my bank account. It was a fine feeling, but the spaghetti lead was still a-dangle and I was avid to use it.

5   About four subsequent articles originated with the spaghetti simile and all four, by the final draft, started some other way. My grouch about the sociologists developed into other more general, less didactic, more amusing, less irritable subjects, and that first lead—for unity's sake—had to go. The spaghetti sentence, until now, never made print. It stopped mattering after a while: having authored several personal essays and other kinds of magazine articles, I no longer felt threatened by sociological de-personification. Nobody could make me feel like a stick of spaghetti, and I was far too busy with writing and housekeeping to ponder over pigeon-holes.

6   That's a personal essay. I wrote it (a) for fun, (b) because the editor asked me for an article about technique, and (c) to use as an example and a basis for discussion.

7   The personal essay is a most satisfactory way to get published. It re· quires no research, no interviews, no scholarship, no legwork. All you need is an interesting (marketable) idea and the ability to present it pungently.

8   Editors like to buy personal essays and, I am told, they have a hard time finding usable ones. Mine fall into the category of "domestic humor," and about twenty of them have been published in half a dozen woman's magazines and newspaper supplements. Last time I looked, *Good House-keeping, McCall's* and *Redbook* were running regular reader-written first-person features. *The Reader's Digest* uses several such features under different names. *Playboy* and *Esquire* use satirical essays. *The Atlantic* and *Harper's* run first-person humor on occasion. Though they are often written by VIP's, personal essays often appear in *Vogue, Harper's Bazaar, Holiday* and *Mademoiselle.*

9   I've gone through some grand markets here, but I should tell you that my earliest anecdotal articles were published in diaper service giveaways, such as *Baby Talk* and *Baby Time.* I was delighted then, too, to get paid for saying something that I wanted to say. I think it's accurate to say that, while the category is special, the market for personal essays is broad.

10   What I'm writing here is a *how-to* article in the tone and shape of a personal essay. I'm using certain principles that I practice in my domestic

humor pieces. The first two of the following principles are probably most applicable to the women's and family field; the last three, I believe, are compulsory in all personal essays.

11   1. *Reader identification.* When a reader says, "It sounds just like me," or he writes, "That's exactly the way it happens in my house," the writer has done a good job. In women's magazines, I deal with fairly typical domestic situations—the problems of party-giving, a slant on sibling rivalry —written from the viewpoint of a fairly typical housewife. In the first sentence or two, I set myself up for quick and easy identification. A lead might go something like this:

12   "When a woman has a six-room house to clean, three choosy children to feed and a hearty husband to keep in step with, she finds it hard to understand that the phrase 'Working Mother' means somebody else."

13   In all my domestic humor pieces, not one line has ever suggested that I do anything other than keep house, raise children, buy clothes, give parties, attend P.T.A. meetings and whatever else is common to all us housewives. Any clowning must be done gently and always with the implication that, though sometimes harassed, I manage to come out ahead, doing a good job at all these things. "Never make a jackass out of yourself," an editor warned me. That's reader identification.

14   Now notice, in the first paragraph of this article, how quickly I introduce myself as a writer. Right off it gives you and me something in common. The clause, "it cannot be more than eight years ago!" not only tells you that I'm experienced, but it also humanizes me. Time goes too quickly for me, too. You're interested because I'm a professional writer; perhaps you'll learn something from me. You're interested because I've confessed a human weakness and am less likely, after such a confession, to bore you with a lecture from a posture of distant superiority. I tell you that my ax was miniature: it's an indication that I am laughing at myself and that what I will say might be amusing as well as informative. The next sentence may have cost me some male readers, but I'm pretty sure that all writing mothers kept with it. In that opening, I achieved reader identification.

15   2. *Intimacy.* If you're going to sit down and share your opinions, observations and/or experiences in a humorous or poignant manner, you need a warm relationship with your reader. Back to my opening anecdote: we are introduced; we find we have something in common. I proceed to talk to you in a frank and friendly way. I even take you into my confidence: "I think I was having an Identity Crisis." I capitalize the fashionable phrase to make it humorous; I append "I think" to make it whimsical; but I am still opening myself up to you when I make that statement. It makes us friends and I continue, as a friend, to tell my story. I can talk about things that interest me on the assumption that they will interest you, too.

16   Here, we must stop to make a distinction. The *I* of the personal essay

is not necessarily the author. The unity required in such an essay makes it almost impossible for the *I* to be completely the author; most of us are multifaceted, far too complex to be single-minded about very much. But once the *I* has set up a relationship with the reader, the author must not interfere with it. At no time should he double-cross his reader by contradicting or questioning himself. To keep his rapport, he should make his points directly. The *I* should say what he means and mean what he says. He should never slip out of his role by turning sarcastic, hostile or obscure to his reader. This is not schizophrenia; it's professionalism.

17   3. *Unity.* One theme is announced, developed, varied and concluded. One idea is proclaimed, clarified, illustrated, modulated and summed up. The personal essay requires disciplined thought and tight writing: no rambling, no diversions. The truth is that you and I are not really friends. You may have to listen to a friend's boring stories, but you can easily turn me off with a flick of the page. Therefore, every sentence that I write should compel you to read the next one. Every sentence must belong to the total structure; that's why my spaghetti line had to be eliminated.

18   Writers are not paid for expressing themselves. The personal essay, like all other professional writing, is meant to entertain, inform or influence—any one, two or three of these aims—and it must be interesting. What you want to say is your business. How you say it is the writing business. Where there are neither important facts nor famous figures to hold your reader's interest, your stated ideas have to do all the work. They have to be tightly organized; only in unity will they have the strength to hold readers.

19   4. *Style.* Style, like personal charm, is an elusive quality, highly individual. Writing style is a combination of language, tone and pace. More than any other kind of writing, except poetry, the personal essay needs to be meticulously worded and phrased, cut and polished. The words are selected by weight and color, as well as meaning. I fool around a lot with my essays, substituting bright words for drab words, trimming flabby sentences, lightening heavy ones, compressing, relaxing. I take pains to find the precisely right word; hardly a piece gets written without consultation of both dictionary and thesaurus.

20   The tone—droll, irate, bewildered, harassed, nostalgic—should be set in the lead and, with minor variations, sustained throughout the essay. If you are ear-minded, it is not difficult to set and maintain a tone. You hear it as you read over what you have written. If not, I suppose reading aloud will help. The tone of my early paragraphs here is, at least to my ears, one of sophisticated amusement. After the first five paragraphs, it turned earnest.

21   Pacing is almost impossible to pin down. If it's right, nobody except a professional notices it. Wrong, it's something like cold chicken soup: the fastidious are distressed and reject it; the apathetic suffer through with vague discomfort. Many writers get by without it. Non-paced novelists, I've noticed, are the ones called storytellers. In most nonfiction, pace

counts as nothing more than an extra added attraction. I'm not even sure that it's compulsory in all essays, though it is a necessary component of the humorous essay. All this leads up to the fact that I can't tell you how to do it. Me, I've always listened a lot to such stand-up comedians as Alan King and Myron Cohen. While I haven't analyzed their timing, I think I've absorbed some of it. Also, I like to read metrical poetry: sonnets, ballades, rondos and villanelles; the footed works of everybody from Chaucer to Ciardi; the crisp couplets of Pope and the iambic pentameter of Shakespeare.

22   My own style, in fiction as in articles, is always under the influence of other writers. I'm particularly impressed by elegant English novelists: Jane Austen, Evelyn Waugh, Nancy Mitford; and American black humorists: Joseph Heller, Shirley Jackson, Bruce Jay Friedman. I would suggest that anybody who wants to develop a style should do a lot of selective reading and listening, always open to the tones and timings and words that please him.

23   5. *Arrogance.* The personal essayist has to be assuming. He has to assume that what he's saying is interesting enough to attract and hold a great many people he's never even met. Modesty and self-doubt have to be set aside as he develops, without reservation or qualification, the theme he arbitrarily chooses to present. Even if, like Leacock in "My Financial Career," you are posing as a bumbler, you can't take a clause to apologize or explain yourself; you must be the complete bumbler, arrogant in your ineptitude. You have to take on an authority that—at least in the beginning of your career—you are hardly likely to feel. What else is there to do? You're the author of the piece, and it's all you—or a projection of you. You have to be authoritative.

24   It takes a certain amount of arrogance plus ardor to get a first personal essay written and off to the editors. A middle-class, public school-educated American is not ordinarily brought up to believe that he is anything special. On the contrary, he (and particularly if he is a woman) is usually led to believe in the virtues of inconspicuousness, humility and keeping his mouth shut. Writing in the first person is not a humble thing to do. It's rather brash, is it not?, to expect to publish a piece of writing based on nothing more than your opinions, experiences and observations. "Why me?" is the question you may ask yourself.

25   The answer is: "Why not?" Actually, none of us is a stick of spaghetti, and nobody else in the world sees things, feels things and can express things exactly as you do. Nobody else can write the personal essay that you can write.

the missing element: moral courage

BARBARA W. TUCHMAN

The problem Tuchman identifies is a national shortage of moral leadership. She dramatizes the problem by showing that our lack of standards leads to crime (paragraphs 3 to 5) and that it is produced by a foolish tolerance (paragraphs 6 to 9). From this point on, she begins to urge the adoption of a new attitude: we need the courage to proclaim the difference between right and wrong (paragraphs 8 to 11). She evaluates the bad effects of our standard-less society—in education (paragraphs 12 to 14), in government (paragraph 15), and in literature and the arts (paragraphs 16 to 20).

It is not necessary for Tuchman to make a formal recommendation at the end. The refrain, "this is excellent and that is trash," appears in one form or another throughout the article. By condemning the wrong, vulgar, and fraudulent, she exemplifies the kind of courage she is recommending.

1 What I want to say is concerned less with leadership than with its absence, that is, with the evasion of leadership. Not in the physical sense, for we have, if anything, a superabundance of leaders—hundreds of Pied Pipers, or would-be Pied Pipers, running about, ready and anxious to lead the population. They are scurrying around, collecting consensus, gathering as wide an acceptance as possible. But what they are *not* doing, very notably, is standing still and saying, "*This* is what I believe. This I will do and that I will not do. This is my code of behavior and that is outside it. This is excellent and that is trash." There is an abdication of moral leadership in the sense of a general unwillingness to state standards.

2 Of all the ills that our poor criticized, analyzed, sociologized society is heir to, the focal one, it seems to me, from which so much of our uneasiness and confusion derive is the absence of standards. We are too unsure of ourselves to assert them, to stick by them, or if necessary, in the case of persons who occupy positions of authority, to impose them. We seem to be afflicted by a widespread and eroding reluctance to take any stand on any values, moral, behavioral, or aesthetic.

3 Everyone is afraid to call anything wrong, or vulgar, or fraudulent, or just bad taste or bad manners. Congress, for example, pussyfooted for months (following years of apathy) before taking action on a member convicted by the courts of illegalities; and when they finally got around to unseating him, one suspects they did it for the wrong motives. In 1922, in England, a man called Horatio Bottomley, a rather flamboyant character and popular demagogue—very similar in type, by the way, to Adam Clay-

Source. Barbara Tuchman, "The Missing Element: Moral Courage," from *In Search of Leaders.* G. Kerry Smith, ed. Washington, D.C.: American Association for Higher Education, 1967. Reprinted by permission of the American Association for Higher Education.

ton Powell, with similarly elastic financial ethics—who founded a paper called *John Bull* and got himself elected to Parliament, was found guilty of misappropriating the funds which his readers subscribed to victory bonds and other causes promoted by his paper. The day after the verdict, he was expelled from the House of Commons, with no fuss and very little debate, except for a few friendly farewells, as he was rather an engaging fellow. But no member thought the House had any other course to consider: out he went. I do not suggest that this represents a difference between British and American morality; the difference is in the *times*.

4   Our time is one of disillusion in our species and a resulting lack of self-confidence—for good historical reasons. Man's recent record has not been reassuring. After engaging in the Great War with all its mud and blood and ravaged ground, its disease, destruction, and death, we allowed ourselves a bare twenty years before going at it all over again. And the second time was accompanied by an episode of man's inhumanity to man of such enormity that its implications for all of us have not yet, I think, been fully measured. A historian has recently stated that for such a phenomenon as the planned and nearly accomplished extermination of a people to take place, one of three preconditions necessary was public indifference.

5   Since then the human species has been busy overbreeding, polluting the air, destroying the balance of nature, and bungling in a variety of directions so that it is no wonder we have begun to doubt man's capacity for good judgment. It is hardly surprising that the self-confidence of the nineteenth century and its belief in human progress has been dissipated. "Every great civilization," said Secretary Gardner last year, "has been characterized by confidence in itself." At mid-twentieth century, the supply is low. As a result, we tend to shy away from all judgments. We hesitate to label anything wrong, and therefore hesitate to require the individual to bear moral responsibility for his acts.

6   We have become afraid to fix blame. Murderers and rapists and muggers and persons who beat up old men and engage in other forms of assault are not guilty; society is guilty; society has wronged them; society beats its breast and says *mea culpa*—it is our fault, not the wrongdoer's. The wrongdoer, poor fellow, could not help himself.

7   I find this very puzzling because I always ask myself, in these cases, what about the many neighbors of the wrongdoer, equally poor, equally disadvantaged, equally sufferers from society's neglect, who nevertheless maintain certain standards of social behavior, who do *not* commit crimes, who do not murder for money or rape for kicks. How does it happen that they know the difference between right and wrong, and how long will they abide by the difference if the leaders and opinion-makers and pacesetters continue to shy away from bringing home responsibility to the delinquent?

8   Admittedly, the reluctance to condemn stems partly from a worthy instinct—*tout comprendre, c'est tout pardonner** and from a rejection

* To understand everything is to pardon everything—Eds.

of what was often the hypocrisy of Victorian moral standards. True, there was a large component of hypocrisy in nineteenth-century morality. Since the advent of Freud, we know more, we understand more about human behavior, we are more reluctant to cast the first stone—to condemn—which is a good thing; but the pendulum has swung to the point where we are now afraid to place moral responsibility at all. Society, that large amorphous, nonspecific scapegoat, must carry the burden for each of us, relieving us of guilt. We have become so indoctrinated by the terrors lurking in the dark corridors of the guilt complex that guilt has acquired a very bad name. Yet a little guilt is not a dangerous thing; it has a certain social utility.

9   When it comes to guilt, a respected writer—respected in some circles—has told us, as her considered verdict on the Nazi program, that evil is banal—a word that means something so ordinary that you are not bothered by it; the dictionary definition is "commonplace and hackneyed." Somehow that conclusion does not seem adequate or even apt. *Of course,* evil is commonplace; *of course* we all partake of it. Does that mean that we must withhold disapproval, and that when evil appears in dangerous degree or vicious form we must not condemn but only understand? That may be very Christian in intent, but in reality it is an escape from the necessity of exercising judgment—which exercise, I believe, is a prime function of leadership.

10   What it requires is courage—just a little, not very much—the courage to be independent and stand up for the standard of values one believes in. That kind of courage is the quality most conspicuously missing, I think, in current life. I don't mean the courage to protest and walk around with picket signs or boo Secretary McNamara which, though it may stem from the right instinct, is a group thing that does not require any very stout spirit. I did it myself for Sacco and Vanzetti when I was about twelve and picketed in some now forgotten labor dispute when I was a freshman and even got arrested. There is nothing to that; if you don't do that sort of thing when you are eighteen, then there is something wrong with you. I mean, rather, a kind of lonely moral courage, the quality that attracted me to that odd character, Czar Reed, and to Lord Salisbury, neither of whom cared a rap for the opinion of the public or would have altered his conduct a hair to adapt to it. It is the quality someone said of Lord Palmerston was his "you-be-damnedness." That is the mood we need a little more of.

11   Standards of taste, as well as morality, need continued reaffirmation to stay alive, as liberty needs eternal vigilance. To recognize and to proclaim the difference between the good and the shoddy, the true and the fake, as well as between right and wrong, or what we believe at a given time to be right and wrong, is the obligation, I think, of persons who presume to lead, or are thrust into leadership, or hold positions of authority. That includes—whether they asked for it or not—all educators and even, I regret to say, writers.

12   For educators it has become increasingly the habit in the difficult cir-

cumstances of college administration today to find out what the students want in the matter of curriculum and deportment and then give it to them. This seems to me another form of abdication, another example of the prevailing reluctance to state a standard and expect, not to say require, performance in accord with it. The permissiveness, 'the yielding of decision to the student, does not—from what I can tell—promote responsibility in the young so much as uneasiness and a kind of anger at *not* being told what is expected of them, a resentment of their elders' unwillingness to take a position. Recently a student psychiatric patient of the Harvard Health Services was quoted by the director, Dr. Dana Farnsworth, as complaining, "My parents never tell me what to do. They never stop me from doing anything." That is the unheard wail, I think, extended beyond parents to the general absence of a guiding, reassuring pattern, which is behind much of society's current uneasiness.

13   It is human nature to want patterns and standards and a structure of behavior. A pattern to conform to is a kind of shelter. You see it in kindergarten and primary school, at least in those schools where the children when leaving the classroom are required to fall into line. When the teacher gives the signal, they fall in with alacrity; they know where they belong and they instinctively like to *be* where they belong. They like the feeling of being in line.

14   Most people need a structure, not only to fall into but to fall out of. The rebel with a cause is better off than the one without. At least he knows what he is "agin." He is not lost. He does not suffer from an identity crisis. It occurs to me that much of the student protest now may be a testing of authority, a search for that line to fall out of, and when it isn't there students become angrier because they feel more lost, more abandoned than ever. In the late turmoil at Berkeley, at least as regards the filthy speech demonstration, there was a missed opportunity, I think (however great my respect for Clark Kerr) for a hearty, emphatic, and unmistakable "No!" backed up by sanctions. Why? Because the act, even if intended as a demonstration of principle, was in this case, like any indecent exposure, simply offensive, and what is offensive to the greater part of society is anti-social, and what is anti-social, so long as we live in social groups and not each of us on his own island, must be curtailed, like Peeping Toms or obscene telephone calls, as a public nuisance. The issue is really not complicated or difficult but, if we would only look at it with more self-confidence, quite simple.

15   So, it seems to me, is the problem of the CIA.[1] You will say that in this case people have taken a stand, opinion-makers have worked themselves into a moral frenzy. Indeed they have, but over a false issue. The CIA is not, after all, the Viet Cong or the Schutzstaffel in blackshirts. Its initials do not stand for Criminal Indiscretions of America. It is an arm of the American government, our elected, representative government (whatever

---

[1] The Central Intelligence Agency was apparently giving financial support to certain student groups.

may be one's feelings toward that body at the moment). Virtually every government in the world subsidizes youth groups, especially in their international relations, not to mention in athletic competitions. (I do not know if the CIA is subsidizing our Equestrian Team, but I know personally a number of people who would be only too delighted if it were.) The difficulty here is simply that the support was clandestine in the first place and not the proper job of the CIA in the second. An intelligence agency should be restricted to the gathering of intelligence and not extend itself into operations. In armies the two functions are distinct: intelligence is G2 and operations is G3. If our government could manage its functions with a little more precision and perform openly those functions that are perfectly respectable, there would be no issue. The recent excitement only shows how easily we succumb when reliable patterns or codes of conduct are absent, to a confusion of values.

16   A similar confusion exists, I think, with regard to the omnipresent pornography that surrounds us like smog. A year ago the organization of my own profession, the Authors League, filed a brief *amicus curiae* in the appeal of Ralph Ginzburg, the publisher of a periodical called *Eros* and other items, who had been convicted of disseminating obscenity through the mails. The League's action was taken on the issue of censorship to which all good liberals automatically respond like Pavlov's dogs. Since at this stage in our culture pornography has so far gotten the upper hand that to do battle in its behalf against the dragon Censorship is rather like doing battle today against the bustle in behalf of short skirts, and since I believe that the proliferation of pornography in its sadistic forms is a greater social danger at the moment than censorship, and since Mr. Ginzburg was not an author anyway but a commercial promoter, I raised an objection, as a member of the Council, to the Authors League's spending its funds in the Ginzburg case. I was, of course, outvoted; in fact, there was no vote. Everyone around the table just sat and looked at me in cold disapproval. Later, after my objection was printed in the *Bulletin,* at my request, two distinguished authors wrote privately to me to express their agreement but did not go so far as to say so publicly.

17   Thereafter, when the Supreme Court upheld Mr. Ginzburg's conviction, everyone in the intellectual community raised a hullaballoo about censorship advancing upon us like some sort of Frankenstein's monster. This seems to me another case of getting excited about the wrong thing. The cause of pornography is *not* the same as the cause of free speech. There *is* a difference. Ralph Ginzburg is *not* Theodore Dreiser and this is not the 1920's. If one looks around at the movies, especially the movie advertisements, and the novels and the pulp magazines glorifying perversion and the paperbacks that make de Sade available to school children, one does not get the impression that in the 1960's we are being stifled in the Puritan grip of Anthony Comstock. Here again, leaders—in this case authors and critics—seem too unsure of values or too afraid of being unpopular to stand up and assert the perfectly obvious difference between smut and free

speech, or to say "Such and such is offensive and can be harmful." Happily, there are signs of awakening. In a *Times* review of a book called *On Iniquity* by Pamela Hansford Johnson, which related pornography to the Moors murders in England, the reviewer concluded that "this may be the opening of a discussion that must come, the opening shot."

18   In the realm of art, no less important than morals, the abdication of judgment is almost a disease. Last fall when the Lincoln Center opened its glittering new opera house with a glittering new opera on the tragedy of Anthony and Cleopatra, the curtain rose on a gaudy crowd engaged in energetic revels around a gold box in the shape of a pyramid, up whose sides (conveniently fitted with toe-holds, I suppose) several sinuous and reasonably nude slave girls were chased by lecherous guards left over from "Aida." When these preliminaries quieted down, the front of the gold box suddenly dropped open, and guess who was inside? No, it was not Cleopatra, it was Anthony, looking, I thought, rather bewildered. What he was doing inside the box was never made clear. Thereafter everything happened —and in crescendos of gold and spangles and sequins, silks and gauzes, feathers, fans, jewels, brocades, and such a quantity of glitter that one began to laugh, thinking that the spectacle was intended as a parody of the old Shubert revue. But no, this was the Metropolitan Opera in the vaunted splendor of its most publicized opening since the Hippodrome. I gather it was Mr. Bing's idea of giving the first night customers a fine splash. What he achieved was simply vulgarity, as at least some reviewers had the courage to say next day. Now, I cannot believe that Mr. Bing and his colleagues do not know the difference between honest artistry in stage design and pretentious ostentation. If they know better, why do they allow themselves to do worse? As leaders in their field of endeavor, they should have been setting standards of beauty and creative design, not debasing them.

19   One finds the same peculiarities in the visual arts. Non-art, as its practitioners describe it—the blob school, the all-black canvasses, the paper cutouts and Campbell soup tins and plastic hamburgers and pieces of old carpet—is treated as art, not only by dealers whose motive is understandable (they have discovered that shock value sells); not only by a gullible pseudocultural section of the public who are not interested in art but in being "in" and wouldn't, to quote an old joke, know a Renoir from a Jaguar; but also, which I find mystifying, by the museums and the critics. I am sure they know the difference between the genuine and the hoax. But not trusting their own judgment, they seem afraid to say no to anything, for fear, I suppose, of making a mistake and turning down what may be next decade's Matisse.

20   For the museums to exhibit the plastic hamburgers and twists of scrap iron is one thing, but for them to *buy* them for their permanent collection puts an imprimatur on what is fraudulent. Museum curators, too, are leaders who have an obligation to distinguish—I will not say the good from the bad in art because that is an elusive and subjective matter dependent on the eye of the time—but at least honest expression from phony.

a glossary of terms

Abstract words: words that name a general quality or property of a thing (e.g., the coldness of snow), usually contrasted with *concrete words:* words that name a specific quality or property of a thing (e.g., an individual snowflake has a temperature of 28° F.).

Analogy: resemblance between some features of otherwise unlike things, used in explanations of unfamiliar things by means of familiar things (see p. 119). For example, the remark attributed to Einstein, "God does not play at dice with the world," involves an analogy between God (the unfamiliar) and a gambler (the familiar).

Analysis: process of breaking a whole thing into parts in order to understand its nature or essential features. See *Synthesis.*

Analysis of cause and effect: a technique of definition in which X, the thing to be defined, is explained in terms of what causes it or what its effects are (see p. 31).

Anecdote: a brief narrative, often humorous, of an event involving human interest and often suggesting some lesson.

Antithesis: a sharp contrast of ideas, as in "We must go to war to secure peace."

Argument: 1. a coherent presentation of reasons or facts to establish a point of view; see deductive arguments (p. 174) and inductive arguments (p. 177). 2. a complete piece of writing that aims at persuading readers of the rightness of its point of view; in this book, "argument" is divided into Substantiation, Evaluation, and Recommendation.

Assertion: a statement declaring that something is the case. "You're late again" is an assertion. "Ouch!" is not. (It's an exclamation.)

Assumption: something taken for granted. "Shut the door" assumes, for instance, that there is a door, and that it open. "Human beings are basically good" assumes that we know what "good" means.

Attribution: a statement asserting that something or some quality belongs to a person or object.

Audience: the group of potential readers by whom a writer hopes his work will be read and whose characteristics partly determine how he expresses his ideas.

Authority, appeal to: citation of professional opinions—the opinions of people who are acknowledged authorities on a subject—to support an assertion.

Beginning: see *Introduction.*

Bibliography: a list of published writings related to a subject.

Cause and effect: see *Analysis of Cause and Effect.*

Chronological order: presentation of events or things in normal time sequence, usually contrasted with "chronological displacement," in which time is disrupted by flashbacks or depiction of future events.

Classification: see *Division.*

Cliché: a trite, overused, or stereotyped expression.

Coherence: the inner connectedness of an argument, essay, or paragraph: each part contributes to the unity of the whole.

Colloquial: conversational, as distinct from formal, language.

Comparison and contrast: a technique of definition in which the similarities and differences between things are clarified; often used to identify the unknown by separating it from the known.

Conclusion: 1. the final statement of a logical argument; 2. the ending of an essay, which may summarize, demonstrate the significance of the material, or in some other way bring the piece of writing to its goal and let us know that we have in fact arrived.

Concrete: see *Abstract.*

Connotation and denotation: connotation signifies the emotion associated with a word or expression; denotation signifies the literal meaning of a word or expression. For example, the word "mother" *connotes* all the emotions that we associate with that unique and necessary person; the word *denotes* simply "female parent."

Context: the sentences or paragraphs that surround a word or group of words and give them a particular meaning or connotative value.

Contrast: see *Comparison.*

Criterion (plural, criteria): a standard on which judgments or evaluations may be based (see pp. 296–299).

Deduction: the process of deriving conclusions from premises (see p. 173).

Definition: 1. determination of a word's meaning by stating the class of items to which it belongs (genus) and supplying terms (differentia) to distinguish it from the other items in its class; 2. in this book, "definition" includes all pieces of writing in which the writer's primary purpose is to explain the meaning of his subject.

Denotation: see *Connotation.*

Description: 1. verbal depiction of the sensory characteristics of things, or of the intellectual characteristics of ideas; 2. in this book, "description" is presented as a method of defining (see p. 24).

Development: the use of examples, arguments, and so forth, to support a proposition or to make an idea advance ("develop"); see *Paragraph.*

Dialogue: a record of direct speech; conversation.

Dichotomy: a division of something into two parts.

Diction: a writer's choice of words. Good diction means words chosen for their effectiveness and clarity, taking into account the subject, audience, and occasion.

Division and classification: a technique of definition in which a subject is divided into its main parts and the parts are arranged (classified) according to some principle, for example, simple to complex (see p. 30).

Documentation: evidence (usually in the form of footnotes or appendices) furnished to verify facts, support theories, or identify the sources of information.

Emphasis: special significance given to some element(s) of a piece of writing for logical effect or emotional appeal. Means of giving emphasis include position (the beginning and end are usually emphatic positions), repetition, or such stylistic devices as the capitalization of words.

Ending: see *Conclusion.*

Essay: literally an "attempt" or "trial," an attempt to translate thought into language; a composition that defines, interprets, or advocates.

Evaluation: a composition in which the writer's primary purpose is to justify his judgment about something, often by means of stated criteria. In this book, evaluations are "moral" if the criteria are defined in ethical terms, "utilitarian" if the criteria are defined in practical terms (see p. 295).

Evidence: any fact, opinion, or idea that serves to prove something else. Evidence ranges from the report of a personal experience, to extensive statistical data, to summaries of the viewpoints of authorities.

Exposition: writing that presents, explains, describes, and so forth; called "Definition" in this book.

Fallacy: an erroneous idea or conclusion that may seem plausible but is based on invalid argument or incorrect inference. It is a fallacy, for example, to claim that since B follows A, B is a *result* of A ("She smoked for twenty years and then died of cancer: the smoking must have caused the cancer"). It is possible that B resulted from some other factor (radiation?) altogether.

Fiction: experience, revised and edited.

Functional definition: defining a thing in terms of how it works or what it does, rather than what it is (see p. 31).

Generalization: a principle or concept derived from particular information (see p. 170).

Hypothesis: a tentative proposition asserted in order to discover whether it can be validated by facts or reasons (see p. 171).

Illustration: the use of examples to develop a generalization or prove a thesis (see p. 27).

Implication: an idea suggested, not stated. "Run, here comes Mama!" suggests (but does not state) that the speaker has done something Mama will not like.

Induction: a process of reasoning in which particular observations or other forms of evidence are assembled and then summarized in a conclusion that is more general than the evidence (see p. 176). The movement from the evidence to the conclusion is called the *inductive leap* (see p. 177).

Interpretation: a statement that goes beyond a simple record or report of an experience to explain what the experience means. A report: "A man slapped a child between the shoulder blades." An interpretation: "The man was angry at the child." An alternative interpretation: "The man was trying to dislodge a cherry pit the child had swallowed."

Intrinsic: a trait that naturally belongs to someone or something, as opposed to *extrinsic,* a trait imposed or acquired from outside. A love of warmth is an intrinsic quality of cats; a fondness for automobile travel is an extrinsic quality that some cats acquire.

Introduction: a beginning; not simply *any* beginning but one designed to lead us toward whatever is coming next (etymologically, the word means "a leading into"). You could begin a car journey by driving off in any direction, but a wiser plan is to choose roads that lead where you want to go.

Intuition: a nonrational (or partly rational) way of knowing, usually used to describe a sudden understanding of a problem or an unsupported expectation. "My intuition tells me that the new mailman will bite the dog instead of vice versa." (See p. 181.)

Irony: statements that say one thing

but mean the opposite (see p. 504).

Irrelevant: see *Relevant.*

Jargon: a special vocabulary known only to a small group of people. Jargon may be legitimate in speaking or writing to an audience consisting only of those people; otherwise it is out of place. Example: "interdigitational encounter" for "holding hands."

Judgment: a conclusion drawn about something, usually about the value of something. *"Tom Sawyer* is a marvelous book" is a judgment. (So is *"Tom Sawyer* is *not* a marvelous book.") A judgment is *premature* when it is made before all of the evidence has been considered ("I'm only half through *Tom Sawyer* but I can tell you it's marvelous" is premature; the only judgment justified so far would be "the first half is marvelous").

Justifying the criteria: defending the choice of criteria being used in an evaluation—usually explaining why the criteria are fair (see p. 297). If you are using a criterion of usefulness to evaluate kangaroos, for most American readers you will need to defend that criterion.

Logic: reasoning according to certain accepted patterns, specifically *deduction* and *induction* (see pp. 173–177), in contrast to non-rational ways of knowing such as *intuition* (see p. 181).

Major premise: the first statement of a deductive argument (see p. 174), usually a general statement such as "All men are mortal."

Matters of fact, matters of inference, matters of opinion: a *matter of fact* concerns a simple statement of experience ("I ate six bananas yesterday"), while a *matter of inference* or a *matter of opinion* concerns our responses to experience ("You're a pig"). (See p. 172.)

Metaphor: a figure of speech in which one thing stands for another; an implied likeness. In the phrase "the milk of human kindness," milk stands for all the intangible forms of kindness; the implied likeness is that both milk and kindness nourish.

Minor premise: the second statement of a deductive argument (see p. 174), usually a statement about some particular person or thing, such as "Socrates is a man."

Moral evaluation: see *Evaluation.*

Narration: the retelling of a sequence of events; *narrative* is frequently a synonym for "story." In this book, narration is presented as a way of defining or clarifying something.

Negative detail: the technique of describing something by negatives, providing details of what it is *not,* usually in order to eliminate misconceptions. "A whale is not a fish."

Objective/subjective: objective statements involve a minimal amount of our own personalities ("It's forty degrees out today"), while *subjective* statements involve our personal likes and dislikes ("It's too cold to go swimming"—maybe for us, but not for walruses). On objective and subjective definition, see p. 25.

Outline: a division of a piece of writing into its parts so that its themes and structure become apparent.

Parable: a brief fictional narrative told to make a point about how people should (or should not) behave.

Paradox: an apparent contradiction, as in "a false truth."

Paragraph: a unit of writing that is also a unit of thought or idea; one full step in the development of an idea. Compare the stones of a stone wall: they may differ in size and shape, but each contributes something necessary to the whole structure. Unlike the single sentence, the paragraph develops its idea. Typical forms of *paragraph development* include the simple-to-complex pattern (and vice versa), chronological sequence, spatial arrangement (near-to-far, top-to-bottom, etc.), and the "thesis-sentence" pattern in which the paragraph opens with a general summarizing statement followed by the evidence on which that statement depends.

Parallel structure: the repetition of words or grammatical sequences to emphasize the relatedness of ideas, as in "I spent the morning writing my uncle a mad letter, and the afternoon regretting it." The grammatical parallelism of "writing" and "regretting" (both are gerunds) helps link the ideas.

Parody: an exaggerated and mocking imitation, usually one that ridicules something by emphasizing a few peculiarities and ignoring all normal characteristics.

Personification: the presentation of a thing or an animal as if it were a person, as in "That collapsible chair lay in wait for me, rejoicing silently in its nasty yellow canvas heart as it watched me approach."

Persuasion: a form of writing in which the primary purpose is to convince readers that they should share the author's desires or convictions. In this book, three types of persuasion are presented separately: *substantiation,* in which the author tries to make his readers accept his logical conclusions; *evaluation,* in which he tries to make his readers accept his value judgments; *recommendation,* in which he tries to make his readers accept his proposals for change.

Prediction: a statement about the future based on our knowledge of the present and the past.

Recommendation: a form of writing in which the writer proposes changes in action or attitude to solve some problem (see p. 425).

Refutation: the process of arguing successfully against someone else's theories.

Relevant/irrelevant: a detail or a paragraph or any ingredient in writing is *relevant* if it contributes to the main purpose or idea, *irrelevant* otherwise (no matter how interesting it may be). If your purpose is to define "the mayor-council form of municipal government," the fact that you first learned about this form of government in a course taught by a descendant of the Spanish monarchy, while interesting, is not relevant.

Reports: statements of observation ("The car's gas gauge reads 'empty' and the engine won't start"), in contrast to statements of interpretation ("The car is out of gas").

Rhetorical question: a question to which the answer is obvious, such as God's question to Job: "Is it *you* who commands the morning to dawn?" (Here the answer is so obviously "No" that Job does not need to reply to the question.)

Satire: a witty, ironic, or sarcastic piece of writing that makes use of exaggeration, simplification, or stereotypes to ridicule, scorn, deride, or expose some evil, outworn convention, or eccentricity. It may be applied to both individuals and societies, and its purpose may range from advocating reform to merely affording insight.

Sensory evidence: see *Evidence.*

Simple to complex: see *Paragraph.*

Spatial development: see *Paragraph.*

Specification: an assertion about a specific individual or thing (as opposed to a *generalization,* which is an assertion about a whole category). (See p. 170.)

Stereotype: a conventionalized description of a group of people, animals, and the like usually used thoughtlessly without testing its accuracy.

Style: all qualities of language beyond what is strictly necessary to "do the job." (Both a brand new Rolls Royce and a 1955 Chevrolet will get you to town; the difference is style.) Options which help a writer individualize his style—make his style reflect his personality—include diction, punctuation, organization, even the decision to leave certain things out.

Subjective: see *Objective/Subjective.*

Substantiation: a form of writing in which the writer's primary purpose is to demonstrate the soundness of his reasoning and the validity of his conclusion (thesis).

Sufficiency: one of the criteria for evaluating evidence. The evidence is sufficient if it is complete or if it is a representative sample (see p. 178).

Summary: 1. a brief overview of ideas and information more fully developed elsewhere; the final paragraph of an essay is sometimes a summary; 2. a statement that adds up the evidence and tries to avoid interpretation.

Syllogism: a pattern of *deduction;* it usually consists of two premises and a conclusion (see p. 174).

Symbol: an individual, object, or event used to stand for a general or abstract idea. Symbols may be divided into *natural,* in which basic qualities of the symbol suggest its meaning (the sea naturally suggests flux), *conventional,* in which culturally shaped qualities suggest the meaning (to Eskimos, the sea may be a symbol of nourishment), and *personal,* in which individual experience determines the meaning (to you, the sea may suggest the end of a love affair).

Syntax: the arrangement of words into sentences. Each language has its own patterns of syntax, which help determine the meanings of sentences. In English, for example, the standard syntactical pattern *Subject* plus *Verb* plus *Complement* helps us know what the sentence "Wilhelmina bit the dentist" means: Wilhelmina did the biting, and the dentist needs the bandage. A writer can choose among various syntactical patterns in order to individualize his style.

Synthesis: process of combining different things into a coherent whole. see *Analysis.*

Theme: 1. often a synonym for a written composition or essay; 2. the subject of a piece of writing.

Thesaurus: a book listing approximate synonyms for words.

Thesis: 1. the central idea of a composition. *Thesis sentence:* a sentence that summarizes the main

of having all elements coherent with each other and contributing to a central purpose.

Utilitarian evaluation: see *Evaluation.*

Validity: the quality of being probable beyond a reasonable doubt, the quality of conforming to the evidence. A statement that is valid may nevertheless not be *true;* "truth" implies an absolute right-ness, rarely available to us. (In everyday language, however, "truth" is often used for "valid-ity." We say "It's true that he's coming tomorrow" when a strict use of the words would require us to say "It is valid—it con-forms to all the evidence we now have—to say that he will come tomorrow.")

Verification: the process of confirm-ing the validity or accuracy of an assertion. Verification often in-volves the collection of further evidence or the practical testing of a theory.

idea. 2. the conclusion of a logi-cal argument. A hypothesis (see p. 171) becomes a "thesis" when its validity has been tested and sustained.

Tone: accent or inflection of a speaker or writer that signifies his atti-tude toward his subject and his audience, usually conveyed by level of diction (e.g., formal or colloquial) and choice of syntax. Tone is sometimes used as a syn-onym for style, but more fre-quently, tone is associated with the writer's emotions ("an angry tone"), while style includes a wider range of qualities.

Transition: words and expressions that connect and show relationships between elements of a composi-tion, such as "therefore" (indicat-ing that what follows is a logical outgrowth of what precedes), or "however" (signalling a turn).

Truth: see *Validity.*

Unity: literally, "oneness"; the quality

a thematic
table of contents

The primary organization of this book is rhetorical—in other words, the selections are arranged by types of writing rather than by subject matter. However, the readings can be chosen so as to form subject matter "clusters," groups of four or five or more selections about the same major theme. The Thematic Table of Contents below presents 14 such clusters. You may find them useful for a thematically organized course or for the preparation of longer compositions requiring reference to several published articles on one subject.

591